Lecture Notes of the Institute for Computer Sciences, Social-Informatics and Telecommunications Engineering 50

Sushil Jajodia   Jianying Zhou (Eds.)

Security and Privacy in Communication Networks

6th International ICST Conference
SecureComm 2010
Singapore, September 7-9, 2010
Proceedings

 Springer

Volume Editors

Sushil Jajodia
George Mason University
Center for Secure Information Systems
4400 University Drive, Fairfax, VA, 22030-4422, USA
E-mail: jajodia@gmu.edu

Jianying Zhou
Institute for Infocomm Research
1 Fusionopolis Way, 21-01 Connexis, South Tower
138632 Singapore
E-mail: jyzhou@i2r.a-star.edu.sg

Library of Congress Control Number: Applied for

CR Subject Classification (1998): C.2, K.6.5, D.4.6, E.3, H.4, D.2

ISSN   1867-8211
ISBN-10 3-642-16160-X Springer Berlin Heidelberg New York
ISBN-13 978-3-642-16160-5 Springer Berlin Heidelberg New York

springer.com

© ICST Institute for Computer Science, Social Informatics and Telecommunications Engineering 2010
Printed in Germany

Typesetting: Camera-ready by author, data conversion by Scientific Publishing Services, Chennai, India
Printed on acid-free paper   06/3180   5 4 3 2 1 0

Preface

These proceedings contain the papers selected for presentation at the 6th International Conference on Security and Privacy in Communication Networks - SecureComm 2010 - held on September 7–9, 2010 in Singapore.

In response to the call for papers, 112 papers were submitted to the conference. These papers were evaluated on the basis of their significance, novelty, and technical quality. Each paper was reviewed by at least three members of the program committee. The program committee meeting was held electronically, with intensive discussions over a period of two weeks. Finally, 28 papers were selected for presentation at the conference, giving an acceptance rate of 25%.

There is a long list of people who volunteered their time and energy to put together the symposium and who deserve acknowledgment. Success of any conference depends on the quality of the selected papers. We are grateful to the members of the program committee and external reviewers for all their hard work during the review and the selection process. Feng Bao, SecureComm 2010 General Chair, deserves our special thanks for his support and suggestions. Thanks are due also to our keynote speakers, Pierangela Samarati and Robert H. Deng, and to Ying Qiu for managing the submission/review system and the conference website. Last, but certainly not least, our thanks go to all the authors who submitted papers and all the attendees.

We hope that you will find the contributions stimulating and a source of inspiration for future research.

September 2010

Sushil Jajodia
Jianying Zhou

SecureComm 2010

6th International Conference on
Security and Privacy in Communication Networks

Singapore
September 7–9, 2010

Organized and Sponsored by

Institute for Computer Sciences, Social-Informatics
and Telecommunications Engineering (ICST)

General Chair

Feng Bao   Institute for Infocomm Research, Singapore

Technical Program Chairs

Sushil Jajodia   George Mason University, USA
Jianying Zhou   Institute for Infocomm Research, Singapore

Publicity Chair

Sara Foresti   UniMi, Italy

Workshop Chair

Javier Lopez   University of Malaga, Spain

Local Arrangements Chair

Shen Tat Goh   Institute for Infocomm Research, Singapore

Web Coordinator

Ying Qiu   Institute for Infocomm Research, Singapore

Technical Program Committee

Claudio Ardagna	UniMi, Italy
Vijay Atluri	Rutgers University, USA
Steve Barker	King's College London, UK
Raheem Beyah	Georgia State University, USA
Marina Blanton	University of Notre Dame, USA
Carlo Blundo	University of Salerno, Italy
David Chadwick	University of Kent, UK
Ee-Chien Chang	NUS, Singapore
Hao Chen	UC Davis, USA
Kefei Chen	Shanghai Jiao Tong University, China
Mauro Conti	VU Amsterdam, The Netherlands
Frederic Cuppens	Télécom Bretagne, France
Nora Cuppens-Boulahia	Télécom Bretagne, France
Anupam Datta	Carnegie Mellon University, USA
Sabrina De Capitani di Vimercati	UniMi, Italy
Roberto Di Pietro	Università di Roma Tre, Italy
Tassos Dimitriou	AIT, Greece
Xuhua Ding	SMU, Singapore
Josep Ferrer-Gomila	UIB, Spain
Joe Giordano	Utica College, USA
Dieter Gollmann	TU Hamburg-Harburg, Germany
Vanessa Gratzer	Uni. Pantheon Sorbonne, France
Yong Guan	Iowa State University, USA
Lucas Hui	University of Hong Kong, China
Michiharu Kudo	IBM Research Tokyo, Japan
Miroslaw Kutylowski	Wroclaw Uni. of Tech., Poland
Brian LaMacchia	Microsoft Research, USA
Costas Lambrinoudakis	Uni. of Piraeus, Greece
Jun Li	University of Oregon, USA
Yingjiu Li	SMU, Singapore
Dongdai Lin	Institute of Software, China
Peng Liu	Penn State University, USA
John Mitchell	Stanford University, USA
Yi Mu	University of Wollongong, Australia
David Naccache	ENS, France
Leonardo Oliveira	University of Campinas, Brazil

Jose Onieva	University of Malaga, Spain
Raphael Phan	Loughborough University, UK
Radha Poovendran	University of Washington, USA
Indrakshi Ray	Colorado State University, USA
Rodrigo Roman	University of Malaga, Spain
Chunming Rong	University of Stavanger, Norway
Rei Safavi-Naini	University of Calgary, Canada
Kouichi Sakurai	Kyushu University, Japan
Shiuhpyng Shieh	NCTU, Taiwan
Krishna Sivalingam	Uni. Maryland Baltimore, USA
Jessica Staddon	Google, USA
Angelos Stavrou	George Mason University, USA
Vipin Swarup	The MITRE Corporation, USA
Patrick Tague	Carnegie Mellon University, USA
Tsuyoshi Takagi	Kyushu University, Japan
Patrick Traynor	Georgia Tech, USA
Vijay Varadharajan	Macquarie University, Australia
Guilin Wang	University of Birmingham, UK
Haining Wang	College of William and Mary, USA
Duncan Wong	City University of Hong Kong, China
Avishai Wool	Tel Aviv University, Israel
Yanjiang Yang	I2R, Singapore
Zhenyu Zhong	McAfee, USA
Bo Zhu	Concordia University, Canada
Sencun Zhu	Penn State University, USA

External Reviewers

Tolga Acar	Roberto Gallo	Przemyslaw Kubiak
Mina Askari	Deepak Garg	Hoi Leh
Mira Belenkiy	Maciek Gebala	Hao Lei
Przemyslaw Blaskiewicz	Dimitris Geneiatakis	Fagen Li
Jeremiah Blocki	Steven Gianvecchio	Hui Li
Shaoying Cai	Amy He	Yan Li
Gabriel Cavalcante	Islam Hegazy	Zhichun Li
Sambuddho Chakravarty	Yoshiaki Hori	Yiyuan Luo
Patrick Chan	Henry Jerez	Xianping Mao
Kefei Chen	Yoon-Chan Jhi	Luciana Marconi
Tat Chim	Limin Jia	Krystian Matusiewicz
Yoon-Ho Choi	Quan Jia	Jose A. Montenegro
Tom Chothia	Zoe Jiang	Eduardo Morais
Eleni Darra	Henrique Kawakami	Lan Nguyen
Bruce DeBruhl	Dilsun Kaynar	Son T. Nguyen
Prokopios Drogkaris	Marcin Kik	Takashi Nishide
Eduardo Ellery	Jongsung Kim	Yossi Oren

Table of Contents

Systems Security – I

Network Security – I

Security Protocols – I

System Security – II

Security Protocols – II

Network Security – II

SAS: Semantics Aware Signature Generation for Polymorphic Worm Detection

Deguang Kong[1,3], Yoon-Chan Jhi[2], Tao Gong[1], Sencun Zhu[2],
Peng Liu[3], and Hongsheng Xi[1]

[1] School of Information Science & Technology, University of Science & Technology of China,
Hefei, China
{kdg,jiangt}@mail.ustc.edu.cn, xihs@ustc.edu.cn
[2] Dept. of Computer Sicence and Engineering, Pennsylvania State University,
University Park, PA 16802
{jhi,szhu}@cse.psu.edu
[3] College of Information Sciences and Technology, Pennsylvania State University,
University Park, PA 16802
pliu@ist.psu.edu

Abstract. String extraction and matching techniques have been widely used in generating signatures for worm detection, but how to generate effective worm signatures in an adversarial environment still remains challenging. For example, attackers can freely manipulate byte distributions within the attack payloads and also can inject well-crafted noisy packets to contaminate the suspicious flow pool. To address these attacks, we propose SAS, a novel *Semantics Aware Statistical* algorithm for automatic signature generation. When SAS processes packets in a suspicious flow pool, it uses data flow analysis techniques to remove non-critical bytes. We then apply a Hidden Markov Model (HMM) to the refined data to generate state-transition-graph based signatures. To our best knowledge, this is the first work combining semantic analysis with statistical analysis to automatically generate worm signatures. Our experiments show that the proposed technique can accurately detect worms with concise signatures. Moreover, our results indicate that SAS is more robust to the byte distribution changes and noise injection attacks comparing to Polygraph and Hamsa.

Keywords: Worm Signature Generation, Machine Learning, Semantics, Data Flow Analysis, Hidden Markov Model.

1 Introduction

The computer worm is a great threat to modern network security despite various techniques that have been proposed so far. To thwart worms spreading out over Internet, pattern based signatures have been widely adopted in many network intrusion detection systems; however, existing signature-based techniques are facing fundamental countermeasures. Polymorphic and metamorphic worms (for brevity, hereafter, we mean both polymorphic and metamorphic when we say polymorphic) can evade traditional signature-based detection methods by either eliminating or reducing invariant patterns

S. Jajodia and J. Zhou (Eds.): SecureComm 2010, LNICST 50, pp. 1–19, 2010.

in the attack payloads through attack-side obfuscation. In addition, traditional signature-based detection methods are forced to learn worm signatures in an adversarial environment where the attackers can intentionally inject indistinguishable noisy packets to misled the classifier of the malicious traffic. As a result, low quality signatures would be generated.

Although a lot of efforts have been made to detect polymorphic worms [1], existing defenses are still limited in terms of accuracy and efficiency. To see the limitations in detail, let us divide existing techniques against polymorphic worms into two categories. The first type of approach is the pattern based signature generation, which uses patterns to identify the worm traffic from the normal traffic as a signature of the invariant part of malicious packets, such as substring and token sequence, etc. For example, systems such as Autograph [2], Honeycomb [3], EarlyBird [4], Polygraph [5], and Hamsa [6] extract common byte patterns from the packets collected in the suspicious flow pool. This approach enables fast analysis on live traffic, but can be evaded by polymorphic worms since the instances of a well-crafted polymorphic worm could share few or no syntactic patterns in common. Moreover, such a syntactic signature generation process can be misled by the allergy attack [7], the red herring and pool positioning attacks [8], and also by the noisy packets injected into the suspicious flow pool [9]. The second approach is to identify the semantics-derived characteristics of worm payloads, as in Cover [10], TaintCheck [11], ABROR [12], Sigfree [13], Spector [14], and STILL [15]. Existing techniques in this approach perform static analysis and/or dynamic analysis (e.g., emulation-based analysis [16]) on the packet payloads to detect the invariant characteristics reflecting semantics of malicious codes (e.g., behavioral characteristics of the decryption routine of a polymorphic worm). This approach is robust to the above evasion attempts because it considers more about semantics. However, the semantics analysis [17] may introduce non-trivial performance overheads, which is often intolerable in network-based on-line detection. Also, the payload analysis could be hindered by anti-static techniques [15] or anti-emulation techniques [18,19]. Our technique aims at a novel signature that is more robust than the pattern-based signatures and lighter than the prior behavior-based detection methods.

In this paper, we focus on the polymorphic worms can be locally or remotely injected using the HTTP protocol. To generate high quality signatures of such worms, we propose SAS, a novel *Semantics Aware Statistical* algorithm that generates semantic-aware signatures automatically. SAS introduces low overhead in signature matching process, thus it is suitable for the network-based worm detection. When SAS processes packets in the suspicious flow pool, it uses data flow analysis techniques to remove non-critical bytes irrelevant to the semantics of the worm code. We then apply a Hidden Markov Model (HMM) to the refined data to generate our *state-transition-graph (STG)* based signatures. Since modern polymorphic engines can completely randomize both the encrypted shellcode and the decryptor, we use a probability STG signature to defeat the absence of syntactic invariants. STG, as a probability signature, can adaptively learn token changes in different packets, correlate token distributions with states, and clearly express the dependence among tokens in packet payloads. Besides this, after a signature is generated, the detector is free of making sophisticated semantic analysis, such as emulating executions of instructions on the incoming packets to match attacks. Our experiments show that our technique exhibits good performance with low false positives and false negatives, especially when attackers can indistinguishably inject noisy bytes to mislead the signature extractor. SAS places itself between the pattern-based signatures and the semantic-derived detection methods, by balancing between security and the signature matching speed. As a semantic-based technique, SAS is more robust than most pattern-based signatures, sacrificing a little speed in signature matching. Based on the statistical analysis, SAS might sacrifice subtle part of security benefits of in-depth semantic analysis, for which SAS gains enough acceleration to be a network-based IDS.

Our contribution is in three-fold.

- To our best knowledge, our work is the first one combining semantic analysis with statistical analysis in signature generation process. As a result, the proposed technique is robust to the (crafted) noisy packets and the noisy bytes.
- We present a state-transition-graph based method to represent different byte distributions in different states. We explore semantics-derived characteristics beyond the byte patterns in packets.
- The signature matching algorithm used in our technique introduces low overhead, so that we can apply SAS as a network-based worm detection system.

The rest of this paper is organized as follows. In Section 2, we summarize the attacks to prior automated signature generation techniques. We then present our semantics-aware polymorphic worm detection technique in Section 3. In Section 4, we discuss the advantages and limitations of SAS, before presenting the evaluation results in Section 5. The related works are reviewed in Section 6, followed by the conclusion in Section 7.

2   Attacks on Signature Generation

2.1   Techniques to Evade Detection

Metamorphism and polymorphism are two typical techniques to obfuscate the malicious payload to evade the detection. Metamorphism [20] uses instruction replacement, equivalent semantics, instruction reordering, garbage (e.g., NOP) insertion, and/or register renaming to evade signature based detectors. Polymorphism [20] usually uses a built-in encoder to encrypt original shellcode, and stores the encrypted shellcode and a decryption routine in the payload. The encrypted shellcode will be decrypted during its execution time at a victim site. The decryption routine can be further obfuscated by metamorphic techniques; the attack code generated by polymorphic engine TAPION [21] is such an example. We note that traditional signature based detection algorithm is easily to be misled by applying byte substitution or reordering. We also doubt if the invariants always exist in all the malicious traffic flows. In fact, we found that for the instances of the polymorphic worm Slammer [22] mutated by the CLET polymorphic engine, the only invariant token (byte) in all of its mutations is "\x04", which is commonly found in all SQL name resolution requests.

2.2   Techniques to Mislead Signature Generation

Besides the obfuscation techniques which aim to cause false negatives in signature matching, there are also techniques attempting to introduce false positives and false

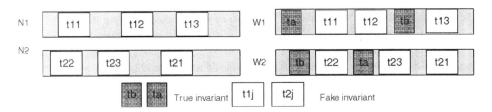

Fig. 1. Suspicious packet flow pool

signatures. For example, the allergy attack [7] is a denial of service (DoS) attack that misleads automatic signature generation systems to generate signatures matching normal traffic flows. Signature generation systems such as Polygraph [5] and Hamsa [6] include a flow classifier module and a signature generation module. The flow classifier module separates the network traffic flows during training period into two pools, the innocuous pool and the suspicious pool. The signature generation module extracts signatures from the suspicious flow pool. A signature consists of tokens, where each token is a byte sequence found across all the malicious packets that the signature is targeting. The goal of a signature generation algorithm is to generate signatures which match the maximum fraction of network flows in the suspicious flow pool while matching the minimum fraction of network flows in the innocuous pool. Generally, existing signature generation systems have two limitations. First, the flow classifier module is not perfect; thus, noise can be introduced into the suspicious flow pool. Second, in reality, the suspicious flow pool often contains more than one type of worms, thus a clustering algorithm is needed to first cluster the flows that contain the same type of worm. Polygraph [5] uses a hierarchical clustering algorithm to merge flows to generate a signature which introduces the lowest false positive rate at every step of clustering process. Hasma [6] uses a model-based greedy signature generation algorithm to select those tokens as a signature which has the highest coverage over the suspicious flow pool.

Let us illustrate the vulnerability of signature generators such as Polygraph and Hamsa when crafted noises are injected in the training traffic as shown in Figure 1. Here N_i denotes normal packets and W_i ($1 \leq i \leq 2$) denotes the true worm packets. Let us assume the malicious invariant (i.e., the true signature) in the worm packets consists of two independent tokens t_a and t_b, and each of them has the same false positive rate p ($0 < p < 1$) if taken as a signature. Let the worm packets also include the tokens t_{ij} ($1 \leq j \leq 3$), each of which has the same false positive rate p as a token in a true signature, thus an attacker can craft normal packets N_is to contain t_{ij} ($1 \leq j \leq 3$). If all these four flows end up being included in a suspicious flow pool, the signature generation process would be misled.

Setting 1: Let the ratio of the four flows (W_1, W_2, N_1, N_2) in the suspicious flow pool be (99:99:1:1). That is, there is only 1% noise in the suspicious flow pool. According to the clustering algorithm in Polygraph, it will choose to merge the flows that will generate a signature which has the lowest false positive rate. In this example shown in Figure 1, the false positive rate of using signature (t_{i1}, t_{i2}, t_{i3}) by merging flows (W_i, N_i) is p^3 and that of signature (t_a, t_b) by merging flows (W_1, W_2) is p^2. The

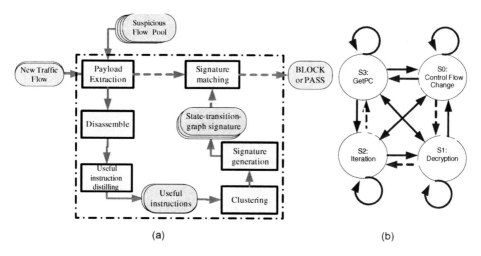

(a)   (b)

Fig. 2. (a) System architecture. (b) State-transition-graph (STG) model.

former is smaller and thus the hierarchical clustering algorithm will merge the flows of W_i with N_i, and it will terminate with two signatures (t_{i1}, t_{i2}, t_{i3}).

Setting 2: Let the ratio of the flows (W_1, W_2, N_1, N_2) in the suspicious flow pool be (99:99:100:100). According to Hasma's model-based greedy signature generation algorithm, Hamsa selects the tokens with the highest coverage in the suspicious flow pool. In our example, the coverages for signature (t_{i1}, t_{i2}, t_{i3}) and (t_a, t_b) are 50% and 49.7%, respectively. Thus, Hamsa first selects token (t_{i1}), then (t_{i1}, t_{i2}), and (t_{i1}, t_{i2}, t_{i3}) as a signature as long as the false positive rate of signature (t_{i1}, t_{i2}, t_{i3}) is below a threshold.

From the above two cases, we can clearly see that if an attacker injects noises into the suspicious flow pool, the wrong signatures will be generated.

3 Our Approach

3.1 Why STG Based Signature Can Help?

The fake blending packets mixed in a suspicious flow pool usually do not have many **useful** instruction code embedded in the packet unless they are truly worms. It is found that byte sequences that look like code sequences are highly likely to be dummies (or data) if the containing packet has no code implying function calls [13]. We use semantic analysis to filter those "noisy" padding and substitution bytes and thus improve the signature quality. Under some conditions, the suspicious flow pool can contain no invariants if we compute the frequency of each token by simply counting them. We find the distributions of different tokens are influenced by the positions of the tokens in packets, which are instruction-level exhibitions of semantics and syntax of the packets. In order to capture such semantics, we use different states to express different token distributions in different positions in the packets. It is more robust to the token changes in different positions of the packets, which correlates the tokens' distributions with a state, making token dependency relationships clear. One issue we want to emphasize here is that different from but not contrary to the claim in [23], our model is based on the remaining code extracted from the whole packets instead of on the whole worm packets.

3.2   System Overview

In Figure 2, we describe the framework of our approach. Our framework consists of two phases, *semantic-aware signature extraction phase* and *semantic-aware signature matching phase*. The signature extraction phase consists of five modules: payload extraction, payload disassembly, useful instruction distilling, clustering, and signature generation. The signature matching phase is comprised of two modules: payload extraction and signature matching module. **Payload extraction module** extracts the payload which possibly implements the malicious intent, from a a flow which is a set of packets forming a message. For example, in a HTTP request message, a malicious payload only exists in Request-URI and Request-Body of the whole flow. We extract these two parts from the HTTP flows for further semantics analysis. **Disassembly module** disassembles an input byte sequence. If it finds consecutive instructions in the input sequence, it generates a disassembled instruction sequence as output. An instruction sequence is a sequence of CPU instructions which has only one entry point. A valid instruction sequence should have at least one execution path from the entry point to another instruction within the sequence. Since we do not know the entry point of the code when the code is present in the byte sequences, we exploit an improved recursive traversal disassembly algorithm introduced by Wang et al. [13] to disassemble the input. For an N-byte sequence, the time complexity of this algorithm is $O(N)$. **Useful instruction distilling module** extracts useful instructions from the instruction sequences. Useless instructions are identified and pruned by control flow and data flow analysis. **Payload clustering module** clusters the payloads containing similar set of useful instructions together. **Signature generation module** computes STG based signatures from the payload clusters. Upon completion of training, **Signature matching module** starts detecting worm packets by matching STG signatures against input packets. Shortly we will discuss these four modules in detail.

3.3   Useful Instruction Extraction

The **disassembly** module generates zero, one, or multiple instruction sequences, which do not necessarily correspond to real code. From the output of the **disassembly** module, we distill useful instructions by pruning useless instructions. Useless instructions are those illegal and redundant byte sequences using the technique introduced in SigFree [13]. Basically, the pruned useless byte sequences correspond to three kinds of dataflow anomalies: *define-define*, *define-undefine*, and *undefine-reference*. When there is an undefine-reference anomaly (i.e., a variable is referenced before it is ever assigned with a value) in an execution path, the instruction which causes the "reference" is a useless instruction. When there is a define-define anomaly (i.e., a variable is assigned a value twice) or define-undefine anomaly (i.e., a defined variable is later set by an undefined variable), the instruction that caused the former "define" is also considered as

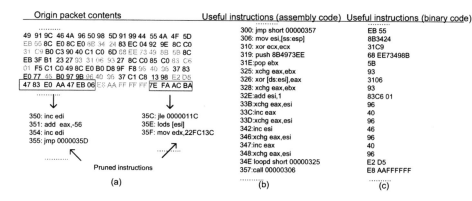

Fig. 3. (a) Original packet contents. (b) Useful instructions (assembly code). (c) Useful instructions (binary code).

a useless instruction. Since normal packets and crafted noisy packets typically do not contain useful instructions, such packets injected in the suspicious flow pool are filtered out after the useful instruction extraction phase. The remaining instructions are likely to be related to the semantics of the code contained in the suspicious packets. An example of polymorphic payload analysis is shown in Figure 3. Here the leftmost part is the original packet content in binary, the middle one is the disassembly code of the useful instructions after removing the useless one, and the rightmost part is its corresponding binaries. For example, in Figure 3, the disassembly code *inc edi* appeared in address *350* is pruned because *edi* is referenced without being defined to produce an *undefine-reference* anomaly.

3.4   Payload Clustering

The useful instruction sequences extracted from polymorphic worms normally contain the following features: (F_1) GetPC: Code to get the current program counter. GetPC code should contain opcode "*call*" or "*fstenv.*" We explain the rationale shortly; (F_2) Iteration: Obviously, a polymorphic worm needs to perform iterations over encrypted shellcode. The instructions that can characterize this feature include *loop*, *rep* and the variants of such instructions (e.g., *loopz*, *loope*, *loopnz*); (F_3) Jump: A polymorphic code highly likely to contain conditional/unconditional branches (e.g., *jmp*, *jnz*, *je*); (F_4) Decryption: Since the shellcode of a polymorphic worm is encrypted when it is sent to a victim, a polymorphic worm should decrypt the shellcode during or before execution. We note that certain machine instructions (e.g., *or*, *xor*) are more often found in decryption routine. The reason why we use these four features is that from our observations, nearly all self-modifying polymorphic worm packets contain such features even after complicated obfuscations.

A decryption routine needs to read and write the encrypted code in the payload, therefore, a polymorphic worm needs to know where the payload is loaded in the memory. To our best knowledge, the only way for a shellcode to get the absolute address of the payload is to read the PC (Program Counter) register [15]. Since the IA-32 architecture does not provide any instructions to directly access PC, attackers have to play a trick to obtain the value in the PC register. As far as we know, currently three methods are known in the attacker community: one method uses *fstenv*, and the other two use relative calls to figure out the values in PC.

In a suspicious flow pool, there are normally multiple types of worm packets. For a given packet, we first extract the instructions indicating each of the four features of polymorphic worms. However, simply counting such instructions is not sufficient to characterize a polymorphic shellcode. In reality, some feature may appear multiple times in a specific worm instance, while some others may not appear at all. This makes it complicated for us to match a worm signature to a polymorphic shellcode. If we measure the similarity between a signature and a shellcode based on the bare sequence of the feature identifying instructions, an attacker may evade our detection by distributing dummy features in different byte positions within the payload or by reordering instructions in the execution path. On the other hand, if we ignore the structural (or sequent) order of the feature-identifying instructions and consider them as a histogram, it might result in an inaccurate detection. So in this work we consider both of the structural and statistical informations in packet classification, and use a parameter δ to balance between them.

Specifically, we define two types of distances: (D_1) the feature distance; and (D_2) the histogram distance. We keep the sequent order of the features appearing in an instruction sequence, in a *feature vector*. Let $D_1(v_1, v_2)$ denote the feature distance between two feature vectors v_1, v_2. When v_1 and v_2 are of the same length, we define $D_1(v_1, v_2)$ as the Hamming distance of v_1 and v_2. For example, the feature vector of the instruction sequence shown in Figure 3 is $S = \{F_3, F_4, F_2, F_1\}$. Given another feature vector $S' = \{F_3, F_4, F_1, F_1\}$, the distance between S and S' is computed as $D_1(S, S') = 1$. When two feature vectors are of different lengths, we define the distance of the two feature vectors as $D_1(v_1, v_2) = \max(\text{length}(v_1), \text{length}(v_2)) - \text{LLCS}(v_1, v_2)$, where $\text{LLCS}(v_1, v_2)$ denotes the length of the longest common subsequence of v_1 and v_2 and $\text{length}(v_1)$ denotes the length of v_1. For example, if we are given $S'' = \{F_3, F_4, F_1, F_3, F_1\}$, distance $D_1(S, S'') = 1$. We also measure the histogram distance, the similarity based on the histograms of two feature vectors. Let $D_2(v_1, v_2)$ denotes the histogram distance between two feature vectors v_1, v_2. For example, the histogram of S above is $(1, 1, 1, 1)$ because every feature appears exactly once. Let us assume that the histogram of feature vector S' is given as $(1, 2, 0, 1)$. Then, we define $D_2(S, S')$ as the Hamming distance of S and S', which is 2.

Given two useful instruction sequences, we use both D_1 and D_2 to determine their similarity. We define the distance between two useful instruction sequences as $D = \delta D_1 + (1 - \delta)D_2$, where δ is a value minimizing the clustering error. Suppose there are M clusters in total. Let L_m be the number of packets in cluster m, where m ($1 \leq m \leq M$) denotes the index of each cluster. When a new packet in a suspicious flow pool is being clustered, we determine whether to merge the packet into an existing cluster or to create a new cluster to contain the packet. We start by calculating the distance between the new packet and every packet in existing clusters. If we find one or more clusters with average distance below threshold θ, we add the new packet to the cluster with the

---

Algorithm 1. State-Transition-Graph Model Learning Algorithm

Input: A cluster of the useful instructions of the payload $O_{[1..T]}$
Output: STG Signature $\lambda = \{\pi, A, B\}$ for the input cluster
Procedure:
1: map tokens $O_t \in X(1 \leq t \leq T)$ to the corresponding states $S_i \in \{S_0, S_1, S_2, S_3\}(0 \leq i \leq N - 1)$
2: calculate initial probability distribution π based on the probabilities of the first token O_1 being on each state $S_i \in \{S_0, S_1, S_2, S_3\}$ // get π
3: generate the frequent token set for each state $S_i \in \{S_0, S_1, S_2, S_3\}$ and calculate $b_i(k)(1 \leq k \leq |X|)$ // get B
4: **for** $i = 0$ to $N - 1$ **do**
5:     **for** $j = 0$ to $N - 1$ **do**
6:         $a_{ij} \leftarrow \dfrac{number(O_t \in Si \wedge O_{t+1} \in Sj)}{number(O_t \in S_i)}$ // get A, here predicate $number$ denotes the frequency of a token

---

minimum distance among them. Otherwise, we create a new cluster for the new packet. We repeat this process until all packets in the suspicious flow are clustered.

3.5 STG Based Signature Generation

After clustering all the packets in the suspicious pool, we build a signature from each of the clusters. Unlike prior techniques, our signature is based on a state transition graph in which each state is mapped to each of the four features introduced above (Figure 2). In our approach, the tokens (either opcode or operands in a useful instruction sequence) are directly visible. The tokens can be the output of any state, which means each state has a probability distribution over the possible output tokens. For example, in Figure 3, "EB" and "55" are tokens observed in different states. This matches exactly with the definition of Hidden Markov Model (HMM) [24], thus we use HMM to represent the state transition graph for our signature.

More formally, our STG model consists of four states ($N = 4$), which forms state space $S = \{S_0, S_1, S_2, S_3\}$. Let $\lambda = \{\pi, A, B\}$ denote this model, where A is the state transition matrix, B is a probability distribution matrix, and π is the initial state distribution. When a STG model is constructed from a polymorphic worm, we use the model as our STG-based signature. Our STG model is defined as follows:

- State space $S = \{S_0, S_1, S_2, S_3\}$, where state S_0 is the *control flow change state*, which correspond to the feature F_3. State S_1 is the *decryption state*, which corresponds to the feature F_4. State S_2 is the *iteration state*, which corresponds to the feature F_2. State S_3 is the *GetPC state*, corresponding to F_1.

- Transition matrix $A = (a_{ij})_{N \times N} = \begin{pmatrix} a_{00} & a_{01} & a_{02} & a_{03} \\ a_{10} & a_{11} & a_{12} & a_{13} \\ a_{20} & a_{21} & a_{22} & a_{23} \\ a_{30} & a_{31} & a_{32} & a_{33} \end{pmatrix}$ where $a_{ij} = $ $P(next\ state\ is\ S_j|$ $current\ state\ is\ S_i)$, $a_{ij} \in \{S \times S \rightarrow [0,1]\}$, and a_{ij} satisfies $\sum_j a_{ij} = 1$ ($0 \leq i, j \leq N - 1$).

- Let Y be the set of a single byte and Y^i denote the set of i-byte sequences. $X = \{Y, Y^2, Y^3, Y^4\}$ is the token set in our system because a token in a useful instruction contains at most four bytes (e.g., "AAFFFFFF"), which corresponds to the word size of a 32-bit system. Let O_t ($1 \leq t \leq |X|$) be a token that is visible

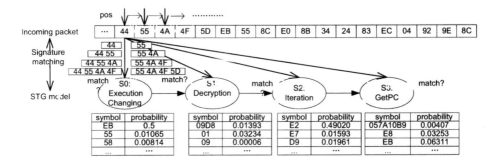

Fig. 4. *STG* signature matching process

at a certain state, and $O = \{O_t | O_t \in X\}$ be the visible token set at the state. For a real instruction sequence with T tokens in the useful instruction sequence, the t-length visible output sequence is defined as $O_{[1..t]} = \{O_1, O_2, ..., O_t\}$ $(t \leq T)$. Then, we can define the probability set B as $B = \{b_i(k)\}$, where $b_i(k) = P(visible\ token\ is\ O_k | current\ state\ is\ S_i)$. $b_i(k)$ is the probability of X_k on state S_i, thus satisfying $\sum_{1 \leq k \leq |X|} b_i(k) = 1$.

– Initial state distribution $\pi = \{\pi_0, \pi_1, \pi_2, \pi_3\}$, where $\pi_i = P(the\ first\ state\ is\ S_i)$.

Algorithm 1 is adopted from the segment K-means algorithm [24] to learn the structure of Hidden Markov Model. As the same token can appear at different states with different probabilities, we manage our model to satisfy $O_t \in S_i$ if $b_i(O_t) > b_j(O_t)$ for all $j \neq i$ (step 2 and step 3). We also remove noises by setting a threshold to discard less-frequent tokens. For example, if $\max_i b_i(O_t)$ is below the threshold (e.g.,θ_0), we ignore this token O_t while constructing a STG model.

3.6   Semantics Aware Signature Matching Process

After we extract STG-based signatures from the suspicious flow pool, we can use them to match live network packets. Given a new packet to test, our detector first retrieves the payload of the packet. Assuming that the payload length is m bytes, the detector checks whether this m-byte payload matches any of the existing signatures. If it does not match any signature (i.e., their deviation distance is above a threshold θ_2), it is considered as a benign packet. If it matches a single signature of certain type of a worm, it will be classified as the type of worm associated with the signature. If the packet matches multiple signatures, the detector classifies the packet as the one with the smallest distance among the matching signatures. An advantage of our approach is that we need not make complicated analysis on the live packets but match the packets byte after byte.

To measure the distance between an m-byte (input) payload and a signature, we try to identify the first token, starting from the first byte of the payload. We form four candidate tokens of length i (i=1, 2, 3, 4), where the i-th candidate token consists of

Table 1. Comparison of SAS with Polygraph and Hamsa

Comparison	Polygraph	Hamsa	SAS
Content (behavior) detection	content	content	content
Semantic related	semantic free	semantic free	semantic related
On-line detection speed	fast	fast	fast
(Crafted) noise tolerance	some	medium	good
Token-fit attack resilience	nearly no	medium	good
Coincidental attack resilience	nearly no	medium	good
Allergy attack resilience	some	some	good
Signature simplicity	simple	simple	complicated

the first i bytes of the payload. As is shown in Figure 4, we first select (44), (44,55), (44,55,4A), (44,55,4A,4F) as the candidate tokens. Then, for each candidate token O_t, we calculate its probability to appear in each of the four states in our STG model, and assign it to the state which gives the largest probability $b_i(O_t)$. Let $max(P_i)$ denotes the maximum of the four $b_i(O_t)$. If $max(P_i)$ is above a threshold θ_1, we choose the candidate token yielding $max(P_i)$ as the real token, and ignore the others. Otherwise, all of the four candidate tokens are ignored. In either case, we move to the next four bytes of the payload. As for the case in Figure 4, we will start to check the next four tokens (55), (55,4A), (55,4A,4F), (55,4A,4F,5D). We will repeat the above process until all m bytes are processed. Finally, we sum up the $max(P_i)$ and calculate its distance from the signature. The deviation distance D is defined as $D = \|\log P[O_{[1...m]}|\lambda] - mean\|$ where $\log P[O_{[1...m]}|\lambda]$ is the matching probability value for a m-byte packet, $mean$ is an average matching value for a certain type of training packets. Assuming that there are l packets in a cluster of the same type, and the byte length for each packet is T_i ($1 \leq i \leq l$), we have $mean = \frac{1}{l}\sum_{k=1}^{l}\log P[O_{[1...T_k]}|\lambda]$. We do not show the detailed algorithm here due to the limited space.

4   Security Analysis

4.1   Strength

Our semantic based signatures can filter the noises in the suspicious flow pool and prune the useless instructions which are otherwise possibly learned as signature, thus it has good noise tolerance. As the STG signature is more complicated than previous signatures (e.g., token-sequence signature), it is much harder for attackers to ruin our automatic signature generation by crafting packets bearing both the tokens of normal and attack packets compared with previous signatures. Moreover, even if the hackers change the contents of the attack packets a lot, they can hardly evade our detection since our signature is not based on syntactic patterns but based on semantic patterns. In addition, the STG signature can match unknown polymorphic worms (which our detector has not been trained with) since it has learned certain semantics of the decryption routine from existing polymorphic worms. Our STG signature matching algorithm introduces low overhead (analysis throughput is more than 10Mbps), thus our detector is fast enough to match live packets. Some anti-disassemble techniques like junk byte

Useful instruction (assembly code)	Bianry code
....	
sub cl,2	80E9 02
dec ecx	49
dec ecx	49
je short 00000261	74 07
jmp short 00000206	EB AA
call 00000201	E8
	A0FFFFFF
....	....

Fig. 5. STG signature example. The bytes used by the signature are marked in *red* color.

insertion, opaque predicate, and code overlap all aim to immobilize linear sweep disassembly algorithms. The disassembler of the STG signature generation approach is a recursive traversal algorithm, which makes our approach robust to such types of antidisassemble techniques. In Table 1, we summarize our benefit in comparison with other signature generation approaches. For STG, it is robust to the attacks filling crafted bytes in the wildcard bytes of the packets (e.g., coincidental-pattern attack [5] and the token-fit attack [6]) since these packets usually fail to pass our semantic analysis process. It is robust to the innocuous pool poisoning [5] attack and allergy attack [7] because our technique can filter the normal packets out for signature generation. As it is a probability based algorithm, the long-tail attack [5] will not thwart our matching process. Finally, by discovering meanings of each token (i.e., which token is exhibiting which feature), our approach explores beyond traditional signatures which leverage only the syntactic patterns to match worm packets.

4.2 Limitations

Here we discuss about the limitations of the proposed technique and possible methods to mitigate these limitations. First, based on static analysis which can not handle some state-of-the-art code obfuscation techniques (e.g., branch-function obfuscation, memory access obfuscation), we can not generate appropriate signatures if the semantic analysis fails to analyze the suspicious flow pool. This can be solved through more sophisticated semantic analysis such as symbolic execution and abstract interpretation techniques. Second, our technique can be evaded if smart attackers use more sophisticated encryption and obfuscation techniques such as doubly encrypted shellcode with invariant substitution. Also, for the non self-contained code [16], there may be absence of features for clustering to generate the signatures. To address these issues, emulation-based payload analysis techniques can be used in the signature extractor and the attack detector, however, state-of-the-art emulation-based techniques are still lack of performance to be used in a live packet analysis. Although one may doubt the utility of byte-level signatures (e.g., it could not handle the packed code), its performance is good for practical deployment compared with the emulation based approaches.

5   Evaluation

We test our system offline on massive polymorphic packets generated by real polymorphic engines used by attackers (i.e., CLET, ADMmutate, PexFnstenvMov) and on normal HTTP request/reply traces collected at out lab PCs. Both CLET and ADM-mutate are advanced polymorphic engines which obfuscate the decryption routines by metamorphism such as instruction replacement and garbage insertion. CLET also uses spectrum analysis to counterattack the byte distribution analysis. PexFnstenvMov is a polymorphic engine included in Metaspoit [25] framework. Opcode of the "*xor*" instruction is frequently found in the decryption routine of PexFnstenvMov. PexFnstenv-Mov also uses the "*fnstenv*" instruction for the GetPC code.

In evaluation, we also use 100,000 non-attack HTTP requests/responses for two purposes: to compute false positive rate and to derive noisy flows to attack signature extraction. The normal HTTP traffic contains 100,000 messages collected for three weeks at seven workstations owned by seven different individuals. To collect the traffic, a client-side proxy monitoring incoming and outgoing HTTP traffic is deployed underneath the web server. Those 100,000 messages contain various types of non-attack data including JavaScript, HTML, XML, PDF, Flash, and multimedia data, which render diverse and realistic traffic typically found in the wild. The total size of the traces is over 1.77GB. We run our experiments on a 2.4GHz Intel Quad-Core machine with 2GB RAM, running Windows XP SP2.

5.1   Comparison with Polygraph and Hamsa

In this section, we evaluate the accuracy (in terms of false positives and false negatives) of our algorithm in comparison with Polygraph and Hamsa. We compare the three systems in two cases: without noise injection attack, with noise injection attack.

Parameter Settings. The parameters of Polygraph are set as follows. The minimum token length α is set to 2, the minimum cluster size is set to 2, and the maximum acceptable false positive rate during the signature generation process is set to 1%. Hamsa in our experiments is built from the source that we downloaded from the Hamsa hompage. The minimum acceptable false positive rate of Hamsa is set to $u = 0.01$ during the signature generation process. In our approach, the parameters θ_0, θ_1 are used to prune the tokens which have little probability to match with the STG signature; and parameter θ_2 is used to label the deviation distance during the packet matching process. These parameters are configured as follows: $\theta_0 = 0.016$, $\theta_1 = 0.016$, $\theta_2 = 12.000$.

Polymorphic Engine. In this experiment, we use CLET because it implements spectrum analysis to attack the byte distribution analysis performed by existing signature extractors. We generate 1,000 worm instances from CLET, among which 400 instances are used as the training data to generate signatures, and 600 instances are used to compute the false negative rate. We also use 100,000 non-attack HTTP requests/responses to compute false positive rate.

Comparison Without Noise Injection. We compare our method with Polygraph and Hamsa, without considering noise injection. Fed with the same 400 attack messages, the signatures generated by Hamsa and the conjunction signature generated by Polygraph are all '\x8b':1,'\xff\xff\xff':1,'\x07\xeb':1. The state transition path of our signature is $(S_0 \rightarrow S_1 \rightarrow S_0 \rightarrow S_3)$. Token sequences '\xff\xff\xff' and '\x07\xeb' are the only invariant tokens appearing in the useful instruction sequences (Figure 5).

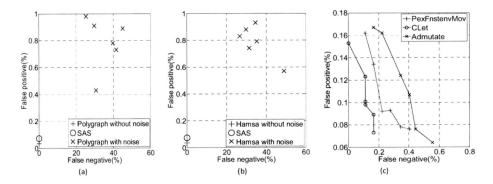

Fig. 6. (a) Comparison of SAS and Polygraph (b) Comparison of SAS and Hamsa (c) Impact of parameters

Comparison Under Noise Injection. We compare SAS, Polygraph, and Hamsa, assuming 1:1 attack-to-noise ratio in the suspicious flow pool. To add the crafted noise to the suspicious flow pool, we adopt the method used by Perdisci et. al. [9]. For each malicious packet w_i, we create the associated fake anomalous packet f_i by modifying the corresponding packet w_i. The way to make crafted noisy packet f_i is divided into the following six steps. (Step 1) f_i^0: create a copy of w_i. (Step 2) f_i^1: permute bytes f_i^0 randomly. (Step 3) $a[\ ]$: copy k substrings of length l from w_i to array a, but do not copy the true invariant. (Step 4) f_i^2: copy the fake invariant substring into f_i^1. (Step 5) f_i^3: inject m-length substring of string v into (f_i^2), we generate n $(n > m)$ bytes of string $v = \{v_1, v_2, ..., v_n\}$ by selecting the contiguous bytes in the innocuous packet which satisfy $0.05 < \mathrm{P}(v|\text{innocuous\quad packets}) < 0.20$. (Step 6) f_i^4: obfuscate the true invariant by substituting the true invariant bytes in the packet.

To craft non-attack derived noises, we use our 10,000 normal HTTP messages. The suspicious flow pool are composed of 400 CLET-mutated instances and 400 crafted noises. We configure the parameters of noise generator as $k = 3$, $l = 5$, $n = 6$, and $m = 3$. The parameters for SAS, Polygraph, and Hamsa are set as the same as in Case-1.

When we compare SAS with Polygraph, we ignore "true invariants" in Step 3 and 6 because we do not know the true invariants until the signature is generated. Instead, we permute the bytes more randomly to separate and distribute contiguous bytes before copying substrings of w_i in Step 3. Atop this, we use even more sophisticated noise injection when we compare SAS with Hamsa. Specifically, in Step 5, we choose a string v which satisfies $\mathrm{P}(v|\text{innocuous\quad packets}) < u$ (u is parameter). Since we set u as described above, Hamsa's false positive rate will not exceed u even if the injected noises are taken as signatures.

Comparison Results. Figure 6(a) and Figure 6(b) show the false positive and false negative rates of SAS, Polygraph, and Hamsa in both experiment cases. In Case-1 experiment (i.e., without noise injection), all the three systems show similar accuracy. Although SAS shows slightly higher false positive rate than Polygraph and Hamsa, the false positive rates of all three systems are already very low (< 0.0008). In Case-2 experiment (i.e., with noise injection), the false positive and the false negative rates of SAS has not been affected by the crafted noise injected to the suspicious flow pool. In contrast, the signature generation process of Polygraph and Hamsa has been greatly misled to add fake invariants taken from the crafted noises, which results in extremely high false negative rate. As a result, the signatures generated by Polygraph and Hamsa miss more than 20% of attack messages. The false positive and false negative rates of Polygraph and Hamsa are still lower than 1%, which is because they have a threshold of maximum false positive rate (say 1%).

5.2   Per-polymorphic Engine Evaluation

In this experiment, we evaluate the impact of different parameter settings on our approach. We use 3,000 worm instances generated by CLET, Admutate, and PexFnstenv-Mov. We feed our signature extractor with 1,200 out of the 3,000 worm instances (400 instances from each type of worm) to generate STG-based signatures. Then, we use the remaining worm instances to evaluate the extracted signatures. We also inject 10,000 normal packets into the suspicious flow pool to make the packet clustering more difficult.

The parameter δ is first set to an initial value, and then adjusted until all the packets are clustered correctly. In our setting, we find the structural information is more important than statistical information. When we set parameter $\delta = 0.8$, all the packets in the suspicious pool are grouped in the right cluster. We aim to find an appropriate δ for the right clustering. The δ can be tuned based on the feedback of clustering result. We test the false negative and false positive rates using the remaining 1,800 attack instances and the 100,000 normal HTTP messages respectively (Table 2). We also evaluate the influence of parameter changes on signature matching as shown in Figure 6(c), where each data point stands for one group of parameter settings. We change the value of θ_1, θ_2 to see how false positive rate and false negative rate vary. In our experiment, we observe the lowest false positve rate when we set the parameters as $\theta_1 = 0.018$, $\theta_2 = 12.000$. Altough we do not present entire results due to page limit, our experiment results show that the false negative rate decreases as θ_1 increases. Also, the false positive rate increases as θ_2 increases. These observations are confirmed from the design of our Algorithm, as higher θ_1 would filter more noises while a higher θ_2 would block more normal packets. The parameters, in practice, can be tuned based on the feedback from training and testing datasets, so that we get a locally optimized false positive rate. Table 2 shows the best configurations obtained by the above method.

Table 2. Accuracy of the STG-based signatures generated by SAS

Polymorphic engine	False positive	False negative	State transition path of STG-based signature
PexFnstenvMov	0.075%	0.40%	$(S_3 \rightarrow S_1 \rightarrow S_2)$
CLet	0.072%	0.42%	$(S_0 \rightarrow S_1 \rightarrow S_0 \rightarrow S_3)$
Admutate	0.062%	0.55%	$(S_0 \rightarrow S_1 \rightarrow S_2 \rightarrow S_3)$

Table 3. Performance evaluation

Polymorphic engine	Training time(sec)	Matching time(sec)	Analysis throughput(Mbps)
PexFnstenvMov	22.901	1.783	10.534
CLet	31.237	2.879	13.655
Admutate	24.833	1.275	12.901

5.3 Performance Evaluation

The time complexity of the signature learning algorithm is $O(N^2TP)$, where T is the length of token sequence, P is the number of the suspicious packets in a clustering, and N is the number of states. The time complexity of our signature matching algorithm is $O(N^2S \cdot L)$, where L is the average length of token sequences in a signature, S is the total length of input packets to match, N is the number of states. The signature matching algorithm can be easily adapted to satisfy the requirements of online detection. The training time, matching time, and analysis throughput for each polymorphic engine are shown in Table 3. The training time includes the time to extract useful instructions from packets. The matching time is the total elapsed time to match 600 mutations generated by each polymorphic engine.

6 Related Work

Pattern Extraction Signature Generation. There are a lot of work on pattern based signature generation, including honeycomb [3], earlybird [4], and autograph [2], which had been shown not to be able to handle polymorphic worms. Polygraph [5] and Hamsa [6] are pattern based signature generation algorithms, and they are more capable of detecting polymorphic worms, but vulnerable to different kinds of noise injection attacks. There are also rich researches on attacks against pattern-extraction algorithms. Perdisci et al. [9] present an attack which adds crafted noises into the suspicious flow to confuse the signature generation process. Paragraph [8] demonstrates that Polygraph and Hamsa are vulnerable to attacks as long as attackers can construct the labeled samples randomly to mislead the training classifier, and this attack can also prevent or severely delay generation of an accurate classifier. Allergy attacks [7] force the signature generation algorithm to generate signatures that could match the normal traffic, thus introducing high false positive rate. Gundy et al. [26] present a class of feature omission attacks on signature generation process that are poorly addressed by Autograph and Hamsa. Polymorphic blending attacks [27] are presented by matching the byte frequency statistics with normal traffic to evade detection. Theoretical analysis of limits of different signature generation algorithms are given in [28]. Gundy et al. [29] show that web based polymorphic worms do not necessarily have invariant bytes. A game-theoretical analysis on how a detection algorithm and an adversary could adapt to each other in an adversarial environment is introduced in [30]. Song et al. [23] studied the possibility of deriving a model for representing the general class of code that corresponds to all possible decryption routines, and concludes that it is infeasible. Our work combines the semantic analysis with the signature generation process, making it robust to many noise-injection attacks (e.g., allergy attack, red herring attack).

Semantic Analysis. Researches have presented semantic based techniques by making static and dynamic analysis on the binary code. Polychronakis et al. [16] have presented emulation-based approach to detect polymorphic payloads by emulating the code and detecting decryption routines through dynamic analysis. Libemu [17] is another attempt to achieve shellcode analysis through code emulations. Compared with their works, our approach has higher throughput and can not be attacked by anti-emulation techniques. Brumley et al. [31] propose to automatically create vulnerability signatures for software. Cover [10] exploits the post-crash symptom diagnosis and address space randomization techniques to extract signatures. TaintCheck [11] exploits dynamic dataflow and taint analysis techniques to help find the malicious input and infer the properties of worms. ABROR [12] automatically generates vulnerability-oriented signatures by identifying typical characteristics of attacks in different program contexts. Sigfree [13] detects the malicious code embedded in HTTP packets by disassembling and extracting useful code from the packets. Spector [14] is a shellcode analysis system that uses symbolic execution to extract the sequence of library calls and low-level execution traces generated by shellcode. Christodorescu et al. [32] present a malware detection algorithm by incorporating instruction semantics to detect malicious program traits. Our motivation is similar, but our work is specific to network packet analysis instead of for file virus. STIIL [15] uses static taint and initialization analysis to detect exploit code embedded in data streams/requests targeting at web services. Kruegel et al. [33] present a technique based on the control flow structural information to identify the structural similarities between different worm mutations. Contrast to their work, our work is to generate signatures based on semantic and statistic analysis.

7   Conclusion

In this paper, we have proposed a novel semantic-aware probability algorithm to address the threat of anti-signature techniques including polymorphism and metamorphism. Our technique distills useful instructions to generate state transition graph based signatures. Since our signature reflects certain semantics of polymorphic worms, the proposed signature is resilient to the noise injection attacks to thwart prior techniques. Our experiment have shown that our approach is both effective and scalable.

Acknowledgments. The authors would like to thank Dinghao Wu for his help in revising the paper. The work of Zhu was supported by CAREER NSF-0643906. The work of Jhi and Liu was supported by ARO W911NF-09-1-0525 (MURI), NSF CNS-0905131, AFOSR FA 9550-07-1-0527 (MURI), NSF CNS-0916469, and AFRL FA8750-08-C-0137. The work of Kong, Xi was supported by Chinese High-tech R&D (863)Program 2006AA01Z449, China NSF-60774038.

References

1. Moser, A., Kruegel, C., Kirda, E.: Limits of static analysis for malware detection. In: Proceedings of the 23rd Annual Computer Security Applications Conference (2007)
2. Kim, H.A., Karp, B.: Autograph: Toward automated, distributed worm signature detection. In: Proceedings of the 13th Usenix Security Symposium (2004)

3. Kreibich, C., Crowcroft., J.: Honeycomb: creating intrusion detection signatures using honeypots. In: Proceedings of the Workshop on Hot Topics in Networks, HotNets (2003)
4. Singh, S., Estan, C., Varghese, G., Savage, S.: Earlybird system for real-time detection of unknown worms. Technical report, Univ. of California, San Diego (2003)
5. Newsome, J., Karp, B., Song, D.: Polygraph: Automatic signature generation for polymorphic worms. In: IEEE Symposium on Security and Privacy (2005)
6. Li, Z., Sanghi, M., Chen, Y., Kao, M.Y., Chavez, B.: Hamsa: Fast signature generation for zero-day polymorphic worms with provable attack resilience. In: IEEE Symposium on Security and Privacy (2006)
7. Chung, S.P., Mok, A.K.: Advanced allergy attacks: Does a corpus really help. In: Kruegel, C., Lippmann, R., Clark, A. (eds.) RAID 2007. LNCS, vol. 4637, pp. 236–255. Springer, Heidelberg (2007)
8. Newsome, J., Karp, B., Song, D.: Paragraph: Thwarting signature learning by training maliciously. In: Zamboni, D., Krügel, C. (eds.) RAID 2006. LNCS, vol. 4219, pp. 81–105. Springer, Heidelberg (2006)
9. Perdisci, R., Dagon, D., Lee, W.: Misleading worm signature generators using deliberate noise injection. In: Proceedings of the 2006 IEEE Symposium on Security and Privacy (2006)
10. Liang, Z., Sekar., R.: Fast and automated generation of attack signatures: A basis for building self-protecting servers. In: Proceedings of the 12th ACM Conference on Computer and Communications Security (2005)
11. Newsome, J., Song, D.: Dynamic taint analysis for automatic detection, analysis, and signature generation of exploits on commodity software. In: Proceedings of Network and Distributed System Security Symposium (2005)
12. Liang, Z., Sekar., R.: Automatic generation of buffer overflow attack signatures: An approach based on program behavior models. In: Proceedings of the Annual Computer Security Applications Conference (2005)
13. Wang, X., Pan, C.C., Liu, P., Zhu, S.: Sigfree: A signature-free buffer overflow attack blocker. In: 15th Usenix Security Symposium (2006)
14. Borders, K., Prakash, A., Zielinski., M.: Spector:automatically analyzing shell code. In: Proceedings of the 23rd Annual Computer Security Applications Conference, pp. 501–514 (2007)
15. Wang, X., Jhi, Y.C., Zhu, S., Liu, P.: Still: Exploit code detection via static taint and initialization analyses. In: Proceedings of Anual Computer Security Applications Conference, ACSAC (2008)
16. Krügel, C., Lippmann, R., Clark, A.: Emulation-based detection of non-self-contained polymorphic shellcode. In: Kruegel, C., Lippmann, R., Clark, A. (eds.) RAID 2007. LNCS, vol. 4637, pp. 87–106. Springer, Heidelberg (2007)
17. Baecher, P., Koetter, M.: Getting around non-executable stack (and fix), http://libemu.carnivore.it/
18. Szor, P.: The Art of Computer Virus Research and Defense, pp. 112–134. Addison-Wesley, Reading (2005)
19. Bania, P.: Evading network-level emulation, http://www.packetstormsecurity.org/papers/bypass/pbania-evading-nemu2009.pdf
20. Collberg, C., Thomborson, C., Low, D.: A taxonomy of obfuscating transformations. Technical Report 148, University of Auckland (1997)
21. Detristan, T., Ulenspiegel, T., Malcom, Y., Superbus, M., Underduk, V.: Polymorphic shellcode engine using spectrum analysis, http://www.phrack.org/show.php?p=61&a=9
22. Ray, E.: Ms-sql worm, http://www.sans.org/resources/malwarefaq/ms-sql-exploit.php

23. Song, Y., Locasto, M.E., Stavrou, A., Keromytis, A.D., Stolfo., S.J.: On the infeasibility of modeling polymorphic shellcode. In: Proceedings of the 14th ACM conference on Computer and communications security (CCS), pp. 541–551 (2007)
24. Rabiner, L.R.: A tutorial on hidden markov models and selected applications in speech recognition. Proceedings of the IEEE 77(2), 257–286 (1999)
25. Moore, H.: The metasploit project, http://www.metasploit.com
26. Gundy, M.V., Chen, H., Su, Z., Vigna, G.: Feature omission vulnerabilities: Thwarting signature generation for polymorphic worms. In: Proceeding of Annual Computer Security Applications Conference, ACSAC (2007)
27. Fogla, P., Sharif, M., Perdisci, R., Kolesnikov, O., Lee, W.: Polymorphic blending attacks. In: Proceedings of the 15th USENIX Security Symposium (2006)
28. Venkataraman, S., Blum, A., Song., D.: Limits of learning-based signature generation with adversaries. In: Proceedings of the 15th Annual Network and Distributed System Security Symposium (2008)
29. Gundy, M.V., Balzarotti, D., Vigna, G.: Catch me, if you can: Evading network signatures with web-based polymorphic worms. In: Proceedings of the First USENIX Workshop on Offensive Technologies (WOOT), Boston, MA (2007)
30. Pedro, N.D., Domingos, P., Sumit, M., Verma, S.D.: Adversarial classification. In: 10th ACM SIGKDD Conference On Knowledge Discovery and Data mining, pp. 99–108 (2004)
31. Brumley, D., Caballero, J., Liang, Z., Newsome, J., Song, D.: Towards automatic discovery of deviations in binary implementations with applications to error detection and fingerprint generation. In: Proceedings of the 16th USENIX Security (2007)
32. Christodorescu, M., Jha, S., Seshia, S., Song, D., Bryant, R.: Semantics-aware malware detection. In: 2005 IEEE Symposium on Security and Privacy (2005)
33. Krugel, C., Kirda, E.: Polymorphic worm detection using structural information of executables. In: 2005 International Symposium on Recent Advances in Intrusion Detecion (2005)

Analyzing and Exploiting Network Behaviors of Malware

Jose Andre Morales[1], Areej Al-Bataineh[2], Shouhuai Xu[1,2], and Ravi Sandhu[1]

[1] Institute for Cyber Security, University of Texas at San Antonio
{jose.morales,ravi.sandhu}@utsa.edu
[2] Department of Computer Science, University of Texas at San Antonio
{aalbata,shxu}@cs.utsa.edu

Abstract. In this paper we address the following questions: From a networking perspective, do malicious programs (malware, bots, viruses, etc...) behave differently from benign programs that run daily for various needs? If so, how may we exploit the differences in network behavior to detect them? To address these questions, we are systematically analyzing the behavior of a large set (at the magnitude of 2,000) of malware samples. We present our initial results after analyzing 1000 malware samples. The results show that malicious and benign programs behave quite differently from a network perspective. We are still in the process of attempting to interpret the differences, which nevertheless have been utilized to detect 31 malware samples which were not detected by any antivirus software on Virustotal.com as of 01 April 2010, giving evidence that the differences between malicious and benign network behavior has a possible use in helping stop zero-day attacks on a host machine.

1 Introduction

The ever growing sophistication of malware, especially zero-day attacks, with faster distribution and stealthier execution has forced signature based detection in an uphill battle that is difficult to win. Behavior based detection is increasingly being used by commercial software vendors with some success but is partially reliant on understanding the behavior of known malware to attempt detecting future attacks.

This research analyzes known malicious and benign samples in an attempt to exploit differences in their network behavior to accomplish accurate behavior based malware detection. The data set consisted of 1000 malware samples, including 31 not detected by any antivirus software on Virustotal.com on 01 April 2010 and 123 benign samples. The analyzed data included DNS, NetBIOS, TCP, UDP, ICMP and other network traffic. For each analyzed malware and benign sample, we collected occurrence amounts of basic network functions such as total number of DNS queries and NetBIOS query requests. Observations of captured network activity and occurrence amounts were analyzed and correlated to identify network behaviors occurring mostly in malware. We use clustering and classification algorithms to evaluate how effectively our observed network behaviors can differentiate malware from benign samples.

Given our observed network behaviors, our clustering and classification produced minimal false positives and false negatives. In addition, 31 malware samples not

S. Jajodia and J. Zhou (Eds.): SecureComm 2010, LNICST 50, pp. 20–34, 2010.

identified by any antivirus software on Virustotal.com on 01 April 2010 were correctly clustered and classified using our observed network behaviors. These results give evidence that the observed differences between malicious and benign network behavior can be useful in stopping zero-day attacks on a host machine.

The principal contributions of this research are:

1. Identification of network behaviors occurring mostly in malware usable in behavior based malware detection.
2. Discovery of novel malicious uses of network services by malware.
3. Evaluating the effectiveness of observed network behaviors in identifying malware and benign processes with clustering and classification.

This research presents early results of one perspective of an ongoing project dealing with malware behavior based on a sample size of 1000 malware and 41 benign processes. The benign processes were executed three times each for a total of 123 instances which were used as samples for our analysis. The goal of this ongoing research is a real time behavior based malware detection system incorporating several perspectives capable of detecting known and unknown malware on host machines.

The rest of this paper is organized as follows: Section 2 gives related work, Section 3 describes our data set, Section 4 presents our network behaviors, Section 5 gives our clustering and classification results, Section 6 discusses our approach and results, Section 7 gives limitations and Section 8 is conclusions and future work.

2 Related Work

The research of Bayer et. al. [3] presents a dynamic malware analysis platform called Anubis which is used to collect behaviors of known malware samples in a controlled environment. This system inputs a binary executable and records API invocation, network activity, and data flows. The results are used to report observed behaviors principally on the file system, registry, and network activity. The reported network activity only provides data on usage of protocol traffic, connections to remote servers, file downloads, port scanning and other typical network tasks. The results give direction as to which forms of network activity should be monitored closely for malicious events. Using Bayer et. al. as motivation, we analyzed and produced occurrence amounts of basic network functions which were used to aid in defining our set of network behaviors.

Malware binary analysis platforms such as Anubis [1], Malheur [13], Bitblaze [4] and CwSandbox [24] are designed primarily to run known malware samples in a controlled environment and record execution behavior. Recording is done via various techniques from API hooking to monitoring modifications and data flows in various OS components. These platforms record general network activity behavior which are reported to the user. The reports do not include sufficient detailed information to identify malware's precise implementation and use of network services making it difficult to discover novel malicious acts captured in network activity. Our research fills this gap by capturing finely grained network behavior facilitating detailed analysis which was key in our discovery of novel network behaviors that successfully detected several malware samples.

The research presented by Morales et. al. [15] analyzes a specific form of network activity behavior called RD-behavior which is based on a combination of DNS activity and TCP connection attempts. The authors found bot processes often use reverse DNS queries (rDNS) possibly to harvest new domain names. The rDNS often fails and is then followed by a TCP connection attempt to the input IP address of the failed rDNS, the authors regard this as an anomalous behavior. This anomalous behavior is successfully used by the authors to detect bots and non-bot malware. The approach in [15] was limited when the authors removed one of their defined behavior: a failed connection attempt to the returned IP address of a successful DNS query. Our results revealed an almost total absence of rDNS usage and several instances where malware used the removed behavior. Using this behavior helped raise our detection accuracy.

The research of Zhu et. al. [28] detected bots with a host-based technique based on high number of failed connection attempts. Measuring the connection failure rate of bots and benign processes showed that successful bot detection is achievable using only this metric. Measuring failed connection attempts may only be effective with bots that are totally or partially inactive while fully active up to date bots and other malware with little or no failed connection attempts may go undetected by this approach. Our research relates failed connection attempts with DNS, NetBIOS and other network behaviors creating a more robust approach to malware analysis and detection.

A broad corpus of research exists analyzing and detecting malware samples, families and categories [8,17,11,9,22,6,14,12,16,18,7,2,23]. All use different perspectives to measure, analyze and detect malware using host-based, network-based and hybrid approaches. Our research enhances the current literature by relating different specific network activities together to define network behaviors mostly used by malware.

3   Data Set Analysis

Our analysis is based on 1000 known malware samples and 41 benign samples. The benign samples were executed three times each for a total of 123 instances which were used as samples for our analysis. The malware samples were acquired by downloading the first 969 samples from the CWSandbox sample feed on 27 October 2009 [24]. The upload date was arbitrarily chosen. The set contains a broad range of malware types including: bots, backdoors, malware downloaders, keyloggers, password stealers and spyware amongst others, Table 1 lists prominent malware in the data set. Uploading the MD5 sums to Virustotal.com provided malware names from Kaspersky, McAfee and Symantec. We also downloaded 31 malware samples from the 31 March 2010 upload on CWSandbox malware repository. These 31 were chosen because their MD5 sums, listed in Table 2, were reported as undetected by all antivirus software used by Virustotal.com on 01 April 2010 and we were capable of executing and capturing their network behavior in our testing environment. The majority of our malware samples had successful network activity during the collection period connecting with remote hosts and conducting malicious deeds.

The benign test set, also listed in Table 1, covered a wide range of popular and daily used network active applications including: web browsers, FTP clients, RSS readers, social network clients, antivirus software, Peer-to-Peer (P2P) clients and standard network tools amongst others. We captured network activity in VMWare Workstation with

Table 1. Prominent malware and benign samples in data set

Prominent malware samples in data set			
Downloaders	**Bots**	**Worms**	**Hybrids**
Bifrose.bmzp	Koobface.d	Iksmas.bqs	Krap.n
PcClient.ahqy	Padobot.m	Mydoom.m	PolyCrypt.b
Poison.pg	Virut.by	Allaple.a	Refroso.qj
Turkojan.il	Zbot.acnd	Bacteraloh.h	Scar.hez
Genome.cehu	Buzus.amsz	Palevo.ddm	
CodecPack.ill			
Lipler.fhm			
Adware	**Scareware**	**Rootkits**	**Viruses**
FenomenGame	SystemSecurity.cc	Tdss.f	Sality.aa
BHO.nby	XpPoliceAV.apd		
Monderd.gen			
Benign samples in data set			
Adobe Reader	Ares	Avant	BitTorrent
Chrome	CuteFtp	DeskTube	Facebook Desktop
FileZilla	FireFox	FlickRoom	Flock
Google Talk	Google Update	IE explorer	Kaspersky Security
K-Meleon	LimeWire	Ping	PPLive
PPStream	RSSBandit	Skype	Snarfer
Snitter	SopCast	Spyware Dr.	Stream Torrent
Streamer radio	TortoiseSVN	Traceroute	TVants
Tvkoo	TVUPlayer	TweetDeck	Twhirl
uTorrent	UUSee	Win Player	Win Update
Zultrax			

Windows XP SP2 using Windows Network Monitor along with proprietary network layer monitors to record the network activity for an execution period of 10 minutes for each data set sample. The individual samples were manually executed one at a time in VMWare Workstation with our monitors collecting all network traffic and the captured data was saved to a local repository for analysis. The benign processes were installed, used under normal conditions and updated (when available) during testing.

The network activity of the group of 969 malware samples was collected between 27 October 2009 and 01 November 2009, the network activity of the group of 31 malware samples was collected on 01 April 2010, and the network activity of the group of 41 benign samples was collected between 01 April 2010 and 03 April 2010. Collecting network behavior of the malware samples was done immediately after downloading the samples to assure the samples were still active, meaning the malware would still connect with remote hosts and conduct malicious deeds producing network traffic. The vast majority of our malware samples, over 95%, produced network traffic which was the basis of our analysis.

Table 2. MD5 sums of data set malware samples not detected on VirusTotal.com

31 malware not detected on Virustotal.com - 01 April 2010	
732e014e309ffab8ed9a05198d060a0b	ce1cd380910e28092f880643ec1f809d
94004413140e2022c0880f3828a1c0ee	cbed573de18b900cd91cc9e4558fb645
bcebf381a36099f697d2e00f3ec4f26e	7a84fd3ff0aa487ae2142e7130c78d9f
2fbea182c4c7d47419b2c25d72eb64bc	6d25e4a5db130cda772e09d458afacad
8a98176d289e099ccf359aaed06daf9e	bdd7bd56d65471b594c0822dd434a84f
037629b54b5714457ff2abefdab0c349	6b24b3779730f4add8d562daa1bc0ddf
7407c24f17d7c582901623c410ab7a91	8189e6f967b612e5ee7a74981278de4a
36a256686620fa7d3b9433af19cf57a2	5cfb57eac56c8639329d9ecab7b7f4ac
cde17b3c02d6143a9c1fa22eedad65ac	fbc377f7010b6a3216f7fd330dcfe69e
2e3108689a758c629286ef552e89b858	0b15d6658f306cfea3fe20bd32c91a0d
ae7d5ad001c26bbda2f32610f28484b9	9207e79e1f2191d3d44343482ab58a4e
25181c8ed97357b52ea775bc5dca353c	2bbb004cc926a071bda327ca83bf03fb
b0c89519569ce2e310958af0e5932ed1	e73da6feae4fabd251bb19f39c1a36d3
d2ebbc7609672d46e7bb8b233af585aa	e38c4a027b5a570eae8c57de8e26fcbb
bc8aa3e072fbec4045bf94375ac53be9	018197ab7020625864e6f4ff65611fc7
5dae2c8bf87e6a9ad44e52d38ac341le	

4   Network Behavior

This research analyzes known malware and benign samples in an attempt to exploit
differences in their network behavior to accomplish accurate behavior based malware
detection. Differences in network behavior were identified through manual post analysis
of collected network traffic. The captured network activity of our data set contained
typical protocols such as TCP, UDP, and DNS but they were not always used in the
normal expected way, most notably in our malware samples. We were able to collect
occurrence totals of basic network functions and correlate together different occurrence
amounts of specific network activity to identify network behaviors which, according
to our results, occurred more often in malware than benign samples. The identified
network behaviors, defined as B_n where n is an identification number, are described
below.

4.1   DNS and NetBIOS

The Domain Name System (DNS) and Network Basic Input/Output System (NetBIOS)
provide services to acquire IP addresses when a domain name is provided and vice
versa [5,19]. Coarse-grain occurrence amounts of both protocols by known malware
has been previously shown [3,15]. Table 3 summarizes our occurrence amounts for DNS
queries, reverse DNS queries and NetBIOS name requests. The analysis revealed 100%
of benign processes and 77% malware issuing DNS queries mostly due to malware's
use of other network services, such as NetBIOS and ICMP, to acquire IP addresses for
connection attempts. The benign samples with failed DNS queries were web browsers
unable to reach third party content and P2P video and audio streamers unable to locate

remote hosts for a specific stream. Several malware samples had failed DNS queries, most were domain names of malware servers that were either not active or previously discovered and shut down. Reverse DNS queries (rDNS) were notably absent with only 2% of malware and no benign samples. This contradicts the findings of [15] which documented bots and non-bot malware performing rDNS and conjectured these queries were an essential component to establish malicious network activity. It can be inferred, from testing our samples, that the current generation of malware may possibly be less reliant on rDNS in favor of other techniques providing the same IP address and domain name related information.

Analyzing the occurrence totals of NetBIOS name requests (NBTNS) revealed 56% of malware and 4% of benign samples implemented this activity. The benign samples with NetBIOS name requests were the web browsers Google Chrome with fifteen name requests and Firefox with six name requests. Further analysis revealed the domain names used in the NetBIOS name request of Google Chrome and Firefox had first been used in a DNS query with some failing and others succeeding. The malware samples revealed two distinct forms of NetBIOS name request usage: (i) expected usage, same as benign, and (ii) performing NetBIOS name requests on domain names that were not part of a captured DNS or rDNS query. To our knowledge, the second form is a novel observation of NetBIOS use by malware not presented in previous research. Of the 1000 malware samples, 49% exhibited the second NetBIOS usage described here. We concluded this was a network behavior occurring mostly in malware and usable for detection. Based on this, we define the following network behavior:

- B_1: A process performs a NetBIOS name request on a domain name that is not part of a DNS or rDNS query.

Table 3 shows B_1 occurring only in malware, with 49%. Using online malware databases such as MalwareURL.com, we found many domain names used by our malware samples in B_1 identified as malware servers, but several other domains did not show up leading us to believe they were recently created and registered, inactive, had avoided detection, were infected hosts, or newly activated servers. We conjecture malware uses behavior B_1 in an attempt to acquire remote host information while avoiding detection by anti-malware that may not monitor NetBIOS but most probably does monitor DNS.

Table 3. Samples with DNS, NetBIOS, & B_1

Samples with	Malware 1000 samples	Benign 123 samples
DNS queries	77%	100%
Reverse DNS queries	2%	0%
NetBIOS name requests	56%	4%
Behavior B_1	49%	0%

4.2   RD-Behavior

This network behavior as originally defined [15] was primarily based on frequent usage of reverse DNS queries (rDNS) by bots. The authors defined four network behavior paths of which three included rDNS. Their results implied rDNS combined with TCP connection attempts was sufficient to detect malware and eliminated false positives by omitting the only behavior path dealing solely with DNS queries. Our analysis revealed a notable absence of rDNS and a high occurrence of DNS queries, see Table 3, many of which exhibited the omitted behavior. We conjecture better detection can be achieved by including all four behaviors from [15] redefined as follows:

- B_2: Failed connection attempt to an IP address obtained from a successful DNS query.
- B_3: Failed connection attempt to the input IP address of a successful rDNS query.
- B_4: Connection attempt to the input IP address of a failed rDNS query.

In [15] behavior path P_5 is defined as: A successful connection to an IP address used in a failed rDNS query and behavior path P_6 is defined as: A failure to connect with an IP address used in a failed rDNS query. We reduced the number of network behaviors by combining behavior paths P_5 and P_6 into one network behavior B_4. Behavior B_2 implies a successful connection should occur to IP addresses obtained in successful DNS queries, a failed connection attempt indicates something is not right and should be investigated. Malware can exhibit this behavior when domain names have been shut down or taken offline and their DNS records have not been updated or removed. Behavior B_3 has the same implication as B_2 but with the input IP address of rDNS queries. Behavior B_4 is assumed to only occur in malware. We assuem an input IP address failing an rDNS query as unreachable and should not be used for connection attempts. Table 4 shows total number of processes with behaviors B_2, B_3 and B_4. Our occurrence amounts showed 21% of malware and no benign samples with B_2 and no occurrences of B_3 and B_4 due to very low rDNS usage. These results imply rDNS may be used less often by malware in favor of other techniques providing the same information in a more clandestine manner.

Table 4. Samples with behaviors B_2, B_3 & B_4

Samples with	Malware 1000 samples	Benign 123 samples
Behavior B_2	21%	0%
Behavior B_3	0%	0%
Behavior B_4	0%	0%

4.3   UDP and ICMP

Traffic between local and remote hosts using captured User Datagram Protocol (UDP) [25] did not serve a significant role, except for DNS and rDNS, in our analysis due to similar occurrence amounts of network activity in both malware and benign. Previous research [3] has documented coarse-grain UDP occurrence amounts by malware, but does not include a comparison with benign processes. Identifying network activity behaviors in the UDP protocol is part of our ongoing research.

The occurrence amounts of Internet Control Message Protocol (ICMP) [10] activity, which focused on ICMP echo requests and replies, revealed an elevated usage by the malware samples in comparison to the benign samples. Further analysis concluded that malware was using ICMP echo requests in the same manner as the Ping network utility [20] to decide if a remote host was reachable, thus being a candidate for a connection attempt. Malware use of ICMP has been previously observed [27] but was not distinguished as a behavior frequently used by malware in comparison to benign. Our analysis showed malware never attempted connections to IP addresses not receiving a reply to an ICMP echo request and almost always attempted to connect with IP addresses that did have a successful reply. Furthermore, the input IP address of the echo requests were never part of a DNS or rDNS query or NetBIOS name request leading to conclude these IP addresses were hardwired, dynamically generated, or downloaded from a malware server. Based on these observations, we define two network behaviors as follows:

- B_5: ICMP only activity, ICMP echo requests for a specific non-local network IP address with no reply or a returned error message.
- B_6: TCP/ICMP activity, TCP connection attempts to non-local IP addresses that received a successful reply to their ICMP echo requests.

We assume the IP addresses used in B_5 and B_6 are never part of DNS, rDNS or NetBIOS activity. This assumption is supported by our observations of the captured network activity. The results of this analysis are listed in Table 5. B_5 occurred more often in benign than malware but the benign samples also used ICMP less than malware, perhaps favoring other similar and more conventional services such as DNS queries, see Table 3. B_6 was exhibited in 11% of malware and only 2% benign samples. This supports our claim that malware frequents ICMP use to identify IP addresses for connection attempts. Our observations of B_5 and B_6 are, to our knowledge, novel in the literature not being previously reported.

Table 5. Samples with behaviors B_5 & B_6

Samples with	Malware 1000 samples	Benign 123 samples
Behavior B_5	3%	4%
Behavior B_6	11%	2%

4.4   Other Network Activity

This encapsulates other less occurring activities which were considered significant since they rarely occurred in any of our data set samples or were implemented in a non-conventional way. We consider these network activities to be anomalous and not necessarily malicious behaviors. The value of recording occurrences of these behaviors is in cases where a novel and never before observed, or rarely used malicious behavior occurs in a malware sample. We encompass this idea with the following behavior:

Table 6. Samples with behavior B_7

Samples with	Malware 1000 samples	Benign 123 samples
TCP connection attempts to IP addresses never used in DNS, NetBIOS, ICMP	10%	2%
Listen connections on non-typical port numbers	2%	7%
Successful DNS queries returning local network IP addresses	1%	0%
Use of non-typical network protocols and commands	4%	0%
Behavior B_7	18%	9%

– B_7: Network activity that is rarely occurring or implemented in an anomalous manner.

Table 6 lists the amount of samples exhibiting the different types of observed network activity and B_7. TCP connection attempts to IP addresses which were not part of DNS, NetBIOS or ICMP activity were the most prominent in this group with 10% in malware and only 2% in benign. These malware, upon initial execution, immediately attempted connections to IP addresses ranging from a few to over one hundred different addresses which appeared to have been hardwired or dynamically generated. The benign sample with this activity was the video chat program Skype which connected to a server during installation.

Second most prevalent network activity was use of non-typical protocols and network commands with 4% in malware none in benign. The malware attempted connections using either FTP or SMB or RTCP. These were the only samples from our data set using these protocols except for FTP which is a typical protocol; the reason we documented FTP usage is the malware had a very small amount of FTP activity download from a remote server along with a much lager amount of TCP and UDP traffic.

One malware sample used the authentication system KerebosV5 and one other malware sample used the network command suite Andx. Interestingly, the Andx commands were attempting to authenticate and access local network IP addresses in search of a file server perhaps to host inappropriate content. Listening TCP connections using non-typical port numbers occurred in 2% malware and 7% benign samples. Malware listened on non-typical or private ports [21] such as port numbers: 19178, 24450, 25254, 27145 and 36975; benign also listened on non-typical or private ports such as port numbers: 19396, 33680, 36363 and 58480. Two malware samples performed successful DNS queries on domain names returning local network IP addresses: gogog029.100webspace.net - 127.0.0.1 and probooter2009.no-ip.org - 0.0.0.0. It is unclear if these DNS query results were modified by the malware or if these were intentionally returned by the DNS server. B_7 was exhibited in 18% malware and 9% benign, suggesting rarely or anomalous occuring network activity may be useful in differentiating malware and benign.

5   Clustering and Classification

To evaluate how effectively our observed network behaviors can differentiate between malicious and benign samples, we input the data through clustering and classification algorithms using the Weka data mining software [26]. Clustering and classification algorithms are extensively used in the literature to evaluate proposed host, network and hybrid detection approaches and are well established as accurate indicators of effectiveness and efficiency of a proposed detection approach. Our data set consisted of the occurrence amounts of network behaviors B_1 through B_7, discussed in Section 4, for each malware and benign sample. The complete data set was used for clustering; for classification, the training set contained the first 700 malware samples and 40 benign with the test set containing the remaining samples. The 31 undetected malware samples were not part of the training set. Some of the samples in the test set not found in the training set are listed in Table 7.

Table 7. Some of the malware and benign samples in test set and not in training set

Malware samples	Benign samples
BHO.nby	Adobe Reader
Mabezat.b	BitTorrent
Monderd.gen	Chrome
Poison.pg	CuteFtp
Swizzor.a (2)	Facebook Desktop
Turkojan.il	FlickRoom
VB.bfo	Kaspersky Security
VB.vr	Skype
31 undetected malware	SopCast
	TVants

Table 8. Top three clustering results with 1000 malware and 123 benign samples

Clustering algorithm	Number of clusters	True positives	True negatives	False positives	False negatives	FP rate	FN rate
DBScan	8	119	1000	4	0	0.4%	0%
Expectation maximization (EM)	4	123	988	0	12	0%	1%
Xmeans	3	123	1000	0	0	0%	0%

5.1   Clustering Results

The data set was input to the complete suite of clustering algorithms in Weka. The top three results are listed in Table 8. False positives and false negatives were determined by observing if the majority of a cluster was composed of malware or benign samples. If malware was the majority then the benign samples were classified as false positives; if benign was the majority then the malware samples were classified as false negatives.

DBScan and EM algorithms produced encouraging results with no false negatives in the first and no false positives in the second algorithm. The four false positives produced by DBScan were SopCast, TVUPlayer, UUsee media center, and TVants. All of these are video streamers whose content source comes from several IP addresses which are constantly changed and removed, making it difficult to keep up to date. This is very similar to IP addresses used by malware authors, especially in botnets [18], which constantly change primarily to avoid detection. All four were grouped in one cluster with many different classes of malware, the samples in this cluster exhibited many instances of behaviors B_1, B_2 and B_7. The main reason why the four false positives were grouped in this cluster was due to having between 3 and 8 instances of behavior B_2. In each case, we attempted to access several video streams. Many of these were unreachable and analyzing the network activity showed the failed connection attempts to IP addresses of successful DNS queries. Further investigation into these IP addresses revealed they were temporary video content servers where the specific video streams were no longer available. The IP was taken offline but the records pointing to them had not been removed from the software's database of active streamers.

The twelve false negatives produced by the EM algorithm consisted of nine malware downloaders, three of which belong to the packed.win32.krap family, one worm, one bot (koobface) and one of the 31 undetected malware samples with MD5 hash value *7407c24f17d7c582901623c410ab7a91*. Three samples: koobface and two malware downloaders were seemingly inactive having no successful connection attempts with remote hosts and only four samples exhibited at most a single instance of just one of the following behavior symptoms: B_1, B_2, B_6, B_7. The small amount of network behaviors produced by these malware led to their false negative production since their network traffic was very similar to the benign samples.

The Xmeans algorithm produced no false positives and no false negatives, with all malware grouped in two clusters and benign in one cluster. The 31 undetected malware samples, see Table 2, were correctly clustered by both Xmeans and DbScan while EM correctly clustered 30 implying our network behaviors can detect malware missed by commercial antivirus software and may be usable in stopping zero-day attacks. Overall, the clustering suggest our network behaviors are capable of detecting malware with minimal false positives and false negatives.

5.2   Classification Results

Several classification algorithms were applied on the test set with BayesNet, NNge, Random Forest and Rotation Forest producing the best results listed in Table 9. The false negative rates for all four algorithms were low ranging from 0.6% to 1%, the false positives were also very low ranging between 0% to 2%. All the algorithms had the same two malware samples, VB.vr and one of the 31 undetected malware (MD5 hash value *25181c8ed97357b52ea775bc5dca353c*) as false negatives. Both of these malware were not part of the training set, exhibited 3 or less instances of behavior B_5 with different IP addresses and had successful network activity with remote hosts whose IP addresses were acquired through successful DNS queries. The third false negative produced by BayesNet was one of the 31 undetected malware (MD5 hash value

$cbed573de18b900cd91cc9e4558fb645$) which was active, had two instances of behavior B_5 on two different IP addresses and was not in the training set.

TVants and SopCast were the only two processes flagged as false positives. These two samples were also clustered as false positives. The reason was again their failed connection attempts to IP addresses which were no longer online hosting a video stream thus producing instances of behavior B_2. Only one of the 31 undetected malware was flagged as false negative by all four of our algorithms, with one more being flagged by BayesNet. The other 29 undetected malware were all correctly classified by all four algorithms. This result further confirms the capability of our behaviors and occurrence amounts to detect malware not detected by commercial antivirus software and gives further evidence to their use in helping stop zero-day attacks. Overall, the classification results further suggest our network behaviors can correctly classify both known and unknown malware.

Table 9. Top four classification test set results with 300 malware and 83 benign samples

Classification algorithm	False positives	False negatives	FP rate	FN rate
BayesNet	1	3	1%	1%
NNge	1	2	1%	0.6%
Random forest	0	2	0%	0.6%
Rotation forest	2	2	2%	0.6%

6 Discussion

According to our results in Section 4, of the seven defined behaviors, B_1 occurred the most in the malware samples with 49% followed by B_2 with 21% and B_7 with 18%. All three are considered behaviors more likely to occur in malware than in benign processes with B_7 initially assumed anomalous and not necessarily malicious. Behaviors B_1, B_5 and B_6 are, to our knowledge, novel observations implemented by malware to locate active remote hosts for connection attempts and, in our tests, occurred more in malware than benign. Behavior B_7 is particularly interesting due to its subjective nature which can encapsulate any network activity considered significant and rarely occurring. Therefore it is easy to add activities which degrade detection accuracy. A knowledge expert is best suited to compose activities which comprise this behavior.

Our clustering results were better than expected with perfect results in the case of Xmeans, implying our network behaviors are capable of providing accurate malware detection. Our data set covered a wide spectrum of known malware and benign classes and was able to train our classifiers to correctly identify the majority of malware in the test set with minimal false positives and false negatives.

The most interesting aspect of the results was the highly accurate clustering and classification of the 31 undetected malware. The MD5 sums of all 31 samples were not detected by any antivirus software on Virustotal.com on 01 April 2010 yet our testing correctly identified them with minimal exceptions. This detection accuracy gives strong evidence that our behaviors can help stop zero-day attacks on a host machine, especially in cases where signature-based detectors fail to identify a zero-day attack.

A robust detection system encompasses several malware detection perspectives. This research has only studied one of these perspectives, network activity, in a behavior based way to avoid implementing a detection methodology dependent on malware signatures. Part of our ongoing research is to combine our findings of the network activity perspective with other perspectives to produce a more complete behavior based malware detection system.

7   Limitations

Several protocols such as ARP and SMB were not studied. Their value to enhance our detection accuracy is being analyzed and added to current results. All analysis was done in a virtual machine which forcibly excluded interesting malware samples that are VM aware and ceased to execute or masqueraded as benign upon VM detection. The data set consisted only of malware samples which are initially executed by a mouse double click. Malware packaged as a dll file, kernel system service, or non-executable were not used. We are developing tools allowing the execution of any malware sample regardless of its format.

8   Conclusion and Future Work

This research analyzes known malware and benign samples in an attempt to exploit differences in their network activity behavior to accomplish accurate behavior based malware detection. By analyzing and comparing known malware and benign processes, we have successfully exploited differences in their network activity behavior and produced accurate and effective malware detection with minimal false positives and false negatives. This was accomplished by producing a set of behaviors which occurred most often in our analyzed malware samples during which two novel behaviors frequently used by malware were discovered.

Our analysis results successfully clustered a diverse group of malware and benign process with very high accuracy and minimal false positives and false negatives. Classification algorithms correctly detected newly introduced malware samples also with minimal false negatives and false positives. Most interestingly, our data set included 31 malware samples whose MD5 sums were not detected by any antivirus software on Virustotal.com on 01 April 2010. These undetected malware were correctly identified using our analysis in both clustering and classification algorithms with few exceptions. This provides strong evidence that our identified behaviors can be used together with existing anti-malware solutions, especially signature-based antivirus software, to help stop zero-day attacks on a host machine. This research has presented early results on one perspective, namely network activity, of a larger ongoing project to develop a behavior based malware detection system.

Future work includes examining a suite of protocols for yet-to-be observed activity usable in creating new behaviors and refining our current behavior set and evaluation methodology to further increase detection effectiveness. Alos implementing our network behaviors in a real time detection prototype to measure the efficiency of such an approach including resource usage in collecting data in heavy traffic flows and precise measurements of elapsed time used to detect a malicious process.

Acknowledgement

This work is partially supported by grants from AFOSR, ONR, AFOSR MURI, and the State of Texas Emerging Technology Fund.

References

1. http://anubis.iseclab.org/
2. Balatzar, J., Costoya, J., Flores, R.: The real face of koobface: The largest web 2.0 botnet explained. Technical report, Trend Micro (2009)
3. Bayer, U., Habibi, I., Balzarotti, D., Kirda, E., Kruegel, C.: A view on current malware behaviors. In: LEET 2009: Usenix Workshop on Large-scale Exploits and Emergent Threats (2009)
4. http://bitblaze.cs.berkeley.edu/
5. http://tools.ietf.org/html/rfc1034
6. Ellis, D.R., Aiken, J.G., Attwood, K.S., Tenaglia, S.D.: A behavioral approach to worm detection. In: WORM 2004: Proceedings of the 2004 ACM workshop on Rapid malcode, pp. 43–53. ACM Press, New York (2004)
7. Gu, G., Perdisci, R., Zhang, J., Lee, W.: BotMiner: Clustering analysis of network traffic for protocol- and structure-independent botnet detection. In: Proceedings of the 17th USENIX Security Symposium, Security 2008 (2008)
8. Gupta, A., Kuppili, P., Akella, A., Barford, P.: An empirical study of malware evolution. In: COMSNETS 2009: Proceedings of the First international conference on COMmunication Systems And NETworks, pp. 356–365. IEEE Press, Piscataway (2009)
9. Holz, T., Steiner, M., Dahl, F., Biersack, E., Freiling, F.: Measurements and mitigation of peer-to-peer-based botnets: a case study on storm worm. In: LEET 2008: Proceedings of the 1st Usenix Workshop on Large-Scale Exploits and Emergent Threats, pp. 1–9. USENIX Association, Berkeley (2008)
10. http://tools.ietf.org/html/rfc792
11. Jiang, X., Xu, D.: Profiling self-propagating worms via behavioral footprinting. In: WORM 2006: Proceedings of the 4th ACM workshop on Recurring malcode, pp. 17–24. ACM, New York (2006)
12. Kolbitsch, C., Comparetti, P.M., Kruegel, C., Kirda, E., Zhou, X., Wang, X.: Effective and efficient malware detection at the end host. In: 18th Usenix Security Symposium (2009)
13. http://www.mlsec.org/malheur/
14. Moore, D., Shannon, C., Claffy, K.: Code-red: a case study on the spread and victims of an internet worm. In: IMW 2002: Proceedings of the 2nd ACM SIGCOMM Workshop on Internet measurment, pp. 273–284. ACM, New York (2002)
15. Morales, J.A., Al-Bataineh, A., Xu, S., Sandhu, R.: Analyzing dns activities of bot processes. In: MALWARE 2009: Proceedings of the 4th International Conference on Malicious and Unwanted Software, pp. 98–103 (2009)
16. Morales, J.A., Clarke, P.J., Deng, Y., Kibria, B.G.: Identification of file infecting viruses through detection of self-reference replication. Journal in Computer Virology Special EICAR conference invited paper issue (2008)
17. Moskovitch, R., Elovici, Y., Rokach, L.: Detection of unknown computer worms based on behavioral classification of the host. Comput. Stat. Data Anal. 52(9), 4544–4566 (2008)
18. Nazario, J., Holz, T.: As the net churns: Fast-flux botnet observations. In: 3rd International Conference on Malicious and Unwanted Software, MALWARE 2008, pp. 24–31 (2008)
19. http://tools.ietf.org/html/rfc1001#ref-2

20. http://en.wikipedia.org/wiki/Ping
21. http://en.wikipedia.org/wiki/List_of_TCP_and_UDP_port_numbers
22. Rabek, J.C., Khazan, R.I., Lewandowski, S.M., Cunningham, R.K.: Detection of injected, dynamically generated, and obfuscated malicious code. In: WORM 2003: Proceedings of the 2003 ACM workshop on Rapid malcode, pp. 76–82. ACM Press, New York (2003)
23. Stinson, E., Mitchell, J.C.: Characterizing bots' remote control behavior. In: Hämmerli, B.M., Sommer, R. (eds.) DIMVA 2007. LNCS, vol. 4579, pp. 89–108. Springer, Heidelberg (2007)
24. http://www.sunbeltsoftware.com/
    Malware-Research-Analysis-Tools/Sunbelt-CWSandbox/
25. http://tools.ietf.org/html/rfc768
26. Witten, I.H., Frank, E.: Data Mining: Practical machine learning tools and techniques, 2nd edn. Morgan Kaufmann, San Francisco (2005)
27. Yin, H., Song, D., Egele, M., Kruegel, C., Kirda, E.: Panorama: capturing system-wide information flow for malware detection and analysis. In: CCS 2007: Proceedings of the 14th ACM conference on Computer and communications security, pp. 116–127. ACM, New York (2007)
28. Zhu, Z., Yegneswaran, V., Chen, Y.: Using failure information analysis to detect enterprise zombies. In: 5th International ICST Conference on Security and Privacy in Communication Networks, Securecomm 2009 (2009)

Inexpensive Email Addresses
An Email Spam-Combating System

Aram Yegenian and Tassos Dimitriou

Athens Information Technology,
19002, Athens, Greece
aramyegenian@alumni.cmu.edu, tdim@ait.edu.gr

Abstract. This work proposes an effective method of fighting spam by developing Inexpensive Email Addresses (IEA), a *stateless* system of Disposable Email Addresses (DEAs). IEA can cryptographically generate exclusive email addresses for each sender, with the ability to re-establish a new email address once the old one is compromised. IEA accomplishes proof-of-work by integrating a challenge-response mechanism to be completed before an email is accepted in the recipient's mail system. The system rejects all incoming emails and instead embeds the challenge inside the rejection notice of Standard Mail Transfer Protocol (SMTP) error messages. The system does not create an out-of-band email for the challenge, thus eliminating email backscatter in comparison to other challenge-response email systems. The system is also effective in identifying spammers by exposing the exact channel, i.e. the unique email address that was compromised, so misuse could be traced back to the compromising party. Usability is of utmost concern in building such a system by making it friendly to the end-user and easy to setup and maintain by the system administrator.

Keywords: Email spam, disposable email addresses, stateless email system, proof-of-work, email backscatter elimination.

1 Introduction

Unsolicited bulk emails, or more commonly known as spam, reached 180 billion emails of total emails sent per day in June 2009 [1]. The cost of handling this amount of spam can be as much as 130 billion dollars [2]. These costs are borne by the email receivers and the enterprises in the form of lost productivity and/or taxing the network for unproductive bandwidth.

Existing anti-spam systems can be successful in combating spam until the moment spammers adapt and find a way around them. Other anti-spam systems add cost to each sent email such that spam would be economically infeasible. However until now these efforts have not seen wide scale adoption and it is believed that they will not be effective in combating spam even if deployed on a large scale. The merits and costs associated with each such method are outlined below:

S. Jajodia and J. Zhou (Eds.): SecureComm 2010, LNICST 50, pp. 35–52, 2010.
© Institute for Computer Sciences, Social Informatics and Telecommunications Engineering 2010

Email Filtering: Email filters examine emails *after* they have been accepted into the local mail system to find patterns of a spam email. The costs [2] involved with this solution include: *False negatives*, *False positives*, *Help desk running costs* for handling complaints about spam or lost emails, and *Storage/Processing costs* since i) emails have to be accepted into the local queue, and ii) have to be processed by the filters, consuming both CPU and IO resources.

Domain Name System Blacklist: Email servers consult a published list of the IPs of suspected servers and determine if an incoming email is originating from a spam generating server [3]. However, the operators of such systems are criticized of being too aggressive, listing legitimate email servers by mistake or on purpose, or lacking clear guidelines in listing and de-listing a server. Any of these actions would destroy the trust that is required to make such a system useful.

Greylisting: This is a method of fighting spam by temporarily rejecting incoming emails from a server that the mail server does not recognize [4]. Properly functioning mail servers would retry delivery of the email contrary to spammers who can not afford wasting the time to retry delivery of a failed email. The main advantage of greylisting is that the incoming email is never accepted into the local mail system.

Proof-of-Work systems: There have been proposals to attach cost to each email sent. Hashcash [9] and Microsoft's Penny Black [10] are two such systems by which an email sender would expend an amount of CPU time to calculate a computationally-expensive puzzle before an email is accepted. This, however has two implications: i) Computer processing power varies immensely between different machines. ii) Spammers have access to botnets, which can be used as computing clouds, or rather spam generating clouds. In this work, we argue that proof-of-work functions could be very effective in fighting spam; however, having challenges based on image recognition instead of computational effort would make it harder for spammers to automate email delivery.

Our Contribution: Email addresses are expensive in the sense that they are tied to a person's identity. It would be impractical for people to change their email address once it is compromised since that would entail informing all of their contacts, updating their business card and updating their web site in order to reflect the change.

IEA, Inexpensive Email Addresses, is a system that successfully uncouples a person's identity from their email address. An *exclusive* email address is cryptographically generated per sender that is used instead of a regular email address. However this exclusive email address can be easily disposed of and re-established once it has been compromised.

The system extends the use of Disposable Email Addresses (DEAs) by integrating a proof-of-work function into the standard mail protocol. The username part of the IEA system serves as a publicly known token whereby an email sender would query to generate an exclusive email address, *provided* that a proof-of-work function is solved before revealing that exclusive address. Meanwhile incoming emails are *rejected* during the SMTP session header transmission, ensuring that emails are not bounced at a later stage, something which would constitute email backscatter. IEA has been developed as a *proxy* server, relaying messages to the SMTP server once all validity checks has passed, thus making the system easily *pluggable* to existing e-mail infrastructure. Finally, the system is user friendly, since creating new disposable email addresses is easy and transparent, requiring minor intervention from the email recipient.

The rest of the paper is organized as follows. Sections 2 and 3 unravel the design details of IEA. Implementation details and experimental results can be found in Section 4. Section 5 contains a comparative study of our system against existing work. Section 6 offers a discussion and critique of IEA, while Section 7 concludes the paper.

2   Inexpensive Email Addresses: IEA

Before we delve into the details of the system, we give a high level overview of IEA. IEA makes it easy for a person to publish an email address for the entire world to use but still retain control of what is delivered to their inbox. The username of an IEA user is used as a token to be queried. An email sender would send an email to this token to establish a new and a unique email communication channel for themselves, however, the new custom email address is only revealed *after* going through a proof-of-work process.

Incoming emails are rejected with a notice containing a challenge-response function that, when solved, reveals a customized email address per email sender. The challenge is embedded in the description of the SMTP error message, which is parsed by the sending MTA, eliminating email backscatter. The challenge-response process limits the number of incoming unsolicited emails since proof-of-work is integrated into the mail protocol. If an email address is compromised, a user has the option to "Roll" or "Ban" the email address which disposes that email address and forces any incoming mails to that address to go through a new challenge-response process.

Outgoing emails that are generated by a user of the IEA system are processed by the IEA daemon to replace the original user's email address by a DEA generated specifically to that recipient. The DEA is then committed to the database of DEA-to-email mappings. Incoming emails using this new DEA are not subject to a challenge-response process, since the IEA user was responsible for initiating the communication channel with the other party.[1]

IEA is transparent to the end-users of the system in the sense that it is compatible with any Mail User Agent (MUA), without any changes needed. Essentially any mail client can be used with IEA, because the IEA daemon is a compliant SMTP server and would handle all emails and perform any required processing transparently. The only case that a user might need to interact with

---

[1] Some critics of challenge-response email systems point out the counter-intuitive process of forcing an email receiver to go through a challenge-response mechanism when the email initiator is the other party, this is why we have opted to allow incoming emails to go through when the email is *initiated* from the local system.

the system is when a user decides to "Roll" or "Ban" an email address. Currently, we have extended an open source webmail client, SquirrelMail [5], to provide that functionality to the user, however, most popular desktop mail clients, like Mozilla Thunderbird or Microsoft Outlook, can also be extended to have the ability to interact with the IEA system.

2.1   How IEA Makes Use of SMTP

SMTP is the standard protocol used by all mail servers to relay emails across the Internet. SMTP is a simple text-based protocol and has preset error codes to handle abnormal circumstances. The IEA system uses the SMTP error messages to embed the challenge inside it. The following is an SMTP session showing an email sent from `alice@example.com` to `bob@iea_system.com`. Alice has not established proof-of-work yet (the sender's MTA is signified by text in italics and the lines are numbered for demonstration purposes).

1. 220 smtp.iea_system.com ESMTP
2. *HELO smtp.example.com*
3. 250 Hello smtp.example.com, pleased to meet you
4. *MAIL FROM:<alice@example.com>*
5. 250 Ok
6. *RCPT TO:<bob@iea_system.com>*
7. 553 <bob@iea_system.com>: Hello, a custom email address has been created for you, please resubmit your email to this new email address. Please visit the following URL to access it:
http://mailhide.recaptcha.net/d?k=01G_n_x4ZFpi4AOgYj6phw bg==&c=C2HSZaHRWBC vz-9zzfqlsDsZ9Ko8NdH5SXgclfm9QQSy4jAYL T6nvOP7UrK8oMRTiS-iBmyF3_RyGBuIzm-cT w==
8. *QUIT*
9. 221 BYE

It should be emphasized that at step number 7, the IEA system rejects the email with an SMTP error code, 553 which means "Requested action not taken - Mailbox name invalid" [6], and embeds the challenge inside the description notice. The sending MTA would close the connection since it has encountered an error message, and deliver the notice to the sender. Also note that the *sending MTA never reached the data sending part*, which can be used to deliver huge attachments in an effort to waste bandwidth or to be used as an attack vector.

2.2   IEA Step-by-Step Walkthrough

Now we present a typical use case of a person sending/receiving an email to/from an IEA system user. When `alice@example.com` sends an email to an IEA system user with the email address `bob@iea_system.com`, the sender's MTA would initiate the SMTP session with the IEA daemon. The IEA daemon system would receive the following email headers:

```
...
From: "Alice" <alice@example.com>
To: "Bob" <bob@iea_system.com>
...
```

At this stage the IEA system checks if the recipient exists in its database and the sender is allowed to use this address, otherwise it checks if the alias used is a valid one by decrypting it. In this case `"bob"` is a token used to generate a custom DEA, so it should be rejected and a challenge is embedded in the rejection notice. The IEA daemon generates a new DEA as previously discussed resulting in an exclusive email address, much like the following:

```
jTYtOowmrE_omtyfMTNSWrT32gyRR-HT@iea_system.com
```

The IEA daemon then creates a URL that would only reveal the DEA after a CAPTCHA is solved, by using the Mailhide API[13] to encrypt the newly created DEA inside the URL:

```
http://mailhide.recaptcha.net/d?k=01G_n_x4ZFpi4AOgYj6phwbg==&c=C2HSZaHRWBC
vz-9zzfqlsDsZ9Ko8NdH5SXgclfm9QQSy4jAYLT6nvOP7UrK8oMRTiS-iBmyF3_RyGBuIzm-cT
w==
```

The IEA daemon then embeds this URL in the description part of the rejection notice and delivers it to the sender's MTA and ends the connection. In turn the sender's MTA delivers the rejection notice immediately to the sender, `alice@example.com`. The sender would receive a message in their inbox from the MTA, the "Mail Delivery Subsystem", stating that the email was not delivered with the subject: "Returned mail: see transcript for details".

Upon opening the email, the following message will be displayed, although the exact message may be different depending on the sender's MTA.

```
...
This is the Postfix program at host iea_system.com. I'm sorry to have
to inform you that your message could not be delivered to one or more
recipients. It's attached below. For further assistance, please send mail
to <postmaster> If you do so, please include this problem report. You can
delete your own text from the attached returned message.
The Postfix program <bob@iea_system.com>: host iea_system.com said:
553 <bob@iea_system.com>: Hello, a custom email address has been created
for you, please resubmit your email to this new email address. Please
visit the following URL to access it:
http://mailhide.recaptcha.net/d?k=01G_n_x4ZFpi4AOgYj6phwbg==&c=C2HSZaHRWB
Cvz-9zzfqlsDsZ9Ko8NdH5SXgclfm9QQSy4jAYLT6nvOP7UrK8oMRTiS-iBmyF3_RyGBuIzm-
cTw==
                  (in reply to RCPT TO command)
...
```

It must be noted that this process is *stateless*, as the DEA is not yet stored in a database. Only *after* the CAPTCHA is solved and an email is resubmitted using this new DEA would the IEA daemon commit the alias into its database. We can clearly see that the email was never accepted in the local mail queue,

(a)   (b)

Fig. 1. (a) Mailhide displaying the challenge. (b) Mailhide displaying the DEA.

since the SMTP header transmission was never completed to reach the data transfer stage thus eliminating any possible attacks or email backscatter.

The sender could now establish proof-of-work by solving the CAPTCHA that is presented to her when she accesses the Mailhide URL (Figure 1(a)). If the sender successfully solves the reCAPTCHA challenge, Mailhide will display the DEA for the sender (Figure 1(b)).

When the sender resubmits the email with the new recipient address, the sender's MTA would reconnect to the IEA daemon to deliver the email, as follows:

```
...
From: "Alice" <alice@example.com>
To: "Bob" <jTYtOowmrE_omtyfMTNSWrT32gyRR-HT@iea_system.com>
...
```

The IEA daemon would check the validity of the alias and decrypt it to reveal the original recipient of the email. The email would only be accepted if the sender information passes the validity checks. The IEA daemon then changes the email headers back to the real recipient's email address, as follows:

```
...
From: "Alice" <alice@example.com>
To: "Bob" <bob@iea_system.com>
...
```

After applying the changes to the email headers then the IEA daemon relays the email to the back-end MTA for delivery to the user's mailbox, bob. Since the IEA daemon acts an SMTP proxy and relays emails to the back-end MTA it never stores email locally, therefore extra storage is not required for the proper functioning of the IEA daemon.

If the IEA sender replies to the message it will also go through the IEA daemon, since it is configured as the default SMTP server for outgoing emails.

The IEA daemon processes the headers of the incoming email that is generated from bob to alice.

```
...
From: "Bob" <bob@iea_system.com>
To: "Alice" <alice@example.com>
...
```

The IEA daemon will first search its database for a DEA associated with alice@example.com and use that if available, otherwise it would create a DEA for alice and store it in the database. Next the IEA daemon would process the headers by changing the "From" field to the DEA that is associated with alice, as follows:

```
...
From: <jTYtOowmrE_omtyfMTNSWrT32gyRR-HT@iea_system.com>
To: "Alice" <alice@example.com>
...
```

This guarantees that when the other party receives the email, the return addresses are correct such that if the receiver is to reply then the correct DEA address is used, and the sender is not subjected to a further challenge-response process.

2.3   Rolling and Banning

An IEA user has a choice of either rolling or banning a DEA once it has been compromised. Rolling a DEA would force only the sender of the email to re-establish a new DEA by going through a proof-of-work process again. A new key (this will become clear in Section 3.2) is generated for that sender and that key is used to generate the new DEA for that sender.

Banning on the other hand would dispose of that DEA for all senders that were allowed to use it and would generate new keys for everyone using that DEA, thereby forcing all the senders of that DEA to go through a proof-of-work process. This would channelize mail communication with all parties, by having the option to only dispose of a DEA per sender, or for everyone that is using it.

3   System Design

3.1   The IEA Sub-systems

IEA is composed of three sub-systems as illustrated in Figure 2(a). A *daemon* that is responsible for mail reception, mail processing, DEA creation, and sub-mission to a back-end MTA for mail delivery. A *web interface*, which exposes the features of the system to the end-user in a user-friendly manner, and a *database* containing validated DEAs and encryption keys used to generate the DEAs.

The IEA Daemon: The IEA daemon acts as a proxy SMTP server which handles incoming and outgoing emails and processes them according to the rules in its database. IEA was designed such that the daemon would be a standalone server, as opposed to be being a mail filter that extends the functionality of the MTA.

This design was chosen for two reasons. First, having a standalone server that uses SMTP to communicate with other MTA servers would make the IEA daemon *inter-operable* with any MTA server running in the back-end. Second, IEA extends the SMTP protocol error message descriptions by embedding the challenge inside the rejection notice that is delivered to a sender's MTA. MTAs do not expose that ability through an API to developers since extending the error descriptions of a mail server is an unorthodox requirement.

The IEA daemon relays the emails that pass the validity checks to the back-end MTA for final delivery. The validity checks are performed during the SMTP session header transmission, and email destined to invalid DEAs would be rejected before the sending MTA reaches the data transmission stage. This would ensure that no emails are accepted in the local queue before the sender has solved the proof-of-work function.

Regarding incoming emails, the IEA daemon rejects all of them and a challenge is embedded in the rejection notice in response. When the challenge is solved, the new DEA is revealed to the sender and will be stored in a database when the sender resubmits the email using the new DEA. On the other hand, senders who are responding to emails that originated from users of the IEA system *are not subjected* to a challenge-response mechanism and their emails are accepted for delivery.[2] This is accomplished by generating a DEA when an email is originated from the local system that specifies a new external recipient. The new DEA is substituted in place of the user's email address in the "From" field and it is also committed to the database so that further communication with that party does not result in a challenge-response request.

The IEA Database. The IEA database contains the DEA-to-sender mapping and their corresponding keys. Since almost 90% of all emails are spam [7], storing a DEA for each incoming email would overwhelm the database in the long run. This can be used as an attack vector by generating a large number of forged email senders and targeting such a system. However, IEA generates a stateless DEA by embedding *inside* the DEA all the data needed to deliver an email. The database is only populated with the new DEA *after* a sender has established proof-of-work.

The database also contains the encryption keys used to generate the DEAs. We distinguish between two keys: i) a *master encryption key* that is used initially per IEA user (say bob) to generate all new DEAs for that user, and ii) *roll encryption keys* that get stored in the database only after the user (Bob) has decided to roll an existing DEA.

---

[2] This is useful when the IEA user wants to generate DEAs on demand, for example to register to a conference or obtain access to a news site. This allows the user to receive emails to that DEA for as long it is desired.

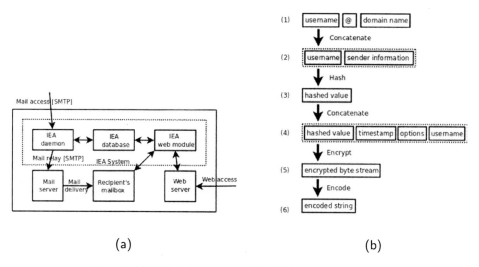

Fig. 2. (a) IEA sub-systems. (b) DEA generation flow.

The master encryption key is associated with Bob's account and is generated when a new account is *first* created for that user. The key is used to produce the initial DEAs for the conversation between Bob and external correspondents. When `bob` chooses to "Roll" an existing email address, a new encryption key (roll key) is generated for that sender only (say `alice`), a new DEA is generated using that key and `alice` has to re-establish proof-of-work (alternatively, instead of a new key an increasing counter value can be used to generate the new DEA in association with the master key). It is only at this point that this new roll key is committed to the database of DEAs already kept by Bob. Similarly, when a user chooses the "Ban" option, the IEA system generates new keys for all the senders that are using that DEA, and they are required to re-establish proof-of-work.

The IEA Web Module. The IEA web module is an interface for users to manage the IEA system. The web module was built as an extension to the popular SquirrelMail webmail client (figure omitted due to space restrictions). However, *any* MUA could be used instead and extended to implement the required features, including desktop email clients like Mozilla Thunderbird or Microsoft Outlook, since the IEA daemon is a fully compliant SMTP server.

The SquirrelMail interface implements the following features:

– *Rolling of a DEA*: A user can choose to tag an incoming email as compromised and "Roll" it. The sender would have to establish a new DEA.
– *Banning of a DEA*: A user can choose to ban a DEA thereby all parties using that DEA would have to re-establish a new DEA.
– *DEA creation*: A user of this system can create a DEA that would be used as an alias to give out to senders or to be used at e-commerce sites. Also the user would have the option to create a DEA that has an *exclusive* user, or

a DEA that allows all senders to deliver emails which is the default (this is used in conjunction with banning above).

- *Specifying an expiration date for a DEA*: This is useful for users who would like to have an email address expire after a certain time has passed.

3.2   The DEAs

A DEA that is generated by the IEA server constitutes an encrypted byte array of the data needed to validate an alias and successfully deliver the email to its intended recipient. The encrypted string is the result of concatenating the username of the recipient with the hashed value of the sender address along with the username of the recipient. The hashed value is used to verify the integrity of the alias at later stages. Each user has a master key that is used to generate the DEAs. The master key is only changed if the user chooses to "Roll" an email address, whereby a new key is generated for that specific sender thus making the old DEA invalid. Figure 2(b) describes how a DEA is generated by the IEA system.

- At first, the domain name part of the recipient email address is stripped away to get the username.
- The hashed value is created by concatenating the sender's email address with the username of the email recipient. MD5 is used to generate the hash value. The hashed value is used to check the integrity of a DEA since we need to verify that an incoming email address is a valid DEA for that specific user.
- The hashed value is then concatenated with the username of the email recipient, a time stamp, and a byte array that contains the option settings for that specific DEA. It is necessary to embed the username of the recipient within the generated DEA because the system is stateless and does not store a DEA-to-username mapping before the challenge is solved; otherwise the intended recipient would be lost. The timestamp is used to determine if the challenge is expired, by default IEA allows a grace period of four days to solve the challenge and resubmit an email using the newly created DEA. The byte array contains option settings (Table 1) that could be used to signify that a DEA is an exclusive one per user, or to verify the domain name of the sender instead of the email address, which is used in the case of correspondence with an e-commerce site.

Table 1. Option settings for a DEA

Options	Values
sender_info_type (default: 0)	0: Sender's e-mail address 1: Sender's e-mail domain 2: mailing list address
dea_type (default: 1)	0: exclusive per sender 1: allow all senders

– The concatenated byte array is encrypted using a master encryption key that was generated *per IEA user* when the user's account was first created. The master encryption key is used to generate all incoming emails per user. Only when the user chooses to "Roll" or "Ban" an email address a new encryption key is generated thus invalidating the old DEA and generating a new DEA for that sender. The encryption scheme used for the IEA system is Blowfish, however any encryption scheme could be used instead. Authenticated encryption, as discussed in [8], was investigated as a faster mode of operation but was not implemented in the current version of the IEA system.

– Finally, the encrypted form is transformed to a string by encoding it using base 64 encoding. It should be noted that we use a safe base 64 encoding that is suitable for the SMTP protocol. Since the characters '+' and '/' are not safe to use with SMTP, they are substituted with '-' and '_' respectively.

4   Implementation

The system was developed and deployed on a virtual machine instance running Linux. The test machine had 64MB of RAM dedicated to it with 128MB of swap space and was powered by an Intel Core 2 CPU running at 2.1GHz.

The prototype IEA system was built using the Python language. The standard Python library `smptd` module was extended to implement the IEA daemon. The IEA system does not require much memory or disk space since it does not accept emails in its local queue. The database to store the generated DEAs and keys was MySQL.

Postfix was used as the back-end MTA to deliver the emails to the user's mailbox and handle outgoing emails. Postfix was setup to run on the same machine as the test machine, although it could be setup to run on a separate machine.

An Apache server was used to run the webmail client. The webmail client, SquirrelMail, is a popular open source client. SquirrelMail is easy to extend and we developed the features required for the IEA system as a plug-in for it.

It should be noted that none of the components used are tightly coupled to the IEA system. Apache, MySQL, Postfix, SquirrelMail and even the operating system, Linux, can be easily replaced with similar functioning components. Although the IEA system was not explicitly designed to be multi-platform or have pluggable architecture, we did rely on standard protocols which make the replacement of components possible.

4.1   Benchmarks

The IEA daemon was benchmarked to measure how many SMTP connections would it be able to handle per unit of time. The IEA daemon was subjected to incoming emails such that it would generate a DEA and create a Mailhide URL for it as we believe that this condition would expose the daemon to the most possible load. The IEA daemon was able to process 252 SMTP sessions *per second.* It should be noted that the running IEA system is a development version, which contains debug code and is *not optimized for performance.*

For comparison reasons we subjected the Postfix server to a similar test. We configured Postfix such that it rejects all incoming emails, as the IEA daemon previously did. The Postfix server was able to process 951 SMTP sessions per second on the same machine. Of course Postfix is a high performance optimized mail server and was configured to reply with just a rejection notice for testing purposes; whereas the IEA daemon is a prototype that had to go through an SQL query, generate a DEA then encrypt the DEA inside a URL. We believe that proper optimization would significantly increase the performance of the IEA system.

While benchmarking the performance of the IEA daemon we noticed that the MySQL server was undergoing increased load. This behavior is understandable since the IEA daemon consults the database to check if the alias already exists as a legitimate alias for a recipient. However, we decided to replace the MySQL server with a lighter database system and to run the benchmarks again to see the difference. SQLite was chosen as a lightweight alternative to MySQL. SQLite is not a standalone client-server SQL server, instead the SQLite library is linked within the Python library thus the overhead of connecting to a back-end SQL does not exist. The benchmarks were performed again, and the IEA daemon was able to process 294 SMTP sessions per second. That constitutes a 16% increase in performance versus using the MySQL server. This further proves that proper optimization could be made to the IEA daemon and better performance would be achieved.

The encryption and decryption speed of DEAs by the IEA daemon was also measured. Test results showed that roughly 6950 encryption and 8720 decryption operations can be performed per second, respectively. This indicates that DEA generation has very little impact on the system as a whole. The validation speed of a DEA was also measured. MD5 was used to create the hash values to verify the integrity of the DEA. Test results showed that roughly 414900 integrity check operations can be performed per second. This also indicates that DEA validation has no impact on the system as a whole.

5   Related Work

In this section, we compare IEA with existing approaches to limit spam. The IEA system borrows some characteristics from these works, however, it refines them and adds some of its own to create a unique and more viable spam-limiting system. What particularly distinguishes IEA is that it does not generate *out-of-band* emails in the challenge-response process, it is not susceptible to a *Denial-of-Service (DoS)* attack and cannot be used as an attack vector to generate spam and/or *email backscatter.* We hope this list of desired properties will prove the viability of IEA and stimulate further research in the area.

Hashcash [9] and the Penny Black Project [10] propose the inclusion of cryptographic puzzles in the SMTP protocol to limit the speed at which spammers deliver emails. However a proof-of-work challenge that relies on computer intensive puzzles will make spammers use botnets to generate and deliver spam.[3] Another problem with this approach is the need for all MUAs and MTAs to be compatible with the protocol. The IEA system uses a human solvable puzzle rather than a cryptographic challenge. Also, the IEA system does not require that the MTA or MUA on the other end to be modified, since it relies on human effort to solve the challenge and it is delivered using the standard SMTP protocol.

Similarly, in [12], the authors propose a system in which a challenge contained inside a URL is distributed alongside one's email address, to be solved prior to sending the email. One critique of this system is that emails that lack the solution to the challenge are silently discarded, which could mean that two users of such a system would get into a deadlock as they do not get any notices about it (the authors, however, propose an alternative solution whereby all MTAs must be modified to cater for discarding emails). In contrast, IEA delivers the challenge through the sending MTA, thereby being compatible with the current mail protocol while also being instantaneous.

Mailhide [13] is a subset of Carnegie Mellon's reCAPTCHA project. Mailhide is very effective in hiding an email address from spambots that scan the web for addresses, however, once the email address has been compromised there is no way back to a safe, no-spam state. The IEA system incorporates Mailhide to deliver the challenge that contains the newly generated DEA. be directly connected to the Mailhide servers. It should be noted, however, that the IEA system could be easily modified to use *any* CAPTCHA generating component.

Rolling Email Address Protocol or REAP [14], is based on a very interesting concept called "Rolling". Rolling basically means that a user has the capability to dispose of an email address and agree upon a new one with the sending party once the current one is compromised and starts receiving spam. The problem with REAP, however, is that it requires too much *manual* intervention from both parties. Therefore what we propose is once a user tags an email address as compromised, all incoming emails to that alias be challenged and a new DEA be created instead. This would channelize the email communication such that each sender would have a unique DEA for itself.

Tagged Message Delivery Agent [15], is an open source mail system that employs a challenge-response function to reduce spam. Three main drawbacks of this system include the generation of an out-of-band email and hence the possibility of email backscatter, the storage of emails into the local queue which may be used as DoS attack vector, and finally the possibility of recovering the challenge (simply a random character array) by spambots.

---

[3] Laurie and Clayton in [11] presented an economic study of the effectiveness of using cryptographic puzzles to fight spam. In their paper they conclude that spammers will not be affected by these systems, instead legitimate email senders would be harmed the most. However, they suggest puzzles based on human effort, CAPTCHAs, as a viable solution to attaching a "cost" to emails.

A "Remailer" component has been presented in [16] that automatically creates new aliases for incoming emails and either bounces or relays emails based on acceptance criteria for that alias in order to fight spam. The Remailer system is responsible for storing all incoming emails that are undeliverable in a special mailbox until the Remailer goes through them and bounces invalidated emails. This, however, opens the system for abuse by senders with forged email addresses to send emails to non-existing aliases which in effect would be bounced by the Remailer, generating email backscatter. The IEA system never accepts any incoming emails that could later be bounced by the back-end MTA. Validity checks are performed during the SMTP session header transmission, and emails are rejected *before* the sender is allowed to transmit the actual data part of the message.

MIDEA [17], proposes a method of eliminating lookup tables for DEA management on the server side by embedding the data needed for the DEA management into the email address. The paper mainly considers limited functionality devices, as mobile phones, to send emails, however it does not delve into spam control.

In addition to the characteristics outlined above, IEA achieves a unique set of properties that distinguish it from past work. These are summarized below:

- *Stateless System:* IEA is a stateless system by avoiding storing a sender's email address at the beginning of establishing a DEA so as to conserve resources and avoid DoS attacks. The DEA is effectively used as a cookie to distinguish a sender that has solved the challenge. Only well intentioned users would go through a challenge-response process, and the DEA would be committed to a database *after* the new DEA has been used for the first time.
- *Email Backscatter Elimination:* Email Backscatter [18,19] is a side-effect of spam emails that get accepted in a mail system having *forged sender* identity then bounced by the email server back to the forged address. This happens since mail filtering checks are done *after* an email is accepted into the queue. IEA was designed to eliminate backscatter by rejecting all incoming emails. The challenge is delivered to the sender by simply embedding it inside the description part of the rejection notice of SMTP error messages.
- *Traceability:* When a DEA starts receiving spam, IEA allows the user to dispose of that particular DEA and tag it as compromised. This would make the system start the challenge-response mechanism on the compromised DEA, ensuring all parties that were using it would establish a new one. If one of these new DEAs is also compromised, that DEA would expose the spamming party since each new party has established a new unique DEA for its own channel.
- *Guaranteed Delivery:* Current challenge-response mail systems generate an out-of-band email that contains the challenge-response function in response to an incoming email. Thus the mail server could be abused to generate backscatter as described before. Also the challenge email is not guaranteed to be delivered since it is effectively an unknown server to the sending mail server. More importantly two users of such a system could end up in a deadlock, where each user's Mail Transport Agent (MTA), sends a challenge email in response of the other party's challenge email.

☆☆☆ None – ★☆☆ Poor – ★★☆ Good – ★★★ Great

	TMDA	Mailhide	REAP	Remailer	MIDEA	Hashcash PennyBlack	IEA
Proof-of-Work	★☆☆	★★★	☆☆☆	★★☆	n/a	★★☆	★★★
Rolling	☆☆☆	n/a	★★★	☆☆☆	☆☆☆	n/a	★★★
Stateless Protocol	★☆☆	★★★	★☆☆	★☆☆	★★★	★☆☆	★★★
Email Backscatter Elimination	☆☆☆	n/a	☆☆☆	☆☆☆	n/a	n/a	★★★
Traceability	★☆☆	☆☆☆	★★☆	★☆☆	★★☆	★☆☆	★★☆
Usability	★★☆	★★★	★★☆	★★☆	★★☆	☆☆☆	★★★
Guaranteed Delivery	☆☆☆	n/a	★☆☆	☆☆☆	n/a	n/a	★★★
Overhead Mail Queue Elimination	☆☆☆	n/a	★☆☆	☆☆☆	n/a	n/a	★★★
Use of Existing Mail Infrastructure	★★★	★★★	★★★	★★★	★★★	☆☆☆	★★★

Fig. 3. Summary of features per system

IEA was designed to reject all new emails and instead embed the challenge function inside the SMTP rejection notice during the mail protocol's header transmission. This would guarantee delivery of the challenge-response notice to the sender's inbox since it is handled by the MTA of the sending party and it is the only authority that can successfully deliver emails into a user's inbox without going through spam filters. Also since the email is rejected and the challenge-response function is embedded in the rejection notice, there is no fear of entering a deadlock between two users of this system.

– *Overhead Mail Queue Elimination:* Current challenge-response mail systems accept all incoming emails to the local mail queue and store the email locally until the generated challenge-response is solved. This constitutes wasted storage and could also be used to attack a mail infrastructure by *mail bombing* the mail server with numerous emails having large attachments..

IEA avoids this problem by rejecting any incoming email that is not a valid DEA, *before* the actual data of the message is transmitted.

– *Usability:* The system limits spam in a non-obtrusive way for the end-user. The system is user friendly, and creating new disposable email addresses is easy and transparent. Switching to a new disposable email address, if the original were compromised, requires minor intervention from the email recipient. Most of that burden is shifted to the sender of the email.

– *Ease of Implementation and Deployment:* The IEA system easily integrates with existing email infrastructure. IEA has been developed as a *proxy server* that operates as a front-end and only relays emails back to the SMTP server once all the validity checks have been passed, therefore making this system easily pluggable into an existing mail infrastructure.

Finally, the system was designed such that emails are kept on the sender's side as much as possible, so an email is not accepted in the local mail queue unless the sender has solved the challenge function. This would relieve the local mail system, and the administrator, from the resources needed for storing the mail in the local queue.

A summary of these properties and a comparison with existing systems is shown in Figure 3. It should be noted that some systems, like TMDA and Remailer, generate backscatter and do nothing to eliminate it.

6   Discussion and Critique of the IEA System

As previously discussed, IEA is a challenge-response system where the challenge is delivered to the sender by embedding it into the description part of the SMTP error message. Strictly speaking this does not follow the SMTP specification since the error codes were implemented to return error messages as opposed to be used in a challenge-response mechanism. However, this was chosen to overcome the problem of generating an out-of-band email or generating email backscatter in response of an incoming email. It must be noted that some mail providers also use the description part of the error code to deliver information, notably Yahoo! Mail servers [20] specify a URL to be visited in the description part of the error message in an effort to enforce Greylisting [4].

IEA incorporates proof-of-work into the standard SMTP protocol, but unlike Hashcash and the Penny Black Project IEA uses the existing mail infrastructure (MTAs and MUAs) to achieve its goals and does not require the other end to be upgraded or changed to fully utilize the protocol.

IEA uses the sender's email address that is sent during the SMTP header transmission as a token to be embedded in the generated DEA. IEA could be criticized as relying on information that can easily be forged to create this token. However, it must be noted that IEA does *not* generate an email using a forged email address which would constitute email backscatter. Instead, the challenge is immediately delivered to the sender's MTA and does not rely on the return path of the MTA or the sender to be correct: the challenge will be delivered to the sending party whether the sender is forged or not. IEA could also make use of frameworks like [21,22] to identify a sender. Although it is not strictly necessary for the successful operation of IEA, it could be used to lessen the load on IEA by identifying the sender before the IEA system process the sender information.

A critical note about IEA is the ability to sign up in mailing lists, or automated systems which might not have a human operator to solve the challenge. Users who are using the IEA system can generate a DEA for specific senders that would pass through to their mailbox without having to go through the challenge-response process, as in the case where a sender wants to send a broadcast email (say) to a class of 100 students.

The inclusion of a challenge-response mechanism in the SMTP protocol whereby proof-of-work is established before accepting emails slows down spammers crippling their operation. However, it will also slow down mail delivery for legitimate users, until they solve the CAPTCHA. Users have come to expect a near-instantaneous operation of email, although email was never designed to function like that. Email was designed to be relayed across servers until it reaches its destination without any specification in the protocol for instantaneous delivery. Some users would object to the delay exhibited by the IEA system, but we believe that users would accept the idea of a little delay knowing that their inbox would be clear of spam, and they would not spend time on filtering their legitimate emails from spam.

7 Conclusions and Future Work

In this work we proposed Inexpensive Email Addresses (IEA), a *stateless* system of Disposable Email Addresses (DEAs) that can be used to channelize email communication in order to fight spam. A challenge-response mechanism is applied to the SMTP protocol such that proof-of-work is established *before* emails are accepted into the local queue and delivered to the mail recipient. DEAs are cryptographically generated per sender and can be used to trace compromising parties.

During the design of the IEA system similar systems were studied and their drawbacks revealed in an effort to design a system that does not generate *email backscatter* or that is vulnerable to *Denial-of-Service* attacks. We believe that decoupling a person's identity from their email address would make establishing and disposing email addresses an effective mechanism to fight spam.

The system we developed uses the description notice of SMTP error messages to embed the challenge, thereby using *existing* mail infrastructure to achieve better spam control. We believe that subjecting mail senders to proof-of-work before accepting an email is better than traditional mail filters that could generate false negatives and/or false positives. A challenge-response system would stifle the operation of spammers by increasing the cost and slowing down the effectiveness of sending mass mail.

There are, however, certain possible expansions and works that can be added to the system to enhance its functionality. Currently the IEA prototype is tightly coupled to the email domain of the user; a user has to have a local mailbox on the IEA system server. A more general solution would have the ability to decouple a user's domain from the IEA system; this way any user at any domain could sign up to an IEA service and an IEA username could be created for that user that acts as a proxy and relays valid emails to the subscriber's address. This would make the system more viable for commercial deployment, providing it as a service for any email user.

Desktop mail applications could be extended to have the features necessary for the IEA system that are currently implemented by the webmail client. Having those options inside the desktop mail application would also make it easier for the users to fully utilize the system.

References

1. Messaging Anti-Abuse Working Group: Email Metrics Program: The Network Operators' Perspective. Report #11 – First and Second Quarter 2009 (2008),
   `http://www.maawg.org/sites/maawg/files/news/`
   `MAAWG_2009-Q1Q2_Metrics_Report_11.pdf` (Retrieved October 27, 2009)
2. Ferris Research: Industry Statistics (2009),
   `http://www.ferris.com/research-library/industry-statistics`   (Retrieved October 27, 2009)
3. Cole, W.K.: DNS-Based Lists: an overview (2007),
   `http://www.scconsult.com/bill/dnsblhelp.html#2-7` (Retrieved November 5, 2009)

4. Harris, E.: The Next Step in the Spam Control War: Greylisting (2003), http://projects.puremagic.com/greylisting/whitepaper.html (Retrieved October 20, 2009)
5. SquirrelMail. SquirrelMail - Webmail for Nuts!, http://www.squirrelmail.org/ (Retrieved September 15, 2009)
6. RFC-1893. Enhanced Mail System Status Codes (1996), http://www.ietf.org/rfc/rfc1893.txt (Retrieved September 10, 2009)
7. Symantec. The State of Spam A Monthly Report (October 2008), http://eval.symantec.com/mktginfo/enterprise/other_resources/ b-state_of_spam_report_10-2008.en-us.pdf (Retrieved Sepember 4, 2009)
8. Rogaway, P., Bellare, M., Black, J.: OCB: A block-cipher mode of operation for efficient authenticated encryption. In: ACM TISSEC (November 2001)
9. Back, A.: Hashcash - a denial of service counter-measure (2002), http://hashcash.org/papers/hashcash.pdf (Retrieved October 10, 2009)
10. Microsoft: The Penny Black Project (2003), http://research.microsoft.com/research/sv/PennyBlack/ (Retrieved October 10, 2009)
11. Laurie, B., Clayton, R.: 'Proof of work' proves not to work. In: Workshop on Economics and Information Security, Minneapolis, MN (May 2004)
12. Roman, R., Zhou, J., Lopez, J.: An Anti-Spam Scheme Using Pre-Challenges. Computer Communications 29(15), 2739–2749 (2006)
13. Mailhile: Carnegie Mellon University. reCAPTCHA Mailhide: Free Spam Protection, http://mailhide.recaptcha.net/ (Retrieved September 30, 2009)
14. Seigneur, J.M., Jensen, C.D.: Privacy Recovery with Disposable Email Addresses. IEEE Security and Privacy 1(6), 35–39 (2003)
15. Mastaler, J.: Tagged Message Delivery Agent (TMDA) Homepage, http://www.tmda.net/ (Retrieved Sepember 30, 2009)
16. Gburzynski, P., Maitan, J.: Fighting the spam wars: A remailer approach with restrictive aliasing. ACM Transactions on Internet Technology (TOIT) 4(1), 1–30 (2004)
17. Ochi, D.: MIDEA: Management of Disposable E-Mail Addresses for Mobile Systems. In: International Symposium on Applications and the Internet Workshops, SAINTW 2007 (2007)
18. Postfix: Postfix Backscatter Howto, http://www.postfix.org/BACKSCATTER_README.html (Retrieved September 31, 2009)
19. Frei, S., Ollmann, G., Silvestri, I.: Mail DDoS Attacks through Non-Delivery Messages (2004), http://www.techzoom.net/papers/ mail_non_delivery_notice_attacks_2004.pdf (Retrieved October 24, 2009)
20. Yahoo: 421 Message temporarily deferred - [numeric code], http://help.yahoo.com/l/us/yahoo/mail/postmaster/errors/ (Retrieved October 17, 2009)
21. Sender Policy Framework: SPF: Project Overview (2008), http://www.openspf.org/ (Retrieved October 17, 2009)
22. DKIM.org. DomainKeys Identified Mail (DKIM), http://www.dkim.org/ (Retrieved October 17, 2009)

Privacy Administration in Distributed Service Infrastructure

Nabil Ajam, Nora Cuppens-Boulahia, and Frederic Cuppens

Institut Télécom
Telecom Bretagne, 2 rue de la Chataigneraie Cesson-Sevigne 35576
LUSSI Department
{nabil.ajam,nora.cuppens,frederic.cuppens}@telecom-bretagne.eu

Abstract. In this paper, we propose a framework to administrate privacy policies in distributed service infrastructure. We define new administrative capabilities that model user preferences and specify how data owners can access to them. We investigate a distributed administration of the privacy policy where three different administrative policies can coexist and one can dominate the other. We define the data collector practices, the legal organisation policies, such as emergency service's policies, and the negotiated policy between the data collector and services providers. We finally specify how to manage these three distributed privacy administration policies.

Keywords: Privacy administration, privacy policy model, access control model, legal policy, user preferences, interoperability, SLA.

1   Introduction

Privacy can be defined as the demands from individuals, groups and institutions to determine by themselves when, how and to what extent information about them is to be communicated to others [1]. By personal data we mean any information that can be used to identify directly or indirectly a person, who is the data subject or the owner of the information. Privacy concerns raise more and more scientist's attention, especially in infrastructures of distributed service providers, such as location-based service (LBS) providers. We stress that the data controller, which collects sensitive information, is different from the service provider, which is the requestor that uses this information to offer services.

Access control models provide a scalable solution to specify privacy policies. Related works mainly proposed an extended RBAC model based on the definition of purposes and obligations [6,17,21]. They chose RBAC to integrate privacy policy because it is a widely deployed model in information systems. However, since RBAC is intrinsically not expressive to handle privacy requirements, this leads to many extensions of RBAC that handle different aspects of privacy. By contrast, we argue that the OrBAC model [8] is natively expressive enough to handle dynamic privacy parameters thanks to contexts in order to implement

S. Jajodia and J. Zhou (Eds.): SecureComm 2010, LNICST 50, pp. 53–70, 2010.
© Institute for Computer Sciences, Social Informatics and Telecommunications Engineering 2010

user privacy preferences. In [3], we have focused on the specification of the privacy policy based on the data owner's preferences. In this paper, we propose an administration model of privacy policies.

Administration tasks of a security policy refer to the specification of the privileges and rules that monitor the whole policy. For example in OrBAC policies, administration capabilities are defined through different administrative views that are responsible for specifying who can add or remove new roles or new privileges to the security policy. Usually, only the policy administrator has access to those views, so the administration is centralized. In our case study, we have three different entities that may handle administrative capabilities, namely the data owners, the data collector and the requestors. The data owners are the subscribers that the collected sensitive data refer to. The data collector is the mobile operator that collects the data, stores it and manages the privacy policy. The requestors are the service providers that need that sensitive information to offer their services, such as location-based services (LBS), or legal organisation that needs the information for security purpose or for legal interception. Each of these actors has its specific privacy requirements. We define and show how to manage this distributed administration, which is composed of different requirements defined by different entities.

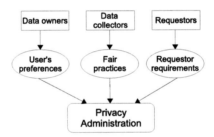

Fig. 1. The distributed administration

This paper is organised as follows. Second section introduces a concrete example to motivate our approach. Third section briefly recalls our privacy-aware approach based on the OrBAC model. Section four is dedicated to our new administration approach of privacy policies. Section five introduces related works. Concluding remarks are presented in section six.

2   Motivating Example

LBS are services that make use of sensitive location information. We can categorize them in two types: the services that use the location information computed and stored within the mobile terminal and the services that need the position collected and managed by the mobile networks. Available positioning techniques depend on the mobile equipment features and the mobile network architecture.

If the location is computed by the mobile equipment itself, a privacy policy can be managed thanks to the P3P framework. However, if the mobile organisation computes and holds these sensitive data, we proposed to use the OrBAC model to define the privacy policy [3].

Let us consider the following example. Suppose that Alice and Bob are mobile subscribers. Alice owns a location-enabled mobile device. The Alice location can be computed locally thanks to its equipment. However, Bob is only located by the mobile network, so the location is stored and managed by the mobile operator. Alice uses the P3P framework to control which third parties may access to her location. For this, she stores her privacy preferences in her user agent, her mobile device in this example, through the APPEL language [20]. And when a third party submits an access request to the user agent, it declares its privacy policy through the P3P language. Next, Alice's user agent will evaluate and compare the privacy preferences with the third party policy and if they are consistent then it discloses the location information to the requestor. Notice that the sensitive information is still under the control of the data owner until the policy check. So, the data owner has full control over her data since she stores the data until the privacy verification.

By contrast, Bob's privacy data protection is slightly different. The mobile operator controls Bob's data until the privacy verification. We need to assume that mobile subscribers trust this mobile operator. An agreement is signed between them to provide the location service. A trustworthy relation exists between them since they already signed an agreement for voice services. But this framework provides an interesting security pledge to the owners. The mobile operator naturally enforces stronger security mechanisms to protect subscriber's data compared to the mobile device. The location data can be easily stolen from the mobile device if it is hijacked, especially when users install unknown applications from Internet. The mobile operator can also prevent data owners from specifying weak privacy policies since user behaviours sometimes do not reflect their needs of privacy protection and they may ignore privacy protection when service are provided to them [2, 18]. So, we argue that an intermediary authority like the mobile operator can prevent users from disclosing excessive information. The last point that motivates our approach, using an intermediary entity, is that when Bob's sensitive data must be used for emergency cases or for legal interception. In this case, Alice's privacy policy can prohibit the access to her data even if it is useful for security purposes that can save lives. She manipulates the device's firmware to prohibit access to the location information. By contrast, Bob's preferences can be bypassed by the mobile operator according to a legal procedure such as legal interception (which is a requirement in many countries), since the operator controls such data. Users must trust the operator to allow such privacy exceptions and we assumed that in our case.

In this paper, we are concerned about the privacy policy administration in that context, namely how the mobile operator will integrate data owner's preferences within its fair information practices. The legal procedures and data owner preferences must coexist without conflict generation. Moreover, does the service requestor has the opportunity to negotiate some privacy parameters with the mobile operator?

We opted for three possible administration enforcements due to the specificity of the privacy requirements. Mobile users can subscribe to the location service, so the privacy preferences can be embedded to this agreement or administrated on the fly through the management of the privacy views. Requestors can also specify some privacy requirements. The privacy policy is a trade-off between those requirements and the operator's fair practices. Furthermore, the trustworthy relation is a relevant parameter. It impacts the administration model of privacy policies. In our case study, mobile operators are trusted enough to provide users with confidence on the manner that their privacy policies are managed. So, we can propose such a privacy framework based on these trusted entities.

We identify three cases of privacy administration enforcement. First, the operator organisation will define and enforce its policy that other actors must agree with. Second, the legal organisations, such as emergency services and intelligence departments, can bypass the operator policy and impose their policy without generating policy conflicts since they have prioritised privileges for security purposes. Third case is when the operator looks for a compromise between the different requirements. This case is modeled using the interoperability approach O2O (Organization to Organization) [10] between service provider's organisations and the operator to negotiate the resulting policy. The privacy policy is a deal between the mobile operator and the service provider based on data owner preferences.

3   The Privacy-Aware OrBAC Model

3.1   The OrBAC Model

In the Organization-Based Access Control model (OrBAC) [15], security policies of an organisation *org* are specified at the abstract organisational level through four privileges: permission, prohibition, obligation and dispensation. Instead of directly specifying security policies using concrete subject, action and object entities, these privileges are applied to three abstract entities: roles, activities and views. Moreover, every privilege may depend on some context. For example, *Permission(org, r, a, v, c)* means that the role r is permitted to perform the activity a on the view v in context c. To derive the concrete security rules, the model introduces three basic built-in predicates:

- *Empower* is a predicate over domains $Org \times S \times R$. If *org* is an organisation, s a subject and r a role, then *Empower(org, s, r)* means that s is assigned to the role r within *org*,
- *Consider* is a predicate over domains $Org \times A \times A$. If *org* is an organisation, α an action and a an activity, then *Consider(org, α, a)* means that *org* considers that α is implementing the activity a,
- *Use* is a predicate over domains $Org \times O \times V$. If *org* is an organization, o is an object and v is a view, then *Use(org, o, v)* means that *org* uses the object o in the view v.

The correspondent derived concrete privileges are *Is_permitted*, *Is_prohibited*, *Is_obliged* and *Is_dispensed*. They apply to the concrete entities: subjects, actions and objects. *Is_obliged* means that the subject is obliged to perform the action. It has two contexts: activation context and violation context. *Is_dispensed* is the dual of *Is_obliged*.

Contexts are introduced to take into account the dynamic parameters of the security policy, such as the spatial location of subjects. An OrBAC built-in predicate *Hold* is used to specify contexts:

- *Hold* is a predicate over domains $Org \times S \times A \times O \times C$. If *org* is an organization, *s* is a subject, α is an action, *o* is an object and *c* is a context, then *Hold(org, s, α, o, c)* means that context *c* holds between subject *s*, action α and object *o* within *org*.

The OrBAC model defines five types of contexts [8]:

- Spatial context: that depends on the subject position,
- Temporal context: that depends on the time of the subject request,
- User-declared context: that depends on parameters declared by the subject,
- Prerequisite context: that depends on a relation between the subject, the action and the object,
- Provisional context: that depends on the previous actions of the subject.

3.2 OrBAC Administration

The OrBAC model is self-administrated, i.e. the OrBAC model may be used to specify administrative security policies. Initially, the administration model AdOrBAC [9] consists in the definition of roles and the corresponding privileges. AdOrBAC defines two administrative views for that. An assignment of a subject to a role is modelled by an insert of an object in the *role_assignment* view. Similarly, granting a privilege to a role is modelled by an insert of an object in the *licence* view. The administrator in AdOrBAC specifies which role is permitted to access those administrative views and in which contexts.

Objects belonging to the *role_assignment* view have two attributes: *assignee* is the subject to which the role is assigned and *assignment* is the role to be assigned. Objects belonging to the *licence* view have four attributes: *grantee* is the subject (or role) to which the licence is granted, *privilege* is the action (or activity) permitted by the licence, *target* is the object (or view) to which the licence grants an access to and *context* is the condition that must be satisfied to use the licence.

Delegation model is based on AdOrBAC and aims to transfer privileges and rights from one role to another [4]. We distinguish between the partial delegation and total delegation. The former delegates some rights whereas the latter delegates roles. So, two more administrative views are defined the *licence_delegation* view and the *role_delegation* view. Objects belonging to these views have the same attributes as *licence* and *role_assignment* objects. But, they have an extra attribute, the *grantor*, which represents the subject who is creating the licence or the role. Inserting objects in these views allows a grantor to respectively delegate permission and role to a grantee. The administrator manages access to the delegation views and to the administrative views. So, a subject may delegate her rights only if some administrator grants her permission to delegate these rights by creating a license delegation (and similarly for the delegation of roles through the role delegation view).

Administrators are also responsible for managing conflict. Conflicts are solved in OrBAC thanks to the prioritised-OrBAC model [11]. The assignment of priorities is still under the control of the administrator. When a conflict is detected by the model and cannot be solved since two opposite privileges, prohibition and permission, are assigned to the same subjects and for the same actions on objects, the administrator has the privileges to specify the precedence of one policy over the other.

3.3   Privacy Contextual Management

In order to specify and manage privacy requirements, we need to model subject's consent over its personal data, accuracy of location objects and purpose for which some access is performed. We proposed in [3] to respectively model the subject's consent as a context, object's hierarchy based on the accuracy of objects, the purpose as a user-declared context and provisional obligation following the access to some sensitive information. Also, we propose to add a current state context and an enhanced spatial context.

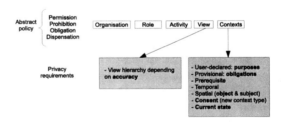

Fig. 2. Contextual privacy management in the OrBAC model

The idea behind our proposal is to include the subject's privacy preferences into the contexts of the security policy of the organisation. The result is one policy for the access control and the privacy management.

A new context type, called consent, is used to model if the object owner gives its consent to the subject, who requests the access to that object. Users store their consent preferences in the *consent_preference* view. Each object in this view corresponds to a particular data owner preference and has three attributes: *Requestor*, who is the subject who requests the access to the object, *Target*, which is the requested object, and *NeedConsent*, which is a Boolean parameter and if its value is *true* so the consent is needed. The user consent context is specified as follows:

$Rule_{consent}$: $\forall org \in Org, \forall s \in S, \forall \alpha \in A, \forall o \in O, \forall v \in V, \forall cp \in O,$
$Hold(org, s, \alpha, o, Consent\_context) \leftarrow Use(org, cp, Consent\_preference) \wedge$
$Requestor(cp, s) \wedge Target(cp, v) \wedge Use(org, o, v) \wedge NeedConsent(cp)$

Then, we suggested that private objects, of each data owner, have different accuracy levels. A private object has four attributes: *data-owner, longitude, latitude* and *accuracy*. A hierarchy is established between the root view, which contains the collected private data, and sub-views consisting of derived objects based on different accuracies. Those accuracies are defined by the data owner, so she can define different privacy preferences based on the accuracy of the object. The accuracy is specified by the couple *(anonymity level, k)*. *Anonymity level* defines the accuracy of the identity attribute of location information. However, k determines the accuracy of the location attributes, which are the longitude and the latitude. So, the operator can apply *k-anonymity* algorithms ([12], [16] and [14]) to derive the longitude and the latitude of the derived objects. The issue of choosing the optimal algorithm is out of the scope of this work.

We modeled the purpose of the access request by a user-declared context. Each data owner can create purpose objects to specify the purposes for which access to private objects are allowed. The purpose objects are grouped in a *Purpose* view. Each purpose object has two attributes [8]. *Recipient* defines who takes advantage of the declared purpose (a service provider in our case), and *declared_purpose* associates a purpose value with the declared purpose object. Purpose values range over the purpose value domain *PV*. On the other hand, the service provider declares the purpose to be provided. So, *user_declared* is a function over the *PV* domain. It returns the value of the context entered by the service provider.

$Rule_{purpose}$ $\forall org \in Org, \forall s \in S, \forall \alpha \in A, \forall o \in O, \forall po \in PO, \forall pv \in PV,$
$Hold(org, s, \alpha, o, user\_declared(pv)) \leftarrow Use(org, po, Purpose) \wedge Recipient(po, s)$
$\wedge Declared\_purpose(po, pv)$

That is, in organisation *org*, subject s performs action α on object o in the user declared context *user_declared(pv)*, if there is a purpose object *po* used in view *Purpose* by organisation *org* such that s is the recipient associated with *po* and *pv* is the declared purpose associated with *po*.

Provisional obligations [5] are introduced to oblige subjects to perform some action following its access to the location information. We need obligations to enforce privacy principles of accountability. So, an obligation may be automatically triggered as a counterpart of the access to some private information. The obligation is expressed thanks to two types of contexts *context_activation* and *context_violation*:

$Obligation(org, r, a, v, context\_activation, context\_violation)$

meaning that subjects empowered in role r are obliged to perform actions implementing activity a on objects used in view v when *context_activation* is activated. This actually corresponds to an organizational obligation. Concrete obligations that apply to subjects, actions and objects are derived when *context_activation* is activated. If subjects actually do not perform the obliged actions on the objects before *context_violation* is activated, then the obligation is violated. See [5] for more details about expression and management of obligations in the OrBAC model.

The *current state context* is used for location privacy policy when the data owner allows service provider to access her location only if she initiated a call or a session data with it. It is necessary to evaluate the current state in this context. The current state indicates if the user has initiated a call or a session to the service provider or not. We assume that *preferred-states* view contains data owner's preferences regarding authorized current states. The data owner specifies its preference by adding new entry to that view. Objects belonging to that view have three attributes: *calling, state-type* and *called.*

Physical and logical spatial contexts are relevant features for privacy policy. In addition to using it to locate the subject who asks for an access, spatial contexts are also useful to locate objects. As suggested by [13], we extend the semantic of spatial context to include the possibility to consider the object positions. The predicate *Is_within* determines if a given object or subscriber is within a location area or not. *Is_within* is a predicate over the domains $O \times LA$, where LA is a set of *location areas*. So, *Is_within(o, la)* means that the object o is within the location area *la*. The spatial context can now be defined using this new predicate.

Rule$_{SpatialObject}$ $\forall org \in Org, \forall s \in S, \forall \alpha \in A, \forall o \in O, \forall la \in LA$
$Hold(org, s, \alpha, o, position(la)) \leftarrow Is\_within(o, la)$

4   The Privacy Distributed Administration

We propose in this section three administration enforcement approaches of the privacy policies. Before, we shall present the new administrative views related to the management of these privacy policies. Based on privacy principles, the owners would have access to these views to specify their privacy preferences. However, this is actually not the case for the two first approaches. In the first case, the dominant operator policy is deployed and the mobile subscribers delegate all privacy administrative tasks to the operator. This alternative ensures a consistent privacy policy with minimal policy updates. We model this alternative through regular administrative tasks: *role assignment, licence definition* and delegation. The characteristic of this alternative is the delegation of the management of the privacy administrative views to the operator. When the mobile subscriber signs an SLA with the operator, it implicitly delegates its rights to the operator. By doing so, the operator can define an optimal privacy policy by enabling or disabling privacy contexts. The operator can offer premium services based on the level of the privacy. This will increase its productivity (for example, it offers a cheaper service to subscribers who accept to be located by advertisers).

The second alternative states that there are prioritised policies. Our objective is to assign a higher priority to the policy defined by legal organisations, for legal interception. This case is useful to enforce security laws that override other privacy requirements. All mobile operators should authorize such conflicts, so we propose a conflict management solution based on the prioritised-OrBAC model [11] to manage conflicts when third parties override user's preferences.

The third alternative proposes an enhanced management of the privacy preferences. Privacy preferences are propagated to the service provider. The established SLA between the mobile subscriber and the operator includes privacy preferences and how the requestors must protect the sensitive data. For example, if the data owner specifies that purpose context must be declared before accessing the location information, this preference must be propagated to the service provider organisation. When another requestor asks for location information from the service provider, the purpose context will be checked. This alternative provides a single privacy policy definition that can be propagated to the service provider. So, it offers the simplest way for data owners to define a universal privacy policy that is enforced by all the interoperable organisations. For this purpose, we use the O2O approach [10]. So, O2O must be supported by the service providers to allow this generalised privacy protection.

4.1 Privacy Administrative Views

Our privacy policy model is mainly based on the definition of contexts. The operator organisation, which enforces privacy preferences of its subscribers, has to administrate the access to those views. In this section, we list the views related to the privacy preferences. Access to these views is controlled by the OrBAC model itself.

Definition *Privacy-administrative views*
Data owners' preferences are implemented in the privacy-aware OrBAC thanks to the views:
- Consent_preference: is responsible for storing if a consent is needed or not,
- Purpose: contains the available purposes that can be declared,
- Preferred-states: contains the preferred states of the connection between the requestor and the data owner at the moment of the access request,
- Spatial_preferences: contains the location areas where data owners can be located.

Logically, data owners have the full privileges over those views when they act in the *owner* role. We define the *management* activity allowing them to add, insert, modify or suppress objects on these privacy administrative views.

Rule$_{preferenceAdministration}$
$Permission(org, owner, management, Consent\_preference, consent\_owner)$
$Permission(org, owner, management, Purpose, subscription)$
$Permission(org, owner, management, Preferred\_states, subscription)$
$Permission(org, owner, management, Spatial\_preferences, default)$
where the *consent_owner* and the *subscription* contexts are defined as follows:
$\forall org \in Org, \forall s \in S, \forall s' \in S, \forall \alpha \in A, \forall o \in O, \forall position \in O, \forall po \in PO,$
$Hold(org, s, \alpha, o, consent\_owner) \quad \leftarrow \quad use(org, o, Consent\_preference) \wedge$
$Target(o, position) \wedge Data\text{-}owner(position, s)$
$Hold(org, s, \alpha, po, subscription) \leftarrow Use(org, po, Purpose) \wedge Recipient(po, s') \wedge$
$Subscribed(s, s')$

consent_owner context is triggered if the consent object *o* belongs to the privacy view *consent_preference* and it has the attribute *position* as target. This position is owned by *s*, who is the data owner.

  subscription context is triggered when a subject *s* performs action α on a purpose object *po* and if this purpose object *po* has *s'* as a recipient and where *s'* is subscribed to *s*. This is represented by the application-dependent predicate *Subscribed*.

  On the other hand, data owners have the right to modify their locations. Precisely, they can define several accuracies of their locations to define different privileges to service providers depending on the location accuracy. This is modeled as follows:

$Permission(org, owner, modify, location, owning)$

owning is a provisional context defined as:

$\forall org \in Org, \forall s \in S, \forall \alpha \in A, \forall o \in O$

$Hold(org, s, \alpha, o, owning) \leftarrow Data\text{-}owner(o, s) \wedge Consider(org, \alpha, modify)$
$\wedge Empower(org, s, owner)$

It means that in organisation *org* the subject *s* performs α, which is considered a *modify* activity, on the object *o* only if *s* is *owning* the sensitive object. The data owner can modify only the *Accuracy* attribute of the location. Then, the operator will apply the obfuscation algorithms to compute the new *Identity*, *Longitude* and *Latitude* attributes. Note that *Data-owner* is an attribute of the location data.

4.2   First Case: Dominance of the Mobile Operator Policy

When users subscribe to a location service, an agreement is established between them and the operator. The latter, which is the data collector, proposes its fair practices. They include the privacy policy that will be enforced by the mobile operator. In other terms, that policy specifies how privacy contexts are managed by the data controller. If the user accepts this management, she delegates the contextual management of her privacy policy to the operator. The mobile operator organisation defines its access control policy based on its privacy fair practices without the intervention of data owners. The data owner tasks are implicitly delegated to the data controller when the agreement is established between them. To specify this procedure, we define first the delegation privilege given to the owners then we specify the licence delegation. The owners are permitted to delegate their rights to the mobile operator. It is ensured by the next privilege:

$Permission(org, owner, delegate, licence\_delegation, default)$

That is in the organisation *org*, subjects who act in the *owner* role have the right to *delegate* licences in the default context.

  The *operator* organisation can be divided into several departments, each of them being responsible for providing one service, such as the location service. Let *administrator_location* be the administrator role of the location service department. When owners sign an SLA with the operator, the following delegations are performed transparently. For example, the permission derived from the delegation on the *Purpose* view is specified by:

Rule$_{delegation Purpose}$
$Permission(operator, administrator\_location, management, Purpose, default)$
$\leftarrow use(L, licence\_delegation) \wedge grantor(L, data\text{-}owner) \wedge privilege(L, manage$-
$ment) \wedge target(L, Purpose) \wedge grantee(L, administrator\_location)$
That is, the *administrator_location* is permitted to perform the *management* activity on the *Purpose* view if there is a licence *L*, belonging to the *licence_delegation*, where the grantor is the *data-owner* role, the target is the *Purpose* view and the grantee is the *administrator_location*.

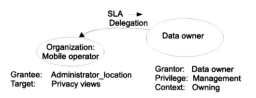

Fig. 3. Privacy policy delegation

Similarly, data owners delegate to the data collector the management of other privacy views, *Consent_preference*, *Preferred-states* and *Spatial_preferences*, when they subscribe to the location service of the operator. The operator provides several privacy packages to the users. Each package defines how the user privacy will be managed and which contexts will be activated.

For example, when the user delegates the management of the *Consent_preference* view to the *administrator_location*, the data owner will no longer be notified for its consent. The mobile operator can fix consent to *false* by default. However, the management of the *Spatial_preferences* by the mobile operator is useful since it can reuse its existing location areas without defining new ones according to subscriber preferences (its existing location areas are zone areas used for the mobility management of the voice service).

4.3 Second Case: Prioritised Third Party Policy

Some legal organisations have the right to access sensitive information and to override the operator policy and user preferences. But to be effective, operator organisations have to define how and in which cases that policies are prioritised. Let *legal_org* be the role of legal organisations. Operator assigns those organisations to that role thanks to the rule:
Rule$_{role\_assignment}$
$Use(mobile\text{-}operator, legal\_org, role\_assignment)$
Data collector shall define the contexts when those organisations are allowed to enforce their policies. Two contexts correspond to this situation: *legal interception* and *emergency*. The former represents the case where there is a legal decision made by a court. The requestor should justify that decision before accessing the sensitive information. The *emergency* state requires an immediate

access to the sensitive information. The proof of emergency can be delayed after the access since the location information can be used for example to save lives or prevent unwanted effects. *Emergency* is a provisional context because it implies an obligation to be fulfilled by the legal organisations after accessing private data. The obligation consists of a proof of the *emergency*, such as voice records of an emergency call. Thanks to the **Rule**$_{licence}$, the *administrator_ location* adds the *legal* licence:

$Permission(mobile\text{-}operator, legal\_org, read, location, emergency)$ $\leftarrow$
$use(mobile\text{-}operator, legal, licence)$ $\wedge$ $authority(legal, mobile\text{-}operator)$ $\wedge$
$grantee(legal, legal\_org) \wedge privilege(legal, read) \wedge target(legal, location) \wedge$
$context(legal, emergency)$

That is the providers that act in *legal_ org* role, can read the objects belonging to the *location* view in the *emergency*. A similar rule applies to manage the *legal interception* context.

This latter permission can introduce conflicts with the data owner preferences. For example, suppose that *Bob* is a privacy fundamentalist who refuses to let any requestor read its location information. The OrBAC model derives the privilege:

$Prohibition(mobile\text{-}operator, service\text{-}provider, read, Bob\text{-}location, default)$

That is all subjects assigned to the *service-provider* role are prohibited to *read* objects in *Bob-location* view. This will lead to a conflict between the privileges given to the legal organisations and the data owner preferences. We propose to manage such conflicts through the Prioritised OrBAC model [8]. The strategy to solve conflicts in OrBAC is the assignment of priorities to security rules. Privileges with higher priority take precedence over the other security privileges. We first consider a set Π of priority levels associated with a partial order relation $\prec$. The OrBAC model is then enriched by the following predicates. $O - Permission(org, r, a, v, c, p)$ and $O - Prohibition(org, r, a, v, c, p)$ define an organization permission or prohibition respectively and are associated with a priority p. The legal organisations have a policy that overrides the data owner preferences and take precedence over the mobile operator policy itself.

Let Π be $\{p1, p2\}$, the set of priority levels. In the prioritised OrBAC, privacy fundamentalist preferences are expressed as follows:

$\forall r \in R, \forall a \in A,$
$O - Prohibition(mobile\text{-}operator, r, a, fundamentalist\text{-}location, default, p1)$

This privilege prohibits any role to access their location information. However, the *legal-organisation* policy has to override such preferences. The following privilege defines their policy:

$\forall a \in A, \forall v \in V$
$O - permission(mobile\text{-}operator, legal\text{-}organisation, a, v, emergency, p2)$

By applying the separation constraints and the potential conflict condition, there is a conflict between previous rules. To prevent such case, priorities will be: $p1 \prec p2$.

The priority assignment is ensured by the administrator. When a legal organisation specifies its policy, the mobile operator shall accept it but it replaces privileges predicates by adding the priority component which is higher than the priorities assigned to data owners.

4.4   Third Case: Policy Negotiation through the O2O Approach

In this section, we will use the interoperability approach to allow the mobile operator to negotiate the access control policy of the location information with service providers based on the privacy preferences of the data owners. We will consider that data owners are the managers of Virtual Private Organizations (VPOs). Each VPO controls the sensitive information of one data owner. As for the first case, the service level agreement (SLA) signed between users and the mobile operator will be used. It guides how the interoperability is controlled.

O2O Basis. O2O is based on virtual organisations. When an organisation aims to cooperate with another organisation, it creates a VPO. Each organisation, that needs to interoperate with other organisations, has to manage the access control and has to administrate its VPO. So, the administration of a VPO is totally decentralized [7].

First, in O2O we mention that there are three kinds of organisations:

- *O_ grantor*: it is the organisation that owns the resource. We name its policy the local policy,
- *O_ grantee*: it is the organisation that requires resource access,
- *VPO*: it is the organisation that administrates the interoperability policy between two organisations. The VPO controls the privileges of the O_grantee when accessing O_grantor resources.

Always, the organisation that provides the resource is the one that administrates the security policy of the VPO. This represents its authority space. We differentiate between the authority and the managing spaces:

- Authority space: an *O_ grantee* organisation is in the authority space of another *O_ grantor* organisation if the security policy, enforced by the *O_ grantee*, is defined and administrated by the O_grantor,
- Managing space: by default, the *O_ grantor* organisation manages its interoperability policy but it can delegate this task to another entity. So the managing space includes the entities that manage the interoperability policies of an organisation.

Assigning subjects to roles, actions to activities and objects to views, must comply with the following constraints to preserve the *O_ grantor* control:

- The subjects belong to the *O_ grantee* organisation. Thus, the VPO is defined to control the access of subjects, which belong to *O_ grantee*, and require resources from *O_ grantor*,
- The objects belong to the *O_ grantor* organisation,
- The actions are under the control of the organisation that provides the access. This organisation is the *O_ grantor*, but *O_ grantee* can initiate them [7].

The goal of the VPO is to extend the authority of the grantor organisation to resources that need interoperability with other organisations. So, the security

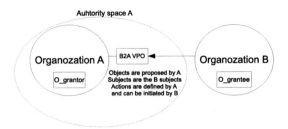

Fig. 4. The O2O approach

policy of the VPO is derived from the local policy of the O_grantor. This policy will manage the access requests coming from other organisations, named *O_grantee*. Since OrBAC enables the definition of hierarchies, the VPOs can be seen as sub-organisations of the *O_grantor*.

Proposed Interoperability Approach for Distributed Privacy Policy Management. From the point of view of the operator, each subscriber can be seen as an organisation, called subscriber organisation. We argue that the mobile operator is the central trusted entity that manages all subscribers' policies because it holds the sensitive information of its subscribers. Each subscriber organisation will create a VPO for each service provider. Service providers are the organisations that require the access to the VPOs of the subscriber organisations.

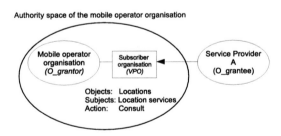

Fig. 5. Management of the subscriber organisation within the operator organisation

According to the O2O approach, the O_grantor is the operator organisation and the O_grantee is the service provider. Each data owner constitutes its own VPO. It defines its privacy policy thanks to the privacy administrative views defined before. The operator also specifies the interoperability policy of that user thanks to the SLA signed with her when she subscribes to the location service. It is a decentralised manner to define the privacy policy. However, the management of the VPOs, belonging to the subscribers of the organisation, is centralized since the operator is the central entity (it is a trusted one).

Policy Propagation and VPO Hierarchy. We stressed the fact that the policies of the VPOs are deduced from the local policy of the *O_grantor*, which is the mobile operator in our case. This means that the dominant policy, which is the local policy that we specified in the first administration, is the root policy of those VPOs. A VPO encompasses the privacy preferences of one mobile subscriber according to the privacy package fixed by the SLA. When, the service provider, which is the *O_grantee*, will access the VPO, it has to enforce the policy of this VPO. By this manner, when another requestor connects to the service provider organisation, the privacy policy of the subscriber will be applied to it. So, it is propagated to the *O_grantee*. The first administration and O2O approach cooperate to spread user preferences.

The definition of a hierarchy of VPOs simplifies the management of the VPOs of the data owner and the specification of the SLA agreement. The data owner will define common privacy preferences within the root VPO, say data_ownertoProvider that is derived from the local policy. The remaining privacy parameters, which depend on the service provider organisation (and are based on the SLA), will be entered to a dedicated VPO, which is a sub-VPO of that data_ownertoProvider. So, the data owner specifies a fine-grained privacy policy for those sub-VPOs.

For example, the data owner can define different accuracies for sensitive data whereas other policy parameters, such as consent requirement and purpose specification, are the same for all service providers. Let Alice be a data owner within the operator organisation. She has three different privacy policies depending on the service provider a, b or c. So, Alice's root VPO has three sub-VPOs allowing the data owner to define different data accuracies depending on service providers.

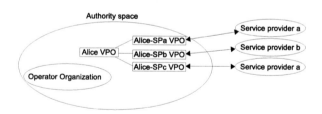

Fig. 6. VPOs hierarchy

This approach simplifies the spreading of the privacy requirements thanks to O2O. By contrast, related works fail to propose a complete framework to propagate user's preferences. In next section, we compare our administration proposal to related works.

5   Related Works

Existing privacy models and languages focused on the definition of the privacy components and how they are expressed but fail to propose a distributed administration model to allow the interoperation between user preferences, data collector practices and legal interception.

The Platform for Privacy Preferences (P3P) [19] is a declarative language that allows web sites specify the fair information practices. The web sites indicate through P3P which personal information is collected and how it will be used. The privacy policy can be attached to some web resources, like web pages and cookies. User agent will compare the P3P privacy policy to client preferences and decides about the access of web sites to client data. P3P defines a standard base data schema, which is a set of data elements that all P3P user agents should understand [19]. P3P defines also a vocabulary for defining privacy practices and statements. It allows essentially web sites to publish their privacy practices in both machine and human readable formats that can be treated by user agents. The ultimate goal of P3P is the automation of the decision in client side through P3P user agent instead of reading privacy policy at every site's visit. It does not provide means to negotiate user preferences and fair information practices. User agent, on behalf of users, uses the P3P Preference Exchange Language (APPEL) [20] to compare user preferences with the fair information practices of web sites. A user can express her preferences in a set of preference-rules, known as ruleset. So, user agent can run the semi-automated or automated decision about the privacy policy from P3P enabled web sites. User agent could be Web browsers, browser plug-ins or proxy servers. The policy evaluation is made by the user agent locally, so the approach does not consider the distributed administration tasks neither a whole policy that includes web site's practices and the user's preferences.

Qui Ni et al. proposed RBAC extensions to incorporate constraints and conditions that are related to privacy. They define a family of privacy-aware RBAC (P-RBAC) models. Privacy policies are expressed thanks to permission assignments. Those permission assignments differ from permissions in RBAC because of the presence of new components: purposes and conditions of the access. A customized language, LC_0, was proposed to allow the definition of conditions. A privacy permission explicitly defines: the intended purposes of the action, under which conditions, and what obligations have to be performed after the access. This work also develops conflict analysis algorithms to detect conflicts among different permission assignments. So, the three main extensions are: purpose component, obligation definition and a dedicated language for conditions. The privacy permission assignment is modelled through privileges, which have the general form: *role* × *action* × *data* × *purpose* × *conditions* × *obligation*.

In our work, we reason differently about contexts. We explicitly define several types of contexts that belong to different administrative privacy views. We proposed also a distributed administration to take into account operator and requestor requirements. To our best knowledge, these issues were not addressed before.

6   Conclusion

In this paper, we proposed an administration framework of privacy policies. We identified three cases where a privacy policy is administrated differently. The resulting administration is distributed since requirements are issued by different entities. The three alternatives are not mutually exclusive. It means that the data collector can deploy all of them simultaneously. Each of them provides precise functionalities and cooperates to provide all privacy needs.

In this paper, we assumed that owners trust the mobile operator since there is already an agreement between them. We should investigate the case where there is no agreement, and if the data owners can sign an SLA on the fly to define how their privacy preferences will be managed. The specification of the SLA is planned in future work.

References

1. 3rd Generation Partnership Project: Open Service Access; Application Programming Interface (API); Part 3: Framework, 3GPP TS 29.198-3
2. Acquisti, A., Grossklags, J.: Privacy Rationality in Individual Dicision Making. IEEE Security and Privacy 1(1), 26–33 (2005)
3. Ajam, N., Cuppens, N., Cuppens, F.: Contextual Privacy Management in Extended Role based Access Control Model. In: The Proceedings of the DPM workshop, DPM-ESORICS, Saint-Malo, France (September 2009)
4. Ben Ghorbel-Talbi, M.: Decentralized Administration of Security Policies, PhD thesis, Télécom Bretagne (2009)
5. Ben Ghorbel-Talbi, M., Cuppens, F., Cuppens-Boulahia, N., Bouhoula, A.: An Extended Role-Based Access Control Model for Delegating Obligations. In: Fischer-Hübner, S., Lambrinoudakis, C., Pernul, G. (eds.) Trust, Privacy and Security in Digital Business. LNCS, vol. 5695, pp. 127–137. Springer, Heidelberg (2009)
6. Byun, J., Bertino, E., Li, N.: Purpose Based Access Control of Complex Data for Privacy Protection. In: Symposium on Access Control Models and Technologies (SACMAT), Stockholm, Sweden, pp. 102–110 (2005)
7. Coma, C.: Interopérabilité et Cohérence de politiques de sécurité pour les Systèmes Auto-organisant, PhD thesis, Télécom Bretagne (2009)
8. Cuppens, F., Cuppens-Boulahia, N.: Modeling Contextual Security Policies. International Journal of Information Security 7(4), 285–305 (2007)
9. Cuppens, F., Miège, A.: An Administration Model for Or-BAC. International Journal of Computer Systems Science and Engineering 19(3), 151–162 (2004)
10. Cuppens, F., Cuppens-Boulahia, N., Coma, C.: O2O: Virtual Private Organizations to Manage Security Policy interoperability. In: Bagchi, A., Atluri, V. (eds.) ICISS 2006. LNCS, vol. 4332, pp. 101–120. Springer, Heidelberg (2006)
11. Cuppens, F., Cuppens-Boulahia, N., Ben Ghorbel, M.: High Level Conflict Management Strategies in Advanced Access Control Models. Electronics Notes in Theoretical Computer Science, vol. 186, pp. 3–26. Elsevier, V., Amsterdam (2007)
12. Duckham, M., Kulik, L.: Location Privacy and Location-aware Computing. In: Dynamic and Mobile GIS: Investigating Change in Space and Time, pp. 34–51. CRC press, Boca Raton (2006)
13. Gabillon, A., Capolsini, P.: Dynamic Security Rules for Geo Data. In: Garcia-Alfaro, J., Navarro-Arribas, G., Cuppens-Boulahia, N., Roudier, Y. (eds.) Data Privacy Management and Autonomous Spontaneous Security. LNCS, vol. 5939, pp. 136–152. Springer, Heidelberg (2009)

14. Gedik, B., Liu, L.: Protecting Location Privacy with Personalized k-Anonymity: Architecture and Algorithms. IEEE Transactions on Mobile Computing 7(1), 1–18 (2008)
15. Abou El Kalam, A., El Baida, R., Balbiani, P., Benferhat, S., Cuppens, F., Deswarte, Y., Miège, A., Saurel, C., Trouessin, G.: Organization Based Access Control. In: Proceedings of the 4th International Workshop on Policies for Distributed Systems and Networks (Policy 2003), Como, Italy (June 2003)
16. Krumm, J.: A Survey of Computational Location Privacy. Journal: Personal and Ubiquitous Computing 13(6), 391–399 (2008)
17. Ni, Q., Trombetta, A., Bertino, E., Lobo, J.: Privacy-aware Role Based Access Control. In: 12th ACM symposium on Access control models and technologies, Session Privacy management, pp. 41–50 (2007)
18. Spiekermann, S., Grossklags, J., Berendt, B.: E-Privacy in Second Generation E-Commerce: Privacy Preferences versus Actual Behaviour. In: Proceedings of the ACM Conference Electronic Commerce (EC 2001), Florida, USA, pp. 38–47 (October 2001)
19. World Wide Web Consortium (W3C), The Platform for Privacy Preferences 1.0 (P3P) Specification (April 2002)
20. World Wide Web Consortium (W3C), A P3P Preference Exchange Language 1.0 (APPEL), Working draft (April 2002)
21. Yang, N., Barringer, H., Zhang, N.: A Purpose-Based Access Control Model. In: The third International Symposium on Information Assurance and Security, pp. 143–148 (2007)

On the Formation of Historically k-Anonymous Anonymity Sets in a Continuous LBS

Rinku Dewri[1], Indrakshi Ray[2], Indrajit Ray[2], and Darrell Whitley[2]

[1] University of Denver, Denver, CO 80208, USA
rdewri@cs.du.edu
[2] Colorado State University, Fort Collins CO 80523, USA
{iray,indrajit,whitley}@cs.colostate.edu

Abstract. Privacy preservation in location based services (LBS) has received extensive attention in recent years. One of the less explored problems in this domain is associated with services that rely on continuous updates from the mobile object. Cloaking algorithms designed to hide user locations in single requests perform poorly in this scenario. The historical k-anonymity property is therefore enforced to ensure that all cloaking regions include at least k objects in common. However, the mobility of the objects can easily render increasingly bigger cloaking regions and degrade the quality of service. To this effect, this paper presents an algorithm to efficiently enforce historical k-anonymity by partitioning of an object's cloaking region. We further enforce some degree of directional similarity in the k common peers in order to prevent an excessive expansion of the cloaking region.

Keywords: historical k-anonymity, continuous LBS, anonymity sets.

1 Introduction

Application domains are potentially endless with location-tracking technology. These applications deliver customized information based on the location of a mobile object. The services can be classified into two types – *snapshot* LBS where the current location of the mobile object is sufficient to deliver the service, and *continuous* LBS where the mobile object must periodically communicate its location as part of the service agreement. For example, a Pay-As-You-Drive insurance service must receive location updates from the mobile object to bill the consumer accurately. A serious concern surrounding their acceptance is the potential usage of the location data to infer sensitive personal information about the mobile users. With access to the location data, sender anonymity can be violated even without the capability to track a mobile object. We refer to this class of adversaries as *location-unaware adversaries*. Such adversaries use external information to perform attacks resulting in restricted space identification, observation identification and location tracking [1].

S. Jajodia and J. Zhou (Eds.): SecureComm 2010, LNICST 50, pp. 71–88, 2010.
© Institute for Computer Sciences, Social Informatics and Telecommunications Engineering 2010

1.1   Motivation

Location obfuscation is one of the widely researched approaches to safeguard location anonymity. This technique guarantees that the location data received at the LBS provider can be associated back to more than one object – to at least k objects under the *location k-anonymity* model [1]. For this, a *cloaking region* is communicated to the service provider instead of the actual location. A k-anonymous cloaking region contains at least $k-1$ other mobile objects besides the service user. However, this approach is not sufficient to preserve privacy in a continuous LBS. In the continuous case, an object maintains an ongoing session with the LBS, and successive cloaking regions may be correlated to associate the session back to the object. Such *session associations* reveal the trajectory of the involved object, and any sensitive information thereof. Assuring that every cloaking region contains k objects is not sufficient since the absence of an object in one of the regions eliminates the possibility that it is the session owner. Performing such elimination is much easier for a *location-aware adversary* who has the capability to monitor users. This class of adversaries has exact location information on one or more objects and uses it to eliminate possibilities and probabilistically associate the session to consistently existing objects. It may seem that these attacks can be avoided by using a different identifier for every cloaking region. However, location data can still be correlated using techniques such as multi-target tracking [2]. Besides, the provider needs to be able to distinguish updates from the same object in order to maintain service quality [3].

Session association attacks can be avoided if it can be assured that every cloaking region in a session contains k common objects. This is referred to as *historical k-anonymity* [4]. However, as a result of the movement of objects, a historically k-anonymous cloaking region is very likely to grow in size over time, thereby deteriorating service quality. Without the proper strategies to control the size of the cloaking region, historical k-anonymity is only a theoretical extension of k-anonymity for continuous LBS. The work presented in this paper is the first known attempt that identifies the issues in effectively enforcing historical k-anonymity.

1.2   Related Work

While significant research has gone into algorithms that enforce k-anonymity [1,5,6,7], very few of them address historical k-anonymity. Gruteser and Liu specifically investigate privacy issues in continuous LBS [8]. They introduce the location inference problem where an adversary can infer supposedly hidden locations from prior or future location updates. Hoh and Gruteser propose a perturbation algorithm to cross paths of objects (by exchanging their pseudonyms) when they are close to each other [9]. Kido et al. use false dummies to simulate the movement of mobile nodes in order to hide the trace of an actual object [10]. Xu and Cai propose using historical traces of objects to derive a spatio-temporal cloaking region that provides trajectory protection [11].

Bettini et al. first introduced historical k-anonymity and proposed a spatio-temporal generalization algorithm to enforce it [4]. The generalization algorithm enlarges the area and time interval of the request to increase the uncertainty about the real location, while including k common objects. The method fails to account for mobility of the objects, without which the generalized area can easily cross acceptable limits. Chow and Mokbel argue that spatial cloaking algorithms should satisfy the *k-sharing* and *memorization* properties to be robust against session associations [12]. Although the focus of their work is query privacy, the two properties together imply historical k-anonymity. Their algorithm maintains groups of objects based on the two properties, along with query types involved with the objects. However, a query may not be equally significant at all locations occupied by a group's members. Xu and Cai propose an information theoretic measure of anonymity for continuous LBS [13]. They define a *k-anonymity area* as the cloaking region whose entropy is at least k. However, the algorithm is prone to *inversion attacks* where an adversary uses knowledge of the anonymizing algorithm to breach privacy. The most recent of algorithms in this domain is *ProvidentHider* [14]. It uses a maximum perimeter constraint to ensure that cloaking regions are not too large, and the starting set of objects is as big as possible (to take care of leaving objects). This algorithm is later used in our comparative study.

1.3   Contributions

The drawbacks present in the above algorithms point out three issues that must be addressed before historical k-anonymity can be efficiently enforced. Our first contribution in this paper is the identification of these issues, namely *defunct peers*, *diverging trajectories* and *locality of requests*. Our second contribution is an anonymization algorithm, called Continuous ANONymizer (CANON), that implements explicit strategies to resolve each of the three identified issues. In particular, we argue that a cloaking region should be determined using direction information of the objects and show how this restricts the inferences that can be made about the issuer of the request. Large cloaking regions are also avoided by this process. Further, we propose using multiple cloaking regions while issuing a query in order to maintain better service quality.

The remainder of the paper is organized as follows. Section 2 highlights the issues related to historical k-anonymity. Our approach to resolve the issues, the CANON algorithm, is presented in section 3. Section 4 details the experimental setup and results from the comparative study. Finally, section 5 concludes the paper.

2   System Architecture

Figure 1 depicts our system consisting of three layers – (i) *mobile objects*, (ii) a *trusted anonymity server*, and (iii) a *continuous LBS provider*. The trusted ano-nymity server acts as a channel for any communication between mobile objects

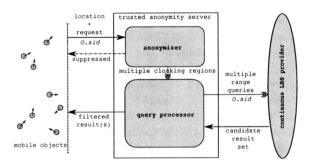

Fig. 1. Schematic of the system architecture

and continuous LBS providers. A mobile object $\mathcal{O}$ initiates a service session by registering itself with the anonymity server. The registration process includes the exchange of current location information ($\mathcal{O}.loc$) and service parameters signifying the request to forward to the LBS provider, as well as the anonymity level ($\mathcal{O}.k$) to enforce while doing so. The anonymity server issues a pseudo-identifier and uses it both as a *session identifier* ($\mathcal{O}.sid$) with the mobile object and as an *object identifier* when communicating with the LBS provider. A set of cloaking regions is then generated for the requesting object and multiple range queries are issued to the LBS provider for these regions. Communication between the anonymity server and the LBS provider is always referenced using the object identifier so that the LBS can maintain service continuity. The candidate results retrieved from the LBS provider are filtered at the anonymity server and then communicated to the mobile object. Subsequent location updates from the mobile object are handled in a similar fashion (with the pre-assigned session identifier) until the anonymity level cannot be satisfied or the service session is terminated. A request is *suppressed* (dropped) when the anonymity requirements can no longer be met within the same service session. A new identifier is then used if the mobile object re-issues the same request. We further assume that an object does not change its service parameters during a session. A separate session is started if a request with different service parameters is to be made. Therefore, an object can have multiple sessions running at the same time, each with a different session identifier.

2.1 Historical k-Anonymity

The primary purpose of a cloaking region is to make a given mobile object $\mathcal{O}$ indistinguishable from a set of other objects. This set of objects, including $\mathcal{O}$, forms the *anonymity set* of $\mathcal{O}$. Objects in the anonymity set shall be referred to as *peers* of $\mathcal{O}$ and denoted by $\mathcal{O}.peers$. A cloaking region for $\mathcal{O}$ is usually characterized by the minimum bounding rectangle (MBR) of the objects in $\mathcal{O}.peers$. Larger anonymity sets provide higher privacy, while at the same time can result in reduced service quality owing to a larger MBR. Therefore, the cloaking region is typically required to achieve an acceptable balance between anonymity and service quality.

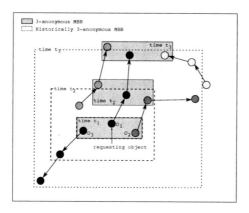

Fig. 2. Conventional k-anonymity and historical k-anonymity

As demonstrated in a number of prior works [5,6,7], achieving reasonable levels of anonymity and service quality is not difficult in the case of a snapshot LBS. However, in our assumed architecture for a continuous LBS system, maintaining the two properties is significantly difficult.

Consider the movement pattern of the objects depicted in figure 2. A 3-anonymous MBR is computed for O_1 during three consecutive location updates. If O_1's requests at the three time instances are mutually independent from each other (as in a snapshot LBS), then the privacy level of O_1 is maintained at 3-anonymity across the different MBRs. However, when the same identifier is associated with all the MBRs (as in a continuous LBS), it only requires an adversary the knowledge of O_1, O_2 and O_3's positions at time t_1, t_2 and t_3 to infer that the requests are being issued by object O_1. This is because O_1 is the only object common across the anonymity sets induced by the cloaking regions. We refer to this as a case of *full disclosure*. Assuming that each object is equally likely to be included in another object's cloaking region, the probability of full disclosure is unacceptably high.

Remark 1: Let $A_1, \ldots, A_n$ be a sequence of anonymity sets corresponding to $n > 1$ consecutive k-anonymous cloaking regions for a mobile object $\mathcal{O}$, generated from a collection of N mobile objects. Then, the probability that the intersection of the anonymity sets $\mathcal{S}_n = \cap_i A_i$ has at least p objects, $p > 1$, is $\left(\prod_{i=1}^{p-1} \frac{k-i}{N-i}\right)^n$.

Remark 2: If $k \leq \frac{N+1}{2}$ then the probability of full disclosure is at least $\frac{3}{4}$. The full disclosure risk is given as $\mathcal{D}_{full} = Pr(|\mathcal{S}_n| = 1) = Pr(|\mathcal{S}_n| \geq 1) - Pr(|\mathcal{S}_n| \geq 2)$. Since intersection of the anonymity sets contain at least one object, we have $Pr(|\mathcal{S}_n| \geq 1) = 1$. Hence, $\mathcal{D}_{full} = 1 - (\frac{k-1}{N-1})^n$. With $k \leq \frac{N+1}{2}$, or $\frac{k-1}{N-1} \leq \frac{1}{2}$, we have $\mathcal{D}_{full} \geq 1 - \frac{1}{2^n} \geq 1 - \frac{1}{2^2} = \frac{3}{4}$.

We also observe in figure 2 that it does not require knowledge on the objects' locations at all three time instances in order to breach O_1's privacy. In fact, location knowledge at time instances t_1 and t_2 is sufficient to lower O_1's privacy to 2-anonymity. This is referred to as a *partial disclosure*. Such disclosures occur when the intersection of anonymity sets (corresponding to the same object) contain less than the desired number of peers (the anonymity level k).

A straightforward extension of the conventional k-anonymity model that can counter risks of full and partial disclosures in a continuous LBS is to ensure that all anonymity sets within a service session contain at least k common objects.

Remark 3: **Historical k-anonymity.** Let $A_1, \ldots, A_n$ be a sequence of anonymity sets corresponding to the cloaking regions with the same identifier and at time instants $t_1, \ldots, t_n$, $t_i > t_j$ for $i > j$, respectively. The anonymity set A_i is then said to satisfy historical k-anonymity if $|A_1 \cap \ldots \cap A_i| \geq k$.

In other words, the sequence of anonymity sets preserve historical k-anonymity if all subsequent sets after A_1 contain at least k same objects from A_1. Figure 2 depicts how the cloaking regions should change over time in order to ensure that object O_1 always has historical 3-anonymity.

2.2 Implications

The privacy guarantees of historical k-anonymity in a continuous LBS is similar to that of k-anonymity in a snapshot LBS. In addition, historical k-anonymity also impedes session association attacks by location-aware adversaries. However, maintaining acceptable levels of service can become increasingly difficult in case of historical k-anonymity. We have identified three issues for consideration that impact the practical usage of historical k-anonymity.

1) **Defunct peers:** A defunct peer in an anonymity set is an object that is no longer registered with the anonymity server. As a result, it can no longer be ascertained that a cloaking region includes the peer. If the first cloaking region generated during a particular session contains exactly k objects, then every other anonymity set in that session must contain the same k objects for it to be historically k-anonymous. A defunct peer in this case does not allow subsequent cloaking regions to satisfy historical k-anonymity and introduces possibilities of partial disclosure.

2) **Diverging peer trajectories:** The trajectories of peers influence the size of a cloaking region (satisfying historical k-anonymity) over time. Refer to figure 2. The MBR for object O_1 becomes increasingly larger owing to the trajectory of object O_3. Bigger cloaking regions have a negative impact on service quality. In general, the more divergent the trajectories are, the worse is the effect. Algorithms that use a maximum spatial resolution will not be able to facilitate service continuity as spatial constraints will not be met.

3) **Locality of requests:** The significance of a particular service request can often be correlated with the locality where it originated. For instance, let us assume that the region shown in figure 2 corresponds to a urban locality. Further, object O_1 issues a request to periodically update itself with information (availability, price, etc.) on the nearest parking garage. At time instance t_1, an adversary cannot infer which object (out of O_1, O_2 and O_3) is the actual issuer of the request. However, as O_3 moves away from the urban locality (suspiciously ignoring the high concentration of garages if it were the issuer), an adversary

---

Procedure 1. CANON(Object $\mathcal{O}$)

Input: Mobile object $\mathcal{O}$ (includes all associated data).
Output: A set of peer groups (one of them includes $\mathcal{O}$); **null** if request is suppressed
    (cannot satisfy anonymity).
1: **if** ($\mathcal{O}.sid =$ **null**) **then**
2:   $\mathcal{O}.peers = CreatePeerSet(\mathcal{O})$
3:   $\mathcal{O}.sid =$ new session identifier
4: **else**
5:   remove defunct objects in $\mathcal{O}.peers$
6: **end if**
7: **if** ($|\mathcal{O}.peers| < \mathcal{O}.k$) **then**
8:   $\mathcal{O}.sid =$ **null**
9:   **return null**
10: **end if**
11: $peerGroups = PartitionPeerSet(\mathcal{O})$
12: **if** ($\exists g \in peerGroups$ such that $|g| < 2$) **then**
13:   $\mathcal{O}.sid =$ **null**
14:   **return null**
15: **end if**
16: **return** $peerGroups$

---

can infer that the issuer of the request is more likely to be O_1 or O_2. We say that these two objects are still in the *locality of the request*. If historical k-anonymity is continued to be enforced, O_3 (and most likely O_2 as well) will be positioned in different localities, thereby allowing an adversary infer with high confidence that O_1 is the issuer of the request.

Note that these three issues are primarily applicable in the context of a continuous LBS. Defunct peers is not an issue in snapshot LBS since the set of peers can be decided on a per request basis. Further, since the same peers need not be present in subsequent anonymity sets, their trajectories do not influence the size of the next privacy preserving cloaking region. Differences in locality also do not provide additional inferential power to an adversary. However, in a continuous LBS, these three issues are direct residues of providing privacy by historical k-anonymity.

3   The CANON Algorithm

CANON is an anonymization algorithm that enforces historical k-anonymity for use with a continuous LBS. The algorithm defines explicit procedures to handle each of the three potential issues identified in the previous section. An overview of the algorithm is shown in Procedure 1.

CANON is initiated by the anonymity server whenever it receives a request from a mobile object $\mathcal{O}$. The algorithm starts by first checking if $\mathcal{O}$ has an open session with respect to the current request. If it finds one then the set of peers is updated by removing all defunct peers from the set. Otherwise, a peer set is generated for $\mathcal{O}$ through the procedure *CreatePeerSet* and a session identifier is assigned. The newly generated (or updated) peer set must have at least $\mathcal{O}.k$ objects in order to continue to the next step; otherwise the request is suppressed and the session is terminated. Historical k-anonymity is ensured at the end of Line 10 since at least k objects inserted into $\mathcal{O}.peers$ by *CreatePeerSet* are still registered with the anonymity server. The next step is to divide the peer set into groups over which the range queries will be issued. A *peer group* is defined as a subset of $\mathcal{O}.peers$. *PartitionPeerSet* divides $\mathcal{O}.peers$ into disjoint peer groups. We shall often use the term "object's peer group" to signify the group that contains $\mathcal{O}$. Each peer group defines a smaller cloaking region than that defined by the entire peer set and reduces the impact of diverging trajectories on service quality. The peer groups returned by CANON are used to issue multiple range queries (one for each) with the same object identifier. Line 12 checks that each peer group contains at least two objects in order to avoid the disclosure of exact location information (of any object) to location-unaware adversaries.

All object agglomerations, namely into peer sets and then into peer groups, are performed so that the *reciprocity* property is satisfied. This property states that the inclusion of any two objects in a peer set (group) is independent of the location of the object for which the peer set (groups) is being formed. Reciprocity prevents inversion attacks where knowledge of the underlying anonymizing algorithm can be used to identify the actual object. The *Hilbert Cloak* algorithm [7] was first proposed in this context for the conventional k-anonymity model. Hilbert Cloak orders the objects according to their Hilbert indices (index on a space filling curve) and then groups them into buckets of size k. The peer set of an object is the bucket that contains the object. The peer set is the same for any object in the same bucket. Further, objects close to each other according to their Hilbert indices also tend to generate smaller (not necessarily optimal) cloaking regions. *CreatePeerSet* and *PartitionPeerSet* thus use Hilbert-sorted lists to incorporate these properties.

3.1   Handling Defunct Peers

As mentioned earlier, defunct peers can influence the lifetime of a service session by reducing the peer set size to below the limit that satisfies historical k-anonymity. The resolution is to include more than k objects in the first peer set. An indirect way to achieve this is to specify a maximum spatial boundary around the requesting object's location and then include all objects within that boundary into the peer set. This is the method used in *ProvidentHider*. However, this approach cannot account for the varying density of objects across time and space. Using spatial boundaries also cannot account for the relative differences in MBR sizes corresponding to varying anonymity requirements. For example, an area of $1\ km^2$ may be sufficient to have enough peers to satisfy a historical 2-anonymity requirement, but may not be so to satisfy a stronger requirement (say historical 50-anonymity).

A more direct method to resolve the issue is to specify the desired peer set size explicitly. This removes any dependency on how the objects are distributed and the area required to cover a reasonable number of them. We can specify the size as a sufficiently big constant. However, this strategy favors objects with weaker anonymity requirements as their peer sets are allowed a comparatively higher number of peers to defunct. For instance, a constant peer set size of 20 would allow the anonymizer to tolerate up to 18 defunct peers to preserve historical 2-anonymity, but only 5 defuncts to preserve historical 15-anonymity. Therefore, the strategy adopted in CANON uses an *oversize factor* τ that relatively specifies the number of extra peers that must be included in the peer set. The minimum initial size of the peer set of an object $\mathcal{O}$ is equal to $(1+\tau)\times\mathcal{O}.k$ with this strategy. We say "minimum" because other parameters introduced later can allow more peers to be included. Use of an oversize factor prevents the problem associated with constant peer set sizes. Note that since CANON partitions the peer set into further groups before issuing a query, the area of the cloaking region defined by the enlarged peer set has little or no influence on service quality. However, we would still not want the area to expand extensively in order to curb the issue of request locality.

3.2   Deciding a Peer Set

The *CreatePeerSet* procedure determines the initial peer set for an object. At this point, we need to ensure that majority of the objects in the peer set are in the locality of the request. We believe there are two requirements to address in this regard.

1. Objects in the peer set should define an area where the request is *equally significant* to all the peers.
2. Objects in the peer set should move so that the defined area does not expand *too much*.

The first requirement will prohibit the inclusion of peers that are positioned in a locality where the issued request is unlikely to be made. The second requirement addresses locality of requests in the dynamic scenario where the trajectories of the peers could be such that they are positioned in very different localities over time. Preventing the MBR of the peer set from expanding prohibits peers from being too far away from each other. The first requirement can be fulfilled by choosing peers according to the Hilbert Cloak algorithm. Peers chosen according to Hilbert indices will induce a small MBR, thereby ensuring that they are more likely to be in the same locality. However, a peer set generated by this process cannot guarantee that the second requirement will be fulfilled for long. This is because the neighbors of an object (according to Hilbert index) may be moving in very different directions.

It is clear from the above observation that the direction of travel of the objects should be accounted for when selecting peers. The direction of travel is calculated as a vector from the last known location of the object to its current location, i.e. if $\mathcal{O}.loc_1 = (x_1, y_1)$ and $\mathcal{O}.loc_2 = (x_2, y_2)$ are the previously and currently known positions of $\mathcal{O}$ respectively, then the direction of travel is given as $\mathcal{O}.dir = \mathcal{O}.loc_2 - \mathcal{O}.loc_1 = (x_2 - x_1, y_2 - y_1)$. $\mathcal{O}.dir$ is set to $(0, 1)$ (north) for

---

Procedure 2. CreatePeerSet(Object $\mathcal{O}$)

Input: Mobile object $\mathcal{O}$ (includes all associated data), and system globals τ, θ and
     α_{full}.
Output: A set of peer objects (including $\mathcal{O}$).
  1: $\mathcal{L}$ = set of available mobile objects sorted by their Hilbert index
  2: $k_{of} = (1 + \tau) \times \mathcal{O}.k; \mathcal{P} = \phi$
  3: **repeat**
  4:     $\mathcal{L}_c = \phi$
  5:     **for all** ($l \in \mathcal{L}$ in order) **do**
  6:         **if** ($|\mathcal{L}_c| \geq k_{of}$ and $AreaMBR(\mathcal{L}_c \cup \{l\}) > \alpha_{full}$) **then**
  7:             **break**
  8:         **end if**
  9:         $\mathcal{L}_c = \mathcal{L}_c \cup \{l\}$
 10:     **end for**
 11:     $\mathcal{P}_{prev} = \mathcal{P}; f = 1; \mathcal{O}_{pivot}$ = first object in $\mathcal{L}_c$
 12:     **repeat**
 13:         $\mathcal{P} = (f\theta)$-neighbors of $\mathcal{O}_{pivot}$ in $\mathcal{L}_c$
 14:         $f = f + 1$
 15:     **until** ($|\mathcal{P}| \geq \min(k_{of}, |\mathcal{L}_c|)$)
 16:     $\mathcal{L} = \mathcal{L} - \mathcal{P}$
 17: **until** ($\mathcal{O} \in \mathcal{P}$)
 18: **if** ($|\mathcal{P}| < k_{of}$) **then**
 19:     $\mathcal{P} = \mathcal{P} \cup \mathcal{P}_{prev}$
 20: **else if** ($|\mathcal{L}| < k_{of}$) **then**
 21:     $\mathcal{P} = \mathcal{P} \cup \mathcal{L}$
 22: **end if**
 23: **return** $\mathcal{P}$

---

newly registered objects. A *θ-neighborhood* for $\mathcal{O}$ is then defined as the set of
all objects whose direction of travel is within an angular distance θ (say in de-
grees) from $\mathcal{O}.dir$. Therefore, a 0°-neighborhood means objects traveling in the
same direction, while a 180°-neighborhood contains all objects. If all peers are
chosen within a 0°-neighborhood then it is possible that the area defined by the
initial peer set will more or less remain constant over time. However, the initial
area itself could be very large due to the non-availability of such peers within a
close distance. On the other hand, using a 180°-neighborhood essentially allows
all objects to be considered and hence the area can be kept small by including close objects. Of course, the area may increase unwantedly over time. Peer
set generation is therefore guided by two system parameters in CANON - the
neighborhood step size θ and the *full-MBR resolution* α_{full}. The neighborhood
step size specifies the resolution at which the θ-neighborhood is incremented
to include dissimilar (in terms of travel direction) peers. The full-MBR resolution specifies some area within which the issued request is equally likely to
have originated from any of the included objects, thereby making it difficult for
an adversary to eliminate peers based on position and request significance. For
small values of θ and some α_{full}, all objects in a peer set would ideally move

in a group, in and out of a locality. Procedure 2 outlines the pseudo-code of *CreatePeerSet*. We assume the existence of a function *AreaMBR* that returns the area of the minimum bounding rectangle of a set of objects.

CreatePeerSet first creates a sorted list $\mathcal{L}$ of all registered objects according to their Hilbert indices. It then continues to divide them into buckets (starting from the first one in the sorted list) until the one with $\mathcal{O}$ is found (Lines 3-17). Every time a bucket is formed, $\mathcal{L}$ is updated by removing all objects in the bucket from the list (Line 16). Lines 5-10 determine a set $\mathcal{L}_c$ of candidate objects that can potentially form a bucket. Starting from the first available object in $\mathcal{L}$, we continue to include objects in $\mathcal{L}_c$ as long as the minimum peer set size (denoted by k_{of} and decided by the oversize factor) is not met, or the area of the MBR of included objects is within the full-MBR resolution. Note that, as a result of this condition (Line 6), the minimum required size of the peer set receives more prominence than the resulting area. Hence, the full-MBR resolution is only a guiding parameter and not a constraint. Next, Lines 12-15 select k_{of} objects from the candidate set to form a bucket. The first object in $\mathcal{L}_c$ is chosen as a pivot and all objects in the θ-neighborhood of the pivot are included in the bucket. If the bucket is not full up to its capacity (k_{of}) and more objects are present in $\mathcal{L}_c$, then the neighborhood is increased by the step size θ. By the end of this process, the bucket would either contain k_{of} objects or there are less than k_{of} objects in $\mathcal{L}_c$. The latter is only possible when list $\mathcal{L}$ contains less than k_{of} objects, i.e. the last bucket is being created. Note that object $\mathcal{O}$ is not explicitly used anywhere to decide the buckets, thereby guaranteeing reciprocity. Once the bucket with $\mathcal{O}$ is found, two more checks are required (Lines 18-22). First, if $\mathcal{O}$'s bucket has less than k_{of} objects (possible if it is the last one), then it is merged with the previous bucket. Second, if the number of objects remaining in $\mathcal{L}$ is less than k_{of} (implying $\mathcal{O}$'s bucket is second to last), then the remaining objects are included into $\mathcal{O}$'s bucket to maintain reciprocity.

CreatePeerSet uses θ-neighborhoods and the full-MBR resolution to balance between dissimilar peers and the resulting MBR area. While the step size θ allows incremental selection of dissimilar peers, α_{full} guides the extent of increment admissible to generate a localized peer set. Note that the creation of a peer set is a one time procedure every service session. Hence, a good estimation of the direction of travel is required to avoid diverging trajectories. One possibility is to obtain destination points of objects and generate an average direction of travel. An average direction can also be calculated based on the displacement vector of the object from its starting position. One can also estimate a direction of travel based on a set of last known locations. CANON uses an instantaneous direction vector. We believe this method performs reasonably well in road networks, although the efficacy of other techniques remains to be determined.

3.3   Handling a Large MBR

The full-MBR resolution parameter is used to control breaches related to request localities. Typical values are in the range of 10 to 50 km^2. The parameter is therefore not intended to help generate cloaking regions with small MBRs.

Procedure 3. PartitionPeerSet(Object $\mathcal{O}$)

Input: Mobile object $\mathcal{O}$ (includes all associated data) and system global α_{sub}.
Output: A set of peer groups.
 1: Sort objects in $\mathcal{O}.peers$ by their Hilbert index
 2: $peerGroups = \phi$
 3: $bucket = \phi$
 4: **for all** $(l \in \mathcal{O}.peers$ in order) **do**
 5:    **if** $(AreaMBR(bucket \cup \{l\}) \leq \alpha_{sub})$ **then**
 6:      $bucket = bucket \cup \{l\}$
 7:    **else**
 8:      $peerGroups = peerGroups \cup \{bucket\}$
 9:      $bucket = \{l\}$
10:    **end if**
11: **end for**
12: $peerGroups = peerGroups \cup \{bucket\}$
13: **return** $peerGroups$

A continuous LBS would require a much finer resolution to deliver any reasonable service. Further, depending on variations in velocity and the underlying road network, some extent of expansion/contraction of the MBR is very likely. The MBR of a peer set is therefore not a good candidate to issue the range queries. Instead, the peer set is partitioned into multiple disjoint groups by *PartitionPeerSet*. Partitioning of the peer set eliminates empty spaces between peers (introduced in the first place if trajectories diverge) and produces smaller MBRs for the range queries [15]. This partitioning can be done either in a way such that each peer group has a minimum number of objects or each peer group has a maximum spatial resolution. The former approach cannot guarantee that the resulting MBR will have an acceptable area. The latter method is adopted in CANON where the maximum spatial resolution of a peer group is specified as the *sub-MBR resolution* α_{sub}. α_{sub} is relatively much smaller than α_{full}. Procedure 3 outlines the partitioning method.

The partitioning is performed in a manner similar to Hilbert Cloak, with the difference that each bucket now induces an area of at most α_{sub} instead of a fixed number of objects. Starting from the first object in the Hilbert-sorted peer set, an object is added to a bucket as long as the sub-MBR resolution is met (Line 6); otherwise the current bucket is a new peer group (Line 8) and the next bucket is created (Line 9). Reciprocity is preserved as before. Note that the pseudo-code in Procedure 3 does not handle the case when a peer group contains only one object. Procedure 1 checks that such groups do not exist (safeguard against location-unaware adversaries); otherwise the request is suppressed. However, the partitioning algorithm itself can relax the sub-MBR resolution when a peer group with a single object is found. One possible modification is to merge any peer group having a single object with the group generated prior to it. Another parameter-less technique is to create partitions that result in the minimum average peer group MBR with the constraint that each group must have at least two objects. We have kept these possibilities open for future exploration.

4 Empirical Study

The experimental evaluation compares the performance of CANON with the *ProvidentHider* algorithm. For every new request, *ProvidentHider* first groups all available objects from a Hilbert-sorted list such that each bucket holds $\mathcal{O}.k$ objects; more if adding them does not violate a maximum perimeter (P_{max}) constraint. The peer set of an object is the bucket that contains the object. A range query is issued over the area covered by the objects in the peer set only if the maximum perimeter constraint is satisfied; otherwise the request is suppressed. Refer to [14] for full details on the algorithm. We measure a number of statistics to evaluate the performance.

- *service continuity:* average number of requests served in a session
- *service failures:* percentage of suppressed requests
- *safeguard against location-unaware adversaries:* average size of the peer group to which the issuing object belongs

4.1 Experimental Setup

We have generated trace data using a simulator [6] that operates multiple mobile objects based on real-world road network information available from the National Mapping Division of the US Geological Survey. We have used an area of approximately $168\,km^2$ in the Chamblee region of Georgia, USA for this study. Three road types are identified based on the available data – expressway, arterial and collector. Real traffic volume data is used to determine the number of objects in the different road types [1].

The used traffic volume information (table 1) results in 8,558 objects with 34% on expressways, 8% on arterial roads and 58% on collector roads. The trace data consists of multiple records spanning one hour of simulated time. A record is made up of a time stamp, object number, x and y co-ordinates of object's location, and a status indicator. The status indicator signifies if the object is registered to the anonymity server. An object's status starts off randomly as being active or inactive. The object remains in the status for a time period drawn from a normal distribution with mean 10 minutes and standard deviation 5 minutes. The status is randomly reset at the end of the period and a new time period is assigned. The granularity of the data is maintained such that the Euclidean distance between successive locations of the same object is approximately 100 meters. Each object has an associated k value drawn from the range $[2, 50]$ by using a Zipf distribution favoring higher values and with the exponent 0.6. The trace data is sorted by the time stamp of records.

During evaluation, the first minute of records is used only for initialization. Subsequently, the status of each record is used to determine if the object issues a request. Only an active object is considered for anonymization. If the object was previously inactive or its prior request was suppressed, then it is assumed that a new request has been issued. Otherwise, the object is continuing a service session. The anonymizer is then called to determine the cloaking region(s), if possible.

Table 1. Mean speed, standard deviation and traffic volume on the three road types

road type	traffic volume	mean speed	standard deviation
expressway	2916.6 cars/hr	90 km/hr	20 km/hr
arterial	916.6 cars/hr	60 km/hr	15 km/hr
collector	250 cars/hr	50 km/hr	10 km/hr

The process continues until the object enters an inactive (defunct) state. Over 2,000,000 anonymization requests are generated during a pass of the entire trace data.

Default values of other algorithm parameters are set as follows: $\tau = 0.0$, $\alpha_{full} = 25\,km^2$, $\alpha_{sub} = 1\,km^2$, $\theta = 180°$ and $P_{max} = 5000\,m$. A $5000\,m$ perimeter constraint for *ProvidentHider* is approximately an area of $1.6\,km^2$. Compared to that, α_{sub} has a smaller default value. The precision is around $1000\,m$ (assuming a square area) which serves reasonably well for a Pay-As-You-Drive insurance service. The full-MBR resolution of $25\,km^2$ evaluates to a locality about $\frac{1}{32}^{th}$ the size of New York City. The entire map is assumed to be on a grid of $2^{14} \times 2^{14}$ cells (a cell at every meter) while calculating the Hilbert indices [16]. Objects in the same cell have the same Hilbert index.

4.2 Comparative Performance

Figure 3a shows the average number of requests served in a session for different anonymity requirements. *ProvidentHider* demonstrates poor performance for higher k values, almost to the extent of one request per session. Comparatively, CANON maintains much better service continuity. As mentioned earlier, using a fixed area for varying anonymity requirements makes it difficult for *ProvidentHider* to keep the peer set within the required size. The task is more difficult for bigger peer sets as the algorithm does not consider the issue of diverging trajectories. In fact, more than 50% of the requests are suppressed for $k > 25$ (figure 3b). CANON's performance also seems to fluctuate depending on the oversize factor. In general, a maximum peer set size slightly larger than the minimum required (for example $\tau = 0.25$) gives the best performance, while any further increase degrades it. While a few extra peers is useful to handle defunct peers, having a much larger peer set implies having objects over a larger area and often far away from each other (over time). Therefore, it is possible that some peer groups are formed with a single object owing to the sub-MBR constraint. Requests are then suppressed in the absence of a strategy to handle such peer groups. This is also corroborated by the similar trend in request suppression.

4.3 Impact of Parameters

Each parameter in CANON is intended to address a specific issue with the use of historical k-anonymity. We performed some parametric studies to demonstrate the consequences of varying these parameters. The neighborhood step size is

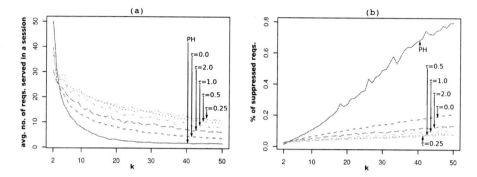

Fig. 3. Comparative performance of CANON with ProvidentHider (PH) for different anonymity requirements (k) and oversize factors (τ). (a) Average number of requests served in a session. (b) Percentage of requests suppressed.

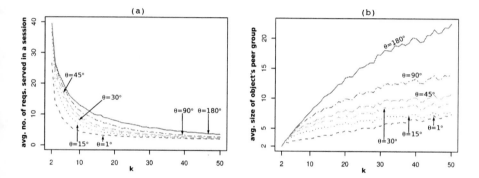

Fig. 4. Impact of different neighborhood step size θ on CANON. (a) Average number of requests served in a session. (b) Average size of requesting object's peer group.

varied between $1°$ and $180°$, and performance is observed for three different settings of the sub-MBR ($\alpha_{sub} = 0.25, 1.0$ and $4\ km^2$) and full-MBR ($\alpha_{full} = 10, 25$ and $50\ km^2$) resolutions. Note that increasing/decreasing the full-MBR resolution will have no impact on peer sets if the required number of objects is always present within a small area. We therefore use a neighborhood step size of $15°$ while observing the impact of α_{full}. All parameters other than the ones mentioned take their default values.

Neighborhood Step Size θ. Performance in terms of service continuity does not differ a lot for varying step size (figure 4a). Some differences are observed for lower ranges of k ($2-15$) where larger step sizes show a better performance. Differences are more prominent in terms of peer group size where a bigger neighborhood improves the safeguard against location-unaware adversaries (figure 4b). This behavior is expected since bigger neighborhood sizes allow the inclusion of more dissimilar peers, thereby inducing bigger peer groups due to the possibly

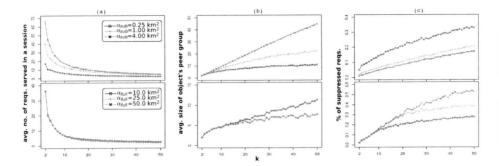

Fig. 5. Impact of spatial resolution parameters on CANON – top: sub-MBR area α_{sub} and bottom: full-MBR area α_{full} with $\theta = 15°$. (a) Average number of requests served in a session. (b) Average size of requesting object's peer group. (c) Percentage of suppressed requests.

close proximity of objects. The statistic of interest is the size of the MBR area defined by the objects in the peer set. We found that this area remains almost constant for the smaller step sizes, specifically for the more frequently requested anonymity levels (higher k), implying that the objects in a peer set move together as a group. Further, the area increases by more than two folds (across different anonymity requirements) when direction of travel is ignored ($\theta = 180°$).

Sub-MBR Resolution α_{sub}. Smaller sub-MBR resolutions mean higher precision in the range queries. However, they also mean higher chances of smaller peer groups, often ones with a single object. With reference to figure 5 (top row), a smaller α_{sub} results in a higher rate of failures, inducing shorter service sessions. Services requiring high location precision will therefore fail to provide longer service continuity. An object's peer group size is also comparatively smaller. Improvements in service continuity is more prominent for weaker anonymity requirements as α_{sub} is increased. However, improvements in peer group size is more noticeable in higher k values. In effect, finding a suitably balanced α_{sub} can help achieve good overall performance. α_{sub} is decided by the service requirements in most cases. Nonetheless, depending on how stringent the requirement is, both privacy (from location-unaware adversaries) and service quality may have scope for improvement.

Full-MBR Resolution α_{full}. The full-MBR resolution is observed to have little or no influence on the average number of requests served in a session (figure 5 bottom row). However, larger areas tend to have higher percentage of failures. A possible explanation is as follows. A larger area with a small step size means similar objects are preferred over the proximity of objects. As a result, a peer set includes objects distributed far apart. This leads to the suppression of requests when the sub-MBR constraint is imposed on the formation of peer groups. Objects far apart cannot be grouped without violating the constraint. This also results in a comparatively smaller peer group size. On the other hand, a smaller area allows inclusion of close proximity objects at the expense of similarity. The sub-MBR constraint is therefore easier to meet and suppression rate is lower.

4.4 Summary

The following points summarize the results from the experimental study.

- CANON has a superior performance compared to *ProvidentHider* in maintaining longer service sessions across a wide range of anonymity requirements. More requests are also successfully anonymized by CANON.
- Including a small number of extra objects in a peer set is advantageous in handling defunct peers. However, extremely large peer sets can be detrimental.
- Use of direction information during the formation of a peer set does help avoid peers drifting away from each other over time. Choice of a too small neighborhood affects service quality, but is not necessary to balance performance across different measures.
- Performance is better with larger sub-MBR resolutions. However, performance in high precision services may be improved with a good strategy to relax the constraint.
- Service continuity is marginally different for different full-MBR resolutions. However, failure to serve new requests is much lower with smaller resolutions.

5   Conclusions

Owing to the limitations of k-anonymity in a continuous LBS, an extended notion called historical k-anonymity has been recently proposed for privacy preservation in such services. However, all known methods of enforcing historical k-anonymity significantly affects the quality of service. In this paper, we identified the factors that contribute towards deteriorated service quality and suggested resolutions. We proposed the CANON algorithm that delivers reasonably good service quality across different anonymity requirements. The algorithm uses tunable parameters to adjust the size of a peer set, trajectories of peers and cloaking regions over which range queries are issued. Immediate future work includes optimizing the performance of CANON in terms of better usage of directional information. We believe this optimization is crucial in order to have similar performance across all levels of anonymity requirements. Merging location anonymity and query privacy in a continuous LBS is a natural extension of this work.

Acknowledgment

This work was partially supported by the U.S. Air Force Office of Scientific Research under contract FA9550-07-1-0042. The views and conclusions contained in this document are those of the authors and should not be interpreted as representing official policies, either expressed or implied, of the U.S. Air Force or other federal government agencies.

References

1. Gruteser, M., Grunwald, D.: Anonymous Usage of Location-Based Services Through Spatial and Temporal Cloaking. In: Proceedings of the First International Conference on Mobile Systems, Applications, and Services, pp. 31–42 (2003)
2. Reid, D.: An Algorithm for Tracking Multiple Targets. IEEE Transactions on Automatic Control 24(6), 843–854 (1979)
3. Beresford, A.R., Stajano, F.: Location Privacy in Pervasive Computing. IEEE Security and Privacy 2, 46–55 (2003)
4. Bettini, C., Wang, X.S., Jajodia, S.: Protecting Privacy Against Location-Based Personal Identification. In: Proceedings of the 2nd VLDB Workshop on Secure Data Management, pp. 185–199 (2005)
5. Bamba, B., Liu, L., Pesti, P., Wang, T.: Supporting Anonymous Location Queries in Mobile Environments with Privacy Grid. In: Proceedings of the 17th International World Wide Web Conference, pp. 237–246 (2008)
6. Gedik, B., Liu, L.: Protecting Location Privacy with Personalized k-Anonymity: Architecture and Algorithms. IEEE Transactions on Mobile Computing 7(1), 1–18 (2008)
7. Kalnis, P., Ghinita, G., Mouratidis, K., Papadias, D.: Preventing Location-Based Identity Inference in Anonymous Spatial Queries. IEEE Transactions on Knowledge and Data Engineering 19(12), 1719–1733 (2007)
8. Gruteser, M., Liu, X.: Protecting Privacy in Continuous Location-Tracking Applications. IEEE Security and Privacy 2(2), 28–34 (2004)
9. Hoh, B., Gruteser, M.: Protecting Location Privacy Through Path Confusion. In: Proceedings of the First International Conference on Security and Privacy for Emerging Areas in Communication Networks, pp. 194–205 (2005)
10. Kido, H., Yanagisawa, Y., Satoh, T.: An Anonymous Communication Technique Using Dummies for Location-Based Services. In: Proceedings of the IEEE International Conference on Pervasive Services 2005, pp. 88–97 (2005)
11. Xu, T., Cai, Y.: Exploring Historical Location Data for Anonymity Preservation in Location-Based Services. In: IEEE INFOCOM 2008, pp. 1220–1228 (2008)
12. Chow, C.Y., Mokbel, M.: Enabling Private Continuous Queries for Revealed User Locations. In: Papadias, D., Zhang, D., Kollios, G. (eds.) SSTD 2007. LNCS, vol. 4605, pp. 258–275. Springer, Heidelberg (2007)
13. Xu, T., Cai, Y.: Location Anonymity in Continuous Location-Based Services. In: Proceedings of the 15th International Symposium on Advances in Geographic Information Systems, p. 39 (2007)
14. Mascetti, S., Bettini, C., Wang, X.S., Freni, D., Jajodia, S.: ProvidentHider: An Algorithm to Preserve Historical k-Anonymity in LBS. In: Proceedings of the 10th International Conference on Mobile Data Management: Systems, Services and Middleware, pp. 172–181 (2009)
15. Tan, K.W., Lin, Y., Mouratidis, K.: Spatial Cloaking Revisited: Distinguishing Information Leakage from Anonymity. In: Mamoulis, N., Seidl, T., Pedersen, T.B., Torp, K., Assent, I. (eds.) Advances in Spatial and Temporal Databases. LNCS, vol. 5644, pp. 117–134. Springer, Heidelberg (2009)
16. Liu, X., Schrack, G.: Encoding and Decoding the Hilbert Order. Software-Practice and Experience 26(12), 1335–1346 (1996)

Securing Personal Health Records in Cloud Computing: Patient-Centric and Fine-Grained Data Access Control in Multi-owner Settings

Ming Li[1], Shucheng Yu[1], Kui Ren[2], and Wenjing Lou[1]

[1] Department of ECE, Worcester Polytechnic Institute, USA
{mingli,yscheng,wjlou}@ece.wpi.edu
[2] Department of ECE, Illinois Institute of Technology, USA
kren@ece.iit.edu

Abstract. Online personal health record (PHR) enables patients to manage their own medical records in a centralized way, which greatly facilitates the storage, access and sharing of personal health data. With the emergence of cloud computing, it is attractive for the PHR service providers to shift their PHR applications and storage into the cloud, in order to enjoy the elastic resources and reduce the operational cost. However, by storing PHRs in the cloud, the patients lose physical control to their personal health data, which makes it necessary for each patient to encrypt her PHR data before uploading to the cloud servers. Under encryption, it is challenging to achieve fine-grained access control to PHR data in a scalable and efficient way. For each patient, the PHR data should be encrypted so that it is scalable with the number of users having access. Also, since there are multiple owners (patients) in a PHR system and every owner would encrypt her PHR files using a different set of cryptographic keys, it is important to reduce the key distribution complexity in such multi-owner settings. Existing cryptographic enforced access control schemes are mostly designed for the single-owner scenarios.

In this paper, we propose a novel framework for access control to PHRs within cloud computing environment. To enable fine-grained and scalable access control for PHRs, we leverage attribute based encryption (ABE) techniques to encrypt each patient's PHR data. To reduce the key distribution complexity, we divide the system into multiple security domains, where each domain manages only a subset of the users. In this way, each patient has full control over her own privacy, and the key management complexity is reduced dramatically. Our proposed scheme is also flexible, in that it supports efficient and on-demand revocation of user access rights, and break-glass access under emergency scenarios.

Keywords: Personal health records, cloud computing, patient-centric privacy, fine-grained access control, attribute-based encryption.

1 Introduction

In recent years, personal health record (PHR) has emerged as a patient-centric model of health information exchange. A PHR service allows a patient to create,

S. Jajodia and J. Zhou (Eds.): SecureComm 2010, LNICST 50, pp. 89–106, 2010.
© Institute for Computer Sciences, Social Informatics and Telecommunications Engineering 2010

manage, and control her personal health data in a centralized place through the web, from anywhere and at any time (as long as they have a web browser and Internet connection), which has made the storage, retrieval, and sharing of the the medical information more efficient. Especially, each patient has the full control of her medical records and can effectively share her health data with a wide range of users, including staffs from healthcare providers, and their family members or friends. In this way, the accuracy and quality of care are improved, while the healthcare cost is lowered.

At the same time, cloud computing has attracted a lot of attention because it provides storage-as-a-service and software-as-a-service, by which software service providers can enjoy the virtually infinite and elastic storage and computing resources [1]. As such, the PHR providers are more and more willing to shift their PHR storage and application services into the cloud instead of building specialized data centers, in order to lower their operational cost. For example, two major cloud platform providers, Google and Microsoft are both providing their PHR services, Google Health[1] and Microsoft HealthVault[2], respectively.

While it is exciting to have PHR services in the cloud for everyone, there are many security and privacy risks which could impede its wide adoption. The main concern is about the privacy of patients' personal health data and who could gain access to the PHRs when they are stored in a cloud server. Since patients lose physical control to their own personal health data, directly placing those sensitive data under the control of the servers cannot provide strong privacy assurance at all. First, the PHR data could be leaked if an insider in the cloud provider's organization misbehaves, due to the high value of the sensitive personal health information (PHI). As a famous incident, a Department of Veterans Affairs database containing sensitive PHI of 26.5 million military veterans, including their social security numbers and health problems was stolen by an employee who took the data home without authorization [2]. Second, since cloud computing is an open platform, the servers are subjected to malicious outside attacks. For example, Google has reported attacks on its Gmail accounts in early 2010. Although there exist administrative regulations such as the Health Insurance Portability and Accountability Act of 1996 (HIPAA) [3], technical protections that effectively ensure the confidentiality of and proper access to PHRs are still indispensable.

To deal with the potential risks of privacy exposure, instead of letting the PHR service providers encrypt patients' data, PHR services should give patients (PHR owners) full control over the selective sharing of their own PHR data. To this end, the PHR data should be encrypted in addition to traditional access control mechanisms provided by the server [4]. Basically, each patient shall generate her own decryption keys and distribute them to her authorized users. In particular, they shall be able to choose in a fine-grained way which users can have access to which parts of their PHR; for the unauthorized parties who do not have the corresponding keys, the PHR data should remain confidential. Also, the

---

[1] https://www.google.com/health/
[2] http://www.healthvault.com/

patient should always retain the right to not only grant, but also revoke access privileges when they feel it is necessary [5]. Therefore, in a "patient-centric" PHR system, there are *multiple owners* who encrypt according to their own ways, using different sets of cryptographic keys.

Essentially, realizing fine-grained access control under encryption can be transformed into a key management issue. However, under the multi-owner setting, this problem becomes more challenging. Due to the large scale of users and owners in the PHR system, potentially heavy computational and management burden on the entities in the system can be incurred, which will limit the PHR data accessibility and system usability. On the one hand, for each owner her PHR data should be encrypted so that multiple users can access at the same time. But the authorized users may come from various avenues, including both persons who have connections with her and who do not. Those users are of potential large number and their access requests are generally unpredictable. Should all the users be directly managed by each owner herself, she will easily be overwhelmed by a linear increase of the key management overhead with the number of users. On the other hand, since there are multiple owners, each user may have to obtain keys from every owner whose PHR she wants to read, limiting the accessibility since not every patient will be always online. Yet, in a straightforward solution where all the users are managed by some central authority (CA) instead of each owner, the CA will have the ability to decrypt all the owners' data, such that owners have no full control over their data and their privacy will still be at risk. While various previous works proposed techniques for cryptographically enforced access control to outsourced data [4,6,7,8,9], they focused on single-owner architecture which cannot directly solve the above challenges under multi-owner scenario in PHR system. Therefore, a new framework for patient-centric access control suitable for multi-owner PHR systems is necessary.

In this paper, we propose a novel and practical framework for fine-grained data access control to PHR data in cloud computing environments, under multi-owner settings. To ensure that each owner has full control over her PHR data, we leverage attribute-based encryption (ABE) as the encryption primitive, and each owner generates her own set of ABE keys. In this way, a patient can selectively share her PHR among a set of users by encrypting the file according to a set of attributes, and her encryption and user management complexity is linear to the number of attributes rather than the number of authorized users in the system.

To avoid from high key management complexity for each owner and user, we divide the system into multiple security domains (SDs), where each of them is associated with a subset of all the users. Each owner and the users having personal connections to her belong to a personal domain, while for each public domain we rely on multiple auxiliary attribute authorities (AA) to manage its users and attributes. Each AA distributively governs a disjoint subset of attributes, while none of them alone is able to control the security of the whole system. In addition, we discuss methods for enabling efficient and on-demand revocation of users or attributes, and break-glass access under emergence scenarios.

2   Related Work

2.1   Traditional Access Control for EHRs

Traditionally, research on access control in electronic health records (EHRs) often places full trust on the health care providers where the EHR data are often resided in, and the access policies are implemented and enforced by the health providers. Various access control models have been proposed and applied, including role-based (RBAC) and attribute-based access control (ABAC) [10]. In RBAC [11], each user's access right is determined based on his/her roles and the role-specific privileges associated with them. The ABAC extends the role concept in RBAC to attributes, such as properties of the resource, entities, and the environment. Compared with RBAC, the ABAC is more favorable in the context of health care due to its potential flexibility in policy descriptions [10]. A line of research aims at improving the expressiveness and flexibility of the access control policies [12].

However, for personal health records (PHRs) in cloud computing environments, the PHR service providers may not be in the same trust domains with the patients'. Thus *patient-centric privacy* is hard to guarantee when full trust is placed on the cloud servers, since the patients lose physical control to their sensitive data. Therefore, the PHR needs to be encrypted in a way that enforces each patient's personalized privacy policy, which is the focus of this paper.

2.2   Cryptographically Enforced Access Control for Outsourced Data

For access control of outsourced data, partially trusted servers are often assumed. With cryptographic techniques, the goal is trying to enforce that who has (read) access to which parts of a patient's PHR documents in a *fine-grained* way.

Symmetric key cryptography (SKC) based solutions. Vimercati *et.al.* proposed a solution for securing outsourced data on semi-trusted servers based on symmetric key derivation methods [13], which can achieve fine-grained access control. Unfortunately, the complexities of file creation and user grant/revocation operations are linear to the number of authorized users, which is less scalable. In [4], files in a PHR are organized by hierarchical categories in order to make key distribution more efficient. However, user revocation is not supported. In [6], an owner's data is encrypted block-by-block, and a binary key tree is constructed over the block keys to reduce the number of keys given to each user.

The SKC-based solutions have several key limitations. First, the key management overhead is high when there are a large number of users and owners, which is the case in a PHR system. The key distribution can be very inconvenient when there are multiple owners, since it requires each owner to always be online. Second, user revocation is inefficient, since upon revocation of one user, all the remaining users will be affected and the data need to be re-encrypted. Furthermore, users' write and read rights are not separable.

Public key cryptography (PKC) based solutions. PKC based solutions were proposed due to their ability to separate write and read privileges. Benaloh *et. al.* [4] proposed a scheme based on hierarchical identity based encryption (HIBE), where each category label is regarded as an identity. However, it still has potentially high key management overhead. In order to deal with the multi-user scenarios in encrypted search, Dong *et.al.* proposed a solution based on proxy encryption [14]. Access control can be enforced if every write and read operation involve a proxy server. However, it does not support fine-grained access control, and is also not collusion-safe.

Attribute-based encryption (ABE). The SKC and traditional PKC based solutions all suffer from low scalability in a large PHR system, since file encryption is done in an one-to-one manner, while each PHR may have an unpredictable large number of users. To avoid such inconveniences, novel one-to-many encryption methods such as *attribute-based encryption* can be used [15]. In the seminal paper on ABE [16], data is encrypted to a group of uses characterized by a set of attributes, which potentially makes the key management more efficient. Since then, several works used ABE to realize fine-grained access control for outsourced data [17,18,19,20]. However, they have not addressed the multiple data owner settings, and there lacks a framework for patient-centric access control in multi-owner PHR systems. Note that, in [21] a single authority for all users and patients is adopted. However, this suffers from the key escrow problem, and patients' privacy still cannot be guaranteed since the authority has keys for all owners. Recently Ibraimi *et.al.* [22] applied ciphertext policy ABE (CP-ABE) [23] to manage the sharing of PHRs. However, they still assume a single public authority, while the challenging key-management issues remain largely unsolved.

3 Patient-Centric Data Access Control Framework for PHR in Cloud Computing

3.1 Problem Definition

We consider a PHR system where there exist multiple PHR owners and multiple PHR users. The owners refer to patients who have full control over their own PHR data, i.e., they can create, manage and delete it. The users include readers and writers that may come from various aspects. For example, a friend, a caregiver or a researcher. There is also a central server belonging to the PHR service provider that stores all the owners' PHRs, where there may be a large number of owners. Users access the PHR documents through the server in order to read or write to someone's PHR. The PHR files can be organized by their categories in a hierarchical way [4].

Security Model. In this paper, we consider honest but curious cloud server as those in [13] and [20]. That means the server will try to find out as much secret information in the stored PHR files as possible, but they will honestly follow the protocol in general. The server may also collude with a few malicious users in the system. On the other hand, some users will also try to access the files beyond their privileges. For example, a pharmacy may want to obtain the prescriptions of patients for marketing and boosting its profits. To do so, they

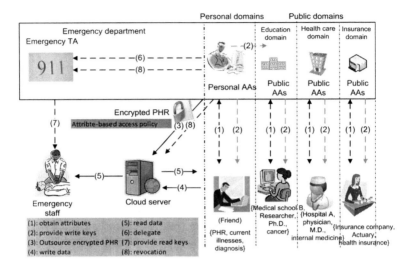

Fig. 1. The proposed multi-owner, multi-authority, and multi-user framework for access control of PHR in cloud computing

may even collude with other users. In addition, we assume each party in our system is preloaded with a public/private key pair, and entity authentication can be done by challenge-response protocols.

Requirements. In "*patient-centric privacy*", we envision that each patient specifies her own privacy policy. The owners want to prevent the server and unauthorized users from learning the contents of their PHR files. In particular, we have the following objectives:

- Fine-grained access control should be enforced, meaning different users can be authorized to read different sets of files. Also, we shall enable multiple writers to gain write-access to contribute information to PHR with accountability.
- User revocation. Whenever it is necessary, a user's access privileges should be revoked from future access in an efficient way.
- The data access policies should be flexible, i.e., changes to the predefined policies shall be allowed, especially under emergency scenarios.
- Efficiency. To support a large and unpredictable number of users, the system should be highly scalable, in terms of complexity in key management, user management, and computation and storage.

3.2 The Proposed Framework for Patient-Centric Data Access Control

Since the cloud server is no longer assumed to be fully trusted, data encryption should be adopted which should enforce patient-specified privacy policies.

To this end, each owner shall act as an authority that independently generates and distributes cryptographic keys to authorized users. However, as mentioned before, the management complexities may increase linearly with the number of users and owners.

Our proposed framework can solve this problem well. The key idea is two-fold. First, in order to lower the complexity of encryption and user management for each owner, we adopt attribute-based encryption (ABE) as the encryption primitive. Users/data are classified according to their attributes, such as professional roles/data types. Owners encrypt their PHR data under a certain access policy (or, a selected set of attributes), and only users that possess proper sets of attributes (decryption keys) are allowed to gain read access to those data.

Second, we divide the users in the whole PHR system into multiple *security domains* (SDs), and for each SD we introduce one or more authorities which govern attribute-based credentials for users within that SD. There are two categories of SDs: *public domains* (PUDs) and *personal domains* (PSDs). Each owner is in charge of her PSD consisting of users personally connected to her. A PUD usually contains a large number of professional users, and multiple *public attribute authorities* (PAA) that distributively governs a disjoint subset of attributes to remove key escrow. An owner encrypts her PHR data so that authorized users from both her PSD and PUDs may read it. In reality, each PUD can be mapped to an independent sector in the society, such as the health care, education, government or insurance sector. Users belonging to a PUD only need to obtain credentials from the corresponding public authorities, without the need to interact with any PHR owner, which greatly reduces the key management overhead of owners and users.

The framework is illustrated in Fig. 1, which features multiple SDs, multiple owners (personal AAs), multiple PAAs, and multiple users (writers and readers). Next, we describe the framework in a conceptual way.

Key distribution. Users first obtain attribute-based keys from their AAs. They submit their identity information and obtain secret keys that bind them to claimed attributes. For example, a physician in it would receive "hospital A, physician, M.D., internal medicine" as her attributes, possibly from different AAs. This is reflected by (1) in Fig. 1. In addition, the AAs distribute write keys that permit users in their SD to write to some patients' PHR ((2)). A user needs to present the write keys in order to gain write access to the cloud server.

PHR Access. First, the owners upload ABE-encrypted PHR files to the cloud server ((3)), each of them is associated with some personalized access policy, enforced by encryption. Only authorized users can decrypt the PHR files, excluding the server. For example, a policy may look like $\mathcal{P}:=$ "(profession=physician)$\wedge$ (specialty=internal medicine)$\wedge$(organization=hospital A)". The readers download PHR files from the server, and they can decrypt the files only if they have suitable attribute-based keys ((5)). The writers will be granted write access to someone's PHR, if they present proper write keys ((4)).

User revocation. There are two types of user revocation. The first one is revocation of a user's attribute, which is done by the AA that the user belongs to, where the actual computations can be delegated to the cloud server to improve efficiency ((8)). The second one is update of an owner's access policy for a specific PHR document, based on information passed from the owner to the server ((8)).

Break-glass. When an emergency happens, the regular access policies may no longer be applicable. To handle this situation, break-glass access is needed to access the victim's PHR. In our framework, each owner's PHR's access right is also delegated to an emergency department (ED, (6)). To prevent from abuse of break-glass option, the emergency staff needs to contact the ED to verify her identity and the emergency situation, and obtain temporary read keys ((7)). After the emergency is over, the patient can revoke the emergent access via the ED.

4   Flexible and Fine-Grained Data Access Control Mechanisms

In this section, we present mechanisms to achieve cryptographically enforced fine-grained data access control for PHRs in cloud computing, under our patient-centric access control framework. We adopt attribute-based encryption (ABE) as the cryptographic tool. ABE [16,23] is a collusion resistant, one-to-many encryption method, where only users possessing proper attributes can decrypt a ciphertext. ABE potentially allows patients to define their own access policies conveniently, eliminates the need to know the user list of each PHR file, and is scalable with the number of users.

The central issue here is how to achieve strong privacy guarantee for the owners. Consider a straightforward application of the CP-ABE scheme [23], where each AA in a PUD corresponds to an organization such as a health care provider, who defines all the attributes of its staffs and runs an independent ABE system. It is simple for an owner to realize complex access policies. If she wants to allow physicians from multiple hospitals to view one of her PHR file (e.g., Fig. 2 (a), $\mathcal{P}$), she can include multiple sets of ciphertext components, each set encrypted using one of the hospital's ABE public keys. However, if any of the authorities (hospitals) misbehave, it can decrypt all the data of owners who allow access to users in that hospital. This is clearly against the patient-centric privacy concept. In addition, this method is not efficient since the policies for the three hospitals are duplicated, which makes the ciphertext long. Ideally the same literals should be collapsed into one (Fig. 2 (a), $\mathcal{P}'$).

To solve the above problems, we adopt the multi-authority ABE (MA-ABE) proposed by Chase et.al. [24], where each authority governs a disjoint set of attributes distributively. An independent MA-ABE system is ran for each PUD, where there are multiple AAs in each of them; while each PSD (owner) runs the KP-ABE proposed by Goyal et.al [16] (GPSW). In each PUD, there is no longer a central authority (CA) and any coalition of up to corrupted $N - 2$ AAs cannot break the security of the system thanks to MA-ABE.

$\mathcal{P}$:=(physician$\wedge$internal medicine$\wedge$hospital A)
$\vee$(physician$\wedge$internal medicine$\wedge$hospital B)
$\vee$(physician$\wedge$internal medicine$\wedge$hospital C)...

$\mathcal{P}'$:=(physician$\wedge$internal medicine$\wedge$
(hospital A$\vee$hospital B$\vee$hospital C))

(a)

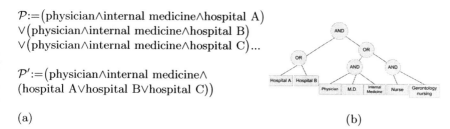

(b)

Fig. 2. (a): A patient-defined access policy under the naive way of authority arrangement. (b): An example policy realizable using MA-ABE under our framework.

Table 1. Frequently used notations

$\mathcal{A}$	The universe of data attributes
$\mathbb{A}$	The universe of role attributes
$\mathcal{A}_u$	User u's data attribute set
$\mathbb{A}_k^C$	A set of role attributes (from the kth AA) associated with a ciphertext
$\mathbb{A}_k^u$	A set of role attributes that user u obtained from the kth AA
$\mathcal{P}$	Access policy for a PHR file
P	An access policy assigned to a user
MK, PK	Master key of an AA and its public key for ABE
SK	A user's secret key
$rk_{i\rightarrow i'}$	Re-encryption key for the server to update attribute i to its current version i'

However, in MA-ABE the access policies are enforced in users' secret keys, and the policies are fixed once the keys are distributed which is not convenient for owners to specify their own policies. By our design, we show that by agreeing upon the formats of the key-policies and specifying which attributes are required in the ciphertext, the supported policy expressions enjoy some degree of flexibility from the encryptor's point of view, such as the one in Fig. 2 (b). In addition, it is a well-known challenging problem to revoke users/attributes efficiently and on-demand in ABE. We adapt the most recent techniques in ABE revocation [19,20], so that an owner/AA can revoke a user or a set of attributes on-demand by updating the ciphertexts and (possibly) user's secret keys, and part of these operations can be delegated to the server which enhances efficiency.

4.1 Definitions, Notations and Preliminary

There are two types of attributes in the PHR system, namely *data attribute* and *role attribute*. The former refers to the intrinsic properties of the PHR data, such as the category of a PHR file. The latter represents the roles of the entities in the system, such as the professional role of a user in an organization. The main notations are summarized in Table. 1.

Key-policy Attribute-Based Encryption (KP-ABE) Schemes. The KP-ABE associates a set of attributes with the ciphertext, and the access policies are enforced in the keys distributed to each user.

First, we briefly review the multi-authority ABE (MA-ABE) [24] which will used in this paper. Assume there are N AAs in total. The MA-ABE consists of the following four algorithms:

Setup This algorithm is cooperatively executed by all of the N AAs. It takes as input a security parameter λ, an attribute universe $\{\mathbb{A}_k\}_{k \in \{1,...,N\}}$ where $\mathbb{A}_k = \{1, 2, ..., n_k\}$ and outputs public keys and a master key for each AA. It defines common bilinear groups $\mathbb{G}_1$, $\mathbb{G}_2$ with prime order q and generators g_1, g_2 respectively, and a bilinear map $e : \mathbb{G}_1 \times \mathbb{G}_2 \to \mathbb{G}_T$. The PK and AA_k's master key MK_k are as follows:

$$MK_k^{MA-ABE} = \langle msk_k, \{t_{k,i}\}_{i \in \mathbb{A}_k}\rangle,$$

$$PK^{MA-ABE} = \langle Y = e(g_1, g_2)^{\sum_k v_k}, \{y_k, \{T_{k,i} = g_2^{t_{k,i}}\}_{i \in \mathbb{A}_k}\}_{k \in \{1,...,N\}}\rangle$$

where msk_k is AA_k's master secret key used only in key issuing, y_k is only used by the AAs, and $t_{k,i} \in \mathbb{Z}_q$ and $T_{k,i} \in \mathbb{G}_2$ are attribute private/public key components for attribute i.

Key issuing In this algorithm, the AAs collectively generate a secret key for a user. For a user with ID[3] u, the secret key is in the form

$$SK_u^{MA-ABE} = \langle D_u = g_1^{R_u}, \{D_{k,i} = g_1^{p_k(i)/t_{k,i}}\}_{k \in \{1,...,N\}, i \in \mathbb{A}_k^u}\rangle,$$

where R_u is a random number for user u, and $p_k(\cdot)$ is a d_k degree polynomial generated by the kth AA.

Encryption This algorithm takes as input a message M, public key PK, and a set of attributes $\{\mathbb{A}_1^C, ..., \mathbb{A}_N^C\}$, and outputs the ciphertext E as follows. The encryptor first chooses an $s \in_R \mathbb{Z}_q$, and then returns

$$\langle E_0 = M \cdot Y^s, E_1 = g_2^s, \{C_{k,i} = T_{k,i}^s\}_{i \in \mathbb{A}_k^C, k \in \{1,...,N\}}\rangle.$$

Decryption This algorithm takes as input a ciphertext E, PK, and a user secret key SK_u. If for each AA k, $|\mathbb{A}_k^C \cap \mathbb{A}_k^u| \geq d_k$, the user pairs up $D_{k,i}$ and $C_{k,i}$ and reconstructs $e(g_1, g_2)^{sp_k(0)}$. After multiplying all these values together with $e(D_u, E_1)$, u recovers the blind factor Y^s and thus gets M.

Second, we use the GPSW KP-ABE scheme [16] for each PSD, where all the attributes and keys come from single personal AA. There are also four algorithms. The setup generates group $\mathbb{G}_1$ with generator g_1, and $e : \mathbb{G}_1 \times \mathbb{G}_1 \to \mathbb{G}_T$. The MK/PK are as follows.

$$MK^{GPSW} = \langle \{y, t_i\}_{i \in \{1,...,n\}}\rangle,$$

$$PK^{GPSW} = \langle Y = e(g_1, g_1)^y, \{T_i = g_1^{t_i}\}_{i \in \{1,...,n\}}\rangle$$

where $n = |\mathcal{A}|$. In key generation, the $SK_u^{GPSW} = \langle \{D_i = g_1^{p(i)/t_i}\}_{i \in \mathcal{A}^u}\rangle$. The encryption is the same except $k = 1$, while the decryption is similar.

---

[3] This ID is a secret only known to u.

Table 2. Sample attribute based keys for three public users in the health care domain

Attribute authority	AMA		ABMS	AHA
Attribute type	Profession	License status	Medical specialty	Organization
$\mathbb{A}^{u_1}$: user 1	Physician *	M.D. *	Internal medicine *	Hospital A *
$\mathbb{A}^{u_2}$: user 2	Nurse *	Nurse license *	Gerontology *	Hospital B *
$\mathbb{A}^{u_3}$: user 3	Pharmacist *	Pharm. license *	General *	Pharmacy C *
Key policy	2-out-of-n_1		1-out-of-n_2	1-out-of-n_3

4.2 Key Distribution

An essential function of key distribution is to enable patients' control over their own access policies. The owners distribute keys only to the users in their PSD, while the AAs in a PUD distribute keys to their PUD. For the former, it is easy for owner to generate each user's key directly so that it enforces that user's access right based on a set of data attributes; however, for a PUD, the challenge is how to allow different owners to specify different personalized user access policies while each user's secret key enforces a fixed access policy pre-distributed by the PAAs. In our solution, the access policies in public users' secret keys conform to some predefined format agreed between the owners and the PAAs, which enables an owner to enforce her own policy through choosing which set of attributes to be included in the ciphertext.

For each PSD, there is the same, pre-defined data attribute universe $\mathcal{A}$, where each attribute is a category of the PHR files, such as "basic profile", "medical history", "allergies", and "prescriptions". When an owner first registers in the PHR system, an end-user software will run its own copy of GPSW's setup algorithm to generate a public key PK and a master key MK for herself, with each component corresponding to one data attribute. After the owner creates her PHR, she invites several person in her PSD to view it. For each invited user, she defines an access policy based on the data attributes, and generates a corresponding secret key SK and sends it securely. Those users are usually personally known to the owner, such as her family member, friends or primary doctors. A family member's policy may look like "basic profile" ∨ "medical history", which gives access to files belonging to either categories. In order to enable the owner themselves to decrypt all files in their PHRs, each owner retains only one secret key component, the data attribute "PHR" which is the root of the category hierarchy.

For each PUD, MA-ABE is adopted. The PAAs first generate the MKs and PK using setup. Each AA k defines a disjoint set of role attributes $\mathbb{A}_k$, which are relatively static properties of the public users. These attributes are classified by their types, such as profession and license status, medical specialty, and affiliation where each type has multiple possible values. Basically, each AA monitors a disjoint subset of those types. For example, in the healthcare domain, the American Medical Association (AMA) may issue medical professional licenses like "physician", "M.D.", "nurse", "entry-level license" etc., the American Board of Medical Specialties (ABMS) certifies specialties like "internal medicine", "surgery" etc;

and the American Hospital Association (AHA) may define user affiliations such as "hospital A" and "pharmacy D". In order to represent the "do not care" option for the owners, we add a *wildcard attribute* "*" in each type of the attributes. The format of the key-policies is restricted to threshold gates, i.e., d_k out of n_k where $n_k = |\mathbb{A}_k^u \cap \mathbb{A}_k^C|$ for the kth AA. Thus, there needs an agreement between the AAs and the owners (encryptors) about what how to implement owners' policies. The AA's part of the agreement is that:

at lease one attribute should be required from each category of attributes, and the wildcard associated with each category shall always be included[4].

After key distribution, the AAs can almost remain offline. A detailed key distribution example is given in Table. 2.

In summary, a user u in an owner's PSD has the following keys: $SK_u^{GPSW} = \langle \{g_1^{\frac{q_i(0)}{t_i}}\}_{i \in \mathcal{A}_u} \rangle$ where $q_x(\cdot)$ is the polynomial for node x in u's access tree. For a user u in a PUD, $SK_u^{MA-ABE} = \langle D_u, \{D_{k,i}\}_{k \in \{1,...,N\}, i \in \mathbb{A}_k^u} \rangle$.

4.3   Enforcement of Access Privileges

Achieving Fine-grained Read Access Control through PHR Encryption. After an owner creates her PHR files, she will be allowed to specify her own privacy policy. The personal users and public users are dealt with differently. For the former, since GPSW is adopted which is based on data attributes, the policy is actually defined per personal user, i.e., what types of files each user can access (denoted as P_{per}). For the latter, the policy is defined per file, i.e., what kinds of users can access each file (denoted as $\mathcal{P}_{pub}$)

For the PSDs, the form of a user's key-policy is unrestricted, i.e., can be any tree structure consisting of threshold gates [16]. So for encryption, the owner simply associates a set of intrinsic data attributes, $\mathcal{A}_F$, with the ciphertext of each PHR file F. $\mathcal{A}_F$ always includes all the data attributes of F on the branch from the root to the leaf node in the category tree, in order to give hierarchical read access to personal users. An example is "PHR, medical history, influenza history". In this way, a user with key corresponding to single attribute "medical history" can view all files under this category.

However, for the public users, the problem is more intricate. Since in MA-ABE it is the AAs that govern role attributes, and the key-policies are set by the AAs rather than the owners, we shall also impose some rules on owners when encrypting each file, to enforce their personalized $\mathcal{P}_{pub}$. The owner's part of the agreement is, she must *include at least one attribute value from each attribute type (column) in the ciphertext*. In this way, AND logic across attribute types is realized by MA-ABE, while OR logic among different values within the same attribute type is realized by including corresponding multiple attribute components in the ciphertext.

For more expressive policies, the AA's part of the protocol needs to be enhanced. For example, if an owner includes {"physician", "M.D.", "internal medicine",

---

[4] Here we are assuming that each medical professional either possess one or none of the attributes of each type.

"hospital A", "nurse", "*", "Gerontology nursing", "hospital B" }, she meant the following policy: (("physician"∧"M.D."∧"internal medicine")∨("nurse"∧"any level"∧"Gerontology nursing"))∧("hospital A"∨"hospital B"). However, since the "*" is the only and same one for attribute type "license status", a physician without a "M.D." attribute but with a "*" can also decrypt the message. To solve this problem, we observe that the set of "license status" of different professions are disjoint in reality. Therefore we can further classify the wildcard attributes in "license status" by its associated profession. For example, there would be a different "*" for physicians and nurses. In this way, the policy in Fig. 2 can be realized.

We note that the expressibility of the above approach is somewhat limited by MA-ABE, which only supports policies in the "AND" form. For example, if an owner chooses hospital A and hospital B as organization attributes, the policies over the rest of the attribute types have to be the same for the two hospitals. However, our scheme does allow different policies for different organizations, in which the owner needs to attach multiple sets of ciphertext components, each corresponding to one organization. This may result in longer ciphertext lengths. Nevertheless, we argue that in reality most patients will not differentiate access policies across the same type of organizations.

If $\mathcal{P}_{pub}$ involves multiple PUDs, then $\mathcal{P}_{pub} = \cup_{pub_j}\{\mathcal{P}_{pub_j}\}$, and multiple sets of ciphertext components needs to be included. Since in reality, the number of PUDs is usually small, our encryption method is much more efficient than the straightforward way in which the length of ciphertexts grows linearly with the number of organizations. Note that, for efficiency, each file is encrypted with a randomly generated symmetric key (FSK), which is then encrypted by ABE.

In summary, the ciphertext for FSK of file F is:
$E_F(FSK) = \langle E_{per}(FSK), E_{pub}(FSK)\rangle$, where

$$E_{per}(FSK) = \langle \mathcal{A}_F, E_0^{per} = MY_{per}^s, E_1^{per} = g_{1,per}^s, \{C_i^{per} = T_{per,i}^s\}_{i \in \mathcal{A}_F}\rangle$$

$$E_{pub}(FSK) = \langle \mathbb{A}_F = \cup_{pub_j}\{\mathbb{A}_F^{pub_j}\}, \{E_0^{pub_j} = MY_{pub_j}^s\}, \{E_1^{pub_j} = g_{2,pub_j}^s\},$$
$$\{C_{pub_j,k,i} = T_{pub_j,k,i}^s\}_{k \in \{1,...,N_j\}, i \in \mathbb{A}_{F_k}}\rangle$$

where pub_j is the jth PUD, $j \in \{1, ..., m\}$ and m is the number of PUDs.

Grant Write Access. If there is no restrictions on write access, anyone may write to someone's PHR using only public keys, which is undesirable. By granting write access, we mean a writer should obtain proper authorization from the organization she is in (and/or from the targeting owner), which shall be able to be verified by the server who grants/rejects write access.

A naive way is to let each writer obtain a signature from her organization every time she intends to write. Yet this requires the organizations be always online. The observation is that, it is desirable and practical to authorize according to time periods whose granularity can be adjusted. For example, a doctor should be permitted to write only during her office hours; on the other hand, the doctor must not be able to write to patients that are not treated by her. Therefore, we combine signatures with the hash chain technique to achieve our goals.

Suppose the time granularity is set to Δt, and the time is divided into periods of Δt. For each working cycle (e.g. a day), an organization generates a hash chain $\mathcal{H} = \{h_0, h_1, ..., h_n\}$, where $H(h_{i-1}) = h_i$, $1 \leq i \leq n$. At time 0, the organization broadcasts a signature of the chain end h_n ($\sigma_{org}(h_n)$) to all users in its domain. After that it multicasts h_{n-i} to the set of authorized writers at each time period i. Note that, the above method enables timely revocation of write access, i.e., the authority simply stops issuing hashes for a writer at the time of revocation. In addition, an owner needs to distribute a time-related signature: $\sigma_{owner}(\text{ts}, \text{tt})$ to the entities that requests write access (which can be delegated to the organization), where ts is the start time of the granted time window, and tt is the end of the time window. For example, to enable a billing clerk to add billing information to Alice's PHR, Alice can specify "8am to 5pm" as the granted time window at the beginning of a clinical visit. Note that, for writers in the PSD of the owner, they only need to obtain signatures from the owner herself.

Generally, during time period j, an authorized writer w submits the following to the server after being authenticated to it:

$$\breve{E}_{pk_{server}}(\text{ts}||\text{tt}||\sigma_{owner}(\text{ts}||\text{tt})||h_n||\sigma_{org}(h_n)||h_{n-j}||r)$$

where $\breve{E}_{pk_{server}}$ is the public key encryption using the server's public key, and r is a nonce to prevent replay attack. The server verifies if the signatures are correct using both org's and $owner$'s public keys, and whether $H^j(h_{n-j}) = h_n$, where $H^j()$ means hash j times. Only if both holds, the writer is granted write access and the server accepts the contents uploaded subsequently.

4.4   User Revocation

A user needs to be revoked on-demand when her attributes change or an owner does not want the user to access parts of her PHR anymore. For the PAAs, they revoke a user's role attributes that deprive her all the read access privileges corresponding to those attributes; an owner revokes data attributes possessed by a user that prevent her from accessing all the PHR files labeled with those attributes. In ABE, traditional revocation schemes [17,25] are not timely, which require non-revoked users to frequently obtain key updates issued by the authorities. Here we apply the revocation method proposed by Yu et.al. [19,20]. The idea is to let an authority actively update the affected attributes for all the remaining users. To this end, the following updates should be carried out by the AA: (1) all the public key components for those affected attributes; (2) all the secret key components corresponding to those attributes of a remaining user. (3) Also, the server shall update all the ciphertext components corresponding to those attributes.

In order to reduce the potential computational burden for the AAs/servers, based on [19,20] we adopt proxy re-encryption to delegate operations (2) and (3) to the cloud server, and use lazy-revocation to reduce the overhead. In particular, for GPSW used by each owner, each data attribute i is associated with a version number ver_i. Upon each revocation event, if i is an affected attribute, the owner submits a re-key $rk_{i,i'} = t'_i/t_i$ to the server, who then updates the affected ciphertexts and increases their version numbers. The remaining users' secret key components are updated similarly; note that a dummy attribute needs to be additionally defined by the owner which is always ANDed with each user's key-policy to prevent secret key leakage. By lazy-revocation, we mean the affected ciphertexts and user secret keys may only be updated when a user logs into the system next time. And by the form of the re-key, all the updates can be aggregated from the last login to the most current one. The process is done similarly for MA-ABE. Due to space limitations, we do not present the details in this paper.

In addition, for each specific PHR file, an owner can temporarily revoke one type of user from accessing it after it is uploaded to the server, which can be regarded as changing her access policy for that file. For example, a patient may not want doctors to view her PHR after she finishes a visit to a hospital, she can simply delete the ciphertext components corresponding to attribute "doctor" in her PHR files. In order to restore the access right of doctors, she will need to reconstruct those components. This can be achieved by keeping the random number s used for each encrypted file on her own computer.

4.5   Handling Break-Glass

For certain parts of the PHR data, medical staffs need to have temporary access when an emergency happens to a patient, who may become unconscious and is unable to change her access policies. Since the data is encrypted, the medical staffs need some trapdoor information to decrypt those data. Under our frame-work, this can be naturally achieved by letting each patient delegate her trapdoor to the emergency department (ED). The ED needs to authenticate the medical staff who requests for a trapdoor. Specifically, a patient's trapdoor for her PHR is in the following form: $TPD = g_1^d$, where d is randomly chosen from $\mathbb{Z}_q$. For each of her PHR file that she wants to be accessed under emergency, she appends an additional ciphertext component: $\tilde{E} = M \cdot e(g_1^s, TPD) = M \cdot e(g_1, g_1)^{ds}$. The patient then sends TPD to the ED who keeps it in a database of patient directory. Upon emergency, the medical staff requests and obtains the corresponding patient's TPD from ED (the ED encrypts TPD using the staff's public key), and then decrypts the PHR file by computing $\tilde{E}/e(g_1^s, TPD) = M$. After the patient recovers from the emergency, she can restore the normal access by com-puting a re-key: d'/d, and then submit it to the ED and the server to update TPD and $\tilde{E}$ to their newest versions.

5   Scheme Analysis

5.1   Security Analysis

In this section, we analyze the security of proposed access control mechanisms. First, the GPSW and MA-ABE schemes are proven to be secure in [16] and

Table 3. Scheme analysis and comparison

	Our proposed scheme			[22]		
Privacy guarantee	Resistant to AA collusion			Only resistant to user collusion		
Key distribution	$O(\|PSD\|)$ (Owner)	$O(1)$ (user)	$O(\|PUD_i\|)$ (PAA)	$O(\|PSD\|)$ (Owner)	$O(1)$ (user)	$O(\sum_{i=1}^{m} \|PUD_i\|)$ (Public auth.)
Revocation	Efficient and on-demand			N/A		
Public key size	$\|\mathbb{A}\|_k + N_i$ [24] (PUD_k)	$\|\mathcal{A}\| + 1$ (Owner)		$\bigcup \|\mathbb{A}\|_k$ (The PUD)	$\|\mathcal{A}\|$ (Owner)	
Secret key size	$\|\mathcal{A}_u\| + 1$ (Public user)	$\|\mathcal{A}_u\| + 1$ (personal user)		$\|\mathcal{A}_u\|$ (public user)	$\|\mathcal{A}_u\|$ (personal user)	
Ciphertext length	$\|\mathcal{A}^C\| + \|\mathbb{A}^C\| + 2 \times m$			$\geq \|\mathcal{A}^C\| + \|\mathbb{A}^C\| + 3$		
Decryption complexity	$O(1)$ (w/ delegation)			$O(\mathcal{A}_u \cap \mathcal{A}^C)$ or $O(\mathbb{A}_u \cap \mathbb{A}^C)$		
Policy expressibility	CNF, enhanced with wildcards			Any monotonic boolean formula		

[24], respectively. Especially, the encrypted data is confidential to non-authorized users. Also, they are both resistant to user collusion, and MA-ABE is further resistant to collusion among up to $N - 2$ AAs in one PUD. This implies that strong privacy guarantee is achieved through file encryption. Second, for the write access enforcement, the one-way property of the hash chain ensures that a writer can only obtain write keys for the time period that she is authorized for. Also, writer can hardly forge a signature of the hash chain end according to the unforgeability of the underlying signature scheme. Third, the revocation scheme is secure, which is proven in [20] under standard security assumptions. Finally, for the break-glass access, an adversary is not feasible to obtain TPD given $\tilde{E}$ and g_1^s, due to the security properties of bilinear pairing.

5.2   Performance Analysis

The performance analysis is summarized in Table. 3. We compare our solution with that of [22] which uses CP-ABE, and a single public authority is used. m is the number of PUDs, while N_i is the number of PAAs in the ith PUD. Note that, the key management complexity is in terms of the number of interactions during key distribution. For ciphertext length comparison, for our scheme the access policy for each PUD is restricted to conjunctive form: $\mathcal{P}_{pub} := \mathcal{P}_1 \wedge ... \wedge \mathcal{P}_m$, where each $\mathcal{P}_i$ is a boolean clause consisting of "∧" and "∨". The number of ciphertext components related to the PUDs is

$$\|\mathbb{A}^C\| = \sum_{j=1}^{m} \left(\sum_{k=1}^{N_i} \|\mathbb{A}_{k,i}^C\| \right),$$

which is linear to the number of PUDs and the number of PAAs. In practice, there are usually a few PUDs (e.g., <5) and a few PAAs and types of attributes in each of them (e.g., 5). Therefore the additional storage overhead for the server created by each ciphertext (encryption of the file encryption key) is usually in the order of tens of group elements, which typically equals to a few hundred bytes if 160-bit ECC is adopted. This is acceptable compared with the length of a PHR document (usually in the order of KB). Apart from those, for each owner, to change access policies and enable emergency access, 2 additional group elements (s and d) shall be locally stored for each encrypted PHR file, which is quite small. The result for [22]'s scheme is derived based on the same access policy to that in our scheme; it is a lower bound due to the lack of wildcard.

Finally, the computational overhead in our scheme is low, since the decryption operation can be mostly delegated to the server. A user can submit all the $D_{k,i}$s to the server and only computes one bilinear pairing: $e(D_u, E_1)$. This is secure because the server does not know D_u.

6 Conclusion

In this paper, we have proposed a novel framework of access control to realize patient-centric privacy for personal health records in cloud computing. Considering partially trustworthy cloud servers, we argue that patients shall have full control of their own privacy through encrypting their PHR files to allow fine-grained access. The framework addresses the unique challenges brought by multiple PHR owners and users, in that we greatly reduce the complexity of key management when the number of owners and users in the system is large. We utilize multi-authority attribute-based encryption to encrypt the PHR data, so that patients can allow access not only by personal users, but also various users from different public domains with different professional roles, qualifications and affiliations. An important future work will be enhancing the MA-ABE scheme to support more expressive owner-defined access policies.

Acknowledgements. This work was supported in part by the US National Science Foundation under grants CNS-0716306, CNS-0831628, CNS-0746977, and CNS-0831963.

References

1. Armbrust, M., Fox, A., Griffith, R., Joseph, A.D., Katz, R., Konwinski, A., Lee, G., Patterson, D.A., Rabkin, A., Stoica, I., Zaharia, M.: Above the clouds: A berkeley view of cloud computing (February 2009)
2. At risk of exposure – in the push for electronic medical records, concern is growing about how well privacy can be safeguarded (2006), http://articles.latimes.com/2006/jun/26/health/he-privacy26
3. The health insurance portability and accountability act of 1996 (1996), http://www.cms.hhs.gov/HIPAAGenInfo/01_Overview.asp
4. Benaloh, J., Chase, M., Horvitz, E., Lauter, K.: Patient controlled encryption: ensuring privacy of electronic medical records. In: CCSW 2009: Proceedings of the 2009 ACM workshop on Cloud computing security, pp. 103–114 (2009)
5. Mandl, K.D., Szolovits, P., Kohane, I.S.: Public standards and patients' control: how to keep electronic medical records accessible but private. BMJ 322(7281), 283 (2001)
6. Wang, W., Li, Z., Owens, R., Bhargava, B.: Secure and efficient access to outsourced data. In: CCSW 2009, pp. 55–66 (2009)

7. Damiani, E., di Vimercati, S.D.C., Foresti, S., Jajodia, S., Paraboschi, S., Samarati, P.: Key management for multi-user encrypted databases. In: StorageSS 2005, pp. 74–83 (2005)
8. Atallah, M.J., Frikken, K.B., Blanton, M.: Dynamic and efficient key management for access hierarchies. In: CCS 2005, pp. 190–202 (2005)
9. Blundo, C., Cimato, S., De Capitani di Vimercati, S., De Santis, A., Foresti, S., Paraboschi, S., Samarati, P.: Managing key hierarchies for access control enforcement: Heuristic approaches. In: Computers & Security (2010) (to appear)
10. Scholl, M., Stine, K., Lin, K., Steinberg, D.: Draft security architecture design process for health information exchanges (HIEs). Report, NIST (2009)
11. Ferraiolo, D.F., Sandhu, R., Gavrila, S., Kuhn, D.R., Chandramouli, R.: Proposed NIST standard for role-based access control. ACM TISSEC 4(3), 224–274 (2001)
12. Jin, J., Ahn, G.-J., Hu, H., Covington, M.J., Zhang, X.: Patient-centric authorization framework for sharing electronic health records. In: SACMAT 2009, pp. 125–134 (2009)
13. di Vimercati, S.D.C., Foresti, S., Jajodia, S., Paraboschi, S., Samarati, P.: Over-encryption: management of access control evolution on outsourced data. In: VLDB 2007, pp. 123–134 (2007)
14. Dong, C., Russello, G., Dulay, N.: Shared and searchable encrypted data for untrusted servers. In: DBSec 2008, pp. 127–143 (2008)
15. Li, M., Lou, W., Ren, K.: Data security and privacy in wireless body area networks. IEEE Wireless Communications Magazine (February 2010)
16. Goyal, V., Pandey, O., Sahai, A., Waters, B.: Attribute-based encryption for fine-grained access control of encrypted data. In: CCS 2006, pp. 89–98 (2006)
17. Boldyreva, A., Goyal, V., Kumar, V.: Identity-based encryption with efficient revocation. In: CCS 2008, pp. 417–426 (2008)
18. Ibraimi, L., Petkovic, M., Nikova, S., Hartel, P., Jonker, W.: Ciphertext-policy attribute-based threshold decryption with flexible delegation and revocation of user attributes (2009), http://purl.org/utwente/65471
19. Yu, S., Wang, C., Ren, K., Lou, W.: Achieving secure, scalable, and fine-grained data access control in cloud computing. In: IEEE INFOCOM 2010 (2010)
20. Yu, S., Wang, C., Ren, K., Lou, W.: Attribute based data sharing with attribute revocation. In: ASIACCS 2010 (2010)
21. Liang, X., Lu, R., Lin, X., Shen, X.S.: Patient self-controllable access policy on phi in ehealthcare systems. In: AHIC 2010 (2010)
22. Ibraimi, L., Asim, M., Petkovic, M.: Secure management of personal health records by applying attribute-based encryption. Technical Report, University of Twente (2009)
23. Bethencourt, J., Sahai, A., Waters, B.: Ciphertext-policy attribute-based encryption. In: IEEE S& P 2007, pp. 321–334 (2007)
24. Chase, M., Chow, S.S.: Improving privacy and security in multi-authority attribute-based encryption. In: CCS 2009, pp. 121–130 (2009)
25. Liang, X., Lu, R., Lin, X., Shen, X.S.: Ciphertext policy attribute based encryption with efficient revocation. Technical Report, University of Waterloo (2010)

A Study on False Channel Condition Reporting Attacks in Wireless Networks*

Dongho Kim and Yih-Chun Hu

Electrical and Computer Engineering, University of Illinois at Urbana-Champaign
{dkim99,yihchun}@illinois.edu

Abstract. Wireless networking protocols are increasingly being designed to exploit a user's measured channel condition; we call such protocols *channel-aware*. Each user reports its measured channel condition to a manager of wireless resources and a channel-aware protocol uses these reports to determine how resources are allocated to users. In a channel-aware protocol, each user's reported channel condition affects the performance of every other user. A possible attack against channel-aware protocols is *false feedback* of channel condition. The deployment of channel-aware protocols increases the risks posed by false feedback. In this paper, we study the potential impact of an attacker that falsely reports its channel condition and propose a defense mechanism to securely estimate channel condition. We analyze our mechanism and evaluate the system performance deploying our mechanism through simulation. Our evaluation shows that our mechanism effectively thwarts channel condition misreporting attack.

Keywords: Wireless Network, Opportunistic Scheduler, Cooperative Relay.

1 Introduction

Many protocols in modern wireless networks treat a link's channel condition information as a protocol input parameter; we call such protocols *channel-aware*. Examples include opportunistic schedulers [1, 2], cooperative relaying network architectures [3, 4], and efficient ad hoc network routing metrics [5, 6]. Even though each different application exploits the channel-condition information in different ways, the main goal of a channel-aware protocol is to enhance system throughput by selecting a user or a path with good channel condition in a given time instance.

Most work on channel-aware protocols has mainly focused on how channel condition information can be used to more efficiently utilize wireless resources. An implicit assumption of most past study is that each user correctly reports channel condition information. However, this assumption can induce a security vulnerability since channel condition can be asymmetric [7]; specifically, due to

---

* This material is based upon work partially supported by USARO under Contract No. W-911-NF-0710287 and the NSF under Grant No. CNS-0953600.

S. Jajodia and J. Zhou (Eds.): SecureComm 2010, LNICST 50, pp. 107–124, 2010.

possible channel condition asymmetry, channel condition to a user *can only be measured and reported by that user*. An attacker that misreports its measured channel condition might allow the attacker to steal another users' service opportunities, for example in a setting where a centralized scheduler schedules each user based on its channel condition. In another setting, a user chooses a next-hop forwarder based on the relayer's channel condition, in which case an attacker can misreport its channel condition to generate a sinkhole [8] to lure packets to itself possibly for the purpose of dropping those packets.

In this paper, we reveal the possible effects of false channel condition reporting in various channel-aware network protocols and propose a defense mechanism that provides secure channel condition estimation. Our contributions are:

- We propose a secure channel condition estimation algorithm that is generally applicable to any channel-aware protocol.
- We analyze our algorithm in terms of performance and security, and we perform a simulation study to verify our performance analysis.
- We analyze the effect of misreported channel condition on reference systems with opportunistic schedulers and cooperative relaying protocols. We also show through simulation that our defense mechanism thwarts the attack effect on those systems.

The false channel condition reporting attack that we introduce in this paper is difficult to identify by existing mechanisms, since our attack is mostly protocol compliant; an attacker need to modify only the channel-condition measurement mechanism. Our attack can thus be performed using modified user equipment legitimately registered to a network.

To the best of our knowledge, we are the first to study the false channel condition reporting attack in a variety of network settings. Racic et al. [9] consider attacks based on false feedback to the PF scheduler. In their work, as in our work, PF effectively resists false feedback, so their attack primarily works by exploiting the handover process rather than the channel-aware nature of PF scheduler. They propose a secure handover algorithm that is orthogonal to our approach of secure channel condition estimation.

The rest of our paper is organized as follows. In Section 2, we introduce the concept of our attack. Then, we develop a defense mechanism called *secure channel condition estimation* against the false reporting attack in Section 3. We evaluate our algorithm through analysis and simulation in Section 4. In Section 5, we briefly review related work. Section 6 concludes this paper.

2   Attack Overview

Threat Model. Our study assumes that a network protocol exploits the channel condition information reported by each user and each user reports to enhance network performance. In this setting, a user can falsely report its channel condition. There are two different types of false reports: *underclaiming* (reporting a channel condition that is worse than that actually measured by the user) and *overclaiming* (reporting a channel condition that is better than that actually measured by the user). The effectiveness of a false channel condition reporting attack depends on the way the attacked protocol uses the reported channel condition, and an attacker's ability to exploit the protocol. We use the term 'channel condition' to refer to all aspects impacting a node's ability to receive a packet.

Attack Purpose. Generally, an attacker's goal in a network is to greedily raise its own bandwidth share or to maliciously downgrade other users' bandwidth share without regard to its own bandwidth share. For these purposes, an underclaiming action is not desirable since underclaiming merely forfeits an attacker's service opportunity. Hence, we focus only on overclaiming actions in this paper. An overclaiming receiver may lose its throughput since the overclaiming receiver may induce a higher order (more aggressive) modulation, possibly resulting in excessive loss. As a result, this paper focuses on attackers that are malicious rather than selfish. We demonstrate through simulation the attack's effect on specific systems in Section 4.3.

Attack Feasibility. An attacker can easily implement false channel condition reporting attack by modifying only a subcomponent that reports channel condition. This subcomponent of user equipment can be implemented in hardware or software. One recent trend of user equipment implementation is to move increasing amount of functionality into software in order to improve adaptability [10, 11, 12]. The increasing software control of user equipment makes false channel condition reporting attack an increasingly practical attack.

3   Defense

In this section, we discuss possible solutions for the false channel feedback attack introduced in Section 2. We argue that to fundamentally defend against attacks that involve false channel condition reports, we need a scheme to securely estimate channel condition. Then, we develop our secure channel condition estimation algorithm.

3.1   Solution Spectrum

To defend against an attack that misreports the channel condition, there are possible approaches. One possible approach is anomaly detection. Anomaly detection is a tool that monitors each user's performance to identify attackers. A response mechanism then disconnects the attacker from the network. A second possible approach is to devise a fair scheduler to provide fair share of a network bandwidth while exploiting channel-aware property. A third possible approach is to measure throughput of a node and compare the measured throughput and the theoretically calculated throughput based on reported channel condition.

Even though these approaches can mitigate the effectiveness of the attack, they have fundamental drawbacks. Anomaly detection mechanisms are subject to detection errors, which could result in incorrect termination of a normal user's service or failure to detect an attacker. When a fair scheduler is used to reduce the effect of the attack, we can frustrate the original goal of channel-aware protocol which is to use resources most efficiently. A scheduler considering fairness will substantially reduce the efficiency when compared to the original protocol, since fairness requires allocation of resources to less-capable channels. We will see the throughput difference between most efficient scheduler and fair scheduler in Section 4.3. In a setting where a sender chooses a relayer with good channel condition, a receiver can calculate a theoretical throughput based on a relayer's reported channel condition and compare the theoretical throughput and actually received throughput. However, this method assumes that a receiver is honest. A receiver can be an attacker not acknowledging that an honest relayer does not forward its packets.

To more effectively prevent the false channel condition reporting attack, we need a mechanism that does not impede the efficiency of channel-aware protocols even under the false reporting attack. We observe that the false reporting attacks are possible because we allow a non-trustable entity to report the channel condition. Our basic approach is to replace non-trustable-entity-driven channel-condition reporting with trustable-entity-driven channel-condition estimation. For example, in a cellular network, base station is a trustable entity and users are non-trustable entities. In this paper, we do not develop whole specific protocols for such networks; rather, we develop a generic algorithm that can be integrated into any channel-aware protocol. We leave protocol integration and design as future work.

3.2   Scope of Our Algorithm

There are two cases to consider an channel condition misreporting attack. The first case is that a trusted entity gets the report of a node's channel condition to the trusted entity. The second case is that a trusted entity can get the report of a node's channel condition to the other node from an untrusted node. The latter case can happen in the deployment of an efficient ad hoc network routing metrics [5,6]. In the first case, the trusted entity can securely examine the channel condition using our algorithm. However, for the latter case, it is difficult for a trusted entity to identify an attacker since the trusted entity may not trust the reports from an untrusted node. In this paper, we focus on the first case as an initial step toward a complete defense against an attack.

3.3   Secure Channel Condition Estimation

In this section, we present our secure channel estimation scheme to prevent an attacker from overclaiming. We do not consider underclaiming, as explained in Section 2, because an attacker gains no benefit from underclaiming, and because an attacker can always reduce its actual channel condition, for example by modifying his antenna. The purpose of this paper is not to propose a whole system but to describe how our mechanism defends against an attacker that overclaims the condition of a single link. We start by presenting the intuition of our approach.

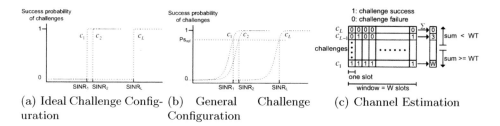

(a) Ideal Challenge Config-   (b)   General   Challenge   (c) Channel Estimation
uration   Configuration

Fig. 1. Secure Channel Estimation

Intuition. For convenience of presentation, we call the trustable entity a "base station" and the non-trustable entity a "user". The base station's goal is to securely and accurately estimate each user's channel condition. We first present our solution to a simplified problem in which a base station wants to know whether or not a user experiences channel condition at least as good as some specified SINR. To solve this simplified problem, the base station sends a *challenge* to a user. This challenge is a packet that can be correctly decoded with high probability only when the channel condition exceeds some specified SINR. The challenge includes a value known only to the base station. Upon receiving the challenge, a user returns the value in that challenge to the base station, which can then compare the received value to the transmitted value. The base station considers the channel condition to exceed the specified SINR if and only if the received value is correct. This challenge mechanism prevents a user with poorer channel condition than the specified SINR from correctly decoding the challenge packet. Our channel condition estimation scheme extends this single challenge scheme to multiple challenges in order to more finely estimate the channel condition.

System Model. We consider a network cell consisting of a base station and N users served by the base station. $\mathcal{N} = \{1, 2, \ldots, N\}$ denotes the set of all users in the system. The base station estimates channel conditions of each user in each time slot using L challenges. A time interval $[dt - d, dt), t \in \mathbb{Z}$ is called time slot t where d is the duration of a time slot. At each time slot t, the base station uses our channel condition estimation to determine a user's channel condition as an element in a set $\mathcal{E} = \{E_1, E_2, \ldots, E_{L+1}\}$ with cardinality $L + 1$. Each element $E_i \in \mathcal{E}$ represents an SINR range of $\text{SINR}_{i-1} \leq \text{SINR} < \text{SINR}_i$, where $\text{SINR}_0 = -\infty$ and $\text{SINR}_{L+1} = \infty$.

Construction of Challenges. In our scheme, the base station sends challenges to users so that users cannot overclaim their channel condition. To prevent the overclaiming attack, a challenge must have the following properties: unpredictability of the value included in a challenge and a well-designed success probability curve of the challenge. If a user receiving a challenge is able to guess the challenge value, the user can return the correct value even without successfully decoding the challenge. To make the challenge value unpredictable, we use a pseudorandom number generator.

To make a challenge that can be successfully decoded only by users with channel condition above a specified SINR, the success probability curve of a challenge must be appropriately designed. The ideal success probability curve would have zero success probability for channel condition worse than a specified SINR and zero error probability for channel condition better than that specified SINR as shown in Fig. 1(a). The dotted lines represent the success probability of reception of challenges according to SINR. With these ideal challenges, the successful reception of a challenge c_i and the failure of the reception of c_{i+1} implies that a given channel condition is $\text{SINR}_i \leq \text{SINR} < \text{SINR}_{i+1}$. We could then estimate the channel condition as E_{i+1}. These ideal challenges enable us to easily and accurately estimate the channel condition with only a single transmission. However, ideal challenges require infinitely large challenges. Our scheme considers non-ideal challenges, as shown in Fig. 1(b). For each challenge c_i, a node with channel condition as the threshold SINR_i for that challenge will successfully decode the challenge with probability $Ps_{ref(i)}$. Even though the shapes of the success probabilities of each challenge look same in Fig. 1(b), our scheme does not require the shape of each success probability to be the same. We discuss the choice of $Ps_{ref(i)}$ for the optimal performance in Section 4.1.

An immediate method to construct multiple challenges having appropriate success probability is to use different modulation and coding techniques for each challenge. However, from a practical point of view, a particular system may not provide various modulation and coding options. In such cases, we need a method to construct challenges with the limited number of modulation and coding options available. In order to not interrupt the flow of presentation, we explain such methods in more detail in Section 3.5.

Transmission of Challenges. The base station periodically broadcasts a set of challenges to users. The period is one parameter of our scheme. One extreme is to send a set of challenges in a single time slot, which allows rapid channel condition estimation and can respond to rapid variations in channel condition. However, sending so many challenges results in significant overhead. In an environment where the channel condition is slowly changing, we can reduce the frequency with which a base station sends challenges.

Estimation. After the base station transmits a challenge to a user, the user returns the challenge value to the base station to prove that the channel to the user is good enough to receive the corresponding challenge. When the base station receives the value from the user, the base station checks that the value is identical to the one that it sent. Then, the base station stores the result of this check. We denote a check result for challenge c_i at time slot t by $F_i(t)$.

$$F_i(t) = \begin{cases} 0 \text{ if challenge } c_i \text{ failed} \\ 1 \text{ if challenge } c_i \text{ succeeded} \end{cases}$$

With ideal challenges, only a single set of check results is enough to estimate channel condition. Since our scheme uses non-ideal challenges, we need multiple sets of check results to reduce the error in the estimated channel condition.

We call the set used for estimating channel condition a window, and we denote the window size as W. Intuitively, a larger window size results in more accurate estimated channel condition but slower adaptation. In Section 4.1, we theoretically analyze the impact of window size on the performance of our algorithm. When a base station finishes collecting a window of check results $F_i(t - W + 1), \ldots, F_i(t), \forall i \in \{1, \ldots, L\}$ at time slot t, the base station sums the check results for each challenge $c_i, \forall i \in \{1, 2, \ldots, L\}$ as follows.

$$S_i(t) = \sum_{j=0}^{W-1} F_i(t - j) \qquad \forall i \in \{1, 2, \ldots, L\}$$

Based on the values of $S_i(t)$, the base station estimates channel condition using a decision function D. In other words, the base station decides which element in the set $\mathcal{E} = \{E_1, E_2, \ldots, E_{L+1}\}$ most accurately characterizes corresponding user's channel condition. We denote the estimated channel condition at time slot t by $E_c(t)$.

$$E_c(t) = D(S_1(t), S_2(t), \ldots, S_L(t))$$

We use a simple threshold-based comparison for our decision function D. Fig. 1(c) shows the comparison procedure. We choose a threshold $T \in [0, 1]$. First, we see how any of the lowest rate challenges (c_1s) are successfully received by a user; it is likely that nearly all of these challenges are received by the user because it checks the lowest SINR range. When all c_1s are successfully received, $S_1(t) = W$. If $S_1(t) \leq WT$, we proceed to check $S_2(t)$. We repeat until we reach $S_i(t) < WT$. That is, we pick $i = \min j, \text{s.t.} S_j(t) < WT$. The base station then estimates the channel condition $E_c(t) = E_i$. For this threshold-based comparison, it is important to choose a proper threshold T. We analyze the impact of T on performance of our algorithm in Section 4.1.

3.4   Application of Our Secure Estimation Algorithm

There are two application types of our secure channel condition estimation algorithm. First, our algorithm can be used to detect and penalize an attacker by comparing reported channel condition to estimated channel condition. We do not pursue this approach further since it suffers from false detection like anomaly detection. Second, our algorithm can be used to select a node with good channel condition. The purpose of this approach is not to penalize an attacker but to provide a fair service to every node. After a node is chosen by our secure estimation algorithm, a sender node can determine modulation order by seeing reported channel condition to reduce loss probability. In this approach, an overclaiming attacker does not gain any benefit since the attacker will the same amount of service opportunity as other users (if all users experience same channel condition) and loss probability will be higher than other users due to higher modulation order.

3.5   Implementation of Multiple Challenges

As discussed in Section 3.3, we need a way to construct multiple challenges having different success probability curves using the limited number of given modulation and coding options. In this section, we introduce two methods to reshape the success probability of a challenge.

The first method is processing gain [13] which improves SINR by transmitting the same signal multiple times; when these copies add up, the signal energy increases by more than the noise power, thus increasing the SINR and shifting the success probability curve higher. To explain the concept of processing gain more formally, we rely on communication theory. We assume that a signal $s(t)$ is transmitted through an Additive White Gaussian Noise (AWGN) channel $n(t)$. The AWGN channel is a channel model which distribution is normal distribution. We assume that in our channel, mean is zero and variance is σ^2 ($\sim N(0, \sigma^2)$). The variance is considered to be noise power. SINR is calculated in symbol time (T) basis. When two identical signals are transmitted, the signal energy is $\int_0^T |2s(t)|^2 \, dt = 4 \int_0^T |s(t)|^2 \, dt$. Hence, the energy of two signals is four times (6dB) higher than that of a single signal. The addition of two AWGN sources is considered to be the sum of two normal distributions ($N(0, \sigma^2) + N(0, \sigma^2) = N(0, 2\sigma^2)$). Hence, the noise power ($2\sigma^2$) of two signals is two times (3dB) higher than that (σ^2) of a single signal. Consequently, the ratio of signal energy to noise power of the sum of two signals is two. With the addition of two signals, we can shift a success probability curve of a challenge to left by 3dB. With the larger number of signal additions, we can shift the success probability curve further to left.

The second method is to add noise in a signal at the transmitter. By adding a noise to a signal, we can reduce the ratio of signal energy to noise power of a signal. Hence, we can shift a success probability curve a challenge to right.

4   Evaluation

In this section, we evaluate the performance and the security of our algorithm. First, we analyze the impact of algorithm parameters on the performance of our algorithm. This analysis can be used to guide our parameter choices. We then perform simulations and compare the result of our analysis to those of our simulation. Second, we integrate our algorithm into a network simulator and evaluate the effect of our algorithm on system performance. We show that our algorithm securely and effectively estimates channel condition through most of its parameter space. Third, we analyze the security of our algorithm. In this analysis, we show that an attacker cannot, by guessing the value of a challenge, cause the channel condition estimate to be higher than if the attacker decoded the challenge in the same way as a normal user. In other words, *regardless of the length of a challenge value*, an attacker and a normal user that experience equivalent channel conditions will receive equal channel estimates in expectation. This paper does not include an evaluation of the overhead that our algorithm imposes. We leave as future work an exploration of the trade-off between the accuracy of estimation and system overhead.

4.1   Performance Analysis

In this section, we analyze the effect of parameter choices on our channel condition estimation algorithm. Specifically, we derive average estimation error $E[|\text{CQI} - \widehat{\text{CQI}}|]$ based on algorithm parameters such as window size (W), threshold (T), the size of a challenge and $Ps_{ref(i)}$ of a challenge. CQI (Channel Quality Indicator) in the average estimation error equation represents an actual CQI-level. $\widehat{\text{CQI}}$ represents an estimated CQI-level.

Assumptions. Our analysis assumes that the channel condition does not change. To analyze variable channel condition, we need to enumerate all possible cases for channel conditions in multiple slots. This analysis requires excessive amounts of computing power. Hence, we use simulation to consider the effect of variable channel condition in Section 4.2. The equations in our analysis do not assume the same values of challenge size and $Ps_{ref(i)}$ for each challenge. However, allowing different values of challenge size and $Ps_{ref(i)}$ increases the parameter space substantially. So when we plot figures, we use the same challenge size and $Ps_{ref(i)}$ for all challenges.

Analysis. Given a target SINR which is mapped to a CQI, we calculate the probability distribution on the estimated CQI ($\widehat{\text{CQI}}$), and then we calculate average estimation error.

We start by assuming that we have functions $R_i(\text{SINR}, Ps_{ref(i)}), \forall i \in \{1, 2, \ldots, L\}$ representing the probability that a bit of a challenge c_i is successfully received given an SINR. This function depends on the modulation and coding method used for constructing challenges, and is well-understood in communication theory [14]; we later illustrate numerical results with a specific modulation and coding scheme. The probability P_{cs_i} that a challenge c_i is successfully received is calculated as

$$P_{cs_i} = R_i(\text{SINR}, Ps_{ref(i)})^{SC_i}$$

where SC_i is the length in bits of challenge c_i. The number of successful challenges in a window of size W for challenge c_i is binomially distributed with probability P_{cs_i}. Hence, the probability $P_{c_i}(n)$ of exactly n successful challenges can be expressed as

$$P_{c_i}(n) = \binom{W}{n} P_{cs_i}^n (1 - P_{cs_i})^{W-n}$$

We can now calculate the probability $P_{ec}(i, \text{SINR})$ that CQI is estimated to be i given SINR. $\widehat{\text{CQI}} = i$ represents that E_{i+1} is chosen by our algorithm. Our algorithm estimates CQI by comparing the number of successful challenge receptions to the product of window size and threshold WT. Counting the number of successful challenge receptions from the lowest CQI-level, our algorithm determines $\widehat{\text{CQI}} = i$ when the number of successful challenge receptions for CQI-level i is less than WT. For CQI-level less than i, the number of successful challenge receptions is greater than or equal to WT. Hence, $P_{ec}(i, \text{SINR}), \forall i \in \{0, \ldots, L-1\}$ is calculated as

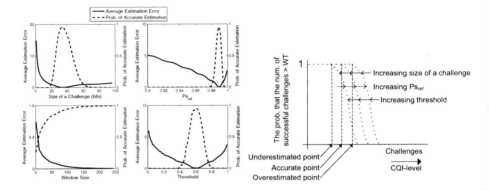

Fig. 2. Average estimation error and estima-   **Fig. 3.** Analyzing parameter design
tion accuracy for various parameters

$$P_{ec}(i, \text{SINR}) = \prod_{j=1}^{i} \left(P_{c_j}(\lceil WT \rceil) + P_{c_j}(\lceil WT \rceil + 1) \cdots + P_{c_j}(W) \right)$$
$$\times \left(1 - P_{c_{i+1}}(\lceil WT \rceil) - P_{c_{i+1}}(\lceil WT \rceil + 1) \cdots - P_{c_{i+1}}(W) \right)$$

For CQI-level L, we have a different form.

$$P_{ec}(L, \text{SINR}) = \prod_{j=1}^{L} \left(P_{c_j}(\lceil WT \rceil) + P_{c_j}(\lceil WT \rceil + 1) + \cdots + P_{c_j}(W) \right)$$

With $P_{ec}(i, \text{SINR})$, we can obtain the average estimation error as follows.

$$E[|\text{CQI} - \widehat{\text{CQI}}|] = \sum_{i=0}^{L} |\text{CQI} - i| \, P_{ec}(i, \text{SINR})$$

Using this analysis on average estimation error, we now want to properly set window size, threshold, the size of a challenge, and reference probability $Ps_{ref(i)}$ of a challenge so that the average estimation error is minimized. As discussed in our assumptions, we use the same values of challenge size and $Ps_{ref(i)}$ for different challenges for ease of performance comparison. To obtain specific numerical results, we use the same definition of CQI as in the 3GPP standard [15].

$$\text{CQI} = \begin{cases} 0 & \text{SINR} \leq \text{-16dB} \\ \lfloor \frac{\text{SINR}}{1.02} + 16.62 \rfloor & \text{-16dB} < \text{SINR} < 14\text{dB} \\ 30 & \text{SINR} \geq 14\text{dB} \end{cases}$$

This CQI configuration is also used for following simulations. Since P_{ec} has a non-continuous function (ceil function), it is difficult to apply optimization theory. To search for optimal parameters in the discontinuous space, we used

Table 1. block size (bits) for channel condition

cqi	block	cqi	block	cqi	block	cqi	block	cqi	block
1	137	2	173	3	233	4	317	5	377
6	461	7	650	8	792	9	931	10	1262
11	1483	12	1742	13	2279	14	2583	15	3319
16	3565	17	4189	18	4664	19	5287	20	5887
21	6554	22	7168	23	7168	24	7168	25	7168
26	7168	27	7168	28	7168	29	7168	30	7168

a hill-climbing approach [16]. First, we set initial values for each parameter intuitively. We then iteratively picked a parameter, optimized this parameter leaving all other parameters fixed, and repeated this process until we converged on a locally optimal parameter set. In the following results, we started with this parameter set and varied parameters one at a time to explore the impact of each parameter on system performance. Our calculation uses the reception probability for QPSK as $R_i(\text{SINR}, Ps_{ref(i)})$. We choose target SINR to allow for equal amounts of overestimation and underestimation in terms of CQI-level; in UMTS, this corresponds to a CQI level of 15 and an SINR of -1.19dB.

Fig. 2 shows our calculated average estimation error and the probability of accurate estimation. The results show an optimal point for each parameter: the size of a challenge, reference probability of a challenge, window size, and threshold. To demonstrate why the optimal points exist, we show the probability that the number of successful challenge transmission is greater than WT for each challenge in Fig. 3. As the size of a challenge increases, the probability curve slides towards the direction of underestimation. Increasing the threshold moves the probability curve in the same direction as the size of a challenge. With increasing reference probability, the probability curve moves towards the direction of overestimation. For window size, larger window size provides a better accuracy. This is intuitively obvious, since the large window size provides larger number of test samples for estimating channel condition.

4.2   Simulation

We performed a simulation study to verify our analysis and consider the effect of variable channel condition on the performance of our algorithm. We start with the case of a static channel condition.

Static Channel Condition. We implemented our algorithm in the NS-2 simulator [17] patched with EURANE [18], a UMTS system simulator. Our reference system is a UMTS system. To obtain specific numerical results, we use the same CQI configuration as we used to obtain numerical results for our analysis. Table 1 shows the transmission block sizes for each corresponding CQI [15]. As in the numerical results of our analysis, we consider the verification process for an SINR of -1.19dB which is a CQI of 15, and modulation using QPSK. We use the same optimal parameter selection as we used in the analysis in Section 4.1. We use the default UMTS time slot duration of 2ms, and our algorithm estimates the channel condition in each time slot. We vary window size and threshold,

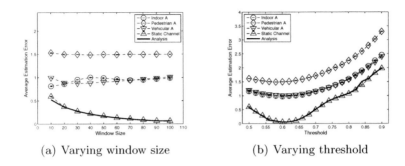

(a) Varying window size   (b) Varying threshold

Fig. 4. Simulation results

fixing $Ps_{ref(i)}$ and the length of each challenge value. We perform five runs for each value of window size and threshold.

For each estimation, we record the difference between actual CQI and estimated CQI (in absolute value). Fig. 4(a) and Fig. 4(b) show the average value of the differences, and validate the results of our analysis. As window size increases, the average estimation error decreases as expected. For all values of window size, the estimation error is below 1 CQI-level, and decreases to 0.05 CQI-levels as the window size grows to 100. Even larger windows would further reduce the error. However, our results show that our algorithm performs accurately with a reasonable window size.

Variable Channel Condition. Even though we can adjust parameters to optimize estimation accuracy in environments with static channel condition, the same parameter setting does not guarantee the same accuracy under a variable channel condition. We use a variable condition channel model to evaluate the effectiveness of our algorithm under a variable channel condition. We repeat the previous simulations, replacing the static channel condition with three UMTS channel models [19]: Indoor A with velocity 3km/h, Pedestrian A with velocity 15km/h and Vehicular A with velocity 120km/h. Fig. 4(a) shows the effect of window size on average estimation error. The average estimation error in variable channel conditions is greater than the error in a static channel condition, and the window size has significantly less impact on accuracy than in a static channel condition; this shows that the variability of the channel condition prevents our algorithm from achieving arbitrary precision by indefinitely increasing the window size. Nonetheless, in most cases, our algorithm's error is not greater than 1 CQI-level. Furthermore, both legitimate nodes and attacking nodes experience similar errors, further reducing the effectiveness of overclaiming. Fig. 4(b) shows the average estimation error for various values of threshold. Again, the estimation error in a static channel condition is less than the errors in variable channel conditions. However, our result shows that we can find a value of threshold that limits the estimation error less than 1.5 CQI-levels, and that the optimal parameters for static channel condition confies to be effective under variable channel conditions.

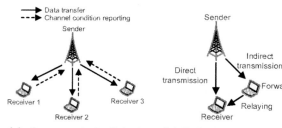

(a) Opportunistic Sched- (b) Relaying Network: A
uler: Scheduler chooses a sender forwards a packet
receiver in each time slot to a relayer when the
based on users' channel relayer has better chan-
conditions. nel condition than the receiver.

Fig. 5. Example Networks For System Performance Evaluation

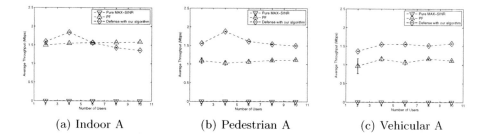

(a) Indoor A   (b) Pedestrian A   (c) Vehicular A

Fig. 6. The effect of our algorithm on opportunistic scheduler

4.3   System Performance

So far, we have evaluated the performance of our secure channel estimation algorithm. Now, we evaluate the impact of our secure channel condition estimation
algorithm on system performance. This evaluation provides an understanding on
how much the estimation error of our algorithm affects the system performance.
Our reference system is the system that we used for the previous simulation in Section 4.2. We implement opportunistic scheduler and cooperative relaying in this
reference system. As we mentioned in Section 3.2, our algorithm works in the case
where a trustable entity gets the report of channel condition of a node to the entity. Hence, we consider single-hop cooperative relaying network where each user
reports its channel condition to base station. We do not consider an efficient routing metric [5,6] in ad hoc network where channel condition between intermediate
nodes are reported to a source node.

Opportunistic Scheduler. Figure 5(a) shows how opportunistic scheduler [1,2]
works in a wireless network. An opportunistic scheduler is a centralized resource
scheduler that exploits the channel condition information of each user for efficient

resource management. One simple example of an opportunistic scheduler is an efficiency-oriented scheduler that allocates resources to only the user with the best channel condition in a time slot. We call this scheduler MAX-SINR. It is obvious that this scheduler achieves the maximum possible system throughput. However, this scheduler may give so few opportunities to a user with poor channel condition that it induces a fairness problem. The Proportional Fair (PF) scheduler [1] is a widely known scheduler that addresses the fairness problem. The PF scheduler collects channel condition information from each user at each time slot t. The PF scheduler uses channel condition feedback from each user to determine which user to serve by calculating metrics $R_i(t)/T_i(t)$ for each user, where $T_i(t)$ is user i's average throughput calculated as

$$
T_i(t) = \begin{cases} (1 - 1/t_c)T_i(t-1) + 1/t_c R_i(t) & \text{if user } i \text{ is chosen} \\ (1 - 1/t_c)T_i(t-1) & \text{if user } i \text{ is not chosen} \end{cases}
$$

and t_c represents the time constant of a low pass filter. In each time slot, the PF scheduler serves the user with the largest metric.

Our simulated network consists of one base station serving several users, half of which are attackers. The attackers choose a simple attack: overclaiming their channel condition to be the best possible condition. The base station reacts by choosing a high bit-rate modulation for each transmission to any attacker, which can induce a high error rate when the actual channel condition is poor. In EU-RANE's implementation, a node that is unable to receive a packet would not send back an ack to the base station, triggering an internal control mechanism in UMTS that stops any connection failing to acknowledge several contiguous transmissions. We modified the attacker to send an ack for every received packet, whether or not that packet was received without error. Our channel model for each user is the same variable channel models (Indoor A, Pedestrian A, and Vehicular A) that we used for performance analysis. We sourced 11 Mbps of CBR traffic to each user. We measure the throughput of normal users under three scheduling policies: PF, MAX-SINR without our algorithm and MAX-SINR with our algorithm. In MAX-SINR with our algorithm, a base station does not use user-reported CQI-level to pick which user has the best channel condition in a give time slot. Instead, the base station uses the CQI-level estimated by our algorithm. Figure 6 shows that MAX-SINR is vulnerable to overclaiming attack and PF prevents attackers from stealing normal users' throughput. However, our simulation results show that MAX-SINR with our algorithm can achieve higher throughput than PF scheduler in most cases. Occasionally PF outperforms MAX-SINR, because our algorithm occasionally overestimates the receiver's channel condition, in which case the base station may choose a modulation scheme that is too aggressive, resulting in packet loss.

Cooperative Relaying Network. In a mobile wireless network, mobile nodes can experience different channel conditions due to their different locations. Though a node experiences a channel condition too poor to receive packets from a source node, a third node may have a good channel condition to both the source and the intended destination. *Cooperative relaying* network architectures (e.g., [3,4,20,21]) shown in Figure 5(b) help a node that has poor channel condition to route its packet through a node with a good channel condition, thus improving system throughput. In order to find such routes, a cooperative relaying protocol must distribute channel condition information for each candidate path, find the most appropriate relay path, and provide incentives to motivate nodes to forward packets for other nodes. Specifically, in UCAN [4], user equipment has two wireless adaptors, one High Data Rate (HDR) cellular interface and one IEEE 802.11 interface. The HDR interface is used for communication with a base station and the IEEE 802.11 interface is used for peer-to-peer communication with other user equipment in a network.

In our simulated network, the base station is the traffic source. The victim node chooses a relayer node if the relayer has a better channel condition. An attacking relayer node overclaims its channel condition to intercept packets to the victim node. As shown in Section 4.2, the channel model can affect the estimation error of our algorithm. Hence, we use the three channel models (Indoor A, Pedestrian A, and Vehicular A) that we used for the simulation of variable channel condition. These results will show us how the estimation error due to varying channel condition affects the system performance. As we vary the distance between the base station and the victim node, we measure the victim's throughput under the false channel condition reporting attack.

Figure 7 shows the measured results in the case of a single relayer for the victim node. Hence, the attacker node is the only relayer for the victim node. In Figure 8, there are two relayers and one relayer is an attacker node. We consider three different cases: overclaiming by 1, overclaiming by 2 and defense with our algorithm. For the cases of overclaiming by 1 and 2, we plot the results without deployment of our algorithm. For the case of defense with our algorithm, we deployed our algorithm to compare the cases with defense and without defense. When the victim node is close to the base station, the throughput of the case with defense is much greater than the throughput of the case without defense. As the victim node is farther from the base station, the throughput difference between defense case and non-defense case is reduced. It is because the degraded channel condition for the victim node far from the base station induces small capacity for the victim node. In the case of two relayers, we can see that due to the redundant relayer, the attack effect is reduced. Over three different channel models, we can see that the throughput results are similar to each other. With these results, we believe that the estimation error of our algorithm does not affect the system performance so much.

4.4   Security Analysis

The security of our scheme for securely estimating channel condition relies on the assumption that the attacker cannot predict the challenge values generated by a pseudo-random number generator. An attacker, then, has two strategies by which he can generate replies: either the attacker can guess the challenge value, or the attacker can attempt to decode the received challenge value as a normal user would. In this section, we will show that when the challenge values are chosen using a pseudo-random number generator, decoding is the dominating strategy of an attacker.

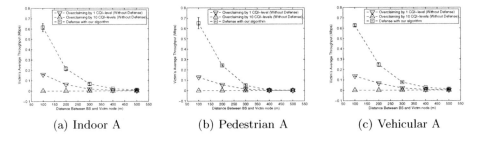

(a) Indoor A   (b) Pedestrian A   (c) Vehicular A

Fig. 7. The effect of our algorithm on a relaying network example (one relayer)

(a) Indoor A   (b) Pedestrian A   (c) Vehicular A

Fig. 8. The Effect of Our Algorithm on A Relaying Network Example (Two Relayers)

We assume that a data symbol experiences an Additive White Gaussian Noise (AWGN) channel, which is a typical model. The optimal (maximum-likelihood) decoder under AWGN takes the input signal and provides the data symbol most likely to correspond to that signal. An attacker that guesses ignores the input signal entirely, and as such, throws away any information contained in the input signal. Discarding this information could not improve the attacker's expected performance, because otherwise the optimal decoder would not be optimal. In other words, the attacker gains no advantage by guessing instead of decoding.

To illustrate, we consider BPSK coding with a received power level of 1 and AWGN power σ. In this environment, the sender sends +1 to send a 1-bit and -1 to send a 0-bit. The receiver receives the sender's value plus a random value drawn from $N(0, \sigma^2)$. The optimal decoder decodes a 1-bit if the received value is greater than 0 and a 0-bit otherwise, which has probability of success $Q(-\frac{1}{\sigma})$. Since $\sigma > 0$, $Q(-\frac{1}{\sigma}) > 0.5$. By simply guessing a bit, an attacker is successful with probability 0.5. The success probability of decoding is always greater than or equal to the success probability of guessing. Hence, if the challenge values are randomly generated, the optimal strategy is to use the optimal decoder. This result shows that an attacker cannot outperform a normal user.

5   Related Work

In this section, we review attacks related to our reference systems.

Attacks on Opportunistic Schedulers. Bali et al. [22] reveal a vulnerability in the PF scheduler that can be induced by a malicious traffic pattern. Bursty traffic enables a single flow to occupy several consecutive slots. They measure this attack's effect on real EV-DO network. The work by Racic et al. [9] on PF scheduler is the closest work to ours in the sense that they consider the effect of falsely reporting channel condition. They conclude that falsely reporting channel condition alone does not do harm other users very much in networks using a PF scheduler. They do find that falsely reporting combined with handover can occupy many consecutive time slots, thereby stealing other user's opportunity to be served. Unlike this work, we find cases where false reporting channel condition alone can significantly affect other user's performance in other network settings.

Attacks on Hybrid Networks. A hybrid network is one that implements cooperative relaying using two distinct data link technologies. Carbunar et al. [20] propose JANUS for defending against selfish or malicious behavior in establishing routes in hybrid networks. They consider the possibility of a rate inflation attack in which a node reports a higher bandwidth to base station than the node can provide. However, their attack overclaims the output rate of a link rather than the channel quality. In JANUS a base station sends request packets to nodes, and uses the fact that an overclaimed link will experience congestive losses. However, JANUS' request packets are not cryptographically secured, so the attacker can guess when it needs to send a response packet to hide the attack from the base station. Our approach differs from the JANUS' in that our algorithm uses cryptographic security to protect challenge messages. More fundamentally, because our verification is conducted at the physical layer, it allows for a more fine-grained verification of channel condition. Haas et al. [21] propose SUCAN, which defends against Byzantine behaviors in hybrid networks. However, they do not consider attacks that misreport channel condition.

6   Conclusion and Future Work

In this paper, we have studied the threat posed by attacks that falsely report their channel condition. Our false channel-feedback attack can arise in any channel-aware protocol where a user reports its own channel condition. To counter such attacks, we propose a secure channel condition estimation algorithm to prevent the overclaiming attack. Through analysis and simulations, we show that with proper parameters, we can prevent the overclaiming attack.

The protocol we describe requires that a trusted entity sends each challenge message, and we present two case studies, the opportunistic scheduler and the single-hop cooperative relaying, in which the trusted entity naturally arises within the environment. In a multi-hop channel-aware protocol, an intermediate hop may have no incentive to correctly estimate channel condition or to correctly relay another link's estimated channel condition. In this paper, we have focused on the single-hop channel estimation environment as an initial step towards defense against channel condition misreporting attack, and we leave secure multi-hop estimation and reporting to future work.

References

1. Jalali, A., Padovani, R., Pankaj, R.: Data throughput of cdma-hdr a high efficiency-high data rate personal communication wireless system. In: Proc. IEEE VTC, vol. 3, pp. 1854–1858 (May 2000)
2. Viswanath, P., Tse, D.N.C., Laroia, R.: Opportunistic beamforming using dumb antennas. IEEE Transactions on Information Theory 48(6), 1277–1294 (2002)
3. Sendonaris, A., Erkip, E., Aazhang, B.: Increasing uplink capacity via user cooperation diversity. In: Proceedings of IEEE International Symposium on Information Theory, p. 156 (August 1998)
4. Luo, H., Ramjee, R., Sinha, P., Li, L.E., Lu, S.: Ucan: a unified cellular and ad-hoc network architecture. In: ACM MobiCom, pp. 353–367. ACM, New York (2003)
5. De Couto, D.S.J., Aguayo, D., Bicket, J., Morris, R.: A high-throughput path metric for multi-hop wireless routing. In: ACM MobiCom, pp. 134–146. ACM, New York (2003)
6. Draves, R., Padhye, J., Zill, B.: Comparison of routing metrics for static multi-hop wireless networks. In: ACM SIGCOMM, pp. 133–144. ACM, New York (2004)
7. Jing, T., Wang, H.J., Hu, Y.C.: Preserving location privacy in wireless lans. In: Proc. ACM MOBISYS (June 2007)
8. Karlof, C., Wagner, D.: Secure routing in wireless sensor networks: Attacks and countermeasures. In: First IEEE International Workshop on Sensor Network Protocols and Applications, pp. 113–127 (2002)
9. Racic, R., Ma, D., Chen, H., Liu, X.: Exploiting opportunistic scheduling in cellular data networks. In: NDSS (2008)
10. Odyssey 8500, http://www.wavesat.com/pdf/OD-8500-IC-PB.pdf
11. Airspan, http://www.airspan.com/products_wimax.aspx
12. Sdr, http://en.wikipedia.org/wiki/Software-defined_radio
13. Smith III, J.O.: Spectral Audio Signal Processing. In: Center for Computer Research in Music and Acoustics, CCRMA (2009)
14. Proakis, J.: Digital Communications, 4th edn., McGraw-Hill Science/Engineering/Math (August 2000)
15. Physical layer procedures (fdd), release 5. 3GPP TS25.214 V5.5.0 (June 2003), http://www.3gpp.org/ftp/Specs/archive/25_series/25.214/25214-550.zip
16. Russell, S.J., Norvig, P.: Artificial Intelligence: A Modern Approach. Pearson Education, London (2003), http://portal.acm.org/citation.cfm?id=773294
17. ns-2: Network simulator, http://www.isi.edu/nsnam/ns/
18. eurane: Enhanced umts radio access network extensions for ns-2, http://eurane.ti-wmc.nl/eurane/
19. Selection procedures for the choice of radio transmission technologies of the umts. ETSI TS UMTS 30.03 V3.2.0
20. Carbunar, B., Ioannis, I., Nita-Rotaru, C.: Janus: A framework for scalable and secure routing in hybrid wireless networks. IEEE Transactions on Dependable and Secure Computing (2008)
21. Haas, J.J., Hu, Y.C.: Secure unified cellular ad hoc network routing. In: IEEE Globecom (2009)
22. Bali, S., Machiraju, S., Zang, H., Frost, V.: A measurement study of scheduler-based attacks in 3G wireless networks. In: Uhlig, S., Papagiannaki, K., Bonaventure, O. (eds.) PAM 2007. LNCS, vol. 4427, pp. 105–114. Springer, Heidelberg (2007)

Characterizing the Security Implications of Third-Party Emergency Alert Systems over Cellular Text Messaging Services

Patrick Traynor

Georgia Institute of Technology
traynor@cc.gatech.edu

Abstract. Cellular text messaging services are increasingly being relied upon to disseminate critical information during emergencies. Accordingly, a wide range of organizations including colleges, universities and large metropolises now partner with third-party providers that promise to improve physical security by rapidly delivering such messages. Unfortunately, these products do not work as advertised due to limitations of cellular infrastructure and therefore provide a false sense of security to their users. In this paper, we perform the first extensive investigation and characterization of the limitations of an Emergency Alert System (EAS) using text messages as a security incident response and recovery mechanism. Through the use of modeling and simulation based on configuration information from major US carriers, we show emergency alert systems built on text messaging not only can not meet the 10 minute delivery requirement mandated by the WARN Act, but also potentially cause other legitimate voice and SMS traffic to be blocked at rates upwards of 80%. We then show that our results are representative of reality by comparing them to a number of documented but not previously understood failures. Finally, we discuss the causes of the mismatch of expectations and operational ability and suggest a number of techniques to improve the reliability of these systems. We demonstrate that this piece of deployed security infrastructure simply does not achieve its stated requirements.

1   Introduction

Text messaging allows individuals to transmit short, alphanumeric communications for a wide variety of applications. Whether to coordinate meetings, catch up on gossip, offer reminders of an event or even vote for a contestant on a television game show, this discreet form of communication is now the dominant service offered by cellular networks. In the United States alone, over five billion text messages are delivered monthly [25]. While many applications of this service can be considered non-critical, the use of text messaging during emergency events has proven to be far more utilitarian.

With millions of people attempting to contact friends and family on September 11th 2001, telecommunications providers witnessed tremendous spikes in cellular voice service usage. Verizon Wireless, for example, reported voice traffic rate increases of up to 100% above typical levels; Cingular Wireless recorded an increase of up to 1000% on calls destined for the Washington D.C. area [28]. While these networks are engineered to handle elevated amounts of traffic, the sheer number of calls was far greater than

S. Jajodia and J. Zhou (Eds.): SecureComm 2010, LNICST 50, pp. 125–143, 2010.
© Institute for Computer Sciences, Social Informatics and Telecommunications Engineering 2010

capacity for voice communications in the affected areas. However, with voice-based phone services being almost entirely unavailable, SMS messages were still successfully received in even the most congested regions because the control channels responsible for their delivery remained available. Similar are the stories from the Gulf Coast during Hurricanes Katrina and Rita. With a large number of cellular towers damaged or disabled by the storms, text messaging allowed the lines of communication to remain open for many individuals in need, in spite of their inability to complete voice calls in areas where the equipment was not damaged and power was available.

Accordingly, SMS messaging is now viewed by many as a reliable method of communication when all other means appear unavailable. In response to this perception, a number of companies offer SMS-based emergency messaging services. Touted as able to deliver critical information colleges, universities and even municipalities hoping to coordinate and protect the *physical security* of the general public have spent tens of millions of dollars to install such systems. Unfortunately, these products will not work as advertised and provide a false sense of security to their users.

In this paper, we explore the limitations of third party *Emergency Alert Systems* (EAS). In particular, we show that because of the currently deployed cellular infrastructure, such systems will not be able to deliver a high volume of emergency messages in a short period of time. *This identifies a key failure in a critical security incident response and recovery mechanism (the equivalent of finding weaknesses in techniques such as VM snapshots for rootkits and dynamic packet filtering rules for DDoS attacks) and demonstrates its inability to properly function during the security events for which it was ostensibly designed.* The fundamental misunderstanding of the requirements necessary to successfully deploy this piece of security infrastructure are likely to contribute to real-world, human-scale consequences.

In so doing, we make the following contributions:

- **Emergency Event Characterization:** Through modeling and simulation based on real provider deployments, we provide the first public characterization of the impact of an emergency event on a cellular network. This contribution is novel in that it explores a range of realistic emergency scenarios and provides a better understanding of their failure modes.
- **Measure EAS over SMS for multiple emergency scenarios:** We provide data to debunk the common assertion made by many third-party vendors that large quantities of text messages can be delivered within a short period of time (i.e., seconds to minutes). We evaluate a number of different, realistic emergency scenarios and explain why a number of college campuses have reported "successful" tests of their systems. Finally, we provide a real-world example that very closely mirrors the results of our simulations.
- **Quantify Collateral Damage:** We characterize the presence of the additional traffic generated by third-party EAS over SMS and show that such traffic causes increased blocking of normal calls and text message, potentially preventing those in need of help from receiving it. We also discuss a number of ways in which these networks can cause unexpected failures (e.g., message delay, message reordering, alert spoofing).

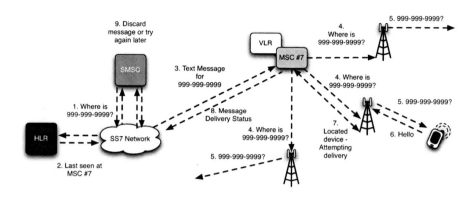

Fig. 1. Before a message can be delivered, a mobile device must be located. To do so, the MSC requests that towers within a given area all transmit paging requests. If an when a device is found, the MSC forwards the message to the appropriate tower, which attempts to deliver it wirelessly. The status of the delivery attempt is then returned to the SMSC. If delivery failed, the SMSC will attempt delivery at a later time.

2   Network Architecture

We specifically examine GSM networks in these discussions as they represent the most widely deployed cellular technology in the world; however, it should be noted that message delivery for other technologies such as CDMA, IDEN and TDMA are very similar and are therefore subject to similar problems.

2.1   Cellular Network Architecture

Sending a Message. While most users are only familiar with sending a text message from their phone, known as *Mobile Originated SMS* (MO-SMS), service providers offer an expanding set of interfaces through which messages can be sent. From the Internet, for instance, it is possible to send text messages to mobile devices through a number of webpages, email and even instant messaging software. Third parties can also access the network using so-called SMS Aggregators. These servers, which can be connected directly to the phone network or communicate via the Internet, are typically used to send "bulk" or large quantities of text messages. Aggregators typically inject messages on behalf of other companies and charge their clients for the service. Finally, most providers have established relationships between each other to allow for messages sent from one network to be delivered in the other.

After entering a provider's network, messages are sent to the *Short Messaging Service Center* (SMSC). SMSCs perform operations similar to email handling servers in the Internet, and store and forward messages to their appropriate destinations. Because messages can be injected into the network from so many external sources, SMSCs typically perform aggressive spam filtering on all incoming messages. All messages passing this filtering are then converted and copied into the necessary SMS message format and encoding and then placed into a queue to be forwarded to their final destination.

Finding a Device. Delivering messages in a cellular network is a much greater challenge than in the traditional Internet. Chief in this difficulty is that users in a cellular network tend to be mobile, so it is not possible to assume that users will be located where we last found them. Moreover, the information about a user's specific location is typically limited. For instance, if a mobile device is not currently exchanging messages with a base station, the network may only know a client's location at a very coarse level (i.e., the mobile device may be known to be in a specific city, but no finer-grained location information would be known). Accordingly, the SMSC needs to first find the general location for a message's intended client before anything else can be done.

A server known as the *Home Location Register* (HLR) assists in this task. This database acts as the permanent repository for a user's account information (i.e., subscribed services, call forwarding information, etc). When a request to locate a user is received, the HLR determines whether or not that device is currently turned on. If a mobile device is currently powered off, the HLR instructs the SMSC to store the text message and attempt to deliver it at another time. Otherwise, the HLR tells the SMSC the address of the *Mobile Switching Center* (MSC) currently serving the desired device. Having received this location information, the SMSC then forwards the text message on to the appropriate MSC.

Wireless Delivery. As mentioned earlier, even the MSC may not know more information about a targeted device's location. In order to determine whether or not the current base station serving this device is known, the MSC queries the *Visitor Location Register* (VLR), which temporarily stores information about clients while they are being served by the MSC. In most cases, this information is not known, and so the MSC must begin the extensive and expensive process of locating the mobile device. The MSC completes this task by generating and forwarding paging requests to all of its associated base stations, which may number in the hundreds. This process is identical to locating a mobile device for delivery of a voice call.

Upon receiving a paging request from the MSC, a base station attempts to determine whether or not the targeted device is nearby. To achieve this, the base station attempts to use a series of *Control Channels* to establish a connection with the user. First, the base station broadcasts a paging request over the *Paging Channel* (PCH) and then waits for a response. If the device is nearby and hears this request, it responds to the base station via the *Random Access Channel* (RACH) to alert the network of its readiness to receive information. When this response is received, the network uses the *Access Grant Channel* (AGCH) to tell the device to listen to a specific *Standalone Dedicated Control Channel* (SDCCH) for further exchanges. Using this SDCCH, the network is able to authenticate the client, perform a number of maintenance routines and deliver the text message. By limiting the operations necessary to deliver a text message to the control channels used for call setup, such messages can be delivered when all call circuits, known as *Traffic Channels* (TCHs) are busy.

When the attempt to deliver the message between the targeted device and the base station is complete, the device either confirms the success or failure of delivery. This status information is carried back through the network to the SMSC. If the message was successfully delivered, the SMSC deletes it. Otherwise, the SMSC stores the message until a later period, at which time the network re-attempts delivery. Figure 1 offers an overview of this entire process.

2.2 Third-Party Provider Solutions

In the past few years, a significant number of third-parties offering to deliver alert messages (and other information services) via text messaging have appeared. Citing the need for improved delivery targeted to a highly mobile population, many such services advertise text messaging as an instant, targeted disseminator capable of delivering of critical information to tens of thousands of mobile phones when it is most needed. These systems have been extensively deployed on college and university campuses throughout the United States.

The architecture of these systems is relatively simple. Whether activated through a web interface [7,10,35,45,46], directly from a phone [18], or as software running on a campus administrator's computer [34,29], these services act as SMS aggregators and inject large numbers of text messages into the network. Colleges and universities subscribing to these services then collect mobile phone numbers from students, faculty and staff. In the event of an alert, all or a subset of the collected numbers can be targeted. While network providers may offer some limited information back to the third party, aggregators are largely unaware of conditions in the network or the geographic location of any specific individual.

3 Modeling Emergency Events in Real Environments

To determine whether there exists a mismatch between the current cellular text messaging infrastructure and third party EAS, it is necessary to observe such systems during an emergency. However, because large scale physical security incidents are rare, we apply a number of modeling techniques to help characterize such events.

3.1 Location Selection and Characterization

The events that unfolded at the Virginia Polytechnic Institute and State University ("Virginia Tech") on April 16, 2007 have become one of the primary motivations behind the calls to use SMS as the basis of an emergency system. Many argue that had such a system been in place during what became the deadliest campus shooting in US history, countless lives could have been saved. However, a thorough examination of such claims has not been conducted. In particular, it is not clear whether or not the messages transmitted by such a system would have reached all students before the Norris Hall shootings. Accordingly, we have selected Virginia Tech as our location to characterize.

Located in southwestern Virginia, this land grant university is home to over 32,000 students, faculty and staff [48]. For the purposes of this work, we assume that just under half (15,000) of these individuals subscribe to a GSM network. As is shown by the red triangles in Figure 2, the major GSM provider in this area provides service to the campus of Virginia Tech from four base stations.[1] Given that each base station has

---

[1] This is the actual configuration of the major GSM carrier in this area, as confirmed through conversations with this provider.

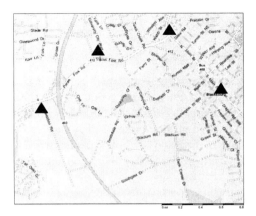

Fig. 2. The placement of base stations (red triangles) for a major GSM provider near Virginia Tech. Given that each base station has three sectors, the campus itself receives service from approximately eight total sectors.

three sectors (each covering a 120 degree range), we assume that the campus itself is covered by 8 of the 12 total sectors in the area.

3.2 Mathematical Characterization of Emergencies

The first step in characterizing a cellular network during an emergency is determining capacity. In particular, we are interested in understanding the minimum time required to deliver emergency messages. If this time is less than the goal of 10 minutes set forth in by the current public EAS policies and the WARN Act [40], then such a system may indeed be possible. However, if this goal can not be met, current networks can not be considered as good candidates for EAS message delivery.

Given that most sectors have a total of 8 SDCCHs, that it takes approximately four seconds to deliver a text message in a GSM network [9,28] and the information above, the capacity of the GSM network serving the campus of Virginia Tech would require the following amount of time to deliver a single message to 15,000 recipients:

$$C = 15,000 \text{ msgs} \times \frac{1 \text{ campus}}{8 \text{ sectors}} \times \frac{1 \text{ sector}}{8 \text{ SDCCHs}}$$
$$\times \frac{4 \text{ secs}}{1 \text{ message}}$$
$$\approx 938 \text{ sec}$$
$$\approx 15.6 \text{ mins}$$

Because the contents of emergency messages are likely to exceed the 160 character limit of a single text message, providers and emergency management officials have estimated the number of messages is likely to increase by at least four times:

$$C = 15,000 \text{ msgs} \times \frac{4 \text{ msgs}}{\text{user}} \times \frac{1 \text{ campus}}{8 \text{ sectors}}$$

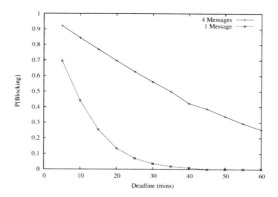

Fig. 3. Calculated blocking probabilities versus delivery windows for emergency SMS traffic

Table 1. Simulation parameters

μ_{TCH}^{-1}	120 sec [32]
$\mu_{SDCCH,call}^{-1}$	1.5 sec [32]
$\mu_{SDCCH,SMS}^{-1}$	4 sec [28,9]
$\lambda_{call,regular}$	10,000 calls/campus/hr .347 calls/sector/sec
$\lambda_{SMS,regular}$	21K msgs/campus/hr 0.75 msgs/sector/sec

$$\times \frac{1 \text{ sector}}{8 \text{ SDCCHs}} \times \frac{4 \text{ secs}}{1 \text{ msg}}$$
$$\approx 3752 \text{ secs}$$
$$\approx 62.5 \text{ mins}$$

The above calculations represent an optimistic minimum time for the delivery of all messages. For instance, it is highly unlikely that all eight SDCCHs will be available for delivering text messages as these channels are also used to establish voice calls and assist with device mobility. Moreover, contention between emergency messages for SDCCHs will also be a significant factor given that the SMSC is unaware of traffic conditions in individual sectors. Finally, depending on conditions within the network, each message is likely to experience different delays. To better characterize these factors, we apply a simple Erlang-B queuing analysis of the system. In a system with n servers and an offered load of $A = \frac{\lambda}{\mu^{-1}}$, where λ is the intensity of incoming messages and signaling traffic and μ is the rate at which a single server can service incoming requests, the probability that an incoming emergency message is blocked is:

$$P_B = \frac{\frac{A^n}{n!}}{\sum_{l=0}^{l=n-1} \frac{A^l}{l!}} \tag{1}$$

Figure 3 compares an imposed deadline for delivering all SMS-based emergency messages against the expected blocking. We note that while Poisson arrival is not appropriate for modeling traffic on the Internet, it is regularly used in telecommunications. Like the capacity equations, *this calculation shows that such large volumes of messages can not be delivered in a short period of time, even without the presence of traffic from normal operations.*

4   Simulating Emergency Events

EAS over SMS traffic may still improve the physical security of its intended recipients even though it can not be delivered to the entire population within a 10 minute time period. If such information can be sent *without interfering with other traffic*, it could be argued that it would remain beneficial to at least some portion of the receiving population.

To better understand the impact of this security incident response and recovery mechanism on other traffic, we further characterize a number of emergency scenarios. While the calculations provided in the previous section and a post-9/11 government study on national text messaging capacity[28] are a good start, neither of these approximations help us understand the complex dynamics of the range of emergency scenarios. We therefore use a GSM simulator developed in previous work [41,42,44] and extend it for our needs. This tool focuses on the wireless portion of the network and allows the interaction between various resources to be characterized. This simulator was designed according to 3GPP standards documents, input from commercial providers and given optimal settings where applicable [22] so that our results are as conservative as possible.[2] Table 1 provides a summary of additional parameters representing busy hour load conditions (i.e., rush hour) and channel holding/service times. All experiments represent the average of 500 runs, the inputs for which were generated according to an exponential interarrival time using the Mersenne Twister Pseudo Random Number Generator [16]. Confidence intervals of 95% for all runs were less than two orders of magnitude from the mean, and are therefore too small to be shown. Given this system, we are able to explore the details of an emergency without having to wait for such an event occur or requesting log data from cellular providers. In the following subsections, we offer views of normal operations, surges of messages and a full emergency situation with EAS over SMS deployed.

4.1   Normal Traffic

Our first set of experiments represent normal network behavior. Figure 4 shows the robustness of these networks to high traffic, illustrating very low SDCCH utilization rates for all of the offered loads. This graph reinforces the case for using SDCCHs for SMS delivery. Even in the 25,000 calls per hour case, during which nearly more than 55% of incoming calls can not be completed, SDCCHs are utilized at approximately 18%.

---

[2] We note that some providers configure their network such that incoming text messages use four of the eight SDCCHs to decrease delivery time. However, this configuration results in higher blocking during busy periods, so we do not consider it further.

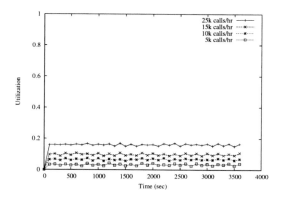

Fig. 4. The average utilization of control channels (SDCCHs) for a variety of traffic intensities

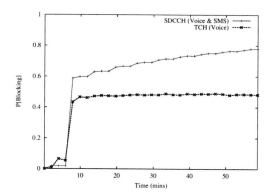

Fig. 5. The average blocking experienced during a large-scale emergency. Note that blocking on TCHs remains steady in spite of increasing call loads due to increased blocking on the SDCCH.

4.2   Emergency Scenarios

Users having received notification of an emergency are unlikely to maintain normal usage patterns. In particular, users are likely to attempt to contact their friends and/or family soon after learning about such conditions. Whether by text message or phone call, however, such instinctual communication leads to significant congestion in cellular networks. This phenomenon lead to a spike in the number of attempted calls to the Washington D.C. are by over 1000% percent on September 11th [28]. Accordingly, increases of varying intensities and characteristics representing reactionary usage must be considered when designing text messaging-based EAS. We explore two such scenarios, which assume that the third-party EAS over SMS provider has configured their system to deliver all messages within the WARN Act's 10 minute requirement [40], that SMSCs retransmit previously undeliverable messages once every 15 minutes and assume that 4 messages per user are transmitted by the EAS over SMS system when an emergency occurs.

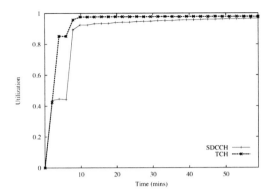

Fig. 6. Channel utilization observed during a large-scale emergency. The network becomes saturated almost immediately after the emergency event is realized.

Large-Scale Emergencies. Whereas small events may have a gradual increase in the volume of traffic, large-scale emergencies are often characterized by substantial and rapid spikes in usage, followed by continued gradual growth. We explore this worst case to understand the full extent of the problems such third party solutions may create. We therefore model a Virginia Tech-like event in which normal traffic increases by 1000% [28], with a 500% increase occurring over the course over a few minutes and the outstanding 500% being distributed across the remaining hour. Like the previous scenario, we conduct these experiments with and without the presence of EAS over SMS.

As expected, the sudden surge of traffic during the emergency almost immediately makes communications difficult. Figure 5 shows blocking rates of approximately 47% for TCHs and between 59% and 79% for SDCCHs. With both SDCCHs and TCHs experiencing near total utilization as shown in Figure 6, the network is already significantly overloaded and unable to deliver additional traffic.

The presence of traffic generated by an EAS over SMS system makes this scenario considerably worse. As shown in Figure 7, call and SMS blocking on SDCCHs almost immediately reaches between 80 and 85%. Like the previous scenario, call blocking on TCHs actually decreases. Such a decrease can again be attributed to the elevated blocking on the SDCCHs, as Figure 8 demonstrates that TCHs remain idle in spite of an increased call volume.

4.3   Testing Campus Alert Systems

The discrepancy between the scenarios presented thus far and the reports of successful tests of deployed systems is a result of a number of factors. As previously mentioned, the 160 character limit per text message often requires the transmission of multiple text messages during an emergency. Most system tests, however, typically involve sending a single message. Traffic in these tests is therefore sent at one-forth the volume of more realistic emergency scenarios. The second difference is the size of the affected population. While many universities offer these systems as an optional service to their

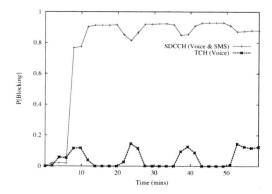

Fig. 7. Average blocking during a large-scale emergency in the presence of EAS over SMS. The network experiences blocking rates of approximately 90% when EAS messages are transmitted.

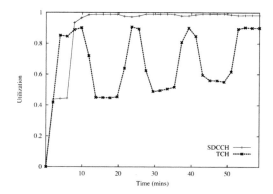

Fig. 8. Channel utilization during a large-scale emergency with EAS over SMS. TCH utilization falls significantly when EAS messages are sent, meaning fewer voice calls are delivered.

students, an increasing number are beginning to make enrollment mandatory. Accordingly, *current tests attempt to contact only a subset of students with a smaller volume of traffic than would be used in a real emergency.*

We use reports of successful tests as input for our final set of experiments. In particular, we attempt to recreate the environment in which these tests are occurring. We site information from officials at the University of Texas Austin [20] and Purdue University [31], each of which have reported transmitting messages to approximately 10,000 participants. Note that this represents roughly 25% of the undergraduate student body at these institutions. We therefore reduce the receiving population at Virginia Tech to 7,500, of which only half are subscribers to the GSM provider.

Figure 9 shows the probability of blocking for this scenario. With approximately 18% blocking, such a system would appear to replicate current deployments - over 80% of recipients are reached within the first 10-minute long transmission. However, as is shown in Figure 10, by increasing the number of messages sent to this small group

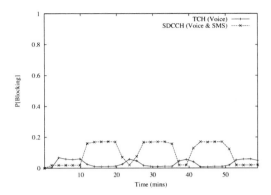

Fig. 9. The average blocking observed during a test (one message) of a third-party EAS over SMS system with only 25% of students registered

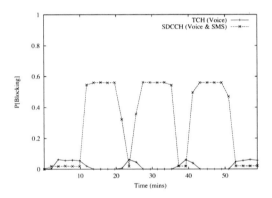

Fig. 10. The average blocking observed when four messages are transmitted and all other traffic remains constant

by a factor of four to allow for a longer emergency message, the probability of blocking increases to 58%. Because the transmission of multiple messages is more likely, campus emergency coordinators should test their systems based on this setting to gain a realistic view of its performance and behavior.

These two cases provide a more complete picture of the issues facing these systems. Whereas a third-party security response and recovery system may be able to deliver a small number of messages to one quarter of the students on campus, attempts to send more messages and therefore more meaningful communications quickly result in high blocking. Such systems are simply unable to support the rapid delivery of emergency messages to the entire population of the campus.

As corroboration of this final assertion and to further ground our results in reality, we note the results of a campus alert system deployed on the campus of Simon Fraser University in Burnaby, British Columbia, Canada. In April 2008, the University attempted to send test alert messages to 29,374 people; however, only 8600 were able to receive these messages [37]. Only 6500 of those having received the message were able to do so within five hours of it being sent, representing nearly an 80% rate of blocking. Worse still, many students reported an elevated rate of busy signals for many hours. These results are very similar to those shown in Figure 7, which while showing a slightly higher load, shows extremely close levels of blocking (approximately 85%). The analysis in this paper, in concert with this real-life test, clearly explains the failure of this security response and recovery mechanism to meet its requirement.

5 Discussion

5.1 3G Networks

We profiled the use of GSM networks in this work because they represent the most widely used cellular technology in the world. However, much faster third generation (3G) cellular systems are beginning to be deployed. With high speed data service available in many metropolitan areas, it would appear as if the analysis made in this paper will not remain relevant.

The migration to these new systems will not address these issues for a number of reasons. First, all cellular networks expend significant effort when establishing a connection. As demonstrated in Section 2, these operations include locating a targeted mobile device and performing significant negotiations before a single packet can be delivered. While the delivery rates of cellular data services have been steadily improving over the past decade, this setup and delivery of the first bit of information remains a significant bottleneck in the process. This means that while it is possible to download large files relatively quickly using such networks, beginning the download remains expensive. Second, many providers currently configure their 3G networks for the circuit switched delivery of text messages. Accordingly, such messages will continue to compete with voice calls for resources, leading to the same kinds of blocking conditions.

5.2 Message Delivery Order

Implicit in the misunderstanding of text messaging as a real-time service are misconceptions about the order in which messages will be delivered to targeted devices. Specifically, it is often assumed that messages will be delivered in the order in which they were injected by the sender. Message delivery order is in fact not always predictable.

The order in which messages are delivered can be affected by a number of factors. For instance, Traynor et al [41] showed that the SMSCs of different providers implement a variety of service algorithms, including FIFO and LIFO service disciplines. Accordingly, it is possible for two providers to deliver the same stream of messages in opposite order. Even if all carriers implemented the same delivery algorithm, congestion in the network can cause further disordering of packets. If an incoming text message is unable to be delivered due to a lack of resources on the air interface, the SMSC will store the message for a later attempt. However, if subsequent messages have been sent before this message fails and manage to gain the required resources, they will be delivered out of the sender's intended order. In an emergency such as a tornado, which may frequently change directions, such out of order delivery may actually send subscribers directly into the storm as opposed to away from it.

There are a number of emergency scenarios in which the above has occurred. During a wildfire evacuation at Pepperdine University in 2007, multi-part messages were transmitted to students and faculty to provide relocation instructions. However, some reported that the messages were not useful. One student later noted that "Each notification that was sent came through in six to eight text messages... And they were jumbled, not even coming in in order" [4]. More serious conflicts in message delivery order were noted at the Georgia Institute of Technology [6]. After a chemical spill in 2007, a message alerting students and faculty to evacuate campus was transmitted. Later, instructions to ignore the evacuation notification were also sent. However, a number of students noted receiving the messages out of order [36], adding greater confusion to the situation. Similar problems have been reported at a number of other universities [8,14].

5.3 Message Delay

Examples of the delay that can be experienced during times of high volume are most easily observed during New Years Eve celebrations or the most recent US Presidential Inauguration. As hundreds of millions of users around the globe send celebratory greetings via SMS, service providers often become inundated with a flood of messages. Accordingly, the delivery of such messages has been noted to exceed more than six hours [11]. Even though providers often plan and temporarily deploy additional resources to minimize the number of blocked calls, the sheer volume of messages during such an event demonstrates the practical limitations of current systems. In spite of temporarily deploying additional towers, such delays are experienced even when cellular providers are aware that a high volume event will take place.

Why then has SMS been a successful means of communication during other national emergencies such as September 11th and Hurricanes Katrina and Rita? Numerous sources cite SMS as an invaluable service when both man-made and natural disasters strike [15,26]. The difference between these events and other emergencies is the magnitude of messages sent. For instance, at the time of the attacks of September 11th, text messaging was still largely a fringe service in the United States. Had most users across the country attempted to communicate using SMS as their primary mode of communication, however, a report by the National Communications System estimates that current network capacities would need to be expanded by 100-fold [28] in order to support such a volume. The reliability of text messaging during Hurricane Katrina is due to similar reasons. Because only a very small number of people were communicating via text messaging, the towers undamaged by the storm were able to deliver such messages without any significant competition from other traffic. Moreover, because the network automatically attempted retransmission, users were more likely to receive text messages than calls. If SMS use during these events approached emergency levels, it would have experienced delays similar to those regularly observed on New Years Eve.

6 Improving Incident Response Communications

From the discussions, mathematical characterizations and simulations in the previous sections, the mismatch between the current cellular infrastructure and current response mechanisms is clear. Accordingly, such systems can not currently form the basis of a reliable alert system in the timescales required by the WARN Act, regardless of promises made by third party systems. However, the ubiquity of cellular phones gives them a potential role in the delivery of critical information during an emergency. This role would be complementary to the other platforms of the Emergency Broadcasting System (Television, radio, etc.).

There are a number of solutions currently under consideration that may help in this space. The most well known is *cell broadcast*. Unlike the point to point operations required for the delivery of messages in current networks, cell broadcast would allow the rapid dissemination of emergency information through point to multipoint communications. Such a system could ideally reach the majority of cellular users in an area and would not require knowledge of each particular user's location. This option is backed by the Commercial Mobile Service Alert Advisory Committee, which is currently working on developing standards documents. However, while cell broadcast will significantly improve communications over current mechanisms, a number of critical problems remain. First, like traditional text messaging, information delivered via cell broadcast will not be authenticated. Second, the channels used for cell broadcast are relatively bandwidth limited. The rate with which complex messages can be delivered during highly dynamic situations (e.g., an on-campus gunman) may therefore be lower than desired. Third, cell broadcast does little to address issues of coverage, which may become exacerbated during an emergency. For instance, in the event of a natural disaster or attack, it is highly likely that some cellular towers will be damaged or unpowered. Third, cell broadcast does not currently provide special options for hearing or visually impaired users. Finally, while cell broadcast is designed to deal with the overload of many simultaneous point to point connections, this technology is still relatively immature (i.e., standards are pending) and has not been deployed and measured in any large scale, public, scientific fashion. When this mechanism is deployed it may indeed improve communications during such scenarios; however, it is critical to recognize that our widely deployed current infrastructure is a deeply flawed information system when used for emergency communications.

The increasing capabilities of mobile devices could potentially be leveraged to improve the reach of communications during an emergency. For instance, cell broadcast could potentially be used to signal mobile phones equipped with 802.11 wireless cards to connect to a specific website containing regularly updated information. This information could potentially include sound or video clips similar to traditional EAS broadcasts to assist hearing and visually impaired users. The presence of 802.11 cards could also assist in improving coverage. Borrowing techniques from delay tolerant networking [13,19,50] may allow phones passing through areas with poor or no cellular reception to inform other devices of the current alert. The recent addition of AM/FM radio tuners in a variety of phones [30,17] may further assist in this process. Specifically, mobile devices could be used to immediately tune into the more traditional Emergency Broadcast system, ensuring consistent dispersal of information. The presence of AM/FM radios would also significantly improve the robustness of communications in a large scale emergency as cellular or 802.11 outages in a user's immediate vicinity would not prevent information from continuing to be delivered.

These suggestions also face a number of research questions. Like the cell broadcast case, a strong method of authenticating incoming notifications would be necessary. This issue may potentially be addressed by directing phones to an SSL-based webpage run by the university. Moreover, studies focused on latency and data provenance for delay tolerant networks in densely populated urban areas and campuses would also need to be conducted. Until such systems are realized, however, legislators and the general public should not rely upon text messaging or third party EAS providers for delivering emergency information.

7   Related Work

Following the events of September 11th, 2001, curiosity about the ability to use text messaging as the basis of a reliable communications system during times of crisis arose. In response, the National Communications System (NCS) conducted an investigating the use of text messaging during a nation-wide emergency, which through simple calculations concluded that current systems would require "100 times more capacity to meet [the] load" created by widespread use of text messaging [28]. A related study by the European Telecommunications Standard Institute (ETSI) identified the increasing prevalence of spam as a significant threat to the operation of cellular networks during an emergency [12]. However, both studies were limited to high-level calculations of a single emergency scenario and neither considered the use of third party EAS over SMS systems. Our study conducted the first characterization and simulation of multiple scenarios for EAS over cellular services and compared them directly to real-world, on-campus testing.

The specific impacts on the reliability and security of such networks under torrents of text messages have also been explored. Traynor el al. [41,43] noted that an attacker could exploit connections between the Internet and cellular networks to cause significant outages. With the bandwidth available to a cable modem, an attacker could send a small but targeted stream of text messages to a specific geographic region and prevent legitimate voice and text messages from being delivered. While subsequent research was able to better characterize and provide mitigations against such attacks [42], it was ultimately discovered that a more basic problem was responsible. Instead of simply being a matter of using a low-bandwidth channel to deliver data, the real cause of such attacks was a result of fundamental tension between cellular networks and the Internet. Specifically, because cellular networks can not amortize the significant cost of connection establishment when delivering data, they are fundamentally vulnerable to such attacks [44]. Accordingly, as long as text messages are delivered in the point to point fashion as is done now, the expense of establishing connections with each and every phone in an area will remain prohibitively expensive.

Whether as an unintended consequence or deliberate act, the flooding behavior exhibited in this above work closely resembles Denial of Service (DoS) attacks on the Internet. The research community has responded with attempts to classify [27] and mitigate [1,2,3,5,21,23,24,33,39,38,47,49] such attacks. However, such attacks are only beginning to be understood in the context of cellular networks, making the direct application of these solutions unsuitable.

8   Conclusion

Cellular networks are increasingly becoming the primary means of communication during emergencies. Riding the widely-held perception that text messaging is a reliable method of rapidly distributing messages, a large number of colleges, universities and municipalities have spent tens of millions of dollars to deploy third-party EAS over cellular systems. However, this security incident response and recovery mechanism simply does not work as advertised. Through modeling, a series of experiments and corroborating evidence from real-world tests, we have shown that these networks can not meet the 10 minute alert goal mandated by the public EAS charter and the WARN Act. Moreover, we have demonstrated that the extra text messaging traffic generated by third party EAS will cause congestion in the network and may potentially block upwards of 80% of normal requests, potentially including calls between emergency responders or the public to 9-1-1 services. Accordingly, it is critical that legislators, technologists and the general public understand the fundamental limitations of this mechanism to safeguard physical security and public safety and that future solutions are thoroughly evaluated before they are deployed.

Acknowledgements

This work was supported in part by 3G Americas. Any opinions, findings, conclusions or recommendations expressed in this publication are those of the authors and do not necessarily reflect the views of 3G Americas. We would also like to thank the cellular providers that helped us more accurately model this issue. This work was also supported in part by the US National Science Foundation (CNS-0916047). Any opinions, findings, conclusions or recommendations expressed in this publication are those of the authors and do not necessarily reflect the views of the National Science Foundation.

References

1. Andersen, D.: Mayday: Distributed Filtering for Internet Services. In: Proceedings of the USENIX Symposium on Internet Technologies and Systems (USITS) (2003)
2. Anderson, T., Roscoe, T., Wetherall, D.: Preventing Internet Denial of Service with Capabilities. In: Proceedings of ACM HotNets (2003)
3. Argyraki, K., Cheriton, D.R.: Scalable Network-layer Defense Against Internet Bandwidth-Flooding Attacks. ACM/IEEE Transactions on Networking (TON) (2009)
4. Blons, S.: Emergency team aids efforts (2007), http://graphic.pepperdine.edu/special/2007-10-24-emergencyteam.htm
5. Casado, M., Cao, P., Akella, A., Provos, N.: Flow Cookies: Using Bandwidth Amplification to Defend Against DDoS Flooding Attacks. In: Proceedings of the International Workshop on Quality of Service, IWQoS (2006)
6. Christensen, T.: Ga. Tech Building Cleared After Blast (2007), http://www.11alive.com/news/article_news.aspx?storyid=106112
7. CollegeSafetyNet. Campus Alert, Campus Security, Emergency Warning, college safety Crisis notification, Reverse 911, Mass emergency notification, Emergency Alert System, Cell phone alerts, Email alerts, Text Message Alerts, Student warning system, Student notification, campus notification, and Mass notification at CollegeSafetyNet.com (2008), http://www.collegesafetynet.com/

8. Courant.com. University Emergency SMS service doesn't deliver, `http://www.courant.com` (November 13, 2007).
9. Daly, B.K.: Wireless Alert & Warning Workshop, `http://www.oes.ca.gov/WebPage/oeswebsite.nsf/ClientOESFileLibrary/Wireless%20Alert%20and%20Warning/file/ATT-OES-2`
10. e2Campus. Mass Notification Systems for College, University & Higher Education Schools by e2Campus: Info On The Go! (2008), `http://www.e2campus.com/`
11. Elliott, A.-M.: Texters to experience 6 hour delays on New Year's Eve (2007), `http://www.pocket-lint.co.uk/news/news.phtml/11895/12919/palm-new-years-text-delay.phtml`
12. European Telecommunications Standards Institute. Analysis of the Short Message Service (SMS) and Cell Broadcast Service (CBS) for Emergency Messaging applications; Emergency Messaging; SMS and CBS. Technical Report ETSI TR 102 444 V1.1.1
13. Fall, K.: A Delay-Tolerant Network Architecture for Challenged Internets. In: Proceedings of the Conference on Applications, Technologies, Architectures and Protocols for Computer Communications, COMM (2003)
14. Ganosellis, L.: UF to test texting alerts after LSU glitch (2008), `http://www.alligator.org/articles/2008/01/08/news/uf_administration/lsu.txt`
15. Geer, D.: Wireless victories. Wireless Business & Technology, 2005 (September 11, 2001)
16. Hedden, J.: Math::Random::MT::Auto - Auto-seeded Mersenne Twister PRNGs. Version 5.01, `http://search.cpan.org/~jdhedden/Math-Random-MT-Auto-5.01/lib/Math/Random/MT/Auto.pm`
17. HTC Corporation. HTC Tattoo Specifications (2009) `http://www.htc.com/europe/product/tattoo/specification.html`
18. Inspiron Logistics. Inspiron Logistics Corporation WENS - Wireless Emergency Notification System for Emergency Mobile Alerts (2008), `http://www.inspironlogistics.com/`
19. Jain, S., Fall, K., Patra, R.: Routing in a Delay Tolerant Network. In: Proceedings of the Conference on Applications, Technologies, Architectures and Protocols for Computer Communications, COMM (2004)
20. Jaramillo, E.: UT director: Text alerts effective (2008), `http://www.dailytexanonline.com/1.752094`
21. Keromytis, A., Misra, V., Rubenstein, D.: SOS: Secure Overlay Services. In: Proceedings of ACM SIGCOMM (2002)
22. Luders, C., Haferbeck, R.: The Performance of the GSM Random Access Procedure. In: Vehicular Technology Conference (VTC), pp. 1165–1169 (June 1994)
23. Mahajan, R., Bellovin, S.M., Floyd, S., Ioannidis, J., Paxson, V., Shenker, S.: Controlling High Bandwidth Aggregates in the Network. Computer Communications Review 32(3), 62–73 (2002)
24. Mahimkar, A., Dange, J., Shmatikov, V., Vin, H., Zhang, Y.: dFence: Transparent Network-based Denial of Service Mitigation. In: Proceedings of USENIX Networked Systems Design and Implementation (NSDI) (2007)
25. Maney, K.: Surge in text messaging makes cell operators, `http://www.usatoday.com/money/2005-07-27-text-messaging_x.htm` (July 27, 2005)
26. McAdams, J.: SMS does SOS (2006), `http://www.fcw.com/print/12_11/news/92790-1.html`
27. Mirkovic, J., Reiher, P.: A Taxonomy of DDoS Attacks and DDoS Defense Mechanisms. ACM SIGCOMM Computer Communication Review 34(2), 39–53 (2004)
28. National Communications System. SMS over SS7. Technical Report Technical Information Bulletin 03-2 (NCS TIB 03-2) (December 2003)

29. National Notification Network (3n). 3n InstaCom Campus Alert - Mass Notification for Colleges and Universities (2008), http://www.3nonline.com/campus-alert
30. Nettles, C.: iPhone 3 to have Broadcom BCM4329, 802.11N/5GHzWireless, FM transmitter/receiver (2009),
http://www.9to5mac.com/broadcom-BCM4329-iphone-802.11n-FM
31. Nizza, M.: This is only a (text messaging) test (2007), http://thelede.blogs.nytimes.com/2007/09/25/this-is-only-a-text-messaging-test/?scp=5&sq=Emergency%20Text%20Messaging&st=cse
32. Nyquetek, Inc. Wireless Priority Service for National Security (2002), http://wireless.fcc.gov/releases/da051650PublicUse.pdf
33. Parno, B., Wendlandt, D., Shi, E., Perrig, A., Maggs, B.: Portcullis: Protecting Connection Setup from Denial of Capability Attacks. In: Proceedings of ACM SIGCOMM (2007)
34. Reverse 911. Reverse 911 - The only COMPLETE notification system for public safety (2008), http://www.reverse911.com/index.php
35. Roam Secure (2008), http://www.roamsecure.net/
36. shelbinator.com. Evacuate! Or Not (2007), http://shelbinator.com/2007/11/08/evacuate-or-not/
37. Simon Fraser University. Special Report on the April 9th Test of SFU Alerts (2008), http://www.sfu.ca/sfualerts/april08_report.html
38. Stavrou, A., Cook, D.L., Morein, W.G., Keromytis, A.D., Misra, V., Rubenstein, D.: WebSOS: An Overlay-based System For Protecting Web Servers From Denial of Service Attacks. Journal of Computer Networks, special issue on Web and Network Security 48(5), 781–807 (2005)
39. Stavrou, A., Keromytis, A.: Countering DOS Attacks With Stateless Multipath Overlays. In: Proceedings of ACM Conference on Computer and Communications Security (CCS) (2005)
40. The 109th Senate of the United States of America. Warning, Alert, and Response Network Act (2005), http://thomas.loc.gov/cgi-bin/query/z?c109:H.R.1753:
41. Traynor, P., Enck, W., McDaniel, P., La Porta, T.: Exploiting Open Functionality in SMS-Capable Cellular Networks. Journal of Computer Security (JCS) (2008)
42. Traynor, P., Enck, W., McDaniel, P., La Porta, T.: Mitigating Attacks on Open Functionality in SMS-Capable Cellular Networks. IEEE/ACM Transactions on Networking (TON) 17 (2009)
43. Traynor, P., Lin, M., Ongtang, M., Rao, V., Jaeger, T., La Porta, T., McDaniel, P.: On Cellular Botnets: Measuring the Impact of Malicious Devices on a Cellular Network Core. In: Proceedings of the ACM Conference on Computer and Communications Security (CCS) (2009)
44. Traynor, P., McDaniel, P., La Porta, T.: On Attack Causality in Internet-Connected Cellular Networks. In: Proceedings of the USENIX Security Symposium (2007)
45. TXTLaunchPad. TXTLaunchPad provides Bulk SMS text message alerts to businesses, schools, and advertisers (2007), http://www.txtlaunchpad.com/
46. Voice Shot. automated emergency alert notification call - VoiceShot (2008), http://www.voiceshot.com/public/urgentalert.asp?ref=uaemergencyalert
47. Walfish, M., Vutukuru, M., Balakrishnan, H., Karger, D., Shenkar, S.: DDoS Offense by Offense. In: Proceedings of ACM SIGCOMM (2006)
48. Wikipedia. Virginia Polytechnic Institute and State University (2008), http://en.wikipedia.org/wiki/Virginia_Tech
49. Yang, X., Wetherall, D., Anderson, T.: TVA: A DoS-limiting Network Architecture. IEEE/ACM Transactions on Networking (TON) (2009)
50. Zho, W., Ammar, M., Zegura, E.: A message ferrying approach for data delivery in sparse mobile ad hoc networks. In: Proceedings of the International Symposium on Mobile Ad Hoc Networking & Computing, MOBIHOC (2004)

Saving Energy on WiFi with Required IPsec

Youngsang Shin, Steven Myers, and Minaxi Gupta

School of Informatics and Computing
Indiana University
Bloomington, IN 47405, USA
shiny@cs.indiana.edu, samyers@indiana.edu, minaxi@cs.indiana.edu

Abstract. The move to a pervasive computing environment, with the increasing use of laptops, netbooks, smartphones and tablets, means that we are more reliant on wireless networking and batteries for our daily computational needs. Specifically, this includes applications which have sensitive data that must be securely communicated over VPNs. However, the use of VPNs and mobile, wireless computing creates conflicting needs: VPNs traditionally assume a stable network connection, which is then secured; in contrast, wireless computing assumes a transitory network connection due to mobility or energy-saving protocols. In this work we study the ability to use traditional VPN protocols, specifically IPsec, in mobile environments while permitting for energy savings. Energy savings come from power-cycling the wireless radio when it is not in use.

More specifically, we develop a mathematical model for determining potential power savings on mobile devices when power-cycling the radio in IPsec use settings. Next, we perform performance measurements on IPsec session resumption protocols IKEv2 [1], MOBIKE [2], and IPsec Gateway Failover (IGF) [3] to provide data for our model. We apply the model to over 3000 wireless sessions, and determine the optimal power savings that could be achieved by power-cycling the radio while maintaining an IPsec connection. We show that there is a high-potential for energy savings in the best case. Finally, we develop an efficient and simple real-world online scheduling algorithm that achieves near optimal results for a majority of users.

Keywords: WiFi, VPN, IPsec, IPsec gateway failover, energy saving, security.

1 Introduction

Mobile devices such as laptops, netbooks, Personal Data Assistants (PDAs), tablets and smartphones typically come equipped with WiFi and/or cellular network radios. This allows them to easily connect to the Internet, motivating their pervasive use with IP-based user applications in conducting business. According to [4], more than 50 million US workers are spending more than 20 percent of the time away from their primary workspace. Yet, with mobile users connecting over untrusted networks to organizations' sensitive resources comes the need for secure communication. Virtual Private Networks (VPN) are widely adopted and used for this purpose, and Internet Protocol Security (IPsec) [5, 6] is perhaps the most commonly used VPN protocol. Most organizations now require that mobile employees use a VPN connection for all connections to the Internet via mobile devices for security and auditing reasons.

S. Jajodia and J. Zhou (Eds.): SecureComm 2010, LNICST 50, pp. 144–161, 2010.

When an IPsec connection is built over WiFi in mobile devices, the usability of secure communication is significantly affected by two important factors: battery power and mobility. Mobile devices are presumed to be operated by battery power and studies have shown that the power usage of the WiFi interface and radio is a major fraction ($\approx 18\%$) of the power used in mobile devices [7]. Further, VPNs often require intensive use of the CPU in the computation of asymmetric cryptography while building the IPsec connection, which is known to consume considerable power. Since mobility and power-cycling radios can frequently force the asymmetric cryptographic operations to be recomputed, examining power-saving opportunities in these scenarios is crucial.

1.1 Scenarios

To help visualize issues, we consider several scenarios:

Academic at a coffee shop: An academic is writing a paper at the coffee shop. She occasionally needs access to the Internet to look up references, find papers, email, etc., but does not need continuous access, nor does she want to continuously re-authenticate to the VPN server.

Roaming Tablet User: A user with a mobile tablet computer (e.g., iPad, iPod-Touch) is traveling through a city, using available free WiFi connections whenever they appear. Since open connections cannot be trusted, a VPN connection must be maintained.

Business at the Airport: While waiting between flights, a business user gets work done. She needs to occasionally update and modify files on servers, but mostly uses local files and apps. She may have to move locations several times due to eating or gate-changes. There is no available power-plug. Her corporation requires all connections be through the VPN.

In each of these cases, the users will need to continuously reestablish VPN connections whether or not they use the VPN a frequent amount of the time. However, manually turning off the WiFi radio is probably too time consuming and frustrating to be done manually; this is especially true when a VPN connection must be re-established with each cycling. Therefore, WiFi is left on, and battery life severely reduced.

1.2 Power Saving Mode (PSM)

The 802.11 standard defines two possible operating modes for wireless interfaces: *active* mode and *power saving mode (PSM)*. In *active* mode, wireless devices can exchange data while being in receive, transmit, or idle states. The PSM is an optional mode. It lowers the energy consumption of the mobile device compared to the *active* mode. If PSM is used, a mobile client's wireless interface goes into PSM when the device is idle. Upon doing so, it informs the access point (AP) so the AP can buffer incoming data. Periodically, usually $100msec$, the AP sends a special frame, called the *Beacon*, which contains a *Traffic Indication Map* (TIM) to inform the client about buffered frames. The clients periodically wake up and receive the Beacon to get buffered frames. A more detailed description of PSM can be found in [8].

Under our usage scenarios PSM has several problems. First, the power consumption in PSM is still close to 250mW, which is around 30% of that in *active* mode [9]. It is nontrivial and unnecessary when there is no network traffic. Second, it is hard to assume that PSM can be continuously supported when users change their location. When users move and transition across APs, the PSM support is not handed over between APs. Further, the user can encounter various APs administrated by different organizations and many old APs in use today do not support the PSM standard. For these reasons, we do not consider PSM subsequently in this paper.

A number of research papers including [10], present techniques to utilize 802.11's PSM to reduce power use. Some works [11] have suggested using proxies at the AP to look at incoming connections and respond to those connections that do not need to wake the client, and can be trivially handled by the proxy. This clearly cannot be done in the case that the data is encrypted, and the proxy is not trusted. Regardless, due to the non-trivial power consumption and inefficiencies of WiFi's PSM protocol, the works of [12, 9, 7] suggest saving power by shutting-down the WiFi radio when the WiFi interface is not actively used. These works use a lower powered radio to forewarn of an incoming WiFi signal and to awaken the WiFi interface. However, in most deployments today, such alternate low-power radios are not deployed on at least one, if not both sides of the wireless connection. We consider a situation in which the radio is predictively power-cycled, without the aid of a low-powered radio to warn of incoming traffic. This may prevent the use of push-based protocols that attempt to access a client. Nonetheless, based on our large number of wireless traces we show this is still an effective strategy for a large number of users, and power savings are achievable without additional hardware.

1.3   Our Contributions

Shutting down the radio is an effective way to save energy, but it comes with important side effects. Specifically, a disconnection in higher layer protocols and/or a change of IP address. Mobility means that the device may be communicating with many different APs over time with transition periods where no connection is available. This results in exactly the same side effects. Since one's IP address is used as a means of identification at the network layer, its change may significantly affect higher layer protocols. We are specifically interested in its effect on IPsec. When a device's IP address is modified, the IPsec connection needs to be reestablished, causing delay and energy consumption. This is particularly true due to CPU-intensive asymmetric cryptographic operations.

To the best of the our knowledge, no prior works have investigated the time and energy impacts of IPsec key reestablishment and session resumption on higher layer energy preservation protocols that power-cycle the wireless radio. We consider three protocols for IPsec session resumption: IKEv2 [1], MOBIKE [2] and IPsec Gateway Failover (IGF) [3].

We develop a mathematical model for calculating the power savings possible with the use of IPsec in the presence of radio cycling under clairvoyant scheduling. In order to populate the model with appropriate parameters on timing and power usage, we compute performance measurements for both clients and servers for IKEv2, MOBIKE and IGF and measure power usage rates and costs for different hardware and protocol executions. Next, we apply this model to over 3000 wireless sessions from Indiana university's campus. The results demonstrate that in the presence of an IPsec connection there is a strong potential for energy savings by power cycling the wireless radio. In scenarios of interest, the hybridization of MOBIKE and IGF gives the best result, implying IGF should be considered for mobility situations. We also show that a simple and efficient algorithm can be deployed that predictively power-cycles the radio based on past network usage. We show that this algorithm achieves near-optimal results for a large fraction of users, while having minor power penalties for a negligible fraction.

Finally, we note that none of the protocols were designed for saving power on mobile devices via power cycling radios, but all three can be used as such.

2   Background on IPsec and Related Protocols

The IPsec protocol allows for private and authenticated communication over an open network. IPsec, as it is typically deployed, works in roughly two phases, a computationally intensive key-exchange phase in which asymmetric cryptographic operations are performed to share secret random keys between the client and server. Other shared state between the client and the server is also amassed and the collection is called the the Security Association (SA). The SA is used to establish a secure session, through the use of symmetric key cryptography, in a second phase. Importantly, the IP addresses of the client and server are embedded in the SA, so *historically* any modifications to the server' or client's IP address require recomputing the first, expensive, phase to acquire a new SA.

2.1   Internet Key Exchange (IKE) Protocol

IKE is the name of the asymmetric cryptographic handshake most commonly used in phase one of IPsec. Technically, there are two version of IKE: IKEv1 [13] and IKEv2 [1]. IKEv1 is inefficient and is being deprecated, all references to IKE herein refer to IKEv2. Other technical details of the protocol are beyond the scope of this paper. Importantly, MOBIKE [2] and IGF [3]—the other protocols we consider— are only designed to interact with IKEv2. IKE can itself use several asymmetric primitives (e.g., RSA or Diffie-Hellman) with different security parameters, and the choice of these parameters have an effect on performance. In our measurements we use RSA keys with 2048 bits, as RSA is the more frequently deployed primitive, and a 2048-bit key length is now considered required for many security objectives. RSA is also preferable to Diffie-Hellman due to the ability to choose small exponents, decreasing computation time at the mobile client at the expense of time on the powered server.

In regards to session resumption, by simply starting a new IPsec session from scratch each time the radio is powered on, we can of course perform a primitive form of 'session resumption'.

Dead Peer Detection(DPD). In practice most IPsec servers run the dead peer detection (DPD) [14] protocol, to determine when clients are no longer present in order to reclaim resources dedicated to the IPsec connection. The DPD protocol is needed since many IPsec clients do not actively notify of a disconnect. However, wireless clients can be perceived as dead due to power cycling the radio or because they are in transit between

APs. DPD determines whether a client is alive or not by waiting for a fixed amount of time for a reply to a keep-alive query. If there is no response, it disconnects the session, deletes any associated state and recovers any associated resources.

2.2   IPsec Gateway Failover (IGF)

IPsec Gateway Failover (IGF) [3] is an extension to IKEv2 designed for the fast, near simultaneous, resumption of a large number of interrupted IPsec connections due to server failures. It was designed to allow IPsec servers that have failed to quickly reestablish the connections with many clients once the servers are back online. This is done without needing to re-execute the computationally expensive IKE protocol with each client. The IGF protocol was not designed with mobility in mind, and we believe we are the first to recognize its potential application in mobility settings. The main scheme is based on the stateless TLS session resumption protocol [15].

In IGF, the server sends a (symmetrically) encrypted and authenticated version of its IKE SA information, called a *ticket*, to the client. The ticket's cryptographic keys are not known to the client; thus, the ticket can only be decrypted or modified by the server. The client simply stores the ticket and presents it to the server when the client needs to restore a failed connection, reestablishing the SA. Importantly, all encryption and authentication of the ticket is done strictly with *efficient symmetric key cryptographic primitives*, and thus, in a given time frame, a server can reactivate many more SAs from tickets, than it could by repeating IKE protocols. Thus, in the scenarios of interest herein, even if an IPsec server decides that a connection has been severed via the DPD protocol and deletes the session's SA, an IPsec session can be re-established via IGF.

2.3   MOBIKE

MOBIKE (IKEv2 Mobility and Multihoming Protocol) [2] is a mobility and multihoming extension to IKE, allowing IP addresses in a previously established SA to change. Thus, it enables a mobile IPsec client *that has already established a SA via IKE or IGF* to keep a connection with a server alive while changing its IP address.

MOBIKE allows mobile IPsec clients who have previously established a SA through other means, such as IKE or IGF, to change IP addresses while maintaining a connection, instead of requiring the establishment of a new IPsec connection via IKEv2. However, this protocol works only when both client and server maintain an existing IPsec connection state. In cases where the connection is lost due to DPD (or some other reason), MOBIKE cannot be used to resume a client's IPsec session. In such situations, MOBIKE can default to IKEv2 or IGF.

We therefore consider three cases relating to MOBIKE i) MOBIKE by itself, where the state of every client would need to be maintained for each client more-or-less indefinitely (i.e., we assume DPD is not run and connections live forever); ii) MOBIKE+IKEv2 and iii) MOBIKE+IGF, where in the latter two cases it is assumed that sessions that are inactive for short periods of time (several minutes) are reinitiated with MOBIKE, but sessions that are inactive for longer periods of time, and thus likely disconnected by the server, are resumed through IKEv2 or IGF respectively.

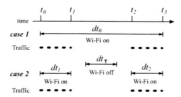

Fig. 1. Scenarios with WiFi on and off during idle times

3   Power Savings for Session-Resumption Protocols

We develop a deployable mathematical power-saving model for IPsec over WiFi for different session resumption protocols. Next, we use it to analyze real world wireless sessions to determine the potential for the power saving schemes. We show that in the optimal case substantial power savings can be achieved using clairvoyant scheduling. We realize that such omniscient optimal scheduling is not possible in real life, but if optimal scheduling does not provide savings there is no potential for a more limited algorithm. Our results provide an upper bound on potential power savings. Finally, we present a practical online scheduler that achieves near optimal power-savings.

3.1   Mathematical Model

In Figure 1 we consider two cases. In case 1 the WiFi radio is on from time t_0 to t_3 but has a large idle gap between t_1 and t_2, and therefore could have potentially been switched off to save power. Equation 1 gives the cost of case 1 for time period $dt_0 = t_3 - t_0$, where $WiFi_M$ represents the maintenance cost per second of keeping on the WiFi radio while it is idle.

We are interested in cases in which the WiFi radio is instantly switched off if it were going to stay idle for some period longer than dt_τ, where dt_τ represents the minimal amount of time a radio needs to be off for it to have been cost effective in terms of power consumption. Note that the power savings have to account for the costs of cycling the wireless radio off and on, and then reestablish an IPsec connection.

Let $WiFi_C, IPsec_C, WiFi_D$ and $IPsec_D$ represent the respective energy costs of connecting and disconnecting WiFi and IPsec connections, where $IPsec_C$ and $IPsec_D$ are dependent on the session resumption protocol in question. Equation 2 calculates the break-even time, $dt_{\tau'}$ of switching the wireless radio on and off and resuming an IPsec session *assuming that setting up IPsec and WiFi connections are instantaneous actions*. In reality, there is a time associated with each, call them $WiFi_t$ and $IPsec_t$, and during that time the device is wasting extra base-line power at a rate of $WiFi_M$ to remain on. So, to truly capture the costs one calculates dt_τ, as in Equation 3.

In Figure 1 case 2, we denote the same traffic scenario as case 1, but with a power saving scheduler. The idle time occurs between t_2 and t_1, since $(t_2 - t_1) > dt_\tau$ the IPsec connection is disconnected and the wireless radio is switched off to save power. At time t_2, the WiFi radio is enabled again as the client needs to use the WiFi connection again. When the WiFi interface is enabled, the VPN connection needs to be reconnected. We consider the reconnection costs of the IPsec connection via IKE, MOBIKE or IGF.

dt_τ	idle-time/power savings cross over point
$WiFi_M$	idle WiFi maintenance cost per second
$WiFi_C$ & $WiFi_D$	WiFi startup and shutdown costs
$IPsec_C$ & $IPsec_D$	IPsec connection and disconnection costs
$WiFi_t$ & $IPsec_t$	time to establish WiFi and IPsec connections

$$dt_0 \cdot WiFi_M \quad (1)$$

$$dt_{\tau'} = \frac{\sum_{i \in \{C,D\}} (WiFi_i + IPsec_i)}{WiFi_M}. \quad (2)$$

$$dt_\tau = dt_{\tau'} + (WiFi_t + IPsec_t). \quad (3)$$

$$\sum_{i \in \{C,D\}} (WiFi_i + IPsec_i) \quad (4)$$
$$+ (dt_1 + dt_2) \cdot WiFi_M$$

The cost of case 2 is given by Equation 4 where $dt_1 = t_1 - t_0$ and $dt_2 = t_3 - t_2$. We do not charge for a user's network traffic during dt_1 and dt_2 since they are the same in both cases. Clearly, *whenever Equation 4 is valued strictly smaller than Equation 1, the power saving scheme is beneficial.*

3.2   Patterns in Real-World WiFi Traffic

To investigate how effective radio-cycling power saving schemes can be, we collected one day of anonymized NetFlow data from Indiana University's *wireless APs*. The data spans 3098 client connections to the *wireless APs* and contains packet headers, packet sizes, and timing information for IP packets going through them. For privacy reasons, the packet headers have source and destination IPs anonymized but port numbers are intact. In cases where only the start and stop time for a flow of multiple packets is known, we assume that the packets were distributed evenly over that time. This is a worst-case assumption that underestimates the potential times the wireless radio can be deactivated in any schedule. It should be noted that no effort was made to have any of the clients run any traffic shaping protocols to optimize the amount of time the radio could be disconnected. The data represents average wireless usage of mobile users at our University.

In Figure 2 we present two sample idle-time patterns that we collected by subjecting network traffic generated by a few real-world users using Wireshark. They show the very different patterns wireless traffic can take for different users. We note that the idle time between most packets, for almost all users, is well under a minute in each case but there are large gaps of several minutes between some of the packets of many users', as is demonstrated by User 1 in the figure. This implies significant power savings are conceivable for such users. With the longest gap between packets of User 2 being 21 seconds, power savings are less likely for users with such behavior. Our goal is to save energy in the cases of users like 1, while not penalizing users with usage patterns similar to 2.

3.3   Measuring Variables for the Mathematical Model

To estimate power savings with our model, we need to estimate the cost of each variable in Equations 1 & 4. Works in [12, 9, 7] used multimeters to gauge power usage. Instead, we determine the battery usage by querying the mobile device through the Linux Advanced Configuration & Power Interface (ACPI) [16]. ACPI is an abstraction layer that enables OS-directed configuration, power, and thermal management of mobile, desktop, and server platforms. ACPI does not provide as high a resolution of energy measurement as multimeters, but it is simpler to measure and it might be argued

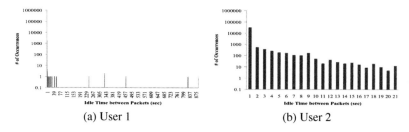

(a) User 1   (b) User 2

Fig. 2. Idle time between packets for two users over an hour period

Table 1. Configuration of machines used for measuring energy usage

Device	CPU/RAM	Network Connection	Operating System
Client	Pentium M 1.86Ghz/512M	Intel Pro/Wireless 2200bg (802.11g)	Linux kernel 2.6.18
Server	Pentium IV 1.3Ghz/640M	10Mbps Ethernet	Linux kernel 2.6.22

is a more effective tool for evaluating our benefits of power saving scheme, because *it represents the information that a typical operating system, and thus scheduling algorithm, will have to measure power-usage.* We use standard laptops to perform energy measurements. Specifics of the configuration of devices are shown in Table 1.

The resolution of the Linux ACPI measurement may be deemed low due to the fact that it cannot directly obtain the power usage of each operation independently. This is due to overhead of the operating system, and other processes running on the machine during calls to the API. Therefore, we measure the average energy usage over 25 iterations for each of the operations. We measure what the API returns as the differential between the battery life before and after the operation. Of course, we must normalize these values to compensate for the fact that there is a base-line power consumption for each mobile device. Through repeated measurements, we found that the baseline rate of energy consumption for the laptop was approximately 18Watts when it was on with the WiFi interface off, and when its LCD's brightness was set to the highest value. This baseline power-consumption is needed, since the proposed power saving scheme incurs an additional waiting time as the WiFi and IPsec connections are established and torn-down and one must charge the power-saving schedule for the extra baseline power consumed during these times. For $WiFi_M$, we measure the energy usages with and without the WiFi connection for 10 minutes. We conduct this experiment 25 times and then calculate an average.

We measured the costs of $WiFi_C$ & $WiFi_D$ and $WiFi_t$ at six different locations and APs to determine if the costs depend on the configuration of APs. The locations include libraries, restaurants, coffee houses, and book stores. The results are shown in Figure 3. For 5 of the 6 locations the costs of $WiFi_C$ & $WiFi_D$ were within $46 \pm 1J$ and $WiFi_t$ was within 2 ± 0.5 *seconds*. An outlying data point, at $61J$ for $WiFi_C$ & $WiFi_D$ and at 4.5 *seconds* for $WiFi_t$, seemed to be due to the fact that there were many APs with the same Service Set Identifier (SSID) at the location. Elsewhere, there were many SSIDs, but each was served by only one AP. We assume that $46J$ for $WiFi_C$ & $WiFi_D$ and 2 *seconds* for $WiFi_t$. Unlike the measurements for $WiFi_C$ & $WiFi_D$

Operations & Steady States	Cost
$WiFi_M$	2.29 W
$IPsec_C$ & $IPsec_D$ with IKE	13.14 J
$IPsec_C$ & $IPsec_D$ with IGF	9.2 J
$IPsec_C$ & $IPsec_D$ with MOBIKE	0.40 J
$WiFi_C$ & $WiFi_D$	46 J
$WiFi_t$	2 seconds

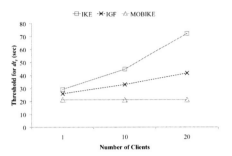

Fig. 3. Energy usages obtained through Linux ACPI and time for WiFi association with AP

Fig. 4. Changes in threshold dt_τ for different session resumption protocols as the number of concurrent connections increase

and $WiFi_t$, we measured the cost of $IPsec_C$ & $IPsec_D$ at only one location because these costs are independent of the WiFi client and its relation to the AP. These measurements were averaged over 25 runs. Lastly for $IPsec_t$, we use the latency numbers in Figure 10. Figure 3 presents the measured values of model variables.

We calculated the threshold value dt_τ for IKE, IGF, and MOBIKE as defined by Equation 3 using the measured values for $IPsec_C, IPsec_D, WiFi_C, WiFi_D, WiFi_M, WiFi_t,$ and $IPsec_t$. The only location dependent values are $WiFi_C, WiFi_D,$ and $WiFi_t$, and since they do not appear to vary much, dt_τ *is effectively location invariant.* The value $IPsec_t$ is dependent on the load on the IPsec server: the higher the server load, the longer the latency experienced by the client (c.f. Sec. 4). While the client is latent and waiting for a server response to the IPsec protocol, it pays a cost of energy at the rate of $WiFi_M$. Figure 4 summarizes the approximate thresholds for each protocol for 1, 10 and 20 simultaneous clients. As expected, the threshold increases with the number of clients for all protocols but MOBIKE, which has no real computational costs.

3.4   Power Savings under Optimal Scheduling

We investigated the optimal power savings for various session-resumption protocols using the 3098 WiFi traffic logs. We assumed that the scheduler deactivates the wireless card immediately upon detecting inactivity and invokes it so it is functioning just in time for a packet to arrive, assuming such power-cycling saves power.

Recall that in our model, power savings depend on dt_τ, which in turn depends on both the number of concurrent connections the server is handling, and the AP that the user is accessing. We consider three cases where the IPsec server is serving 1, 10, and 20 concurrent connections. We chose 20 as the maximal number of concurrent clients due to the limitation of the strongSwan software[1], which does not permit larger configurations than 20. We consider five variants of session-resumption protocols: i) IKE, ii) MOBIKE, iii) IGF, iv) MOBIKE+IKE and v) MOBIKE+IGF. With the hybrid protocols iv) and v) we assume that MOBIKE is used to resume sessions that are idle for

---

[1] *strongSwan* is an open source IPsec implementation for Linux.

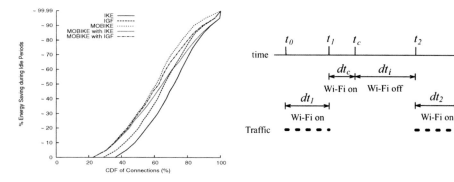

Fig. 5. Energy savings for real-world WiFi sessions under optimal scheduling with different session-resumption protocols

Fig. 6. Idle-time scenario for the prediction algorithm

less than 2 minutes and then the alternate protocol (IKE or IGF respectively) is used otherwise. We chose 2 minutes as it is the default disconnect time for the DPD protocol in strongSwan. To compute model variables for hybrid cases, we use the appropriate $IPsec_C$, $IPsec_D$, and $IPsec_t$ dependent on the protocol for session resumption.

In the case where the VPN server is handling 20 concurrent session-resumption requests, we note that 78% of WiFi connections reap some benefits of power savings. The differences among the various session-resumption protocols is shown in Figure 5. The cumulative distribution function (CDF) of the percentage of connections that reap energy savings is given. As expected, MOBIKE has the best performance but this is under the unrealistic assumption that the DPD protocol never terminates sessions. DPD is in fact used to release sessions specifically so servers do not become overwhelmed reserving resources for dead connections. However, when MOBIKE is combined with IGF (and DPD), we get only slightly worse performance than MOBIKE by itself. We skip presenting the results for 1 and 10 concurrent clients for brevity but note that as the number of concurrent clients drops to one, the CDFs for all of the protocols cluster close to the MOBIKE curve.

3.5 A Real-World Scheduler

Having shown that optimal scheduling permits potentially great energy savings, we now provide a simple prediction algorithm that uses a user's previous network usage history to predict future network usage requirements, and to decide if and when the radio should be power-cycled. When the radio is on but idle we estimate the probability that the tentative remaining idle time is longer than dt_τ, the minimal time period the radio can be off to save power. If the estimated probability is higher than a given predefined threshold α, the radio is power-cycled. In cases where there is no historical data yet, say during device initiation, the protocol uses a threshold value determined by calculating the average of users' history on our real world data traces. We re-enable the WiFi radio only when the client again attempts to send a packet. This can result in lost

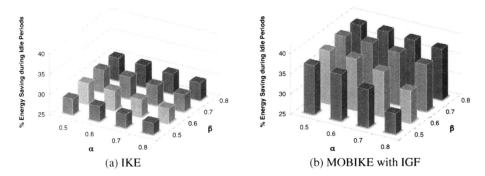

(a) IKE   (b) MOBIKE with IGF

Fig. 7. Average energy savings for 100 WiFi sessions using worst and best session-resumption protocols under varying α and β

t_c	current time
m_{t_c}	# of idle periods in user history where length $\geq dt_c$.
n_{t_c}	# of idle periods in user history where length minus $dt_c \geq dt_\tau$.
$m_{avg\_t_c}$	# of idle periods in average user's history where length $\geq dt_c$.
$n_{avg\_t_c}$	# of idle periods where length minus $dt_c \geq dt_\tau$.

$$P_{t_c} = n_{t_c}/m_{t_c} \qquad (5)$$

$$P_{avg\_t_c} = n_{avg\_t_c}/m_{avg\_t_c} \qquad (6)$$

$$P_{t_c} > \alpha \qquad (7)$$

$$P_{avg\_t_c} > \beta \qquad (8)$$

incoming packets if the WiFi radio is off. We consider two scenarios: i) all such packets are lost, and ii) the IPsec server acts as a proxy for basic networking protocols.

To help demonstrate the scheduler operation, we depict a scenario in Figure 6. Here, an idle time starts at time t_1. The current time is t_c, and we must make a decision as to whether or not to power-cycle the radio. The prediction algorithm estimates the probability, P_{t_c} that the tentative remaining idle time dt_i will be longer than dt_τ, based on historical network usage patterns. If the estimated probability is greater than a threshold value α the WiFi is turned off.

The probability, P_{t_c} can be calculated in Equation 5. When it is greater than a threshold, α in Equation 7, the WiFi radio is turned off. One issue with the proposed scheme is that if a user's network usage history does not contain any idle period whose length is longer than at least dt_τ, P_{t_c} is always 0. For this case, we adopt a probability, $P_{avg\_t_c}$ calculated from average users' network usage history in Equation 6. Thus, when P_{t_c} is 0, the algorithm checks if $P_{avg\_t_c}$ is greater than a threshold, β in Equation 8. The values are tabulated by taking into account all of the network trace-data we have, minus 100 traces we have randomly chosen and separated to use for independent performance evaluation.

Scheduler Performance. To evaluate the scheduler, we chose 100 different sessions in our wireless traces uniformly at random. We also calculated the average users' network-usage history from all the sessions excluding the 100 test sessions. We simulate α and β with values 0.5, 0.6, 0.7, and 0.8, where the greater value the more conservative our power-saving is. In Figure 7, we present the average energy savings for worst (IKE) and second-best (IGF+MOBIKE) of the resumption protocol we considered. MOBIKE has the best savings, but the need to keep an unlimited number of sessions open is unrealistic

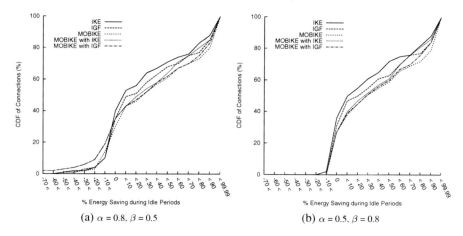

(a) $\alpha = 0.8$, $\beta = 0.5$ (b) $\alpha = 0.5$, $\beta = 0.8$

Fig. 8. CDF of percentage energy savings under the history-based scheduling with different resumption protocols

and thus discounted as a potential protocol. As α increases, the average savings decrease. This means that the conservative prediction misses energy-saving opportunities based on user's historical usage patterns. In contrast, as β increases (the threshold based on average user's data), better average savings are achieved. This is because an average users' network-usage history does not reflect each user's usage accurately and the conservative prediction avoids false positives.

In Figure 8, we show the percentage energy savings with different resumption protocols when α and β are 0.8 and 0.5, and 0.5 and 0.8 respectively. In Figure 8a, When β is 0.5 , less than 15% of users actually spend more energy due to such false positives in the prediction. However, when β is 0.8 in Figure 8b, only around 2% of users spend less than 10% more energy under IKEv2 protocol. We get the best energy saving results with $\alpha = 0.5$ and $\beta = 0.8$. *The prediction algorithm achieves energy savings that are within 3.5% difference from the optimally-scheduled case. That is, it achieves over 90% of the maximum energy savings which can be obtained in the optimal scheduling.*

Estimating dt_τ: The scheduler needs access to several measured values. The measured energy usage values in Figure 3 are relatively constant and can be embedded in to the client. On the other hand dt_τ depends on the IPsec server's load. To estimate an effective dt_τ, the client should be able to approximate the server's current load. However, it makes the client implementation too complicated for the client to measure and maintain such server's response time. Instead, the IPsec server can efficiently measure statistics on the number of concurrent clients it serves over time and broadcast this information to the clients. For example, the server can generate semi-hourly statistics estimating its loads based on previous usages on previous days and send them to the client when the client establishes an IPsec connection to the server for the first time each day. However, the estimates might be off, resulting in over- or under-estimates due to sporadic or unusual activities at the server. Thus, it is crucial to investigate what effect a false

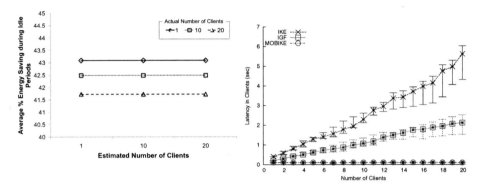

Fig. 9. Average energy savings on real-world WiFi session for potential misestimation of the number of concurrent clients in MO-BIKE+IGF

Fig. 10. Client latencies for various session resumption protocols

estimation of dt_τ would have on the energy savings or costs for the client. Figure 9 shows the effects of such false estimation. Due to space restrictions, we show only IGF+MOBIKE, which can be seen to be fairly immune to poor estimation of dt_τ. This is because an approximate threshold value for dt_τ changes very slowly in IGF as the number of concurrent clients is changed (Figure 4). Further, in MOBIKE, it is almost invariable.

Efficiently Computing Variables for the Scheduler: In practice a network card could not keep track of a data-structure that maintained all historical idle-times longer than dt_τ, and then compute P_{t_c} on the fly. However, in practice there are only two issues one cares about i) the value of t_c for which $P_{t_c} = \alpha$, as a network card can just wait until it is idle for such a time t_c, and then power-off the radio; and ii) how to determine the new value t_c such that $P_{t_c} = \alpha$ when a new idle period longer than dt_τ is recorded. This can be done by discretizing time, and making a set of buckets, one for each discrete time interval. We have a counter for each bucket to represent the number of idle-times whose length fell in to the interval defined by the bucket. When a new idle time of length t is processed, we increment the bucket corresponding to t.

We must simultaneously keep track of which bucket has the $\alpha \cdot N$th element (and thus which bucket corresponds to the time interval t_c for which $P_{t_c} = \alpha$). For purposes of example let $\alpha = 0.5$. We need to keep track of the bucket containing the median. This is done by keeping an index to the current bucket containing the median, the size of that bucket, and the position within that bucket of the median. If a new idle length is put in a smaller (larger) bucket than the median bucket, the relative position in the bucket is increased (decreased resp.) by one. If the new idle length goes in the same bucket as the median, then its index is increased by $1/2$ and the bucket size is increased by 1. Should the index go below 0, or above the bucket-size, the median is moved to the next bucket and the process repeated.

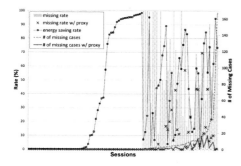

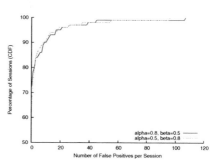

Fig. 11. Comparative depiction of energy savings and missed packets in the 100 test sessions

Fig. 12. CDF for false positives per session

False Negatives & Positives: It is important to calculate the false positives (missed opportunities to cycle the radio) and false negatives (the radio is power-cycled, but incoming packets are dropped) of our scheduler. Due to space limitations, we provide these for the MOBIKE+IGF scheduler only. The false positive rate is quite low and depicted in missed power-cyclings per session in Figure 12, with 90% of the sessions have fewer than 10 false positives. This leaves little room for improvement.

Since the radio is only power-cycled back on when the client sends packets, incoming packets can be lost. They are the false negatives. We consider two scenarios: i) all missed packets are simply dropped, and ii) the IPsec server acts as a simple proxy responding for the client to simple network protocols that do not actually need the client's presence. Specifically, it responds to DHCP, DNS, and MICROSOFT-DS. Such proxies have been well studied when used at AP's [11], but their use must be incorporated in to the IPsec server due to the encrypted traffic. In Figure 11 we show the results. We clearly see that 60% of users suffer no dropped packets in scenario i), and 70% of users suffer no dropped packets in scenario ii) with the proxy. Without specific packet information in the traces, it is impossible to determine how important the missed packets were in the 30% to 40% of cases we missed at least one packet. However, it suggests that a simple user-interface can be devised that allow users to quickly switch from an energy-saving mode of IPsec to a performance mode, where users can quickly decide if they want power-savings. In such scenarios, users can default to power-savings, and if they notice performance issues they can toggle the device to an alternate mode. We consider more advanced schedulers as future work.

4   Comparison of Performance of IPsec Session-Resumption Protocols

We evaluate and compare the performance of the IGF, IKE and MOBIKE protocols, from both the server and client perspectives, as the number of concurrent connections that are actively trying to be established (or re-established) increases. This comparison

Table 2. Configuration of machines for multiple client connection measurements

Device	CPU/RAM	NIC	Operating System
Server	2.8Ghz, 2G	100Mbps	Linux kernel 2.6.25
Client 1-20	3.2Ghz, 2G	100Mbps	Linux kernel 2.6.18

not only provides *the first performance data on concurrent use of the IGF protocol*, it also provides essential validated data on which to base the mathematical power saving model in Section 3.

4.1 Methodology

We implemented the IGF protocol as an extension to strongSwan [17], which is an open source IPsec implementation for Linux. StrongSwan already implements traditional IKE and its extension MOBIKE. For our evaluation, we use two different versions of strongSwan: 4.2.4 for IPsec clients and 4.1.8 for an IPsec server[2].

For the experiments, we used twenty one x86 Dell Optiplex GX Pentium IV machines which were connected through Ethernet switches. Table 2 shows their specifications. To observe the effects of connection (re)initiation on an overloaded server, we chose an inferior hardware configuration for our server so it was easier to stress. Although the measured latencies include message transfer times over the network, such factors are not important for comparisons between different server loads as the communication costs stay essentially constant. This is because the network is far from capacity, while the computational load of the server increases. We perform experiments over the wired network to obtain (nearly) constant latencies. For IKE security settings, we used a 2048-bit RSA key and a 128-bit AES key, a minimum requirement in today's security contexts. We considered cases of multiple clients simultaneously (re)connecting to the IPsec server. We report average latency over 25 independent experiments.

4.2 Performance Evaluation

Figure 10 gives average *client* latencies for up to 20 concurrent connections in IKE, IGF, and MOBIKE respectively. In the case of IKE and IGF, the data points represent latencies incurred when concurrent connections are being formed or reformed respectively. In the case of MOBIKE, we see latencies involved in updating the IP address associated with a client without establishing a new session. MOBIKE incurs the least latency. This is expected since MOBIKE needs to only update the client IP address and does not perform any cryptographic operations, symmetric or asymmetric. Its very low overhead enables the latency to stay essentially constant irrespective of the number of concurrent clients. As a result of avoiding computationally expensive asymmetric key cryptographic operations, the latency of IGF is also almost half that of IKE when only a single client is connecting to the server. But the gap between IKE and IGF increases

---

[2] We tested various versions of strongSwan between 4.1.8 and 4.2.5. However, only the given combination allowed up to 20 *simultaneously initiating* clients.

with the number of concurrent clients. This data shows that re-connection through IGF easily outperforms IKE, with increasing performance benefits as the number of simultaneously initiating clients increases.

The *server side* processing times of the IPsec server for concurrent IPsec client connections are not shown due to space constraints. However, as expected, they are nearly identical to client latencies, but with tighter variance due to the lack of noise in the network measurements. The processing times were measured by computing the difference between time-stamps of the first network message to arrive from a client to the end of last operation of the protocol for said client.

5   Related Work

A formal security analysis of IGF and a evaluation of the performance of a prototype implementation is presented in [18]. The authors simulate a large number of connections with file transfer, as opposed to actual concurrent connections. Hence, the evaluation does not effectively demonstrate the performance of IGF and IKE with concurrent clients.

For fast IPsec reconnections, work in [19] introduced zero address-set functionality (ZASF) for MOBIKE. ZASF allows a mobile client with a predicted long idle period to notify the IPsec server that it will temporarily disable its radio. The server acknowledges, and temporarily disables all related IPsec states, concurrently dropping any packets destined to the client. This approach is similar to our approach (excluding our proxy), but further requires indefinitely Security Association storage for each of its clients and requires the disabling of DPD and the enabling of a local policy which terminates connections that are disabled for too long of a period. The IPsec server must also store all associated SA state information for all clients that are asleep. Our scheme, in comparison would use IGF to recover from sessions terminated by DPD, and no SA state information need be stored at the server when clients are disabled.

[20] proposes a scheme to transfer an IPsec connection state through Context Transfer Protocol (CXTP) [21] when a mobile IPsec client needs to connect to a different gateway due to changes in physical and thus network location. This scheme does not consider the case where the initial gateway does not maintain an IPsec connection due to transient connections on mobile clients. It therefore does not deal with mobile clients as we consider herein.[3]

[22] extends Multi-Layered IPsec (ML IPsec) [23] to support mobility by integrating ML IPsec with Mobile IP as presenting an efficient key distribution protocol between Foreign Agents (FA) for Mobile IP. However, they do not discuss the issues in building trust between FAs managed by different organizations; furthermore, they do not support a fast IPsec reconnection after relatively long absence in network.

A number of research papers, such as [10], present a technique to effectively utilize power saving mode (PSM) in the 802.11 WiFi standard [8] to reduce radio energy usage by clients. The work of [10] presents a scheme in which PSM can effectively be

---

[3] In cases where both servers are for the same organization and implicitly trust each-other, then by having a common secret keys between servers, IGF could resume sessions between gateways.

used to save time and energy costs by switching power modes. However, this work assumes that each network application will provide somewhat accurate predictions about its network usage. Based on the predictions the scheme decides when to activate the PSM. However, due to non-trivial power consumption and inefficiencies of the PSM itself, [12, 9, 7] propose different power saving strategies that turn off the WiFi interface when it is not used, and concurrently activate a lower power/lower bandwidth radio. This radio is used to signal the activation of the WiFi radio when there is traffic to be communicated. The work of [9] utilizes Bluetooth as the low power radio not only for activating a WiFi connection, but also for low bandwidth data transfer where WiFi is not needed. However, the power saving schemes in [12, 9, 7] require a dual access point as an infrastructure, making incremental deployment difficult. Furthermore, none of them have considered the effect on the connection-oriented security protocols such as IPsec.

A number of research papers [11] have considered using proxies at APs to allow APs to drop or respond to traffic that is destined for sleeping clients. In the IPsec scenario, such proxies must be at the IPsec server, since the AP would be unable to read the encrypted packets.

6   Conclusions

Our results show the clear and practical potential for energy savings on mobile devices through power cycling the wireless radio, even in the presence of mandatory IPsec connections. While IPsec allows some energy savings, servers that handle many clients do much better when they consider more appropriate protocols. While using MOBIKE by itself, without dead-peer detection (DPD), gives the best potential savings, this scenario seems rather unlikely to be practical in large organizations due to the potentially large state and committed resources a server would need to maintain with many clients. For large organizations, MOBIKE+IGF hybrid represents a close second in terms of performance, even when a server needs to continuously handle multiple concurrent session resumptions. In fact, a simple implementation of our scheduling algorithm achieves extremely rare energy-penalties, but over 50% of network sessions could save 20% or more of their wireless energy costs for idle times! Further, the algorithm performs nearly optimally in terms of potential energy savings. Simple modifications to the servers to broadcast estimates on their load, and clients to predict when they power-cycle their radios are relatively easy to implement in either hardware or software.

References

1. Kaufman, C.: Internet Key Exchange (IKEv2) Protocol. RFC4306 (December 2005)
2. Eronen, P.: IKEv2 Mobility and Multihoming Protocol (MOBIKE). RFC4555
3. Sheffer, Y., Tschofenig, H., Dondeti, L., Narayanan, V.: IPsec Gateway Failover Protocol. draft-sheffer-ipsec-failover-04.txt (July 2008)
4. Palumbo, S., Dyer, N.: Maximizing Mobile Worker Productivity. Yankee Group Research, Inc. (January 2008)
5. Kent, S., Seo, K.: Security Architecture for the Internet Protocol. RFC4301 (2005)

6. Housley, R.: Using Advanced Encryption Standard (AES) CCM Mode with IPsec Encapsulating Security Payload (ESP). RFC4309 (December 2005)
7. Agarwal, Y., Schurgers, C., Gupta, R.: Dynamic power management using on demand paging for networked embedded systems. In: Asian and South Pacific Design Automation Conference, ASP-DAC (2005)
8. IEEE Computer Society: Wireless LAN medium access control (MAC) and physical layer (PHY) specifications. IEEE Standard 802.11, 1999 Edition (1999)
9. Pering, T., Agarwal, Y., Gupta, R., Want, R.: CoolSpots: Reducing the Power Consumption of Wireless Mobile Devices with Multiple Radio Interfaces. In: ACM MobiSys (2006)
10. Anad, M., Nightingale, E.B., Flinn, J.: Self-Tuning Wireless Network Power Management. In: ACM MobiCom (2003)
11. Nedevschi, S., Chandrasheka, J., Liu, J., Nordman, B.: Skilled in the art of being idle: Reducing energy waste in networked systems. In: ACM/USENIX Symposium on Networked Systems Design & Implementation, NSDI (2009)
12. Shih, E., Bahl, P., Sinclair, M.J.: Wake on Wireless: An Event Driven Energy Saving Strategy for Battery Operated Devices. In: ACM MobiCom (2002)
13. Harkins, D., Carrel, D.: The Internet Key Exchange (IKE). RFC2409 (November 1998)
14. Huang, G., Beaulieu, S., Rochefort, D.: A Traffic-Based Method of Detecting Dead Internet Key Exchange (IKE) Peers. RFC3706 (February 2004)
15. Salowey, J., Zhou, H., Eronen, P., Tschofenig, H.: Transportation Layer Security (TLS) Session Resumption without Server-Side State. RFC4507 (May 2006)
16. Linux/ACPI project: Linux ACPI, http://www.lesswatts.org/projects/acpi
17. strongSwan project: strongSwan, http://www.strongswan.org/
18. Tegeler, F.: Security analysis, prototype implementation, and performance evaluation of a new IPSec session resumption method. Master's thesis, University of Goettingen (2008)
19. Kivinen, T., Tschofenig, H.: Design of the IKEv2 Mobility and Multihoming Protocol (MOBIKE). RFC4621
20. Allard, F., Bonnin, J.M.: An application of the context transfer protocol: IPsec in a IPv6 mobility environment. Int'l. Journal of Communication Networks and Distributed Systems 1(1) (2008)
21. Loughney, J., Nakhjiri, M., Perkins, C., Koodli, R.: Context Transfer Protocol (CXTP). RFC4067 (July 2005)
22. Choi, H., Song, H., Cao, G., Porta, T.L.: Mobile multi-layered IPsec. In: IEEE Infocom (March 2005)
23. Zhang, Y., Singh, B.: A multi-layer IPsec protocol. In: USENIX Security Symposium (August 2000)

Transparent Protection of Commodity OS Kernels Using Hardware Virtualization

Michael Grace[1], Zhi Wang[1], Deepa Srinivasan[1], Jinku Li[1], Xuxian Jiang[1], Zhenkai Liang[2], and Siarhei Liakh[1]

[1] Department of Computer Science, North Carolina State University
[2] School of Computing,
National University of Singapore

Abstract. Kernel rootkits are among the most insidious threats to computer security today. By employing various code injection techniques, they are able to maintain an omnipotent presence in the compromised OS kernels. Existing preventive countermeasures typically employ virtualization technology as part of their solutions. However, they are still limited in either (1) requiring modifying the OS kernel source code for the protection or (2) leveraging software-based virtualization techniques such as binary translation with a high overhead to implement a Harvard architecture (which is robust to various code injection techniques used by kernel rootkits). In this paper, we introduce hvmHarvard, a hardware virtualization-based Harvard architecture that transparently protects commodity OS kernels from kernel rootkit attacks and significantly reduces the performance overhead. Our evaluation with a Xen-based prototype shows that it can transparently protect legacy OS kernels with rootkit resistance while introducing $< 5\%$ performance overhead.

Keywords: Virtualization, Harvard Architecture, Split Memory.

1 Introduction

Kernel rootkits are among the most insidious threats to computer security today. Embedding themselves within the operating system kernel, these rootkits enjoy unfettered access to the entire system and adopt various techniques to make themselves stealthy and "sticky," thus preventing them from being detected and removed. Given the effectiveness of this approach, it is not surprising that there has been explosive growth in the number of new rootkit families over recent years [2,4].

Kernel rootkit countermeasures have attracted a commensurate amount of attention in the research community. In particular, there are two main categories of existing efforts. The first category aims to detect the rootkit presence by looking for abnormalities or symptoms of rootkit infection. For example, Copilot [28] uses a special PCI card to grab a memory image of the kernel and then scans for any possible manipulation of kernel code or system-critical data structures. The follow-up efforts [29,30] extend it to detect any violation from semantic specifications of static and dynamic kernel data or

S. Jajodia and J. Zhou (Eds.): SecureComm 2010, LNICST 50, pp. 162–180, 2010.

deviation from the normal kernel control flow graph. However, these systems by design are all based on detecting rootkits *after* they have already installed themselves in the kernel.

In contrast, the second category strives to prevent rootkit infection in the first place by enforcing some security property. For example, SecVisor enforces a $W \oplus X$ property on kernel memory pages. The $W \oplus X$ property states that a given memory page can be either writable or executable, but not both at the same time. $W \oplus X$ enforcement is complicated by legacy OS kernels that contain mixed kernel pages with both code and data [20,21,22]. To handle such pages, SecVisor modifies the kernel source code to make the OS kernel memory layout conform to the $W \oplus X$ property. From another perspective, NICKLE [31] takes a software virtualization (i.e., binary translation) approach to emulate a Harvard architecture on x86, which essentially creates a separate memory space to reliably store authorized kernel code. By transparently redirecting kernel instruction fetches to the separate memory space, NICKLE is able to support unmodified kernels and guarantee their kernel code integrity, which effectively defeats most existing rootkits. However, from another perspective, the presence of a dedicated code memory and the need for transparent redirection of kernel instruction fetches require intercepting and redirecting every single kernel instruction execution, which unfortunately causes significant performance overhead [31].

In this paper, we introduce *hvmHarvard*, a hardware virtualization-based Harvard architecture on x86 that can not only transparently support commodity OSs without modification, but also effectively reduce the performance overhead. Specifically, we observe that the high performance overhead of implementing software-based Harvard architecture is mainly caused by *instruction-level* interception and redirection (of kernel instruction fetches) to the code memory. As such, we propose *page-level* redirection in hvmHarvard so that the performance overhead can be significantly reduced without unnecessarily sacrificing the security guarantee.

There are two main challenges involved in changing from instruction-level redirection to page-level redirection of kernel instruction fetches. The first one comes from the fact that x86 is not designed to support the Harvard architecture. To address that, we make an unconventional use of split code and data TLBs on x86 in combination with recent hardware-based tagged TLB support [3]. In particular, with separate code and data TLBs, we can dynamically adjust the page table to virtualize the Harvard architecture on top of x86 (so that code and data each have its own memory address space). The tagged TLB support is essential here as it avoids flushing the code/data TLBs in a virtualized environment (e.g., VM exits – Section 3.1), thus allowing the hypervisor to safely intervene and manipulate the guest page table in use for the Harvard architecture creation. With the separation of code memory and data memory, our Harvard architecture can naturally handle the mixed code and data pages in commodity OS kernels while still strictly enforcing $W \oplus X$. In the meantime, we also observe that the majority of existing kernel memory pages are not mixed. As a result, there is no need for hvmHarvard to keep a shadow copy of these pages, nor does it need to intervene on instruction fetches from them. By doing so, no processing overhead will be incurred on these pages and no extra memory space will be wasted, as they no longer need to be shadowed [31].

The second challenge stems from the need to perform *mode-sensitive* page-level redirection since we are interested in redirecting kernel instruction fetches only. In other words, we need to first determine the current running mode and then decide whether the corresponding instruction fetch should be redirected or not. This imposes a strict requirement to intercept every mode-switching event (e.g., including system calls) in the redirection logic. Intercepting these events at the hypervisor will cause significant performance overhead. Our solution to this problem involves altering the guest's view of memory at each privilege level (or mode): all of user memory becomes non-executable when a process is executing at the kernel mode, and vice versa. For brevity, we call this a mode-sensitive view (Section 3.2). During the normal operation of the guest, hvmHarvard does not intercept and mediate the change between different views of memory. Instead, our system injects trampoline code to switch between these two views of memory upon the mode-switching event inside the guest. The trampoline mechanism leverages an Intel hardware virtualization extension called the CR3 Target Value List (Section 3.2) to avoid being trapped by the hypervisor and to achieve better performance.

We have implemented a Xen[9]-based proof-of-concept prototype. The prototype can transparently support a number of commodity systems including legacy Red Hat 8.0 (with a Linux 2.4.18 kernel) and recent Ubuntu 9.04 (running Linux 2.6.30-5). Our evaluation shows that our system is effective in preventing eight kernel attacks (including six real-world rootkits and two synthetic attacks) against legacy OS kernels that do not have the $W \oplus X$ support. Such protection is achieved with only a small performance overhead (i.e., $< 5\%$). To summarize, our paper has the following contributions:

- We propose a hardware virtualization-based Harvard architecture to effectively protect commodity OS kernels from kernel rootkit attacks. Compared with existing approaches, our system can not only achieve a similar protection guarantee, but also significantly reduce the performance overhead suffered by previous approaches.
- The first key technique in our approach is *page-level* redirection of instruction fetches, which departs from prior efforts that perform instruction-level redirection. Our technique significantly reduces the performance overhead in the creation of the Harvard architecture on top of x86.
- The second key technique enables *mode-sensitive* redirection by redirecting *only* kernel instruction fetches. In this way, we can effectively avoid hypervisor intervention in the guest's mode-switching events. As these events occur frequently inside the guest, this technique also contributes to reducing the overall performance overhead.
- Finally, we present a Xen-based system prototype. The evaluation results with the prototype confirmed the practicality and effectiveness of our approach.

The rest of the paper is structured as follows. We briefly describe necessary background on the Harvard architecture and hardware virtualization in Section 2. Our system design and implementation are then presented in Section 3 and Section 4, respectively. After that, we present the evaluation results in Section 5, which is followed by the discussion on possible limitations and their improvement in Section 6. Finally, we discuss related work in Section 7 and conclude our paper in Section 8.

2   Background

In this section, we briefly review some key concepts that are essential to our system but may be unfamiliar to some readers: the Harvard architecture and shadow paging in virtualization. Readers with sufficient background can safely skip this section.

2.1   Harvard Architecture

Modern computers use a single address space to refer to working memory. This model of memory is commonly known as the von Neumann architecture. Interestingly, some of the very earliest computers used two utterly separate working memories, one for instructions and one for data. This arrangement is known as the Harvard architecture (Figure 1). In a pure Harvard architecture machine, data accesses and instruction accesses are treated as accessing totally distinct address spaces. From a security standpoint, this addressing scheme eliminates code injection attacks. For example, some buffer overflow attacks use an overlong memory copy operation to overwrite memory that will be executed as code. A pure Harvard architecture machine is not vulnerable to this class of attacks, as their addressing scheme does not allow code and data to be referred to interchangeably.

This work focuses on a widely deployed processor family, *x86*, which has a unified address space for main memory and is thus a von Neumann architecture. However, x86 processors typically have separate caches for instructions and data. When executing from cache, the processor behaves like a Harvard architecture machine[1]. Only when main memory must be consulted, does x86 look like a von Neumann architecture. This observation is the foundation of our page-level redirection technique for the creation of the Harvard architecture on top of x86 (Section 3.1).

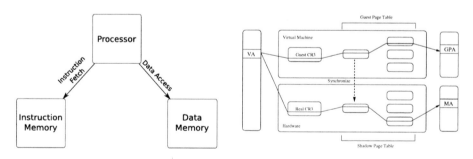

Fig. 1. The Harvard architecture   **Fig. 2.** Guest page table vs. shadow page table

2.2   Virtualization and Shadow Paging

Virtualization involves running a guest operating system in an environment that provides the illusion of complete access to a physical machine. All the resources used to construct such an illusory machine constitute a Virtual Machine (VM), while the

---

[1] This hybrid architecture is known as a *modified* Harvard architecture; many processors with the caching feature use such an arrangement today.

software that maintains one or more VMs is known variously as a hypervisor or a Virtual Machine Monitor (VMM). The hypervisor is commonly considered to be part of Trusted Computing Base (TCB) as it is strictly isolated from the VMs it manages and is often much smaller than modern operating systems.

There are several ways to virtualize a guest operating system. Since our work is based on hardware virtualization, we focus on its operation here. In particular, based on certain processor extensions, hardware virtualization operates a "trap-and-emulate" model. When a guest OS wishes to perform a privileged operation, the hardware has two options: either it can handle the request based on the processor extension for hardware virtualization, or if that is not possible, it can pass control to the hypervisor for handling. Handling the latter case constitutes a goodly portion of the hypervisor's workload and is typically an involved process.

Shadow paging is one such example. To better describe it, we first review how memory management works on an un-virtualized machine. Recall that x86 supports two memory protection mechanisms: segmentation and paging. They protect memory in a similar way by essentially permitting a higher-privilege piece of software to put blinders on a lower-privilege program, thus restricting its view of memory to only those things it is supposed to be able to access. Since segmentation support is being phased out in the new 64-bit long mode, we focus on the paging protection mechanism. In essence, paging uses page translation tables, or page tables for short, to remap memory for a given process. Virtual addresses are translated into physical addresses by these tables. These tables are also used by the hardware to enforce certain permissions policies (e.g., NX [1]) on the types of accesses allowed.

Virtualization has not changed this picture of the process; it has merely added another layer underneath it. By leveraging paging, the hypervisor divides the machine's memory into distinct logical machine memories. The guest OS in a VM then treats the memory it is given in the traditional way, dividing it up between the applications running in the guest. Under hardware virtualization, however, the OS itself does not know the *real* machine addresses that make up its allotted memory. With shadow paging, the hypervisor solves this problem by introducing an extra layer of indirection. In particular, a shadow table is created for a guest and maintained in the hypervisor. An unsuspecting guest OS kernel is allowed to maintain its own page tables, but they are not actually used by the hardware. Instead, the hypervisor marks these guest page tables read-only. Any attempt to write to them therefore generates a page fault, which is trapped by the hypervisor. The hypervisor, in turn, emulates the write request, eventually outputting the equivalent entry into the "real" page table used by the hardware. The guest can never see this real page table, which is assiduously kept synchronized with the one it can see – thus the name "shadow page table."

This arrangement is illustrated graphically in Figure 2. In the diagram, a virtual address (VA) is translated through both the guest's and the hardware's page tables. The guest's page tables eventually lead to a guest physical address (GPA) – the address the guest thinks of as being a hardware address. The shadow page tables instead translate the same virtual address into the real machine address (MA). The tables are kept synchronized by the hypervisor; this synchronization is represented by the dotted lines in the figure.

3   Design

In this work, we aim to develop a hardware virtualization-based Harvard architecture that can efficiently support unmodified legacy OS kernels and protect them from kernel rootkit attacks. Specifically, the presence of two distinct memory spaces for code and data in a Harvard architecture is useful for blocking code injection attacks and enforcing the $W \oplus X$ property. In this work, we propose to take a step further by enforcing mode-sensitive $W \oplus X$, also known as $W \oplus KX$. Due to our focus on OS kernel protection, $W \oplus KX$ requires that a user-level memory page will not be executable from the kernel mode and vice versa. Commodity hardware by default allows the execution of user-level memory pages at kernel privilege, which opens up "interesting" opportunities for kernel rootkit infection. As our defense, $W \oplus KX$ is proposed to effectively block this infection vector.

Threat Model and System Assumption. In this paper, we assume an adversary model where attackers or kernel rootkits are able to exploit software vulnerabilities in an OS kernel to launch code injection attacks. Accordingly, we also assume kernel rootkits have the highest privilege level inside the victim VM (e.g., the *root* privilege in a UNIX system) and have full access to the VM's memory space (e.g., through /dev/mem in Linux). However, the goal of a kernel rootkit is to stealthily maintain and hide its presence in the victim system; to do so, it will need to execute its own (malicious) code in the kernel space. We note that such a need exists in most kernel rootkits today, and we will discuss possible exceptions in Section 6.

In the meantime, our system assumes a trustworthy hypervisor as the necessary trusted computing base (TCB) to provide strict VM isolation. This assumption is shared by many other hypervisor-based security research efforts [13,14,17,25,43] and being hardened by existing hypervisor-protection solutions [26,41]. We will discuss possible attacks (e.g., VM escape) in Section 6. With this assumption, we consider the threat from layer-below attacks launched from physical hosts outside of the scope of this work.[2]

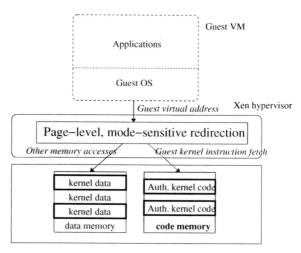

Fig. 3. Page-level mode-sensitive redirection enables an efficient implementation of the Harvard architecture on top of x86

---

[2] There exists another type of layer-below or specifically hardware DMA attack that is initiated from within a guest VM. However, since the hypervisor itself virtualizes or mediates guest DMA operations, recent hardware support for IOMMU can be readily adopted to intercede and block them. Therefore, we do not consider them in this paper.

3.1   Page-Level Redirection for $W \oplus X$

The central scheme of our approach is to efficiently create a Harvard architecture (Figure 3) on x86 by virtualizing one memory space for code and another for data. To achieve our goal, we observe the presence of separate TLBs for instruction fetches and data accesses. Note that each TLB entry caches the translation result from a virtual address to a physical address. When a memory access or an instruction fetch occurs, the virtual address lookup will go through the corresponding TLB first. Should that TLB not contain an entry for the requested translation (called a TLB miss), the hardware walks through the page table entries in main memory to do the lookup, then constructs such an entry. As a result, from the TLB's perspective, the hardware itself thinks in terms of two address spaces. However, in normal operation, these address spaces are kept synchronized and thus describe a unified memory space. Fortunately, to our benefit, there is no hardware requirement that this must be the case. In other words, to emulate a pure Harvard architecture, we can take advantage of these two TLBs by desynchronizing and loading them with two different page table entries for the same virtual address, thus creating two distinct memory spaces for code and data.

Unfortunately, the de-synchronization of these two TLBs is a delicate process, which is complicated by the fact that a TLB entry has a relatively limited lifespan. First, the TLBs are not large enough to cache all translation results at the same time, which means that older entries are eventually overwritten by newly-requested translations. Second, when an OS kernel either alters a page table or switches address contexts, these caches are implicitly flushed. Third, x86 provides very few instructions for interacting with the TLBs. In fact, after enabling the paging mode, the provided instructions are mainly used for removing one or all entries from *both* TLBs, which means the only way for us to populate a TLB entry will be by performing an address translation that eventually winds up in that cache.

To deal with the above challenges, we need to effectively intercept the hardware's attempts to re-populate TLBs. In particular, for the virtual addresses of interest, when there is a TLB miss, the hardware consults the page table and checks the permission bits of the entry it loads. If those permissions are violated, a page fault (or #PF) exception will be thrown. When there is a TLB hit, the cached entry's permissions are directly checked without consulting the page table. As a result, in the case of a TLB miss, we need to carefully prepare the page table in a way that will load the desired translation results as well as related permissions into respective TLBs.

There are three permission bits that can cause useful faults: the USER bit, the PRESENT bit and the NX bit. The USER bit only faults when a user-mode instruction fetch references a kernel page. With our focus on kernel protection, we are not interested in using this bit. The PRESENT bit, if not set, traps *any* access – which would lead to many expensive world switches. The NX bit causes a fault on any instruction fetch from pages with this bit set. In our system, we naturally leverage the NX bit.

In particular, to use the NX bit to cause one virtual address to map to two context-sensitive memory pages, we map the address to its data memory page and set its NX bit. If execution branches to an address within the page, the page fault handler substitutes its entry to code memory page and clears the NX bit. In order to load the entry into the instruction TLB (ITLB), the page fault handler must allow the guest to execute an

Algorithm 1. TLB de-synchronization algorithm

Input: Redirected Page Address (addr), Page table Entry for addr (pte)

```
/* handling NX-based page fault */ ;          /* handling TF-based fault */ ;
    pte = the_code_page (addr);                   pte = the_data_page (addr) ;
    set_trap_flag ();                             unset_trap_flag ();
    return_to_guest ();                           return_to_guest ();
```

instruction using this entry. However, once the code page entry has been loaded, the system needs to regain control to restore the map back to the data memory page. If this is not done, the data TLB (DTLB) may wind up being populated with the code page entry, routing data reads to the code page and thus violating the Harvard architecture. Note that the code page entry is marked as *read-only* and there is no way to cause a page to be executable yet not readable on the *x86* architecture.

To ensure that the page table is restored to the corresponding data entry as soon as possible, our design relies on the x86 single-step execution feature. Specifically, by setting the *trap* flag (or TF) of the EFLAGS register, the processor will generate an exception after every instruction. This feature allows us to execute one instruction, and then restore the data page entry in the TF handler. The process is shown in pseudo-code in Algorithm 1.

In this way, our design can populate the ITLB with one record and DTLB with another record without interfering each other. Here, we point out that if by trapping the execution of a guest VM to the hypervisor, a VM exit (or VMEXIT) occurs. In some processors, VM exits will flush the TLBs, which defeat our purpose of de-synchronizing TLBs. In our prototype, we leverage a hardware feature called tagged TLB [3] that is available in all recent hardware-virtualized AMD processors as well as Intel processors based on the new Nehalem architecture. This hardware feature essentially adds an extra field or an identification "tag" to each TLB entry that specifies the VM context within which the entry is valid. When a VM exit occurs, these entries will not be flushed. More details about our system will be presented in Section 4.1.

3.2   Mode-Sensitivity for $W \oplus KX$

By effectively creating a Harvard architecture on x86, our page-level redirection technique is able to enforce $W \oplus X$ while accommodating mixed kernel pages in commodity OS kernels. However, the $W \oplus X$ enforcement is still insufficient due to the need to block the execution of user-level pages from the kernel level. In other words, we need to enforce a stronger $W \oplus KX$ policy. As mentioned earlier, this is necessary as commodity OS kernels disallow the access of kernel memory pages from user mode, but do permit the execution of user memory pages from kernel mode.

To elaborate on this, the *x86* architecture has two related concepts in this vein: the USER page table permission bit and the Current Privilege Level (CPL) bits in the CS register. The CPL simply determines what instructions are valid – including access right checking on instruction fetches. The most-privileged CPL (or ring 0 where the kernel runs) has all the capabilities of the least-privileged CPL (or ring 3 where user-level applications run). Therefore, while it is illegal for a program executing at the ring 3 privilege to access kernel space, it is perfectly acceptable for a ring-0 kernel to branch its execution to user space.

With $W \oplus KX$, we aim to define a new Kernel eXecute (KX) mode of operation. In this mode, instruction fetches only succeed if the privilege level of the machine matches the privilege level of the page table entry. In other words, if USER is cleared for a page table entry, it is only executable at CPL=0, and when USER is set, it is only executable at CPL=3.

To achieve this, we propose maintaining *two* shadow page tables instead of one in the normal situation: one for user-privilege (or mode) execution and one for kernel-privilege execution. Each has the NX bit set for the opposite privilege's pages. A straightforward approach would require the hypervisor to intervene and swap the shadow page table upon every mode switch, from user to kernel and vice versa. Unfortunately, this scheme would induce a large number of costly VMEXITs – two for every system call. To reduce this overhead, note that modern processors introduce special instructions – sysenter/sysexit to enable fast transfers between user and kernel. As these instructions use registers to point to the entry point of the system call handler, by redirecting that register to our trampoline code, we can handle a large number of mode switches in a performance-efficient fashion. More specifically, our approach leverages a hardware feature known as the "CR3 Target Value List."[5] This feature is designed to allow a hypervisor to whitelist a set of expected CR3 values: when a guest changes CR3 to one of these values, the hypervisor is not consulted, saving a significant number of cycles that would be wasted on a world switch. In our prototype, our system injects a trampoline into the guest that simply switches page tables upon each mode switch, before the actual OS system call handler is invoked. Similarly, we use this trampoline to switch the page tables again before the system call handler returns back to user mode.

We assert that this optimization does not harm the $W \oplus KX$ security guarantee offered by our system. Specifically, the trampoline code is located on a page that the hypervisor prevents the guest from modifying. Also, if the guest invokes the trampoline code in an unintended way, it will always wind up either transferring control to the sysenter/syscall handler or executing the corresponding return instruction. From the OS kernel's perspective, the $W \oplus X$ property is not violated. More detailed discussion will be presented in Section 6.

Finally, it is worth mentioning that our system follows the same steps proposed in NICKLE to support loadable kernel modules (LKMs) [31]. In particular, we simply verify the hash signature of such drivers (and the main kernel) when they are being loaded. For example, for Linux kernels, we leverage the fact that the kernel's module loader calls the init() method of a module when it is being loaded. As this will cause a page fault due to our page-redirection technique, we can check the instruction pointer (IP register) to see if it matches an address within the kernel's module loader. If it does, the system can locate the module definition structure and use that information to determine how to verify the module. Falsifying the module structure information would inevitably result in a hash signature inconsistent with the trusted version of the module, causing the falsified module to be simply rejected by our system. Note that we do not need to modify the guest operating system; our system simply needs to know how to find the information it needs in the guest operating system's memory. Such knowledge can be provided in a number of ways, e.g., either directly compiled into the hypervisor, loaded in the VM's metadata or indirectly hinted to the hypervisor from a hypercall within the VM.

4   Implementation

We have developed a proof-of-concept prototype on top of Xen 3.3.1, targeting fully-virtualized 32-bit legacy guests running under a 32-bit PAE hypervisor. Our development was tested against a Red Hat 8.0 image (running a Linux 2.4.18 kernel) and an Ubuntu 9.04 image (running a Linux 2.6.30-5 kernel). Our development machine had a Core i7-930 Nehalem processor with recent hardware virtualization support. Our current prototype only supports a single virtual CPU for one guest and the support of SMPs are left to future work. In the following, we present additional implementation details for the two key techniques in our approach.

4.1   Page-Level Redirection

As mentioned earlier, our scheme virtualizes a pure Harvard architecture machine on x86 by using a hypervisor to desynchronize the processor's TLBs. Naturally, our prototype mainly deals with various particulars of the x86 paging mechanism and related TLB operations. In particular, our experience indicates that there is a strong correlation between the frequency with which the TLBs must be fixed up and the performance overhead of the system as a whole. Note the process of de-synchronizing or splitting a page's TLB entries is a costly operation. Each time a page needs to be split, there are two associated VMEXITs: one caused by the NX-based page fault to populate the ITLB, and another from the single step fault handler to populate the DTLB. Because of that, it is critical to avoid generating these events if possible.

In our prototype, we implement an optimization that is akin to the traditional copy-on-write (COW) technique. Recall that one main purpose of our system is to ensure $W \oplus X$. As such, if some kernel pages in commodity OSs are already amenable for $W \oplus X$ enforcement, we can simply enforce it without needing to create two separate copies (one for code and one for data) in the first place. By doing so, we can not only avoid allocating additional memory spaces in storing copies, but also reduce the number of VMEXITs that would otherwise be needed to maintain the separate presence of code and data copies.

To further elaborate that, consider the impact of splitting a kernel page[3]. If the kernel page is never used as code, the additional overhead will be incurred when generating and maintaining the two copies, though there is little or no performance impact. However, if the kernel page is never used as data, then we will be splitting the page every time it is executed and the translation is not cached in the ITLB (or already flushed from the ITLB). As mentioned earlier, this process will involve the hypervisor and cause VMEXITs, resulting in a high performance overhead.

---

[3] Xen's concept of kernel pages can be different than the guest OS'. For example, Xen does not internally use 2M or 4M "superpages"; if the guest OS allocates these, Xen treats them as a large number of normal 4K pages.

In our prototype, to determine the liveness of a kernel page, we perform basic reference-counting and dynamically track the number of times a given kernel page is referenced by the guest's page tables. In addition, by counting the number of writable mappings to a given kernel page, our system can intelligently choose *not* to split the page if that count is zero. In this way, we can further avoid unnecessary VMEXITs for better performance.

4.2   Mode-Sensitivity Support

To make the page-level redirection mode-sensitive, we implement two shadow pages tables: one for guest user-mode and another for guest kernel-mode. As a result, every time the guest OS wishes to make a change to its page tables, the hypervisor intercepts the change and synchronizes it with the two shadow pages. As synchronization will require the hypervisor to walk through the shadow page tables and make the corresponding hardware-visible change, the presence of two shadow page tables will double the cost of synchronization. To reduce the cost, our prototype opts to interleave two page tables; this allows a single walk through them to find both entries related to a particular page table update. Specifically, for each page table bifurcated in this way, twice the normal amount of memory for shadow page tables is allocated. The low-order version of the page table is used for the guest kernel mode, and the high-order version is for the guest user mode. With that, one walk is needed to find the location to alter, followed by a privilege-level check that determines which changes to make and where to look for the second copy of that page.

With the two shadow page tables in place, our prototype further takes another optimization. Considering the fact that page tables are laid out in a layered hierarchy, we can trade granularity for ease of updating, simply by having two distinct top-level page tables map down to the same set of level-1 page tables (see Figure 4). The top levels of the page table are

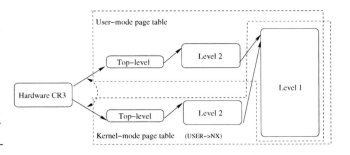

Fig. 4. Two shadow page tables: the user-mode page table and the kernel-mode page table share the same level-1 entries, but *not* top-level and level-2 entries

not altered as frequently as the lower levels are, leading to disproportionately less update overhead. They are also smaller (as there are fewer such top-level entries), leading to less cache pressure when compared to the case where all entries had to be maintained separately. Using a 32-bit Linux guest as an example, the Linux kernel occupies the top one gigabyte of address space. As the shadow page tables are 32-bit PAE tables, this neatly corresponds to one of the four top-level entries. Though the top-level entries do not have the NX permission bit, we can maintain two sets of the level-2 page tables instead that have the NX permission bit.

Table 1. Effectiveness of our system

Rootkit	Attack Vector	Prevented?	Result
adore-ng 0.56	LKM	Yes	Module fails to load
superkit	/dev/kmem	Yes	Crashes
mood-nt 2.3	/dev/kmem	Yes	Crashes
sk2rc2	/dev/kmem	Yes	Crashes
eNYeLKM 1.2	LKM	Yes	Module fails to load
Phalanx b6	/dev/mem	Yes	Crashes
synthetic-1	LKM	Yes	Module fails to modify itself
synthetic-2	LKM	Yes	insmod crashes

Afterwards, the two shadow pages will be switched based on the current running mode of the guest VM. In our prototype, we hook the handler for the sysenter instruction (by detouring the corresponding Model Specific Register or MSR content) to capture the user-to-kernel mode switch. Similarly, we also detour the sysexit execution by performing a kernel-to-user switch. We point out that such detouring happens inside the guest context with a trampoline without involving the hypervisor, thus avoiding unnecessary VMEXITs. However, from another perspective, our prototype can still function properly without hijacking them because the hypervisor will simply step in and switch page tables itself, though at a lower pace.

An astute reader may observe that the trampoline code will essentially change CR3, the page table base address register. Changes to CR3 will typically be trapped by the hypervisor. Fortunately, a recent hardware feature, i.e., the CR3 Target Value List, allows our page table switch without being trapped by the hypervisor if the new CR3 value is on the target value list. However, the CR3 update is still considered a context switch, which unfortunately causes an unnecessary TLB flush – purging any split entries from the instruction TLB. Interestingly, the related level-1 page table entries contain a GLOBAL bit that can prevent a TLB flush from purging a particular entry.

There is a subtle issue in the interplay between the CR3 Target Value List and the GLOBAL bit. By definition, the hypervisor is not alerted if CR3 is changed to a value on the list. Likewise, if a split entry in the TLB is not purged, the page tables will not be consulted upon an instruction fetch to its virtual address. Therefore, if our user-mode CR3 value is loaded from a page that is marked GLOBAL, execution could branch to user land while still at high privilege! Fortunately, there are only two ways that CR3 can take a new value: via hardware task switching (ltr) or through the explicit assignment (mov cr3, <general register>). Hardware task switching is not used by either Windows or Linux.[4] For the more common mov cr3 operation, we ensure that the instruction pointer, after a mov cr3, <register> operation, will always point to a virtual address that does not map to a TLB entry with the GLOBAL bit set. To assure that, we can scan each page as it is being split, ensuring that the opcode for this dangerous operation does not occur. In other words, we look for that string of bytes

---

[4] Note that even if it is used, the ltr operation acts on tables that are privileged and hardware virtualization allows for trapping the ltr operation. In other words, we can still prevent hardware task switching from breaking our $W \oplus KX$ guarantee.

throughout the split page. If it is found, the split code will ensure that upon every insertion to the ITLB, that split page's entry will not have the GLOBAL permission bit set.[5]

5   Evaluation

To test the effectiveness of our prototype, we run six real-world rootkits and two synthetic exploits (both violate $W \oplus KX$) against a default Ubuntu 9.0.4 system. These attacks were selected as representative of the infection vectors used by existing kernel rootkits. In every case, our system was able to defeat the infection and protect the system. In the following, we present details of two representative experiments.

Mood-NT Rootkit Experiment. Some rootkits install themselves by directly writing to mixed pages in kernel memory. In this experiment, the *mood-nt* rootkit [31] uses the /dev/kmem interface to access kernel memory through the file system. Specifically, the rootkit uses the interface to copy its resident logic into kernel memory, and then overwrites function pointers to hijack the kernel's control flow.

When the test system is protected under our prototype, code injection appears to work fine as the injected content is directly written into the data page. However, when one of the rootkit's function pointers is called, our page-level redirection technique immediately causes the resulting instruction fetch to a code page, *not* the data page that contained the injected content. As a result, instead of fetching the rootkit's code, the processor attempts to execute whatever is in the code page, eventually leading to a crash in our experiment.

Synthetic Attacks. In this experiment, we intentionally play with the $W \oplus KX$ protection by redirecting kernel control flow to user-space code. Since we do not have a rootkit sample that was developed in this way, we simply synthesize an attack that would execute user code at kernel privilege.

Specifically, we implemented a branch-to-userspace exploit as a loadable kernel module. In the module's initialization function, we create a pointer to an address within insmod's address space. This address in user space contains an instruction sequence that copies the top of the stack into EBX and then returns. Therefore, after successfully executing it, EBX should equate to EIP. Running under hvmHarvard, the execution faults to the hypervisor when the first user instruction is fetched. From the page fault handler, it reports the fault as a NX violation and relays it to the guest OS kernel, which then terminates the insmod process.

Performance Overhead. To evaluate the impact on system performance, we have performed benchmark-based measurements. In particular, we use two application-level benchmarks and one microbenchmark to evaluate the system. They are (1) a normal

---

[5] Note that there are a few corner cases worth mentioning. The mov cr3, <register> instruction is translated to 0f 22 d? in machine code. If the split page ends neatly with 0f 22 d?, then it would put the instruction pointer onto the next page, whose GLOBAL property is uncertain. Fortunately, that case does not occur in the Linux kernels we have examined. Such a special case can also be handled upon insertion into the TLB, by proactively re-populating the next page's TLB entry as ¬GLOBAL.

Table 2. Software configuration for performance evaluation

Item	Version	Configuration
Ubuntu	9.0.4	Using Linux 2.6.30
Apache	2.0.59	Using the default high-performance configuration file
Kernel	2.6.30	Standard kernel compilation
ApacheBench	2.0.40-dev	ab -c3 -t 60 <url/file>
LMbench	3.0alpha	Using the default configuration

compilation of the Linux 2.6.30 kernel, (2) network throughput test on the Apache web server using the ApacheBench [8], and (3) a standard system benchmark toolkit called LMbench [24]. Our tests were performed on a Dell Optiplex, which runs the Ubuntu 8.04 system and has an Intel Core i7-920 (2.66GHz) CPU and 4GB RAM. The guest VM runs Ubuntu 9.04 with Linux kernel 2.6.30-5 and 1GB of memory. For comparison, we run the guest VM on Xen 3.3.1 twice, with and without protection. The software configuration for our evaluation is shown in Table 2. The benchmark programs were run ten times and averaged. Our results are shown in Table 3.

Table 3. Application benchmark results. For make, lower is better; for Apache, higher is better.

Benchmark	Without protection	with protection	Overhead
make kernel	41.289 s	43.312 s	4.9%
ApacheBench	11728.68 req/s	11497.24 req/s	2.0%

In our first application benchmark, we compiled our guest VM's kernel with the command 'make kernel', using time to measure how long the process took. The system under protection takes 44.275 seconds to complete, which is 4.9% longer than the compilation time in an unprotected system. In our next application benchmark, we set up an Apache [7] web server. The ApacheBench program, ab, was run against a small (15K) html file on that server. We then collected the network throughput and the results show a 2.0% slowdown. We also evaluated our system with LMbench [24], which is a micro-benchmark for OS kernel performance. The tasks include process creation, basic arithmetic operations, context switching, file system operation, local communication, and memory latency. Among these results, the maximum overhead of our system is 4.70% when doing context switching. The overhead comes from updating the CR3 Target Value List that is used for later switching of the two shadow page tables. Other tasks such as performing basic arithmetic or floating-point operations incur the lowest overhead, which is nearly zero.

6   Discussion

In this section, we discuss several issues related to our system. First, our goal here is to efficiently create a Harvard architecture on x86 and enable $W \oplus KX$ for kernel code integrity protection. As a result, our system is not able to protect the kernel control-flow integrity. In other words, an attacker could possibly launch a "return-into-libc" style attack or the so-called return-oriented attack [10,16,37] within the kernel by leveraging only the existing authenticated kernel code. Fortunately, solutions exist for protecting control flows [6,15,30,42] and data flow integrity [11] for user-level applications, which could be potentially extended to complement our system for kernel protection.

Second, as with existing systems for kernel code integrity, our current implementation does not support self-modifying kernel code. This limitation can be removed by intercepting the self-modifying behavior (e.g., by trapping and validating the self-modification behavior) and re-authenticating and updating the kernel code in the code memory after the modification.

Third, our system currently does not support kernel page swapping. Linux does not swap out kernel pages, but Windows does have this capability when under heavy memory pressure. Supporting kernel page swapping would require intercepting swap-out and swap-in events and ensuring that the page being swapped in has not been maliciously tampered with.

Fourth, hvmHarvard cannot take advantage of the hardware-assisted paging mechanisms built into modern AMD and Intel processors [3,5]. These schemes do not require the hypervisor to intervene when the guest wishes to alter its page table (as in shadow paging), resulting in superior performance. Unfortunately, our page-level redirection scheme requires page table updates be registered with the hypervisor. Consequently, further work would be required to adapt our scheme to use hardware-assisted paging.

Finally, we point out that our scheme assumes a trustworthy hypervisor to enforce $W \oplus KX$. This assumption is needed because it essentially establishes the root-of-trust of the entire system and secures the lowest-level system access. We also acknowledge that a VM environment can potentially be fingerprinted and exploited [18,33] by attackers. Fortunately, recent solutions on hypervisor protection [19,23,41] can be employed to thwart these attacks. Also notice that as virtualization continues to gain popularity, the concern over VM detection may become less significant as attackers' incentive and motivation to target VMs increase.

7 Related Work

Kernel Rootkit Detection. A number of systems have been proposed to detect the presence of kernel rootkits. Some of them passively validate kernel code and examine kernel data for signs of infection. For example, System Virginity Verifier [34] validates the integrity of the Windows instance that it runs within. As running inside a compromised operating system is dangerous, Copilot [28] copies operating system memory onto a PCI card for analysis by a dedicated co-processor. Further extensions allow it to detect breaches of kernel data semantic integrity [29] and state-based control flow integrity [30]. Strider GhostBuster [40] and VMwatcher [17] aim to look for discrepancies between an internal and external view of a system to detect the hiding behavior from rootkits.

Recently, Lares [27] and its in-VM equivalent, SIM [38], attempt to create secure kernel hooks that can be used to monitor system events. In particular, SIM is capable of installing hooks into a virtualized guest that run code safely *without* hypervisor intervention. SIM uses the same Intel CR3 Target Value List feature that our work does, but uses it to create a safe introspection environment instead of a new paging feature as in our system.

Kernel Rootkit Prevention. Rather than detecting rootkits already resident in an OS kernel, other systems attempt to protect the kernel from being infected in the first place. Livewire [14] is among the first in using virtualization techniques for this purpose, though the system mainly focuses on the protection of static kernel code and data structures. SecVisor [36] is a small security hypervisor that aims to securely enforce a $W \oplus X$ guarantee over memory but it requires modifying the OS kernel for the support. In other words, it is not able to support legacy OSs such as Redhat 8.0. Also note that SecVisor implemented a similar KX paging mode, but its shadow page table implementation uses a single page table per process, which leads to considerable performance overhead [36]. Instead, our approach proposes two page tables. Further, with the CR3 Target Value List hardware virtualization feature, our system allows a guest running under our system to switch between these two page tables without hypervisor intervention. In the same vein, NICKLE [31] aims to protect the integrity of the kernel code with a software-based implementation of the Harvard architecture. The software implementation is based on instruction-level redirection, which has a high performance overhead. In comparison, our approach proposes a page-level, mode-sensitive redirection that substantially reduces the performance overhead.

More recently, Overshadow [12] is another related system. Its basic premise is that the kernel cannot be trusted with sensitive user data, even if it is not compromised or actively malicious. Like our system, Overshadow captures the mode-switching changes to alter the view of memory inside a protected VM. However, the differences are twofold: (1) First, our system switches between user and kernel page tables on each mode switch but do not attempt to encrypt user memory pages. In comparison, Overshadow makes the user memory appear encrypted to the operating system kernel, yet acts as normal when at user privilege; (2) Second, the goal of our system is to protect the kernel from malicious user applications while Overshadow does the exact reverse.

In addition to these techniques, there have been attempts to use lightweight virtual machines in place of processes. For example, the Qubes [35] operating system uses Xen to manage AppVMs each containing an application and a small Linux environment. AppVMs are treated analogously to processes, instead of as full-on virtual machines: functions such as storage and networking are handled centrally in dedicated, hardened virtual machines. While the isolation guarantees from such methods are potentially very strong, they are not a drop-in solution for legacy systems, due to their radically different interface.

TLB Manipulation. Finally, the presence of separate TLBs has been recognized and exploited in other contexts for different applications. For example, Wurster et al. [44] proposes using different ITLB and DTLB mappings to attack self-checksumming code. Almost simultaneously, Sparks and Butler [39] shows a rootkit prototype called Shadow Walker that could elude existing detection using the de-synchronized TLB. Later, Rosenblum et al. [32] demonstrates a system that used a modified version of Xen to instrument a tamper-resistant process within a VM. While the version of Xen used is unclear, it appears that their system operated on para-virtualized guests. In contrast, our system is mainly concerned with fully-virtualized guests and aims to defeat existing kernel rootkits. To the best of our knowledge, no other system has exploited recent hardware virtualization features to efficiently implement the Harvard architecture on x86, including the use of tagged TLBs to manipulate the TLBs of a guest from outside as well as the unique hardware feature of the CR3 Target Value List.

8   Conclusion

In this paper, we present hvmHarvard, a hardware virtualization-based, efficient implementation of the Harvard architecture on top of x86. The Harvard architecture has two memory spaces (one for code and one for data) and is thus inherently robust to code injection attacks employed by most existing kernel rootkits. Different from prior efforts in using the instruction-level redirection to virtualize the Harvard architecture, our approach proposes a page-level, mode-sensitive scheme to achieve the same goal but with a significantly reduced performance overhead. We have implemented a Xen-based prototype. Our evaluation shows that it allows for transparent support of legacy OSs (without modification) as the guest and protects them from existing kernel rootkit attacks with a small performance overhead ($< 5\%$).

Acknowledgments. The authors would like to thank the anonymous reviewers for their numerous, insightful comments that greatly helped improve the presentation of this paper. This work was supported in part by the US Army Research Office (ARO) under grant W911NF-08-1-0105 managed by NCSU Secure Open Systems Initiative (SOSI) and the US National Science Foundation (NSF) under Grants 0852131, 0855297, 0855036, 0910767, and 0952640. Any opinions, findings, and conclusions or recommendations expressed in this material are those of the authors and do not necessarily reflect the views of the ARO and the NSF.

References

1. W^X, http://en.wikipedia.org/wiki/W_xor_X
2. Rootkit Numbers Rocketing UP, McAfee Says (2006),
   http://news.cnet.com/2100-7349_3-6061878.html
3. AMD Virtualization (AMD-V) Technology (2009),
   http://sites.amd.com/us/business/it-solutions/usage-models/
   virtualization/Pages/amd-v.aspx
4. Cooperation Grows in Fight Against Cybercrime (2010),
   http://www.avertlabs.com/research/blog/index.php/category/
   rootkits-and-stealth-malware/
5. Intel 64 and IA-32 Architectures Software Developers Manual, Volume 3B: System Programming Guide (2010),
   http://www.intel.com/assets/pdf/manual/253669.pdf
6. Abadi, M., Budiu, M., Erlingsson, U., Ligatti, J.: Control-Flow Integrity Principles, Implementations, and Applications. ACM Transactions on Information and System Security 13(1), 1–40 (2009)
7. Apache Http Server Project, http://httpd.apache.org/
8. ab - Apache Benchmarking Tool,
   http://httpd.apache.org/docs/2.2/programs/ab.html
9. Barham, P., Dragovic, B., Fraser, K., Hand, S., Harris, T.L., Ho, A., Neugebauer, R., Pratt, I., Warfield, A.: Xen and the Art of Virtualization. In: SOSP 2003: Proceedings of the 19th ACM Symposium on Operating Systems Principles, pp. 164–177. ACM, New York (2003)

10. Buchanan, E., Roemer, R., Shacham, H., Savage, S.: When Good Instructions Go Bad: Generalizing Return-Oriented Programming to RISC. In: CCS 2008: Proceedings of the 15th ACM Conference on Computer and Communications Security, pp. 27–38. ACM, New York (2008)

11. Castro, M., Costa, M., Harris, T.: Securing Software by Enforcing Data-Flow Integrity. In: OSDI 2006: Proceedings of the 7th Symposium on Operating Systems Design and Implementation, pp. 147–160. USENIX Association, Berkeley (2006)

12. Chen, X., Garfinkel, T., Lewis, E.C., Subrahmanyam, P., Waldspurger, C.A., Boneh, D., Dwoskin, J., Ports, D.R.: Overshadow: A Virtualization-based Approach to Retrofitting Protection in Commodity Operating Systems. In: ASPLOS XIII: Proceedings of the 13th International Conference on Architectural Support for Programming Languages and Operating Systems, pp. 2–13. ACM, New York (2008)

13. Dunlap, G.W., King, S.T., Cinar, S., Basrai, M.A., Chen, P.M.: ReVirt: Enabling Intrusion Analysis Through Virtual-Machine Logging and Replay. In: OSDI 2002: Proceedings of the 5th Symposium on Operating Systems Design and Implementation, pp. 211–224. ACM, New York (2002)

14. Garfinkel, T., Rosenblum, M.: A Virtual Machine Introspection Based Architecture for Intrusion Detection. In: Proceedings of the Network and Distributed Systems Security Symposium, pp. 191–206 (2003)

15. Grizzard, J.B.: Towards Self-Healing Systems: Re-establishing Trust in Compromised Systems. Ph.D. thesis, Georgia Institute of Technology (2006)

16. Hund, R., Holz, T., Freiling, F.C.: Return-Oriented Rootkits: Bypassing Kernel Code Integrity Protection Mechanisms. In: Security 2009: Proceedings of the 18th USENIX Security Symposium (2009)

17. Jiang, X., Wang, X., Xu, D.: Stealthy Malware Detection through VMM-based "Out-of-the-Box" Semantic View Reconstruction. In: CCS 2007: Proceedings of the 14th ACM Conference on Computer and Communications Security, pp. 128–138. ACM, New York (2007)

18. Klein, T.: ScoopyNG (2010), http://www.trapkit.de/research/vmm/scoopyng/

19. Kortchinsky, K.: Honeypots: Counter Measures to VMware Fingerprinting (2004), http://seclists.org/lists/honeypots/2004/Jan-Mar/0015.html

20. Liakh, S., Jiang, X.: [2/4,tip:x86/mm] Set First MB as RW+NX (2010), https://patchwork.kernel.org/patch/90048/

21. Liakh, S., Jiang, X.: [3/4,tip:x86/mm] NX Protection for Kernel Data (2010), https://patchwork.kernel.org/patch/90046/

22. Liakh, S., Jiang, X.: [4/4,tip:x86/mm] RO/NX Protection for Loadable Kernel Modules (2010), https://patchwork.kernel.org/patch/90047/

23. Liston, T., Skoudis, E.: On the Cutting Edge: Thwarting Virtual Machine Detection (2006), http://handlers.sans.org/tliston/ThwartingVMDetection_Liston_Skoudis.pdf

24. LMbench - Tools for Performance Analysis (1998), http://www.bitmover.com/lmbench/

25. Lombardi, F., Di Pietro, R.: KvmSec: A Security Extension for Linux Kernel Virtual Machines. In: SAC 2009: Proceedings of the 2009 ACM Symposium on Applied Computing, New York, NY, pp. 2029–2034 (2009)

26. Murray, D.G., Milos, G., Hand, S.: Improving Xen Security through Disaggregation. In: VEE 2008: Proceedings of the 4th ACM SIGPLAN/SIGOPS International Conference on Virtual Execution Environments, pp. 151–160. ACM, New York (2008)

27. Payne, B.D., Carbone, M., Sharif, M.I., Lee, W.: Lares: An Architecture for Secure Active Monitoring Using Virtualization. In: Oakland 2008: IEEE Symposium on Security and Privacy (S&P 2008), pp. 233–247. IEEE Computer Society, Los Alamitos (2008)

28. Petroni Jr., N.L., Fraser, T., Molina, J., Arbaugh, W.A.: Copilot - A Coprocessor-based Kernel Runtime Integrity Monitor. In: Security 2004: Proceedings of the 13th USENIX Security Symposium, pp. 179–194. USENIX Association, Berkeley (2004)
29. Petroni, Jr., N.L., Fraser, T., Walters, A., Arbaugh, W.A.: An Architecture for Specification-based Detection of Semantic Integrity Violations in Kernel Dynamic Data. In: Security 2006: Proceedings of the 15th USENIX Security Symposium, pp. 289–304. USENIX Association, Berkeley (2006)
30. Petroni, Jr., N.L., Hicks, M.: Automated Detection of Persistent Kernel Control-Flow Attacks. In: CCS 2007: Proceedings of the 14th ACM Conference on Computer and Communications Security, pp. 103–115 (2007)
31. Riley, R., Jiang, X., Xu, D.: Guest-Transparent Prevention of Kernel Rootkits with VMM-Based Memory Shadowing. In: Lippmann, R., Kirda, E., Trachtenberg, A. (eds.) RAID 2008. LNCS, vol. 5230, pp. 1–20. Springer, Heidelberg (2008)
32. Rosenblum, N.E., Cooksey, G., Miller, B.P.: Virtual Machine-provided Context Sensitive Page Mappings. In: VEE 2008: Proceedings of the 4th ACM SIGPLAN/SIGOPS International Conference on Virtual Execution Environments, pp. 81–90. ACM, New York (2008)
33. Rutkowska, J.: Red Pill (2004), http://invisiblethings.org/papers/redpill.html
34. Rutkowska, J.: System Virginity Verifier: Defining the Roadmap for Malware Detection on Windows System (2005), http://www.invisiblethings.org/papers/hitb05_virginity_verifier.ppt
35. Rutkowska, J., Wojtczuk, R.: Qubes OS Architecture (2010), http://qubes-os.org/
36. Seshadri, A., Luk, M., Qu, N., Perrig, A.: SecVisor: A Tiny Hypervisor to Provide Lifetime Kernel code Integrity for Commodity OSes. In: SOSP 2007: Proceedings of the 21st ACM SIGOPS Symposium on Operating Systems Principles, pp. 335–350. ACM, New York (2007)
37. Shacham, H.: The Geometry of Innocent Flesh on the Bone: Return-into-libc without Function Calls (on the x86). In: CCS 2007: Proceedings of the 14th ACM Conference on Computer and Communications Security, pp. 552–561. ACM, New York (2007)
38. Sharif, M.I., Lee, W., Cui, W., Lanzi, A.: Secure In-VM Monitoring Using Hardware Virtualization. In: CCS 2009: Proceedings of the 16th ACM Conference on Computer and Communications Security, pp. 477–487. ACM, New York (2009)
39. Sparks, S., Butler, J.: Shadow Walker.: Raising the Bar for Rootkit Detection. In: Black Hat Japan (2005)
40. Wang, Y.M., Beck, D., Vo, B., Roussev, R., Verbowski, C.: Detecting Stealth Software with Strider GhostBuster. In: DSN 2005: Proceedings of the 2005 International Conference on Dependable Systems and Networks, pp. 368–377. IEEE Computer Society, Los Alamitos (2005)
41. Wang, Z., Jiang, X.: HyperSafe: A Lightweight Approach to Provide Lifetime Hypervisor Control-Flow Integrity. In: Oakland 2010: IEEE Symposium on Security and Privacy (S&P 2010), pp. 380–398. IEEE Computer Society, Los Alamitos (2010)
42. Wang, Z., Jiang, X., Cui, W., Ning, P.: Countering Kernel Rootkits with Lightweight Hook Protection. In: CCS 2009: Proceedings of the 16th ACM Conference on Computer and Communications Security, pp. 545–554. ACM, New York (2009)
43. Wang, Z., Jiang, X., Cui, W., Wang, X.: Countering Persistent Kernel Rootkits through Systematic Hook Discovery. In: Lippmann, R., Kirda, E., Trachtenberg, A. (eds.) RAID 2008. LNCS, vol. 5230, pp. 21–38. Springer, Heidelberg (2008)
44. Wurster, G., Oorschot, P.C.v., Somayaji, A.: A Generic Attack on Checksumming-Based Software Tamper Resistance. In: Oakland 2005: Proceedings of the 2005 IEEE Symposium on Security and Privacy (S&P 2005), pp. 127–138. IEEE Computer Society, Los Alamitos (2005)

A Generic Construction of Dynamic Single Sign-on with Strong Security

Jinguang Han[1,3], Yi Mu[1], Willy Susilo[1], and Jun Yan[2]

[1] Centre for Computer and Information Security Research
School of Computer Science and Software Engineering
[2] School of Information Systems and Technology
University of Wollongong, NSW2522, Australia
[3] College of Science, Hohai University, Nanjing 210098, China
{jh843,ymu,wsusilo,jyan}@uow.edu.au

Abstract. Single Sign-On (SSO) is a core component in a federated identity management (FIM). Dynamic Single Sign-on (DSSO) is a more flexible SSO where users can change their service requirements dynamically. However, the security in the current SSO and DSSO systems remain questionable. As an example, personal credentials could be illegally used to allow illegal users to access the services. It is indeed a challenging task to achieve strong security in SSO and DSSO. In this paper, we propose a generic construction of DSSO with strong security. We propose the formal definitions and security models for SSO and DSSO, which enable one to achieve the security of SSO and DSSO with the underlying (standard) security assumptions. We also provide a formal security proof on our generic DSSO scheme.

Keywords: Single Sign-on, Authentication, Security.

1 Introduction

With an increasing use of personalized/protected services, users need to maintain more and more usernames and the corresponding passwords in order to access the entitled services. This imposes a burden on users. Single Sign-on (SSO) provides a good remedy to this problem, as it allows a single password to be used to access multiple services. A traditional SSO system comprises three entities: an identity provider (IdP), a group of users (Us) and a group of service providers (SPs). The IdP manages the user's personally identifiable information (PII), authenticates network users and issues credentials to them. SPs provide services to users once they are authenticated by the IdP. SSO is a system where a user authenticates himself to the IdP and can access the designated SPs without the need for further authentication [24]. SSO can shift the great administrative burden of the numerous users profiles from SPs to the IdP. Hence, SSO plays a core role in the federated identity management (FIM) where the exchange of the user's identity-related information can be optimized [5].

Unfortunately, current SSO systems have some obvious flaws. For instance, they are fragile to resist single point of failure [16,22,23]. The main reason for this

S. Jajodia and J. Zhou (Eds.): SecureComm 2010, LNICST 50, pp. 181–198, 2010.
© Institute for Computer Sciences, Social Informatics and Telecommunications Engineering 2010

is that the IdP must always be online, otherwise users cannot be granted services from SPs. They are not well protected from illegally using a personal credential, where a credential could be used for an illegitimate user to gain the services which should not be accessed by him. These systems are subject to impersonation attacks. When a password is compromised, the attacker can impersonate the user and log in using the compromised account. This is mainly due to the missing of individual participation principle provided in the thirteenth principle of Organization for Economic CO-Operation and Development (OECD) [20] and the missing of the user control and consent principle for the laws of identity [6]. All these flaws stem from the lack of active/dynamic control over the process by the user, after the user has entered the correct password. In the following, we review some existing SSO systems. Although those systems provide elegant solutions to SSO, they suffer from various attacks.

Released 1999, Microsoft .NET Passport is one of the most widely deployed SSO systems, where a passport server acts as the IdP [22]. It uses cookies to store and convey user's PII. When a user access to an SP, the SP redirects the user to the passport server for authentication. After authentication, the passport server creates three cookies: ticket cookie, profile cookie and visited sits cookie. The ticket cookie contains the unique identifier and a timestamp. The profile cookie consists of the user's profile information. The visited sits cookie contains the lists sites the user has accessed. All cookies created by the passport server are encrypted with the triple DES encryption algorithm under the shared key between the passport server and all SPs. The passport server sends these cookies to the user. The user redirects them to the SP. The SP decrypts the cookies and obtains the user's authentication information. .Net Passport incurs some attacks, such as single point of failure, key management failure, misuse of cookies, etc. [16,22,23].

In September 2001, the Liberty Alliance Project was launched [17]. This project was aimed to create an open, federated, SSO solution for the digital economy via any device connected to the Internet. The Liberty project does not use cookies to transfer information between IdPs and SPs. Instead, it transfers information through HTTP redirects and URL encodings. In Liberty Alliance, an SSO Service (SSOS) provides users an Identity Web Services Framework (ID-WSF)-based means to obtain Liberty authentication assertions enabling them to interact with SPs [18]. In this system, the user only shows his credentials to the SP, without proving the ownership of them. Therefore, it is unable to prevent credential transfer, namely the user can share his credentials with other illegal users.

Proposed in 2005, OpenID is an open, decentralized standard for authenticating users. In OpenId, users are allowed to access to different services with the same digital identity where the SPs trust the IdP. OpenID solves the problem without relying on any centralized IdP to confirm digital identity. There are more than one IdP in OpenID system, users can get their OpenID from any IdP in the system. OpenID can be used as an effective mean for cross company authentication as well as for SSO. OpenID has two major modes of operation: Dumb mode and Smart mode [21,28]. In the Dumb mode, the SP needs to compare the authentication assertion received from the user with the initial one stored in the IdP to prevent the malicious attackers. While in the Smart mode, the IdP encrypts the authentication assertion under the shared key between the SP and the IdP. Therefore, in both modes, the IdP must always be online to enable users authentication.

In 2003, Pahalidis and Mitchell presented a taxonomy of SSO system [24]. They divided SSO systems into four categories: local pseudo-SSO systems, proxy-based pseudo-SSO systems, local true SSO systems and proxy-based true SSO systems. They designed two SSO systems based on trusted platforms and GSM/UMTS, respectively [25,26]. In order to resolve the single point of failure, two distributed SSO systems Cornell SSO (CorSSO) and Threshold Passport (Thres-Passport) were proposed by Josephson and Chen in 2004 and 2005, respectively [7,15]. In these systems, the authentication key is split into n different shares, and each share is sent to an authentication server. Only authenticated by at least t authentication servers, can the user get services from an SP. Recently, user-centric federated identity management systems have been proposed to protect user's PII [30,27]. In 2009, based on a private credential mechanism, Suriadi and Foo proposed a user-centric federated SSO system (UFed SSO), in which the user can minimize the release of his PII [31]. Although, every system mentioned above has its merits, they did not provide a security proof.

In 2006, Bhargav-Spantzel and Camenisch [30] proposed a taxonomy and raised some open issues on user centric federated identity management systems. They classified the existing systems into two predominant variants: credential-focused systems and relation-focused systems. In credential-focused systems, the IdPs must be offline and issue long-term credentials. While in relationship-focused systems, users need to maintain the relationship with the online IdPs that create short-term credentials for them during transactions. They defined an universal user centric FIM which should have long-term as well as short-term credentials, online and offline IdP. However, this scheme has not been investigated thoroughly.

Our Contribution
In this paper, we propose a novel dynamic SSO scheme, which resists against all the previously described attacks. We formalize the definitions and the security models for SSO and DSSO. It is the first time that the formal definitions and security models for SSO and DSSO are formally defined. We give a generic construction of DSSO systems based on three building blocks: (1) CCA-secure broadcast encryption, (2) strongly existentially unforgeable signature, and (3) zero knowledge proof. We provide a formal security proof for our generic construction.

Paper Organization
The rest of this paper is organized as follows. In Section 2, we propose the formal definitions and security models for SSO and DSSO. We review the three building blocks which are used to construct DSSO in Section 3. In Section 4, a generic

construction for DSSO is described. In Section 5, we reduce the security of our construction to the underlying assumptions. Section 6 concludes this paper.

2   Formal Definitions and Security Models

In this section, we provide a formal definition and a security model for SSO and DSSO.

2.1   Single Sign-on

In SSO systems, a user needs to authenticate himself to the IdP once for access to multiple SPs without the need to re-authentication. In order to protect the PII of the user, an ideal SSO system should satisfy the basic requirement that only the intended SPs can check the user's PII. Now we formalise the definition of SSO as follows:

Definition 1. *A Single Sign-on system consists of five algorithms: system setup algorithm* Setup$(\cdot)$, *enrollment algorithm* Enrol$(\cdot)$, *credential generation algorithm* CreGen$(\cdot)$, *credential verification algorithm* CreVer$(\cdot)$, *and proof of knowledge algorithm* PK$(\cdot)$.

- *Setup(λ): Taking as input a security parameter $\lambda \in \mathbb{N}$, it returns public parameters PP and a public-secret key pair $(K_{IP}, K_{IS}) \leftarrow \mathcal{G}(1^\lambda)$ for the IdP.*
- *Enrol(PP, RI): Taking as input public parameters PP, SP_i's registration information RI_{SPi} or U's registration information RI_U, it returns (ID_{SP_i}, K_{SP_i}) to SP_i, and (ID_U, A_U) to U, where ID_{SP_i} and ID_U are the identifiers of SP_i and U in the circle of trust (CoT)[1], K_{SP_i} is SP_i's verification key and A_U is U's access right which is a set consisting of the identifiers of the service providers that the user has selected. U generates his public-secret key pair $(K_{UP}, K_{US}) \leftarrow \mathcal{G}(1^\lambda)$.*
- *CreGen$(K_{IS}, M_U, ID_U, T_U, K_{UP}, PP)$: Taking as input the IdP's secret key K_{IS}, an authentication assertion M_U, user's identifier ID_U, user's public key K_{UP}, a timestamp T_U and public parameters PP, it returns a credential Cre_U.*
- *CreVer$(K_{SP_i}, Cre_U, M_U, ID_U, K_{UP}, T_U, K_{IP}, PP)$: Taking as input the service provider SP_i's verification key K_{SPi}, the user's credential Cre_U, the authentication assertion M_U, the user's identifier ID_U, user's public key K_{UP}, IdP's public key K_{IP}, the timestamp T_U and public parameters PP, it returns True if and only if the service provider $ID_{SP_i} \in A_U$ and the credential Cre_U is created by the IdP. Otherwise it returns False.*
- *PK$((K_{US}, K_{UP}), \gamma)$: Taking as input the user's public-secret key pair (K_{UP}, K_{US}) and a random number γ, it returns a number s such that Accept $\leftarrow PKVer(s, K_{UP}, \gamma)$ if and only if K_{US} is the user's secret key corresponding to the public key K_{UP}, where $PKVer(\cdot)$ is the verification algorithm in the proof of knowledge. Otherwise it returns Reject.*

---

[1] A circle of trust consists of the identity provider and service providers, where each service provider trusts the identity provider.

2.2   The Security of Single Sign-on

In SSO systems, three types of attacks should be considered: collusion credential forging attacks, collusion impersonation attacks and coalition credential forging attacks. In the collusion credential forging attacks, malicious users can collaboratively forge a credential for the target user. They can impersonate the target one to get services from the service providers whose identifiers are listed in the forged credential. In the collusion impersonation attacks, we assume that the malicious service providers have checked the credentials of a user and therefore obtained the corresponding proof information on the user. Hence, malicious service providers can collaboratively mimic the owner of the credentials. In the coalition credential forging attacks, malicious users and service providers can collaboratively forge a credential for the target user, in which the identifiers of the malicious service providers are not included.

In order to formalise our notions of security for SSO systems, we define a series of games between two Turing machines: Challenger and Adversary $\mathcal{A}$.

Game 1: Collusion Credential Forging Attacks.

Init. Let $\mathcal{A}$ be all malicious users. $\mathcal{A}$ begins by outputting the target user U^* for whom it wants to forge a credential.

Setup. The challenger runs Setup(λ) to generate the public parameter PP and the public-private key pair (K_{IP}, K_{IS}). It sends $\mathcal{A}$ the public parameter PP and the public key K_{IP}.

Enrollment queries. $\mathcal{A}$ can adaptively issue enrollment queries $\{RI_{U_1}, RI_{U_2}, \cdots, RI_{U_{qe}}\}$, where $RI_{U_i} \neq RI_U^*$, $qe \leq (|\mathbb{U}| - 1)$, $\mathbb{U}$ is the set consists of all users in the CoT. The challenger returns $\{(ID_{U_1}, A_{U_1}), (ID_{U_2}, A_{U_2}), \cdots, (ID_{U_{qe}}, A_{U_{qe}})\}$.

Credential generation queries. $\mathcal{A}$ can adaptively issue credential generation queries $\{(ID_{U_1}, K_{UP_1}), (ID_{U_2}, K_{UP_2}), \cdots, (ID_{U_{qc_1}}, K_{UP_{qc_1}})\}$, where $(ID_{U_i}, K_{UP_i}) \neq (ID_U^*, K_{UP}^*)$. The challenger returns $\{Cre_{U_1}, Cre_{U_2}, \cdots, Cre_{U_{qc_1}}\}$.

Credential verification queries. $\mathcal{A}$ can adaptively issue credential verification queries $\{(ID_{U_1}, K_{UP_1}, Cre_{U_1}), (ID_{U_2}, K_{UP_2}, Cre_{U_2}), \cdots, (ID_{U_{qc_2}}, K_{UP_{qc_2}}, Cre_{U_{qc_2}})\}$. Upon receiving a query, the challenger returns $True$ or $False$.

Output. $\mathcal{A}$ outputs a credential Cre_U^* for U^*. $\mathcal{A}$ wins the game if

1. $True \leftarrow$ CreVer $(K_{SP_i}, Cre_U^*, ID_U^*, K_{UP}^*, T_U^*, K_{IP}, PP)$ and
2. $(ID_U^*, Cre_U^*) \notin \{(ID_{U_1}, Cre_{U_1}), (ID_{U_2}, Cre_{U_2}), \cdots, (ID_{U_{qc_1}}, Cre_{U_{qc_1}})\}$.

Definition 2. *A Single Sign-on system is $(t, qe, qc_1, qc_2, \epsilon)$-secure against collusion credential forging attacks if no t-time adversary, who makes at most qe enrollment queries, qc_1 credential generation queries and qc_2 credential verification queries, has advantage at least ϵ in* Game 1.

Game 2. Collusion Impersonate Attacks.

Init. Let $\mathcal{A}$ be all malicious service providers in the CoT. $\mathcal{A}$ begins by outputting a user U^* whom it wants to impersonate.

Setup. The challenger runs Setup(λ) to obtain the public parameters PP and the public-secret key pair (K_{IP}, K_{IS}). It sends $\mathcal{A}$ the public parameter PP and the public key K_{IP}.

Proof of Knowledge queries. $\mathcal{A}$ can adaptively issues proof of knowledge queries $\{(K_{UP_1}, \gamma_1), (K_{UP_2}, \gamma_2), \cdots, (K_{UP_{qp}}, \gamma_{qp})\}$, where $K_{UP_i} \neq K_{UP}^*$. The challenger returns $\{s_1, s_2, \cdots, s_{qp}\}$.

Challenge. The challenger sends a challenge (K_{UP}^*, γ^*) to $\mathcal{A}$.

Output. $\mathcal{A}$ outputs s^*. $\mathcal{A}$ wins the game if

1. $Accept \leftarrow PKVer(s^*, K_{UP}^*, \gamma^*)$ and
2. $K_{UP}^* \notin \{K_{UP_1}, K_{UP_2}, \cdots, K_{UP_{qp}}\}$.

Definition 3. *A Single Sign-on system is (t, qp, ϵ)-secure against collusion impersonation attacks if no t-time adversary, who makes at most qp proof of knowledge queries, has advantage at least ϵ in* Game 2.

Game 3: Coalition Credential Forging Attacks.

Init. Let $\mathcal{A}$ be the coalition, which consists of all malicious users and service providers. $\mathcal{A}$ begins by outputting a user U^* that it wants to impersonate and a service provider SP^* that it wants to attack.

Setup. The challenger runs Setup(λ) to generate the public parameters PP and the public-secret key pair (K_{IP}, K_{IS}). It sends $\mathcal{A}$ the public parameter PP and the public key K_{IP}.

Enrollment queries. $\mathcal{A}$ can adaptively issue enrollment queries $\{RI_{U_1}, RI_{U_2}, \cdots, RI_{U_{qe_1}}\}$ and $\{RI_{SP_1}, RI_{SP_2}, \cdots, RI_{SP_{qe_2}}\}$, where $RI_{U_i} \neq RI_U^*$, $RI_{SP_i} \neq RI_{SP}^*$, $qe_1 \leq (|\mathbb{U}| - 1)$, $qe_2 \leq (|\mathbb{SP}| - 1)$, $\mathbb{SP}$ is the set consists of all service providers in the CoT, and $qe_1 + qe_2 = qe$. The challenger returns $\{(ID_{U_1}, A_{U_1}), (ID_{U_2}, A_{U_2}) \cdots, (ID_{U_{qe_1}}, A_{U_{qe_1}})\}$ and $\{(ID_{SP_1}, K_{SP_1}), (ID_{SP_2}, K_{SP_2}), \cdots, (ID_{SP_{qe_2}}, K_{SP_{qe_2}})\}$.

Credential generation queries. $\mathcal{A}$ can adaptively issue credential generation queries $\{(ID_{U_1}, K_{UP_1}), (ID_{U_2}, K_{UP_2}), \cdots, (ID_{U_{qc_1}}, K_{UP_{qc_1}})\}$, where $(ID_{U_i}, K_{UP_i}) \neq (ID_U^*, K_{UP}^*)$. The challenger returns $\{Cre_{U_1}, Cre_{U_2}, \cdots, Cre_{U_{qc_1}}\}$.

Credential verification queries. $\mathcal{A}$ can adaptively issue credential verification queries $\{(ID_{U_1}, K_{UP_1}, Cre_{U_1}), (ID_{U_2}, K_{UP_2}, Cre_{U_2}), \cdots, (ID_{U_{qc_2}}, K_{UP_{qc_2}}, Cre_{U_{qc_2}})\}$. The challenger returns $True$ or $False$.

Output. $\mathcal{A}$ outputs a credential Cre_U^*. $\mathcal{A}$ wins the game if

1. $True \leftarrow CreVer(K_{SP}^*, Cre_U^*, M_U^*, ID_U^*, K_{UP}^*, T_U^*, K_{IP}, PP)$.

2. $(ID_U^*, Cre_U^*) \notin \{(ID_{U_1}, Cre_{U_1}), (ID_{U_2}, Cre_{U_2}), \cdots, (ID_{U_{qc_1}}, Cre_{U_{qc_1}})\}$.

3. $ID_{SP}^* \in A_U^*$ and $ID_{SP} \notin A_U^*$ if $SP \in \mathcal{A}$.

Definition 4. *A Single Sign-on system is $(t, qe, qc_1, qc_2, \epsilon)$-secure against coalition credential forging attacks if no t-time adversary, who makes at most qe enrollment queries, qc_1 credential generation queries, and qc_2 credential verification queries, has advantage at least ϵ in the* Game 3.

2.3 Dynamic Single Sign-on

DSSO is an SSO system in which the user can change his choice dynamically. We formalise the definition of DSSO as follows:

Definition 5. *A dynamic single sign-on system (DSSO) consists of seven algorithms:* Setup($\cdot$), Enrol($\cdot$), CreGen($\cdot$), CreVer($\cdot$), PK($\cdot$), *an addition algorithm* A($\cdot$) *and a deletion algorithm* D($\cdot$). *Where* Setup($\cdot$), Enrol($\cdot$), CreGen($\cdot$), CreVer($\cdot$) *and* PK($\cdot$) *are the same as in definition 1.*

- A (ID_{SP}) : *Taking as input the service provider SP's identifier ID_{SP}, it returns $A_U \leftarrow A_U \bigcup \{ID_{SP}\}$.*
- D (ID_{SP}) : *Taking as input the service provider SP's identifier ID_{SP}, it returns $A_U \leftarrow A_U \backslash \{ID_{SP}\}$.*

2.4 The Security of Dynamic Single Sign-on

In multiple parties communication and dynamic schemes, because the participants can join or leave frequently, two special attacks should be addressed, namely forward security and backward security. In DSSO, users can be added to or revoked from a service dynamically; therefore a secure DSSO system can resist these attacks. By forward security, we mean that the SP can not validate the credentials, which were issued before he is added to the user's access right A_U. By backward security, we mean that the service providers can not validate the credentials, which are issued after he has been removed from the the user's access right A_U. We formalise these two attacks by the following games.

Game 4: Forward Security.

Setup. Let $\mathcal{A}$ be malicious service providers. The challenger runs Setup(λ) to generate the public parameters PP and the public-secret key pair (K_{IP}, K_{IS}). It sends $\mathcal{A}$ the public parameter PP and the public key K_{IP}.

Credential verification queries. $\mathcal{A}$ can adaptively issue credential verification queries $\{(ID_{U_1}, K_{UP_1}, Cre_{U_1}), (ID_{U_2}, K_{UP_2}, Cre_{U_2}), \cdots, (ID_{U_{qc}}, K_{UP_{qc}}, Cre_{U_{qc}})\}$, which were issued after $\mathcal{A}$ has been joined to A_U. The challenger returns $True$ or $False$.

Challenge. The challenger sends to $\mathcal{A}$ an old credential Cre_U^O, which was issued before he is joined to A_U.

Output. $\mathcal{A}$ outputs $True$ or $False$. $\mathcal{A}$ wins the game if his answer on Cre_U^O is correct.

Definition 6. *A Dynamic Single Sign-on system is (t, qc, ϵ)-forward secure if no t-time adversary, who makes at most qc credential verification queries, has advantage at least ϵ in the* Game 4.

Game 5: Backward Security.

Setup. Let $\mathcal{A}$ be malicious service providers. The challenger runs Setup(λ) to generate the public parameters PP and the public-secret key pair (K_{IP}, K_{IS}). It sends $\mathcal{A}$ the public parameter PP and the public key K_{IP}.

Credential verification queries. $\mathcal{A}$ can adaptively issue credential verification queries $\{(ID_{U_1}, K_{UP_1}, Cre_{U_1}), (ID_{U_2}, K_{UP_2}, Cre_{U_2}), \cdots, (ID_{U_{qc}}, K_{UP_{qc}}, Cre_{U_{qc}})\}$, which were issued before $\mathcal{A}$ is deleted from A_U. The challenger returns $True$ or $False$.

Challenge. The challenger sends $\mathcal{A}$ a new credential Cre_U^N which was issued after he has been deleted from A_U.

Output. $\mathcal{A}$ outputs $True$ or $False$. $\mathcal{A}$ wins the game if his answer on Cre_U^N is correct.

Definition 7. *A Dynamic Single Sign-on system is (t, qc, ϵ)-backward secure if no t-time adversary, who makes at most qc credential verification queries, has advantage at least ϵ in the* Game 5.

3   Building Blocks

In this section, we provide three building blocks, which are used to construct DSSO systems.

3.1   Broadcast Encryption System

The notion of broadcast encryption was proposed by Fiat and Naor in 1993 [10]. A broadcast encryption system consists of three randomized algorithms:

- Setup(n, λ): Taking as input the number of receivers n and security parameter λ, it outputs n secret keys $K_{R1}, K_{R2}, \cdots, K_{Rn}$ and public parameters PP_B.
- Encrypt(S, PP_B): Taking as input a subset $S \subseteq \{ID_1, ID_2, \cdots, ID_n\}$ and public parameters PP_B, it outputs a pair (Hdr, K), where Hdr is called the header and $K \in \mathcal{K}$ is a message encryption key. (S, Hdr) is often called the full header.
- Decrypt(Hdr, K_{Ri}, PP_B): Taking as input the header Hdr, the secret key K_{Ri} for the receiver $ID_i \in S$ and the public parameter PP_B, it outputs the message encryption key $K \in \mathcal{K}$.

3.2   Chosen Ciphertext Security of Broadcast Encryption System

The chosen ciphertext security of broadcast encryption system is defined using the following game between a challenger and an adversary $\mathcal{A}$ [1,9].

Init. The adversary $\mathcal{A}$ outputs a receivers set $S^* \subseteq \{ID_1, ID_2, \cdots, ID_n\}$ which he wants to attack.

Setup. The challenger runs $\mathsf{Setup}(n, \lambda)$ to generate secret keys $K_{R1}, K_{R2}, \cdots, K_{Rn}$ and public parameters PP_B. It sends $\mathcal{A}$ all secret key K_{Ri} for $ID_i \notin S^*$.

Query phase 1. $\mathcal{A}$ issues decryption queries $q_1, q_2, \cdots, q_t$, where $q_i = (Hdr, ID_l)$, $ID_l \in S^*$. The challenger responds with $\mathsf{Decrypt}(Hdr, K_{R_l}, PP_B)$.

Challenge. The challenger runs algorithm $\mathsf{Encrypt}(S^*, PP_B)$ to obtain (Hdr^*, K), where $K \in \mathcal{K}$. The challenger chooses a random $b \in \{0,1\}$. It sets $K_b = K$ and chooses a random $K_{1-b} \in \mathcal{K}$. It sends (Hdr^*, K_0, K_1) to $\mathcal{A}$.

Query phase 2. $\mathcal{A}$ can adaptively issue decryption queries $q_{t+1}, q_{t+2}, \cdots q_d$, where $q_j = (Hdr, ID_l)$, $ID_l \in S^*$. The only constraint is that $Hdr \neq Hdr^*$. The challenger returns $\mathsf{Decrypt}(Hdr, K_{R_l}, PP_B)$.

Guess. $\mathcal{A}$ outputs its guess $b' \in \{0,1\}$ for b. $\mathcal{A}$ wins the game if $b = b'$.

Definition 8. *A broadcast encryption system is* (t, n, q_d, ϵ) *CCA-secure if no* t-*time adversary* $\mathcal{A}$, *who makes at most* q_d *decryption queries, has advantage at least* ϵ *in the above game.*

3.3   Signature Scheme

Digital signature scheme was proposed by Diffie and Hellman [8]. A signature scheme consists of four algorithms:

- $\mathsf{Setup}(\gamma)$: Taking as input the security parameter γ, it outputs the public parameters PP_S.
- $\mathsf{KeyGen}(\gamma, PP_S)$: Taking as input the security parameter γ and the public parameters PP_S, it outputs a public-secret key pair (K_S, K_P).
- $\mathsf{Sign}(K_S, m, PP_S)$: Taking as input the secret key K_S, a message m and the public parameters PP_S, it outputs a publicly verifiable signature σ.
- $\mathsf{Ver}(m, \sigma, K_P, PP_S)$: Taking as input the message m, the signature σ, the public key K_P and the public parameters PP_S, it outputs $True$ if the signature is correct. Otherwise it outputs $False$.

3.4   Strong Unforgeability of Signature

A digital signature system is said to be secure if it is existentially unforgeable under a chosen-message attack [2,13]. The strong unforgeability of signature is defined using the following game between a challenger and an adversary $\mathcal{A}$.

Setup. The challenger runs Setup(γ) and KeyGen(γ, PP_S) to generate the public parameters PP_S and a public-secret key pair (K_P, K_S). It sends public parameters PP_S and public key K_P to $\mathcal{A}$.

Signature queries. $\mathcal{A}$ can adaptively issue up to qs signature queries $\{m_1, m_2, \cdots, m_{qs}\}$. To each query m_i, the challenger runs algorithm Sign(K_S, m_i, PP_S) to produce the corresponding signature σ_i. The challenger responds with message-signature pairs $\{(m_1, \sigma_1), (m_2, \sigma_2), \cdots, (m_{qs}, \sigma_{qs})\}$.

Output. $\mathcal{A}$ outputs a message-signature pair (m^*, σ^*). $\mathcal{A}$ wins the game if
  1. $True \leftarrow Ver(m^*, \sigma^*, K_P, PP_S)$ and

  2. $(m^*, \sigma^*) \notin \{(m_1, \sigma_1), (m_2, \sigma_2), \cdots, (m_{qs}, \sigma_{qs})\}$.

Definition 9. *A signature is (t, qs, ϵ)-strongly existentially unforgeable under adaptive chosen-message attacks if no t-time adversary, who makes at most qs signature queries, has advantage at least ϵ in the above game.*

3.5   Zero Knowledge Proof

Zero knowledge proof (ZKP) was introduced by Goldwasser, Micali and Rackoff in 1985 [14]. It is an interactive protocol by which a prover P (Peggy) can convince a verifier V (Victor) that he knows a secret without revealing any information about it to V. The formal definition of zero knowledge proof is as follows:

Definition 10. *Let (P, V) be a pair of Turing machines and V is polynomially bounded. P and V share the same input and can interact with each other. Let L be a language. We say that a pair (P, V) is zero knowledge proof system, if P and V satisfy the following properties:*

- Completeness: *For any input $x \in L$ to (P, V), $Pr[s \leftarrow (P, V)(x), V(x, s) = 1] \geq 1 - \frac{1}{n^k}$, for each k and sufficiently large n which denotes the length of the input.*
- Soundness: *For any $x \notin L$, and any prover P', $Pr[s \leftarrow (P', V)(x), V(x, s) = 1] < \frac{1}{n^k}$.*
- Zero-knowledge: *For any $x \in L$, and any verifier V', there exists a simulator S such that two distribution $S_{V'}(x)$ and $Vew_{V'}(x)$ are computationally indistinguishable.*

Any language in $\mathcal{NP}$ has an interactive zero knowledge proof system [11,12]. Let (P, V) be an interactive zero knowledge proof system. By $(P, V)(x)$ we denote that the prover P executes an interactive zero knowledge proof protocol with the verifier V to prove that he knows the secret corresponding to x.

4   Generic Construction for Dynamic Single Sign-on

Our generic construction for DSSO consists of three building blocks: a CCA-secure broadcast encryption scheme BroEnc($\cdot$), a strongly unforgeable signature scheme Sign($\cdot$) and a zero knowledge proof scheme (P,V)($\cdot$). In our construction, users can change their choices dynamically, while other participants (users and SPs) in the system do not need to change their credentials. When the user logs in, the IdP creates a credential for him. The user can then use this credential to access all designated SPs, instead of sending different credentials to different SPs. For each logging request, the IdP creates a new credential for the user. At this point of time, a user can also be revoked due to expiry of his membership, for instance. Our construction can prevent illegal credential sharing, which is defined as all-or-nothing non-transferability. By all-or-nothing non-transferability, we mean that all the credentials of a user are shared, once he shares one of them with others [30,3,4,19]. Figure 1 provides the architecture of our construction.

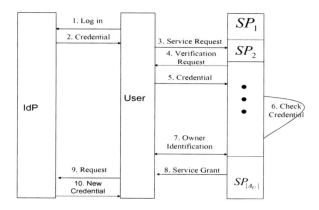

Fig. 1. DSSO Architecture

1. **System Set-up.** Runs the Setup(λ) to generate the public parameters PP, which includes all public parameters in the three underlying building blocks, and a public-secret key pair $(K_{IP}, K_{IS}) \leftarrow \mathcal{G}(1^\lambda)$ for the IdP, where λ is the security parameter.

2. **Enrollment.**

   (a) **Service providers enrollment.** SP_i submits his necessary registration information RI_{SPi} to the IdP. The IdP issues an identifier ID_{SPi} for SP_i, sends a verification key K_{SPi} to him, which is regarded as the receiver key in the broadcast encryption scheme, and stores $(SP_i, ID_{SPi}, K_{SPi})$ for him.

   (b) **User enrollment.** U sends his necessary registration information RI_U to the IdP. The IdP issues an identifier ID_U for him. The user generates his public-secret key pair $(K_{UP}, K_{US}) \leftarrow \mathcal{G}(1^\lambda)$ and sends the public key K_{UP} to the IdP. The IdP decides the user's access right A_U, which is a set that consists of the identifiers of the service providers that the user can access, and stores (ID_U, K_{UP}, A_U) for the user. Note that A_U will be regarded as the receiver set S in broadcast encryption.

3. Single Sign-on.

   (a) Log in. U uses his username and corresponding password to log in the system.

   (b) Credential generation. The IdP runs $\mathsf{BroEnc}(|A_U|)$ to generate the broadcast encryption key K which can only be computed by the service providers whose identifiers are listed in A_U, and encapsulates it in (A_U, Hdr). IdP generates a signature $\delta_U = \mathsf{Sign}(K_{IS}, M_U, ID_U, K_{UP}, T_U)$, where K_{IS} is the secret key of IdP, M_U is an authentication assertion, ID_U is the user's identifier, K_{UP} is the user's public key and T_U is a timestamp. Then, IdP encrypts the signature δ_U under K. The credential for the user is

$$Cre_U = (A_U, Hdr, D), \quad \text{where} \quad D = E_K(\delta_U, M_U, ID_U, K_{UP}, T_U).$$

   (c) Service request. U sends a service request to the service provider SP_i $(ID_{SPi} \in A_U)$.

   (d) Verification request. SP_i asks U to show his credential to him.

   (e) Credential verification. U sends Cre_U to SP_i. SP_i computes the broadcast encryption key K from (A_U, Hdr) using his verification key K_{SPi}, decrypts $D = E_K(\delta_U, M_U, ID_U, K_{UP}, T_U)$ and verifies the signature δ_U. If δ_U is a valid signature on (M_U, ID_U, K_{UP}, T_U), SP_i executes the next step. Otherwise SP_i aborts.

   (f) Owner identification. U executes zero knowledge proof protocol (U, SP_i) (K_{UP}) with SP_i to prove that he knows the secret key K_{US} corresponding the public key K_{UP} included in Cre_U.

   (g) Service grant. If the zero knowledge proof is successful, SP_i grants the services to the user. Otherwise, SP_i rejects the services.

If the user wants to access to other SPs whose identifiers are listed in A_U, he can send Cre_U to them directly, without having to request the IdP to issue a new credential for him, namely step (a) and (b) can be omitted.

4. Dynamic Change.

If the user needs to change his access right, when he logs in, he must submit a request to the IdP. After checking it, the IdP creates a new credential for the user, according to his current status.

   (a) Request. U must submit a request for changing A_U to the IdP. After checking the request, the IdP does the following two changes on A_U.

   (b) Add. The IdP adds a service provider SP_j to the user's access right A_U by setting $A_U \leftarrow A_U \bigcup \{ID_{SP_j}\}$, and updates the broadcast encryption key K.

   (c) Delete. The IdP deletes a service provider SP_j from A_U by setting $A_U \leftarrow A_U \backslash \{ID_{SP_j}\}$, and updates the broadcast encryption key K.

   (d) New credential generation. The IdP uses the updated broadcast encryption key K to generate a new credential for U.

5   Security Analysis

In this section, we prove that our construction for DSSO is secure against collusion credential forging attacks, collusion impersonate attacks and coalition credential forging attacks, and provides forward security and backward security.

Theorem 1. *Our generic construction for DSSO is $(t, qe, qc_1, qc_2, \epsilon)$ -secure against collusion credential forging attacks if the broadcast encryption scheme is (t, n, qc_1, ϵ_1) CCA-secure and the signature scheme is $(t, qc_2, \epsilon.(1 - \epsilon_1)^{qc_2})$-strongly existentially unforgeable.*

Proof. Suppose there exists t-time malicious users $\mathcal{A}$ that $(t, qe, qc_1, qc_2, \epsilon)$ breaks the collusion credential unforgeability of our generic construction for DSSO. We will show that there exists an algorithm $\mathcal{B}$ who can $(t, qc_2, \epsilon.(1 - \epsilon_1)^{qc_2})$ breaks the strongly existential unforgeability of the underlying signature scheme.

Init. Algorithm $\mathcal{B}$ runs $\mathcal{A}$ and receives a user U^* for whom $\mathcal{A}$ wants to forge a credential.

Setup. $\mathcal{B}$ sends the public parameters PP and the IdP's public key K_{IP} to $\mathcal{A}$.

Enrollment queries. $\mathcal{A}$ can adaptively issues at most qe enrollment queries $\{RI_{U_1}, RI_{U_2}, \cdots, RI_{U_{qe}}\}$, where $RI_{Ui} \neq RI_U^*, qe \leq (|\mathbb{U}|-1)$. $\mathcal{B}$ returns $\{(ID_{U_1}, A_{U_1}), (ID_{U_2}, A_{U_2}), \cdots, (ID_{U_{qe}}, A_{U_{qe}})\}$.

Credential generation queries. $\mathcal{A}$ can adaptively issue credential generation queries $\{(ID_{U_1}, K_{UP_1}), (ID_{U_2}, K_{UP_2}), \cdots, (ID_{U_{qc_1}}, K_{UP_{qc_1}})\}$, where $(ID_{U_i}, K_{UP_i}) \neq (ID_U^*, K_{UP}^*)$. $\mathcal{B}$ redirects these queries to the challenger. The challenger returns $\{Cre_{U_1}, Cre_{U_2}, \cdots, Cre_{U_{qc_1}}\}$, where $Cre_{U_i} = (A_{U_i}, Hdr_i, D_i)$, $D_i = E_{K_i}(\delta_i, M_{U_i}, ID_{U_i}, K_{UP_i}, T_{U_i})$ and $\delta_i = \mathsf{Sign}(K_{IS}, M_{U_i}, ID_{U_i}, K_{UP_i}, T_{U_i})$.

Credential verification queries. $\mathcal{A}$ can adaptively issue credential verification queries $\{(ID_{U_1}, K_{UP_1}, Cre_{U_1}), \quad (ID_{U_2}, K_{UP_2}, Cre_{U_2}), \quad \cdots, \quad (ID_{U_{qc_2}}, K_{UP_{qc_2}}, Cre_{U_{qc_2}})\}$. $\mathcal{B}$ redirects these queries to the challenger. The challenger returns $True$ or $False$.

Output. $\mathcal{A}$ outputs a credential $Cre_U^* = (A_U^*, Hdr^*, D^*)$, where $(ID_U^*, Cre_U^*) \notin \{(ID_{U_1}, Cre_{U_1}), (ID_{U_2}, Cre_{U_2}), \cdots, (ID_{U_{qc_1}}, Cre_{U_{qc_1}})\}$

$\mathcal{B}$ sends Cre_U^* to SP_l ($ID_{SP_l} \in A_U^*$). SP_l returns the corresponding plaintext $(M_U^*, ID_U^*, K_{UP}^*, T_U^*)$ or $\bot$ for meaningless ciphertext.

1. If $\bot$ is responded, namely D^* is not the corresponding ciphertext of $(M_U^*, ID_U^*, K_{UP}^*, T_U^*)$ under the encryption key K^* encapsulated in Hdr^*, $\mathcal{B}$ aborts. The simulation fails.

2. If the corresponding plaintext $(M_U^*, ID_U^*, K_{UP}^*, T_U^*)$ is responded, namely $\mathcal{A}$ can get the broadcast encryption key K^* from Hdr^*, $\mathcal{B}$ will abort. $\mathcal{B}$ can use $\mathcal{A}$ to break the broadcast encryption scheme. Due to the broadcast encryption is (t, n, qc_1, ϵ_1) CCA-secure, the probability that $(M_U^*, ID_U^*, K_{UP}^*, T_U^*)$ is received is at most ϵ_1.

3. If $\mathcal{B}$ does not abort, he can obtain a valid signature δ^* on $(M_U^*, ID_U^*, K_{UP}^*,$ $T^*)$ at the same advantage ϵ.

Now we compute the probability that $\mathcal{B}$ does not abort. If the broadcast encryption scheme is (t, n, qc_1, ϵ_1) CCA-secure, then $\mathcal{B}$ can abort at most ϵ_1. Therefore, the probability that $\mathcal{B}$ dose not abort during the qc_2 credential verification queries is at least $(1 - \epsilon_1)^{qc_2}$. Thus, the advantage that $\mathcal{B}$ can break the strongly existential unforgeability of the underlying signature scheme is at least $\epsilon.(1-\epsilon_1)^{qc_2}$ which contradicts the assumption that the underlying signature is $(t, qc_2, \epsilon.(1 - \epsilon_1)^{qc_2})$-strongly existentially unforgeable.

Theorem 2. *Our generic construction for DSSO is secure against collusion impersonation attacks if the zero knowledge proofs scheme is secure.*

Proof. Let $\mathcal{A}$ be malicious service providers to whom U has showed credentials and proved the ownership of these credentials. If $\mathcal{A}$ can impersonate U, we will show that there exists an algorithm $\mathcal{B}$ (knowledge extractor) can break the security of the underlying zero knowledge scheme.

If $\mathcal{A}$ can impersonate U to prove that he is the owner of the credentials which U has showed to him, he must execute the ZKP protocol with some service providers to prove that he knows the secret key K_{US} corresponding to the public key K_{UP}. If $\mathcal{A}$ can do this, $\mathcal{B}$ (knowledge extractor) can use the rewinding techniques to obtain the user's secret key K_{US} from two different challenges sent to U and $\mathcal{A}$. So, $\mathcal{B}$ can use $\mathcal{A}$ to break the security of the underlying zero knowledge proofs scheme.

Note that, in our generic construction, the user can not share his credentials with others. Because, if he wants to share one credential with others, he must reveal his secret key K_{US} to them and all credentials of the user will be shared with others. This is the so-called all-or-nothing non-transferability property mentioned at section 4.

Theorem 3. *Our generic construction for DSSO is $(t, qe, qc_1, qc_2, \epsilon)$ -secure against coalition credential forging attacks if the broadcast encryption scheme is (t, n, qc_1, ϵ_1) CCA-secure, the signature scheme is $(t, qc_2, \epsilon.(1 - \epsilon_1)^{qc_2})$-strongly existentially unforgeable.*

Proof. Suppose there exists t-time coalition $\mathcal{A}$ that $(t, qe, qc_1, qc_2, \epsilon)$ can forge a credential for the target user, in which the identifiers of the malicious service providers are not included. We will show that there exists an algorithm $\mathcal{B}$ who can $(t, qc_2, \epsilon.(1-\epsilon_1)^{qc_2})$- break the strongly existential unforgeability of the underlying signature scheme.

Init. Algorithm $\mathcal{B}$ runs $\mathcal{A}$ and receives a target user U^* for whom $\mathcal{A}$ wants to forge a credential and a target service provider SP^* that $\mathcal{A}$ wants to attack.

Setup. $\mathcal{B}$ sends the public parameters PP and IdP's public key K_{IP} to $\mathcal{A}$.

Enrollment queries. $\mathcal{A}$ can adaptively issue enrollment queries $\{RI_{U_1}, RI_{U_2}, \cdots,$ $RI_{U_{qe_1}}\}$, where $RI_{U_i} \neq RI_U^*$, $qe_1 \leq (|\mathbb{U}| - 1)$, and $\{RI_{SP_1}, RI_{SP_2}, \cdots,$ $RI_{SP_{qe_2}}\}$, where $RI_{SP_i} \neq RI_{SP}^*$, $qe_2 \leq (|\mathbb{SP}| - 1)$, and $qe_1 +$ $qe_2 = qe$. $\mathcal{B}$ redirects these queries to the challenger. The challenger returns $\{(ID_{U_1}, A_{U_1}), (ID_{U_2}, A_{U_2}) \cdots, (ID_{U_{qe_1}}, A_{U_{qe_1}})\}$ and $\{(ID_{SP_1}, K_{SP_1}), (ID_{SP_2}, K_{SP_2}), \cdots, (ID_{SP_{qe_2}}, K_{SP_{qe_2}})\}$ respectively.

Credential generation queries. $\mathcal{A}$ can adaptively issue credential generation queries $\{(ID_{U_1}, K_{UP_1}), (ID_{U_2}, K_{UP_2}), \cdots, (ID_{U_{qe_1}}, K_{UP_{qe_1}})\}$. $\mathcal{B}$ redirects these queries to the challenger. The challenger returns $\{Cre_{U_1}, Cre_{U_2}, \cdots,$ $Cre_{U_{qe_1}}\}$, where $Cre_{U_i} = (A_{U_i}, Hdr_i, D_i)$, $D_i = E_K(\delta_i, MU_i, ID_{U_i}, K_{UP_i}, T_i)$ and $\delta_i = \mathsf{Sign}(K_{IS}, MU_i, ID_{U_i}, K_{UP_i}, T_{U_i})$.

Credential verification queries. $\mathcal{A}$ can adaptively issue credential verification queries $\{(ID_{U_1}, K_{UP_1}, Cre_{U_1}), (ID_{U_2}, K_{UP_2}, Cre_{U_2}), \cdots, (ID_{U_{qc_2}}, K_{UP_{qc_2}}, Cre_{U_{qc_2}})\}$. $\mathcal{B}$ redirects these queries to the challenger. The challenger returns $True$ or $False$ by decrypting D_i and verifying δ_i.

Output. $\mathcal{A}$ outputs a credential $Cre_U^* = (A_U^*, Hdr^*, D^*)$, where $(ID_U^*, Cre_U^*) \notin \{(ID_{U_1}, Cre_{U_1}), (ID_{U_2}, Cre_{U_2}), \cdots, (ID_{U_{qc_1}}, Cre_{U_{qc_1}})\}$, $ID_{SP}^* \in A_U^*$ and $ID_{SP} \notin A_U^*$ if $SP \in \mathcal{A}$.

$\mathcal{B}$ sends Cre_U^* to SP^*. SP^* returns the corresponding plaintext $(M_U^*, ID_U^*,$ $K_{UP}^*, T^*)$ or $\perp$ for meaningless ciphertext.

1. If $\perp$ is responded, namely D^* is not the corresponding ciphertext of $(\delta^*, M_U^*,$ $ID_U^*, K_{UP}^*, T^*)$ under encryption key K^* encapsulated in Hdr^*, $\mathcal{B}$ aborts. The simulation fails.

2. If the corresponding plaintext $(M_U^*, ID_U^*, K_{UP}^*, T_U^*)$ is responded, namely $\mathcal{A}$ can compute the broadcast encryption key K^* from Hdr^*, $\mathcal{B}$ will abort. $\mathcal{B}$ can use $\mathcal{A}$ to break the broadcast encryption scheme. Due to the assumption that broadcast encryption is (t, n, qc_1, ϵ_1)CCA-secure, the advantage that $(M_U^*, ID_U^*, K_{UP}^*, T_U^*)$ is responded is at most ϵ_1.

3. If $\mathcal{B}$ does not abort, he can obtain a valid signature δ^* on $(M_U^*, ID_U^*, K_{UP}^*, T_U^*)$ at the same advantage ϵ.

Now, we compute the probability that $\mathcal{B}$ does not abort at the qc_2 credential verification queries. Due to the broadcast encryption scheme is (t, n, qc_1, ϵ_1)CCA-secure, the probability of $\mathcal{B}$ aborts when he gets the corresponding ciphertext is at most ϵ_1 for each decryption query. Therefore the probability of $\mathcal{B}$ dose not abort at the qc_2 decryption queries is at least $(1 - \epsilon_1)^{qc_2}$. So, the probability that $\mathcal{B}$ can break the strongly existential unforgeability of the underlying signature scheme is at least $\epsilon.(1 - \epsilon_1)^{qc_2}$ which contradicts the assumption that the underlying signature scheme is $(t, qc_2, \epsilon.(1 - \epsilon_1)^{qc_2})$-strongly existentially unforgeable.

Theorem 4. *Our generic construction for DSSO is (t, qc, ϵ)-forward secure if the broadcast encryption scheme is (t, n, qc, ϵ)CCA-secure.*

Proof. Suppose there exists a t-time malicious service provider $\mathcal{A}$ that (t, qc, ϵ) breaks the forward security of our generic construction for DSSO. We will show there exists an algorithm $\mathcal{B}$ who can (t, n, qc, ϵ) breaks the CCA security of the broadcast encryption scheme. By A_U^O, we denote the access right of U before $\mathcal{A}$'s identifier is listed in it.

Setup. $\mathcal{B}$ sends public parameter PP, and the IdP's public key K_{IP} to $\mathcal{A}$.

Credential verification queries. $\mathcal{A}$ can adaptively issue credential verification queries $\{(ID_{U_1}, K_{UP_1}, Cre_{U_1}),\ (ID_{U_2}, K_{UP_2}, Cre_{U_2}),\ \cdots,\ (ID_{U_{qc}}, K_{UP_{qc}}, Cre_{U_{qc}})\}$, which are issued after his identifier has been added to A_U. $\mathcal{B}$ redirects these quires to the challenger. The challenger returns $True$ or $False$.

Challenge. $\mathcal{B}$ sends $\mathcal{A}$ an old credential Cre_U^O, where $Cre_U^O = (A_U^O, Hdr_O, D_O)$, $D_O = E_{K_O}(\delta_O, m_U, ID_U, K_{UP}, T_O)$ and $ID_{\mathcal{A}} \notin A_U^O$.

Output. $\mathcal{A}$ outputs a correct verification result $True$ or $Fals$ on credential Cre_U^O at least ϵ.

If it is, $\mathcal{A}$ can decrypt $D_O = E_{K_O}(\delta_O, m_U, ID_U, K_{UP}, T_O)$ at least ϵ. Namely, $\mathcal{A}$ is not a receiver in the broadcast encryption scheme, but can compute the broadcast encryption key K_O from Hdr_O at least ϵ. So, $\mathcal{B}$ can use $\mathcal{A}$ to break the CCA security of the broadcast encryption scheme at least ϵ.

Theorem 5. *Our generic construction for DSSO is (t, qc, ϵ)-backward secure if the broadcast encryption scheme is (t, n, qc, ϵ) CCA-secure.*

The proof is similar to that of theorem 4. We omit the proof due to the page constraint.

6   Conclusion

The current SSO systems suffer from various security issues such as illegally sharing credentials and difficulties in user revocation. In this paper, we formalised the definitions and security models for SSO and DSSO, and proposed a generic scheme of DSSO. Our generic scheme provides a sound solution to these problems. We also provided a formal security proof of our scheme.

Acknowledgement

The first author was supported by PhD scholarships of Smart Services Cooperative Research Centre (CRC) and University of Wollongong.

References

1. Boneh, D., Gentry, C., Waters, B.: Collusion resistant broadcast ecryption with short ciphertexts and private keys. In: Shoup, V. (ed.) CRYPTO 2005. LNCS, vol. 3621, pp. 258–275. Springer, Heidelberg (2005)

2. Boneh, D., Shen, E., Waters, B.: Strongly unforgeable signatures based on computational diffie-hellman. In: Yung, M., Dodis, Y., Kiayias, A., Malkin, T.G. (eds.)
   PKC 2006. LNCS, vol. 3958, pp. 229–240. Springer, Heidelberg (2006)
3. Camenisch, J., Herreweghen, E.V.: Design and Implementation of the idemix
   Anonymous Credential System. In: Atluri, V. (ed.) ACM CCS 2001, pp. 93–118.
   ACM, Innsbruck (2001)
4. Camenisch, J., Lysyanskaya, A.: An efficient system for non-transferable anonymous credentials with optional anonymity revocation. In: Pfitzmann, B. (ed.)
   EUROCRYPT 2001. LNCS, vol. 2045, pp. 93–118. Springer, Heidelberg (2001)
5. Camenisch, J. and Pfitzmann, B.: Federated identity management. In: Petkovic,
   M. and Jonker, W. (eds.), Preceedings: Security, Privacy, and Trust in Modern
   Data Management. Data-Centric Systems and Applications, vol. 2851, pp 213–
   238. Springer, Heidelberg (2007)
6. Cameron, K.: The laws of identity. Architect of Identity. Microsoft Corporation
   (2005)
7. Chen, T., Zhu, B.B., Li, S., Cheng, X.: Threspassport-A distributed single sign-on
   service. In: Huang, D.-S., Zhang, X.-P., Huang, G.-B. (eds.) ICIC 2005. LNCS,
   vol. 3645, pp. 772–780. Springer, Heidelberg (2005)
8. Diffie, W., Hellman, M.E.: New directions in cryptography. IEEE Transactions on
   Information Theory 22(6), 644–654 (1976)
9. Dodis, Y., Fazio, N.: Public key trace and revoke scheme secure against adaptive
   chosen ciphertext attack. In: Desmedt, Y.G. (ed.) PKC 2003. LNCS, vol. 2567, pp.
   100–115. Springer, Heidelberg (2002)
10. Fiat, A., Naor, M.: Broadcast encryption. In: Stinson, D.R. (ed.) CRYPTO 1993.
    LNCS, vol. 773, pp. 480–491. Springer, Heidelberg (1994)
11. Fiege, U., Fiat, A., Shamir, A.: Zero knowledge proofs of identity. In: ACM STOC
    1987, pp. 210–217. ACM, New York (1987)
12. Goldreich, O., Micali, S., Wigderson, A.: Proofs that yield nothing but their va-
    lidity or all languages in NP have zero-knowledge proof systems. Journal of the
    Association for Comptuing Machinery 38(1), 691–729 (1991)
13. Goldwasser, S., Micali, S., Rivest, R.L.: A digital signature scheme secure against
    adaptive chosen-message attacks. SIAM Journal on Computing 17(2), 281–308
    (1988)
14. Goldwasser, S., Micali, S., Rackoff, C.: The knowledge complexity of interactive
    proof-systems. In: ACM STOC 1985, pp. 291–304. ACM, Providence (1985)
15. Josephson, W.K., Sirer, E.G., Schneider, F.B.: Peer-to-peer authentication with
    a distributed single sign-on service. In: Voelker, G.M., Shenker, S. (eds.) IPTPS
    2004. LNCS, vol. 3279, pp. 250–258. Springer, Heidelberg (2005)
16. Kormann, D.P., Rubin, A.D.: Risks of the passport single signon protocol. Com-
    puter Networks 33(1), 51–58 (2000)
17. Liberty Alliance, http://www.projectliberty.org
18. Liberty Alliance. Liberty ID-WSF Authentication Service and Single Sign-On
    Service Specification Version: v2.0,
    http://www.projectliberty.org/liberty/content/download/871/6189/file/
    liberty-idwsf-authn-svc-v2.0.pdf
19. Lysyanskaya, A., Rivest, R.L., Sahai, A., Wolf, S.: Pseudonym systems. In: Heys,
    H.M., Adams, C.M. (eds.) SAC 1999. LNCS, vol. 1758, pp. 184–199. Springer,
    Heidelberg (2000)
20. OECD. OECD Guidelines on the Protection of Privacy and Transborder Flows of
    Personal Datal (1980), http://it.ojp.gov/documents/OECD-FIPs.pdf

21. OpenID, http://openid.net
22. Oppliger, R.: Microsoft .Net passport: a security analysis. Computer 36(7), 29–35 (2003)
23. Oppliger, R.: Microsoft. Net passport and identity managemen. Information Security Technical Report 9(1), 26–34 (2004)
24. Pashalidis, A., Mitchell, C.J.: A taxonomy of single sign-on systems. In: Safavi-Naini, R., Seberry, J. (eds.) ACISP 2003. LNCS, vol. 2727, pp. 249–265. Springer, Heidelberg (2003)
25. Pashalidis, A., Mitchell, C.J.: Single sign-on using trusted platforms. In: Safavi-Naini, R., Seberry, J. (eds.) ISC 2003. LNCS, vol. 2851, pp. 54–68. Springer, Heidelberg (2003)
26. Pashalidis, A., Mitchell, C.J.: Using GSM/UMTS for single sign-on. In: IEEE SympoTIC 2003, pp. 138–145. IEEE, Bratislava (2003)
27. Perlman, R., Kaufman, C.: User-centric PKI. In: Seamons, K., McBurnett, N., Polk, T. (eds.) IDtrust 2008, pp. 59–71. ACM, Gaithersburg (2008)
28. Rehmant, R.U.: Get Ready for OpenID. Conformix Technologies Inc. (2008)
29. Sahai, A., Waters, B.: Fuzzy Identity-Based Encryption. In: Cramer, R. (ed.) EUROCRYPT 2005. LNCS, vol. 3494, pp. 457–473. Springer, Heidelberg (2005)
30. Spantzely, A.B., Camenisch, J., Gross, T., Dieter Sommer, D.: User centricity: a taxonomy and open issues. In: ACM DIM 2006, pp. 1–10. ACM, Alexandria (2006)
31. Suriadi, S., Foo, E., Jsang, A.: A user-centric federated single sign-on system. Journal of Network and Computer Applications 32(2), 388–401 (2009)

DeCore: Detecting Content Repurposing Attacks on Clients' Systems

Smitha Sundareswaran and Anna C. Squicciarini

College of Information Sciences and Technology,
The Pennsylvania State University
{sus263,acs20}@psu.edu

Abstract. Web 2.0 platforms are ubiquitously used to share content and personal information, which makes them an inviting and vulnerable target of hackers and phishers alike. In this paper, we discuss an emerging class of attacks, namely content repurposing attacks, which specifically targets sites that host user uploaded content on Web 2.0 sites. This latent threat is poorly addressed, if at all, by current protection systems, both at the remote sites and at the client ends. We design and develop an approach that protects from content repurposing attacks at the client end. As we show through a detailed evaluation, our solution promptly detects and stops various types of attacks and adds no overhead to the user's local machine or browser where it resides. Further, our approach is light-weight and does not invasively monitor all the user interactions with the browser, providing an effective protection against these new and powerful attacks.

Keywords: Content Repurposing, Malware, Web 2.0, Same Origin Policy, Information Flow.

1   Introduction

The emergence of Web 2.0 has brought with it an upsurge in the use of Web applications and Web-based communities that allow their users to load, store and share their content with others. These social computing platforms are an easy target of hackers and phishers alike, to whom the user content represents a wealth of information.

User uploaded content may potentially include executable files or malware, which have then the ability to access any other content which resides in the site's domain. Malicious files may harvest users' remotely stored sensitive data, and send them back to the hackers who triggered the attack. Further, when such malware is opened on the browsers of the users, it has the ability to access all the information present on their local machines, such as cookies or password files. To prevent these attacks, Web-sites often prevent users from uploading any executables, such as EXE files, or files which may potentially contain executables, such as XML files. These restrictions can be overcome by subverting the legitimately allowed uploadable file types such as images and text files to contain within them other executables. These attacks are referred to as *repurposing attacks*, and are nowadays proliferating. In fact, a number of attack vectors can be crafted to exploit this vulnerability such as botnets [20], different forms of distributed denial of service attacks [28,2] and various forms of malware exploring the internal structure of the Web 2.0 platform.

S. Jajodia and J. Zhou (Eds.): SecureComm 2010, LNICST 50, pp. 199–216, 2010.

Content repurposing has, however, often been used to allow a particular type of file to carry more information than it otherwise would. Examples are steganography [30], where the image is modified to carry messages, and mimic functions [29], where a file is modified to have the statistical properties of another file type. Hence, content repurposing has very important and legitimate uses, even with respect to security of files. A trivial solution such as never allowing repurposed content to be opened can be detrimental to the usability of these methods.

In this work, we thoroughly investigate the effect of misusing content repurposing. We conduct a preliminary analysis focusing on two specific examples of repurposing attacks, which have gained attention from the media [4,3]. The first attack vector, namely the Gifar [4], uses a form of steganography, combining images or any other file types (such as word file or flash etc) with Jar files. The modified file is used to carry the payloads of various attacks that can be triggered when posted on Web portals [9]. The second attack vector consists of repurposing a Flash-file by modifying its ActionScript and combining it with other file types enabling it to be uploaded to any online content management sites [3]. While some patches have been proposed for the Gifar attack [25], users need to update their system by installing the latest version of Java to install the patch. This is often cumbersome for end users [18] and hence may not be a suitable solution. Further, while specific solution exist for certain attacks, we are unaware of any general solution addressing the class of content repurposing attacks. For example, to date Flash-based attacks have not been patched.

We present a slew of attacks which can be launched easily using Gifars and Flash-file. These attacks help us demonstrate the ability of the repurposed content to manipulate and steal information from the local machine of the victim, when these files are opened in the victim's browser. Existing defense mechanisms do not recognize the repurposed files as malicious, nor do they raise an alarm when the attacks are carried out. Our tests also demonstrate that the Gifars and malicious Flash-files can be uploaded to numerous popular Web-sites, including Picasa, Orkut and Friendster. Surprisingly, even common antivirus or antispyware fail in detecting an ongoing attack.

In light of these observations, we propose a new approach to protect against generic content repurposing attacks. Our approach is to silently monitor the content being served to determine if it is repurposed, and subsequently determine whether the events occurring signal an ongoing attack. An attack is detected based on the analysis of the control flow graph, which given a set of inputs and the current state, can be used to predict possible legitimate actions and thus identify illegitimate states. To capture the users' interactions with the browser we rely on DOM (Document Object Model) Events [8], since the DOM forms a representation of the Web page as shown to the user and accepts asynchronous input from the user.

We design the **DeCore** (**De**tecting **Co**ntent **Re**purposing) system using a client-end architecture, since it effectively allows us to monitor the user's interactions with the browser without invasively monitoring the specifics of the input. Further, if the protection is at the server-end, the attacker can overcome server-based protection by hosting the malicious file on a remote server and launching an attack on the end user's system by tricking the user into clicking the link which launches the applet in the malicious file.

We deploy the DeCore using an add-on for Mozilla Firefox, and Google Chrome. As demonstrated by our test results, the add-on adds no overhead to the users local machine or browser where it resides. It also does not invasively monitor all the user interactions with the browser, in that it is not concerned about specific clicks or other input by the user such as text, user ids or passwords.

The rest of the paper is organized as follows. In the next section, we elaborate on the content repurposing attack, and discuss its applicability in existing Web-sites. In Section 3 we present the design of the DeCore followed by the system's implementation in Section 4. DeCore's evaluation and testing are discussed in Section 5. We discuss related works in Section 6 and conclude in Section 7.

2   Content Repurposing Attacks

In this section, we describe how content repurposing attacks can harm users' systems and remote servers, by focusing on two representative types of attack vectors and on a few examples of attacks. Next, we discuss how the current protection mechanisms fare against these attacks.

2.1   Overview of the Content Repurposing Attacks

Content Repurposing attacks take some particular type of content or file type and then modify it by combining it with active file types which contain executables. This maliciously crafted content remains undetected for two main reasons. First, the repurposed content masquerades itself as a benign file. Second, the operations performed by a repurposed file when it is loaded in the browsers are often the same type of operations needed by the Web applications to genuinely perform their tasks. Two popular types of content repurposing attacks are Gifar-based attacks [4] and Flash-based attacks [3]. While our analysis is intended to be general to all content repurposing attacks, we conduct our preliminary investigation with these attacks in mind, since these are the most recent and harmful attacks identified. Other important attacks falling under the umbrella of content repurposing are the recently announced attack utilizing zip files along with steganography to launch malware via emails [22], and attacks on Flash crossdomain policy files, and sniffing the MIME with images in Internet Explorer [25].

Both Java applets and Flash-files leverage the same origin policy (SOP) in Web browsers. The SOP governs access control among different Web objects (such as HTTP cookies, HTML documents, images, JavaScript, CSS files, XML files, etc) and prohibits a Web object from one origin from accessing Web objects from a different origin[17]. By exploiting this rule, the attacker can upload content able to access all data and files on the domain the repurposed content is served from. The malicious content can even be given the capability to browse through the internal network structure of the domain it is uploaded to and also to attack the local machine of a user via the browser.

In their most common form, Gifar-based attacks exploit the fact that when an image file, such as a *.jpg or a *.gif file, is combined with a JAR file, the resulting file can be rendered as a valid image by the browser, while the Java Virtual Machine is capable of recognizing the same as a JAR file. The JAR files contained in the Gifars are applets, which can be used to exploit the victim whose browser the Gifars are running on.

Specifically, the Gifar is created when the attacker combines some malicious applet in the form of a JAR with an image using the command line's copy command. For the attack to be completed, the attacker needs to be able to invoke the applet using an HTML file, like the one shown below:

```
<!DOCTYPE html PUBLIC "-//W3C//DTD HTML 4.01 Transitional//EN"
"http://www.w3.org/TR/html4/loose.dtd">
<html>
<body bgcolor="#dddddd">
<applet code="localfile.class"
archive="file:///C:/Program%20Files/PostgreSQL/EnterpriseDB%20ApachePhp
/apache/www/ drupal/sites/default/files/images/gifar2.gif"
width="100" height="100">
</applet>
</body>
</html>
```

The browser then opens the image containing the applet as a JAR and executes the code in it. The HTML file includes the Gifar the same way any non-malicious applet is usually included, except that the applet tag refers to the Gifar file.

Gifar-based attacks succeed for a number of reasons. First, the Java Runtime Environment does not check the extension of files before parsing the JARs. Further, browsers run any file in the format specified by the underlying HTML code of a given Web page without verifying what the actual extension of the given file is. Third, the other underlying vulnerability which allows all these attacks to succeed is the fact that the most Web portals allow unverified traffic to flow through it.

Flash-based attacks are similar in that they also exploit the fact that the type of file rendered is not verified by the Flash plugin, and the ActionScript used by Flash-file can be used to execute malicious code. The attackers therefore combine malicious Flash-files with any type of zip files or even poorly formed image files, self-extracting executables, Microsoft Office Open XML documents, XPI files, and, even JAR files. The files are combined similarly as in the case of Gifar-based attacks, that is, by using the command lines copy command. These files can then be uploaded to a large number of sites, while remaining undetected. Zip files, for example, can be sent as attachments or uploaded onto any Web-site which stores such files. In order to be executed, these files are simply passed to an Adobe Flash Player, or in case they are sent as attachments, they simply need to be opened by the recipient.

The attacks carried out by content repurposing attacks target integrity, confidentiality and availability of the user's data. We now provide a few examples of attacks, grouped by the security property being violated.

Attacks to confidentiality: Attacks breaching confidentiality usually circumvent security mechanisms which protect user's data. To accomplish this task, content repurposing attacks can be launched to bypass the control of certain authentication protected information in various ways. First, the Gifar can be used to bypass Web-sites' authentication. The user will have to download the JAR file which completes the attack, that can be delivered using a Gifar image. This Gifar retrieves the saved cookies of the user and subsequently uses them for login, using a second program. The program sending the cookies to the attacker is the one which is delivered to the victim in the form of the Gifar. The victim also needs to "launch" this JAR by clicking on a link. This could be the link to an HTML file on a remote server, which has been posted on a social network (SN) site. In order for the cookies based authentication to succeed, the victim should have persistent cookies (i.e. the "Remember me" option is selected on the browser for any sites which require a password-based login). This attack can also be adapted to send all the saved passwords of the victim to the attacker. If the cookies are persistent, then the passwords are stored in easily reachable files in the end-user's local machine. For example, in Mozilla, the saved passwords Firefox are stored in a file called "signons3.txt" (this file varies by the version of the browser the victim uses) -and in `Microsoft Credential File` in Internet Explorer-. This file combined with the "key.db" file of Firefox can be forwarded from the victims system to the attacker in order to allow him to gain all passwords. The same attack can be perpetrated with Flash-files, where the attacker needs also to ensure that user logs in to their account after the malicious file has been loaded onto their browser.

Another type of attack which poses a threat to confidentiality is a remote intrusion attack. By using a repurposed file, the attacker can open an explorer window which allows him to explore the victim's machine from his remote location. In case of a Gifar, the JAR that allows him to open the window exploits the Java Remote Desktop (JRD) so as to provide the attacker a control of the window. The attack begins when the victim opens the Web page which embeds the Gifar image as an applet. The applet then executes and runs the JRD using the Runtime.exec() function, which opens a remote window and connects to the attacker's, allowing him to remotely explore the victim's system. In case of a Flash-based attack, the ActionScript file can be used to exploit the JRD in a similar fashion. In this case too, the attack begins when the Flash-file is loaded onto the browser.

Attacks to availability: In the context of content repurposing, attacks to availability are of two types. One of them is command and control (C&C), where the attacker tries to take over the victim's system by using it as a bot. A C&C attack basically allows the attacker a surreptitious channel to install and execute the files which turn a machine into a bot. The C&C channels are used by the attacker to remotely control the botnets [10]. The Gifars or Flash-files could provide the attacker a distributed C&C channel for the botnets owned by the attacker. The attackers can easily create and embed their server and/or client programs as the JARS or ActionScript files, such that once the HTML page invoking the applet embedded in the Gifar is loaded or the Flash-file is opened in the browser, botnets receive their commands and begin to carry out the malicious operations. The other type of attack is a form of denial of service, where the attacker tries to choke the victim's browser. The JAR file included in the Gifar launches a series of windows to the victim's profile. The page being opened can be a page on the Web site that the attacker wishes. In case of Flash-based attacks, similar actions are carried out by using an ActionScript based code. This attack can further be modified into a DDoS attack. The Web server hosting the Gifar or the malicious Flash-file can be subjected to a DDoS if the attacker posts a number of Gifars (or Flash-files) on different profiles and also sets the number of windows being opened sufficiently high. The attack can be made more disruptive by choosing a page with "heavy" elements like multiple multimedia files.

204 S. Sundareswaran and A.C. Squicciarini

Attacks to integrity: These attacks aim at changing the content of some of the user's files, and may result in the victim's corrupted data, or in a denial of service of sorts. For example, if the attacker modifies the password files of the victim, when the victim tries to log in using a saved password, the authentication would fail. The attacker can additionally issue the commands in the C&C attacks by modifying files stored on the victim's local machine. Another attack which falls under this category is when the attacker tries to modify the remote profile (say in a social network site) or web space of a user. For this attack to succeed, the attacker first needs to bypass the authentication, which constitutes another attack in itself as discussed below.

To assess the potential of content repurposing attacks, we have extensively tested the attacks in real-world settings. We successfully tried Gifar-based attacks on Orkut, Friendster, LiveJournal, Facebook, the art community DeviantArt[1]. These sites allow us to load the Gifar, directly or indirectly via remote links, and the Gifars are stored without modification.

To test Flash-based attacks, we combined Flash-file with image and zip files. DeviantArt allows both uploading modified images and embedding the files directly, as does Orkut. Both DeviantArt and Orkut are the most susceptible to these types of attacks. As with Gifars, Facebook was one of the most resilient sites against the attacks. However, the malicious Flash-files can be directly embedded on a page, such as profile page, or even by including them as part of an HTML based post by using "fb: swf" tag. Therefore, it is not fully immune against such attacks. In LiveJournal, we cannot embed the Flash-file directly, however, we can upload a modified image. Though the attack is not launched without a Flash player (thus making LiveJournal the safest), it leaves a vulnerability waiting to be exploited. Further, Flash-based attacks have been successfully conducted also against email systems, such as Gmail [3].

Finally, we tested the top 5 Antiviruses and the top 5 AntiSpyware[2] as listed by CNet [6,5], and found that none of these softwares detected any of the Gifar files as malicious, nor were they able to recognize the attacks when they were actually going on. The Antiviruses fail to recognize these attacks because these attacks perform functions which are usually carried out by the browser while loading certain pages. For example, the file modification based attacks are not easily recognized because the `Password Files` are modified whenever the user changes a password or asks the browser to remember another password. The AntiSpywares do not recognize content repurposing attacks because the attacks do not necessarily require any visit to malicious sites or to carry out other suspicious activity like displaying advertisements or scanning for personal user information.

2.2 Existing Protection Mechanisms

Current systems try to cope with content-repurposing attacks in various ways, both at the server end and the client end. However, none of these approaches is satisfactory, as

---

[1] LiveJournal is available at www.livejournal.com, Orkut at www.orkut.com. Facebook's site: www.facebook.com, DevianArt is available at www.devianart.com

[2] The programs tested by us were Lavasoft -Ad Aware, Zone Alarms, Tenebril Spycatcher, Webroot Spy Sweeper (SpyCtacher Express -5.1.2), SpywareDoctor, Symantec Endpoint Protection, Kaspersky, Norton Antivirus, BitDefender, F-Secure Antivirus and Avast.

they all suffer from some significant vulnerabilities. Below is an overview of the most common attack defenses currently implemented.

- Using a "throwaway" server for images. That is, the images and other user-uploaded content are stored on a separate server which is not on the same domain as the rest of the content. This approach thwarts content repurposing attack which exploit the SOP as it does not allow for the SOP to be valid. However, this solution can be adopted only by large popular portals as it is not cost effective for smaller ones. Besides,the malicious repurposed files can still be uploaded to some remote site which is owned by the attacker and the attack can be launched the end user's local machine from that site.
- Ensuring that only authenticated scripts can run in the server space. The server can require any script which runs on the server side or searches the database to be authenticated to it. This however does not ensure that authenticated scripts do no leak data. It also does not prevent the repurposed malicious files from using the stored cookies of the client or running scripts on the client's system when the page hosting the malicious content is visited.
- Scrubbing the images when uploaded. Filtering any content which is being up-loaded to a Web application end involves eliminating any associated data with the images such as any metadata and also stripping the images of any code embedded in them. Such filtering of content can be performed at the client end when the content is being uploaded, as is done by Orkut, or it could be done after the content is uploaded to the server. This technique applies only to Gifar-based attacks; its very difficult to remove the content attached to zip files, since zip files as such are meant to carry other file types. Resizing images often causes the embedded code in the Gifar to be corrupted or lost. While filtering the content before it is saved ensures that no malicious content is saved on the server, this approach could also result in certain types of animation or multimedia files being corrupted or spoiled otherwise as these files often have some sort of associated code in Java, JavaScript or PHP. Besides, scrubbing may not always be sufficient to completely remove all the malicious content attached with the image; a sophisticated attacker would be able to still launch the attack by restoring the corrupted content.

Additionally, there are some easy-to-implement 'shortcuts' solutions [14,25], such as avoid the use of persistent cookies to prevent an attacker from bypassing Web-sites authentication. These approaches, however, cannot be deemed as practical solutions because of the popularity of such persistent cookies. Web portals could also opt for limiting/blocking the HTML links posted on their sites. This, however, is not a suitable solution, since the ability to post arbitrary comments contributes largely to the popularity of many content management portals.

As we return later in the paper, using secure browsers like Chrome does not hinder content repurposing attacks because these browsers do not verify whether the content being served is legitimate with respect to the plugins of the applications they are being served by. Verifying the integrity of content uploaded at the front end or ensuring that applications can only access data legitimately required by them is not sufficient either. These checks can be easily circumvented by attackers who can always use different applications to upload malicious content and further attack applications to leak any data legitimately gathered by them.

At all effects, what we are trying to tackle is an information flow problem rather than simply an information integrity one. Hence, our approach is to detect the information flow violations between the targeted Web site, the local systems and any external Web site which is loaded while the original site is being viewed.

3   The DeCore System Design

To protect from repurposing attacks, we have designed a protection mechanism, referred to as *DeCore* (<u>De</u>tecting <u>Co</u>ntent-<u>Re</u>purposing). While our protection system implementation is primarily tailored for the known attacks described in Section 2.1, the DeCore system design is modular, and constitutes a general protection mechanism for both the victim's local system and, to a certain extent, his remote data. The overall design principle of the DeCore system is to monitor the host's observable properties, such as internal state, state transitions (events), and I/O activity to detect and zero-in possible attacks. The DeCore can be successfully deployed at the user-end, or as a component at remote server. Since most of the content repurposing attacks aim at attacking resources on a end-user's machine, however, a client-based solution offers a higher degree of visibility as it is integrated into the host it is monitoring, as an application.

Our architecture is characterized by two main logical components: the *auditor*, and the *detector*.

The DeCore flow auditor. The DeCore System's Auditor is responsible for sensing an ongoing attack. To this extent, its main task is to detect anomalies in the information flow rules that are originally intended by the Web Portal which is being accessed by the user. These anomalies can either be with respect to the content being served or the expected flow of operations.

The auditor detects anomalies by carrying out three main operations: (i) verifying whether all the files being served on a page have the legitimate extensions supported by the plugins, i.e. a Java Plugin is served only a JAR file while a Flash Plugin is served only files with extensions *.swf, *. fxg, *.fla etc. (ii) capturing all the interactions between the user and the browser (iii) matching these interactions with the changes in the files at the end-user's local machine and also checking the displayed content at the Web server's site.

Task (i) is completed by referring to a list of legitimate plugins, and then checking whether the file type being served is the same as the one requested for. To obtain a list of legitimate extensions supported by each of the plugins, the monitor periodically searches the Web for a list of all possible extensions.

To carry out tasks (ii) and (iii), the auditor relies on a *control-flow graph* (CFG, for short). The CFG is a finite labeled graph, constructed upon the user opening a given Website. The CFG captures all the possible interactions between the browsed Web site, the end-user's machine and a remote site in order to identify flows which result in potentially malicious code being run. The nodes represent various possible states the browser can be in and the edges represent the required user input to make a transition between two

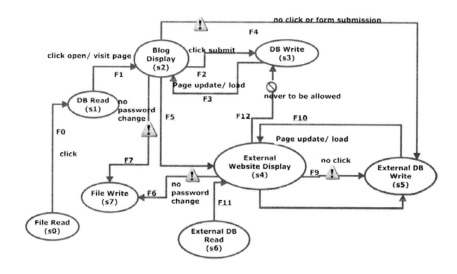

Fig. 1. Example of Control-Flow graph

legitimate states. The CFG is derived by considering all the possible DOM events and JavaScript links by the DeCore after examining the source code of a Web-site.

Example 1. Figure 1 provides an example of a control-flow graph between a blog, the user's local system and an external Web site's domain. In the figure, the edges which are not crossed denote legitimate flows. A crossed edge between the comments or messages, and any entity indicates a malicious operation being performed.

For example, the edge F5 signals a new Web site being opened as a result of the user's click on the blog. A blog could contain a link to a legitimate Web site. Therefore when a connection is launched by clicking the link on the scrap to the external Web site, it may not necessarily be any malicious activity. However, when the external Web site interacts with the user's local machine files using any I/O operation (F6), it signals that an external entity is trying to modify something on the user's local machine.

Once the graph is loaded, the auditor calls the detector which verifies that the information flows from and to legitimate states as prescribed by the graph.

The DeCore Detector. At the heart of the DeCore is the detector. This component interprets CFG violations and reported events from the auditor, and decides whether or not an attack is undergoing. If the system has been compromised, the detector is responsible for responding in an appropriate manner.

The detector has, in turn, several logical subcomponents, each of which checks whether a given type of attack is under progress, and takes some action to either prevent the attack or block it, and to alert the victim. Due to the polymorphic nature of repurposing content attacks, a single approach may not suit all the possible ways according to which this attack vector is exploited. Therefore, similar to an intrusion detection system, with DeCore it is possible to implement several security policies, zeroing-in the different forms of these attacks.

Each policy module leverages the CFG developed by the auditor and runs in tandem with it to detect a particular type of attack. Policy modules can be run stand-alone or in concert with other policy modules. We provide a discussion of three sample policy modules by classifying the attack according to the security property being violated. We chose these policies as examples that illustrate more general paradigms of policy design that can be supported by this architecture.

Attacks to the Integrity: The DeCore System's security policy towards attacks on integrity is to constantly poll the user's data and to notify the user of any seemingly illegitimate change to the data. An illegitimate change is differentiated from a legitimate one by checking if changes to the data take place without explicit input from the user. To avoid false positives in cases where such data may be updated without user interaction, the polling of the data is not done unless the data is located on some location which can be updated only by the user such as the user's local machine or a profile page in a SN or a closed blog.

Attacks to availability: The security policy applied in the case of attacks to availability are based on an event-triggered approach, where any event which can potentially disable the user's control on the system triggers an alarm which stops the event in question from proceeding without the user's approval. Events monitored by this module include the browser choking denial of service attack discussed in Section 2.1.

Attacks to Confidentiality: The security policy for this type of attacks involves monitoring whether any access to the user's data takes place once a page serving suspicious content is opened. Should such an access be detected, the user is notified, to indicate that an attack may be undermining the confidentiality of his documents.

4   The DeCore Implementation

To better understand the implementation difficulties, performance overhead, and practical effectiveness of our architecture, we implemented the DeCore System as a browser plug-in. We purposely encoded most of the add-on in JavaScript and using JAR files, so as to ensure its portability to any browser. All references to the files and file paths were left platform independent, thus making it compatible with different platforms and file systems. To port the DeCore onto a specific browser or OS, the files references must be configured according to the chosen platform. Further, the DeCore is well compatible with sandboxed environments, such as Google Chrome. As long as the source code of the Web-site is visible to the add-on, the DeCore can monitor the response obtained by the HTTP Servlet which allows the getHeader method to obtain a valid response. Therefore it can detect when any repurposed content is being obtained in response to the request.

4.1   The DeCore Auditor Implementation

The DeCore Auditor checks whether the file being served is repurposed by verifying that the file has an extension type supported by the plugin requesting it.To obtain a

Algorithm 1. Algorithm to detect attacks launched using repurposed content

```
 1: Send HTTP GET request
 2: Response.type:= text/html
 3: Enumeration headerNames:= request.getHeaderNames()
 4: plugins − type: = pluginspage[type]
 5: array extensions [] = "http://www.google.com/search?q=".plugins-type."+extensions"
 6: for i ← 1 to length(extensions[]) do
 7:    if extensions[i] == headerNames then
 8:        status:= "No Attack"
 9:    else
10:        status:= "Attack Suspected"
11:    end if
12: end for
```

list of legitimate extensions supported by each of the plugins, the monitor periodically searches the Web for a list of all possible extensions. It determines the type of file being served to the page by running a small Java-based program which sends a request to the domain serving the files on behalf of the Web site using the getHeader method of the HttpServletRequest. The pseudo code for this type of validation is presented in Algorithm 1.

As content repurposing attacks are carried out by completing a few seemingly normal events such as redirection to an external Web site from a source site, or reading of the password file, the auditor verifies that none of the possible states modeled by the CFG is reached without the DOM events which are needed to ensure a legitimate transition to the given state. The DOM is a platform-independent, event-driven interface which accepts input from the user and allows programs and scripts to access and update the content of the page. The CFG itself is derived by the DeCore using a Java program which reads each line of the source code of a Web-site, considers all the JavaScript links, buttons, boxes and form elements, and HTML links, buttons, checkboxes and form elements to derive the CFG. The CFG takes into account all the possible actions which require a user's input and any actions which result in redirection to another page or the opening of a new window or tab. DOM events that are not caused by the user's interaction or input are indicative of a possible attack[3].

For example, the flow monitor checks that all the page load and window load events are actually caused by other DOM events such as mouse clicks. The mouse clicks indicate a user's interaction with the elements on the Web browser.

If any of these two conditions are violated, that is, if the states in the CFG are reached without the required DOM events or there is a violation in the flow, then an attack is assumed to be ongoing. Further, to improve detection accuracy, the auditor, besides correlating DOM events, checks whether DOM events such as keystrokes and mouse clicks are carried on at a legitimate rate for a human user. While it is possible for an attacker to simulate such keystrokes at a reasonable rate, these attacks would entail an

---

[3] An exception to this rule occurs when the user has set some preferences which allow the browser to carry out some actions automatically, such as to automatically launch a prefixed number of tabs upon being opened the first time.

unlikely level of sophistication. Such simulation requires the use of sophisticated HCI models such as GOMS and UIMs besides a huge database of similar activity by a human being [15,26]. Finally, in order to minimize possible attempts of this type, the system requests feedback from the end user upon detecting an attack. For example, DeCore notifies the user when a Gifar attack is suspected through event-delivery notifications. These methods are discussed in detail below.

4.2   The DeCore Detector Implementation

We have four separate JavaScript components which enforce the security policy modules discussed in Section 3. Two of three sample policy modules of the detector consist of an individual JavaScript component (i.e. a single file) that leverages the detector framework, while one policy module is implemented using two JavaScript components. The implementation details of the security policy for each module is given below.

Attacks to the Integrity: Our integrity checker attempts to detect if the victim system files are being modified by periodically using nsIFile functions [23]. A nsIFile instance allows for a cross-platform representation of a location in the file system. Once an nsIFile instance is created, it can be used to navigate to ancestors or descendants of a given file or directory without having to deal with the different path separators used on different platforms. It can also be used to query the state of any file or directory at the position represented by the nsIFile and create, move or copy items in the file system independent of the platform on which the file is located. An nsIFile can be retrieved by either instantiating an nsILocalFile using a platform specific path string or by using cross-platform locations retrieved from the directory service. This approach is particularly well suited to securing files across multiple OS without intrusive monitoring of the user's file system. For example, if files are downloaded from the site which is suspected to host a Gifar attack, and not correlated to the user's event, the attack is deemed as started. The user is then alerted of a possible attack and asked to close the Web site hosting the Gifar. Further, if there is a change to the file system while the attack page is opened, the user is alerted to the changes.

Another example of attack to the victim's integrity is as follows. The attack can target remotely stored user-generated content in social computing platforms, such as SNs, and blogs. Once the malicious file is opened, it can, for example, add spamming content malicious links or modify the user posted content. To prevent this attack, at the time the monitor suspects an attack, the detector periodically checks for unexpected (and not-user driven) modifications in the rendered content, while the Web page hosting the suspected Gifar is open. To limit the scope of the monitoring, the DeCore detects whether the page being served is the user's profile in case of a SN, or some closed site which cannot be modified without the user's input (such as his blog). Specifically, when one of such pages is accessed, a JavaScript-based component checks whether the last modifications occurred upon the user submitting a form, on the Web site, and matches the same to changes in the content. If the modification on the rendered content is not corresponding to some user input and a Gifar is being detected by the monitor, the user is alerted of a possible attack and asked to close the Web site hosting the suspicious Gifar. Notice that this approach in turn helps tracking whether the SN's database is being modified by some external code, while not requiring any interaction with the server, since the detection is based on data collected from the DeCore at the client-end. For other types of sites, the user can create a list of such sites that the DeCore should control, along with a list of sites to be excluded from the controls. In fact, the user can also indicate sites which by nature refresh dynamically their content (without generating DOM events), such as scoreboards or games, and therefore should not be monitored.

Attacks to availability: The module addressing the security policy for this attack takes a event-driven approach, by checking for page load events and mouse click events, and taking action upon certain conditions are verified. To avoid false positives, this detector's module checks whether the number of mouse click events are not only the same as the number of page events, but also that they were executed at the same rate as the loaded pages. If the difference between the mouse click and page load events, say x, is larger than a choking threshold μ (where $\mu << x$), an attack is deemed under way. A choking attack is also assumed to be going on if a very large number of pages (where the number of pages y is greater than a threshold β) is opened within a very short period of time (where the time is less than δ seconds)The user is then alerted to a possible attack and asked whether he wants to continue opening multiple pages.

Attacks to Confidentiality: The DeCore enforces the general security policy for such attacks by monitoring the file systems of the end user's local machine for any access. We use the `FileSystemWatcher` class in Java. This command is run in a loop till such time the window hosting the suspicious files is closed. The `FileSystemWatcher` class has an option called the `notifyfilter`. This option allows us to monitor whether the last access time of any of the files on a file system is changed. Should such a change occur, we notify the user, or depending on the user's confirmation, take more proactive actions such as encrypting the file. While possible to prevent access on the basis of the process accessing the files, we choose not to because doing this requires an invasive level of monitoring.

The JavaScript components used by DeCore are not dependent on the particular approach used by the attack but rather look for specific outcomes or effects produced by an attack. For example, for the choking attack, we check for multiple requests opening multiple pages from the user's system. We do not check for specific pages being opened, nor do we check for the signature of a particular DoS attack. In this way, the DeCore covers the class of attacks where a victim's browser is rendered useless to him as it is taken over by a malicious script.

5   The DeCore Evaluation

Our experiments were performed on a Dell Latitude D630 Laptop, with 2G Ram and a Intel(R) Core(TM)2 Duo CPU T7500 @ 2.20GHz processor. We conducted two separate set of tests. First, we tested the system's overhead. Second, we assessed the accuracy of the DeCore. Both the tests were conducted twice, once for Firefox and once for Google Chrome. The results presented below apply to both the add-on for both the browsers. This is because except the basic construction of the add-on itself, the rest of the code for detecting the various attacks does not change.

In the first set of tests, we compared the execution time for the browser with and without the DeCore add-on. We specifically recorded the time for opening new sessions with multiple tabs. We varied the number of tabs from 0 to 60 and the number of windows from 1 to 6. In order to ensure accurate results, each test run was carried out according to the following steps. First, we disabled the plugin, loaded a page over a quiescent network, and determined how long the page took to load. Next, we cleared the cache for the following run. When collecting data for the DeCore-enabled browser, the same methodology was used, but we first enabled the plugin, at each run. We reported no overhead caused by the DeCore and the exact same time was taken for the operations both with and without the add-on. The time required for Firefox to start was always around 1 ms. This time included only the time it takes for Firefox to start as a process by the system, and did not factor in the time taken to make the Firefox available for use. Further, we checked the maximum CPU usage and found that the difference in the percentage of CPU usage was less than $\pm$ 2 ms (for example, for 0 tabs with 1 window, when the Firefox session is being restored the usage was 47 % with the add-on and 46 % without the add-on. The usage for the Firefox session being restored with 6 windows and 60 tabs was 56 % without the add-on and 54 % with the add-on). We obtained similar results for Chrome. The major difference between the Firefox and Chrome testing was that in Chrome we cannot open multiple windows as in Firefox, so we just opened multiple tabs. Again, we reported no overhead in the case of Chrome either and the same time was taken for the operation with and without the add-on.

Our second set of tests aimed at verifying the accuracy of the DeCore. To this extent, we carried out several different experiments of increasing complexity on both the browsers. First, we begin with assessing false positive rates, i.e. whether the DeCore would falsely detect a page with benign Java and/or JavaScript components as a page hosting a Gifar. The tests were carried out by having the DeCore running while 100 different sites were visited to test the accuracy of our system when it is continuously monitoring for content-repurposing attacks. The sites were selected based on their popularity and on the presence of active components. The sites visited by us included popular gaming sites (such as *Games.com* and *Miniclip Games*), which often utilize JAR files and JVM to allow their users to run the games, magazines (such as *Elle* and *Glamour*) and blogs. With our second round of experiments, the page hosting the malicious files had benign components. Specifically, we created 100 sites, each of which embedded some variant of the attacks, such as the denial of service attacks or remote intrusion attacks. The actual attack code varied for each try, so as to create polymorphic attack code. To create the variations of the attack code, we introduced random NOP blocks in each attack to introduce random delays. Further, we combined one or more attacks with each other. Also, the page invoking the malicious content was different for each try. The elements we included in each page consisted of one or more of the following: images, videos, audio components such as wmv files, other benign JARs carried in applets but not embedded in images, text documents, hyperlinks, Java buttons, JavaScript buttons, JavaScript forms, zip files, Microsoft Office Open XML documents, XPI files, benign SWFs and simple games. The DeCore proved to be accurate in both set of tests, detecting the attacks correctly, regardless of the attack type. Finally, we created a new test case by launching multiple attacks at the same time. We crafted attacks so as to combine more than one content-repurposing attack on a single HTML page. We constructed the attacks in two alternative forms: we either hosted multiple repurposed files in a same page, or created a file which would carry out different attacks in a single file. Both Gifar and Flash-attacks were tested. With this attack, we were not only interested in checking whether the DeCore could identify and stop the launched attacks, but also whether the detection of one attack could slow down the detection of the subsequent ones. We tested 15 different attacks . The different types of attack were constructed by combining the attacks discussed in Section 2.1 with one another. We focused on some non-trivial attacks, namely five attacks with 2 repurposed files hosted at each page, five attacks with 3 repurposed files and 2 combinations of all the 4 repurposed files, resulting a total of 15 different types of attacks. We ran this experiment by hosting web pages on a secure remote PHP server and also on a server hosted on the same local machine where the DeCore system was deployed as a plugin. None of the attacks were successful. For example, the file modification attack was always detected with a delay less than 1 ms. Subtler attacks, such as bypassing the authentication, fail as well, since the victim's hard drives are always protected before the attack can be completed, thereby causing the attack to abort (hence, rendering the combination of attacks useless). The time required to complete any single attack to execute is (order of 100 ms) significantly higher than the time required for our detection script to run (order of 0.01 ms). The only delay was recorded when testing the choking attack in combination with 2 or 3 other attacks. Specifically, the attacks placing the choking attack as the last one being launched, resulted in the attack being started before any warning was raised by the DeCore. We found that unless the delay in detecting the attacks is a magnitude higher than 100ms (which never happens with out implementation), the chance of this attack being successful is negligible. Therefore, we conclude that the DeCore proves to be an effective protection mechanism, with respect to all types of content repurposing attacks.

6   Related Work

In this section we summarize some of the most closely related approaches recently proposed to thwart attacks similar to the ones we tackled in this paper. There are two parallel lines of work that are of interest to us: monitoring-based systems [21,12] and information flow control strategies [1,13].

In [11] an approach similar to ours has been proposed for Ajax intrusion detection. The authors develop a monitor which matches if the series of requests received by the server is similar to an abstract request graph previously derived. While similar to our approach, Guha and colleagues focus on the response to the server from the client. Therefore, they mainly address server-based attacks, while the DeCore is geared toward attacks carried out at the client end. However, we also plan to enable our solution to detect server-based attacks in the future. Further, the proposed system needs to run as proxy between the server and the client, which evaluates the response from the client machine. Our solution is less invasive and does not rely on the response from the client to the server for its detection, thus succeeding at detecting attacks that affect only the client machine and provide feedback to the victim.

A similar approach to the above is taken in [7] by Dhawan et al. The authors develop a system which uses in-browser information tracking to analyze JavaScript extensions.

We borrowed from this work the idea of using information flow by considering the DOM events, to investigate whether sensitive data is being leaked. However, Dhawan's approach is applicable to JavaScript Extensions, and it does not monitor the malicious behavior of any outside code, nor does it detect Java-based attacks. Also, unlike us, the implemented prototype requires modifications to the interpreter of Firefox, viz. Spider-Monkey.

The work by Karlof et al. also looks at attacks which sends the browser malicious JavaScript [17]. The authors focus on *Dynamic Pharming* attacks, that exploit DNS-rebinding vulnerabilities DNS and the name-based SOP to hijack a legitimate session after authentication has taken place. The solution presented, however, is completely different from ours. The authors propose two locked SOPs for web browsers. As opposed to the normal SOP, which regulates cross-object access control in browsers using domain names, the locked SOPs enforce access using servers' X.509 certificates and public keys.

Since content-repurposing attacks can be classified as stemming from information flow problems, the other way to tackle such attacks is by monitoring information flow. One of the widely accepted approaches to information flow monitoring involves using security typed languages such as JIF, Caml etc. JiF (Java - Information Flow) [13] is a security-typed programming language that extends Java with support for information flow control and access control, which is enforced at both compile and run time. Static information flow control could be used to protect the confidentiality and integrity of information as it is being manipulated by computing system. JiF can also be used to reduce the exposure of data to online organizations [13]. However in order for this approach to work, it is essential to know all the parties which are legitimately involved in an exchange and further to know what each party is allowed to receive. Since it is not possible for a third party application, which is situated at the client end, to know about all the information flow requirements without access to the SN's database or client input, this approach is not suitable.

A reference monitor, such as the Shamon architecture[21], has been often used to regulate the flow of information within the system and the between the processes. With the use of remote attestation and virtual machines [12], the traditional guarantees offered by the reference monitor may be extended to provide the same guarantees on multiple machines, and thereby on the Internet scale. The disadvantage with reference monitors is that they are usually very heavy to implement due to their reliance on authentication. Further, they monitor all the system processes, but afford little help in maintaining the information flow in the browser. Sun released a patch to prevent Gifar attacks. Upon testing by installing JRE 6 Update 13 on a Windows XP Dell Latitude D630 Laptop, with 2G Ram and a Intel(R) Core(TM)2 Duo CPU T7500 @ 2.20GHz processor, we found the patch to be ineffective against the attacks. Further, this patch does not solve the general issue of content repurposing attacks and is directed only at attacks which affect the Sun's Java Plugins.

Finally, AjaxScope [19], BrowserShield [24], and CoreScript [31] secure the browsers by rewriting HTML and JavaScript. They convert any embedded scripts into safe equivalents by placing filters at run time to protect against known attacks. While this approach could be adapted so as to include some content repurposing attacks in the list of attacks checked for, it still cannot monitor, detect or prevent the actual attacks on the end-user's machine once an attack is launched.

7   Discussion and Concluding Remarks

In this paper we presented a light-weight and effective tool to protect against an emerging class of attacks, namely, content repurposing attacks. This latent threat is poorly if at all addressed by current protection systems, both at the remote sites and locally by antivirus and antispyware. We designed and developed the DeCore, which tool promptly detects a number of possible content repurposing attacks and adds no overhead to the users local machine or browser where it resides. It also does not invasively monitor all the user interactions with the browser. Further, the DeCore effectively stops any ongoing attack. Next, we will improve the accuracy of our system's detection, by enabling detection for subtle attacks. Currently, we cannot determine whether the malicious applet is trying to steal information from password files or whether it is simply scanning the local machine's file system. We are exploring how to supplement the add-on to detect additional attacks by adding more JavaScript based components.

Acknowledgements. The work reported in this paper has been partially supported by the NSF grant CNS 08-31247 (2008-2012).

References

1. Askarov, A., Sabelfeld, A.: Secure implementation of cryptographic protocols: A case study of mutual distrust. In: di Vimercati, S.d.C., Syverson, P.F., Gollmann, D. (eds.) ESORICS 2005. LNCS, vol. 3679, pp. 197–221. Springer, Heidelberg (2005)
2. Auger, R., et al.: Threat classification - denial of service, http://www.Webappsec.org/projects/threat/classes/denial_of_service.shtml
3. Bailey, M.: Foreground Security.Superior Security. Visible Results - Flash Origin Policy Issues, http://foregroundsecurity.com/MyBlog/flash-origin-policy-issues.html
4. Brandis, R.: Exploring below the surface of the gifar iceberg. Whitepaper (February 2009)
5. CNET. Cnet Antivirus Software, http://download.cnet.com/windows/antivirus-software/?sort=editorsRating+asc&tag=mncol;pm
6. CNET. Top 10 Anti Spyware Software, http://www.top10list.com/top,10,spyware,software/top-ten-spyware-protection.asp
7. Dhawan, M., Ganapathy, V.: Analyzing Information Flow in JavaScript-based Browser Extensions. In: ACSAC 2009: Proceedings of the 2009 Annual Computer Security Applications Conference (December 2009)
8. Document object model (dom) level 2 events specification. W3C Specifications (November 2000), http://www.w3.org/TR/DOM-Level-2-Events/
9. Grossman, J.: Top ten Web hacking techniques of 2008 (official) (February 2009)
10. Gu, G., Zhang, J., Lee, W.: Botsniffer: Detecting botnet command and control channels in network traffic. In: 15th Annual Network and Distributed System Security Symposium, NDSS 2008 (February 2008)

11. Guha, A., Krishnamurthi, S., Jim, T.: Using static analysis for ajax intrusion detection. In: WWW 2009: Proceedings of the 18th international conference on World wide Web. ACM, New York (2009)
12. Haldar, V., Chandra, D., Franz, M.: Semantic remote attestation - a virtual machine directed approach to trusted computing. In: Third virtual Machine Research and Technology Symposium. USENIX (2004)
13. Hicks, B., Ahmadizadeh, K., McDaniel, P.: From languages to systems: Understanding practical application development in security-typed languages. In: 22nd Annual Computer Security Applications Conference (2006)
14. Inferno's blog on application security. Easy server side fix for the gifar security issue (January 2009) http://securethoughts.com/2009/01/easy-server-side-fix-for-the-gifar-security-issue/
15. John, B.E., Vera, A., Matessa, M., Freed, M., Remington, R.: Automating CPM-Goms. In: Computing Human Interaction (2002)
16. Jackson, C., Bortz, A., Boneh, D., Mitchell, J.C.: Protecting browser state from web privacy attacks. In: Proceedings of the 15th ACM World Wide Web Conference (2006)
17. Karlof, C., Shanka, U., Tygar, J.D., Wagner, D.: Dynamic pharming attacks and locked same-origin policies for web browsers. In: 14th ACM Conference on Computer and Communications Security (2007)
18. Keizer, G.: Typical Windows user patches every 5 days Computer World, http://www.computerworld.com/s/article/9165738/Typical_Windows_user_patches_every_5_days
19. Kiciman, E., Livshits, B.: Ajaxscope: A platform for remotely monitoring the client-side behavior of Web 2.0 applications. In: ACM SOSP Symposium on Operating Systems Principles (2007)
20. MacVittie, L.: The Web 2.0 botnet: Twisting twitter and automated collaboration, http://devcentral.f5.com/Weblogs/macvittie/archive/2009/04/13/the-Web-2.0-botnet-twisting-twitter-and-automated-collaboration.aspx
21. McCune, J.M., Jaeger, T., Berger, S., Caceres, R., Sailer, R.: Shamon: A system for distributed mandatory access control. In: Computer Security Applications Conference (2006)
22. Mills, E.: Cnet news. Researchers warn of malware hidden in.zip files (April 2010), http://news.cnet.com/8301-27080_3-20002542-245.html
23. nsIFile - Mozilla development center. Developer's Guide (May 2009)
24. Reis, C., Dunagan, J., Wang, H.J., Dubrovsky, O., Esmeir, S.: Browsershield: Vulnerability-driven filtering of dynamic html. In: USENIX OSDI Symposium on Operating Systems Design and Implementation (2006)
25. Rios, B.: Billy (bk) Rios, Thoughts on security in an uncivilized world. Blog, http://xs-sniper.com/blog/ (Last Accessed: February, 2010)
26. Ritter, F.E., Baxter, G.J., Jones, G., Young, R.M.: Supporting cognitive models as users. ACM Transactions on Computer-Human Interaction 7 (2000)
27. Giffin, J., Sharif, M., Singh, K., Lee, W.: Understanding precision in host based intrusion detection. In: Kruegel, C., Lippmann, R., Clark, A. (eds.) RAID 2007. LNCS, vol. 4637, pp. 21–41. Springer, Heidelberg (2007)
28. Ur, B.E., Ganapathy, V.: Evaluating attack amplification in online social networks. In: W2SP 2009: 2009 Web 2.0 Security and Privacy Workshop (May 2009)
29. Wayner, P.: Mimic Functions. Cryptologia XVI(3) (1992)
30. Wayner, P.: Disappearing cryptography. In: Information Hiding: Steganography & Watermarking, 3rd edn. MK/Morgan Kaufmann Publishers, San Francisco (2009)
31. Yu, D., Chander, A., Islam, N., Serikov, I.: JavaScript instrumentation for browser security. In: ACM SIGPLAN-SIGACT Symposium on Principles of Programming Languages (2007)

Realizing a Source Authentic Internet*

Toby Ehrenkranz[1], Jun Li[1], and Patrick McDaniel[2]

[1] Department of Computer and Information Science
University of Oregon
Eugene, OR 97403 USA
{tehrenkr,lijun}@cs.uoregon.edu
[2] Department of Computer Science and Engineering
Pennsylvania State University
University Park, PA 16802 USA
mcdaniel@cse.psu.edu

Abstract. An innate deficiency of the Internet is its susceptibility to IP spoofing. Whereas a router uses a forwarding table to determine where it should send a packet, previous research has found that a router can similarly employ an incoming table to verify where a packet should come from, thereby detecting IP spoofing. Based on a previous protocol for building incoming tables, SAVE, this paper introduces new mechanisms that not only address a critical deficiency of SAVE when it is incrementally deployed (incoming table entries becoming obsolete), but can also push the filtering of spoofing packets towards the SAVE router that is closest to spoofers. With these new mechanisms, and under the assumption of incremental deployment, we further discuss the security of SAVE, evaluate its efficacy, accuracy, and overhead, and look into its deployment incentives. Our results show incoming-table-based IP spoofing detection is a feasible and effective solution.

Keywords: IP spoofing, IP source address, IP spoofing detection, incoming table, pushback.

1 Introduction

Attackers today can send packets pretending to be from any Internet address. Any host on the Internet can be a victim of such "spoofing" attacks. Even in today's botnet infested Internet, an attacker prefers to use IP spoofing whenever possible. While the attacker may simply spoof a victim's address to hide the real attack source, it is very likely the victim address is the focus of a targeted attack. For example, only through IP spoofing can an attacker perform DNS amplification (subverting DNS servers to perform a bandwidth-based DDoS attack [1,2]),

---

* This material is based upon work supported by the USA National Science Foundation under Grant No. 0520326. Any opinions, findings, and conclusions or recommendations expressed in this material are those of the authors and do not necessarily reflect the views of the National Science Foundation.

S. Jajodia and J. Zhou (Eds.): SecureComm 2010, LNICST 50, pp. 217–234, 2010.

reset a victim's TCP connections (sending spoofed TCP reset packets with in-window sequence numbers [3]), poison a DNS cache (transparently redirecting victims to the attacker's server [4]), or circumvent spam filters (getting around mail blocks an ISP may place on a botnet's zombie machines [5,6]). Although the underlying threat of IP spoofing is not new, the problem continues to worsen: attackers persist in finding new ways of crafting attacks using spoofed IP packets, and attackers can spoof from a greater portion of the Internet than before [6].

If every network in the world was able to coordinate a deployment of even simple ingress filtering [7] and unicast reverse path forwarding [8] checks, the threat would be all but eliminated. Unfortunately due to both technical and logistical reasons, this is an unattainable goal [9]. When even a small percentage of networks do not deploy such basic filtering methods, nobody is safe. Everyone's Internet address is still at risk of being spoofed. Researchers have proposed more sophisticated spoofing prevention mechanisms over the years [9], but all have failed to neutralize the threat of IP spoofing.

Fortunately there has been promising research, showing that if even a *small* percentage of routers on the Internet deploy a more finely grained filtering table to discard packets with a forged source address, a synergistic filtering effect can be achieved to stop a large fraction of spoofed IP packets [10,11]. SAVE [12,13] is a light-weight protocol to build such a filtering table, called an *incoming table*, at routers. As a router has multiple physical interfaces to receive incoming packets, every entry of the incoming table specifies the valid incoming interface for packets from a specific IP address prefix to arrive at the router. A recent survey [9] has further shown that compared to other IP spoofing prevention methods, using an incoming table to filter spoofed packets is the most effective.

Although SAVE provides the incoming tables necessary for effective filtering with only a small deployment, the SAVE protocol itself faces a serious challenge when incrementally deployed. A router's incoming table that is up-to-date at time t may become obsolete at some time after t because of routing changes on the Internet. We describe how a router's incoming table becomes obsolete below.

In the SAVE protocol, every SAVE-capable router that is in charge of a source address space *periodically* sends updates to its downstream routers about the *current* incoming interface for the source address space. Furthermore, when a routing change occurs at any downstream router, that router must send out a new update immediately to ensure routers further downstream learn the new valid incoming interface of the source address space in question. Otherwise, those routers will stay out of date until the next periodical update. However, legacy routers that do not run SAVE will simply do nothing when a routing change occurs; legacy routers will never initiate a SAVE update! As shown by the example in Figure 1(a) and 1(b), if R was a legacy router, the lack of SAVE update from R after its routing change will cause the SAVE-capable router T's incoming table about packets from router S to be out of date (until the next periodic SAVE update from S reaches T).

As SAVE is incrementally deployed, there will be many legacy routers, probably even outnumbering SAVE-capable routers for a long time; *it is highly likely*

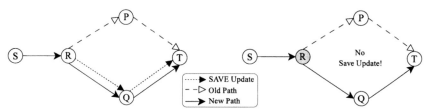

(a) R is a SAVE router and initiates a SAVE update when the link from R to P is broken. T's incoming table is updated to show that packets from S should come from its lower left incoming interface.

(b) R is a legacy router so it does *not* initiate a SAVE update when the link from R to P is broken. T's incoming table is out of date, still showing packets from S should come through upper left incoming interface.

Fig. 1. An example showing how an incoming table can contain obsolete entries

that incoming tables at SAVE-capable routers will often contain obsolete entries. While it is promising to use incoming tables to stop spoofed packets, it is also difficult to use them if they carry obsolete entries.

In this paper we make the following fundamental contributions: We study if we can introduce new mechanisms to enable SAVE-capable routers to reliably discard spoofing packets, even though their incoming table may be obsolete. In particular, we devise and evaluate three new elements that a SAVE-capable router can employ: a blacklist data structure, an on-demand-update mechanism, and a pushback mechanism.

- *Blacklist*: The blacklist complements the incoming table at a router in classifying an incoming packet, including determining if the packet is spoofed.
- *On-demand update*: A SAVE-capable router can request SAVE updates on demand to verify possibly incorrect or outdated information.
- *Pushback*: SAVE-capable routers along the way of a spoofing flow can push the filtering of spoofed packets to the router that is the closest to the spoofer.

In combination, these new elements allow SAVE to function properly even in the presence of legacy routers. Referring back to the example in Figure 1(b), T can request an on-demand update from S, essentially replacing the triggered SAVE update in Figure 1(a). The blacklist gives a router more state information, so the router does not need to request an on-demand update for every packet that does not match the incoming table. Finally, the pushback mechanism serves two purposes. First, it helps to reduce spoofing traffic by dropping spoofing packets as close to the attacker as possible. Second, it tells a router in charge of a source address space when downstream routers have incorrect information in their blacklists regarding its address space.

Also of great importance is the security of SAVE with these new mechanisms. SAVE must secure itself against all possible attacks. Not only may attackers try to evade the IP spoofing detection at SAVE routers, they may also attempt to introduce illegal control messages. For example, an attacker (or a bot machine it controls) could try to establish wrong incoming information at SAVE routers by injecting a SAVE update about a source address it is going to spoof. In this paper, we also discuss how security can be addressed.

Our evaluation demonstrates the viability of these new mechanisms. We perform a detailed simulation to evaluate their effectiveness at detecting spoofing packets, and explore the relationship between efficacy and adoption rates. These Internet-scale simulations show that with as little as 0.08% deployment, attackers cannot spoof protected source addresses in over 90% of all cases. Moreover, we evaluate the storage, traffic, and computational overhead of SAVE with the new mechanisms, showing that the overhead is low.

The rest of the paper is organized as follows. We first describe how a SAVE router can introduce a blacklist alongside the incoming table to help classify incoming packets in Section 2. We then describe the on-demand-update mechanism and the pushback mechanism in Sections 3 and 4, respectively. Section 5 discusses how SAVE can secure itself. We present our evaluation in Section 6, with open issues discussed in Section 7. Finally, we discuss related work in Section 8, and conclude our paper in Section 9.

2   Incoming Table, Blacklist, and Packet Classification

In addition to an incoming table described above, we add to every SAVE-capable router a blacklist data structure. With both the incoming table and the blacklist, a router classifies incoming packets into several different types, and takes some action specific to each of those types. In this section we describe the blacklist data structure and classification mechanism.

2.1   Blacklist

Whereas the incoming table of a router specifies the legitimate incoming interfaces for different source address spaces, the blacklist indicates whether an incoming packet is *spoofing* based on its source address, destination address, and the incoming interface. More specifically, a router's blacklist is maintained through two separate blacklists corresponding to two different ways of matching an incoming packet against a blacklist entry:

SI: Matches the source address and the incoming interface of the packet.
SD: Matches the source address and the destination of the packet.

A router receiving spoofing packets that match its SI blacklist could be on the legitimate path from the spoofed source to the destination, but not from the spoofing packet's incoming direction. A router receiving spoofing packets that match its SD blacklist should not be on the legitimate path from the spoofed source to the destination, and so should never see a packet with such a source and destination.

2.2 Packet Classification

With both its incoming table and blacklist in place, a router classifies an incoming packet as:

- *Valid* if it matches the incoming table but not the blacklist.
- *Suspicious* if it matches neither the incoming table nor the blacklist.
- *Invalid* if it matches the blacklist.
- *Unknown* if there is no information regarding the packet's source address.

Only when the packet is classified as invalid will the router drop the packet. For the other three types the router will forward the packet.

Furthermore, if a packet is suspicious, the router will initiate the on-demand-update mechanism. The packet is suspicious either because the packet is spoofing, or because the packet is legitimate but the router's incoming direction information is outdated. As we described in Section 1, the routing change at a legacy router upstream will not lead to an immediate SAVE update for this router to update its incoming table.

If a packet is invalid, the router will initiate the pushback mechanism. No further actions are taken for valid or unknown packets.

We describe both on-demand-update and pushback in the following sections, including how they deal with obsolete incoming table entries.

3 On-demand Update

When a router classifies a packet as suspicious, it still forwards the packet as usual, but it will also initiate an on-demand update. From the incoming table entry that matches the packet's source address, the router determines the source address space in question and the source router in charge of the source address space. It then requests that the source router sends an on-demand update— which is on behalf of the entire source address space—towards the destination of the suspicious packet.

Following the same design as in SAVE [12,13], the on-demand update will travel the same path as the legitimate packets that originate from the source router's address space. When the on-demand update arrives at the router from a specific incoming interface, this interface is then also the legitimate interface for the source address space in question. The router then makes sure its incoming table records *this* interface as the legitimate incoming interface for the source address space.

If the on-demand update does *not* arrive from the same incoming interface as the suspicious packet, the suspicious packet was in fact spoofing. Furthermore, the router updates its blacklists. Denote the spoofing packet's spoofed source address *space* as S and its incoming interface as i. It adds to the SI blacklist a new entry $\langle S, i \rangle$. If in the future a packet matches the newly added blacklist entry, the router will classify it as invalid. The router does not add a new entry to the SD blacklist, because the router could legitimately see packets from the suspicious packet's source to its destination—just not from the incoming interface that the suspicious packet used.

If the on-demand update *does* arrive from the same direction as the suspicious packet, the packet was not spoofing. Note the router already forwarded the packet earlier so no false positive occurs.

It is also possible the on-demand update never reaches the router. This could be because the router is not on the path from the source to the destination, or because congestion caused the update request or the update itself to be dropped. Since the router cannot know for sure, it takes no action. Assuming similar suspicious packets continue to arrive, the router will continue to request updates. We use a truncated binary exponential backoff scheme for subsequent requests.

4   Pushback of Spoofed Packets

The aim of the pushback is to push the filtering of spoofed packets all the way toward the router that is the closest to the spoofer(s). The pushback procedure is packet-driven and it is triggered when a SAVE router receives an invalid packet.

Once the pushback procedure is triggered by an invalid packet, the router sends pushback messages to immediate upstream SAVE routers that the packet possibly passed through. (The router uses incoming SAVE updates to record upstream SAVE routers along every incoming interface, and can easily identify those upstream along the incoming interface of the packet.) Assume the packet is from source address space S to destination address d. When an upstream SAVE router receives a pushback message, it adds an entry $\langle S, d \rangle$ to its SD blacklist. The incoming interface does not matter—the upstream router is not on the legitimate path from the packet's inscribed source to its destination at all. Upon receiving subsequent packets that match this new blacklist entry, the upstream router will classify them as invalid and continue to propagate the pushback further upstream.

Blacklist entries can become outdated if a routing change causes the legitimate path from the spoofing victim to become the same as that of the spoofing packets. If that happens, the pushback procedure will finally reach the source router in charge of the victim source address space. The source router can in turn send out an update that travels along the path and reaches every SAVE router en route. Every SAVE router can then remove its outdated blacklist entries.

Fig. 2 shows a pushback example. An attacker at legacy router A sends spoofing packets with a source from space S_X (X's source address space) and a destination dst_Z (an address towards which Z is downstream from X and Y). The spoofing packets arrive at router Y along the same interface as legitimate packets from S_X. Y classifies the packets as valid and forwards them. Z however expects packets from S_X to arrive on interface 1 according to its incoming table, so it classifies the first spoofing packet arriving at incoming interface 2 as suspicious. Z requests an on-demand update. Upon receipt of the requested update, Z confirms its incoming table information was correct, and the suspicious packet was in fact invalid (Fig. 2(a)). Z then adds a new entry to its SI blacklist: Based on

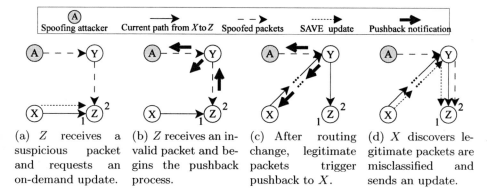

Fig. 2. A pushback example. An attacker, A, sends packets spoofing X's address space, S_X, towards dst_Z.

source S_X and incoming interface 2 of the suspicious packet, the new blacklist entry is $\langle S_X, 2\rangle$.

Z classifies later spoofing packets as invalid, and initiates the pushback process (Fig. 2(b)). Z knows Y is its neighbor along the spoofing packet's incoming interface. Z sends Y a pushback message, instructing Y to add an entry to its SD blacklist for all packets from S_X to dst_Z. When Y receives a packet matching the new blacklist entry, it classifies the packet as invalid and continues the pushback. Y finds all neighbors along the spoofing packet's incoming interface, and propagates the pushback towards such neighbors. Y's neighbors do not see matching packets, so do not further propagate the pushback. Y is the closest SAVE router to the attacker.

Later, if there is a routing change at a legacy router which causes the originally invalid "$X \cdots Y \cdots Z$" path to become valid and legitimate packets begin to flow along the path, SAVE will quickly converge to correct the error. During the transient period, router Y and Z will misclassify valid packets from S_X towards dst_Z as invalid. But now that Y's upstream neighboring SAVE routers also see packets matching the pushback request, the upstream routers will relay the pushback all the way to the source router X (Fig. 2(c)). After X receives the pushback, it realizes that downstream routers have incorrect blacklist entries matching its legitimate traffic. X sends an update towards dst_Z, causing all routers along the newly valid "$X \cdots Y \cdots Z$" path to remove their incorrect blacklist entries (Fig. 2(d)).

5   Security Considerations

SAVE must also be secure. The security of SAVE encompasses securing SAVE itself against attack and keeping attackers from being able to use SAVE to launch attacks. In addition to basic security functions such as confidentiality, integrity, and replay prevention, we must consider (1) *origin authentication* to ensure a router is authorized to speak for a source address space, and (2) *collusion prevention* to ensure attackers cannot collude to manipulate incoming direction information at SAVE routers.

5.1 Origin Authentication

Origin authentication ensures SAVE routers are authorized to speak for their corresponding source address space. This requires a trusted authority to sign a certificate that an address space owner can present. A public key infrastructure as described in [14] can provide such certificates of address ownership. The root certificate authority can be ICANN, with regional Internet registries such as ARIN or RIPE at the next level, and ISPs below. If SAVE is simply deployed inside an AS, the AS can simply use its self-signed certificates.

5.2 Collusion Prevention

Attackers may attempt collusion to manipulate the incoming table stored at a downstream SAVE router. They may collude by masquerading as each other or copying an update from an upstream space to each other, causing downstream routers to receive the update about a source address space along a wrong incoming interface.

Since the original update from the source address space still travels along the correct path[1], such manipulation by attackers can only be temporary. More importantly, such manipulation cannot cause a router to drop legitimate packets. If a router mistakenly classifies a legitimate packet as suspicious, an on-demand update will verify that it is in fact legitimate and fix the incoming direction information. Note the manipulation does not give the attackers further spoofing capabilities either, since attackers can only copy existing upstream updates.

5.3 Confidentiality, Integrity, and Replay Prevention

With a public key infrastructure, confidentiality and integrity is straightforward. If confidentiality is needed, a SAVE router can use the recipient's public key to encrypt its messages; or, it can establish a secure channel with the recipient, and use the session key associated with the channel to encrypt the messages. If integrity is needed, a SAVE router can uses its private key to create digital signatures for its messages.

Replay attacks must be prevented in order to ensure that a previous update cannot be copied and resent at a later time. Downstream routers must receive the most up-to-date incoming direction information. Replay attacks can be prevented by adding a counter to SAVE updates. The counter in an update must be greater than the counter of earlier updates.

---

[1] SAVE security does *not* encompass routing-level security, as that is the job of routing protocols—we assume routers *will* route a packet correctly towards its destination, and will *not* maliciously forward a packet in the wrong direction, nor maliciously drop a packet en route. Every SAVE update is encapsulated inside an UDP packet.

An implementation note. The security issues that SAVE faces are similar to those faced by BGP. Both need to ensure that a router can speak for an address space (SAVE's source address space and BGP's destination address space), both need to prevent conclusion of attackers, and both need to provide integrity, replay prevention, and sometimes confidentiality. In particular, to implement SAVE's security, we can borrow some ideas from IRV [15], an incrementally deployable BGP security solution. Basically, each network can contain a *validation server* to be responsible for security purposes, including keeping track of certificates and keys, performing signature creation and validation for SAVE messages, and managing security policies. Doing so would also maintain a lighter load on SAVE routers, allowing them to focus on its main purpose of receiving, validating, and forwarding packets.

6   Evaluation

In this section we discuss the performance of SAVE with the new mechanisms we introduced in this paper. First we present SAVE's efficacy in catching spoofed packets. We then evaluate SAVE's false positives. Finally we show that SAVE's storage, network, and computational overhead are reasonable.

6.1   Efficacy

Methodology. For efficacy evaluation we use a modified static distributed packet filtering (DPF) [10] simulator. The DPF simulator allows us to evaluate the efficacy of SAVE on Internet-scale topologies by calculating efficacies based on the Internet AS graph and SAVE router locations. It uses Internet Autonomous System (AS) topologies from Route Views [16]. The efficacy metrics are similar to those in [10]. Specifically, we report:

- $\Phi_2(1)$ that represents the percentage of ASes that an attacker cannot send spoofing packets from—any spoofed packets from those ASes would be detected and filtered out;
- $\Phi_3(1)$ that represents the percentage of all attacker-victim AS pairs where the attacker *cannot* send spoofed packets to the victim; and
- $\Psi_1(\tau)$ that represents the fraction of target ASes which can narrow down an attacker's location to within τ possible attack ASes.

We consider a variety of placement strategies of SAVE routers. First, we deploy SAVE routers so they form a vertex cover (as in the original DPF work [10]). Then, we look at random deployments, with deployment percentages between 0% and 100% in 10% increments. Finally, we deploy SAVE routers at the top ASes by degree.

Results and Analysis. The efficacy of SAVE in catching spoofed packets depends upon both the deployment strategy and the percentage of deployment. With a random deployment, the efficacy increases along with the deployment percentage. With deployment at high-degree ASes or using a vertex cover for

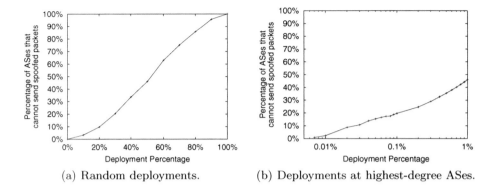

(a) Random deployments.   (b) Deployments at highest-degree ASes.

Fig. 3. $\Phi_2(1)$: The percentage of ASes on an Internet AS topology from which an attacker cannot send spoofed packets

deployment, the efficacy is much higher than a random deployment, even with a much lower percentage of deployment.

Fig. 3 shows $\Phi_2(1)$, the percentage of ASes on an Internet AS topology from which an attacker cannot send *any* packets that spoof a protected source address. We can clearly see that deployment strategies are an important factor. $\Phi_2(1)$ with a vertex cover deployment is around 99% (not shown), where the vertex cover consisted of around 14.5% of all routers. Fig. 3(a) shows $\Phi_2(1)$ for random deployments; with 15% or less deployment percentage, $\Phi_2(1)$ is even no more than 10%. Fig. 3(b) shows $\Phi_2(1)$ for deployments at ASes with the highest degree on the same topology; as a sharp contrast to random deployment, even with less than 1% of ASes deploying SAVE, over 40% of all ASes are unable to spoof *any* protected source.

Fig. 4 shows $\Phi_3(1)$, the percentage of attacker-victim AS pairs where the attacker cannot send spoofed packets to the victim. Deployment strategy, again, plays an important role. A random deployment is not very effective—high efficacy requires high levels of deployment. More targeted deployments, however, can be extremely effective. With a vertex cover deployment the efficacy is over 99.9% (not shown). Even very small targeted deployments can be effective: With deployment at only the top 0.08% of ASes by degree (21 ASes in this case), efficacy is over 90%.

Fig. 5 shows $\Psi_1(\tau)$ with again the same deployments as above. $\Psi_1(\tau)$ is the percentage of destination ASes that can narrow down an attacker's location to within τ source ASes, when intermediate routers were unable to filter the spoofed packet. Note that this percentage is for instantly narrowing down an attacker's location based on the network topology, the location of SAVE routers, and the fact that the spoofed packet reached its destination. Vertex cover deployments (not shown) and high-degree AS deployments have excellent performance, generally being able to narrow down an attacker's actual location to within 5 locations or fewer. More random deployments are not able to reliably narrow down an attacker's location, with possible attacker locations measured in the

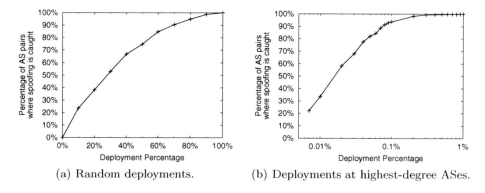

Fig. 4. $\Phi_3(1)$: The percentage of attacker-victim AS pairs where the attacker cannot send spoofed packets to the victim

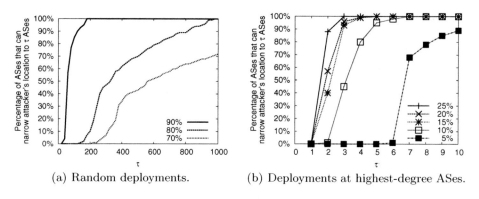

Fig. 5. $\Psi_1(\tau)$: The percentage of destination ASes that can narrow down an attacker's location to within τ source ASes

hundreds. (SAVE includes additional location capabilities through the use of its pushback mechanism, which we plan to evaluate further.)

Finally, the high efficacy with the highest-degree ASes (as shown in Figs. 3(b), 4(b), and 5(b)) shows that such ASes—if they deploy SAVE—can filter spoofing packets and locate attackers very effectively. They thus will have a strong incentive to deploy SAVE. Moreover, doing so provides an incentive for other ASes to follow; with the highest-degree ASes deploying SAVE, when the followers also deploy SAVE they will protect their own address space much more effectively.

6.2   False Positives

False positives only occur when the following conditions are *all* met:

– A pushback path that spoofing packets travel becomes a valid path due to a sudden underneath routing change;

- Legitimate packets begin to flow along the path;
- The SAVE update from the source router of the legitimate packets has not reached SAVE routers along the path to void the blacklist entries that cause the legitimate packets to be dropped.

The transient time that all three conditions are met is short-lived. Assume S is the source router and R is a SAVE router on the path. False positives will occur at R from the time the first legitimate packet arrives along the new valid path to the time R's blacklist is updated. Assuming there is a steady stream of packets from S passing through R, it will take the following amount of time to update R's information:

$$rtt + \sum_{i=next(S)}^{R} C_i + \sum_{i=S}^{prev(R)} P_i + \sum_{i=next(S)}^{R} U_i \qquad (1)$$

rtt is the round trip time between R and S, $next(S)$ is the SAVE router downstream from S towards R, C_i is the time it takes for router i to classify a packet, $prev(R)$ is the SAVE router upstream from R towards S, P_i is the time it takes for router i to process a pushback message, and U_i is the time it takes for router i to propagate an update.

The values of these parameters vary. Assuming values of 20ms for rtt, 100μs for C_i, P_i, U_i, and 10 SAVE hops from S to R, the transient period will be 50ms.

6.3   Overhead

Here we discuss SAVE's storage, network, and computational overhead.

Methodology. For overhead evaluation we use the J-Sim [17] network simulation framework. (Note the DPF simulator cannot calculate SAVE storage or network overheads.) The J-Sim framework simulates all routers, links, and messages in a network topology in order to conduct detailed overhead evaluation. This, however, limits the size of the topology to generally 5,000 nodes—even with our fairly high-end evaluation environment. (We performed all the evaluations on a computer with 16 GB of RAM, dual 2.6 GHz AMD dual-core Opteron 285 CPUs, running CentOS Linux 4.6.) To solve this problem, we note that SAVE can run at two separate levels: intra-AS level and inter-AS level, and we can evaluate the overhead at these two separate levels. At the intra-AS level, although a small number of ASes may have more than 5,000 routers, most ASes will fall into the range that the J-Sim framework can simulate. At the inter-AS level, all border routers of an AS can act as *one* "virtual router" with the entire AS as its source address space, and therefore SAVE's overhead at the inter-AS level can be analyzed using a topology of all virtual routers—which is equivalent to an Internet AS topology. As the Internet has approximately 26,000 ASes, a detailed J-Sim simulation with up to 5,000 nodes should be close enough for us to understand SAVE's overhead at a large scale.

The overhead analyses at intra-AS level and inter-AS level are similar, except that different topology models probably should be used. In this paper, we focus on the inter-AS level where each node is an AS (or a virtual router), and use network topologies generated by shrinking AS topologies with Orbis [18]—such topologies are smaller than the AS topology of the real Internet but they have similar structure patterns.

Also, we again evaluate multiple placement strategies of SAVE routers. We evaluate vertex cover deployments, deployments at the top 1% of routers by degree, and biased 1% deployments consisting of a random half of the top 2% of routers by degree. They are all effective from our efficacy analysis above. We simulate networks ranging in size from 500 to 5,000 nodes (only up to 3,000 nodes for vertex cover deployments due to computation power limitation).

Storage Overhead: In this paper, the blacklist is the only new data structure. We now implement it as a cache of fixed size that runs the Least Recently Used (LRU) algorithm to replace old entries. Further work is needed to evaluate how the size affects the efficacy of the system. We do not worry about losing old blacklist entries; neighboring routers will still filter spoofing traffic, and the on-demand-update mechanism can recreate entries if necessary in any case.

Network Traffic Overhead: Fig. 6 shows the per-router traffic during spoofing attacks. As the network size increases, network overhead decreases—because spoofing traffic, and thus control traffic, is more spread out (Figs. 6(a) and 6(d)). With a fixed network size (1,000 nodes) and increasing spoofing traffic, the network overhead increases linearly (Figs. 6(b), 6(c), 6(e), and 6(f)). This overhead is offset significantly as the SAVE system is also removing spoofing traffic from the network. Instead of the spoofing traffic overloading its target at the edge of the network, routers drop the spoofing traffic and SAVE's traffic overhead is spread out inside the network. Note that due to simulation limitations we cannot simulate a larger number of attackers, but results from Fig. 6 is still indicative about the network overhead effects from the size of the network, the number of attackers, and the number of spoofing packets.

Computational Overhead: SAVE's most crucial computational overhead is the time taken for a router to classify packets, which mainly consists of table lookup operations (using a router's incoming table and blacklist). We do not have actual measurements for computational overhead since the system is only implemented as a simulation, but we expect SAVE will impose only a minimal computational cost. Today's routers are designed for fast, efficient table lookups (a router's main function is forwarding table lookup).

7   Open Issues

Several issues related to incoming-table-based IP spoofing detection warrant further investigation. These issues include incentives for deploying SAVE, spoofing strategies attackers can employ to avoid SAVE, and false positives.

Incentives. As SAVE can only be deployed incrementally, for successful incremental deployment, domains must *want* to deploy SAVE. There must be incentives that

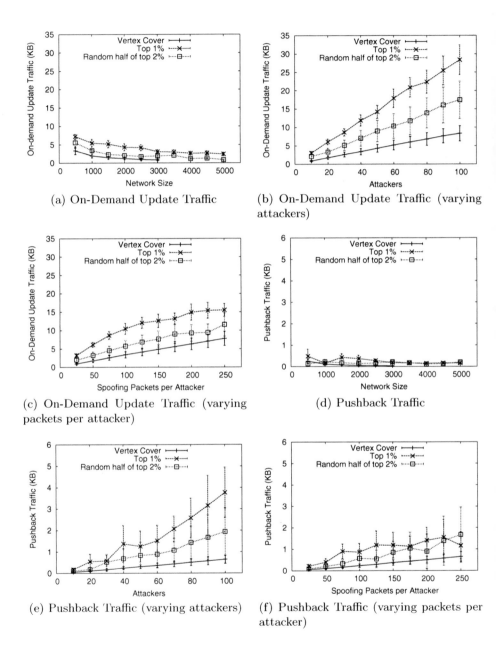

(a) On-Demand Update Traffic

(b) On-Demand Update Traffic (varying attackers)

(c) On-Demand Update Traffic (varying packets per attacker)

(d) Pushback Traffic

(e) Pushback Traffic (varying attackers)

(f) Pushback Traffic (varying packets per attacker)

Fig. 6. Network traffic due to spoofing (with 95% confidence intervals)

include a clear benefit for the deploying domain. "Early adopters" of the protocol should be attracted when the deployment level is still low.

We already know the following incentives for deploying SAVE on a network: Attackers are less likely to successfully spoof source addresses belonging to a SAVE-protected domain, protecting a domain from misplaced blame and reflection style attacks. A protected domain will also allow fewer spoofing packets to enter its network, protecting internal hosts from receiving spoofing packets. Furthermore, SAVE routers can assign higher priorities to packets from SAVE-protected source address spaces, giving clients with protected sources higher quality of service.

What needs to be further studied is how highest-degree ASes can become incentivized to deploy SAVE. From Section 6.1 we know that deployments at highest-degree ASes will be mostly effective while random deployments will be least. One driving force here could be that knowing the correct source of traffic may help large ISPs monitor and manage their traffic more reliably according to contractual agreements with their customers.

Spoofing Strategies. Attackers may employ peculiar spoofing strategies to evade SAVE's filtering. One such spoofing is random source spoofing in which the attacker stamps a random source address on every packet it sends out. When a SAVE router receives any such packet, it will locate the incoming table entry that matches the inscribed source of the packet. Since for each such packet the SAVE router probably has not seen its inscribed source before (i.e., no blacklist entry established), it will treat everyone of them as suspicious, and still forward them. The router will request on-demand updates, but only to confirm that its incoming table is up-to-date.

Fortunately, the damage an attacker could cause with random spoofing is limited. Random spoofing could hide the attacker's true identity, but random spoofing cannot be used in attacks such as DNS amplification [1,2], DNS cache poisoning [4], in-window TCP resets [3], and spam filter circumvention [5,6]. Any type of reflection attack cannot succeed, since traffic triggered by the spoofing packets will spread out through the network instead of becoming concentrated in one area. Similarly, the effect on the SAVE infrastructure is manageable since any requests for on-demand updates will also be spread throughout the network.

We are investigating the most cost-effective way of addressing this spoofing strategy. Our concern with random spoofing is the effect it might have on SAVE itself, so our solution focuses on minimizing the overhead it could generate. In our current solution, described only briefly for space considerations, a router does not request an on-demand update for every suspicious packet. Instead, routers use a truncated binary exponential back off strategy. Initially, a router will request an on-demand update after it sees $n = 1$ suspicious packet. If the requested update shows the incoming table was in fact correct, the router will not request another on-demand update until it sees $n = 2$ more suspicious packets. Every time a requested update arrives, if it agrees with the incoming table, the router subsequently waits for $n = 2n$ more suspicious packets before requesting another on-demand update. We do not allow n to increase over 1024. On the other hand, if the requested update shows the incoming table was incorrect, the router decreases the wait to $n = 1$ suspicious packet. In this manner, random spoofing by attackers cannot cause too much network overhead nor fill up a router's blacklist; at the same time, SAVE can continue to quickly update its incoming table.

False Positives. As discussed in Section 6.2, our pushback mechanism is subject to false positives when certain conditions are met. Although the transient period for false positives to occur is very short, further minimizing them is important and we plan to study this issue further.

8 Related Work

Source address validation is comprised of end-host methods and router-based methods. To validate the source address of newly received packets, an end-host can either actively probe supposed sources, or passively observe the pattern of packets from them [19]. However, although end-host-based detection is easier to deploy, it cannot prevent spoofing packets from reaching their destinations. Router-based solutions can be classified as preventive approaches (e.g., filtering) or reactive approaches (e.g., traceback). Since SAVE is a router-based, filtering-oriented solution, we focus on these below.

Filtering approaches attempt to identify invalid packets by examining certain attributes of incoming packets at a router. Many approaches have been proposed. Network ingress filtering [7] can stop a spoofing attack at its source, but is useless against spoofing attacks once they enter the Internet. With unicast reverse path forwarding (uRPF) [8], a router drops any packet from an address that does not arrive on the interface that the router uses to reach that address. However, Internet routing is frequently asymmetric: the path from a given address is not necessarily the same as the path to that address [20].

SPM [21] proposes that packets from a source AS to a destination AS carry a key bound with that AS pair, but losing the key to an attacker will enable the attacker to successfully deliver spoofed packets from anywhere. As opposed to SAVE, SPM is also specific to BGP and cannot help intermediate routers gain source validity knowledge.

Passport [22] is also BGP specific and uses keys based on AS pairs. It uses multiple keys based on the packet's source AS and each AS along the path to its destination. This allows intermediate ASes to perform validation, in addition to the destination AS. Passport has problems with packets fragmented in the middle of the network; the fragmentation invalidates the Passport header. Routers therefore forward fragmented packets, both legitimate and spoofed, all the way to their destination. More importantly, intermediate ASes never drop invalid packets, only lower their priority. An attacker's spoofing packets will still reach the destination AS.

The authors of the route-based distributed packet filtering (DPF) [10] studied the benefits of DPF for attack prevention and traceback, as well as its partial deployment strategies. Unfortunately, the work did not specify how routers can learn the incoming direction for different source addresses. IDPF [23] attempts to address this gap. It relies on specific BGP forwarding policies and AS peering relationships, but only to learn feasible paths, instead of actual paths, from a given source. BASE [24] is another similar work that relies on BGP, and has yet to effectively address commonly seen AS-level routing asymmetry.

Pi [25] and StackPi [26] provide a hybrid approach: routers mark each packet with an identifier for the path that the packet travels, and end hosts examine packets and classify which paths are attack paths and which are not. Pi/StackPi cannot handle fragmented packets correctly, and a spoofing packet must reach its destination before Pi/StackPi can detect it.

9   Conclusion

Research has shown that if a small percentage of routers throughout the Internet deploy a filtering table to discard packets with a forged source address, a synergistic filtering effect can be achieved to stop a large fraction of spoofed IP packets. Such an approach to IP spoofing has also been found to be the most effective. However, in building such a filtering table, specifically an incoming table, we have found that the previously designed SAVE protocol is susceptible to obsolete incoming table entries as it is incrementally deployed.

We introduce new mechanisms in this paper to address this deficiency. We introduce blacklists at SAVE routers and use both the blacklist and the incoming table to classify and filter incoming packets. Our on-demand mechanism enables a SAVE router to deal with suspicious packets and update its incoming table, and the pushback mechanism further pushes the filtering of spoofing packets toward the SAVE router that is the closest to spoofers. With these new mechanisms, and with both security and performance issues considered, we show that incoming-table-based IP spoofing detection is a viable approach to addressing the critical problem of IP spoofing, and that ASes (beginning with high-degree ASes) will have incentives to deploy such a solution. Simulations show that, for example, with deployment at only the top 0.08% of ASes by degree, the efficacy of catching spoofing packets is over 90%.

References

1. Paxson, V.: An analysis of using reflectors for distributed denial-of-service attacks. ACM Computer Communications Review (CCR) 31(3), 38–47 (2001)
2. Jackson, D.: DNS amplification variation used in recent DDoS attacks (February 2009), http://www.secureworks.com/research/threats/dns-amplification/
3. Touch, J.: Defending TCP against spoofing attacks. RFC 4953 (July 2007)
4. US-CERT: Multiple DNS implementations vulnerable to cache poisoning, Vulnerability Note VU 800113 (July 2008)
5. Morrow, C.: BLS FastAccess internal tech needed (January 2006), http://www.merit.edu/mail.archives/nanog/2006-01/msg00220.html
6. Beverly, R., Berger, A., Hyun, Y., Claffy, K.: Understanding the efficacy of deployed Internet source address validation filtering. In: Proceedings of the ACM Internet Measurement Conference (November 2009)

7. Ferguson, P., Senie, D.: Network ingress filtering: Defeating denial of service attacks which employ IP source address spoofing. RFC 2827 (2000)
8. Baker, F., Savola, P.: Ingress Filtering for Multihomed Networks. RFC 3704 (2004)
9. Ehrenkranz, T., Li, J.: On the state of IP spoofing defense. ACM Transactions on Internet Technology 9(2), 1–29 (2009)
10. Park, K., Lee, H.: On the effectiveness of route-based packet filtering for distributed DoS attack prevention in power-law internets. In: Proceedings of ACM SIGCOMM (2001)
11. Mirkovic, J., Kissel, E.: Comparative evaluation of spoofing defenses. IEEE Transactions on Dependable and Secure Computing 99 (2009) (PrePrints)
12. Li, J., Mirkovic, J., Ehrenkranz, T., Wang, M., Reiher, P., Zhang, L.: Learning the valid incoming direction of IP packets. Computer Networks 52(2), 399–417 (2008)
13. Li, J., Mirkovic, J., Wang, M., Reiher, P.L., Zhang, L.: SAVE: Source address validity enforcement protocol. In: Proceedings of IEEE INFOCOM (June 2002)
14. Kent, S., Lynn, C., Mikkelson, J., Seo, K.: Secure border gateway protocol (S-BGP) — real world performance and deployment issues. In: Proceedings of the Network and Distributed System Security Symposium (2000)
15. Goodell, G., Aiello, W., Griffin, T., Ioannidis, J., McDaniel, P., Rubin, A.: Working around BGP: An incremental approach to improving security and accuracy of interdomain routing. In: Proceedings of the Network and Distributed System Security Symposium (February 2003)
16. University of Oregon: Route Views Project, http://www.routeviews.org/
17. Tyan, H.Y., Sobeih, A., Hou, J.C.: Towards composable and extensible network simulation. In: Proceedings of the International Parallel and Distributed Processing Symposium (2005)
18. Mahadevan, P., Hubble, C., Krioukov, D.V., Huffaker, B., Vahdat, A.: Orbis: rescaling degree correlations to generate annotated Internet topologies. In: Proceedings of ACM SIGCOMM (2007)
19. Templeton, S.J., Levitt, K.E.: Detecting spoofed packets. In: Proceedings of the DARPA Information Survivability Conference and Exposition, vol. 1 (2003)
20. Paxson, V.: End-to-end routing behavior in the Internet. In: Proceedings of ACM SIGCOMM (1996)
21. Bremler-Barr, A., Levy, H.: Spoofing prevention method. In: Proceedings of IEEE INFOCOM (2005)
22. Liu, X., Li, A., Yang, X., Wetherall, D.: Passport: Secure and adoptable source authentication. In: Proceedings of USENIX Symposium on Networked Systems Design and Implementation (2008)
23. Duan, Z., Yuan, X., Chandrashekar, J.: Constructing inter-domain packet filters to control IP spoofing based on BGP updates. In: Proceedings of IEEE INFOCOM (2006)
24. Lee, H., Kwon, M., Hasker, G., Perrig, A.: BASE: An incrementally deployable mechanism for viable IP spoofing prevention. In: Proceedings of the ACM Symposium on Information, Computer, and Communication Security (2007)
25. Yaar, A., Perrig, A., Song, D.: Pi: A path identification mechanism to defend against DDoS attack. In: Proceedings of the IEEE Symposium on Security and Privacy (2003)
26. Yaar, A., Perrig, A., Song, D.: StackPi: New packet marking and filtering mechanisms for DDoS and IP spoofing defense. IEEE Journal of Selected Areas in Communications 24(10), 1853–1863 (2006)

Partial Deafness: A Novel Denial-of-Service Attack in 802.11 Networks*

Jihyuk Choi, Jerry T. Chiang, Dongho Kim, and Yih-Chun Hu

University of Illinois at Urbana-Champaign, USA
{jchoi43,chiang2,dkim99,yihchun}@illinois.edu

Abstract. We present a new denial-of-service attack against 802.11 wireless networks. Our attack exploits previously discovered performance degradation in networks with substantial rate diversity. In our attack, the attacker artificially reduces his link quality by not acknowledging receptions (which we call "partial deafness" because an attacker pretends to have not heard some of the transmission), thereby exploiting the retransmission and rate adaptation mechanisms to reduce Medium Access Control (MAC)-layer performance. As compared to previously proposed attacks, the partial deafness attack is particularly strong because the attacker does not necessarily need any advantage over normal users in terms of transmission power, computation resources, or channel condition.

Previous work has shown that time fairness in sharing the wireless medium can improve network throughput. We show that time-based regulation at the data queue of the access point can similarly mitigate the negative impact of a partial deafness attacker.

Keywords: IEEE 802.11 DCF, MAC retransmission, Rate adaptation, Denial of service attack.

1 Introduction

Wireless networks based on the IEEE 802.11 standard [1] are widely deployed today for governmental, commercial, and personal uses. Attacks against the 802.11 standard can cause widespread security exploits ranging from mere inconvenience to privacy breaches and machine compromise. Much attention is dedicated to both possible attacks and their respective solutions. For example, the original security scheme specified by 802.11, the Wired Equivalent Privacy (WEP), is shown to be susceptible to various attacks against both the encryption mechanism [2,3,4] and the authentication scheme [5]. Many protocols are proposed to fix these weaknesses [6,7,8].

Other aspects of the 802.11 are also shown to be susceptible to attacks. For example, the virtual carrier sense mechanism is susceptible to a type of Denial-of-Service (DoS) attack where an attacker repeatedly reserves the channel for

* This material is based upon work partially supported by USARO under Contract No. W-911-NF-0710287 and the NSF under Grant No. CNS-0953600.

S. Jajodia and J. Zhou (Eds.): SecureComm 2010, LNICST 50, pp. 235–252, 2010.

long transmissions, thereby starving other users of any transmission opportunities [5]. Many attacks target the backoff mechanism of the 802.11 standard by not backing off as much as specified by the standard [9,10,11]. Backing off less than specified allows the attackers to obtain more access opportunities, and hence higher throughput, than legitimate users.

Heusse et al. demonstrate that even without any malicious intent or misbehavior, a slow connection can still significantly impact the transfer speed of a fast connection because of the fairness mechanism implemented by the Distributed Coordination Function (DCF) at the Medium Access Control layer (MAC) [12]. In particular, since the IEEE 802.11 DCF seeks to fairly grant access opportunities to each station, each station has an equal opportunity to be the next station to transmit a data packet, thus a fast connection regularly has to wait until a slow connection finishes its reception. This performance anomaly together with excessive channel reservation can be viewed as head-of-queue blocking at the wireless medium since the DCF cannot schedule the next station until the current transmitter is finished.

In this paper, we present *partial deafness attack*, a novel DoS attack that builds of Heusse et al.'s observation. Our attack is based on the realization that most commercial access points are implemented with only a single data queue since the 802.11 standard does not specify or recommend any queuing behavior. Thus, if a transmitted packet is not acknowledged, the packet triggers retransmissions and possible rate adaptation (i.e. slowing the data rate), thereby creating head-of-queue blocking at the access point. The head-of-queue blocking then drastically degrades the performance of the wireless network.

Like other DoS attacks, our attack does not aim to give better performance to the attacker, but to reduce the performance of other users. In our attack, each attacker *artificially worsens* his link quality by intentionally failing to acknowledge packet receptions. Our attack impacts the system in a manner similar to a legitimate user with a slow connection. However, by exploiting the retransmission mechanism specified by the 802.11 standard, the impact of our attack becomes much more devastating, especially to the Transport Control Protocol (TCP) performance of other users.

Our work is novel and interesting for two reasons. First, the attacker can carry out our attack targeting the MAC protocol without modifying the MAC layer; second, our attack can consistently impact the system regardless of the opportunistic nature of the physical layer.

Our proposed attack targets the MAC-layer protocol but does not require the attacker to modify the MAC protocol implementation at his station. For example, an attacker can suppress an acknowledgment by turning off the network interface card any time between the start and completion of packet reception. In contrast to many previously proposed attacks that require substantial modification of the firmware or the hardware and are thus often deemed impractical, our attack can be easily implemented in several ways, including methods that do not directly modify the MAC-layer implementation. For example, in Section 4, we detail our implementation of a partial deafness attacker by enabling and disabling the acknowledgment function in the driver of a commercial Wireless Local Area Network (WLAN) card. In other words, our attack works even when the attacker abides by the same MAC rules as every other node.

An attacker can simply move farther away from the access point to physically worsen his channel condition and impact other users. However, this approach requires the attacker to find a location such that the channel condition is sufficiently weak to regularly results in retransmission, and yet is not weak enough to result in disassociation. If fading causes the attacker to be disconnected, then the attacker cannot impact other users; on the other hand, if fading improves the attacker's channel condition intermittently, then other users can also experience improved transfer rate intermittently. Our attack suppresses the acknowledgment and thus allows an attacker to be able to consistently worsen his channel condition over time, and cause significant degradation of service to other users.

Since the partial deafness attack relies on head-of-queue blocking at the access point, there are many different methods that can mitigate the attack. We propose implementing time-fairness at the access point instead of relying on a single First-In-First-Out (FIFO) data queue. Our proposed solution can be implemented entirely in software, and does not require any changes to the widely used 802.11 MAC protocol.

The rest of the paper is organized as follows: In Section 2 we review some related work. In Section 3 we detail our attack and analytically show the effect of our attack. We show in Section 4 that our attack is indeed practical and causes severe degradation of network performance. In Section 5 we detail a time-fair mechanism and show that this mechanism mitigates the partial deafness attack. We conclude this paper in Section 6.

2   Related Work

The IEEE 802.11 standard is widely deployed due to the unlicensed spectrum in which it operates and the low cost of client devices and access points. As a result, the security of 802.11 attracts much attention. In particular, most research on MAC security focuses on the requirements of confidentiality and integrity. The original security protocol, WEP, is designed to provide privacy and authenticity of data. However, Fluhrer et al. note that weakness in the encryption algorithm used by WEP can be exploited to allow the discovery of session keys [2]. Numerous related attacks exist in the literature [3,4].

While a cryptographic attack has strong adverse effects on users' privacy and protocol's confidentiality and integrity, our work considers another type of attack where the attacker seeks only to deny service to other users. That is, the attacker aims to reduce a protocol's availability. Specifically, we consider the attacks against the MAC-layer protocol specified in 802.11 rather than the pure resource consumption attacks such as the jamming attack (e.g. jamming attack exploiting clear channel assessment [13]).

Attacks on the 802.11 MAC protocol can exploit management vulnerabilities. Bellardo and Savage implement and demonstrate an attack that targets the authentication/association scheme of 802.11 [5]. Bellardo and Savage note that the deauthentication and disassociation messages are not encrypted, thus an attacker can easily forge these messages. The attacker can then send the deauthentication message to the access point before client's data is received, or the attacker can send the disassociation message to the client before the client's data is transmitted. Ferreri et al. [14] describe DoS attacks against an access point's association and authentication mechanisms.

Attacks on the 802.11 MAC can also exploit media access vulnerabilities. Bellardo and Savage also note that the 802.11 carrier sense mechanism can be easily exploited. For example, in 802.11 networks, a node can only send data during a certain time period after the channel stops being busy. In particular, if not due to retransmission or fragmentation, a user can only transmit data DCF InterFrame Space (DIFS) after channel is available; otherwise the user can transmit data Short InterFrame Space (SIFS) after, where SIFS < DIFS. A very simple method to deny service is to send a short burst every SIFS. Bellardo and Savage present a more sophisticated scheme exploiting the virtual carrier sense mechanism. The 802.11 standard specifies that the MAC frame header of all packets should contain a *duration* field, which specifies how long others have to wait before transmission is allowed in order to avoid collision. Users update their Network Allocation Vector (NAV) with this duration information and keep quiet for the specified duration. Thus an attacker can repeatedly request long channel occupancy time, thereby starving normal clients of channel occupancy.

The benefit of attacking the duration field rather than sending a short burst every SIFS is the amount of power used to carry out the attack. In the duration field attack, an attacker simply initiates a Request to Send (RTS)/ Clear to Send (CTS) handshake along with the specified duration. The handshake in theory would keep the channel busy for roughly 30 ms. The short burst approach, on the other hand, requires sending a short burst every SIFS, or 10 μs in 802.11b/g networks. Our proposed attack performs even better in terms of power saving for the attackers; in particular, our attack can easily occupy 100 ms of channel time without having to send any messages. Moreover, our attack does not require the attacker to have better service, higher power, or closer distance to the access point. Finally, unlike our attack which works on each access point we tested, the duration field attack does not work in many real systems because most vendors do not implement the 802.11 specification correctly [5].

Heusse et al. point out that when a client uses a lower bit rate than others in a 802.11 network, the performance of all clients is considerably degraded [12]. Tan and Guttag subsequently suggest that time fairness can mitigate this performance anomaly and provide better throughput for the WLAN [15]. In this paper, we present an attacker that exploits the conclusion of Heusse et al. by artificially and intentionally creating rate disparities. We show that access point retransmissions exacerbate the anomaly by creating head-of-queue blocking at the access point's data queue. We then adapt the principle of Tan and Guttag's solution and show how to mitigate our attack by implementing time fairness at the access point's data queue.

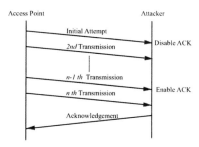

Fig. 1. Partial Deafness Attack

3   The Partial Deafness Attack

3.1   Description

In this section, we present our novel *partial deafness attack*, which exploits the re-transmission mechanism of the 802.11 protocol to reduce the bandwidth of non-attacking nodes. In our attack, the attacker, upon receiving a unicast data frame addressed to it, intentionally fails to send a timely acknowledgment for at least a portion of those data frames. Though previous work has suggested denial-of-service attacks against IEEE 802.11, our attack stands out because it substantially reduces the bandwidth available to legitimate nodes without requiring the attacker to have superior connection quality. That is, an attacker with lower transmission power, fewer computation resources, located farther away than a normal client, can still deny service to all the normal clients within the network.

As illustrated in Fig. 1, when a unicast transmission is not acknowledged, an 802.11 station will normally transmit a frame up to seven times before it gives up and discards the frame. An attacker can thus fail to acknowledge the first six transmissions. In addition, senders in 802.11 employ *rate adaptation* (e.g. Auto Rate Fallback (ARF) [16], SampleRate [17]) to maximize the throughput of the channel. When a receiver repeatedly fails to receive transmissions at one bit rate, the sender chooses a lower bit rate in an attempt to successfully deliver the packet. Eventually the sender will choose the lowest possible rate, called the *base rate*, to deliver packets to the attacker.

Since most 802.11 networks are infrastructure networks in which clients connect directly to an access point, and most traffic is directed to or received from an access point, the behavior of an access point plays an important role in the fairness perceived by a station. The 802.11 standard does not specify or recommend any queuing behavior at the access point, so most commercial access points use a single queue. Thus all packets are treated with the same priority and each packet is completed before subsequent packets can be serviced, regardless of the number of retransmissions, or the rate that is selected for those retransmissions. The attacker can thus induce the access point to spend a large amount of time to transmit to the attacker, thereby drastically decreasing the time allocated to the normal clients, and reducing the overall throughput.

3.2 Analysis

We will first analyze the impact of our attack in 802.11b, where the maximum rate is 11 Mbps and the base rate is 1 Mbps. We then use a theoretical analysis to show that rate diversity exacerbates the problem; thus, in commonly deployed 802.11b/g networks, where the maximum and base rates are 54 Mbps and 1 Mbps respectively, are even more susceptible to our attack.

To quantify the degree of imbalance caused by the partial deafness attack, we consider a case in which a normal client and a malicious client share one base station. We call the normal client Alice; the malicious client, Mallory; and base station, Bob. In our example, Alice and Mallory have the same link quality to Bob, so when Mallory is not performing any attack, Bob can send to both Alice and Mallory at 11 Mbps. That is, if Alice and Mallory started User Datagram Protocol (UDP) downloads, they would each receive approximately half of the available bandwidth.

Let us consider the particular rate adaptation algorithm implemented on a Linksys WRT54G access point. Initially, Bob's rate adaptation chooses 11 Mbps for its first three transmissions and 2 Mbps for its last four retransmissions. If Mallory acknowledges after the 3rd transmission, Bob determines that 11 Mbps is too high an initial rate, and will send the subsequent packet at 5.5 Mbps for the first three transmissions and 1 Mbps for the next four retransmissions. If Mallory again acknowledges after the 3rd transmission, Bob determines that 5.5 Mbps is again too high an initial rate, and will send the subsequent packet at 2 Mbps for the first three transmissions and 1 Mbps for the next four retransmissions. If Mallory again acknowledges after the 3rd transmission, Bob will determine that 2 Mbps is still too high and will send all subsequent packets at 1 Mbps.

If Mallory performs the partial deafness attack, and she does not acknowledge receiving a packet until the 7th transmission, Bob would send packets to Mallory at 1 Mbps in the steady state, but to Alice at 11 Mbps. Thus, it would take Bob 11 times longer to send an identical packet to Mallory than to Alice. In other words, if Bob sends an equal number of packets to Alice and Mallory, without considering retransmission, Mallory is already allocated $\frac{11}{12} = 91.7\%$ of the channel occupancy time as opposed to 50% in a time-fair scheme.

We now consider the additional effect of retransmissions. In the Direct Sequence Spread Spectrum (DSSS) mode of 802.11b, the slot time is 20μs, minimum and maximum contention window size are 31 and 1023. Typically 802.11 networks are configured to allow a maximum transmission unit of around 2304 bytes. In 802.11, a station can fragment larger packets into smaller fragments and transmit each fragment separately. In this case, Mallory allows Bob to send each fragment the maximum number of times before Bob gives up on the fragment. Thus each fragment of the packet is transmitted seven times, which is nearly equivalent to transmitting the entire packet seven times. (There are minor differences because of the interframe spacing used between fragments, but seven retransmissions of one large frame should closely approximate seven retransmissions of each of several smaller fragments).

We now quantify Mallory's per-packet channel occupancy time in steady-state. We assume that every time the sender (in this case Bob) wishes to send a packet, the medium is busy, so the 1st transmission experiences backoff. We further assume that once the medium becomes idle, there are no further transmissions on that medium except those initiated by Bob. We will validate the theoretical results here with implementation results in Section 4, which show that these assumptions provide results comparable to those seen in normal access point behaviors. We will consider a single UDP packet containing 1470 bytes of data, which, after UDP- and Internet Protocol (IP)-layer headers, comes to 1498 bytes. The addition of MAC-layer headers brings the total to 1534 bytes.

If Alice and Mallory both acknowledge reception of a packet by the 3rd transmission, the steady-state data rate is 11 Mbps. In this case, the 1st transmission takes about 1571.6 μs in expectation: 50 μs for DIFS, 310 μs of expected backoff, 96 μs of preamble, and 1115.6 μs of data. Bob would expect an acknowledgment within 126 μs, which represents the sum of: the SIFS that Mallory must wait following reception, the maximum propagation delay between Mallory and Bob, which is defined in 802.11 to be one slot time, and the delay that 802.11 allows between when the radio frequency energy starts impinging on the receiver until that receiver starts receiving a message, which is defined to be the length of the preamble. In expectation, a failed 1st transmission would therefore be detected 1697.6 μs after the medium becomes idle. When the 1st transmission is successful, Mallory waits SIFS and transmits a preamble and a 12 byte acknowledgment at 2 Mbps, which gives an expected time of 1725.6 μs from when the medium is idle until the transmission is received. (We assume the propagation time is negligible; the 20 μs slot time of 802.11 is sufficient for a 6 km transmission, which is well in excess of typical 802.11 transmission distances). In further retransmissions, the one thing that changes is the expected backoff value, which increases from 310 μs to 630 μs to 1270 μs within these first three retransmissions. Also, Bob will not wait DIFS when Bob does not receive an acknowledgment. Thus success after three retransmissions takes $1697.6 + (1647.6 + 320) + (1675.6 + 320 + 640) = 6300.8$ μs. If Mallory forces three retransmissions for each packet while Alice acknowledges every 1st transmission, then Mallory will capture $\frac{6300.8}{6300.8+1725.6} = 78.5\%$ of the channel occupancy time.

When Bob must regularly transmit each packet at least four times in order to reach Mallory, Bob sends every packet to Mallory at 1 Mbps. Thus each data transmission takes 12272 μs for data alone, which, after adding backoff, preamble, and header for the 1st transmission takes 12678 μs. The acknowledgment times out after the same 126 μs, giving a failure time for the 1st transmission of 12804 μs. Thereafter, each failure takes the same amount of time after adjustment for backoff, and when the acknowledgment finally comes, it is transmitted at 1 Mbps, so seven retransmissions takes $50 + 12678 * 7 + 126 * 6 +$ backoff increases $+ 202$ (μs), where 50 μs is DIFS, 12678 μs is the time that each packet transmission takes, 126 μs is the time to detect that an acknowledgment is not forthcoming, and 202 μs is the time to finish receiving an acknowledgment. The total additional backoff for seven retransmissions is 28160 μs in expectation, so the total transmission time is 117914 μs. If Mallory forces six retransmissions (for a total of seven transmissions) for each packet while Alice acknowledges every 1st transmission, then Mallory will capture $\frac{117914}{117914+1725.6} = 98.6\%$ of the channel occupancy time.

Finally, we argue that rate diversification exacerbates the partial deafness attack. In the same scenario, when Alice uses a 54 Mbps link in a 802.11b/g network, Mallory's transmissions take the same amount of time, but Alice's transmissions are now much faster. The DIFS and backoff take 360 μs as before (because it is a mixed-mode 802.11b/g access point), 802.11g does not require a preamble, and Alice's data transmission is now 227.3 μs, for a forward transmission time of 587.3 μs; after a 10 μs 802.11g SIFS and a 30 μs 802.11g acknowledgment, each Alice's packets take 627.3 μs in expectation. Thus Alice's channel occupancy time drops further to 0.53%.

4 Implementation and Evaluation of the Partial Deafness Attack

In this section, we detail our implementation of a partial deafness attacker and observe that the attack does in fact impact the data rate greatly.

4.1 Implementation

We implemented a partial deafness attacker to see the effect of the attack on an 802.11 network. Our implementation uses commercial off-the-shelf 802.11 Network Interface Cards (NICs). Most commodity 802.11 NICs generate and send acknowledgment frames automatically in firmware whenever a packet is received, because of the hard real-time deadlines on generating acknowledgments. The partial deafness attack can then be implemented by building custom hardware, modifying the firmware to defer acknowledgments, or turning off the network interface card any time between the start and completion of packet reception.

In order to simplify the task of deferring packet acknowledgments, we choose to modify the MadWifi driver, which is a Linux kernel device driver for Atheros-based WLAN devices. The Atheros chipset does not load a firmware onto the card, but instead relies on a Hardware Abstraction Layer (HAL) module that is part of the driver. The HAL module defines the interface between the hardware and other software in the device driver to manage many of the chip-specific operations and to enforce any relevant regulations.

We modified MadWifi to control a particular register in the HAL module that allows us to enable and disable packet acknowledgments. As illustrated in Fig. 1, we suppressed acknowledgements from the first $n - 1^{th}$ transmissions by switching the HAL register.

Our evaluation network consists of a traffic source connected to an IEEE 802.11b/g access point. A normal user and an attacker use 802.11 to connect to the access point. This topology is illustrated in Fig. 2. We use two different kinds of access points in our experiment. When we do not need to modify the

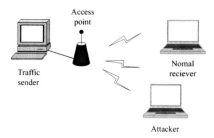

Fig. 2. Network Topology

access point queuing algorithms, we use commercial off-the-shelf access points such as Linksys WRT54G, which uses the Broadcom BCM5352EKPB chipset and supports 802.11b/g mixed mode, because it shows how the rate adaption is practically implemented in real 802.11 system. When we do need to modify the access point queuing algorithms, we use HostAP on a Pentium-III 1 GHz laptop running Linux 2.6.24 because we cannot control queuing behavior in the commercial products to which we have access. The Pentium-III laptop has an Ethernet interface and an Atheros 802.11a/b/g card. We use MadWifi and configure the Atheros NIC to operate in 802.11 master mode. We then use kernel-level bridging to bridge between the 802.11 network interface card and the Ethernet network interface card. For traffic generation, we use iperf; the traffic source generates traffic as an iperf client, which was then sunk at iperf servers running on the normal user and the attacker. We collect our data through an additional machine (not shown in Fig. 2), which captures all 802.11 frames sent on the network.

4.2   Evaluation

Maximum Throughput of Attacker. In order to determine the bit rate that an attacker needs to send to saturate the channel, we first examine the maximum throughput of the attacker using 802.11b when the attacker is the only user of the access point. We perform these measurements and theoretical analysis using UDP because UDP is a non-conforming load and will allow us to set our load regardless of the route's capability to handle that load. When Mallory forces Bob to transmit each packet n times, we compute the amount of time required per packet as described in Section 3; we then translate this into an application-layer rate and present it in Table 1.

As described in Section 3, the rate adaptation mechanism at the access point selects an 11 Mbps rate for users that acknowledge at least once every 3 transmissions and selects a 1 Mbps rate for users that acknowledge less frequently than every 3 transmissions. This contributes to the sharp reduction in maximum throughput between a user who acknowledges every 3 packets and a user who acknowledges every 4 packets.

We then implemented the partial deafness attacker that requires 1 to 7 transmissions before it will send an acknowledgment. We could not consistently require 2 transmissions because the driver we used to enable and disable acknowledgments could not consistently set the register within the real-time requirement between the first and the second transmissions. We ran this attacker both in an outdoor environment without measurable 802.11 interference and in an indoor environment where the 802.11 interference was uncontrolled. Some experimental results are greater than the calculated theoretical values because the access point, in violation of the specification, interleaves a beacon transmission between retransmissions of the original data packet. Because beacons are broadcast, and because broadcast messages are always considered successful, they reset the contention window size to minimum without resetting the retry count. Appendix A provides further details. Our results show that a partial deafness attacker receiving about 115 kbps of traffic can exhaust the entire forwarding capability of an access point.

Impact on UDP victim. We consider the impact on the throughput of a normal client that uses UDP against a partial deafness attacker that only acknowledges the 7th transmission of each packet. Theoretically, if the access point receives α packets destined to the normal user for every packet destined to the attacker, then we would expect that the normal user would get a $\frac{\alpha}{1+\alpha}$ share of the overall throughput, since the access point treats all packets equally.

To test this hypothesis, we gave the attacker a UDP source rate of 200 kbps, which is sufficient to saturate the access point's wireless link under the partial deafness attack; and the normal user, a UDP source rate of 100, 200, then 400 kbps. The resulting throughput is shown in Table 2. As expected, the ratio of throughputs is equal to the ratio of the UDP source rates.

Table 1. Maximum UDP throughput of an attacker. n is the number of transmissions required before the attacker sends an acknowledgment; this table shows results in a theoretical analysis as described in Section 3 and an actual outdoor/indoor experiment without/with any detectable 802.11 interference.

n	Theoretical	Outdoor	Indoor
1	6814.9 (kbps)	6049.0 (kbps)	5782.0 (kbps)
2	3184.2 (kbps)	N/A	N/A
3	1866.4 (kbps)	1563.0 (kbps)	1282.0 (kbps)
4	214.4 (kbps)	209.1 (kbps)	193.3 (kbps)
5	162.3 (kbps)	163.2 (kbps)	159.4 (kbps)
6	123.5 (kbps)	128.8 (kbps)	123.2 (kbps)
7	99.7 (kbps)	115.0 (kbps)	114.0 (kbps)

Table 2. UDP throughputs under partial deafness attack. Attacker's source rate is 200 kbps. Results are averaged over 20 runs.

Normal user's source rate	Normal user's throughput	Attacker's throughput
100 (kbps)	55.7 (kbps)	112.0 (kbps)
200 (kbps)	111.8 (kbps)	111.7 (kbps)
400 (kbps)	219.1 (kbps)	109.3 (kbps)

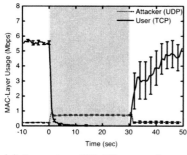 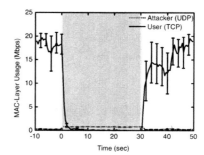

(a) Impact on 802.11b normal user   (b) Impact on 802.11g normal user

Fig. 3. MAC-layer utilization by TCP under the partial deafness attacker. The shaded region (0-30 sec) shows the time of attack; results are averaged over 20 runs, with the error bars (95% confidence interval).

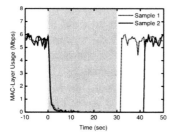 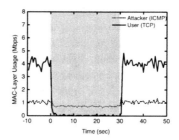

Fig. 4. The differences of TCP recovery time. The shaded region (0-30 sec) shows the time of attack.

Fig. 5. Partial deafness attack using ICMP ping. The shaded region (0-30 sec) shows the time of attack.

Impact on TCP victim. We now consider a normal TCP user competing for bandwidth against a partial deafness attacker. The attacker again uses a UDP source rate of 200 kbps. To show the impact of the attack, we allow TCP to warm up for a period of time before the attack starts; then perform the attack for a period of time, and finally turn off the attack and allow TCP to return to its steady-state behavior. Because we are interested in how nodes share the available bandwidth on the wireless link, we measure MAC-layer bandwidth usage, counting each retransmission as additional channel usage. As shown previously, each transmission to the attacker theoretically takes around 118 ms. We thus quantized each protocol's usage into 500 ms slots so that the normal user has a chance to receive data in each slot, and each slot conveys the granularity of MAC-layer usage. We plotted the MAC-layer usage over time for each scenario. Because we allow a warm-up and cool-down period where the attacker does not perform the partial deafness attack, each plot includes a shaded box covering the 30-second time interval (from 0 to 30) during which the attack took place.

Fig. 3(a) shows the MAC-layer usage when a partial deafness attacker competes against a normal user's TCP flow when both clients use 802.11b. As shown

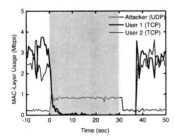

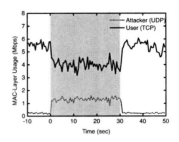

Fig. 6. Partial deafness attack on the network with two 802.11b normal users. The shaded region (0-30 sec) shows the time of attack.

Fig. 7. Partial deafness attack on an access point with fixed rate, 11 Mbps. The shaded region (0-30 sec) shows the time of attack.

in Table 1, a UDP attacker only needs to transmit 115 kbps in order to saturate the link and cause congestion; by allowing the attacker to send 200 kbps traffic would cause the attacker to experience a 43% loss rate without considering a sharing normal user. When a normal TCP user shares the channel with the attacker, the access point treats and drops an equal fraction of UDP and TCP packets, hence the TCP user would experience similar loss rate as the attacker. That is, the normal TCP user would experience at least a 43% loss rate; since TCP is a conforming transport layer protocol, such a high loss rate causes repeated TCP time-out and results in minimal throughput for the normal user, as shown in Fig. 3(a). We observe that TCP has substantial variance in the MAC layer usage during recovery (Fig. 3(a)); to show the cause of this large variance, we plot two sample runs in Fig. 4 and show that the TCP flow in each sample run recovers at substantially different time.

We examined the impact of a partial deafness attacker in the scenario where a normal user connects to the access point using the 802.11g standard. The normal user enjoys a faster connection when the attacker is silent; however, when the attacker carries out the partial deafness attack, the transfer speed of the normal 802.11g user is not significantly faster than that of a normal 802.11b user. This result is consistent with our analysis of rate diversity in a 802.11b/g network at the end of Section 3.

Partial deafness can even be carried out by an unauthenticated station when an access point uses a captive portal to authenticate end points. To attack such an access point, the attacker guests traffic to itself by sending Internet Control Message Protocol (ICMP) ping messages to the captive portal. Fig. 5 shows the impact of the data rate of a normal user when an attacker performs a flood ping (using the '-f' option) where each ping packet contains 1470 bytes of data. Our results shows that an attacker can deny an access point's service, even if the access point uses a captive portal to authenticate users.

The partial deafness attack creates head-of-queue blocking by using retransmission and rate adaptation; thus, a normal user will experience an even higher loss rate when other normal users are also present. This is intuitive since all

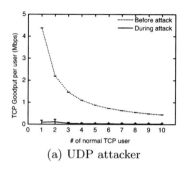

(a) UDP attacker

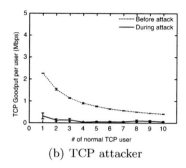

(b) TCP attacker

Fig. 8. ns-2 simulation of the partial deafness attack on a network with multiple 802.11b normal users; results are averaged over 20 runs, with the error bars showing 95% confidence interval

users are going to compete for the limited amount of remaining bandwidth. We performed our partial deafness attack in a network with 2 normal users, and show our results in Fig. 6.

We also performed an ns-2 simulation on the impact of the partial deafness attack in a network with 1 to 10 normal users in addition to the attacker. In our simulation, all users (normal and attacker) are located on a circle 1 m away from the access point. The normal users and the attacker are given identical properties (such as signal and noise power levels), except the acknowledgment policy. That is, the attacker is identical to a normal user except he does not acknowledge receiving a packet until the 7th transmission.

We present our simulation results in Fig. 8. Fig. 8(a) and Fig. 8(b) show the effectiveness of the partial deafness attack when the attacker uses UDP with source rate of 200 kbps and TCP respectively. In both cases, we see the goodput per normal user during attack is minuscule compared to the fair goodput each normal user enjoys without the attack.

The partial deafness attack works by exploiting the retransmission mechanism specified by 802.11 and the rate adaptation implemented at an access point. We thus examined the effectiveness of the partial deafness attack in the scenario where the access point does not support rate diversity. Since a fast connection is impacted by the slow connection partially due to the transfer speed, we expect the impact of partial deafness attack to be alleviated in the case where the access point does not provide rate adaptation. We show our result in Fig. 7.

We examined the effectiveness of the partial deafness attack on two other access points that use different chipsets from that of Linksys WRT54G. Specifically, we examined a Linksys WRT54GC, and a Trendnet TEW-432BRP access points. We present our results in Fig. 9. We observe that both access points are also susceptible to the partial deafness attack. Even though rate adaptation mechanisms of these two access points are different from that of Linksys WRT54G, the partial deafness attack still makes the attacker's traffic use the base rate during attack period. For the Linksys WRT54GC, each packet is

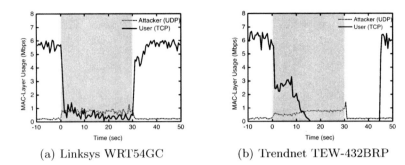

(a) Linksys WRT54GC   (b) Trendnet TEW-432BRP

Fig. 9. MAC-layer utilization by TCP under the partial deafness attacker. The shaded region (0-30 sec) shows the time of attack.

retransmitted only 4 times (we discuss this behavior in Appendix A.3). The rate adaptation mechanism in Trendnet TEW-432BRP decreases the rate slowly as compared to the Linksys WRT54G. This difference results in slower performance degradation, as shown in Fig. 9(b).

5   Countermeasure

In this section, we propose a countermeasure that mitigates the partial deafness attack. The partial deafness attack is based on head-of-queue blocking at the access point that results in starvation of normal users. Thus our intuition for mitigating the attack is to use time fairness to prevent starvation. Time fairness has also been suggested in previous work [15] to increase throughput in a network with rate diversity.

Time fairness can be enforced at the access point by implementing a Time-Based Regulator (TBR) that times each transmission: if user A is allocated time duration t_n in the nth round, then all other users are allocated the same time duration.

We implemented a TBR on HostAP as described in Section 4.1. In particular, we implemented a priority queue at the access point that allows us to select the next client to serve. We also emulated the rate adaptation of the Linksys WRT54G access point in order to obtain consistent comparisons of the data rates between our attack scenarios and our mitigation implementation.

Table 3. UDP throughput of normal user and partial deafness attacker with Time-Based Regulator (TBR). The source rate of attacker and normal user is 11 Mbps. Results are averaged over 20 runs.

	Attacker	Normal user
Normal user only		6.07 (Mbps)
Without TBR	110.9 (kbps)	107.9 (kbps)
With TBR	52.5 (kbps)	2.93 (Mbps)

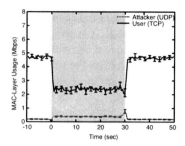

Fig. 10. The TCP user's MAC-layer channel utilization with the countermeasures. The shaded region (0-30 sec) shows the time of attack; results are averaged over 20 runs, with the error bars (95% confidence interval).

We first consider the case where a normal UDP user shares the wireless link with a partial deafness attacker. We gave both the partial deafness attacker and the normal user a UDP source rate of 11 Mbps. The partial deafness attacker is configured to only acknowledge the 7th transmission of every packet. The resulting throughput is shown in Table 3. When there is no attacker, the user can receive 6.07 Mbps of traffic, which is consistent with our previous result in Table 1. Moreover, when the attacker is present, the user still enjoys almost half of this rate, at 2.93 Mbps, which shows a significant improvement over using access opportunity fairness.

We applied a TBR to a TCP user in the presence of a partial deafness attacker who uses UDP at the transport layer. Fig. 10 shows that a TBR allows the user to obtain significantly better service when under attack. In particular, the TCP user ceases to experience heavy packet losses when a TBR is deployed at the access point.

Time fairness can be implemented with 802.11e by choosing appropriate traffic category for each node according to their fair share of channel occupancy time [15]. However, 802.11e itself (i.e. 802.11e without TBR) might not be effective as a countermeasure since 802.11e specifies only four traffic categories (i.e. four queues). As multiple partial deafness attackers can connect to a single access point, the attackers can collectively block all four queues used by 802.11e.

6   Conclusions

In this paper, we presented a denial-of-service attack, called *partial deafness*, against current IEEE 802.11 wireless networks. Our attack targets the 802.11 MAC protocol without modifying the MAC-layer implementation. Furthermore, our attack does not require the attacker to have better resources than a normal user; the attacker can have lower signal strength, slower computation, and be farther from the base station and still negatively impact the normal users. We showed that our attack substantially degrades the performance of normal users that use UDP and can almost completely deny service to users using TCP.

We then proposed and evaluated a countermeasure based on time fairness that mitigates the partial deafness attack. We use time-based regulation to ensure that each client gets an equal fraction of the service provided by the access point. We experimentally showed that this mechanism restores a reasonable level of performance for normal users, whether they use UDP or TCP, when an attacker performs the partial deafness attack.

References

1. IEEE Std. 802.11: Wireless LAN Medium Access Control (MAC) and Physical Layer (PHY) Specifications (2007)
2. Fluhrer, S., Mantin, I., Shamir, A.: Weaknesses in the key scheduling algorithm of RC4. In: Vaudenay, S., Youssef, A.M. (eds.) SAC 2001. LNCS, vol. 2259, pp. 1–24. Springer, Heidelberg (2001)
3. Stubblefield, A., Ioannidis, J., Rubin, A.D.: A key recovery attack on the 802.11b wired equivalent privacy protocol (WEP). ACM Transactions on Information and System Security 7(2), 319–332 (2004)
4. Bittau, A., Handley, M., Lackey, J.: The final nail in WEP's coffin. In: 27th IEEE Symposium on Security and Privacy, pp. 386–400. IEEE Computer Society, Los Alamitos (2006)
5. Bellardo, J., Savage, S.: 802.11 denial-of-service attacks: Real vulnerabilities and practical solutions. In: 12th USENIX Security Symposium, pp. 15–27. USENIX Association, Berkeley (2003)
6. Wi-Fi Alliance: Wi-Fi Protected Access: Strong, standards-based, interoperable security for today's Wi-Fi networks (2003)
7. IEEE Std. 802.11i: Medium Access Control (MAC) Security Enhancements (2004)
8. IEEE Std. 802.1X: Port-Based Network Access Control (2004)
9. Kyasanur, P., Vaidya, N.H.: Selfish MAC layer misbehavior in wireless networks. IEEE Transactions on Mobile Computing 4(5), 502–516 (2005)
10. Cardenas, A.A., Radosavac, S., Baras, J.S.: Performance comparison of detection schemes for MAC layer misbehavior. In: 26th IEEE Conference on Computer Communications, pp. 1496–1504. IEEE Communication Society, Piscataway (2007)
11. Raya, M., Hubaux, J.P., Aad, I.: DOMINO: A system to detect greedy behavior in IEEE 802.11 hotspots. In: 2nd International Conference on Mobile Systems, Applications, and Services, pp. 84–97. ACM, New York (2004)
12. Heusse, M., Rousseau, F., Berger-Sabbatel, G., Duda, A.: Performance anomaly of 802.11b. In: 22nd IEEE Conference on Computer Communications, pp. 836–843. IEEE Communication Society, Piscataway (2003)
13. Denial of service vulnerability in IEEE 802.11 wireless devices, http://www.auscert.org.au/render.html?it=4091
14. Ferreri, F., Bernaschi, M., Valcamonici, L.: Access points vulnerabilities to DoS attacks in 802.11 networks. In: IEEE Wireless Communications and Networking Conference, pp. 634–638. IEEE Communication Society, Piscataway (2004)
15. Tan, G., Guttag, J.: Time-based fairness improves performance in multi-rate WLANs. In: USENIX Annual Technical Conference, pp. 269–282. USENIX Association, Berkeley (2004)
16. Kamerman, A., Monteban, L.: WaveLAN-II: A high-performance wireless lan for the unlicensed band. Bell Labs Technical Journal 2(3), 118–133 (1997)

17. Bicket, J.C.: Bit-rate Selection in Wireless Networks. Master's thesis, Massachusetts Institute of Technology (2005)
18. Han, B., Schulman, A., Gringoli, F., Spring, N., Bhattacharjee, B., Nava, L., Ji, L., Lee, S., Miller, R.: Maranello: Practical partial packet recovery for 802.11. In: 7th USENIX Symposium on Networked Systems Design and Implementation. USENIX Association, Berkeley (2010)

A   Time Distribution of Beacon-Induced Backoff

Each access point periodically broadcasts beacons. Since beacons are broadcast messages, they are not acknowledged, so the 802.11 standard considers all beacon transmissions successful. However, when beacons are transmitted between retransmissions, the perceived success from the broadcast causes the access point to choose a contention window on the interval between $[0, \mathrm{CW_{min}}]$. Furthermore, since the packet waiting for retransmission has not yet been acknowledged, the access point does not reset the retry limit counter. This creates significant discrepancies in the backoff process between what the standard specifies and what actually happens using commercial products.

To demonstrate the discrepancies caused by the periodic beacons, we examine the latency between the 6th and 7th transmission. The 802.11 standard specifies that the 7th transmission wait Short InterFrame Space (SIFS) (10 μs) and then backoff with a value uniformly distributed over $[0, \mathrm{CW[7]}]$. However, if the contention window were reset between the mth and the $(m + 1)^{\mathrm{st}}$ transmission, the resulting backoff between the 6th and 7th transmission would be off by a factor of 2^{m-1}. (We use $m - 1$ instead of m because $\mathrm{CW[6]} = \mathrm{CW[7]}$ in 802.11b.) Therefore, given the beacons are transmitted periodically, we should expect the latency to be distributed geometrically.

A.1   Broadcom Chipset

We examined a Linksys WRT54G (ver. 5) using a Broadcom chipset. By default, this access point sends a beacon message every 100 ms. However, as shown in Section 3, the total time required to send 7 transmissions almost always takes longer than 100 ms. Thus, we change the beacon interval to 200 ms in order to demonstrate the effect of the beacon messages.

Fig. 11(a) shows a histogram of the latency between the 6th and 7th packet transmission with each bin size 100 μs, equaling 5 slot time. We categorized transmissions into two sets: one set contains all the transmissions where a beacon packet had been interleaved between the 1st transmission of this packet and the 7th; the other set contains all the transmissions for which no beacon packet had been interleaved between the 1st transmission of this packet and the 7th. The thin line shows the latency of the second set; that is, when no beacon has been interleaved. In the non-interleaved case, the latency is uniformly distributed, as would be expected from reading the 802.11 standard. The bold line shows our observation of latency from the first set; that is, for packets into which beacons have been interleaved. In this case, the latency is exponentially/geometrically

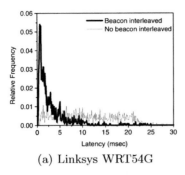 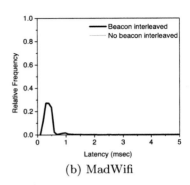

(a) Linksys WRT54G   (b) MadWifi

Fig. 11. Latency between the 2nd to last and last retransmissions of the same packet

distributed, which shows that beacons are interleaved and this interleaving does affect the backoff values chosen.

A.2   MadWifi Driver

As described in Section 4.1, the Hardware Abstraction Layer (HAL) module operates between the hardware and the device driver and is implemented to manage many of the chip-specific operations. The HAL module is distributed with the driver. Thus, the same Atheros Network Interface Card (NIC) may exhibit different behaviors when using different drivers that contain different HALs.

With the same scenario as described in previous section, we tested the Mad-Wifi driver and the Atheros NIC by using HostAP. We observed that the Mad-Wifi driver does not increase its contention window when retransmitting packets as shown in Fig. 11(b). There had been suspicions that MadWifi driver is not backing off properly [18]; moreover, when we used Windows and a Windows driver with the same Atheros NIC in an ad-hoc connection, we did not observe the improper backoff behavior. We thus conclude that MadWifi driver does not perform exponential backoff properly.

A.3   Marvell ARM914 Chipset

We also tested the Linksys WRT54GC access point, which uses the Marvell ARM914 chipset.We found that the maximum number of retransmissions was 4 instead of 7. The 802.11 standard specifies that packets with payload longer than Request to Send (RTS) threshold are transmitted up to the long retry count of 4, and with payload shorter than RTS threshold are transmitted up to the short retry count of 7. Most access points, including the Linksys WRT54GC, set the RTS threshold so that all packets are sent without RTS/Clear to Send (CTS), and thus each packet should be retransmitted up to 7 times. We thus conclude that the WRT54GC improperly set the short retry count to 4.

Attacking Beacon-Enabled 802.15.4 Networks

Sang Shin Jung, Marco Valero, Anu Bourgeois, and Raheem Beyah

CAP Research Group
Department of Computer Science, Georgia State University
Atlanta, GA 30303, USA
{sangsin,mvalero,abourgeois,rbeyah}@cs.gsu.edu
http://www.cs.gsu.edu/cap

Abstract. The IEEE 802.15.4 standard has attracted time-critical applications in wireless sensor networks (WSNs) because of its beacon-enabled mode and guaranteed time slots (GTSs). However, the GTS management scheme's built-in security mechanisms still leave the 802.15.4 MAC vulnerable to attacks. Further, the existing techniques in the literature for securing 802.15.4 either focus on non beacon-enabled mode 802.15.4 or cannot defend against insider attacks for beacon-enabled mode 802.15.4. In this paper we illustrate this by demonstrating attacks on the availability and integrity of a beacon-enabled 802.15.4 sensor network. To confirm the validity of the attacks, we implement the attacks using Tmote Sky Motes for sensor nodes, where the malicious node is deployed as an inside attacker. We show that the malicious node can easily exploit information retrieved from the beacon frames to compromise the integrity and availability of the network. We also discuss possible defense mechanisms against these attacks.

Keywords: Insider attacks, Beacon-enabled 802.15.4, wireless sensor networks, MAC misbehavior.

1 Introduction

Wireless sensor networks (WSNs) have emerged quickly and attracted a number of diverse applications. The use of these applications ranges from residential to government. For example, AlertMe home monitoring [1] is a residential system that enables secure indoor and outdoor home environment monitoring with simple contact and passive infrared (PIR) sensors. If AlertMe detects intruders, it immediately reports the intrusion to the homeowner. The military is also using WSNs to detect an adversary's behavior and location. For example, seismic sensors can be used to detect the movement of heavy artillery (e.g., tanks) in the battlefield. In either case, not receiving information about the environment in a time-sensitive manner can have significant consequences. To provide support for time-sensitive communication, the IEEE 802.15.4 standard provides a beacon-enabled mode. Unlike non beacon-enabled mode, the beacon-enabled mode in 802.15.4 networks facilitates real-time delivery of data using the GTS management scheme during the contention free period (CFP) [2,3,4,5,6,7].

S. Jajodia and J. Zhou (Eds.): SecureComm 2010, LNICST 50, pp. 253–271, 2010.

In the beacon-enabled mode, a centralized node (i.e., personal area network (PAN) coordinator) broadcasts beacon frames to synchronize the nodes in the network, manages GTS allocation/de-allocation requests from the end devices, and assigns dedicated slots for transmission from these nodes. Many researchers have focused on improving the performance or energy efficiency of beacon-enabled 802.15.4. For example, the IPP-HURRY research group has analyzed the delay bound of GTS allocation to maximize the throughput of each GTS allocation for real-time sensor networks [3,4]. In addition, in [5] the authors present a case study of Siemens Industry Automation Division that requires real-time delivery of short alarms/messages. The case study evaluates GTS allocation to maximize low latency of its scheme. Although there has been a significant emphasis on improving the performance of the beacon-enabled 802.15.4 protocol, there has been little work on securing this mode of the 802.15.4 protocol. This is significant, given that the GTS management scheme in beacon-enabled 802.15.4 networks does not verify the ID of each sensor node that requests GTSs. Therefore, an inside attacker can easily compromise the guaranteed data transmissions from the time-sensitive applications in the beacon-enabled network by either impersonating existing legitimate nodes' IDs or creating IDs for nodes that do not exist (i.e., implement a Sybil attack [8] at the MAC layer).

In this paper, we demonstrate four attacks that are possible by an inside attacker who impersonates legitimate nodes or generates multiple fake IDs. This is accomplished by the inside attacker targeting the vulnerabilities of the GTS management scheme in a beacon-enabled 802.15.4 network. The contributions of this paper include the discovery of vulnerable properties of the beacon-enabled mode in the IEEE 802.15.4 standard, the implementation and analysis of four potential insider attacks associated with those vulnerabilities, and the presentation of defense mechanisms against the attacks.

The rest of this paper is organized as follows. We review some related works including several security protocols for WSNs and attacks on beacon-enabled IEEE 802.15.4 in Section 2. In Section 3, we explain the GTS management scheme and its vulnerabilities. In Section 4, we define the network and attack model used to implement four potential attacks. In Section 5, we introduce our four attacks against the GTS management scheme. In Section 6, we describe the implementation of the attacks. In Section 7, we show the result of each attack based on the collected data. We briefly mention possible defenses against these attacks in Section 8 and conclude our work in Section 9.

2   Related Work

In this section we categorize current 802.15.4 defense mechanisms into beaconless mode and beacon-enabled mode according to the literature and highlight their limitations. We also discuss the difference between our attacks on beacon-enabled 802.15.4 networks and others previously demonstrated.

Defense Mechanisms in Beacon-Less Mode
In [9,10,11], the received signal strength indication (RSSI) was proposed to identify nodes conducting a Sybil attack. The basic idea of RSSI-based methods is that sensor nodes at different locations can be differentiated by the different RSSIs. In [10], M. Demirbas et al. calculate the ratio of RSSIs to improve traditional RSSI-based solutions. In [9], J. Yang et al. propose K-means cluster analysis that can be applied to RSSI readings. However, RSSI-based solutions can be evaded by malicious nodes with mobility. Another defense method is a cryptographic approach. Most of these approaches presents either light-weight methods such as light-weight identity certificates [12] or key distribution and management algorithms [13,14,15,16] to distinguish between legitimate nodes and malicious nodes using multiple stolen or forged IDs. However, it is not practical for resource constrained sensor devices to utilize highly expensive key distribution methods. Some link layer secure protocols such as SPINS, TinySec, and MiniSec [17,18,19] respectively are designed specifically for energy constrained sensor nodes and provide data authentication and secrecy at the link layer. However, these protocols are susceptible to failures when a compromised node in the network acquires a shared pair-wise or network-wide secret key. Although the aforementioned protocols have merit, they do not apply to beacon-enabled 802.15.4 networks. Further, they cannot be directly applied to beacon-enabled mode because it utilizes many different features such as time-sensitive GTSs.

Defense Mechanisms in Beacon-Enabled Mode
Few defense methods have been proposed for beacon-enabled mode. One RSSI-based solution for beacon-enabled mode was proposed by F. Amini et al. in [11]. The authors proposed an RSSI solution where they introduced the use of a disc number and a device ID. However, if a malicious node is close enough to a legitimate node in the same personal area network (PAN), its RSSI may be confused with the RSSI of the legitimate node. The IEEE 802.15.4 standard [20] also has built-in security features to provide data secrecy and data authenticity. However, in [21], N. Sastry et al. point out that these security features have vulnerabilities related to the initial vector (IV) management, key management, and integrity protection. Another link layer secure protocol implementation for beacon-enabled mode was presented in [22]. Alim et al. introduce EAP-Sens which provides entity authentication and key management to validate each device ID with an extensible authentication protocol (EAP) [23] and EAP-generalized pre-shared key (EAP-GPSK) [24]. Even though Alim et al. mention that EAP-Sens is not vulnerable to a man-in-the-middle attack due to its shared key method, EAP-Sens is still vulnerable to attacks when there is an inside attacker. Overall, neither the aforementioned detection mechanisms nor secure link layer protocols in beacon-enabled mode are effective in the case of compromised nodes acting as inside attackers.

Attacks on Beacon-Enabled 802.15.4 Networks
In [25], R. Sokullu et al. use ns-2 simulations to demonstrate GTS attacks on the 802.15.4 MAC, particularly in beacon-enabled mode. The GTS attacks

were divided into four different scenarios: One Intelligent Attacker (OIA), One Random Attacker (ORA), Two Intelligent Attackers (TIAs), and Two Random Attackers (TRAs). Both the OIA and TIAs scenarios target the maximum number of GTSs assigned to one legitimate node. In contrast, the ORA and TRAs scenarios attack just one randomly chosen GTS. The main goal of the GTS attacks in [25] is to create collisions during the CFP to deny the use of GTSs. In contrast, our four attacks seek to exploit the beacon-enabled 802.15.4 MAC by providing scenarios of unfairness and exhaustion [26,27].

In addition to presenting different types of attacks compared to those discussed in [25], our attacks were implemented on real devices (i.e., Tmote Sky Motes) rather than in simulation. This latter point is extremely important for 802.15.4 MAC layer attacks, because in addition to the challenge of accurately modeling physical layer interference, simulations do not take into account constraints imposed by the hardware, operating system, and applications, which can lead to simplified attack scenarios. This is especially pronounced in resource-constrained devices (e.g., Tmote Sky Motes). For example, to implement the Sybil attack (at the MAC layer) in TinyOS, we modified the timer function of TinyOS (in TimerC.nc) to make it multithreaded so each fake node could use an instance. Each instance now has to compete internally (within TinyOS) to gain access to the node's resources (e.g., processor, transceiver), making this attack much more difficult to conduct. This small, but noticeable nuance is not present in simulation tools.

3 Problem Statement

In this section, we briefly explain the GTS management scheme of the IEEE 802.15.4 standard and we state three vulnerabilities of the scheme.

3.1 GTS Management Scheme

The IEEE 802.15.4 standard [20] operating in beacon-enabled mode defines the superframe (SF) that consists of contention access period (CAP), contention free period (CFP), and inactive period as shown in Figure 1. According to the standard, the personal area network (PAN) coordinator periodically transmits beacon frames at intervals defined by the *aBeaconOrder* variable. The beacon frames contain the number of GTSs and these directions used by nodes to transmit data during the CFP. The structure of the beacon frame and the GTS field are shown in Figure 2 (a) and (b) respectively. As shown in Figure 1, the PAN coordinator defines that each superframe can have maximum of seven GTSs for the CFP other than *aMinCAPLength* in [20]. The slots of GTSs must be assigned to legitimate nodes issuing GTS allocation requests to the PAN coordinator. Then, the assigned slots should be released by the PAN coordinator after receiving a GTS deallocation request from the same legitimate node.

Below we briefly explain the normal GTS allocation and deallocation processes.

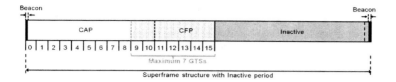

Fig. 1. GTSs in Superframe structure

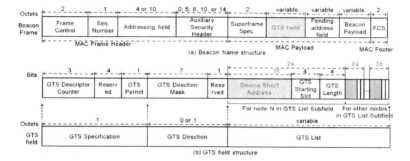

Fig. 2. Details of MAC frame structure: (a) beacon frame structure and (b) GTS field structure in beacon frame

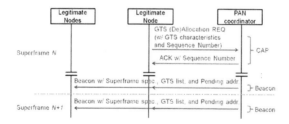

Fig. 3. GTS allocation and deallocation procedure

GTS Allocation: If a legitimate node has data to transmit, it generates a GTS allocation request. The PAN coordinator will allocate an available GTS to the legitimate node, and all subsequent beacon frames will contain the GTS descriptor defining the device address, GTS slot and direction. Upon receiving the beacon with the GTS descriptor, the legitimate node will schedule the pending packet to be transmitted at the allocated GTS. The GTS allocation process is shown in Figure 3.

GTS Deallocation: The GTS deallocation occurs after the GTS descriptor has been transmitted for $aGTSDescPersistenceTime$ beacons by the PAN coordinator or when the legitimate node using the GTS sends an explicit GTS deallocation request. The GTS deallocation process is shown in Figure 3.

3.2   Vulnerabilities of GTS Management Scheme

The PAN coordinator manages a list of GTSs to control the network access during the CFP. However, the GTS management scheme has the following vulnerabilities.

CAP Maintenance: According to the IEEE 802.15.4 standard, the PAN coordinator can perform several preventative actions to keep $aMinCAPLength$. One of these actions is to deallocate unused GTSs within every $2 * n$ SFs, where n is defined as either $2^{(8-macBeaconOrder)}$ $(0 \leq macBeaconOrder \leq 8)$ or $(9 \leq macBeaconOrder \leq 14)$. However, if a malicious node keeps constantly sending either GTS requests or data at the assigned GTSs during the CFP, the preventative action is ineffective.

Verification of Sensor Nodes' IDs: In the 802.15.4 GTS management scheme, the PAN coordinator manages the Identities (IDs) of legitimate nodes requesting one or more GTSs. The PAN coordinator assigns GTSs to the nodes, deallocates the assigned slots, and avoids duplicated GTS requests from the same legitimate node. However, as shown in Figure 4 the PAN coordinator only checks the sensor nodes' IDs (a short 2-octet address) and the sequence number of the packets. Thus, a malicious node can easily evade the verification process for sensor nodes' IDs by using new forged IDs or impersonating legitimate nodes in the network.

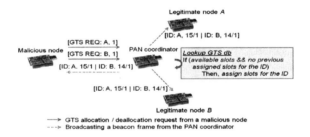

Fig. 4. A malicious node impersonating the IDs of legitimate node A and B

4   Experiment Design

In this section, we present the network design, the attack model, and the hardware and software components used in this work.

4.1   Network Design

In this paper, we use sensor nodes supporting the IEEE 802.15.4 standard in beacon-enabled mode. The nodes performing legal activities in the network are called legitimate nodes, while the bad nodes are called malicious nodes. The nodes are organized in a cluster which has a base station (i.e., PAN coordinator) collecting messages from each sensor. We use Tmote Sky Motes [28] as sensor nodes and PAN coordinator. Tmote Sky Mote has a CC2420 radio chip [29] and supports the 802.15.4 standard [20] in both beacon-less and beacon-enabled mode.

4.2 Attack Model

Similar to the threat models defined in [26] and [30], we assume that a malicious node behaves badly as a mote-class, inside, and active attacker. As a mote-class adversary, a malicious node has the same capabilities as that of any legitimate node. Therefore, we use Tmote Sky Motes for the malicious node. As an inside and active attacker, a malicious node listens to broadcasting beacons and interferes with the communication between legitimate nodes and the PAN coordinator.

4.3 Hardware and Software Components

We used four Tmote Sky Motes [28]: one PAN coordinator, two legitimate nodes, and one malicious node. Our attack experiments use the IEEE 802.15.4 open-ZB open source implementation [31]. In particular, we used version 1.2 of the source code in conjunction with TinyOS v1.15 [32]. In addition, we used the Texas Instruments (TI) CC2420 Evaluation Board/Evaluation Module (EB/EM) [33] in conjunction with the TI Chipcon packet sniffer [34] to capture and analyze packet traffic in the network. Only four nodes were used because the open source implementation used became unstable above four nodes in the network. However, it is important to note that these attacks are *independent* of the number of nodes deployed in the network. Figure 5 shows examples of captured packets from the TI Chipcon packet sniffer. Figure 6 shows Tmote Sky Motes and CC2420 EB/EM.

5 Overview of Attacks

We divided the four attacks into two categories depending on the types of IDs that the malicious node uses to perform the illicit activities. The first category is *existing IDs* in the PAN where a malicious node uses the ID of a legitimate node in the PAN. The second category is *non-existing IDs* in the PAN where malicious nodes use any non-existing ID in the PAN and pretend to be newly deployed nodes in the network. In the former category, the malicious node can affect exhaustion of legitimate nodes. In the latter, it causes exhaustion and unfairness against legitimate nodes.

5.1 Existing Identities in the PAN

In this category, a malicious node impersonates the existing legitimate nodes in the PAN. The attack is of the form of DoS against data transmissions during the

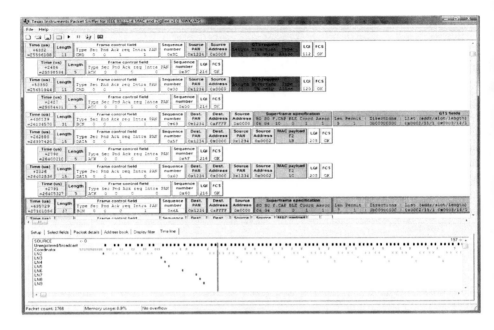

Fig. 5. Captured packets from TI Chipcon packet sniffer

Fig. 6. Tmote Sky Motes and CC2420 EB/EM

CFP. The idea is to block data transmission of legitimate nodes, which denies legitimate nodes requiring GTSs access to the link.

DoS against Data Transmissions during CFP

If a malicious node is in the transmission range of the PAN coordinator, it can eavesdrop on the messages sent by legitimate nodes and also intercept the beacons sent by the PAN coordinator. Since the beacons include the GTS list (Figure 2 (b)), the malicious node can recognize not only how many legitimate nodes are in the PAN, but also what legitimate nodes request and use GTSs to send data during the CFP. In this attack, a malicious node sends GTS deallocation requests using legitimate nodes' IDs to the PAN coordinator. Figure 7 shows an example of this attack where two legitimate nodes send GTS allocation requests

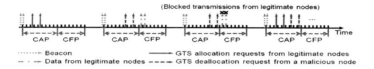

Fig. 7. A malicious node blocking a legitimate node sending data during CFP

before sending data during the CFP of the next SF. However, a malicious node knowing that the two nodes are in the GTS list can terminate the data transmissions of the legitimate nodes by sending a GTS deallocation request with the legitimate nodes' IDs.

False Data Injection

While a legitimate node is not in the GTS list, a malicious node can send a GTS allocation request and try to send data using the legitimate node's ID. Having checked the node's IDs and sequence number, the PAN coordinator accepts the data sent by the malicious node that contain false information. Figure 8 shows how this attack works; if a legitimate node is transmitting current temperature data during the CAP, the malicious node sends a GTS allocation request with the spoofed ID, and pretends to be the legitimate node to inject false data during CFP.

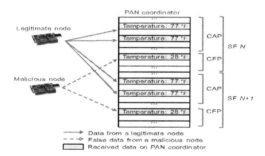

Fig. 8. A malicious node sending false temperature to the PAN coordinator

5.2 Non-existing Identities in the PAN

In this category of attacks, a malicious node forges 7 different IDs depending on the maximum number of available GTSs. Two attacks herein perform exhaustion and unfairness attacks by occupying all 7 GTSs and not allowing legitimate nodes to reserve GTSs.

DoS against GTS Requests

To perform this attack, a malicious node keeps monitoring the available GTS slots with the intent of completely occupying them. Then, the attacker sends

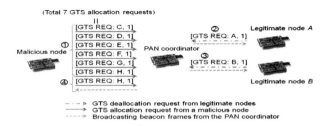

Fig. 9. A malicious node filling up all 7 GTSs. 1: the malicious node sends five GTS allocation requests. 2 and 3: legitimate node A and B send GTS deallocation requests. 4: the malicious node sends the rest of GTS allocation requests.

several GTS allocation requests to fill up all the available GTSs in the SF. The advantage of this attack is that the malicious node can reduce its energy consumption because once it occupies all 7 GTSs, it does not need to send out any data or commands. The malicious node simply dissects beacon frames to see if the PAN coordinator performs the preventative action for the CAP maintenance. Figure 9 shows that after legitimate node A and B send GTS deallocation requests, the malicious node completely fills all 7 GTSs with two additional GTS allocation requests. The goal of this attack is *not* for the attacker to use the bandwidth requested, rather it is to prevent the legitimate nodes from transmitting.

Stealing Network Bandwidth

Similar to the DoS against GTS requests, in this attack, an attacker observes the GTS list in order to eventually occupy the available GTS slots. However, in this attack, the malicious node sends data at the assigned time slots. The purpose of data transmission is to prevent the PAN coordinator from dropping the assigned GTSs. As shown in Figure 10, the second CFP has data transmitted from both legitimate nodes and a malicious node. However, since legitimate nodes send GTS deallocation requests during the second CAP, the malicious node sends a GTS allocation requests to occupy the new free GTS. Eventually, only the malicious node sends data during the fourth CFP. The time slots will never be vacant during the CFP of every SF, which can cause both exhaustion and unfairness against legitimate nodes. This also affects the PAN coordinator who cannot go into sleep mode (denial of sleep attack [35]).

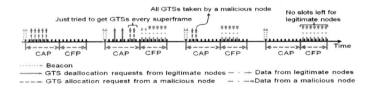

Fig. 10. A malicious node stealing all 7 GTSs during CFP

6   Implementation of Attacks

6.1   Existing Identities in the PAN

We assume that there is one PAN coordinator, two legitimate nodes: LN2 and LN6, and one malicious node: MN4 as shown in Figures 11 and 12. MN4 impersonates the IDs of LN2 and LN6 after eavesdropping on beacon frames.

DoS against Data Transmissions during CFP
As shown in Figure 11, this attack works through two SFs. In the first SF, LN2 and LN6 send GTS allocation requests to the PAN coordinator to reserve one GTS. Then, the PAN coordinator broadcasts the beacon with the GTS list to inform LN2 and LN6 of their assigned slots. Along with LN2 and LN6, MN4 also receives the beacon. Therefore, MN4 knows how many legitimate nodes are in the GTS list and what their IDs are. In the second SF, MN4 sends GTS deallocation requests with the impersonated LN2 and LN6's IDs. The PAN coordinator removes LN2 and LN6 from the GTS list and will not receive data during the CFP of the next SF. Since LN2 and LN6 have no allocated GTSs anymore, they will not able to send their messages during the CFP of the third SF.

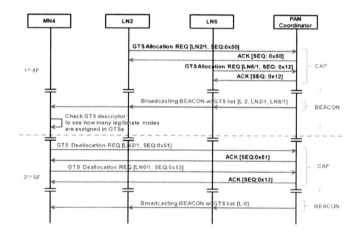

Fig. 11. The sequences of DoS against Data Transmissions During CFP

False Data Injection
Unlike DoS against Data Transmissions During CFP, this attack exploits GTS allocation requests to transmit false data. Figure 12 shows such a case that LN2 has already been assigned to one GTS. In this case, MN4 starts after LN2 sends a GTS deallocation request in the first SF. Then, the PAN coordinator removes LN2's ID on the GTS list of the next beacon. Since MN4 is aware that LN2 is not in the GTS list, it immediately tries to get one GTS by sending a GTS allocation request with LN2's ID. Once MN4 successfully takes the GTS, it starts sending false data with LN2's ID in the third SF.

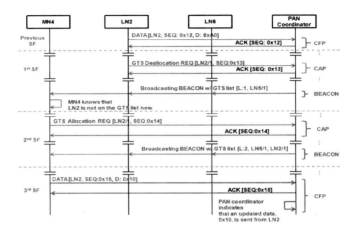

Fig. 12. The sequence of False Data Injection

6.2 Non-existing Identities in the PAN

For forging non-existing IDs, we also have one PAN coordinator, two legitimate nodes: LN2 and LN6, and one malicious node: MN4 that pretends to be a different ID from ones of LN2 and LN6. In this case, MN4 eavesdrops on the beacons to learn what IDs do not belong in the PAN.

DoS against GTS Requests

As shown in Figure 13, this attack needs several superframes to allow MN4 to fill all 7 GTSs. In each SF, MN4 knows how many GTSs are available and sends GTS allocation requests in order to reserve the remaining slots of GTSs. Once MN4 takes all 7 GTSs, it stops sending GTS allocation requests to reduce its

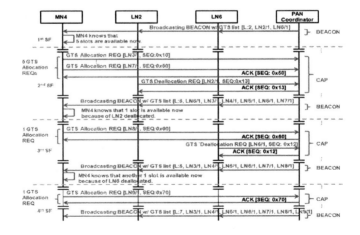

Fig. 13. The sequence of DoS against GTS request

energy consumption and monitors the beacons to start sending GTS allocation requests again if the PAN coordinator drops the unused GTSs by a preventative action for the CAP maintenance.

Stealing Network Bandwidth

Figure 14 shows that a malicious node takes the last slot out of GTSs, 6 slots of which were already assigned to the malicious node. Then, it can utilize all 7 GTSs during the CFP to transmit data. The difference from the previous DoS against GTS Requests is that since this attack continues to transmit data at each time slot of the CFP, the PAN coordinator will not take a preventative action for the CAP maintenance.

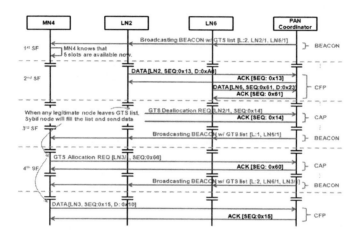

Fig. 14. The sequence of Stealing Network Bandwidth

7   Attack Analysis

We have verified our implementation with the packet sniffer [34] to monitor the packet transmission while each attack is executing. We utilize the PAN coordinator to log humidity and temperature sent by a legitimate node during both the CAP and the CFP. In addition, the throughputs in Figures 15, 16, and 17 are based on the total number of data in bytes divided by the elapsed time. The total data is counted only during the CFP. For each test of the four attacks, we measured the packet transmission for 100 to 400 seconds depending on the complexity of each attack.

DoS against Data Transmission during CFP

Figure 15 shows the decline of data throughputs on LN2 and LN6 while MN4 is sending GTS deallocation requests with LN2 and LN6's IDs. Around the 50-second mark of the experiment, a malicious node sends two GTS deallocation requests back to back. It also sends the same two GTS deallocation requests whenever it receives a beacon-notification. Therefore, the data throughputs from

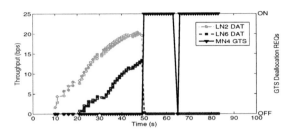

Fig. 15. Legitimate nodes (LN2 and LN6) data throughput during CFP by a malicious node (MN4). LN2 DAT and LN6 DAT: Data from LN2 and LN6 and MN4 GTS: GTS deallocation requests from MN4.

LN2 and LN6 during the CFP are dropped to 0bps. During the moment after 50-second mark, even though LN2 and LN6 try to send GTS allocation requests, the requests cannot be accomplished because of continuously sending GTS deallocation requests from MN4.

False Data Injection
Figure 16 shows the change of humidity and temperature from LN2. We tested this attack inside of a building, the humidity and temperature conditions were approximately 41% and 72°F respectively. However, since MN4 sends false data readings of 90% of humidity and 28°F temperature during the CFP, this results in many fluctuations of data for 20 seconds around the 73 to 93-second mark. Since 28°F is below the freezing point, the false data of temperature might lead to a warning sign in a practical situation.

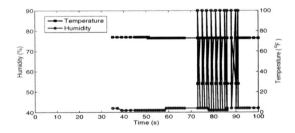

Fig. 16. Fluctuation of humidity and temperature

DoS against GTS Requests
Figure 17 shows two instances of this attack. LN2 and MN4 are started at the same time (around the 20-second mark). By sending a GTS request, LN2 quickly occupies one GTS and transmits data during the CFP. Similarly, MN4 quickly occupies the remaining 6 of the 7 GTSs. While LN2 is transmitting data, MN4 continuously sends GTS allocation requests in an attempt to occupy the last

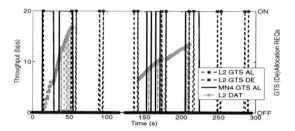

Fig. 17. A malicious node (MN4) filling up all 7 GTSs. LN2 DAT: LN2 Data, LN2 GTS AL: LN2 GTS allocation request, LN2 GTS DE: LN2 GTS deallocation request, and MN4 GTS AL: GTS allocation requests from MN4.

GTS. Once LN2 releases its GTS at the 50-second mark, the coordinator allows MN4 to occupy the last GTS. MN4 now stops sending GTS allocation requests to conserve energy. LN2 sends a GTS allocation request around the 60-second mark and the 90-second mark, but the coordinator does not assign LN2 a GTS (because MN4 has them all). To see another iteration of this, we turn off the PAN coordinator around the 130-second mark to force it to perform the preventative CAP maintenance action manually (this is because the IEEE 802.15.4 source code from the open-ZB does not handle this situation as it should). Accordingly, the PAN coordinator does not have any requested GTSs. Around the 140-second mark, we turn on the PAN coordinator and LN2 successfully is allocated one GTS and it transmits data during the corresponding CFP for about 70 seconds. MN4 now begins sending GTS allocation requests between the 150-second mark and 200-second mark and is able to occupy 6 GTSs. Also, when LN2 releases its GTS around the 200-second mark, MN4 immediately occupies all 7 GTSs again.

Stealing Network Bandwidth

Figure 18 shows the data throughputs of LN2 and MN4 and the GTS allocation requests of MN4. While LN2 has one GTS and transmits data during the CFP, MN4 starts sending GTS allocation requests with 7 forged IDs around 20-second mark and transmits data at the assigned GTSs. One of 7 GTSs

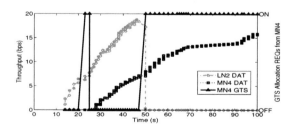

Fig. 18. A malicious node (MN4) stealing GTSs during CFP. LN2 DAT and MN4 DAT: Data from LN2 and MN4 respectively and MN4 GTS: GTS allocation requests from MN4.

allocation requests of MN4 is discarded at the first attempt because one GTS is already assigned to LN2. However, as soon as LN2 releases its GTS around the 50-second mark, MN4 occupies the last GTS immediately and has all 7 GTSs. MN4 probably consumes its energy by itself. However, LN2 and the PAN coordinator can use a lot of energy because LN2 attempts a GTS allocation request to get one GTS, and the PAN coordinator needs to receive data from the nodes.

8 Possible Countermeasures

We can consider several countermeasures against an inside attacker launching attacks in a beacon-enabled 802.15.4 network. [1] Even though light-weight authentication for each node might be a viable solution, authentication with a reliable key distribution and management is a expensive method for resource limited sensor nodes. In addition, the 802.15.4 standard states that key management and entity (e.g., sensor node) authentication can be implemented on top of the MAC layer [20]. Therefore, we present less expensive methods that can defend against our implemented attacks.

Reliable GTS Management Scheme: According to the 802.15.4 standard [20], its security features already have an access control list (ACL) mode. However, the functionality of the ACL mode does not cover the GTS management scheme. The access control should be extended to restrict the available numbers of GTSs to each node and keep track of thine reserved GTSs. The access control mechanism should exam the frequency of sending GTS (de)allocation requests from each node. If the frequency of GTS requests is too high from one node, it may become suspicious that a malicious node is trying to hold the CAP by sending a number of GTS requests (one of the commands in the 802.15.4) because all the commands can be sent during the CAP if there is no contention. In addition, the access control mechanism should keep track of the interval between GTS requests from the same node. If the interval of the same GTS request is too short, this could be an indication that a malicious node is interfering with a legitimate node sending GTS requests.

Multiple Channels: Another possible prevention against an inside attacker either impersonating legitimate nodes or forging new nodes' IDs is that the PAN coordinator might use different pre-defined channels for each legitimate node that may be changed after a short period of time (i.e., frequency hopping). Then, a malicious node would need to take a while to scan the communication channel with each change. Even though the malicious node discovers one proper channel, it can pretend to be a legitimate node for a very short time since the legitimate node can change the communication channel with the PAN coordinator. Moreover, the malicious node will have to spend a large amount of time to scan other channels for other legitimate nodes.

---

[1] Due to space constraints, the countermeasures will be addressed in detail in our future work.

9   Conclusion and Future work

In this paper, we first described some existing vulnerabilities of the GTS management scheme in the IEEE 802.15.4 standard. We also investigated security protocols proposed in the recent years and security features adopted in the standard. However, to date, no method considers insider attacks against beacon-enabled 802.15.4 networks. Therefore, we have targeted the GTS management scheme in a beacon-enabled IEEE 802.15.4 network and implemented four possible attacks on integrity and availability: (1) DoS against sending data during CFP, (2) False data injection, (3) DoS against GTS requests, and (4) Stealing network bandwidth. We also analyzed the results for each attack. For our future work, we will consider ways for malicious nodes to save energy while attacking, develop other types of attacks in the MAC layer, and implement the defense mechanisms discussed in Section 8.

Acknowledgements

This work was partly supported by NSF Grant No. CAREER-CNS-844144.

References

1. Alert Me homepage, http://www.alertme.com/products/home-monitoring
2. Mishra, A., Na, C., Rosenburgh, D.: On Scheduling Guaranteed Time Slots for Time Sensitive Transactions in IEEE 802.15.4 Networks. In: Military Communications Conference, MILCOM 2007, pp. 1–7. IEEE, Los Alamitos (2007)
3. Koubaa, A., Alves, M., Tovar, E.: i-GAME: an implicit GTS allocation mechanism in IEEE 802.15.4 for time-sensitive wireless sensor networks. In: 18th Euromicro Conference on Real-Time Systems, vol. 10, pp. 183–192 (2006)
4. Koubaa, A., Alves, M., Tovar, E.: GTS allocation analysis in IEEE 802.15.4 for real-time wireless sensor networks. In: 20th International Parallel and Distributed Processing Symposium, IPDPS 2006, 8p. (2006)
5. Chen, F., Talanis, T., German, R., Dressler, F.: Real-time enabled IEEE 802.15.4 sensor networks in industrial automation. In: IEEE International Symposium on Industrial Embedded Systems, SIES 2009, pp. 136–139 (2009)
6. Park, P., Fischione, C., Johansson, K.H.: Performance Analysis of GTS Allocation in Beacon Enabled IEEE 802.15.4. In: 6th Annual IEEE Communications Society Conference on Sensor, Mesh and Ad Hoc Communications and Networks, SECON 2009, pp. 1–9 (2009)
7. Mehta, A., Bhatti, G., Sahinoglu, Z., Viswanathan, R., Zhang, J.: Performance analysis of beacon-enabled IEEE 802.15.4 MAC for emergency response applications. In: 2009 IEEE 3rd International Symposium on Advanced Networks and Telecommunication Systems (ANTS), pp. 1–3 (2009)
8. Douceur, J.R.: The Sybil Attack. In: Druschel, P., Kaashoek, M.F., Rowstron, A. (eds.) IPTPS 2002. LNCS, vol. 2429, p. 251. Springer, Heidelberg (2002)
9. Yang, J., Chen, Y., Trappe, W.: Detecting sybil attacks in wireless and sensor networks using cluster analysis. In: 5th IEEE International Conference on Mobile Ad Hoc and Sensor Systems, MASS 2008, 29-October 2, pp. 834–839 (2008)

10. Demirbas, M., Song, Y.: An rssi-based scheme for sybil attack detection in wireless sensor networks. In: International Symposium on a World of Wireless, Mobile and Multimedia Networks, WoWMoM 2006, p. 5, p. 570 (2006)
11. Amini, F., Misic, J., Pourreza, H.: Detection of sybil attack in beacon enabled IEEE 802.15.4 networks. In: International Conference on Wireless Communications and Mobile Computing, IWCMC 2008, pp. 1058–1063 (August 2008)
12. Zhang, Q., Wang, P., Reeves, D., Ning, P.: Defending against Sybil attacks in sensor networks. In: 25th IEEE International Conference on Distributed Computing Systems Workshops, pp. 185–191 (June 2005)
13. Du, W., Deng, J., Han, Y.S., Varshney, P.K.: A pairwise key predistribution scheme for wireless sensor networks. In: CCS 2003: Proceedings of the 10th ACM conference on Computer and communications security, pp. 42–51. ACM, New York (2003)
14. Liu, D., Ning, P.: Establishing pairwise keys in distributed sensor networks. In: CCS 2003: Proceedings of the 10th ACM conference on Computer and communications security, pp. 52–61. ACM, New York (2003)
15. Du, W., Deng, J., Han, Y., Chen, S., Varshney, P.: A key management scheme for wireless sensor networks using deployment knowledge. In: INFOCOM 2004. Twenty-third AnnualJoint Conference of the IEEE Computer and Communications Societies, vol. 1, p. 597 (March 2004)
16. Eschenauer, L., Gligor, V.D.: A key-management scheme for distributed sensor networks. In: CCS 2002: Proceedings of the 9th ACM conference on Computer and communications security, pp. 41–47. ACM, New York (2002)
17. Perrig, A., Szewczyk, R., Wen, V., Culler, D., Tygar, J.D.: SPINS: security protocols for sensor networks. In: MobiCom 2001: Proceedings of the 7th annual international conference on Mobile computing and networking, pp. 189–199. ACM, New York (2001)
18. Karlof, C., Sastry, N., Wagner, D.: Tinysec: a link layer security architecture for wireless sensor networks. In: SenSys 2004: Proceedings of the 2nd international conference on Embedded networked sensor systems, pp. 162–175. ACM, New York (2004)
19. Luk, M., Mezzour, G., Perrig, A., Gligor, V.: MiniSec: a secure sensor network communication architecture. In: IPSN 2007: Proceedings of the 6th international conference on Information processing in sensor networks, pp. 479–488. ACM, New York (2007)
20. Wireless medium access control and physical layer specications for low-rate wireless personal area networks. IEEE Standard, 802.15.4-2003 (May 2003), ISBN 0-7381-3677-5
21. Sastry, N., Wagner, D.: Security considerations for ieee 802.15.4 networks. In: WiSe 2004: Proceedings of the 3rd ACM workshop on Wireless security, pp. 32–42. ACM, New York (2004)
22. Alim, M.A., Sarikaya, B.: EAP-Sens: a security architecture for wireless sensor networks. In: WICON 2008: Proceedings of the 4th Annual International Conference on Wireless Internet, Brussels, Belgium, Belgium, pp. 1–9. ICST (2008)
23. Aboba, L.B.B., Vollbrecht, J.C.J., Levkowetz, H.: Extensible Authentication Protocol EAP (June 2004), http://tools.ietf.org/html/rfc3748
24. Clancy, T., Tschofenig, H.: Extensible Authentication Protocol Generalized Pre-Shared Key EAP-GPSK method (February 2009), http://tools.ietf.org/html/rfc5433
25. Sokullu, R., Dagdeviren, O., Korkmaz, I.: On the IEEE 802.15.4 MAC layer attacks: GTS attack. In: Second International Conference on Sensor Technologies and Applications, SENSORCOMM 2008, pp. 673–678 (August 2008)

26. Roosta, T., Shieh, S., Sastry, S.: Taxonomy of security attacks in sensor networks and countermeasures. In: The First IEEE International Conference on System Integration and Reliability Improvements, Hanoi, pp. 13–15 (2006)
27. Wood, A.D., Stankovic, J.A.: Denial of service in sensor networks. Computer 35, 54–62 (2002)
28. Moteiv Corporation, tmote-sky-datasheet (2006), http://www.moteiv.com
29. Chipcon product from Texas Instruments, CC2420, http://focus.ti.com/lit/ds/symlink/cc2420.pdf
30. Karlof, C., Wagner, D.: Secure routing in wireless sensor networks: Attacks and Countermeasures. In: Proceedings of the First 2003 IEEE International Workshop on Sensor Network Protocols and Applications, pp. 113–127 (May 2003)
31. Open-zb homepage, http://www.open-zb.net/
32. TinyOS homepage, http://www.tinyos.net/
33. Chipcon Products from Texas Instruments, User Manual Rev. 1.0 CC2420DK Development Kit, http://focus.ti.com/lit/ug/swru045/swru045.pdf
34. Texas Instruments Incorporated, SmartRFPacket Sniffer User Manual Rev. 1.9, http://focus.ti.com/docs/toolsw/folders/print/packetsniffer.html
35. Wood, A.D., Stankovic, J.A.: A Taxonomy for Denial-of-Service Attacks. In: Wireless Sensor Networks. CRC Press, Boca Raton (2004)

Supporting Publication and Subscription Confidentiality in Pub/Sub Networks[*]

Mihaela Ion[1], Giovanni Russello[1], and Bruno Crispo[2]

[1] CREATE-NET International Research Center,
via alla Cascata 56D, 38123 Trento, Italy
{mihaela.ion,giovanni.russello}@create-net.org
[2] Department of Information Engineering and Computer Science,
University of Trento, Trento, Italy
crispo@disi.unitn.it

Abstract. The publish/subscribe model offers a loosely-coupled communication paradigm where applications interact indirectly and asynchronously. Publisher applications generate events that are sent to interested applications through a network of brokers. Subscriber applications express their interest by specifying filters that brokers can use for routing the events. Supporting confidentiality of messages being exchanged is still challenging. First of all, it is desirable that any scheme used for protecting the confidentiality of both the events and filters should not require the publishers and subscribers to share secret keys. In fact, such a restriction is against the loose-coupling of the model. Moreover, such a scheme should not restrict the expressiveness of filters and should allow the broker to perform event filtering to route the events to the interested parties. Existing solutions do not fully address those issues. In this paper, we provide a novel scheme that supports (i) confidentiality for events and filters; (ii) filters can express very complex constraints on events even if brokers are not able to access any information on both events and filters; (iii) and finally it does not require publishers and subscribers to share keys.

1 Introduction

The publish/subscribe (pub/sub) model is an asynchronous communication paradigm where senders, known as *publishers*, and receivers, known as *subscribers*, exchange messages in a loosely coupled manner, i.e. without establishing direct contact. The messages that publishers generate are called *events*. Publishers do not send events directly to subscribers, instead a network of interconnected brokers is responsible for delivering the events to the interested subscribers. In fact, publishers do not know who receives their events and subscribers are not aware of the source of information. In order to receive events, subscribers need to register their interest with a broker through a *filter*. When

---

[*] This work was supported by the EU FP7 programme, Research Grant 214859 (project Consequence) and Research Grant 216917(project MASTER).

S. Jajodia and J. Zhou (Eds.): SecureComm 2010, LNICST 50, pp. 272–289, 2010.

a new event is published, brokers forward it to all subscribers which expressed a filter that matches the event.

The pub/sub communication paradigm has the advantage of allowing the full decoupling of the communicating entities [8] which enables dynamic and flexible information exchange between a large number of entities. The communicating parties do not need to know each other or establish contacts in order to exchange content. Moreover, if durable subscription is enabled, publisher and subscribers do not need to actively participate in the interaction at the same time. If a subscriber is offline when a publisher creates an event, the broker will store the event until the subscriber becomes online and the event can be delivered.

Pub/sub is an open communication model, however, in many cases it may be desirable to protect the content of publications and subscriptions from unauthorized accesses. Only intended subscribers should be able to read the events. At the same time, subscribers may wish to keep the details of their filters private. For example, a subscriber may ask to be notified when the price of the quotes of a certain company is below a certain threshold. This information could reveal the subscriber's strategy to a competitor, thus the subscriber will wish to keep it private.

One of the main challenges that pub/sub systems are still facing is protecting the confidentiality of the exchanged information without limiting the decoupling of the paradigm. Publishers and subscribers do not establish contact so they cannot exchange keying material. Moreover, protecting the confidentiality from malicious brokers is very difficult. Brokers should be able to route events by matching them against filters expressed by the subscribers without having access to the actual content of events and filters.

Current solutions for confidentiality in pub/sub systems achieve only partially these goals. For example, in order to support routing based on expressive filters, [12] and [14] encrypt only certain event fields while other fields are left as cleartext so that they can be used for routing. Other solutions [14] require publishers and subscribers to share a group key which hampers the loosely coupling and scalability of pub/sub model. [16] provides confidentiality of events and filters but the filter is restricted to equality with one keyword.

The main contribution of this paper is to present an approach catering for the confidentiality in pub/sub systems such that: (i) it provides confidentiality of events and filters, (ii) it does not require publishers and subscribers to share keys, and (iii) it allows subscribers to express filters that can define any monotonic and non-monotonic conditions. To achieve this, our solution combines attribute-based encryption and an encrypted search scheme.

This paper is structured as follows: Section 2 introduces the pub/sub communication model and provides an example of an application where pub/sub confidentiality is required. Section 3 describes the problem of confidentiality and the properties achieved by our solution and Section 4 introduces the relevant encryption mechanisms. The details of our solution are provided in Section 5. Section 6 revises the application example described in Section 2 implemented with our approach. Section 7 provides the security analysis. Section 8 describes the related work and Section 9 concludes the paper.

2   The Publish/Subscribe Communication Paradigm

Several pub/sub implementations that differ in the granularity used in the definition of the filters have been proposed in the literature. The most simple one is *topic-based*, in which subscribers subscribe to a topic identified by a *keyword* [20]. A topic-based scheme is similar to the notion of group communication. When subscribing to a topic T, a subscriber becomes a member of group T. When an event for topic T is published, the event is broadcasted to all the members of that group. Organizing topics in hierarchies allows a better management of subscriptions [17]. For example, by registering to a topic, a subscriber is also registered to all subtopics.

Topic-based schemes are easy to implement but they offer limited expressiveness. *Content-based* schemes are more flexible and allow expressing subscriptions based on the actual content of the event. To express a filter on the content of an event, subscribers need a query language and understanding of the data formats. For example, in Gryphon [2] and Siena [5] events consist of sets of $(attribute_{name} = attribute_{value})$ pairs and filters are specified as SQL WHERE clauses. Java Message Service (JMS) [11] does not allow filtering on the content of the event, but instead, events carry properties in their headers and subscribers can define filters on them. Filters that apply to the composition of simple events have also been proposed (such as in [1]). When expressing such a filter, subscribers are notified upon the occurrence of the composite event.

Because of its generality and expressiveness, we will focus on content-based filtering. We assume that filters define constrains in the form of *name-op-value* where *op* can be one of the comparison operators such as $=, \leq, <, \geq, >$. Constrains can be logically combined using AND, OR and NOT to form complex subscription patterns.

We motivate the need for confidentiality in pub/sub systems through an example.

2.1   A Case for Pub/Sub Confidentiality

In this section we present an example of an application built using a pub/sub system where confidentiality is of paramount importance. In particular, Figure 1 shows an example of a Financial News Service implemented using a pub/sub system for information delivery. The publishers P are different stock exchanges and financial news agencies which use the Financial News Service to sell their content to customers S. To subscribe to particular content, a customer specifies a filter and contacts the News Service to pay the fee and obtain a token. It then subscribes with a broker B to receive notifications and the broker registers the filter only after the token is verified with the Financial News Service. When a publisher publishes some new content, the network of brokers will deliver the

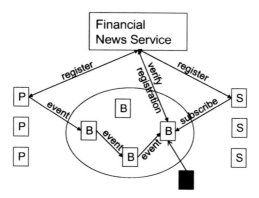

Fig. 1. An attacker who is able to corrupt a broker can listen on filters and events

content to the authorized subscribers. The publisher receives the payment from the Financial News Service without contacting the subscribers directly.

In a typical pub/sub system where confidentiality is not implemented, an attacker who is able to corrupt a broker could read the traffic that comes in and out the broker. The attacker would be able to read the events without paying the fee and then resell them, and read the filters expressed by the subscribers. To protect from this kind of attacks, it is necessary to protect the content of notifications and filters.

3   Confidentiality in Publish/Subscribe Systems

Providing the *publication confidentiality* property ensures that the content of the events is hidden from the broker or any unauthorized third party listening on the network. Only legitimate subscribers should be able to decrypt an event. Providing the *subscription confidentiality* property ensures that the details of the filters are hidden from the brokers (or other unauthorized parties). The broker should be able only to tell if an event matches a filter but gain no other information about the event and the filter. It has already been discussed in [16] that both publication and subscription confidentiality are required to effectively reduce the risk of leaking event or filter information in a pub/sub system. For instance, in providing only subscription confidentiality an attacker who knows the content of the event may infer the subscription filter.

However, providing both publication and subscription confidentiality in pub/sub systems it is still an open issue. On the one hand, a basic encryption scheme would require publisher and subscribers to share a secret key. This is not desirable because it would weaken the referential decoupling property of the paradigm. On the other hand, brokers would need to execute matching operations on encrypted events and filters which is not simple using basic techniques.

The main contribution of this paper is to propose an encryption scheme for pub/sub systems in which the following properties are supported:

(P1) confidentiality of events;

(P2) confidentiality of filters;

(P3) a simplified key management that does not require publishers and subscribers to share keys, hence fully supporting the loosely-coupled model of the pub/sub paradigm;

(P4) allowing brokers to execute matching of encrypted events against complex encrypted filters.[1]

Confidentiality of events (P1) and filters (P2) can be achieved by means of encryption. Encryption mechanisms usually require that publishers and subscribers share a key which means they need to establish contact. However, this is not desirable in pub/sub systems where publisher and subscribers do not communicate with each other directly (loose coupling). What is required is a mechanism that allows authorized subscribers to decrypt events without establishing shared keys with the publishers (e.g., group keys). In our approach, publishers encrypt the content of the event using an attribute-based encryption scheme (such as in [10]) specifying the characteristics that subscribes must satisfy to obtain the cleartext of the event. In this way, we are effectively decoupling the encryption of events at the publisher site from its decryption at the subscriber site and simplifying the key management process (P3).

Because events and filters are encrypted, event filtering at the broker side becomes a more complex task. Indeed, brokers should be able to decide whether an event matches a filter or not, without having access to neither the content of the event nor the filter. In our approach we combine the expressive access control structures supported by attribute-base encryption scheme with encrypted search. This allows our scheme to support encrypted event filtering against complex filters. The only information that the broker can access is which filters are matched by an event (P4).

In the following section, we describe the techniques used in our approach for supporting the above properties.

4   Background

This section provides background information on the techniques that we have combined to achieve confidentiality in pub/sub systems without compromising the loosely-coupled property of the paradigm.

4.1   Attribute-Based Encryption (ABE)

The concept of attribute-based encryption (ABE) was first introduced in [15]. In their construction, both ciphertext and keys are labeled with sets of attributes. A key is able to decrypt a ciphertext if at least k attributes match between key and ciphertext.

---

[1] With complex encrypted filters we mean filters that can express conjunctions and disjunctions of equalities, inequalities and negations in an encrypted form.

[10] extended this construction and introduced Key-Policy ABE (KP-ABE) in which ciphertexts are labelled with sets of attributes and private keys are associated with access structures. A key is able to decrypt a ciphertext if its associated access structure is satisfied by the attributes of the ciphertext. The access structure, represented as a tree, allows expressing any monotone access formula consisting of AND, OR, or threshold gates.

[13] proposed a KP-ABE scheme that can additionally handle negations (i.e., NOT). The data can be decrypted only if a given attribute (embedded in the key) is *not* present among the attributes of the ciphertext.

[4] proposed a construction for ciphertext policy ABE (CP-ABE) in which policies (access structures) are associated with data and attributes are associated with keys. This is similar to the capability model in access control. A key can decrypt some data if its associated attributes satisfy the policy associated with the data. They also show how to construct the access tree in order to additionally handle inequalities.

4.2   Encrypted Search

[18] proposed a mechanism for equality tests on data encrypted with a symmetric key. The advantages are that the searched keyword remains secret and the server cannot learn anything more about the data than the search results. However, the scheme works only for matching single words. The solution of [9] addresses the problem of conjunctions. Documents are stored encrypted together with a list of keywords, also encrypted. To retrieve a document, the user computes a capability for the list of keywords of interest. The server uses the capability to search for documents. The disadvantage of this method is that the server can learn the keywords from the capabilities.

[7] propose a data encryption scheme that allows an untrusted server to perform encrypted searches on data without revealing the data or the keywords to the server. The advantage of this method is that it allows multi-user access without the need for a shared key between users. Each user in the system has a unique set of keys. The data encrypted by one user can be decrypted by any other authorized user. The scheme is built on top of proxy encryption schemes. The idea is that a user defines a set of keywords for each document. The keywords and document are encrypted using proxy encryption and stored on the server. When a user wants to search for a document, it needs to create a trapdoor for each keyword. The trapdoor is used by the server to match the search keywords against the keywords of the stored document. The server can identify a match without learning the keyword.

5   Solution Details

In this section, we discuss in details our scheme for providing confidentiality in pub/sub systems. We assume an honest-but-curious model for publishers, brokers and subscribers, as in [19,16]. This means that the entities follow the protocol, but may be curious to find out information by analysing the messages that are exchanged. For example, a broker may try to read the content of an event or try to learn the filtering constrains of subscribers. Subscribers may want to read the events delivered to other subscribers. We also assume that a passive attacker outside the pub/sub system may be able to listen on the communication and invade the privacy of the participants.

In our approach an event E consists of:(i) the message M that represents the content of the event and (ii) a set of attributes a_i that characterise M and are used for event filtering by the brokers.

To support confidentiality of events (P1), the message M is encrypted using CP-ABE [4]. CP-ABE allows a publisher to specify which attributes a decrypter must have. The goal is to allow only authorised subscribers to decrypt messages. So, a publisher could specify that only who subscribed to IBM market data should read the message. In using CP-ABE to encrypt M, publishers and subscribers do not need to share any secret key (thus achieving property P4).

Filter confidentiality (P2) is achieved by combining KP-ABE [10] with multi-user searchable data encryption (SDE) scheme [7]. In particular, a subscriber S_j can define a filter F_j as KP-ABE access trees. The set of attributes a_i that the publisher defined on an event E is used by the brokers against the filters. When the event E reaches a broker, if the set of attributes associated with the event satisfy the filter F_j, then the broker knows that the event can be forwarded to S_j. However, the broker does not gain any information on the actual content of the event because M is encrypted with CP-ABE.

However, if the KP-ABE scheme is used as proposed in [10], then the broker is still able to obtain information on the filters and attributes associated with events, thus violating the confidentiality of events and filters. In fact, the KP-ABE scheme requires that attributes associated with the ciphertext are not encrypted. To circumvent this limitation, we propose the following modification to the KP-ABE scheme: the set of attributes associated with an event and the access tree representing the filter are encrypted using the scheme from [7]. The scheme supports encrypted search, so it can be used to verify if the encrypted attributes specified by the publisher are the same as those specified by the subscriber in the filter. With this modification, our scheme supports confidentiality of filters (P2) and allows the brokers to perform encrypted event filtering (P4). It should be noted that both KP-ABE and the multi-user SDE do not require that publishers and subscribers share keys thus simplifying the key management and respecting the referential decoupling of the pub/sub paradigm (P3).

In the following, we show the steps that are performed in our scheme.

5.1   Init(1^k)

The initialisation is run by a trusted authority and defines the security parameters for KP-ABE and El Gamal based SDE schemes.

On input 1^k, output two prime numbers p and q such that $q = (p - 1)/2$ and $|q| = k$, and a cyclic group G_1 with generator g such that G_1 is the unique order q subgroup of $\mathbb{Z}_p^*$. Let $e : G_1 \times G_1 \to G_2$ be a bilinear map. In addition,

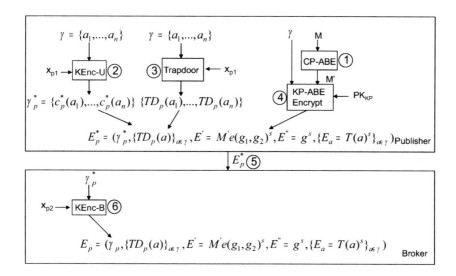

Fig. 2. Event encryption

define the Lagrange coefficient $\Delta_{i,S}$ for $i \in \mathbb{Z}_p$ and a set S of elements in $\mathbb{Z}_p$: $\Delta_{i,S}(x) = \prod_{j \in S, j \neq i} \frac{x-j}{i-j}$. Each attribute will be mapped to a number in $\mathbb{Z}_p^*$ by using a collision resistant function $H_1 : \{0,1\}^* \to \mathbb{Z}_p^*$. This allows using arbitrary strings as attributes and adding them to a user's private key. The event will be encrypted using a set of n^2 elements of $\mathbb{Z}_p^*$.

Choose a random $y \in \mathbb{Z}_p$ and compute $g_1 = g^y$. Also choose a random element g_2 from G_1. Let N be the set $\{1, 2 \ldots, n+1\}$, where n is the number of attributes used for event encryption. Choose $t_1, \ldots, t_{n+1}$ uniformly at random from G_1. Define a function T as:

$$T(X) = g_2^{X^n} \prod_{i=1}^{n+1} t_i^{\Delta_{i,N}(X)}.$$

Publish the public parameters as: $PK_{KP} : g_1, g_2, t_1, \ldots, t_n$, and keep securely the master key $MK_{KP} : y$.

We define the parameters for the El Gamal based SDE scheme in group G_1 as in [7]. Let x be chosen uniformly at random from $\mathbb{Z}_p^*$ and compute $h = g^x$. Let H be a collision resistant hash function, f a pseudorandom function and s_1 a random key for f. Output the public and secret parameters for El Gamal based SDE: publish $PK_{SE} = (G_1, g, p, h, H, f)$, and keep securely $MK_{SE} = (x, s_1)$.

For every user (publisher or subscriber), run $Keygen(MK_{SE}, i)$ as in SDE, where i is the identity of the user. This function chooses x_{i1} random from $\mathbb{Z}_p$ and gives it to the user (publisher or subscriber) and computes $x_{i2} = x - x_{i1}$ and gives to the broker connected to the user the key (i, x_{i2}).

---

[2] With minor modifications, KP-ABE can encrypt to all sets of size $\leq n$.

5.2   Event Encryption

Figure 2 shows the steps needed to encrypt an event. The publisher specifies a set of attributes γ under which the content $M \in G_2$ of the event will be encrypted.

Step 1. To provide confidentiality of M, the publisher encrypts it using the CP-ABE scheme. We call the message encrypted in this way M'.

Step 2. To provide confidentiality of attributes, the publisher encrypts them using the multi-user SDE. A new set γ_p^* will be generated as follows: every attribute a_i of γ is encrypted using KEnc-U(x_{p1}, a_i). KEnc-U(x_{p1}, a_i) performs the following operations. Choose r_i at random from $\mathbb{Z}_p$ and compute $c^*(a_i) = (\hat{c}_1, \hat{c}_2, \hat{c}_3)$ where $\hat{c}_1 = g^{r_i + \sigma_i}$, $\sigma_i = f_{s_1}(a_i)$, $c_2 = \hat{c}_1^{x_{p1}}$, $\hat{c}_3 = H(h^{r_i})$. The encrypted set of attributes γ_p^* contains all $c^*(a_i)$.

Step 3. For every attribute $a \in \gamma$, the publisher computes a trapdoor by calling Trapdoor((x_{p1}, s_1), a) as in multi-user SDE . Trapdoor() chooses a random r in $\mathbb{Z}_q$ and computes $TD_p(a) = (td_1, td_2)$ for each attribute such that $td_1 = g^{-r}g^{\sigma_a}$ and $td_2 = h^r g^{-x_{p1}r} g^{x_{p1}\sigma_a} = g^{x_{p2}r}g^{x_{p1}\sigma_a}$ where $\sigma_a = f_{s_1}(a)$.

Step 4. The publisher encrypts the message M' under γ as in KP-ABE. Choose a random $s \in \mathbb{Z}_p$ and compute the ciphertext as:

$$E^* = \text{Encrypt}(M', \gamma, PK_{KP}) = (\gamma_p^*, \text{E'} = M'e(g_1, g_2)^s, \text{E''} = g^s, \\ \{E_a = T(a)^s)\}_{a \in \gamma})$$

Note that we replaced the unencrypted set of attributes γ (as it appears in KP-ABE) with the encrypted set γ_p^*. The values E', E'' and E_a are computed as in KP-ABE.

Step 5. The publisher sends the encrypted event E^* together with the trapdoors for matching event attributes to the broker:

$$E_p^* = (\gamma_p^*, \{TD_p(a)\}_{a \in \gamma}, \text{E'} = M'e(g_1, g_2)^s, \text{E''} = g^s, \{E_a = T(a)^s)\}_{a \in \gamma}).$$

Step 6. The broker locates the key (p, x_{p2}) corresponding to the publisher and re-encrypts γ_p^* to γ_p by calling KEnc-B($p, x_{p2}, c^*(a)$) for each attribute c_a^* of γ_p^*. KEnc-B() transforms each encrypted attribute $c^*(a)$ in $c(a) = (c_1, c_2)$ so that $c_1 = \hat{c}_1^{x_{p2}} \hat{c}_2 = \hat{c}_1^{x_{p2} + x_{p1}} = (g^{r+\sigma})^x = h^{r+\sigma}$ where $\sigma = f_{s_1}(a)$ and $c_2 = \hat{c}_3 = H(h^r)$. The final encrypted event is:

$$E_p = (\gamma_p, \{TD_p(a)\}_{a \in \gamma}, \text{E'} = M'e(g_1, g_2)^s, \text{E''} = g^s, \{E_a = T(a)^s)\}_{a \in \gamma}).$$

The above operations provide confidentiality of the message and attributes for an event, thus achieving property P1.

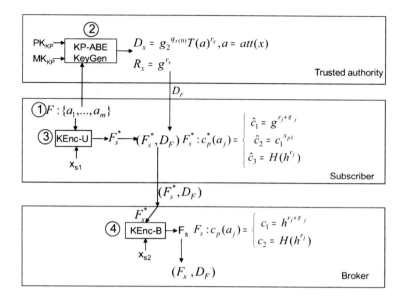

Fig. 3. Filter generation and encryption

5.3   Filter Generation

Figure 3 shows the main steps for generating and encrypting the filter.

Step 1. The subscriber defines the filter as an access tree F. Each non-leaf node of the tree represents a threshold gate described by a value and its children. Let x be a node with num_x children. The threshold value k_x represents the number of children subtrees that need to be satisfied, hence $1 \leq k_x \leq num_x$. When $k_x = 1$ the threshold gate is an OR and when $k_x = num_x$, the threshold gate is an AND. Each leaf node x is described by an attribute and a threshold value $k_x = 1$.

We additionally define the following functions on the tree: parent(x) returns the parent of a node x and att(x) is defined only for a leaf node and returns the attribute associated with x. Further, we define an ordering between the children of every node x and give each child an index from 1 to num_x. The function index(x) returns the index associated to node x.

Step 2. As in KP-ABE, the subscriber sends the filter F to a trusted authority and requests a decryption key D_F. When applying to an event the filter D_F, the result will be a secret value (used for partially decrypting the content M) only if the attributes associated with the event match the filter. Otherwise the returned value will be a null value ($\perp$).

Choose a polynomial q_x for each node x in the tree F_s^*. The polynomials are chosen in a top down manner, starting from the root node r. For each node x in the tree, set the degree d_x of the polynomial q_x to be one less than the threshold value k_x of that node, that is, $d_x = k_x - 1$. Now for the root node r, set $q_r(0) = y$ and d_r other points of the polynomial q_r randomly to define it completely. For any other node x, set $q_x(0) = q_{parent(x)}(index(x))$ and choose d_x other points randomly to completely define q_x.

Once the polynomials have been decided, for each leaf node x, the authority gives the following secret values to the subscriber:

$$D_x = g_2^{q_x(0) \cdot T(a)^{r_x}}, \text{ where a=att}(x)$$
$$R_x = g^{r_x}$$

where r_x is chosen uniformly at random from $\mathbb{Z}_p$ for each node x. The set of the above values is the filter D_F, corresponding to a decryption key in KP-ABE.

Step 3. Encrypt the leaf nodes of the filter using multi-user SDE. For every leaf node x in F run KEnc-U(x_{s1}, a), where a=att(x). Choose r at random from $\mathbb{Z}_p$ and compute $c^*(a) = (\hat{c}_1, \hat{c}_2, \hat{c}_3)$ where $\hat{c}_1 = g^{r+\sigma}$, $\sigma = f_{s_1}(a)$, $c_2 = \hat{c}_1^{x_{s1}}$, $\hat{c}_3 = \dot{H}(h^r)$.

Step 4. The subscriber sends D_F together with F_s^* to the broker. The broker locates the key (s_1, x_{s2}) corresponding to the subscriber and re-encrypts the leaf-node attributes of F_s^*. For each attribute $c^*(a)$ run KEnc-B($s_1, x_{s2}, c^*(a)$). First compute $c(a) = (c_1, c_2)$ such that $c_1 = \hat{c}_1^{x_{s2}} \hat{c}_2 = \hat{c}_1^{x_{s2}+x_{s1}} = (g^{r+\sigma})^x = h^{r+\sigma}$ where $\sigma = f_{s_1}(a)$ and $c_2 = \hat{c}_3$.

The above operations provide confidentiality of the filter, thus achieving property P2. At the same time, the filter is able to express any access formula. We only give the details for expressing any monotone access formula consisting of AND, OR, or threshold gates, bur by extending the construction as in [13] and [4] we are able to represent inequalities and non-monotone access structures, thus achieving property P3.

5.4   Filtering of Events

When a new event E_p is published, for every filter D_F the broker will run the decryption algorithm from KP-ABE to verify if D_F decrypts E_p.

Step 1. Figure4 shows the operations necessary in this step. For each leaf node in D_F check if it belongs to the set of attributes specified by the publisher. In KP-ABE this step is straightforward since the attributes are not encrypted. We will use multi-user SDE to check if the encrypted attributes match the encrypted filters. For every leaf node x with attribute a encrypted as (c_{b1}, c_{b2}) in the filter F_s, check if it is contained in the set of attributes γ_p as follows. For every attribute a in γ_p, the broker retrieves the trapdoor $TD_p(a)$ and the secrete key (p, x_{p2}) and computes $TD = td_1^{x_{p2}} td_2 = g^{x\sigma}$. Then it checks if $c_{b2} = H(c_{b1} \cdot TD^{-1})$. If this is the case, we will have that

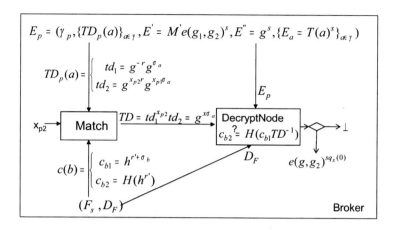

Fig. 4. Event filtering

$$DecryptNode(E_p, D_F, x) = \frac{e(D_x, E")}{e(R_x, E_a)} = \frac{e(g_2^{q_x(0)} \cdot T(a)^{r_x}, g^s)}{e(g^{r_x}, T(a)^s)} = \frac{e(g_2^{q_x(0)}, g^s) \cdot e(T(a)^{r_x}, g^s)}{e(g^{r_x}, T(a)^s)} = e(g, g_2)^{s q_x(0)}$$

otherwise, DecryptNode(E,D_F,x)=$\perp$.

We now consider the recursive case when x is a non-leaf node. The algorithm DecryptNode(E,D_F,x) then proceeds as follows. For all nodes z that are children of x, it calls DecryptNode(E,D_F,z) and stores the output as F_z. Let S_x be an arbitrary k_x-sized set of child nodes z such that $F_z \neq \perp$. If no such set exists then the node was not satisfied and the function returns $\perp$. Otherwise, we compute:

$$F_x = \prod_{z \in S_x} F_z^{\Delta_{i,S'_x}(0)} \quad \begin{cases} \text{where } i = index(z), \\ S' = \{index(z) : z \in S_x\} \end{cases}$$

$$= \prod_{z \in S_x} (e(g, g_2)^{s \cdot q_z(0)})^{\Delta_{i,S'_x}(0)}$$

$$= \prod_{z \in S_x} (e(g, g_2)^{s \cdot q_{parent(z)}(index(z))})^{\Delta_{i,S'_x}(0)} \quad \text{(by construction)}$$

$$= \prod_{z \in S_x} (e(g, g_2)^{s \cdot q_x(0)})^{\Delta_{i,S'_x}(0)} = e(g, g_2)^{s q_x(0)} \quad \text{(using polynomial interpolation)} (1)$$

and return the result. The broker calls the DecryptNode function on the root node of the encrypted filter. $DecryptNode(E, D_F, r) = e(g, g_2)^{ys} = e(g_1, g_2)^s$ if and only if the attributes of the event satisfy the filter. If the result equals $\perp$, it means that the content does not match the filter.

Step 2. In case of a successful match, the broker obtains M' from $E' = M'e(g_1, g_2)^s$ by dividing it with $e(g_1, g_2)^s$ and forwards it to the subscriber.

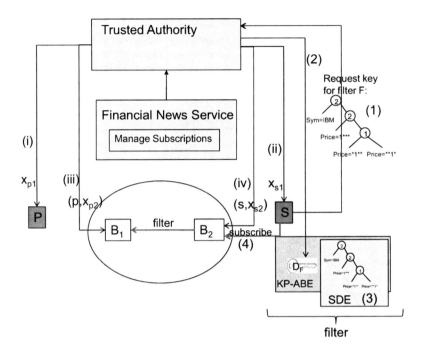

Fig. 5. Key and message exchange for filter generation

5.5   Decryption of the Content

When the subscriber receives M', if its attributes satisfy the requirements defined by the publisher by means of CP-ABE, the subscriber is able to obtain the content M. It should be stressed that although publishers select the attributes, they do not know the subscribers. Publishers are only characterizing the subscribers so it could be the case that a subscriber who receives the event is not able to decrypt the content because it does not satisfy the properties specified by the publisher. For example, a publisher may want to send an event only to people belonging to a particular organization. Subscribers interested in the information but not belonging to that organization will not be able to decrypt the event.

6   Revisiting the Stock Quote Example

In the following we show how the example in Section 2.1 can be extended with the solution described above to provide confidentiality of events and filters.

As part of the initialization (see Section 5.1), the Trusted Authority generates the public(PK) and master (MK) keys for KP-ABE, CP-ABE and SDE. The public keys are published while the master keys are kept securely.

In our example, publisher P and subscriber S register with the Financial News Service. The Service contacts the Trusted Authority to generate the secret keys of the publisher and subscriber that will be used for SDE. The Trusted Authority sends these keys on a secure channel to the publisher (i), subscriber (ii) and also to the brokers (iii, iv). These steps are shown in Figure 5.

Subscriber S expresses the subscription filter: "Sym=IBM" AND "Price>10". The following operations need to be performed (see Figure 5):

1. Construct the access tree corresponding to the filter. The tree representing the filter is shown in Figure 6. To represent the inequality "Price>10" we use the representation introduced in [4] and construct the access tree by expressing conditions on the bit values of the attribute. The threshold values of the nodes represent the number of sub-trees that need to be satisfied. In our example, 2 corresponds to an AND and 1 to an OR.
2. The subscriber sends this filter to the Trusted Authority which will generate a key D_F. This key is able to decrypt any event whose attributes satisfy the filter.
3. To ensure confidentiality of the filter, the attributes expressed in the leaf nodes are encrypted using SDE.
4. The subscriber sends the filter which contains D_F and the encrypted tree to broker B_2. The broker further distributes the encrypted filter in the pub/sub network.

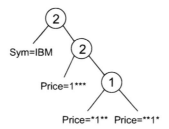

Fig. 6. Access tree for "Sym=IBM" AND "Price>10"

Next, publisher P generates an event with the following attributes: "Sym=IBM" AND "Price=11". This event is to be received only by subscribers with the attribute "Premium customer". The publisher performs the following operations, as shown in Figure 7.

1. Request a CP-ABE key for "Premium customer" from the Trusted Authority.
2. Encrypt the message content M with the received key. This ensure that only subscribers who possess this attribute will be able to read the message.
3. To allow comparisons of numerical values, the publisher creates an attribute for each bit of the numerical attribute (as introduced in [4]). For Price=11 (1011), the attributes are: Price=1***, Price=*0**, Price=**1* and Price=***1.

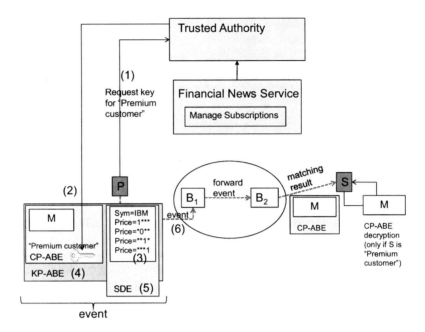

Fig. 7. Key and message exchange for event generation

4. Encrypt the message M using KP-ABE under the defined attributes.
5. To provide confidentiality of the attributes, encrypt all attributes using SDE. Also compute a trapdoor for each attribute (see section 5.2).
6. Send to broker B_1 M encrypted under CP-ABE and KP-ABE and the encrypted attributes with their trapdoors computed as in SDE.

Broker B_1 matches the received event against the stored filters and based on the matching result, it forwards the event to broker B_2. Broker B_2 matches the event against the filter from subscriber S. The matching corresponds to a KP-ABE decryption for which we additionally encrypted the ciphertext attributes and key access tree. When the event from publisher P is matched against the filter from subscriber S, the broker is able to remove the KP-ABE encryption without learning neither the attributes nor the filter. The matching result is the message content M expressed by the publisher encrypted with CP-ABE. B_2 then forwards the matching result to S. The subscriber S is able to decrypt the message only if it possesses the attribute "Premium customer".

7   Security Analysis

This section evaluates the security of the scheme. To ensure confidentiality of events our scheme encrypts both messages and associated attributes to prevent attackers to infer an event from its attributes. Messages are encrypted using CP-ABE encryption [4]; the attributes are encrypted using the multi-user SDE scheme, then encrypted messages are further encrypted by the publisher under the set of attributes by using KP-ABE with non-monotonic filters.

All the used encryption schemes are proved to be at least indistinguishable under chosen plaintext attack (*IND-CPA*). [6] proves CP-ABE to be chosen plaintext (CPA) secure under the Decisional bilinear Diffie-Hellmann (DBDH) assumption, generally considered a hard problem. About multi-user SDE [7] proves that the concrete construction, our scheme uses, built upon El Gamal-based proxy encryption is indistinguishable under chosen plaintext attack (*IND-CPA*) under the assumption the Decisional Diffie-Hellmann problem is hard relative to the group on which El Gamal is defined. Hence the encryption scheme that protects events is IND-CPA secure. About the KP-ABE scheme, [13] proves that the IND-CPA security of KP-ABE with non-monotonic access structures in the attribute-based selective-set model reduces to the hardness of the Decisional bilinear Diffie-Hellmann (DBDH) assumption, generally considered a hard problem.

All encryption primitives used by our scheme are *IND-CPA* secure, what is left is to show their combination is still secure. The different mechanisms are used as multiple layer of encryption and [3] shows that if a cryptosystem is secure in the sense of indistinguishability, then the cryptosystem in the multi-user setting, where related messages are encrypted using different keys, is also secure. In our case each encryption layer uses an independent key so the combination is at least as secure as any individual encryption. Thus, the scheme is at least *IND-CPA* secure.

Filters' confidentiality is achieved by using KP-ABE with multi-user SDE. Thus, using the same argument used for the case of events' confidentiality also in case of filters the multiple layer encryption is *IND-CPA* secure.

8   Related Work

Current solutions for ensuring confidentiality in publish/subscribe systems provide only some of the properties satisfied by our solution, but not all of them at the same time. For example, [12] proposes a scheme that does not require publishers and subscribers to share a key, but does not achieve full confidentiality of events and confidentiality of filters. Events are encoded in XML format, but only specific fields (e.g., price) are encrypted with a symmetric key k. The publisher then encrypts k with its public key. The brokers forward the event based on the fields left unencrypted and a proxy service changes the encryption of k to an encryption with the public key of the subscriber.

In [14] Raiciu and Rosenblum achieve partial confidentiality but they require that publishers and subscribers share a group key which is used to encrypt events and filters. In their model, notifications are composed of (*name, value*) pairs where only value is encrypted which in some scenarios may not provide a sufficient level of confidentiality.

In [19], Srivartsa & Liu propose a specific key management scheme and a probabilistic multi-path event routing to prevent frequency inferring attacks.

The method achieves confidentiality of events and filters, however, filtering is done based on only one keyword. A centralized trusted authority distributes encryption keys to publishers and authorization keys to subscribers. Inequalities are supported by using a hierarchical key structure where each key corresponds to an interval. However, the inequality condition cannot be checked by the brokers, instead, after receiving an event corresponding to the specified keyword, a subscriber will be able to decrypt it only if the numerical value of the event's attribute is in the range corresponding to the subscriber's authorization key.

In [16], Shikfa et al. propose a solution based on multiple layer commutative encryption that achieves content and filter confidentiality, and routing of encrypted data. The advantage of this method is that key management is local and publisher and subscribers do not need to share keys. However, the filter is limited to equality filter with only one keyword.

9   Conclusions and Future Work

In this paper, we presented a solution for providing confidentiality in pub/sub systems. Our solution is an encryption scheme based on CP-ABE, KP-ABE and multi-user SDE. Our scheme supports both the publication and the subscription confidentiality properties while at the same time does not require publishers and subscribers to share secret keys. Although events and filters are encrypted, brokers can still perform event filtering without learning any information. Finally, our scheme allows subscribers to express filters that can define any monotonic and non-monotonic constraints on events.

As future work, we are working on a more formal proof to evaluate the security of the scheme. At the same time, we are planning to implement our scheme and to include it in one of the mainstream implementations of the pub/sub model. This would allow us to assess the impact in performance that such scheme imposes on the resources of the pub/sub system.

Acknowledgements

The work of the second author is supported by the EU project Consequence Research Grant FP7-214859. The work of the third author is partially funded by the EU project MASTER contract no. FP7-216917.

References

1. Bacon, J., Moody, K., Bates, J., Hayton, R., Ma, C., McNeil, A., Seidel, O., Spiteri, M.: Generic support for distributed applications. IEEE Computer 33(3), 68–76 (2000)
2. Banavar, G., Chandra, T., Mukherjee, B., Nagarajarao, J., Strom, R., Sturman, D.: An efficient multicast protocol for content-based publish-subscribe systems. In: International Conference on Distributed Computing Systems, vol. 19, pp. 262–272. IEEE Computer Society Press, Los Alamitos (1999)

3. Bellare, M., Boldyreva, A., Staddon, J.: Multi-recipient encryption schemes: Security notions and randomness re-use. In: Desmedt, Y.G. (ed.) PKC 2003. LNCS, vol. 2567. Springer, Heidelberg (2002)
4. Bethencourt, J., Sahai, A., Waters, B.: Ciphertext-policy attribute-based encryption. In: IEEE Symposium on Security and Privacy, pp. 321–334 (2007) (Citeseer)
5. Carzaniga, A., Rosenblum, D.S., Wolf, A.L.: Design and evaluation of a wide- area event notification service. ACM Transactions on Computer Systems (TOCS) 19(3), 332–383 (2001)
6. Cheung, L., Newport, C.: Provably secure ciphertext policy abe. In: CCS 2007: Proceedings of the 14th ACM conference on Computer and communications security, pp. 456–465. ACM, New York (2007)
7. Dong, C., Russello, G., Dulay, N.: Shared and searchable encrypted data for untrusted servers. In: Atluri, V. (ed.) DAS 2008. LNCS, vol. 5094, pp. 127–143. Springer, Heidelberg (2008)
8. Eugster, P.T., Felber, P.A., Guerraoui, R., Kermarrec, A.M.: The many faces of publish/subscribe. ACM Computing Surveys (CSUR) 35(2), 131 (2003)
9. Golle, P., Staddon, J., Waters, B.: Secure conjunctive keyword search over encrypted data. In: Jakobsson, M., Yung, M., Zhou, J. (eds.) ACNS 2004. LNCS, vol. 3089, pp. 31–45. Springer, Heidelberg (2004)
10. Goyal, V., Pandey, O., Sahai, A., Waters, B.: Attribute-based encryption for fine-grained access control of encrypted data. In: Proceedings of the 13th ACM conference on Computer and communications security, p. 98. ACM, New York (2006)
11. Burridge, R., Sharma, R., Fialli, J., Hapner, M., Stout, K.: Java message service. Sun Microsystems Inc., Santa Clara (2002)
12. Khurana, H.: Scalable security and accounting services for content-based publish/subscribe systems. In: Proceedings of the 2005 ACM symposium on Applied computing, p. 807. ACM, New York (2005)
13. Ostrovsky, R., Sahai, A., Waters, B.: Attribute-based encryption with non- monotonic access structures. In: Proceedings of the 14th ACM conference on Computer and communications security, p. 203. ACM, New York (2007)
14. Raiciu, C., Rosenblum, D.S.: Enabling confidentiality in content-based publish/subscribe infrastructures. In: Securecomm and Workshops. vol. 28, pp. 1–11 (2006)
15. Sahai, A., Waters, B.: Fuzzy identity-based encryption. In: Cramer, R. (ed.) EUROCRYPT 2005. LNCS, vol. 3494, pp. 457–473. Springer, Heidelberg (2005)
16. Shikfa, A., Onen, M., Molva, R.: Privacy-Preserving Content-Based Publish/Subscribe Networks. In: Proceedings of Emerging Challenges for Security, Privacy and Trust: 24th Ifip Tc 11 International Information Security Conference, SEC 2009, Pafos, Cyprus, May 18-20, p. 270. Springer, Heidelberg (2009)
17. Singhera, Z.U.: A workload model for topic-based publish/subscribe systems (2008)
18. Song, D.X., Wagner, D., Perrig, A.: Practical techniques for searches on encrypted data. In: Proceedings of 2000 IEEE Symposium on Security and Privacy, SP 2000, pp. 44–55 (2000)
19. Srivatsa, M., Liu, L.: Secure event dissemination in publish-subscribe networks. In: Proceedings of the 27th International Conference on Distributed Computing Systems, p. 22 (2007) (Citeseer)
20. Zhuang, S.Q., Zhao, B.Y., Joseph, A.D., Katz, R.H., Kubiatowicz, J.D.: Bayeux: An architecture for scalable and fault-tolerant wide-area data dissemination. In: Proceedings of the 11th international workshop on Network and operating systems support for digital audio and video, p. 20. ACM, New York (2001)

CED²: Communication Efficient Disjointness Decision

Luciana Marconi[1], Mauro Conti[2], and Roberto Di Pietro[3]

[1] "Sapienza" Università di Roma, Department of Computer Science,
Roma 00198, Italy
marconi@di.uniroma1.it
[2] Vrije Universiteit Amsterdam, Department of Computer Science,
Amsterdam HV 1081, The Netherlands
mconti@few.vu.nl
[3] Università di Roma Tre, Department of Mathematics,
Roma 00146, Italy
dipietro@mat.uniroma3.it

Abstract. Enforcing security often requires the two legitimate parties of a communication to determine whether they share a secret, without disclosing information (e.g. the shared secret itself, or just the existence of such a secret) to third parties—or even to the other party, if it is not the legitimate party but an adversary pretending to impersonate the legitimate one. In this paper, we propose CED² (Communication Efficient Disjointness Decision), a probabilistic and distributed protocol that allows two parties—each one having a finite set of elements—to decide about the disjointness of their sets. CED² is particularly suitable for devices having constraints on energy, communication, storage, and bandwidth. Examples of these devices are satellite phones, or nodes of wireless sensor networks. We show that CED² significantly improves the communication cost compared to the state of the art, while providing the same degree of privacy and security. Analysis and simulations support the findings.

Keywords: sets disjointness test, communication complexity, privacy, security, probabilistic algorithms.

1   Introduction

Secure communications often require the involved parties to share a secret. As an example, two parties can use a pre-loaded shared symmetric key to encrypt the communication between them [4]. However, a problem arising in such scenarios is for the parties to determine whether they share such a secret. In this paper, we deal with this problem. In particular, we aim at minimizing the communication effort needed by the two parties to discover whether they share any common element from a given set. Note that this approach is mandatory where the communication cost is a driving system parameter. For instance, this is usually the case in satellite communications—where bandwidth can be limited or it has to

S. Jajodia and J. Zhou (Eds.): SecureComm 2010, LNICST 50, pp. 290–306, 2010.

be shared between multiple users at the same time—or when elements exchange is unfeasible because of the set or elements size.

Note that in this paper we present the problem of deciding whether there is an intersection between two sets for a security purpose. However, set intersection operations are required in a wide range of applications, particularly in the area of information integration across databases [1,9]. Further examples of applications are: finding common volumes between large libraries; finding common friends or interests in social networks without exchanging the corresponding lists; and, public welfare survey establishing how many welfare recipients are treated for a specific illness [1,9].

For the majority of these applications, there are often privacy and security concerns requiring the use of privacy-preserving techniques that usually relies on expensive asymmetric cryptographic primitives and a considerable communication cost [8,15]. However, there are scenarios that call for inexpensive cryptographic primitives and reduced communication cost, such as the ones cited before; these are the niche applications where CED^2 comes at hand.

Contribution. In this work, we propose CED^2 (Communication Efficient Disjointness Decision): a probabilistic and distributed protocol for deciding set intersection. We assume that each of the two parties of a communication has a set of secrets (or more generally, elements): the sets being $\mathcal{A}$ and $\mathcal{B}$, with elements from a domain $\mathcal{D}$. CED^2 is particularly concerned in minimizing the communication cost. Hence, focusing on communication complexity means to reduce the bits of information that the two parties exchange until at least one of them discovers whether $\mathcal{A} \cap \mathcal{B} = \emptyset$. The proposed solution does not require the parties to actually send any element of the set. CED^2 leads to a global communication saving compared to the state of the art—that, to the best of our knowledge, is represented by the algorithm by Kurtz and Manber [10] (we later refer to this algorithm as KM). Finally, this improvement is achieved providing the same level of privacy and security of KM—our solution does not disclose more information. The main contribution of this work is in the reduced communication overhead compared to KM, that is a building block protocol for many security settings where two parties need to know (efficiently) whether they share a secret.

Roadmap. The rest of the paper is organized as follows. Section 2 describes the related work in the area. Section 3 presents our solution, that is the CED^2 protocol. Section 4 provides the analysis of CED^2, while Section 5 is devoted to the protocol evaluation and comparison with the state of the art. Finally, Section 6 reports some concluding remarks.

2   Related Work

The literature on set intersection decision problem makes available a wide range of applications from set theory, combinatorial optimization, database searching, circuit complexity and applied cryptography [2,3,5,15]. In this paper, we focus on the evaluation of communication complexity of the disjointness problem. This problem is characterized as follows: two parties, Alice (A) and Bob (B), hold subsets $\mathcal{A}$ and $\mathcal{B}$ respectively, both of n elements from a given domain $\mathcal{D}$. Alice and

Bob follow a protocol to jointly decide whether they share some elements or not. That corresponds to the computation of the disjointness function $Disj(\mathcal{A}, \mathcal{B})$, defined as follows:

$$Disj(\mathcal{A}, \mathcal{B}) = \begin{cases} 1, & \text{if } \mathcal{A} \cap \mathcal{B} = \emptyset \\ 0, & \text{otherwise} \end{cases} \tag{1}$$

The two parties do not know each other's input. To determine the output value, they alternatively exchange bits according to the protocol. In a deterministic protocol, their answer must always be correct, i.e., equal to $Disj(\mathcal{A}, \mathcal{B})$ for every input pair $\mathcal{A}, \mathcal{B}$. In a probabilistic protocol, the algorithms of the parties depend on unbiased coin tosses, and are required to be correct with a bounded probability $(1/2)$ on every input. Interested readers can refer to [11] for a survey.

We briefly remind the notion of the communication complexity, introduced by Yao [14]. The communication complexity of a protocol P is the number of bits exchanged by the involved parties during the protocol run. In general, the communication complexity of a function f is that of the best possible protocol that computes f. The probabilistic communication complexity, denoted by $R(f)$, takes into account also the coin tosses used. Two access models to the random bits distinguish the private coin model, in which each party tosses his private coin, from the common randomness model, in which both parties share a common random bit string. It is known that $R(Disj)$ is $\Theta(n)$: the lower bound $\Omega(n)$ is given in [7], [11]; the upper bound corresponds for both parties of just sending all of their input. More recently, Håstad and Widgerson studied the communication complexity of the disjoint function [6]. They proved that in the model of common randomness:

- $R(Disj_n^k) = O(n)$, for all n;
- $R_0(Disj_n^k) = O(n)$, for instances of disjoint sets, and $R_0(Disj_n^k) = O(n + \log k)$ for not-disjoint sets. $R_0(f)$ represents the number of bits exchanged to compute f with the Las-Vegas type probabilistic algorithm, where the answer is required to be always correct (zero-error) [13].

$Disj_n^k(A, B)$ indicates the disjoint function of sets of size n whose elements are represented as bit strings of length k.

Thus computing $|\mathcal{A} \cap \mathcal{B}|$ requires $\Theta(n)$ communication. Therefore, even without taking any other requirement into consideration (e.g. privacy), the communication complexity of any set intersection algorithm is at least proportional to the input size. Moreover, Freedman et al. [5] showed a reduction from disjointness, proving that the communication cost of an approximation algorithm for the intersection size is lower-bounded by $\Omega(n)$.

The cited works study the formal properties of the disjointness problem considered as a communication problem. However, in order to evaluate the design of our solution and compare its performance, we consider a specific solution to the disjointness problem. This solution is provided by the algorithm from Kurtz and Manber appeared in 1987 [10]. The authors describe a distributed probabilistic algorithm that solves the disjointness problem in $O(\log_2 \log_2 n)$ rounds. The solution requires to exchange a message of $O(cn)$ bits at each round (where c is the number of bits ($O(\log_2 n)$) for the representation of the vector's indexes (see Section 4).

The basic idea of their solution is to reduce sets $\mathcal{A}$ and $\mathcal{B}$ at each round, eliminating all elements that are not in the intersection. The algorithm terminates when either i) no more elements are left—in which case the sets are guaranteed to be disjoint—or ii) when, with high probability, a set of candidates belonging to the intersection is left. The core of the KM solution is to use random hash functions taken from a pre-determined class of hash functions, to establish which elements are not in the intersection. The KM solution can be summarized as follows. At a generic round $i > 0$, the parties agree on a random hash function H_i. The agreement can be reached in several ways. For instance, we can assume that only one party chooses (uniformly at random) the function from the family, and then it sends a description of the function to the other party. Alternatively, if we suppose that the family of hash functions is an ordered set, one party can send to the other just the index of the selected function . Let be x a vector of size n with all values initialized to *false*, and let $\mathcal{A}^i$ denote the elements of $\mathcal{A}$ that are not eliminated after round i. $\mathcal{A}$ computes $H_i(a_s)$ for each $a_s \in \mathcal{A}^i$ and set $x[j] = x[j] \vee (H_i(a_s) = j)$. Note that $x[j]$ is *true* iff there exists at least one element $a_s \in \mathcal{A}^i$ such that $H_i(a_s) = j$ (i.e. a_s is hashed into the jth position). The party B executes the same computation using a vector y. The corresponding vectors x and y (of length n) are then exchanged. This requires sending n bits. A can now eliminate all elements of $\mathcal{A}^i$ that were hashed into position j, such that $y[j] = false$; B does the same for $\mathcal{B}^i$. Intuitively, this is equivalent to a bins and balls model where balls are the set elements and bins are the vector positions. Hashing is assumed to be equivalent to random throwing balls in bins (A throwing in vector x and B throwing in vector y). At each round, the algorithm eliminates all the balls for which the corresponding bin of the other party is an empty bin.

In our solution we use similar techniques. That is, the same probabilistic model (bins and balls) and the same simulation technique of the model (hashing). Exploiting a result on the bins and balls model contained in [12], we consider at each round only the maximum loaded bin. Thus, exchanging only one index at each round we build a protocol that computes the disjointness function with a global saving in the number of bits exchanged.

3   Our Solution: CED²

In this section, we propose CED² (Communication Efficient Disjointness Decision), a communication efficient protocol for deciding whether there are elements in the intersection of two given sets. Section 3.1 introduces the system model and the notation used in the paper. Section 3.2 gives an overview of the proposed solution, while the protocol description can be found in Section 3.3.

3.1   System Model and Notation

Let us consider two sets $\mathcal{A} = \{a_1, a_2, ..., a_n\}$ and $\mathcal{B} = \{b_1, b_2, ..., b_m\}$, with $n, m \in \mathbb{N}$. We can assume w.l.o.g that $\mathcal{A}, \mathcal{B} \subseteq \{0, 1, ..., 2^k - 1\}$ with $k \in \mathbb{N}$ and $m = n$.

$\mathcal{A}$ and $\mathcal{B}$ are stored at two different parties, A and B respectively, that can exchange messages.

We would like to establish whether $\mathcal{A} \cap \mathcal{B} = \emptyset$ or not. Moreover, we would like to establish what is the communication cost payed in terms of total numbers of exchanged bits. Table 1 summarizes the notation used in this paper.

Table 1. Notation Table

$\mathcal{A}$	input set
$\mathcal{B}$	input set
A	(Alice); protocol party
B	(Bob); protocol party
$\mathcal{X}$	$\mathcal{A} \cap \mathcal{B}$
$\mathcal{H}$	family of hash functions
H_i	hash function randomly selected from $\mathcal{H}$ at round i
j_M	index of the max loaded bin
$\mathcal{A}^i$	elements not eliminated from $\mathcal{A}$ after round i
$\mathcal{B}^i$	elements not eliminated from $\mathcal{B}$ after round i
$U_A^i[j]$	elements from $\mathcal{A}$ hashed, at round i, in position j
$U_A[j]$	configuration of j-th bin of A at a generic round
$U_B^i[j]$	elements from $\mathcal{B}$ hashed, at round i, in position j
$U_B[j]$	configuration of j-th bin of B at a generic round
$\log n$	natural logarithm
$\log_2 n$	base 2 logarithm
$R_0(f)$	communication complexity of a Las-Vegas probabilistic protocol for function f
$R(f)$	communication complexity of a Monte Carlo probabilistic protocol for function f
$Disj_n^k$	the disjointness function: $Disj_n^k(A,B) = 1$ iff $\mathcal{A} \cap \mathcal{B} = \emptyset$, $\mathcal{A}$ and $\mathcal{B}$ having n elements
KM	Kurtz and Manber algorithm [10]

3.2   Protocol Overview

CED^2 works through different rounds. In particular, similarly to KM [10], the idea of CED^2 is to reduce the sets $\mathcal{A}$ and $\mathcal{B}$ at each subsequent protocol round. CED^2 also uses the bins and balls concept and, at the beginning of each protocol step, the remaining set's elements (balls) are assigned to bins accordingly to a hash function—different for each round. The basic idea is to eliminate, at each round, elements that are not in the intersection, exchanging the minimum number of bits for this purpose. To achieve the goal, we focus only on one particular bin at each round, the most loaded one. This allows us to cut the maximum number of balls possible with the minimum communication cost (just one index at each time).

Using this technique, we can save a significant amount of communication in the single round, as shown later in the paper. In fact, we exchange a single index (the one of the bin with the max load) instead of the whole vector (pairs index, load), as done by KM. The simple fact that the cost of a single round is less than the one of a single round of KM does not directly implies that the overall cost of CED² is less than the one of KM. In fact, the overall cost depends also on the number of steps, that it is different for the two considered protocols. Analysis and the experimental results show that CED² outperforms KM.

3.3 Protocol Description

CED² can be described via the bins and balls model. At every round i, we assign (throw) the n elements (balls) of each set in n indexes of a vector (bins). The launches are simulated by a hash function H_i, mapping elements of the sets into the vector indexes. In the following, the two vectors U_A and U_B denote bins, while $U_A^i[j]$ $(U_B^i[j])$ denotes the set of values $a_i \in A$ $(b_i \in B)$ mapped to the j-th position at round i. At each round, the parties agree on the hash function H_i—chosen uniformly at random from a family $\mathcal{H}$ of hash functions. In particular, we consider $\mathcal{H} = \{H \equiv \lceil ax + b(mod p)\rceil (mod n)\}$, where $a, b < p$ $(a \neq 0)$ are chosen at random, p is a prime $> 2^k$, and n is the sets cardinality—we remind that we assume that the two sets have the same cardinality. We denote with H_i the hash function randomly selected at round i. Furthermore, $\mathcal{A}^i$ and $\mathcal{B}^i$ denote the elements not eliminated after round i, from A and B respectively. Notation $H_i(a_k) = j$ indicates that the item $a_k \in A$ has been assigned to the bin j, for the round i. Each of the parties involved in the protocol computes the assignment independently—without requiring any communication. However, using both parties the same hash function (even if different for each round) guarantees that elements belonging to $A \cap B$ map to the same position. Let us assume that for a given j, $U_A[j]$ contains v elements (of A) and the corresponding bin (same vector's index j) $U_B[j]$ is empty. This assure that the v elements of A mapped into $U_A[j]$ do not belong to the intersection $A \cap B$. From the hash function definition we have the following two properties:

$$a_s = b_t \in A \cap B \Longrightarrow H_i(a_s) = H_i(b_t) = j \tag{2}$$

$$H_i(a_s) = H_i(b_t) = j \nRightarrow a_s = b_t \in A \cap B. \tag{3}$$

Equation 3 justifies the need for using different hash functions in the subsequent protocol rounds. In fact, let us assume that, at a given round, the randomly selected hash function induces a configuration of the bins such that bin $U_A[j]$ contains elements of A that are not in $A \cap B$, and bin $U_B[j]$ contains elements of B that are not in $A \cap B$ (hash collisions). Intuitively, changing the hash function at the next round gives a different distribution for the balls in the bins. Thus, we have a chance to eliminate the balls that do not belong to the intersection—using randomly chosen functions at each round permits to have launches behave differently at each round.

The behaviour of CED² is described in Algorithm 1. First, A randomly select the hash function used in the current iteration i (line 1). Hence, A maps all the elements A into the n elements vector, using the hash function (line 2). Then, A

sends to B the vector index, j_M, with the maximum number of elements mapped into (line 3). B sends back to A the information whether its own vector is empty at position j_M. If this is the case (line 5), A cuts all the elements mapped in j_M (line 6). Then, it checks whether there are remaining elements (line 7). In the negative case, A can conclude that the intersection is empty, and terminate with output 1 (line 8). Otherwise, if the B vector is not empty at position j_M (line 10), A checks for how many are the consecutive rounds it was not able to eliminate elements (line 11). If these consecutive rounds are more than a predetermined constant q (its value is discussed in Section 5), A terminates with output 0 (line 12). If neither of the two termination conditions are verified (lines 8, 12), A iterates the procedure (line 14).

Algorithm 1. CED^2

Round i; computation made by A

1: A chooses a random H_i from $\mathcal{H}$ and sends a description of H_i (i.e. function parameters a, b, p) to B
2: A computes $H_i(a) = j$ for each $a \in \mathcal{A}^{i-1}$ and stores a in $U^i_{\mathcal{A}}[j]$
3: A sends to B the j_M index, the maximum loaded bin
4: A receives from B the information whether the $U^i_{\mathcal{B}}[j_M]$ is empty or not
5: **if** $U^i_{\mathcal{B}}[j_M] = \emptyset$ **then**
6:     $\mathcal{A}^i = \mathcal{A}^{i-1} \setminus \{a_s \mid a_s \in \mathcal{A} \text{ and } H_i(a_s) = j_M\}$
7:     **if** $(\mathcal{A}^i = \emptyset)$ **then**
8:         output 1: Disjoint
9:     **end if**
10: **else**
11:     **if** i satisfy the condition $\mathcal{A}^{i-q} = \mathcal{A}^{i-q+1} = ... = \mathcal{A}^i$ **then**
12:         output 0: Not-Disjoint
13:     **else**
14:         $i = i + 1$; throwing again
15:     **end if**
16: **end if**

In figures 1 and 2, we depict the two possible scenarios for CED^2: disjoint sets (Figure 1) and not-disjoint sets (Figure 2). For the sake of clarity we do not show the configuration of the entire bins vectors $U^i_{\mathcal{A}}$ and $U^i_{\mathcal{B}}$ but just a sample of them.

Figure 1 shows an example of disjoint sets instances, presented in Figure 1a. Considering these sets, an example of a cutting round is shown in Figure 1b and a not cutting round in Figure 1c. Looking at Figure 1b, let us suppose that position 4 of the A vector is the maximum loaded bin j_M. We can observe that the corresponding position in the vector of B ($U^i_{\mathcal{B}}[4]$) is empty. Thus, at the subsequent round $i + 1$, $\mathcal{A}^{i+1} = \{0, 1, 3, 5, 6, 7, 8\}$. Instead, in the case depicted in Figure 1c the corresponding position in the vector of B is not empty. In fact, $U^i_{\mathcal{B}}[4]$ contains the element labeled 16. Hence, at the subsequent round $i + 1$, $\mathcal{A}^{i+1} = \mathcal{A}^i = \{0, 1, 2, 3, 4, 5, 6, 7, 8, 9\}$.

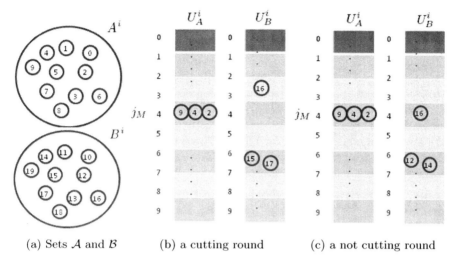

(a) Sets $\mathcal{A}$ and $\mathcal{B}$ (b) a cutting round   (c) a not cutting round

Fig. 1. Example of Disjoint Instances

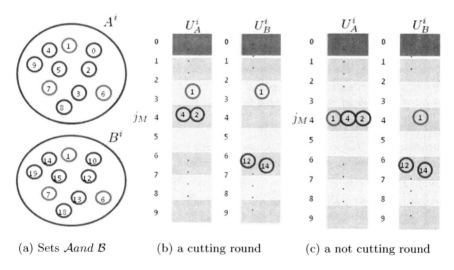

(a) Sets $\mathcal{A}$ and $\mathcal{B}$ (b) a cutting round   (c) a not cutting round

Fig. 2. Example of Not-Disjoint Instances

Similarly to Figure 1, Figure 2 shows an example of two not-disjoint sets, presented in Figure 2a; the green balls indicating elements belonging to the intersection. Considering this case, a cutting launch is shown in Figure 2b and a not cutting launch in Figure 2c. In Figure 2b, the position 4 is the maximum loaded bin j_M of $\mathcal{A}$, it does not contain any intersection element and the corresponding bin $U_{\mathcal{B}}^i[4]$ is empty. Hence, at the subsequent round $i + 1$, $\mathcal{A}^{i+1} = \{0, 1, 3, 5, 6, 7, 8, 9\}$. Instead, in the case depicted in Figure 2c the green ball labeled 1 makes $U_{\mathcal{B}}^i[4]$ not empty. This produces, at the subsequent round $i+1$, $\mathcal{A}^{i+1} = \mathcal{A}^i = \{0, 1, 2, 3, 4, 5, 6, 7, 8, 9\}$. In fact, the green ball belongs to the intersection and falls in the bin $j_M = 4$.

4   Analysis

In this section, we analyze the communication cost of CED^2 and KM. The analysis given in this section only considers the scenario where the two sets are actually disjoint.

We start analyzing the cost for CED^2. The overall result is given in Lemma 4. However, we need the following intermediate results: Lemma 1, Lemma 2 and Lemma 3. Lemma 1 is a result from [12].

Lemma 1.   *When n balls are thrown into n bins, the maximum number of balls in any bin is $O(\frac{\log n}{\log \log n})$ with high probability, i.e., $1 - \frac{1}{n}$.*

Lemma 2.   *When n balls are thrown into n bins the probability of a particular bin being empty is $\frac{1}{e}$ for large n.*

Proof. The probability that a ball does not fall into a particular bin is $1 - \frac{1}{n}$. Therefore: $Pr[bin\ j\ is\ empty] = \left(1 - \frac{1}{n}\right)^n \approx \frac{1}{e}$.   □

Lemma 3.   *Given two sets $\mathcal{A}$ and $\mathcal{B}$ with $\mid \mathcal{A} \mid = \mid \mathcal{B} \mid = n$, if $\mathcal{A} \cap \mathcal{B} = \emptyset$ then the average number of messages exchanged for CED^2 (Algorithm 1) is $O(n \cdot \frac{\log \log n}{\log n})$.*

Proof. From Lemma 1, we know that if at each round it is possible to cut $\frac{\log n}{\log \log n}$ elements. Hence, the expected number of rounds to cut all the elements is $n \cdot \frac{\log \log n}{\log n}$. The expected trials to find empty a given box j is e (Lemma 2). Thus, the total expected number of rounds needed to cut all the elements is $e \cdot n \cdot \frac{\log \log n}{\log n}$.   □

We can now give the following Lemma for CED^2.

Lemma 4.   *Given two sets $\mathcal{A}$ and $\mathcal{B}$ with $\mid \mathcal{A} \mid = \mid \mathcal{B} \mid = n$, if $\mathcal{A} \cap \mathcal{B} = \emptyset$ then the average number of bits exchanged for CED^2 is $O(n \cdot \log \log n)$.*

Proof. From Lemma 3, we know that $e \cdot n \cdot \frac{\log \log n}{\log n}$ is the expected number of rounds required by CED^2 to cut all the elements. At each round CED^2 exchanges a message of $O(\log_2 n)$ bits. Indeed, each party sends one single index using $\log_2 n$ bits for its representation. Hence, the expected CED^2 total bits expenditure is:

$$e \cdot n \cdot \frac{\log \log n}{\log n} \cdot \log_2 n. \tag{4}$$

Substituting $\log_2 n = \frac{\log n}{\log 2}$ in (4), the claim follows.   □

The communication complexity of KM is given by the following Lemma, provided in [10].

Lemma 5.   *Given two sets $\mathcal{A}$ and $\mathcal{B}$ with $\mid \mathcal{A} \mid = \mid \mathcal{B} \mid = n$, if $\mathcal{A} \cap \mathcal{B} = \emptyset$ then the average number of bits exchanged for KM is $O(n(\log_2 n)(\log_2 \log_2 n))$.*

Comparing Lemma 4 to Lemma 5, we conclude that CED^2 communication complexity (Lemma 4) is lower than KM communication complexity (Lemma 5) by a factor $O(\log_2 n)$.

5   Protocol Evaluation

In the previous section we have provided the analysis of both CED^2 and KM for the disjointness case. In this section, we evaluate our solution leveraging both the previous analysis and the results of the simulations we run. We consider both disjointness and not-disjointness cases—and discuss them separately. We compare our solution to the one of Kurtz and Manber that, to the best of our knowledge, is the most efficient solution in the literature. In order to run the simulations shown in this section, we implemented a simulator using Python. The inputs sets are generated as random integers using the Python libraries for randomness. The same libraries have been also employed to implement the family of hash functions described both for CED^2 and KM. Each point plotted in the graphs shown in this section represents the average computed over 500 run of the algorithms.

5.1   Disjoint Sets Instances

We first consider disjoint sets instances as input for the algorithms. Both algorithms work over subsequent rounds by removing elements ("cutting") from the starting sets. The two algorithms both terminate when all elements are removed. Hence, we start investigating how the size of the remaining sets vary with the number of rounds. The results are shown in figures 3a and 3b for CED^2 and KM, respectively. We specify that data for Figure 3b has been obtained fixing a value for the number of rounds, and calculating the average number of elements cut (y-axis value) for that value. Comparing the results for the two protocols, we observe that CED^2 requires a significant higher number of rounds to complete with respect to KM. As an example, for sets of $n = 1000$ elements, CED^2 requires some 600 protocol rounds to complete, while KM terminates in 3 iterations.

From just these results, one might conclude that the communication cost of CED^2 is higher than the one of KM. However, we still need to investigate what

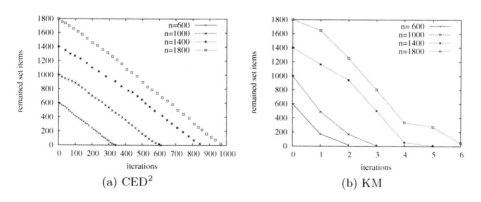

Fig. 3. Disjoint Sets: Cuts Trend

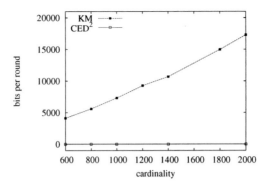

Fig. 4. Disjoint Sets: Average Bits per Round

is the communication cost of each single protocol iteration. Hence, we run our simulator to collect the number of bits exchanged in each single protocol round and we considered the average of all the rounds. The results are shown in Figure 4.

From Figure 4, we observe that the key difference between the two algorithms is the communication bits payed in each single iteration. In fact, while CED^2 requires more rounds than KM (figures 3a and 3b), each round has a very small communication cost—almost negligible compared to a round of KM. In particular, for the sets cardinality considered in the simulation (x-axis of Figure 4), the communication cost of CED^2 varies from 12 to 15 bits per round. Whereas, the cost of KM varies from 4113 bits (for sets of 600 elements), up to some 17276 bits (for sets of size 2000).

We note that "cutting" all the elements provides an answer to the question whether the sets intersect. Hence, this is a zero-error termination criteria for both algorithms. Unfortunately, we do not have the same characterization for the not-disjoint sets, as discussed in Section 5.2.

In the following graph (Figure 5) we report the overall communication complexity for the two protocols; that is, the number of bits required for the two protocols to complete. More specifically, in Figure 5, we give a global view of analysis and simulations for both algorithms showing:

- the expected behaviour from analysis, respectively from Lemma 4 for CED^2 and from Lemma 5 for KM;
- the results of simulations of the two algorithms.

Observing the results shown in Figure 5, we can draw the conclusion that CED^2 (Algorithm 1) performs better than KM algorithm. We underline that the aim of these results is to show a qualitative behaviour without taking into consideration any specific communication protocol. In fact, one might argue that when our solution is used in a practical scenario, the size of the exchanged message might be bigger than the one shown in the figure—due to the message header of the communication protocol used. However, we observe that the advantage provided

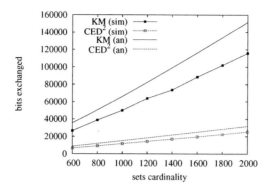

Fig. 5. Disjoint Sets: Analysis (an) and Simulations (sim) of Communication Complexity

by our solution is preserved even when a practical message header is considered. For example, let us consider sets of 1400 elements. Our solution would require an average of 843 messages (see Figure 3a) each of 15 bits of payload (Figure 4). The KM solution would require an average of 5 messages (see Figure 3b), each of 73654 bits of payload (Figure 4). Let us consider a message header of 10 bits—that is a practical choice for setting like WSN, where the header can have a small size that includes the bits required to identify the receiver (e.g. among some 1000 nodes). With 10 bits of header our solution would send about 843 messages, each of 25 bits, while KM would use 5 messages of 73664 bits. Hence, the overall number of bits would be 21075 for our solution, compared to the 368320 required by KM. This example shows that the advantage of our solution compared to KM remains even in practical scenario.

The simulations confirmed that the number of bits sent in the two solutions differs of a $O(\log_2 n)$ factor, as predicted in Lemma 4 and Lemma 5. We note that KM analysis gives an upper bound on the number of exchanged bits based on the $O(\log_2(n))$ bits representation for bins indexes (see Lemma 5). Running the KM simulation produces averaged values for indexes representation expenditure, $\lceil \frac{\log_2(n)+1}{2} \rceil$. This motivates the gap between the two KM curves. Similar argument justifies the fact that indexes representation cost in bits does not affect our solution. In fact, as each party in the protocol sends just one index at a time, the upper bound from analysis (see Lemma 3) and the result of the simulation are likely to be close to each other. We also observe that in the experiment shown in Figure 5 we used an optimized implementation of the KM algorithm. In fact, we send just empty bins indexes to the other party, saving on the total transmitted bits. Actually, the KM algorithm would send the entire vector of size n. In the latter case, the difference between the two compared communication costs would be larger. The conclusion is that in case of disjoint sets instances, choosing to reduce the exchanged bits in the single round provides a global saving in the total communication complexity.

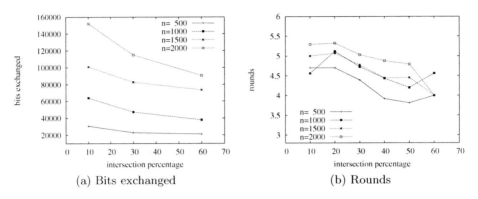

(a) Bits exchanged   (b) Rounds

Fig. 6. Not-Disjoint Sets: KM; $q = 2$

5.2   Not-disjoint Instances

For not-disjoint instances, let us first analyze KM termination that authors left as an open issue. In KM the termination condition occurs at round r when $\mathcal{A}^{r-q} = \mathcal{A}^{r-q+1} = \ldots = \mathcal{A}^r$, for a pre-determined constant q (not specified in [10]). This condition is similar to the one used in CED^2 (see Algorithm 1, line 11), but the value of q is influenced by different underneath stochastic processes. In fact, even though the two algorithms use the same hashing strategy, the stochastic process produced by the choice of the maximum loaded bin at each round (CED^2), is not equal to the one produced by the exchange of all the empty bin indexes (KM).

We argue that $q = 2$ would be a good choice for KM to establish if two sets are disjoint or not. In fact, KM algorithm is likely to cut elements at each round. The only adverse circumstance is the configuration in which all not empty bins indexes, for one party, match all not empty bins indexes for the other party. As it is unlikely that KM algorithm does not cut elements at a given round, if for two rounds it is not possible to cut elements, this means that, with high probability, KM cut all the elements not belonging to the intersection. We report in Figure 6 both the amount of exchanged bits (Figure 6a) and the total rounds employed (Figure 6b) with this termination criteria. From Figure 6b, we can observe that the numbers of rounds employed to end, for all the cardinalities considered, vary in a short range from some 3.8 for $n = 500$ and 50% of common elements between the input sets, up to some 5.4 for $n = 2000$ and 20% of common elements. From Figure 6a, we can observe that the bits expenditure is ranged between some 22000 bits, obtained for $n = 500$ up to nearly 160000 for $n = 2000$. The second hypothesis from KM is to run the algorithm for $c \cdot (\log_2 \log_2 n)$ rounds, with constant $c > 1$. If not all the elements are eliminated, then the sets are not disjoint with an error probability depending on c.

For comparisons with CED^2 we choose this latter hypothesis and set $c = 1.1$ for the simulations. The reason is twofold: on the one hand, as we are focusing

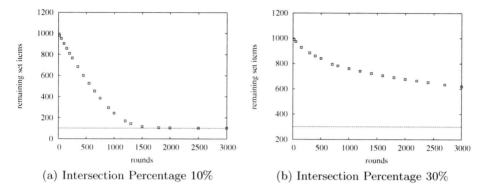

Fig. 7. Not-Disjoint Sets: CED^2; Cuts Trend with respect to Intersection Cardinality; $n = 1000$

on the amount of exchanged bits, we are interested in the scenario in which KM saves more—setting $c = 1.1$ means to have the minimum rounds and thus the minimum bits expenditure for KM. On the other hand, the approach to cut all the elements not belonging to the intersection (like in the first KM hypothesis) is not applicable to CED^2. In fact, for not-disjoint instances, if CED^2 reaches, at some round, a configuration where elements not in the intersection are less than the bin maximum load (see Lemma 1), it will never be able to cut those elements (it would be impossible to find them in the maximum loaded bin). Even if CED^2 may not be able to cut all the elements not belonging to the intersection, still the cuts trend shows meaningful information.

We start observing that the convergence rate to the intersection cardinality is slow (see Figure 7) and goes slower as the intersection cardinality increases. The phenomenon is captured in figures 7a and 7b where we compare the cuts trend—using different intersection percentage—to the real intersection size.

The behaviour of the curves can be explained by observing that the possibility to cut elements, at a certain round, depends on the probability that: no intersection elements fall in the max loaded bin and the corresponding bin of the other party is empty. It is possible to check that this probability is $\leq e^{-\left(\frac{|\mathcal{X}|}{n}+1\right)}$ and that this is congruent with the simulations results depicted in Figure 7. We also observe that, for all the curves in Figure 7, increasing the protocol round number (x-axis), the cardinality of the remaining set (y-axis) decreases slowly than the case for the empty intersection (or disjointness) curve—this is shown in Figure 3a (see the curve for $n = 1000$). This behaviour can be observed even for a small intersections size (e.g. 10% of common elements; see Figure 7a). A direct comparison of these curves can be found in Figure 8a. Looking at Figure 8b, we can check that a similar phenomenon can be recognized in KM, even if it appears a bit less marked. We test CED^2 termination simulating the algorithm with $q = 11$. That is, if for 11 consecutive iterations it is not possible to cut elements, then we conclude that the intersection is not empty and terminate the execution. From simulations results, the choice of the value q resulted to be a good one. In fact (see Figure 10), setting $q = 11$ produces an error rate less than 20%. That is, we obtain the correct answer with a probability $> 4/5$. The optimal value for q and the related error rate appears to be an interesting matter for further investigations.

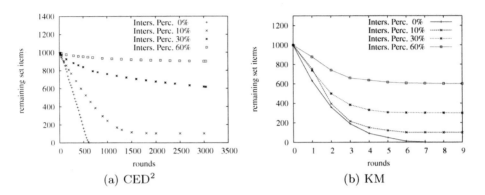

Fig. 8. Not-Disjoint Sets: Cuts Trend; $n = 1000$

Figure 9 shows iterations (see Figure 9b) and communication bits (see Figure 9a) reported by CED^2 simulations to decide if the two sets in input are not disjoint. Since, we want also to be able to avoid errors when disjoint instances are provided as input, we tested the two protocols providing in input to our simulator 50% of disjoint sets input pairs and 50% of not disjoint sets. In such a testing environment, CED^2 terminated with a wrong decision on 4.21% of the input pairs. This value is not plotted in Figure 9.

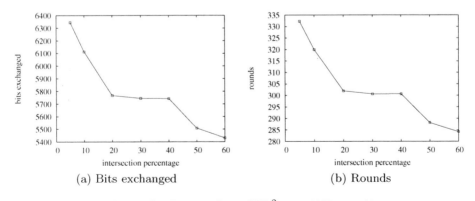

Fig. 9. Not-Disjoint Sets: CED^2; $n = 1000$; $q = 11$

Figure 10 compares CED^2 and KM simulations results using the termination criteria discussed above. In both cases, fixed a protocol parameter (q for CED^2

and c for KM) we can observe that the error rate increases as the cardinality of the sets increases. On the KM side, it is possible to check that setting $c = 1.1$ is equivalent to set the number of rounds for termination to 4. This can be verified substituting the values of the cardinality tested in the termination condition. As we can see in Figure 3b, the average number of rounds required to cut all the elements is at least 6 for $n = 2000$, while it is just 3 considering $n = 1000$. This justifies why, with 4 rounds, KM makes more errors for $n = 2000$ than for $n = 1000$ on disjoint sets instances. On the CED^2 side, the probability to find empty the bin corresponding to the max loaded one at round i, is $e^{-\frac{|A^i|}{n}}$. This value decreases as n increases. This justifies why, as the sets cardinality increases, the number of consecutive launches before cutting elements also increases. As a consequence, also CED^2 makes more errors for $n = 2000$ than for $n = 1000$.

From the performances perspective, Figure 10 shows that even if we consider the scenario with the minimum bits expenditure for KM (i.e. $c = 1.1$), still CED^2 obtains a lower error rate. In fact, in the majority of the cardinality considered, with a single exception, CED^2 requires much less communication bits. This allows us to conclude that the CED^2 strategy to consider a single bin at each round produces a global saving in the communication bits expenditure for both disjoint and not-disjoint input instances.

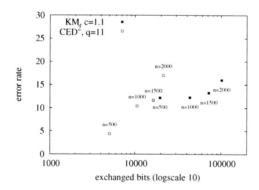

Fig. 10. Not-Disjoint Sets: KM and CED^2 Relation Between Communication Cost and Error Rate

6   Conclusions

In this paper we presented CED^2 (Communication Efficient Disjointness Decision), a probabilistic and distributed protocol that allows two parties to decide about whether they share a secret. CED^2 has been showed to be particularly suitable for devices having constraints on energy, communication, storage, and bandwidth. In particular, CED^2 significantly improves the communication cost compared to the work in the literature, having a communication complexity of $O(n \log \log n)$—improving by $O(\log_2 n)$ the state of the art. While in this paper we focused on the (probabilistic) discovery of shared secrets, our results can be applied to any scenario where two parties need to determine the disjnointness of their sets. Finally, this improvement has been achieved providing the same level of privacy and security of the state of the art solution.

Further ongoing work focus on relaxing the termination criteria—introducing probabilistic termination—and providing probabilistic assurance on the intersection size.

References

1. Agrawal, R., Evfimievski, A., Srikant, R.: Information sharing across private databases. In: Proceedings of the 22th ACM SIGMOD international conference on Management of data (SIGMOD 2003), pp. 86–97 (2003)
2. Barbay, J., López-Ortiz, A., Lu, T., Salinger, A.: An experimental investigation of set intersection algorithms for text searching. Journal of Experimental Algorithmics 14, 3.7–3.24 (2009)
3. Demaine, E.D., López-Ortiz, A., Ian Munro, J.: Adaptive set intersections, unions, and differences. In: Proceedings of the Eleventh Annual ACM-SIAM Symposium on Discrete Algorithms (SODA 2000), pp. 743–752 (2000)
4. Eschenauer, L., Gligor, V.: A key-management scheme for distributed sensor networks. In: Proceedings of the 9th ACM Conference on Computer and Communications Security (CCS 2002), pp. 267–282 (2002)
5. Freedman, M.J., Nissim, K., Pinkas, B.: Efficient private matching and set intersection. In: Cachin, C., Camenisch, J.L. (eds.) EUROCRYPT 2004. LNCS, vol. 3027, pp. 1–19. Springer, Heidelberg (2004)
6. Håstad, J., Wigderson, A.: The randomized communication complexity of set disjointness. Journal Theory of Computing 3(1), 211–219 (2007)
7. Kalyanasundaram, B., Schnitger, G.: The probabilistic communication complexity of set intersection. SIAM Journal on Discrete Mathematics 5(4), 545–557 (1992)
8. Kiayias, A., Mitrofanova, A.: Testing disjointness of private datasets. In: S. Patrick, A., Yung, M. (eds.) FC 2005. LNCS, vol. 3570, pp. 109–124. Springer, Heidelberg (2005)
9. Kissner, L., Song, D.X.: Privacy-preserving set operations. In: Shoup, V. (ed.) CRYPTO 2005. LNCS, vol. 3621, pp. 241–257. Springer, Heidelberg (2005)
10. Kurtz, T.G., Manber, U.: A probabilistic distributed algorithm for set intersection and its analysis. Journal of Theoretical Computer Science 49(2-3), 267–282 (1987)
11. Kushilevitz, E., Nisan, N.: Communication complexity. Cambridge University Press, New York (1997)
12. Mitzenmacher, M., Upfal, E.: Probability and Computing: Randomized Algorithms and Probabilistic Analysis. Cambridge University Press, New York (2005)
13. Motwani, R., Raghavan, P.: Randomized Algorithms. Cambridge University Press, Cambridge (1997)
14. Yao, A.C.-C.: Some complexity questions related to distributive computing. In: Proceedings of the eleventh annual ACM symposium on Theory of computing (STOC 1979), pp. 209–213 (1979)
15. Ye, Q., Wang, H., Pieprzyk, J., Mo Zhang, X.: Unconditionally secure disjointness tests for private datasets. International Journal of Applied Cryptography 1(3), 225–235 (2009)

Impossibility of Finding Any Third Family of Server Protocols Integrating Byzantine Quorum Systems with Threshold Signature Schemes[*]

Jingqiang Lin[1,2], Peng Liu[2], Jiwu Jing[1], and Qiongxiao Wang[1]

[1] The State Key Laboratory of Information Security, Graduate University of CAS, Beijing 100049, China
[2] The Pennsylvania State University, University Park, PA 16802, USA

Abstract. In order to tolerate servers' Byzantine failures, a distributed storage service of self-verifying data (e.g., certificates) needs to make three security properties be Byzantine fault tolerant (BFT): data consistency, data availability, and confidentiality of the (signing service's) private key. Building such systems demands the integration of Byzantine quorum systems (BQS), which only make data consistency and availability be BFT, and threshold signature schemes (TSS), which only make confidentiality of the private key be BFT. Two families of correct or *valid* TSS-BQS systems (of which the server protocols carry all the design options) have been proposed in the literature. Motivated by the failures in finding a third family of valid server protocols, we study the reverse problem and formally prove that it is *impossible* to find any third family of valid TSS-BQS systems. To obtain this proof, we develop a *validity theory* on server protocols of TSS-BQS systems. It is shown that the only two families of valid server protocols, "predicted" (or deduced) by the validity theory, precisely match the existing protocols.

Keywords: Byzantine fault tolerance, Byzantine quorum systems, threshold signature schemes.

1 Introduction

Malicious codes, software bugs or operator mistakes can cause servers' Byzantine (or arbitrary) failures [12], and then compromise the services of network systems. As a result, BFT (Byzantine fault tolerant) systems, which run correctly in the presence of failures and do *not* have any assumptions about the behavior of faulty entities, are increasingly important. Several techniques [5,6,8,12,13] are proposed to provide BFT properties, such as integrity, consensus, consistency, availability and confidentiality. Of these techniques, BQS (Byzantine quorum systems) [13] and TSS (threshold signature schemes) [6] are remarkable.

---

[*] Jingqiang Lin, Jiwu Jing and Qiongxiao Wang were supported by National Natural Science Foundation of China grant 70890084/G021102 and National Science & Technology Pillar Program of China grant 2008BAH22B01. Peng Liu was supported by AFOSR FA9550-07-1-0527 (MURI), ARO W911NF-09-1-0525 (MURI), NSF CNS-0905131, NSF CNS-0916469 and AFRL FA8750-08-C-0137.

S. Jajodia and J. Zhou (Eds.): SecureComm 2010, LNICST 50, pp. 307–325, 2010.

BQS provide distributed storage services by replicating data on multiple servers, despite the Byzantine failures of (a certain number of) servers. To ensure data consistency and data availability, each read/write operation is performed on some quorum of servers (every quorum is a subset of servers; any two quorums have at least one server in common). In particular, in order to tolerate up to f faulty servers, $3f + 1$ servers are needed to compose a *dissemination* BQS storing *self-verifying* data, and every quorum contains $2f + 1$ servers (i.e., each operation is performed on at least $2f + 1$ servers; the intersection of quorums masks the impact of faulty servers and enables clients to obtain the right replica).

TSS are also proposed to tolerate servers' Byzantine failures by distributing a private key among n servers. Each server holds a share (or partition) of the private key. A threshold number (denoted h, $1 < h \leq n$) of servers can cooperatively use the distributed private key to sign messages, while any subset of fewer than h servers cannot. Every server *partially* signs a message (i.e., uses its key share to generate a partial signature), and h partial signatures can be combined into a fully signed message.

Essentially, *a*) the goal of BQS is to make data consistency and data availability be BFT; and *b*) TSS can be viewed as a measure to make confidentiality of the (signing service's) private key be BFT. This key observation provides an intuitive understanding about the merits of *integrating* BQS with TSS, two BFT techniques holding different security properties. In a nutshell, traditional BQS [13,14] make two properties (i.e., data consistency and availability) be BFT, while the integration of BQS and TSS yields three BFT properties (i.e., confidentiality of the private key, data consistency and availability). More specifically, this integration benefits the services that demand Byzantine fault tolerance on all of the three properties instead of two.

Given these nice properties of TSS-BQS systems, people have been trying to design TSS-BQS systems. COCA [26] is a TSS-BQS system for BFT certificate query/update services, and its protocol is adopted in CODEX [15] to store secret data. [10] proposed another server protocol. Their study shows that when BQS (e.g., public key infrastructures or publish/subscribe systems) need to support write operations (e.g., create or update) on self-verifying data, the third property is much useful. From the user point of view, letting confidentiality of the signing service's private key BFT ensures non-repudiation of service signatures; so clients can have full trust in the service. Besides, proactive recovery, not implemented in traditional BQS, is enabled by the integration with TSS [15,26]: the service's private key keeps unchanged while servers are recovered periodically.

This integration provides more assurance than the "sum" of BQS and TSS. In particular, it is recognized that an *integrated* storage service in this manner shall and can ensure two "upgraded" security properties:

Service Availability. In the presence of Byzantine failures, a read/write request from authorized clients still gets a response to it, which is signed using the distributed service private key.

Service Integrity. Each fully signed response guarantees that the requested read/write operation has been performed on some quorum of servers.

These two integrated properties are beyond both BQS and TSS, and cannot be satisfied automatically even when confidentiality of the service private key, data consistency and availability are all ensured. Compared to traditional BQS [13,14], clients can directly update self-verifying data without the assistance of external signing services. Compared to TSS, the implication of a signed response is beyond asserting that the request has been processed by the signing service itself; it also asserts that the requested operation has been performed on a quorum of servers and that Byzantine failures won't affect the correctness.

At first glance, there appear to be lots of options in designing a *valid* TSS-BQS system. For example, *a)* the threshold to sign might be any number between 2 and $3f + 1$; and *b)* integrated with TSS, BQS might construct a response when less than $2f + 1$ servers are examined to have performed the requested operation. Moreover, the comparison of existing TSS-BQS systems [10,26] in terms of communication costs, computation costs and the ability to handle concurrent operations (see Section 6) shows that these options can affect performance of TSS-BQS systems, and suggests that there might be different optimized options or tradeoffs when TSS-BQS systems are applied for specific applications.

However, *only two* valid server protocols [10,26] are proposed in the literature (they have roughly the same client protocol). We had tried to design a different or better one, but the outcome is always similar to [10,26]. The failures suggest that there may *not* exist *any third* family of valid server protocols! This suggestion is hard to believe, but our research shows that this conjecture should be true.

Our main contribution is a *formalization* of this impossibility conjecture and a *proof* asserting that it is true. In particular, we propose a validity theory on server protocols of TSS-BQS systems. To the best of our knowledge, it is the first validity theory on this problem. Using this theory, we prove that there are *only two* families of valid server protocols of TSS-BQS systems. The representatives of these two families are that of COCA [26] (denoted *SP-I* in this paper) and that of [10] (denoted *SP-II*), respectively. The validity theory also shows that SP-I and SP-II are the only two *efficient* (and valid) protocols. Our conclusion advises researchers to *a)* apply TSS-BQS systems through one of these two protocols, and *b)* improve TSS-BQS systems by more efficient TSS, task schedulers or resource management of servers, but *not* by server protocol designs.

The rest of this paper is organized as follows. Section 2 describes the TSS-BQS system model. The problem of server protocol design is formulated in Section 3, followed by the main results of the validity theory in Section 4. In Section 5, we deduce the two existing server protocols based on the proposed theory. Performance is analyzed in Section 6, and related work is presented in Section 7. We conclude in Section 8.

2   System Model

A TSS-BQS system consists of n *servers*, and an arbitrary number of *clients* that are distinct from the servers. Servers can be *correct* or *faulty*. A correct server always follows its protocol, while a faulty one can *arbitrarily* deviate from its protocol (i.e., Byzantine failure). Assume up to f servers can be faulty throughout this paper. We assume that clients always behave correctly.

Data Replication. TSS-BQS systems are demanded by the security requirements arising in maintaining *self-verifying* data (e.g., certificates), whose authenticity (or origin) and integrity can be verified by any entity (server or client). Before being replicated on servers of a TSS-BQS system, each data item is signed by the system to make it self-verifying; thus any modification (by faulty servers or other attackers) can be detected by any entity.

To tolerate servers' Byzantine failures, data are replicated on multiple servers, which can be regarded as variables supporting read/write operations. For a variable x, each server (denoted S_i, $1 \leq i \leq n$) independently stores its replica (consisting of a value v and a timestamp t, which are signed *together* as one replica), denoted $[x, v_i, t_i]$. Timestamps are assigned by a client when it writes the variable, and each client c has its own timestamp set TS_c, not intersecting other $TS_{c'}$ for any other client c' [13]. For example, timestamps can be formed as ascending sequence numbers appended with the name of clients [14].

Quorum. In order to tolerate up to f faulty servers, a dissemination BQS is composed of $n = 3f + 1$ servers, and each quorum contains $2f + 1$ servers [13]. Then, every pair of quorums intersect on at least $f + 1$ servers. This "pervasive intersection" feature enables BQS to achieve data consistency; i.e., a read operation returns the *right* replica, which is written by the most recent write operation. To leverage this feature, a new data item $[x, v, t]$ must be delivered to some quorum of $2f + 1$ servers before the write operation ends. The right replica of variable x is obtained out of the (different) replicas stored on $2f + 1$ servers, by choosing the unmodified one with the highest timestamp [13].

Service Key. A TSS-BQS system holds one system-wide key pair, the *service private key* and the *service public key*. The service private key is split into *service key shares* based on TSS, and distributed among the *same* $3f + 1$ servers composing the dissemination BQS. Any h ($1 < h \leq n$) servers can use their service key shares to sign messages cooperatively. Conspiracies by fewer than h servers cannot compromise the service private key or use it to sign any messages.

The service public key is known to every entity, and clients accept responses and replicas only if they are verifiable using the service public key. That is, servers can use the service private key to sign a) a response to clients, and b) each data item stored in TSS-BQS systems.

Server Key. To prevent outside attackers from impersonating servers of TSS-BQS systems and for secure communications among servers, each server also holds a key pair denoted *server key*, which has *nothing* to do with the service key pair. A server knows others' public keys, and server keys are used to sign and verify messages *only* among servers.

Clients only (need to) know the service public key but *not* any server keys. As a further benefit, they aren't disturbed by proactive recovery [8,27] (i.e., periodic refreshment of service key shares and server keys) against mobile adversaries [19] (which attack and compromise one server for a limited period of time before moving on to another), because the service key pair keeps unchanged while service key shares are refreshed.

Uniformity. All servers are uniform. Given a TSS-BQS system, all (correct) servers follow one same protocol. If a message is delivered to two correct servers, they process it following the same protocol. Servers are *not* assumed to run identically. Each server runs independently according to its own state and messages received, and then they may run to *different* branches of the same protocol. However, there is no sentence with any special servers' identities in the protocol. Note that this uniformity assumption has *not* any constraints on faulty servers, which always run in an arbitrary way.

This assumption is generalized from usual threshold cryptographic schemes and quorum systems. Assuming that all servers are uniform, the threshold to sign and the size of a quorum can depict the condition to fully sign a messages by TSS and to finish a read/write operation in BQS, respectively.

Asynchronous Fair Link. A fair link [15,26] is a channel that doesn't deliver all messages sent, but if an entity sends infinitely many messages to another entity then infinitely many of these messages are correctly delivered. In addition, the link is asynchronous; i.e., there is no bound on message delivery delay or server execution speed.

We assume that only asynchronous fair links are provided among all entities. Adversaries may eavesdrop, delay, delete or alter messages in transmit, and replay or insert messages. However, a message sent sufficiently often by an entity to another will be delivered eventually.

3   Problem Formulation

The problem is to formally prove that it is impossible to design any third family of valid server protocols. To make this problem tangible, we need to define the notion of "validity" and firstly model the activities of clients and servers.

3.1   Client Protocol

When reading/writing variable x, an authorized client of TSS-BQS systems periodically sends a request to at least $f+1$ servers until it receives a signed response verifiable using the service public key. Because up to f servers could be faulty, sending a request to $f + 1$ servers guarantees that at least one correct server receives it eventually, and starts the server protocol.

A credential is generated and included in the read/write request, authorizing this operation. To prevent attackers from replaying the past signed responses, a nonce (e.g., the name of the client and an ascending sequence number) is included in each request and also the corresponding response. For reading, only the right replica is returned in each fully signed response. For writing, a client firstly reads the variable to obtain its current timestamp t', and chooses a higher timestamp $t > t'$ [13]. Then, the new value v and the timestamp t compose the write request, and its response is a signed acknowledgement to it.

3.2   General Model of Server Protocols

We present a general model of server protocols to enable the design space identification for TSS-BQS systems, showing both the flexible and the fixed parts. In our model, every server is abstracted to implement three functions as follows.

Storage. As a server of BQS firstly, S_i maintains its replica of variable x independently. On receiving a read request, S_i replies with its replica $[x, v_i, t_i]$. On receiving a request writing $[x, v, t]$, S_i acknowledges it, and only updates its replica if the data item being written is unmodified (i.e., verifiable using the service public key) and has a higher timestamp than its own (i.e., $t > t_i$).

Delegate. Since clients only know the service public key, some servers shall become *delegates* for each request, performing the requested read/write operation among servers on behalf of the client sending the request [26]. Note that a delegate is *not* a special or additional server; otherwise it will be a vulnerable component not tolerating failures. On receiving a request from clients, each (correct) server becomes a delegate for it. Since each request is sent to $f + 1$ servers, there may be more than one delegate for each operation. These delegates will return same responses, unless there are concurrent read/write operations.

On receiving a request from clients, a delegate constructs a response, cooperates with h servers to sign it, and then sends this signed response to clients. The response (to be signed) is constructed as below: *a)* in the case of read operations, the delegate lets the response be the right replica determined (or chosen) out of the $2f + 1$ replicas read from some quorum of servers; *b)* in the case of write operations, the delegate firstly cooperates with h servers to sign the data item being written to make it self-verifying, writes it to $2f + 1$ servers, and lets the response be an acknowledgement to this write request.

Partial-Signing. The service key pair is used to communicate with clients and create self-verifying data. So, servers can generate partial signatures for *a)* a response to clients, or *b)* a data item being written (to make it self-verifying).

S_i can use its service key share to partially sign a response, when receiving a partial-signing request for it. However, since the delegate sending this request may be faulty, the response (to be signed) may: *a)* be constructed when the requested read/write operation has not been performed on enough servers; sometimes, the corresponding request doesn't even exist; or *b)* return an out-of-date but self-verifying replica, even though the faulty delegate has read $2f + 1$ replicas. To avoid signing such a fake response, before partially signing each response, a (correct) server S_i shall process the corresponding read/write request by itself, and/or carry out some examinations. Messages that are signed using server keys, indicating that some servers have processed the read/write request, can be sent along with the partial-signing request as evidences to convince S_i to partially sign a response.

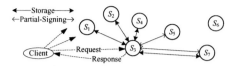

Fig. 1. General Model of Server Protocols

S_i can also generate a partial signature for each data item to make it self-verifying, before delegates write it to some quorum. This *data-signing* requires that: *a*) the service private key is available, and *b*) at least one correct server is involved in checking that the write request is generated by an authorized client (i.e., $h \geq f + 1$). For a *valid* server protocol, these two requirements of data-signing must be satisfied as well as service availability and service integrity (see Section 1). Fortunately, they are satisfied automatically when service availability and integrity are ensured. Otherwise, service availability isn't ensured if the service private key is unavailable, or service integrity isn't ensured if $h \leq f$ and then faulty servers can conspire to sign responses arbitrarily.

So, we skip this data-signing in the remainder due to limited space, focus on how to ensure service availability and integrity, and assume that each data item $[x, v, t]$ has been self-verifying when a client sends the write request.

Figure 1 shows the relationship of these three functions when $f = 2$ and $h = 3$, *not* showing the data-signing. A client sends a request to $f + 1$ servers. Then, S_3 assumes the role of delegate, performs the requested read/write operation on $2f + 1$ servers (including S_3), cooperates with h servers (also including S_3) to sign a response, and sends it to the client. It can be seen that in this flexible model, the server subset of partial-signing can *differ* from that of storage, though they may be the same in some instances or for some server protocols.

3.3   Defining the Validity of Server Protocols

As mentioned in Section 1, to provide BFT storage services as traditional BQS, an integrated TSS-BQS system must provide two upgraded security properties:

Service Availability. A read/write request from authorized clients gets a signed response to it, which is signed using the service private key.

Service Integrity. Each signed response guarantees that the requested operation has been performed on some quorum of servers. That is, a write response is signed only if the request has been delivered to at least $2f + 1$ servers; and a signed read response is derived from (different) replicas of $2f + 1$ servers, returning the right replica which is written by the most recent write operation.

These two security properties produce the definition of *valid* server protocols. On receiving a read/write request from clients, a delegate starts the valid server protocol to perform the requested operation on some quorum of servers, get a response fully signed, and return the signed response to clients.

Definition 1 (Valid Server Protocol). *A valid server protocol guarantees that a response is fully signed using the service private key if and only if a read/write request (generated by an authorized client) is delivered to some correct server (i.e., a delegate) and the requested read/write operation is performed on each server in some quorum.* □

3.4 Existing Valid Server Protocols

Two valid server protocols are proposed in [10,26], ensuring service integrity through different mechanisms. Based on these protocols, we can design similar ones, leading to two families of TSS-BQS systems.

SP-I. COCA [26] is the first system integrating BQS with TSS: *a)* $3f+1$ servers compose a dissemination BQS to provide certificate query/update services; *b)* the service private key is distributed among the exactly same $3f+1$ servers; *c)* the threshold to sign certificates or responses is $f+1$; and *d)* before using its service key share to partially sign a response, each server examines that the corresponding read/write operation has been performed on $2f+1$ servers. Since up to f servers can be faulty, at least one correct server carries out the necessary examinations before partially signing it, ensuring service integrity.

By increasing the threshold to sign of COCA, we can get a family of similar server protocols, where service integrity is still ensured through the examinations by the correct server(s) partially signing responses. For example, $h = f+2$ while all other features keep unchanged. Then, service integrity is ensured repeatedly, because there are at least two correct servers carrying out the examinations.

SP-II. Another valid protocol (SP-II) is suggested in [10]: *a)* the threshold to sign is equal to the size of a quorum (i.e., $h = 2f+1$); and *b)* each server processes the read/write request itself before partially signing a response. Thus, when a response is fully signed, $2f+1$ servers must have performed the requested operation; and service integrity is ensured through the threshold to sign.

By requiring servers of SP-II to carry out additional examinations, we can get another family of server protocols, where service integrity is ensured through the threshold to sign. For example, before partially signing the response, each server processes the read/write request itself and examines that the requested operation has been performed on d ($d < 2f+1$) servers. However, service integrity is still ensured through the threshold to sign (but not the examinations), because the d servers may be a subset of the h servers signing responses and multiple examinations together don't guarantee that the operation has been performed on more than h servers.

3.5 Is It Possible to Find Any Third Family of Valid Protocols?

SP-I and SP-II ensure service integrity of TSS-BQS systems through different mechanisms. Some questions appear when we analyze these protocols. Firstly, are there any valid server protocols ensuring service integrity through mechanisms *essentially* different from SP-I and SP-II? We had tried to design a different one, but the outcome is always similar to SP-I or SP-II. Secondly, can we design valid server protocols with a *combined* mechanism requiring fewer examinations than SP-I while having a smaller threshold to sign than SP-II? Such combined protocols might have advantages of both SP-I and SP-II, and offer balanced performance. Finally, (if such a combined mechanism exists) can we discover the relationship of these two mechanisms to ensure service integrity? The relationship may lead to parameterized TSS-BQS systems with flexible configurations.

4   Main Results

In this section, we present the validity theory on TSS-BQS systems. The "soul" of this theory is to identify the "bonds" between the validity definition (Definition 1) and the design space for server protocols in a mathematically rigorous way so that a formal proof of our impossibility conjecture is derived. In particular, we prove that: *a*) there exist *only two* families of valid server protocols integrating BQS with TSS; *b*) service integrity is ensured through either the threshold to sign or the examinations by the correct server(s) partially signing responses; and *c*) *nobody* can design a combined mechanism, e.g., a server protocol requiring fewer examinations than SP-I and having a smaller threshold than SP-II.

4.1   Design Space for Server Protocols

Based on the general model in Section 3.2, it can be seen that the design flexibilities of server protocols are mainly associated with how servers validate the correctness of a response (to be signed) and partially sign it. We find that the design flexibilities can be "captured" by a rather simple concept called *signing-condition* (i.e., the condition to satisfy when a server partially signs a response).

For example, following some server protocol, a *correct* server S_i can partially sign a response *only if* it receives messages indicating that the corresponding read/write request has been processed by certain servers, e.g., replicas or acknowledgements signed using their server keys. So, when S_i partially signs a response, it is asserted that the operation has been performed on these servers. However, it doesn't mean that all these servers strictly serve the storage function. A read/write operation is defined to be performed on a server of BQS [13], if it receives the request and replies with a replica or acknowledgement.

Definition 2 (Signing-Condition). *Given a server protocol, whenever S_i (either correct or faulty) uses its service key share to partially sign a response, it is asserted that the corresponding read/write operation has been performed on some subset of servers. This specific subset is called one* signing-condition *of S_i, denoted $C(S_i)$.* □

Given one server protocol, the condition enabling a server to partially sign a response can be *not* unique. Rather, alternative signing-conditions exist. In Figure 1, for example, S_5 uses its service key share to partially sign a response after it is convinced that $\{S_1, S_2, S_3, S_4, S_7\}$ have processed the read/write request. However, if the delegate S_3 performs the operation on another quorum of servers (e.g., $\{S_1, S_2, S_3, S_4, S_5\}$ or $\{S_2, S_3, S_4, S_5, S_6\}$), S_5 will also partially sign it. Thus, there are at least three alternative signing-conditions of S_5.

Definition 3 (Signing-Condition-Set). *Given a server protocol, the set of all signing-conditions $C(S_i)$ of S_i is called the* signing-condition-set $\mathscr{C}(S_i)$ *of S_i; i.e.,* $\mathscr{C}(S_i) = \{C(S_i)\}$. $\qquad\square$

Correct and faulty servers often have different signing-condition-sets, because faulty servers can partially sign either correct or fake responses (without satisfying the conditions as correct servers must follow).

4.2 Properties of Valid Server Protocols

Assumption 1. *For a* valid *server protocol, the read/write request from clients is included in the partial-signing request (sent by a delegate to servers).*

Justification. When requesting servers to partially sign a response, a delegate shall firstly convince them that an authorized client has sent the corresponding request. Otherwise, if a response is signed even when clients don't send the request, this response can be cached by faulty servers to launch attacks later. For example, if faulty servers can (convince others to) sign responses returning the *current* right replica with "potential" nonce when there doesn't exist a read request, these signed responses can be accepted by clients later, even when the returned "right" replica is updated by some write operation.

So, it is necessary for (correct) servers to check that the corresponding request exists before they partially sign a response. A safe and straightforward way is to include the intact read/write request in each partial-signing request, and then any server can authenticate it[1]. $\qquad\square$

Assumption 2. *On receiving a read/write request, either forwarded by delegates directly or sent along with a partial-signing request, a* correct *server performs the requested read/write operation.*

Justification. Each *correct* server S_i of TSS-BQS systems is firstly a server of BQS and serves the basic storage function. On receiving a read/write request forwarded by delegates, S_i acts as a server of BQS [13,14]: it replies with its replica or an acknowledgement signed using its *server key*, and only updates its replica if the data item being written has a higher timestamp than its own.

On receiving a read/write request sent along with a partial-signing request (to sign a replica to be returned or an acknowledgement)[2], S_i uses its *service*

---

[1] We can require clients to sign the read/write request; then each server can use clients' public keys to authenticate it. And each client's public key (or certificate) can also be stored in the TSS-BQS system as a self-verifying variable and servers can (act as *read-only* clients to) read it, making the system self-contained.

[2] In the meantime, some signing-condition of S_i must be satisfied.

key share to partially sign *a)* the replica to be returned if it is identical with its own[3], or *b)* the acknowledgement. S_i also updates its replica if the data item being written has a higher timestamp than its own. In this case, S_i *actually acts the same* as that of BQS: serves the storage function and signs the same messages, except that one is signed using its server key and the other is done using its service key share, which are both held by S_i only.   □

Because TSS-BQS systems assume asynchronous channels, this assumption doesn't harm the security. Moreover, it allows more flexible and efficient server protocols. Firstly, it doesn't require a strict order between the read/write operation and the partial-signing of each server. Secondly, the read/write request can be sent along with the partial-signing request to reduce communication costs. In addition, a correct delegate also "sends" the request to itself, then serves the storage function and performs the requested read/write operation.

Lemma 1. *For a* valid *server protocol,* $\forall C(S_i) \in \mathscr{C}(S_i) : S_i \in C(S_i)$.

Proof. This lemma can be directly concluded from Assumptions 1 and 2. When S_i (either correct or faulty) accepts a partial-signing request and replies with a partial signature, this partial-signing means that S_i has *a)* received the corresponding read/write request according to Assumption 1, and *b)* performed the requested operation according to Assumption 2. So, $S_i \in C(S_i)$.   □

In BQS (and TSS-BQS systems), "an operation performed on each server in some quorum" doesn't mean that all these servers strictly follow the server protocol and serve the storage function. As long as $2f + 1$ servers reply with their replicas or acknowledgements (and the *correct* ones of them have accepted and processed the read/write request), data consistency is ensured. Although up to f faulty servers may send fake replicas or acknowledge write requests without updating their replicas, the negative impact of faulty servers and their replies are masked by (the correct ones in) any quorum of $2f + 1$ servers.

Lemma 2. *For a* valid *server protocol,* $\mathscr{C}(S_i) = \{C : S_i \in C\}$ *if* S_i *is faulty.*

Proof. If S_i is faulty, it can uses its service key share to partially sign a response *arbitrarily*, whether with any process or not. Then, a partial signature by S_i may ensure *no* operations on any other servers except *itself* according to Lemma 1. So, any subset C containing S_i ($S_i \in C$) can be a signing-condition of S_i.   □

Theorem 41. $\mathscr{C}(\cdot)$ *of valid server protocols satisfies the following* signing-condition-inequality*:*
For any h-server set $H = \{S_{i_1}, S_{i_2}, \cdots, S_{i_h}\}$ ($|H| = h$), $\forall C(S_{i_e}) \in \mathscr{C}(S_{i_e} : 1 \le e \le h) : \bigcup_H C(S_{i_e}) = C(S_{i_1}) \cup C(S_{i_2}) \cup \cdots \cup C(S_{i_h})$ *contains some quorum of* $2f + 1$ *servers; that is,* $|\bigcup_H C(S_{i_e})| \ge 2f + 1$.

---

[3] If the replica to be returned is unmodified and has a higher timestamp than its own, S_i also partially signs it. This case can be explained as two steps: firstly S_i updates its replica with the one to be returned (which must be written by a more recent write operation), and then partially signs the response returning its replica.

Proof. To prove this theorem by contradiction, assume a server protocol *not* satisfying the inequality, and then we will find that service integrity is *not* ensured either. If the signing-condition-inequality is not satisfied, there must exist an h-server set (denoted H'), $\exists C'(S_{i_e}) \in \mathscr{C}(S_{i_e} : S_{i_e} \in H') : |\bigcup_{H'} C'(S_{i_e})| < 2f + 1$.

On receiving a read/write request, a faulty server can serve as a delegate:

1. Perform the requested operation on servers in $\bigcup_{H'} C'(S_{i_e})$, and construct a response to be signed;

2. Request $S_{i_1} \in H'$ to partially sign the response, and S_{i_1} (either correct or faulty) will partially sign it because the operation has been performed on servers in $C'(S_{i_1}) \subseteq \bigcup_{H'} C'(S_{i_e})$;

3. Request $S_{i_2}, S_{i_3}, \cdots, S_{i_h} \in H'$ to partially sign the response, and collect the partial signatures generated by these h servers; and

4. Combine these h partial signatures into a signed response.

Then, this signed response will be accepted by the client even when the requested operation is performed on fewer than $2f + 1$ servers, i.e., $\bigcup_{H'} C'(S_i)$. Hence, service integrity is *not* ensured. So, the signing-condition-inequality is a *necessary* condition of valid server protocols. □

Theorem 42. *A server protocol is valid if and only if the following conditions are satisfied:*
A. There exists an h-server set H^* ($|H^*| = h$) consisting of correct servers only; and $\exists C^*(S_i) \in \mathscr{C}(S_i)$ for all $S_i \in H^* : |\bigcup_{H^*} C^*(S_i)| \leq n - f = 2f + 1$.
B. Every signing-condition-set $\mathscr{C}(\cdot)$ satisfies the signing-condition-inequality.

Proof. Necessity. Firstly, an h-server set H^* consisting of correct servers only, is necessary to sign responses using the service private key, when faulty servers don't partially sign any messages. Secondly, the subset that performs the requested read/write operation (i.e., $\bigcup_{H^*} C^*(S_i)$), shall be available if f servers are crash, so it cannot contain more than n-f servers. Thus, Condition-A is a necessary condition as well as the signing-condition-inequality.

Sufficiency. On receiving a read/write request from clients, a (correct) delegate can perform the requested operation on servers in $\bigcup_{H^*} C^*(S_i)$, cooperate with the h correct servers in H^* to sign the response, and send it to clients. So, the service is available. Service integrity is also ensured because the signing-condition-inequality is satisfied and $\bigcup_{H^*} C^*(S_i)$ contains some quorum. □

Lemma 3. *For a valid server protocol, $f + 1 \leq h \leq 2f + 1$.*

Proof. Firstly, there exists an h-server set consisting of correct servers only according to Theorem 42, and up to f out of n servers can be faulty, so $h \leq n - f = 2f + 1$. Secondly, let's prove $f + 1 \leq h$ by contradiction. Assume $h < f + 1$; there exists an h-server set consisting of *faulty* servers only (denoted $\bar{H}$). For each $S_j \in \bar{H}$, $\{S_j\}$ is a signing-condition of S_j according to Lemma 2. Then, $|\bigcup_{\bar{H}} C(S_j)| = |\bigcup_{\bar{H}} \{S_j\}| = |\bar{H}| = h < f + 1$, and the signing-condition-inequality is *not* satisfied. Thus, $h \geq f + 1$; i.e., faulty servers cannot conspire to use the service private key to sign responses arbitrarily. □

4.3 Two Families of Valid Server Protocols

We investigate $\mathscr{C}(S_i)$ of valid server protocols under the *uniformity* assumption.

Lemma 4. *Assuming that servers are uniform and S_i is correct, if $C \in \mathscr{C}(S_i)$ and $S_j \in C$, then $C \in \mathscr{C}(S_j)$, where $j \neq i$.*

Proof. According to Lemma 2, C is a signing-condition of S_j ($S_j \in C$) if S_j is faulty. Let's assume S_j is correct. Since C is a signing-condition of S_i, S_i uses its service key share to partially sign a response after examining that the requested operation has been performed on servers in C ($S_i \in C$). Following the same server protocol as S_i, S_j also partially signs it after examining that the requested operation has been performed on the same subset C ($S_j \in C$; the relationship between C and S_i is the same as that between C and S_j). Thus, C is also a signing-condition of S_j; i.e., $C \in \mathscr{C}(S_j)$.   □

Lemma 5. *Assuming that servers are uniform and S_i is correct, if $C \in \mathscr{C}(S_i)$ and $S_j \notin C$, then $\{S_j\} \cup C' \in \mathscr{C}(S_j)$, where $C' = C \setminus \{S_i\}$.*

Proof. According to Lemma 2, $\{S_j\} \cup C'$ is a signing-condition of S_j if S_j is faulty. Let's assume S_j is correct. Since $C = \{S_i\} \cup C'$ is a signing-condition of S_i, S_i uses its service key share to partially sign a response, after it processes the request itself and examines that the requested operation has been performed on servers in C' ($S_i \notin C'$). Following the same server protocol as S_i, S_j also partially signs the response, after it processes the request itself and examines that the requested operation has been performed on the same subset C' ($S_j \notin C'$; the relationship between C' and S_i is the same as that between C' and S_j). Thus, $\{S_j\} \cup C'$ is a signing-condition of S_j; i.e., $\{S_j\} \cup C' \in \mathscr{C}(S_j)$.   □

Theorem 43. *Assuming that servers are uniform, there are* only *two families of valid server protocols as listed below, and it is* impossible *to find any third family:*
1. $2f + 1 > h \geq f + 1$, and for any h-server set H, $\exists S^* \in H : \mathscr{C}(S^*) = \{C : S^* \in C \wedge |C| \geq 2f + 1\}$.
2. $h = 2f + 1$, and $\forall C(S_i) \in \mathscr{C}(S_i) : S_i \in C(S_i)$.

Proof. Two cases are analyzed to find h and $\mathscr{C}(\cdot)$ of valid server protocols. Note that these complementary cases cover *all possible* scenarios.

1. For any h-server set H, $\exists S^* \in H, \forall C(S^*) \in \mathscr{C}(S^*) : |C(S^*)| \geq 2f + 1$.
   The signing-condition-inequality is satisfied without additional constraints because $|\bigcup_H C(S_i)| \geq |C(S^*)| \geq 2f + 1$. Furthermore, since $S_i \in C(S_i)$ according to Lemma 1, $\mathscr{C}(S^*) = \{C : S^* \in C \wedge |C| \geq 2f + 1\}$.

2. There exists an h-server set (denoted $\widetilde{H}$), $\forall S_i \in \widetilde{H}, \exists \widetilde{C} \in \mathscr{C}(S_i) : |\widetilde{C}| < 2f + 1$.
   According to Lemma 3, $h \geq f + 1$ and there is at least one *correct* server $\widetilde{S} \in \widetilde{H}$. There exists $\widetilde{C} \in \mathscr{C}(\widetilde{S}) : |\widetilde{C}| < 2f + 1$. For each $S_j \in \widetilde{C}$, $\widetilde{C}$ is a signing-condition of S_j according to Lemma 4. Select all servers in $\widetilde{C}$, and then

$|\bigcup_{\tilde{C}} C(S_j)| = |\tilde{C} \cup \cdots \cup \tilde{C}| = |\tilde{C}| < 2f + 1$. So, in order to satisfy the signing-condition-inequality, more servers than $\tilde{C}$ are needed to compose a valid h-server set, i.e., $h > |\tilde{C}|$. Then, we can find an h-server set $\tilde{H}^* \supset \tilde{C}$.

For each $S_k \in \tilde{H}^* \setminus \tilde{C}$, $\{S_k\} \cup \tilde{C}'$ is a signing-condition of S_k according to Lemma 5, where $\tilde{C}' = \tilde{C} \setminus \{\tilde{S}\}$; and $|\bigcup_{\tilde{H}^*} C(\cdot)| = |\bigcup_{\tilde{C}} C(S_j) \bigcup_{\tilde{H}^* \setminus \tilde{C}} C(S_k)| = |\tilde{C} \cup \cdots \cup \tilde{C} \bigcup_{\tilde{H}^* \setminus \tilde{C}} (\{S_k\} \cup \tilde{C}')| = |\tilde{C} \bigcup_{\tilde{H}^* \setminus \tilde{C}} \{S_k\}| = |\tilde{H}^*| = h$. So, $h \geq 2f + 1$ to satisfy the signing-condition-inequality.

Thus, $h = 2f + 1$ because $2f + 1 \geq h$ according to Lemma 3; and the signing-condition-inequality is satisfied: $|\bigcup_H C(S_i)| \geq |\bigcup_H \{S_i\}| = |H| = h = 2f + 1$.

These two solutions cover all possible scenarios and there is *no* other solution for the signing-condition-inequality (i.e., Condition-B of Theorem 42), and it can be verified that these solutions also satisfy Condition-A. Therefore, according to Theorem 42, they are the all solutions (or valid server protocols) of TSS-BQS systems, and no other valid protocol exists. ☐

These solutions correspond to two families of valid server protocols, respectively. The first family satisfies the signing-condition-inequality (i.e., ensures service integrity) through the examinations by correct server S^* ($|C(S^*)| \geq 2f + 1$), and the second does through the threshold to sign ($h = 2f + 1$). There is no valid protocol with combined mechanisms requiring fewer examinations than $2f + 1$ while having a threshold $h < 2f + 1$. Although we can design a protocol where $|C(\cdot)| \geq 2f + 1$ for correct servers and $h = 2f + 1$, service integrity is ensured *repeatedly* through each of these two mechanisms, instead of a *combined* one.

5   Efficient Server Protocols

In this section, two existing server protocols [10,26] are deduced by minimizing the computation costs of the solutions predicted in Theorem 43. Two types of computations are reflected in these solutions as follows:

Partial-signing using service key shares. The computation cost is measured by h: h partial signatures are needed to fully sign a response.

Examinations that the requested read/write operation has been performed on certain servers. The computation cost is measured by $|C(\cdot)|$: before partially signing a response, a (correct) server S_i verifies messages which are signed using server keys, to examine that servers in $C(S_i)$ have processed the read/write request. In fact, since $S_i \in C(S_i)$, it can verify only $|C(S_i)| - 1$ messages from other servers.

By minimizing the amount of computations (i.e., choosing the minimal h and $|C(\cdot)|$ allowable), we find two solutions of *efficient* (and valid) server protocols:

1. $h = f + 1$, and for any h-server set H, there exists a (correct) server $S^* \in H : \mathscr{C}(S^*) = \{\{S^*\} \cup C' : |C'| = 2f + 1\}$ (C' may contain S^* or not).
2. $h = 2f + 1$, and $\mathscr{C}(S_i) = \{\{S_i\}\}$ if S_i is correct.

Based on the efficient solutions, we design two server protocols as below. They are essentially the same as SP-I [26] and SP-II [10], which may have additional design details for specific applications (e.g., the means of generating timestamps).

5.1   Server Protocol I

The service private key is shared by $3f + 1$ servers, and the threshold to sign is $f + 1$. Servers use the following protocol, and S_d is a delegate.

A. On receiving a read/write request from clients, S_d forwards it to all servers.

B. On receiving a read/write request from S_d, S_i uses its server key to sign a reply and sends it to S_d. The reply is its replica for reading. For writing, S_i replies with an acknowledgement, and only updates its replica if the data item being written has a higher timestamp than its own.

C. S_d repeats Step-A periodically until it receives replies from $2f + 1$ servers.

D. S_d generates a partial-signing request and sends it to all servers. The partial-signing request includes: the read/write request, the response (to be signed), and those $2f + 1$ replies collected in Step-C. For reading, the response is the right replica (i.e., the unmodified one with the highest timestamp out of those $2f + 1$ replicas). For writing, the response is an acknowledgement.

E. On receiving a partial-signing request from S_d, S_i uses its service key share to generate a partial signature for the response and sends it to S_d, after examining that those included replies are generated by $2f + 1$ servers for the included read/write request. For reading, S_i also examines that the replica to be returned a) is the unmodified one with the highest timestamp out of those included $2f + 1$ replicas, and b) has a timestamp higher than or identical with its own. Otherwise, S_i replies to S_d with a rejection. For writing, S_i also updates its replica if the data item being written has a higher timestamp than its own.

F. S_d repeats Step-D periodically until it receives partial signatures from $f + 1$ servers, or re-starts from Step-A if it receives $f + 1$ rejections for reading (happening when a write operation overlaps the read operation). S_d combines these $f + 1$ partial signatures into a fully signed response and sends it to clients.

5.2   Server Protocol II

The threshold to sign of SP-II is equal to the size of a quorum (i.e., $h = 2f + 1$). Steps for reading and writing are described separately, and S_d is a delegate.

Read

A. On receiving a read request from clients, S_d generates a partial-signing request and sends it to all servers. The partial-signing request includes: the read request, and the response (to be signed) which includes the right replica to be returned. S_d sets the "right" replica to its own replica *tentatively*.

B. On receiving a partial-signing request from S_d, S_i uses its service key share to generate a partial signature for the response and sends it to S_d, after checking that the replica (to be returned) is unmodified and has a timestamp higher than or identical with its own. Otherwise, S_i replies to S_d with a rejection.

C. S_d repeats Step-A periodically until it receives partial signatures from $2f + 1$ servers, or breaks to Step-D if it receives $f + 1$ rejections. S_d combines these $2f + 1$ partial signatures into a fully signed response and sends it to clients.

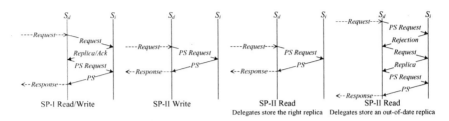

Fig. 2. Communication Costs of SP-I and SP-II

D. S_d forwards the read request (from clients) to all servers. Step-D is executed only if S_d receives $f + 1$ rejections, happening when it doesn't store the right replica and shall collects replicas from other servers to update its own.

E. On receiving a read request from S_d, S_i replies with its replica.

F. S_d repeats Step-D periodically until it receives replicas from $2f + 1$ servers. S_d obtains the right replica out of these $2f + 1$ replicas, updates its own, and re-starts from Step-A.

Write

A. On receiving a write request from clients, S_d generates a partial-signing request and sends it to all servers. The partial-signing request includes: the write request, and the response (to be signed) which is an acknowledgement.

B. On receiving a partial-signing request from S_d, S_i uses its service key share to generate a partial signature for the response and sends it to S_d. S_i also updates its replica if the data item being written has a higher timestamp.

C. S_d repeats Step-A periodically until it receives partial signatures from $2f + 1$ servers. S_d combines these $2f + 1$ partial signatures into a fully signed response and sends it to clients.

6   Performance

In this section, SP-I and SP-II are compared in terms of communication costs, computation costs and the read responses on concurrent read/write operations.

6.1   Communication

Assuming that there are no concurrent read/write operations, Figure 2 shows the communication costs of SP-I and SP-II. It can be seen that SP-I always needs two rounds of communications among servers, while SP-II-write needs only one round, because SP-II doesn't need to collect process results from some quorum as SP-II does before delegates request other servers to partially sign responses.

The communication cost of SP-II-read varies whether delegates store the right replica or not. If S_d stores the right replica, one round is enough. Otherwise, three rounds are needed: after receiving $f + 1$ rejections, S_d collects replicas to update its own, and requests other servers to partially sign the response again.

6.2 Computation

The major computation costs of TSS-BQS systems are public key cryptographic computations [15,26]: signing using server keys and partial-signing using service key shares. Firstly, the computation costs of server key depend on the communications among servers, because they are used to sign messages among servers.

Secondly, while SP-II always needs partial signatures by more f servers than SP-I, the cost of each partial-signing varies with different TSS. The following analysis is specific to the scheme used in [15,26,27]: each partial-signing includes $L_{n,h} = l(n - h + 1)/n$ modular exponentiations of long integer (e.g., 1024 bits), where $l = \binom{n}{h-1}$. It can be verified that $L_{3f+1,f+1} = L_{3f+1,2f+1}$, i.e., each partial-signing of SP-I and SP-II costs approximately equal resources.

6.3 Concurrent Read/Write Operations

Since each read/write operation must be performed on $2f + 1$ servers and may last a long time, concurrent operations can happen usually in TSS-BQS systems. We analyze the responses of the read operations overlapped by a concurrent write operation, and firstly define the windows of operations:

Read. A read operation returning $[x, v_r, t_r]$ from some quorum starts (denoted T_{rs}) when the first server in this quorum receives the read request and replies with its replica, and ends (denoted T_{re}) when the delegate determines to return $[x, v_r, t_r]$, which is eventually signed and sent to clients. Note that the delegate may determine and be rejected for several times before the operation ends.

Write. An operation writing $[x, v_w, t_w]$ on some quorum starts (denoted T_{ws}) when the first *correct* server in this quorum receives the write request and updates its replica, and ends (denoted T_{we}) when the last *correct* one in this quorum does. Variable x really starts to change only when a correct server receives the write request, because even if faulty servers receive the request before T_{ws}, they can drop it maliciously.

Assume that $[x, v_0, t_0]$ is the right replica before the concurrent operation writing $[x, v_w, t_w]$ and $t_w > t_0$. All situations of concurrent operations are analyzed as below.

1. $T_{ws} < T_{rs} < T_{we} < T_{re}$ or $T_{rs} < T_{ws} < T_{we} < T_{re}$

SP-I may return $[x, v_w, t_w]$ or $[x, v_0, t_0]$, while SP-II always returns $[x, v_w, t_w]$ at the cost of (possible) more rounds of communications among servers. Following SP-I, the $2f+1$ replicas sent along with the partial-signing request as evidences, may be collected before T_{we} and contain $[x, v_0, t_0]$ only (e.g., these replicas are collected when only one correct server has updated its replica). And the $f + 1$ servers signing the read response, may contain only another correct server which doesn't receive the concurrent write request or update its replica.

Following SP-II, the $2f+1$ servers signing the read response, must contain one correct server which has received $[x, v_w, t_w]$ when T_{we}, because BQS guarantee that the intersection of any two quorums contains at least one correct server. This correct server partially signs the response only if the replica to be returned has a timestamp higher than or identical with its own (i.e., $t_r \geq t_w$); otherwise, it rejects to sign it, leading to two more rounds of communications.

2. $T_{ws} < T_{rs} < T_{re} < T_{we}$ or $T_{rs} < T_{ws} < T_{re} < T_{we}$

Both SP-I and SP-II may return $[x, v_w, t_w]$ or $[x, v_0, t_0]$. Although at least one correct server has received $[x, v_w, t_w]$ after T_{ws}, it may *not* be involved in the concurrent read operation at all. It is possible that all servers involved in the read operation, store $[x, v_0, t_0]$ only; and then the read response returns $[x, v_0, t_0]$.

7   Related Work

BQS of self-verifying data over asynchronous, authenticated and reliable channels are proposed in [13]; variations of other data or over different channels can be found in [4,13,17]. Dynamic BQS [1,11,16] can reconfigure the number of servers and faulty ones (i.e., dynamic n and f).

Several distributed storage systems [7,9,22,24,25] apply threshold cryptography (e.g., secret sharing, erasure code, etc.) to protect data integrity and confidentiality. In [18] and [23], secret sharing is integrated with quorum systems and BQS, respectively, to provide fault-tolerant storage services.

TSS are utilized to sign messages in state machine replication [2,3,20,21] and distributed storage systems [9,22]: signatures by TSS indicate that enough servers agree with the content of signed messages or have performed the requested operations, masking the impact of faulty servers. COCA [26] is the first work to integrate BQS with TSS, and its protocol is adopted in CODEX [15] to store secret data. [10] proposed another server protocol of TSS-BQS systems.

8   Conclusions

To provide *self-contained* BFT storage services of self-verifying data, traditional BQS are no longer sufficient. Achieving this goal demands the integration of BQS and TSS, and only two *valid* TSS-BQS systems have been proposed in the literature. Based on these two systems, we can find similar server protocols, leading to two families of TSS-BQS systems. We develop a *validity theory* on server protocols of TSS-BQS systems and formally prove that it is *impossible* to find any third family of valid TSS-BQS systems. It is also shown that the *only two* families of valid server protocols "predicted" (or deduced) by the proposed theory precisely match the existing protocols.

References

1. Alvisi, L., Dahlin, M., et al.: Dynamic Byzantine quorum systems. In: Int'l. Conf. Dependable Systems and Networks, pp. 283–292 (2000)
2. Amir, Y., Coan, B., et al.: Customizable fault tolerance for wide-area replication. In: IEEE Symp. Reliable Distributed Systems, pp. 65–82 (2007)
3. Amir, Y., Danilov, C., et al.: Scaling Byzantine fault-tolerant replication to wide area networks. In: Int'l. Conf. Dependable Systems and Networks, pp. 105–114 (2006)
4. Bazzi, R.: Synchronous Byzantine quorum systems. Distributed Computing 13(1), 45–52 (2000)

5. Castro, M., Liskov, B.: Practical Byzantine fault tolerance and proactive recovery. ACM Trans. Computer Systems 20(4), 398–461 (2002)
6. Desmedt, Y.: Society and group oriented cryptography: A new concept. In: Pomerance, C. (ed.) CRYPTO 1987. LNCS, vol. 293, pp. 120–127. Springer, Heidelberg (1988)
7. Goodson, G., Wylie, J., et al.: Efficient Byzantine-tolerant erasure-coded storage. In: Int'l. Conf. Dependable Systems and Networks, pp. 135–144 (2004)
8. Herzberg, A., Jakobsson, M., et al.: Proactive public key and signature systems. In: ACM Conf. Computer Communications Security, pp. 100–110 (1997)
9. Iyengar, A., Cahn, R., et al.: Design and implementation of a secure distributed data repository. In: IFIP Int'l. Information Security Conference, pp. 123–135 (1998)
10. Jing, J., Wang, J., et al.: Research on server protocols of Byzantine quorum systems implemented utilizing threshold signature schemes (accepted to appear). Chinese Journal of Software
11. Kong, L., Subbiah, A., et al.: A reconfigurable Byzantine quorum approach for the Agile Store. In: IEEE Symp. Reliable Distributed Systems, pp. 219–228 (2003)
12. Lamport, L., Shostak, R., et al.: The Byzantine generals problem. ACM Trans. Programming Languages and Systems 4(3), 382–401 (1982)
13. Malkhi, D., Reiter, M.: Byzantine quorum systems. Distributed Computing 11(4), 203–213 (1998)
14. Malkhi, D., Reiter, M.: Secure and scalable replication in Phalanx. In: IEEE Symp. Reliable Distributed Systems, pp. 51–60 (1998)
15. Marsh, M., Schneider, F.: CODEX: A robust and secure secret distribution system. IEEE Trans. Dependable and Secure Computing 1(1), 34–47 (2004)
16. Martin, J.-P., Alvisi, L.: A framework for dynamic Byzantine storage. In: Int'l. Conf. Dependable Systems and Networks, pp. 325–334 (2004)
17. Martin, J.-P., Alvisi, L., et al.: Small Byzantine quorum systems. In: Int'l. Conf. Dependable Systems and Networks, pp. 374–383 (2002)
18. Naor, M., Wool, A.: Access control and signatures via quorum secret sharing. IEEE Trans. Parallel and Distributed Systems 9(9), 909–922 (1998)
19. Ostrovsky, R., Yung, M.: How to withstand mobile virus attacks. In: ACM Symp. Principles of Distributed Computing, pp. 51–59 (1991)
20. Reiter, M., Birman, K.: How to securely replicate services. ACM Trans. Programming Languages and Systems 16(3), 986–1009 (1994)
21. Reiter, M., Franklin, M., et al.: The Ω key management service. In: ACM Conf. Computer and Communications Security, pp. 38–47 (1996)
22. Rhea, S., Eaton, P., et al.: Pond: the OceanStore prototype. In: USENIX Conf. File and Storage Technologies, pp. 1–14 (2003)
23. Subbiah, A., Ahamad, M., et al.: Using Byzantine quorum systems to manage confidential data. Technical Report GIT-CERCS-04-13, Georgia Institute of Technology (2004)
24. Subbiah, A., Blough, D.: An approach for fault tolerant and secure data storage in collaborative work environments. In: ACM Workshop on Storage Security and Survivability, pp. 84–93 (2005)
25. Wylie, J., Bigrigg, M., et al.: Survivable information storage systems. IEEE Computer 33(8), 61–68 (2000)
26. Zhou, L., Schneider, F., et al.: COCA: A secure on-line certification authority. ACM Trans. Computer Systems 20(4), 329–368 (2002)
27. Zhou, L., Schneider, F., et al.: APSS: Proactive secret sharing in asynchronous systems. ACM Trans. Information and System Security 8(3), 259–286 (2005)

Context-Aware Usage Control for Android

Guangdong Bai, Liang Gu, Tao Feng, Yao Guo*, and Xiangqun Chen

Key Laboratory of High Confidence Software Technologies (Ministry of Education),
Institute of Software, School of EECS, Peking University, Beijing, China
{baigd08,guliang05,fengtao09,yaoguo,cherry}@sei.pku.edu.cn

Abstract. The security of smart phones is increasingly important due to their rapid popularity. Mobile computing on smart phones introduces many new characteristics such as personalization, mobility, pay-for-service and limited resources. These features require additional privacy protection and resource usage constraints in addition to the security and privacy concerns on traditional computers. As one of the leading open source mobile platform, Android is also facing security challenges from the mobile environment. Although many security measures have been applied in Android, the existing security mechanism is coarse-grained and does not take into account the context information, which is of particular interest because of the mobility and personality of a smart phone device.

To address these challenges, we propose a context-aware usage control model ConUCON, which leverages the context information to enhance data protection and resource usage control on a mobile platform. We also extend the existing security mechanism to implement a policy enforcement framework on the Android platform based on ConUCON. With ConUCON, users are able to employ fine-grained and flexible security mechanism to enhance privacy protection and resource usage control. The extended security framework on Android enables mobile applications to run with better user experiences. The implementation of ConUCON and its evaluation study demonstrate that it can be practically adapted for other types of mobile platform.

Keywords: security, access control, mobile platform, context-aware, Android.

1 Introduction

During the past few years, smart phones, combining the functionalities of traditional mobile phone and increasing computing and storage capabilities, have become prevalent. They are serving more and more individuals and organizations as extensions of desktop computers. As a result, many critical applications are moved to smart phones. Unfortunately, security risks and attacks on traditional PCs have since shifted to smart phones as well [19,12,15].

Compared to the security of traditional computing platforms, the security of mobile devices faces more challenges [21] because they possess many unique features, including *Personalization, Mobility, Pay-for-service and Limited resources*. These distinct features require special privacy protection and resource usage constraints compared to

---

* Corresponding author.

S. Jajodia and J. Zhou (Eds.): SecureComm 2010, LNICST 50, pp. 326–343, 2010.

PCs. *Personalization* increases the requirement for data confidentiality and privacy. *Mobility* increases the risk of device loss and theft, which leads to privacy exposure, as well the risk of classified information theft in a confidential environment, a business meeting and a military conference, for instance. *Pay-for-service* and *limited resources* make the phone prone to overcharge attacks and DoS attacks.

Android [18], a Google-led open source mobile platform, is one of the most popular mobile platforms. A series of security mechanisms such as UIDs, permission label, application signing and sandbox have been adopted into Android to enhance its security [26]. However, the permission model of Android is coarse-grained and incomplete [22]. For example, an Android application requests a list of permissions at installation; the user can only choose to either allow all these permissions or none. In addition, the user cannot revoke or change the permissions of an application once he grants the permissions, unless the application is re-installed. It cannot provide data protection and resource usage constraints in a fine-grained manner. Furthermore, there is no mechanism for the user to enforce context-aware constraints on data and resources on Android.

Some approaches have attempted to enhance the security of Android (or similar smart phone platforms) through malware detection [8,9,29], application certification [14] and access control [22]. However, to the best of our knowledge, no existing studies have combined context information to provide fine-grained security/privacy measures on smart phone platforms, especially on Android.

To address these challenges, we propose a context-aware usage control mechanism for the Android platform. We first present a Context-aware Usage CONtrol model (ConUCON) based on the previously proposed UCON model [27]. By taking into account the context information, such as the spatial and temporal data during runtime enforcement, ConUCON is able to support flexible data protection and resource usage constraints. Based on ConUCON, we also extend the existing security mechanism to implement a new policy enforcement framework on the Android platform. The new framework offers several new security features, such as allowing the user to grant permissions in a fine-grained manner, and supporting revocations and modifications on an application's permission at runtime.

We make the following main contributions in this paper.

- We propose a context-aware usage control model ConUCON, extending the UCON model to support context-ware protection for mobile platforms. It enables smart phone users to employ fine-grained and flexible security mechanisms to enhance the privacy protection and resource usage control.
- ConUCON provides continuous usage control because its usage decisions are not only performed prior to the access, but also during the access.
- We extend the policy specification interface of Android according to the proposed ConUCON model to provide an interface for the user to express his policy on data and resources in a context-aware and fine-grained manner. As a result it could provide better user experiences with this extended framework.
- Finally, as our extended mechanism is implemented by introducing minimal changes to the existing one, it is transparent and could easily support existing applications.

The rest of this paper is organized as follows: Section 2 describes the background, including the motivating scenarios, UCON model and Android security. Section 3 presents the ConUCON model formally. Section 4 shows the framework based on the ConUCON model. Section 5 presents the implementation and evaluation. Section 6 introduces the related works, and finally, Section 7 concludes this paper.

2   Background

2.1   Motivating Scenarios

Confidentiality and Privacy Protection. A smart phone user may store private data such as photos and calendar on his/her phone. Assume that a user Alice loses her smart phone and it is picked up (or maybe stolen) by Bob. Then Bob takes it home (We can safely assume that it is a strange location) and tries to browse the data for malicious purpose (or just out of curiosity). If this unfamiliar context is detected, or Alice has ever enforced context constraints on her privacy data, an authentication will be required, which would prevent the exposure of Alice's privacy.

Resources Usage Constraints. Some services such as GPRS and voice calls may charge extra fees according to the usage time and user's location, that is, incurring significantly more expenses at a certain time in the day, or if the user roams out of a certain area. Thus, the user may tend to restrict applications' usage on these resources during specific periods or at locations with higher charge rate.

In a government or military meeting, in which confidentiality is specially concerned, the participants are required to disable certain functions of the phone such as audio capture. If the participants' phones can detect the meeting-related contexts (time and location), it would be possible to disable corresponding functions automatically.

2.2   UCON Model

UCON [24,27,23,34] is a generalized security model proposed by Sandhu *et. al* to cover a variety of security aspects including obligations, conditions, continuity and mutability, etc. The UCON model consists of eight components: subjects, subject attributes, objects, object attributes, rights, authorizations, obligations, and conditions. The first five hold similar meanings with the concepts in traditional access control models, while authorizations, obligations and conditions impact on the usage decisions. Authorizations permit or deny an access from a subject to an object with a particular right based on attributes of subject and object. Obligations require the subject to perform specific actions before (pre) or during (ongoing) an access. Conditions are environmental factors.

2.3   Android Security

Android is a software stack for mobile devices, and it contains an operating system, middleware and key applications. The applications in Android consist of four different types of components: activities, services, broadcast receivers and content providers. Most security mechanisms on Android are enforced at the application level. Each application is assigned with a unique UID at install-time. At runtime, by adopting a sandbox mechanism to run applications as separate processes, Android protects them from modifying or controlling each other.

To use some protected resources, such as the dialer or GPRS, an application must include a file named `AndroidManifest.xml`, which contains several `<uses-permission>` tags to declare the required permissions. During installation, the package installer will list these permissions to the user, who can then choose to grant all permissions to the application, or deny all permission requests and withdraw the installation. Once all permissions are granted, the application will be allowed to use the resources without reminding the user all the time. The user cannot revoke the permissions unless the application is reinstalled.

3   ConUCON: A Context-Aware Usage Control Model

This section presents the proposed context-aware usage control model ConUCON, which consists of three major parts: model components, user policy specifications and runtime usage decisions. ConUCON can leverage the context information to enhance the security of mobile computing platforms, and it serves as the foundation of our extended security framework for Android platform.

3.1   Model Components

ConUCON contains the following components: subjects, objects, states (which include subject attributes and object attributes), rights, permissions, obligations, and contexts. We will introduce the definitions and descriptions of these components in this section.

The concepts of subjects and objects remain similar with those in traditional access control models as well as the UCON model.

Definition 1. *(**Subjects** and **Objects**) A **subject** is an entity that holds and exercises certain rights on objects. An **object** is an entity that subjects can access or use. **Subject set** and **object set** are denoted by S and O, respectively.*

Example 1. For example, subjects can be applications and components in Android, while objects can be files, resources, and services.

Definition 2. *(**Attributes**) An **attributes** is a property used in usage decisions,* such as UID, software producer, permission label and path of an object. All attributes are contained in the **attribute set** (AT).

Each subject or object is associated with a corresponding attribute set, which can be queried with the function $\tau : S \cup O \rightarrow \mathscr{P}(AT)$. For a subject or object $so \in S \cup O$ that holds an attribute $at \in \tau(so)$, the value of the attribute $so.at$ can be retrieved with the function $v : (S \cup O) \times \tau(S \cup O) \rightarrow ran(\tau(S \cup O))$, where $ran(a)$ is the value of attribute a.

Example 2. A Telecom Provider may provide a specific number of free SMSes for users every day, and will charge fees for any extra message. As a result, the user may wish to prohibit the corresponding applications to send messages once the quota for a day is exhausted. Thus, the usage history of the SMS service should be recorded as an attribute of the object and be involved in the usage decision process.

Definition 3. *(States) A **state** is defined as a set, whose elements are triples*

$$(so, at, val), where\ so \in S \cup O,\ at \in \tau(so)\ and\ val = v((so, at)).$$

A state element consists of an attribute set, the owner of the attribute set, and the values of these attributes in the set. A state is a subset of the **State Set**(ST), which contains all the attributes and their values.

An update action is defined as a function $\mu : \mathscr{P}(ST) \rightarrow \mathscr{P}(ST)$.

Definition 4. *(Rights) A **right** is an operation that a subject can perform on an object. All Rights comprise the **Right set**(R).*

Rights can be divided into several functional categories. For files and other data, the rights include read, write, delete, etc.; while for resources and services, the rights include use, disable, etc. The Right set is defined by users.

Definition 5. *(Permission Labels) A **permission label** is a credential to allow a subject to perform a specific right on corresponding objects, which are assigned to subjects and objects. All permission labels comprise the **Permission label set**(P).*

For a subject, its permission labels determine which objects it can access, while the labels for an object determine which subjects can access it. Each subject owns a permission label set, which can be retrieved using the function $\varphi_s : S \rightarrow \mathscr{P}(P)$.

Each resource object and service object can be attached with a permission label [26] to declare the permission required to use it. The function $\varphi_o : O \rightarrow P$ is defined to query the label.

It is a bit more complex for data objects. Each of the objects has two labels, one for confidentiality and the other for integrity. The confidentiality label is an element of the **confidentiality label set**(CL), while all integrity labels comprise the **integrity label set**(IL). A subject is also associated with these two labels to indicate its confidentiality level and integrity level, respectively. The orders of the confidentiality level and integrity level are denoted by $\{\leqslant_c, \geqslant_c\}$ and $\{\leqslant_i, \geqslant_i\}$, respectively.

The functions $\varphi_c : S \cup O \rightarrow CL$ and $\varphi_i : S \cup O$ are defined to retrieve the confidentiality and integrity labels of a data object or a subject, respectively.

Definition 6. *(Obligations) An **obligation** is a mandatory action that must be performed before or during an access. It is an element of the **obligation set**(OB).*

Example 3. To avoid privacy exposure caused by trojans such as Pbstealer.A [16], a user may require all applications that access the contacts to disable Bluetooth before and during the access. Thus the obligation for these applications is to disable Bluetooth by themselves or to agree the usage control decision process to disable it.

Definition 7. *(Contexts) A **context** is defined as a property of environment and system. The type of a property is the **context type**, which is an element of **context type set**(CT).*

The examples of context types are CPU rate, battery, device location and time. For ConUCON, We focus on the contexts related with the system and environment. In addition, there is a subtle difference between context and attribute: a context is a property of systems or physical environment, whereas an attribute is a property directly related to a subject or an object.

Continuous evaluation is critical on mobile platforms because of their features mentioned before. Thus, the evaluation of context constraint in ConUCON is performed before (pre) and during (ongoing) an access. For example,

Example 4. A user has required the permission to read a confidential article which is restricted to be read only in a specific area. While browsing the article, the user roams out of the restricted area unconsciously. The smart phone should trigger a warning as soon as it detects this situation.

3.2 Environment Contexts

For a smart phone platform, environment contexts such as spatial and temporal contexts are especially important.

Spatial Context. *A* **spatial context** is defined as a spatial property. **Spatial context** $\in$ CT. We adopt the geometric model of GEO-RBAC [13] to model the positions.

Definition 8. *(**Features and Feature Types**) A **feature** is an object which indicates an entity that occupies a space in real world, which is identified by feature name. The features are included in **feature set**(F). Each feature has a **feature type** contained in **feature type set**(FT).*

*A feature can be mapped to a **geometry** on Earth. A **geometry** is an object in Euclidean space with a coordinate, which is an element in the **geometry set**(GEO).*

The functions $\gamma : F \rightarrow FT$ and $\xi : F \rightarrow GEO$ are used to get the feature type and the geometry of a feature.

Definition 9. *(**Feature Order and Feature Type Order**)*

- ***feature type order** $(\leqslant_{ft})$:* $ft_1 \leqslant_{ft} ft_2$ *iff* $\forall f_1 \in F \wedge \gamma(f_1) = ft_1, \exists f_2 \in F \wedge \gamma(f_2) = ft_2, \xi(f_1) \subseteq \xi(f_2)$
- ***feature order** $(\leqslant_f)$:* $f_1 \leqslant_f f_2$ *iff* $\gamma(f_1) \leqslant_{ft} \gamma(f_2) \wedge \xi(f_1) \subseteq \xi(f_2)$

Example 5. Office 2E315, Pentagon, Arlington, Virginia are examples of features, whose feature types are Room, Building, County, State, respectively. The Room and Building satisfy the $\leqslant_{ft}$ order, while Arlington and Virginia satisfy the $\leqslant_f$ order.

Definition 10. *(**Real Position and Logical Position**) A **real position** is a position on the Earth and can be obtained using a device such as a GPS based equipment, while a **logical position** is a semantic representation of a position. **Real position set** and **logical position set** are denoted as RP and LP, respectively.*

Obviously, a real position corresponds to a geometry and a logical position corresponds to a feature. A real position may correspond to one or more logical positions under different feature types. For example, a region may correspond to a room or part of a city, when assigning it with these two feature types.

The function $\rho_{ft} : RP \rightarrow LP$ is used to map a real position to the corresponding logical position under feature type ft.

Thus, we can define the inclusion relation between a real position and a logical position $\sqsubseteq_p$: $rp \sqsubseteq_p lp$, *where* $rp \in RP \wedge lp \in LP$ *iff* $\rho_{\gamma(lp)}(rp) \leqslant_f lp$.

Temporal Context. *A* **temporal context** is defined as a temporal property. **Temporal context** ∈ CT.

Definition 11. *(Time Instants) A time instant is a time point that has the form*
$$TI := mm/dd/yy\_hh : ii : ss \quad where$$
$mm \in \{1, 2, ..., 12\} \wedge dd \in \{1, 2, ..., 31\} \wedge yy \in \mathbb{N} \wedge hh \in \{0, 1, ..., 23\} \wedge ii,\ ss \in \{0, 1, ..., 59\}$.

The definition of the periodic expression in ConUCON is based on past studies in [6,31,5]:

Definition 12. *(Periodic Expression) The* **periodic expression** *is defined as*
$$PE := Y|W$$
$$Y := R.years|R.years \rhd S.years|R.years + M$$
$$W := weeks|weeks + D$$
$$M := R.months|R.months \rhd S.months|R.months + D$$
$$D := R.days|R.days \rhd S.days|R.days + H$$
$$H := R.hours|R.hours \rhd S.hours|R.hours + M$$
$$M := R.minutes|R.minutes \rhd S.minutes$$
$$where\ R \in 2^{\mathbb{N}} \cup \{all\},\ S \in \mathbb{N}.$$

Example 6. We can use the periodic expression $years + 7.months \rhd 6.months$ to indicate the second half of every year and the expression $weeks + \{1, 2, ...5\} Days + 9.hours \rhd 8.hours$ to indicate working hours of every week.

As a result, we can define the inclusion relation between a time instance and a periodic time [6] $\sqsubseteq_t$: $ti \sqsubseteq_t \langle [begin,\ end],\ P \rangle$ if and only if there exists a time interval $it \in \Pi(P)$ such that $ti \in it$ and $begin \leqslant ti \leqslant end$, where $\langle [begin,\ end],\ P \rangle$ is a periodic time, $begin$ and end are two time instants, $\Pi(P)$ is the set of time intervals corresponding to the periodic expression P.

Example 7. $PT = \langle$ [01/01/2010_00:00:00, 12/31/2012_23:59:59], $weeks + \{1, 2, ...5\}$. $Days + 9.hours \rhd 8.hours \rangle$ indicates the working hours during the year 2010 and year 2012. A time instant 4/19/2010_14:30:00 $\sqsubseteq_t$ PT.

3.3   User Policy Specification

The policy specification allows a user to specify his security policies on usage, i.e. data and resources. The security policies describe:

- Which permission label should be assigned to a resource object? Which confidentiality label and integrity label should be assigned to a data object? Which permission label set should be assigned to a subject?
- If a subject requests to perform a specific action (right) on an object, what authorizations, obligations and contexts should be satisfied before (pre) and during (ongoing) the access?

Definition 13. (*Label Policies*) *Define function* $\varpi_{o_1} : O \to P$ *to impose a permission label to a resource object, function* $\varpi_{o_2} : O \to CL \times IL$ *to impose confidentiality label and integrity label to a data object, and function* $\varpi_s : S \to \mathscr{P}(P)$ *to grant a permission label set to a subject.*

Definition 14. (*Usage Control Policy*) *The* **usage control policy** *is used to specify authorizations, obligations and contexts that should be satisfied before (pre) and during (ongoing) a subject performing a specific action (right) on an object. All the usage control policies are included in the* **usage control policy set** *(UP).*
$$UP \subseteq S \times O \times R \times PreOb \times OnOb \times StateConstraint \times PreContext \times$$
$$OnContext \times Update, \ where$$

- $PreOb, OnOb \in \mathscr{P}(OB)$
- $StateConstraint := (StatePredicate) \mid \neg StateConstraint \mid StateConstraint \vee State$-$Constraint \mid StateConstraint \wedge StateConstraint.$ (*StatePredicate is a relational expression, with form of* $f(\mathscr{P}(S \cup O \times AT))relator\langle value\rangle$, *where* f *is an operation expression using the attributes as operands, while relator is a logical operator.*)
- $PreContext, OnContext \subseteq ContextConstraint,$ **where** $ContextConstraint :=$ $(ContextPredicate) \mid \neg ContextConstraint \mid ContextConstraint \vee ContextConstraint$ $\mid ContextConstraint \wedge ContextConstraint$
  $ContextPredicate := \langle CT\rangle relator\langle value\rangle \mid PeriodicTime \mid LP$

Example 8. Let's consider the *Resources Usage Constraint* scenario in Section 2.1 to illustrate the User Policy Specification. At first, a smart phone user Alice may restrict the usage of the camera in her phone as following:

- To prevent conflict, all applications that apply for using the camera must close or remind the user to close the other application that are using the camera.
- To keep privacy, all applications that are recording video must pause recording when an incoming call comes.
- To preserve battery for more critical functions, the camera should be disabled when the remaining battery power is blow 30%.
- If one application was denied a short time ago(one minute, for instance), its request should be denied automatically.

Now suppose there is a confidential meeting in the company where Alice works during 10:00 to 12:00 every Wednesday and Thursday in 2010, and video recording is not allowed at the meeting. We can specify the policy as in Table 1.

3.4 Runtime Usage Decisions

We employ the Bell-LaPadula model [4] for confidentiality and the Biba model [7] for integrity to express the authorizations in ConUCON. The other appropriate security models can be used to express specific application constraints in ConUCON.

Definition 15. (*Authorizations*) **Authorizations** *are used to check whether a subject is allowed to perform an action on an object, according to specified security model,*

Table 1. An example of usage control policy

Components	Constraints
Subject	All
Object	Camera
Right	Use
Pre-obligation	ObligationID$_1$ (predefined as closing or reminding user to close the other application that is using the camera)
On-obligation	ObligationID$_2$ (predefined as pausing recording if an incoming call comes)
State	$currentTime - lastForbiddenTime \geqslant 1minute$
Pre-context	$(batterypower \geqslant 30\%)$ $\wedge((\neg\langle[01/01/2010\_00:00:00, 12/31/2010\_23:59:59], weeks+$ $\{3,4\}.day + 10hours \rhd 2hours)) \vee (\neg meetingroom))$
Ongoing-context	$(batterypower \geqslant 30\%)$ $\wedge((\neg\langle[01/01/2010\_00:00:00, 12/31/2010\_23:59:59], weeks+$ $\{3,4\}.day + 10hours \rhd 2hours)) \vee (\neg meetingroom))$
Update	$if(forbidden)lastForbiddenTime = currentTime$

such as integrity models and confidentiality models. The function $\Omega : S \times O \times R \to \{true, false\}$, which is used to get the authorization result, is defined as:

$$\Omega(s, o, r) \Rightarrow \begin{cases} \varphi_o(o) \in \varphi_s(s), \textit{if o is a resource object} \\ \varphi_c(s) \geqslant_c \varphi_c(o) \wedge \varphi_i(s) \leqslant_c \varphi_i(o), \textit{if o is a data object, and r = read} \\ \varphi_c(s) \leqslant_c \varphi_c(o) \wedge \varphi_i(s) \geqslant_c \varphi_i(o), \textit{if o is a data object, and r = write} \end{cases}$$

Definition 16. *(Usage Decision) The usage decision determines whether an access should be permitted or an ongoing access should be revoked based on authorizations, obligations, contexts, and states. The usage decision is performed as below:*

- $allow(s, o, r) \Rightarrow \Omega(s, o, r) \wedge fulfill(preOb) \wedge fulfill(preContext) \wedge fulfill(stateConstraint)$
- $revoke(s, o, r) \Leftarrow \neg fulfill(onOb) \vee \neg fulfill(onContext)$
- $update(state)$

4   A Usage Control Framework for Android

Based on the above ConUCON model, we developed a continuous context-aware usage control framework for Android.

4.1   Framework Overview

Figure 1 describes the architecture of the framework. The framework consists of a Policy Enforcement Point (PEP), a Policy Decision Point (PDP), a Policy Information Point (PIP) and a Policy Administration Point (PAP). These components communicate with each other with the messaging mechanism listed in Table 2.

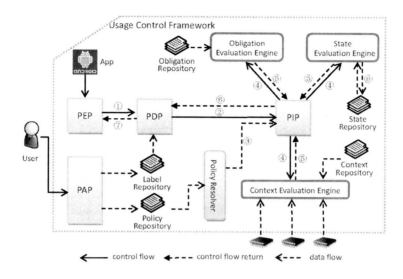

Fig. 1. ConUCON Framework

Table 2. Message types transmitted among components

Message	Source	Destination	Meaning
$request(s,o,r)$	PEP	PDP	The subject s is requesting to perform the right r on the object o.
$permit(s,o,r)$	PDP	PEP	The $request(s,o,r)$ is permitted.
$deny(s,o,r)$	PDP	PEP	The $request(s,o,r)$ is denied.
$terminate(s,o,r)$	PEP	PDP	The subject s terminates access to the subject o.
$revoke(s,o,r)$	PDP	PEP	Revoke the $request(s,o,r)$.
$evaluate(s,o,r)$	PDP	PIP	Perform obligation, state and context evaluation.
$fulfill(s,o,r)$	PIP	PDP	The obligation, state and context policies are enforced.
$violate(s,o,r)$	PIP	PDP	Not all obligations, state and context policies are enforced.
$withdraw(s,o,r)$	PDP	PIP	Withdraw all continuous evaluations.

The circled numbers in the figure indicate the processing flow during one usage decision process. When an application tries to access an object, the PEP perceives the request and invokes the PDP using $request(s,o,r)$. Then the PDP performs authorization and activates the PIP with $evaluate(s,o,r)$. The PIP then invokes the Policy Resolver to resolve predefined policies related to s and o, and then invokes the Evaluation Engines to check the pre-policies. After that, the PIP sends a result(i.e. a $fulfill(s,o,r)$ or $violate(s,o,r)$ message) to the PDP, which synthesizes the received result and the authorization result to decide whether the access should be permitted or denied, and notifies the PEP of the decision by a $permit(s,o,r)$ or a $deny(s,o,r)$ message. The State Evaluation Engine also updates the states accordingly.

Two cases are not illustrated in Figure 1 for the sake of simplicity. The first case is continuous evaluation. After permitting the access, the Evaluation Engines begin to evaluate ongoing policies continuously. Once a violation is detected, the Engines notify the PIP, which then sends a $violate(s, o, r)$ message to the PDP. And the PDP will send a $revoke(s, o, r)$ message to the PEP immediately to revoke the access at once. The other case occurs when an application terminates the access. The PEP notifies the PDP by a $terminate(s, o, r)$ message, which then sends a $withdraw(s, o, r)$ message to the PIP to withdraw the continuous evaluation on this session.

Notice that the PDP can send a $revoke(s, o, r)$ message to the PEP on its own initiative before the PEP sends a $terminate(s, o, r)$ message. Similarly, the PIP can send a $violate(s, o, r)$ message to the PDP once the Engines detect a violation, no matter whether the PDP sends an $evaluate(s, o, r)$ message or not. This is an important improvement upon existing access control research, whose usage decision only occurs before the access.

4.2 Framework Components

Policy Enforcement Point (PEP). The PEP takes charge of perceiving access request and termination, invoking the PDP to perform the usage decision and enforcing the usage control according to the PDP's response.

When the PEP captures a request, it invokes the PDP with a $request(s, o, r)$ message. The PEP allows the access only if the PDP responds a $permit(s, o, r)$ message. After permitting the access, the PEP shifts to a listening state. If any of the ongoing policies is violated, the PEP will be noticed by PDP with a $revoke(s, o, r)$ message to terminates the access. In addition, The PEP should perceive the termination of the access. Once a subject terminates the access, the PEP sends a $terminate(s, o, r)$ message to the PDP, and then the PDP stops monitoring policies.

To capture the access requests to all objects, the PEP should be integrated in the relatively low level, the application framework layer of Android platform, for instance. It should also implement specific messaging mechanism to communicate with the PDP.

Policy Decision Point (PDP). The PDP is the component that performs usage decisions. The PDP is responsible for activating the Policy Resolver and the PIP, authorizing (i.e. checking the permission labels), and notifying the PEP of the usage decision result after merging the authorization result and the responding result of the PIP. The PDP is invoked by the PEP when access actions including request and termination occur.

The PDP is invoked by the PEP using a $request(s, o, r)$ message. After being invoked, the PDP retrieves the permission labels of s and o from label repository and performs authorization based on Definition 15. If the result is true, the PDP then invokes the PIP to gather information related with usage decision (i.e. pre-policy evaluation result). If any policy is violated, the PDP responds a $deny(s, o, r)$ message to the PEP to deny the access. Otherwise, it returns the PEP a $permit(s, o, r)$ message, and listens on both the PEP and the PIP to process the $violate(s, o, r)$ from the PIP and $terminate(s, o, r)$ from the PEP.

Policy Information Point (PIP). The PIP is the component that provides the PDP with evaluation information on obligation, state and context both before (pre) and during (ongoing) the access, with the aid of the Obligation Evaluation Engine, the State Evaluation Engine and the Context Evaluation Engine.

The PIP is invoked by the PDP with an $evaluate(s, o, r)$ message. The PIP then calls Policy Resolver to resolve policies that contain pre-policies and ongoing-policies. After that, the PIP invokes Evaluation Engines to evaluate pre-policies at first. If any engines returns false, the PIP responds a $violate(s, o, r)$ to the PDP. Otherwise, the PIP returns $fulfill(s, o, r)$, then invokes Evaluation Engines to fork daemons to evaluate ongoing polices continuously. If any of ongoing policies is violated, the PIP notifies the PDP of a $violate(s, o, r)$ message. The PIP also listens on the PDP after the pre-policies evaluation. When it receives a $withdraw(s, o, r)$ message from the PDP, it withdraws the ongoing evaluation.

Evaluation Engines. The Evaluation Engines are invoked by the PIP to perform corresponding policy evaluation for obligation, state and context.

The Obligation Evaluation Engine monitors the execution of obligations. If the obligation is an action that can be carried out by the Engine directly, the Engine can require the subject to perform the obligation or carry out directly. Recall Example 8. The Engine can ask for the application to remind the user to close another application that is using the video recorder, or just close it directly. If the obligation can only be observed, the Engine does not return true until the obligation is observed. The obligations defined by Definition 6 are stored in the Obligation Repository, which can be accessed using their obligation IDs or paths specified by the user.

The State Evaluation Engine is invoked to evaluate the state constraints. It first resolves the attribute type from the state constraint expressions, and retrieves the corresponding attribute values from the State Repository. Then it evaluates whether the constraint is satisfied, and notifies the PIP of the evaluation result. Besides, the State Evaluation Engine will update the state values into the state repository if needed.

The Context Evaluation Engine evaluates the context policies and monitors the change of the context. Similarly with the State Evaluation Engine, it first resolves the context types from context constraint expressions. Then it interacts with underlying systems and sensors to retrieve context value such as the coordinate, CPU utilization and battery power.

Policy Administration Point (PAP). The PAP is a component that interacts with the user, which allows the user to administrate the usage policies for the data and resources in his smart phone. The user can impose or deprive the permission labels, confidentiality labels and integrity labels to a subject or an object as Definition 5.

The PAP then formats the user's policy specification and stores the policies into the Label Repository and Policy Repository, respectively. The policies are formatted in XML, which will be discussed in Section 4.3.

4.3   Policy Specification

Through the PAP, the user specifies his usage policies on his data and resources according to Definition 13 and 14. In order to facilitate policy storage and transmission among the components, the policies are represented in an XML format. The primary tags used are listed as follows.

- $\langle$Subject$\rangle$, $\langle$Object$\rangle$ and $\langle$Right$\rangle$ specify the subject, object and right associated with the policy.
- $\langle$Obligation$\rangle$ tag specifies an obligation. The *ObligationTime* specifies whether the obligation must be performed before (pre) or during (ongoing) the access, while the *ObligationID* specifies the ID of the obligation, the Obligation Evaluation Engine retrieves the action stored in Obligation Repository using this ID. The user can specify a new obligation by assigning the action path to the *ObligationID*, and use several $\langle$ Parameter $\rangle$ tags to specify the parameters to execute the action.
- $\langle$State$\rangle$ tag specifies the state constraint in the policy. The $\langle$Attribute$\rangle$ tag indicates the attribute in this state constraint, while the attribute *Owner* indicates owner of this attribute and the *Type* is the attribute type. The $\langle$Expression$\rangle$ tag specifies the logic expression expected, which is defined in Definition 14.
- $\langle$Context$\rangle$ tag specifies the context constraint in the policy. The meaning of *ContextTime* is similar with *ObligationTime*. The context consists of several $\langle$ ContextComposition $\rangle$ tags, which are connected with "∧". Each $\langle$ ContextComposition $\rangle$ consists of several $\langle$ Factor $\rangle$ tags, connected with the *Operator*. The $\langle$Factor$\rangle$ is a context predicate defined in Definition 14, the *Type* specifies the context type defined in Definition 7.
- $\langle$Update$\rangle$ tag specifies an update policy. The *UpdateTime* declares the time to perform this update, which is in {Allow, Deny, Ongoing, Post}. The $\langle$Attribute$\rangle$ tag indicates the attribute to be modified. It is stored in State Repository and identified by *Name*, while the default value of the attribute is *Default*. An $\langle$Expression$\rangle$ tag specifies an assignment expression that is executed to update the state.

Figure 2 illustrates the XML representation of Example 8. The root node $\langle$Policies$\rangle$ contains all the policies. It includes several $\langle$Policy$\rangle$ tags, each indicates a user-specified policy defined in Definition 14.

```
<Policies>                                                      <Fator Type="Temporal">[01/01/2010_00:00:00,
  <Policy Effect="Permit">                                         12/31/2010_23:59:59], weeks ~ {3, 4}.day ~ 10 hours ->
    <Subject>All</Subject>                                         2hours</Fator>
    <Object>Camera</Object>                                    <Fator Type="Spatial">Meeting Room</Fator>
    <Right>Use</Right>                                       </ContextComposition>
    <Obligations>                                            <ContextComposition>
      <Obligation ObligationTime="Previous" ObligationID =     <Fator Type="BatteryPower">batteryPower >= 30%</Fator>
      "com:android:conUcon:obligationID1"></Obligation>     </ContextComposition>
      <Obligation ObligationTime="Ongoing" ObligationID=    </Context>
      "com:android:conUcon:obligationID2"></Obligation>     <Context ContextTime="Ongoing">...</Context>
    </Obligations>                                         </Contexts>
    <States>                                                <Updates>
      <State>                                                 <Update UpdateTime="Deny">
        <Attribute Owner="Camera"                               <Attribute Owner="Camera" Name = "lastForbiddenTime"
          Type = "lastForbiddenTime"></Attribute>               Default="01/01/1900_00:00:00"></Attribute>
        <Expression>System.currentTime-                        <Expression>Camera.lastForbiddenTime
          Camera.lastForbiddenTime>=1</Expression>             =System.currentTime</Expression>
      </State>                                                </Update>
    </States>                                               </Updates>
    <Contexts>                                              </Policy>
      <Context ContextTime="Previous">                    </Policies>
        <ContextComposition Operator="~">
```

Fig. 2. XML representation of Example 8 in Section 3.3

5   Implementation and Evaluation

We have implemented the above framework on Android, which will be described in this section. The framework monitors the accesses to the resources, data and files (i.e. the Objects in ConUCON) performed by the applications and application components (i.e. the Subjects in ConUCON). The identities of subjects and objects, i.e. a subject's UID and an Object's URI, are included in their attribute sets. The attribute sets also contain other information such as the software producer, usage times and attributes defined by the user, like `lastForbiddenTime` in Example 9. The attributes can be retrieved and maintained by the usage decision process. Some frequently used obligations are predefined and hard-coded in the Obligation Evaluation Engine, an interface is also provided to the user to assign a new obligation in the way described in section 4.3. Context types are confined to frequently used property in our implementation, such as temporal, spatial, battery, signal strength, acceleration, Bluetooth state, WiFi state, CPU utilization, and memory amount, which can be easily retrieved in Android.

The framework components are implemented and deployed according to their responsibility. The PEP, PDP and PIP are integrated in the application framework layer on Android. We implement the Policy Resolver as a parser to resolve the `xml` file which stores the policies. The Evaluation Engines are implemented as daemon threads to monitor and evaluate the ongoing policies continuously. The messages described in Section 4.1 can be implemented as procedure calls and inter component communications (ICC). The Repositories are stored in the `\system` directory on Android and are managed using the `Content Provider` component, which provides inherent isolation and protection.

5.1   Usage Decision

The applications in Android retrieve the resources and data using an ICC mechanism. Intent is used to encapsulate the information related to the ICC. An Intent object is passed to `Context.startActivity()`, `Context.startService()`, or other limited number of methods. These methods are implemented by the `ApplicationContext` class, which then transmits control to the `ActivityManagerService` class, where the Intent is resolved to determine the component which will handle it. Then the UID and permission required for accessing the component are used as parameters to call the `checkComponentPermission()`. The `checkPermission()` in `ActivityManagerService`, which is claimed (by the comments in source code) as the only public entry point [22], actually calls the `checkComponentPermission()` to perform permission check. Thus, we hook this function to insert our usage decision `conUconPDP()`.

After performing the existing permission check in the `checkComponentPermission()`, the `conUconPDP()` takes over the control. It first extracts and analyzes the object information from the Intent. If the object is a file object (including the pictures, contacts, and regular files), it retrieves the confidentiality and integrity labels of the subject and object from the label repository and checks the permission. After that, it invokes the `conUconPIP()` to perform evaluation on obligations, states and contexts.

The `conUconPIP()` calls the Policy Resolver to get the policies. For the obligations, the `conUconPIP()` executes the hard-coded instructions according to the `obligationID` or calls the routine specified by the user. For the states, it checks whether the constraint is fulfilled. It also creates representations for the new attributes and maintains them in the State Repository. For contexts, it invokes different managers to get the context information and evaluates it. If the evaluation is passed, it returns true. Meanwhile, if necessary, it may create daemon threads to evaluate the ongoing policies before returning. The daemons periodically check whether the constraints are violated. If a violation is identified, the daemons will terminate the session.

5.2 Policy Specification

An activity `com.android.conUcon.contextDefine` is implemented to provide a usable interface for the user to define his context information such as examples illustrated in Table 3. Besides, we modify the `PackageInstallerActivity` to allow a user to impose his policies on an application at install-time. The existing framework lists the permission that the application requires. We modify this interface to enable the user to set his obligation, state and context constraints on this permission. An activity `com.android.conUcon.policyAdministrator` is implemented to enable the user to specify his policies after installation. This activity lists all the installed applications, all the resources and all the data (i.e. contacts, pictures, files and so on). The user can associate the confidentiality and integrity labels to the subjects and data objects and specify the policy on these applications, resources and data. The specifications are resolved by the activity, which then generates the corresponding data and stores them in the Repositories. The activity even provides an interface for expert users to specify his policies by editing the policy file.

Table 3. A context information stored in the Context Repository

Context Type	Context Name	Context Value
temporal	weekday	$periodic\ expression =$ $''<[0,\infty], weeks + \{1,2,,5\}.days>''$
logic position	my university	$featuretype ='' school'', realposition =$ $''(o = (39.99°N, 116.30°E), r = 1530m)''$
battery power	low power	$''batterypower \leqslant 10\%''$

5.3 Performance Evaluation

Because the usage decision in ConUCON framework performs extra actions to evaluate the obligation, state and context policies, an overhead will be introduced. To evaluate this overhead, we carry out some experiments on the Android emulator to measure the execution time. The actions we choose are frequently used in the daily life.

To keep authenticity, we associate different policies on these actions. For example, The applications starting dialer must perform the obligation to check whether the audio capture is closed. The call duration should be maintained as a state, meanwhile, its constraint should consider restrictions on location and time. The constraints on all these actions come into three categories: Obligation, State and Context in Table 4. If an experiment with ConUCON considers specific types of constraints in its security policy, the corresponding column are marked as"√". The performance contrast between existing mechanism and our framework are illustrated in Table 4. The overhead caused by our usage decision is quite acceptable when we restrict context types within what can be retrieved locally, such as temporal, WiFi and battery power. Other information such as location that needs to be retrieved by querying network or satellite will consume a little longer time (the numbers within parentheses in Table 4). However, if the data and resources are extremely important, it is worthwhile sacrificing a little performance.

Table 4. Performance Comparisons

Actions	Existing mechanism (ms)	ConUCON framework			
		Obligation	State	Context	Time (ms)
sarting WiFi	102.5	√	-	√	117.3 (195.3)
sending SMS	69.8	-	√	√	76.0
starting dialer	49.7	√	√	√	80.6(150.8)
accessing a contact	95.3	-	√	√	116.5
accessing a picture	55.8	√	√	√	68.5(153.8)

6   Related Work

Some literatures have proposed solutions for enhancing the security on smart phone platforms. Malware detection on smart phone is already widely concerned [8,9,29,32]. Zhang et al. [33] proposed an isolation technique for mobile platform by realizing the TCG's Trusted Mobile Phone specification and by leveraging SELinux which provides a generic domain isolation concept at the kernel level. Schmidt et al. [29] demonstrated how to monitor a smart phone running Symbian and Windows Mobile in order to extract features for anomaly detection.

Access control models play an important role in security mechanisms. Some researchers have extended the RBAC model [28], the most popular access control model nowadays, to include context information in authorization decisions. Damiani et.al proposed GEO-RBAC [13] to support spatial roles. Bertino et al. proposed TRBAC [6] to support temporal roles. Other extensions include GRBAC [20,11], STARBAC [1] and LRBAC [25]. Context-awareness has attracted much attention in the security issues of mobile platforms as well, some literatures have already focused on context-aware access control in the networks [10,3,2].

Android security is also widely concerned in recent researches. Asaf Shabtai et.al analyzed and assessed the security mechanisms incorporated in Android by identifying the threats and potential dangers, as well as solutions in Android platform [30]. SCANDROID [17] is a tool for reasoning automatically about the security applications, which checks whether data flows through an application are consistent with its specifications. Enck et al. [14] proposed Kirin security service for Android, which performs lightweight certification of applications to mitigate malware at install-time. Apex [22] presents a policy enforcement framework to enable the the user grant permissions in a fine-grained manner and enforces policy user defined at runtime. However, the context information is not taken into consideration in these approaches. Our work refers to the Apex [22] in policy specification and implementation, yet we focus on performing a continuous usage decision including obligations, states and contexts.

7 Conclusion

The existing security mechanism on the Android platform is facing great challenges because of the mobility and openness of mobile computing environment. This paper proposes a context-aware usage control mechanism to enhance data protection and resource usage constraints on Android. We propose a context-aware Usage CONtrol model ConUCON, which is able to take obligations, states and contexts into consideration at usage decisions. Based on ConUCON, we extend the existing security mechanism to implement a policy enforcement framework on Android, which enables the user to grant permissions in a fine-grained manner and to support revocations and modifications on an application's permissions at runtime. We also evaluate our mechanism with some frequently used actions, which shows that the overhead introduced by the proposed scheme is acceptable. We will further study the application of our ConUCON model on other types of mobile platform.

Acknowledgements. This work is supported by the National Basic Research Program of China (973) under Grant No. 2009CB320703, the Science Fund for Creative Research Groups of China under Grant No. 60821003, National Key S & T Special Projects under Grant No. 2009ZX01039-001-001 and the National High-Tech Research and Development Plan of China under Grant No. 2007AA010304.

References

1. Aich, S., Sural, S., Majumdar, A.K.: STARBAC: Spatio temporal role based access control. In: Meersman, R., Tari, Z. (eds.) OTM 2007, Part II. LNCS, vol. 4804, pp. 1567–1582. Springer, Heidelberg (2007)
2. Al-Muhtadi, J., Ranganathan, A., Campbell, R.H., Mickunas, M.D.: Cerberus: A context-aware security scheme for smart spaces. In: PerCom, p. 489 (2003)
3. Bandinelli, M., Paganelli, F., Vannuccini, G., Giuli, D.: A contextaware security framework for next generation mobile networks. In: MobiSec. Springer, Heidelberg (2009)
4. Bell, D., LaPadula, L.: Secure computer systems: Mathematical foundations. Technical Report ESD-TR-73-278, MITRE Corporation (1973)
5. Bertino, E., Bettini, C., Ferrari, E., Samarati, P.: An access control model supporting periodicity constraints and temporal reasoning. ACM Trans. Database Syst. 23(3), 231–285 (1998)
6. Bertino, E., Bonatti, P.A., Ferrari, E.: TRBAC: A temporal role-based access control model. In: RBAC 2000, July 26-27, pp. 21–30. ACM Press, New York (2000)
7. Biba, K.J.: Integrity considerations for secure computer systems. MTR-3153, Rev. 1, The Mitre Corporation (1977)
8. Bose, A., Hu, X., Shin, K.G., Park, T.: Behavioral detection of malware on mobile handsets. In: MobiSys 2008, pp. 225–238. ACM, New York (2008)

9. Cheng, J., Wong, S.H.Y., Yang, H., Lu, S.: Smartsiren: virus detection and alert for smartphones. In: MobiSys 2007, pp. 258–271. ACM, New York (2007)
10. Covington, M.J., Fogla, P., Zhan, Z., Ahamad, M.: A contextaware security architecture for emerging applications. In: ACSAC, pp. 249–260 (2002)
11. Covington, M.J., Moyer, M.J., Ahamad, M.: Generalized role-based access control for securing future applications (November 03, 2000)
12. Dagon, D., Martin, T., Starner, T.: Mobile phones as computing devices: the viruses are coming! IEEE Pervasive Computing 3(4), 11–15 (2004)
13. Damiani, M.L., Bertino, E., Catania, B., Perlasca, P.: Geo-rbac: A spatially aware RBAC. ACM Trans. Inf. Syst. Secur. 10(1), 2 (2007)
14. Enck, W., Ongtang, M., McDaniel, P.D.: On lightweight mobile phone application certification. In: Proceedings of CCS 2009, pp. 235–245. ACM, New York (2009)
15. F-Secure. Cabir, http://www.f-secure.com/v-descs/cabir.shtml
16. F-Secure. Pbstealer. A.,
    http://www.f-secure.com/v-descs/pbstealer_a.shtml
17. Fuchs, A.P., Chaudhuri, A., Foster, J.S.: Scandroid: Automated security certification of android applications
18. Google. Android, http://www.android.com
19. Hypponen, M.: Mobile Malware. In: USENIX Security Symposium (August 2007), http://www.usenix.org/events/sec07/tech/hypponen.pdf (Invited Talk)
20. Moyer, M.J., Abamad, M.: Generalized role-based access control. In: 21st International Conference on Distributed Computing Systems, pp. 391–398 (April 2001)
21. Mulliner, C.: Security of Smart Phones. Master's thesis, Department of Computer Science, University of California Santa Barbara (June 2006)
22. Nauman, M., Khan, S., Alam, M., Zhang, X.: Apex: Extending android permission model and enforcement with user-defined runtime constraints. In: ASIACCS 2010, Beijing, China, April 13-16. ACM, New York (2010)
23. Park, J., Sandhu, R.: The UCON$_{ABC}$ usage control model. ACM Transactions on Information and System Security 7(1), 128–174 (2004)
24. Park, J., Sandhu, R.S.: Towards usage control models: beyond traditional access control. In: SACMAT, pp. 57–64 (2002)
25. Ray, I., Kumar, M., Yu, L.: LRBAC: A location-aware role-based access control model. In: Bagchi, A., Atluri, V. (eds.) ICISS 2006. LNCS, vol. 4332, pp. 147–161. Springer, Heidelberg (2006)
26. Android reference. Develope Guide,
    http://developer.android.com/guide/index.html
27. Sandhu, R.S., Park, J.: Usage control: A vision for next generation access control. In: MMMACNS (2003)
28. Sandhu, R.S.: Role-based access control. Advances in Computers 46, 238–287 (1998)
29. Schmidt, A.-D., Peters, F., Lamour, F., Albayrak, S.: Monitoring smartphones for anomaly detection. In: MOBILWARE 2008. ICST (2007)
30. Shabtai, A., Fledel, Y., Kanonov, U., Elovici, Y., Dolev, S., Glezer, C.: Google android: A comprehensive security assessment. IEEE Security & Privacy (2010)
31. Stevenne, J., Niezette, M.: An efficient symbolic representation of periodic time. In: Finin, T.W., Yesha, Y., Nicholas, C. (eds.) CIKM 1992. LNCS, vol. 752. Springer, Heidelberg (1993)
32. Xie, L., Zhang, X., Chaugule, A., Jaeger, T., Zhu, S.: Designing system-level defenses against ellphone malware. In: SRDS 2009, pp. 83 –90 (September 2009)
33. Zhang, X., Aciiçmez, O., Seifert, J.-P.: A trusted mobile phone reference architecture via secure kernel. In: STC, pp. 7–14. ACM, New York (2007)
34. Zhang, X., Parisi-Presicce, F., Sandhu, R., Park, J.: Formal model and policy specification of usage control. TISSEC 8(4), 351–387 (2005)

Efficient Isolation of Trusted Subsystems in Embedded Systems

Raoul Strackx, Frank Piessens, and Bart Preneel

IBBT-Distrinet, Katholieke Universiteit Leuven,
Celestijnenlaan 200A, B-3001 Heverlee, Belgium
{raoul.strackx,frank.piessens}@cs.kuleuven.be,
bart.preneel@esat.kuleuven.be

Abstract. Many embedded systems have relatively strong security requirements because they handle confidential data or support secure electronic transactions. A prototypical example are payment terminals. To ensure that sensitive data such as cryptographic keys cannot leak, security-critical parts of these systems are implemented as separate chips, and hence physically isolated from other parts of the system.

But isolation can also be implemented in software. Higher-end computing platforms are equipped with hardware support to facilitate the implementation of virtual memory and virtual machine monitors. However many embedded systems lack such hardware features.

In this paper, we propose a design for a generic and very lightweight hardware mechanism that can support an efficient implementation of isolation for several subsystems that share the same processor and memory space. A prototypical application is the software implementation of cryptographic support with strong assurance on the secrecy of keys, even towards other code sharing the same processor and memory. Secure cohabitation of code from different stakeholders on the same system is also supported.

Keywords: software security, memory protection, isolation.

1   Introduction

Many embedded systems, including for instance payment terminals and other terminals supporting secure electronic transactions, have relatively strong security requirements. In order to meet these requirements, security-critical parts of these systems, like the cryptographic processor, are implemented as separate chips, and hence physically isolated from other parts of the system [1,2,3,4]. This increases the assurance that sensitive data such as cryptographic keys cannot leak.

But isolation can also be implemented in software. Many of the hardware security features of today's higher-end computing platforms – including memory protection hardware and hardware to support virtualization – were designed to enable the software implementation of efficient isolation of components that

S. Jajodia and J. Zhou (Eds.): SecureComm 2010, LNICST 50, pp. 344–361, 2010.

share the computing platform. Based on these hardware building blocks, efficient software implementations of virtual memory, virtual machine monitors or hypervisors are feasible, and these in turn make it possible to have high assurance isolation between several software components sharing the same physical hardware [5,6,7,8].

Several trends in embedded system design make it interesting to investigate to what extent such isolation mechanisms can play a role in secure embedded systems.

First, the desire to minimize cost pushes towards the reuse of one single processor for tasks that were traditionally divided over physically separated hardware. A prime example are the hardware security modules or cryptographic coprocessors mentioned above: the increased computational power of general purpose processors combined with an increased support for high assurance isolation of software components sharing the processor makes it feasible to design software-based cryptographic coprocessors. Obviously, this raises security concerns that need to be investigated. In particular, one would like to maintain the strong assurance on key secrecy that separate hardware security modules provide.

Second, the co-location of different applications owned by different stakeholders on the same embedded system makes it important to provide high-assurance isolation between these applications. Prime examples are third-party applications on mobile phones, multi-application smartcards, or shared sensor networks. While some of the security requirements of such multi-stakeholder embedded platforms are similar to these of high-end multi-user computing platforms, there are also essential differences, and hence it is necessary to re-evaluate and where needed re-design the security mechanisms to provide secure isolation.

This paper proposes *self-protecting modules (SPM)*: based on a minimal form of hardware support for memory access control, we show how trusted subsystems can share the same processor and memory space, while still maintaining strong security properties including strong isolation guarantees between two such subsystems, and high assurance on the confidentiality of subsystem-private data.

More specifically, the contributions of this paper are the following:

- a novel memory access control model, where access to memory locations can also depend on the value of the program counter,
- based on this access control model, the design of self-protecting modules: software modules that can provide strong security guarantees both for the data they handle as well as for how they can be invoked by other modules,
- a proof sketch of the security of this design,
- and a discussion of several application examples.

The remainder of this paper is structured as follows: in the next Section the threat model will be presented as well as the security properties provided. Section 3 will present SPM's in more detail including an overview, layout of an SPM and the required hardware modifications. We also discuss a proof sketch of the security properties of SPM's. In Section 4 we discuss possible applications. Finally we discuss related work and offer a conclusion.

2   Problem Statement

2.1   Threat Model

We assume that an attacker has the ability to inject machine code of his choice into the memory space of the system under attack. This is a realistic assumption: there are several ways in which an attacker can achieve this. First, the attacker can exploit a software vulnerability such as a buffer overflow in one of the applications on the system, and perform a code injection attack [9,10].

Second, the attacker could be one of the stakeholders in a system where several mutually distrusting stakeholders cohabit the same platform. Third, the attacker may have compromised the software layer below (for instance the OS kernel).

We also assume that the attacker does *not* have the ability to perform a physical attack: he can for instance not disconnect memory from the processor, place probes on the memory bus, or perform a hard reset of the system. An example of such an attack is discussed by Halderman [11]: memory chips containing sensitive information are placed in a machine that is under total control of the attacker, and the secrets can be extracted relatively easy. Such attacks are not considered in this paper. If such physical attacks are an important concern, the software-based implementation of security proposed in this paper is not appropriate.

2.2   Security Properties

Under the threat model discussed above, we want to support the execution of software modules that share the same memory address space guaranteeing the following security properties:

- *Restriction of entry points.* Software modules can securely restrict how they can be invoked. In other words, the entry points into the module can be defined by the module provider. An attacker can not jump to an arbitrary location within the module.
- *Security of module data.* Sensitive information, such as keys, managed by the module can only be read or modified by code from the module.
- *Authentication of modules.* Modules have a secure mechanism of identifying other modules in memory.
- *Secure communication between modules.* Modules can communicate efficiently with other modules they have authenticated. Moreover, the integrity and confidentiality of messages passed over this communication channel can be assured.
- *Minimal Trusted Computing Base (TCB).* The correct and secure execution of a module depends only on (1) the hardware, (2) a small part of the boot process of the system (see Section 3.7), and (3) the correct behavior of the code of the module itself and any third-party modules that it calls. In particular, the operating system kernel is excluded from the TCB.

Note that we do not aim to protect a module against vulnerabilities in its own implementation: if a module contains a logical fault (e.g. a faulty API design [12]), or an implementation-level vulnerability (e.g. a buffer overwrite [9], a buffer over-read [13] or other low-level vulnerabilities [10]), then sensitive data may leak. We only protect the module against attacks that are a consequence of malicious code sharing the memory space of the module. Protection against vulnerabilities in the module itself can be provided by other countermeasures [14].

Note also that we do not protect against denial-of-service: malicious code running on the machine can go into an infinite loop, or can install any number of additional modules thus exhausting CPU-time or memory space. In Section 3.10 we discuss some possible mitigations.

3   Self-Protecting Modules

3.1   Overview

A self-protecting module (SPM) is an area of memory with a particular layout and with particular memory protection settings. Many SPM's as well as other code or data can share the same memory address space. Any code outside the SPM, including code in other SPM's, could be potentially hostile. Here is an overview of how SPM's operate.

First, an SPM is structured in three sections. Each section is a contiguous range of memory. The SSecret section will contain data that untrusted code should not be able to access directly. The SPublic section will contain data that can be accessed in a read-only manner, as well as the code of the module. Finally, the SEntry section defines the entry points into the module's code: this is a list of pointers into the SPublic section, and the only way to call the SPM is by jumping to an address in this list.

Second, memory access control restricts the rights to read, write or execute memory locations, based on both the value of the program counter (PC), as well as on the address being accessed. For instance, the SSecret memory will only be readable while the PC is in the SPublic section, and the SPublic section is read-only accessible when the PC is outside the SPM. We discuss the access control rules in more detail further on.

The creation and initialization of an SPM takes several steps and is displayed graphically in Fig. 1a. First, the operating system loads the SPublic and SEntry sections into memory (step 1). This part of the initialization does not need to be trusted: if an attacker interferes with the loading, it will be detected later on.

Second (step 2), a new hardware instruction, setProtected, to create the SPM. This instruction defines the boundaries of the three sections of the SPM, enables memory access control, and clears the SSecret section to all zeros. Memory protection enforces, from this point on, that only the SPM itself can destroy itself, or modify its contents. As a consequence, the identity of SPM's can be securely authenticated from this point on: SPublic and SEntry sections are world-readable, and together they define the identity of an SPM.

Third, loading the secret data of the module in the SSecret section requires the assistance of another trusted SPM that we call the *vault* (step 3). This SPM

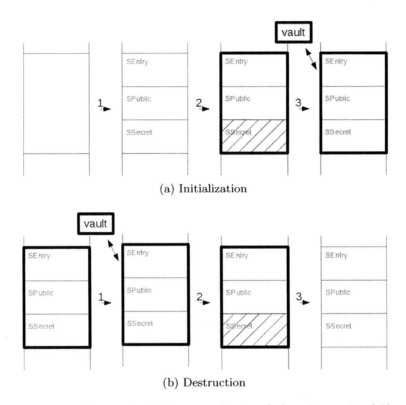

(a) Initialization

(b) Destruction

Fig. 1. The life of an SPM from initialization (1a) to destruction (1b)

will authenticate the identity of the newly loaded SPM and then provision it with its initial secret data.

Of course, the question then remains how the vault itself gets initialized. For that, we trust (a part of) the boot process: the vault gets installed and provisioned with secret data at boot time, and is never unloaded.

Once SPM's are loaded and initialized, they can securely call functionality of other SPM's. That is: an SPM can call an entry point of another SPM with the following guarantees: (1) it is calling into an SPM with the correct identity, and (2) the integrity and confidentiality of parameters and return values is protected.

Destruction of an SPM is similar to initialization. Fig. 1b displays the steps graphically. First, the vault is used to store secret data securely on untrusted storage. In step two, the secret data is overwritten. Finally, access control on the SPM is disabled and the SPM becomes unprotected memory again.

We now discuss several aspects of this design in more detail.

3.2   Layout of an SPM

An SPM is structured in three memory areas or sections (see Fig. 2) with different access control settings. Table 1 gives a schematic overview and should be read as follows: the "from" index is determined by the current value of the PC, and the "to" index is determined by the memory address being accessed. For instance, if the PC is in the SPublic section, then memory locations in the SSecret section of the *same* SPM can be read and modified. An identical instruction issued from any other location will be prevented. Note that access to a section originating from a *different* SPM is treated in the same way as access originating from unprotected memory.

SSecret. Sensitive data of the SPM is stored in this section. This includes cryptographic keys and application-level data such as credit card numbers, but also a return stack to implement an SPM's functionality and other control flow data.

In contrast with the other sections, *any* attempt to access this section from outside the SPM will fail. This provides complete isolation of secret data. Data can only flow out or into this section using the functionality provided by the self-protected module.

In our design, execution of instructions stored in the SSecret section is prevented for the following reasons: (1) the SSecret section is not a part of the identity of the SPM that can be authenticated by other SPM's, and (2) making any the only writable section non-executable has important security advantages from the point of view of protecting against vulnerabilities in the SPM itself [15,16].

SPublic. Contrary to the SSecret section, the SPublic section can be read from any location, including from unprotected memory locations. The instructions implementing the functionality of the SPM are placed in this section, as well as constant non-secret data such as security certificates. The hardware implemented access control will prevent write instructions to this section from *any* location. Therefore, it can't be modified after access control on the module is enabled and SPM's can be authenticated easily (see Section 3.5).

The code in the SPublic section is assumed to be trustworthy. It is responsible for instance to prevent undesired leaking of secret information to untrusted memory locations or to untrusted SPM's. It should also make sure that an attacker cannot inject false data.

SEntry. It is very hard to guarantee good properties of a piece of machine code if one cannot restrict the possible entry points into the code [17]. By carefully choosing the destination of a jump instruction, security sensitive code, such as encryption functions, could be skipped.

To prevent such attacks, direct calls to the SPublic section from outside the SPM are prevented (see Table 1). But jumping to the SEntry section is allowed. This section contains a list of jump instructions to valid locations in the SPublic section. By making SEntry executable from outside the secured section, and SPublic not, entry points are effectively restricted to those listed in the SEntry section. Note that jumping from SEntry to SPublic is allowed by the memory access control model.

Modifications of the SEntry section are prevented by marking it only read and executable, both from within as from outside the secured section.

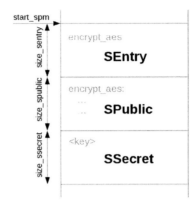

Fig. 2. The layout of an SPM in memory

Table 1. The memory access control matrix

from\to	SEntry	SPublic	SSecret	unprotected
SEntry		x		
SPublic	rx	rx	rw	rwx
SSecret				
Unprotected/other SPM	rx	r		rwx

3.3   Hardware Modifications

In order to use the proposed solution, some hardware modifications are required. Besides the access control model, three instructions need to be supported.

setProtected. Installation of an SPM starts with loading the content of its sections into memory. Up to this point this content is not protected but any modification will be detected later on. Only after successful execution of the setProtected instruction with the correct parameters, access control is enabled and the SPM is protected from hostile code stored at any location outside the SPM, running at any privilege level.

To simplify checks executed before protection is enabled, the setProtected instruction assumes a fixed ordering of the SPM's sections in memory. The SEntry section is always placed at the lower memory locations immediately followed by the SPublic and SSecret sections, respectively. Using this fixed layout, the instruction only requires 4 arguments; start_spm, size_sentry, size_spublic and size_ssecret (see Fig. 2). The first argument, start_spm, provides the address of the lowest memory location that will be protected, the base of the SEntry section. The other arguments provide the length of each section as they are placed in memory.

Before access control can be safely enabled, a check needs to be performed that the new SPM will not overlap with an existing one[1].

When the check succeeds, the content of the SSecret section is blanked with zeros to prevent an attacker from injecting false data. Finally, the SPM is protected by enabling access control on each section.

isProtected. Before secret data can be passed between SPM's securely, they should be able to authenticate one another. The ability to read the code and public data part of an SPM is not sufficient. Its correct installation must be proven. This not only includes that the access control is enabled, but also that the layout of the SPM is as expected.

The `isProtected` instruction takes a memory location as an argument and returns the layout of the surrounding SPM in the same format as expected by the `setProtected` instruction. In case the memory location is not protected an error value is returned.

resetProtected. Once an SPM is created, its protection cannot be disabled from outside the SPM, not even by code running at the processor's highest privilege level. Only the SPM can remove it by executing the `resetProtected` instruction.

To keep data stored in the SSecret section secret from attackers, it should be destroyed before access control is disabled. Since we need to trust the SPM code to correctly clean up for other purposes as well (see Section 3.6), we require the SPM to overwrite the data explicitly rather than blanking it automatically when the `resetProtected` instruction is issued.

3.4   Initialization of SPM's

Initialization of SPM's takes three steps (see Fig. 1a). First, the content of its SEntry and SPublic sections is loaded in unprotected memory (step 1). Next, its SSecret section is blanked by the `setProtected` instruction and access control on all sections is enabled (step 2). Finally, the SPM should initialize its internal data structures (step 3). For example, a new return stack should be created within the SSecret section as control flow data of the SPM should never be stored at an unprotected location. There are two approaches for the initialization of SPM's.

First, it may be possible to initialize it using only public data. This situation occurs when only secure execution is an issue, not secrecy. When the provided data stays the same over time, it could be shipped and placed alongside the code in the SPublic section. To allow its modification by the SPM, it can be copied to the SSecret section. In case the public data changes repeatedly over time and only integrity needs to be protected, the SSecret section could be created and cryptographically signed by a trusted third party and sent to the SPM. After checking the signature, the provided data can be used to initialize the SPM.

---

[1] In principle the SEntry and SPublic sections could be shared by multiple instances of the same SPM to reduce memory consumption. This optimization and its security issues are considered to be out-of-scope for this paper.

Second, the SSecret section could be initialized using secret data stored in a cryptographically encrypted and signed file. As a secret key must be available for decryption and since prior to initialization, an SPM can not contain secret data, help of another trusted SPM is required. Our design proposes a special SPM called *vault* to provide such functionality. We discuss this in Section 3.7.

3.5   Authentication of SPM's

Previous sections described how an SPM could be loaded into memory from an untrusted source. Even when a software module has been received correctly, it may have been modified while it was stored on disk. Before it can be trusted with secret data, its trustworthiness must be validated.

For this purpose, each SPM is shipped with a *security report*. It states that the correct implementation of the SPM has been verified by its issuer. In case that third party is trusted, so can the SPM when the security report is valid. Recall that our threat model assumes that the SPM does not contain logical faults nor implementation-level vulnerabilities (see Section 2.1).

By placing the security report in the SPublic section, it can be accessed easily and efficiently as access control of the SPM allows read access from any location.

Each security report contains following information:

- *Hash of SEntry and SPublic sections*: To be able to establish trust in an SPM, it must be identical to the SPM certified by the trusted third party. By providing a hash result of the SEntry and SPublic sections[2], any modification will be detected.
- *The layout of the SPM*: When incorrect parameters are supplied with the setProtected instruction, the SPM may use unprotected memory locations to store secret data. To avoid such situations, the layout of the SPM is included in the security report. Using the results of the isProtected instruction, the layout of the newly installed SPM can be validated.
- *Cryptographic signature*: The security report is signed with its issuer's private key. An SPM that wishes to verify the trustworthiness of another, has a list of trusted certificate authorities (CA's). When a chain of trust can be built from a CA to the public key of the issuer, the security report can be trusted.

If an SPM A wishes to authenticate SPM B, it should (1) verify the signature of B's security report, (2) verify the hashes of the SEntry and SPublic sections, and (3) verify the SPM layout using the isProtected instruction.

3.6   Secure Communication

The ability to communicate securely between two mutually trusted SPM's does not only result in a more modular system, it is also required to bootstrap the system. Section 3.7 describes how an SPM loaded from an untrusted location

---

[2] The hash of the SPublic section implies knowledge of the security report. To break this circular dependency, the security report is replaced with zeros during calculation.

can be authenticated and provided its secret data. This Section presents how two SPM's can communicate with one another while preserving secrecy and integrity of the exchanged messages. Injection of false data is prevented as well.

Each of the presented protocols assumes that the SPM's know each others location and implemented functionality. In practice this can be accomplished by requiring each SPM to register itself to a centralized service. As this service does not have to be trusted, its inner workings are not considered in this paper.

One-Way Authentication. Some applications only require that one endpoint of the communication channel is authenticated. Consider for example an SPM *SecureRandom*, providing the service of secure random number generation. For obvious security reasons, the client needs to authenticate the service. SecureRandom in turn, has no need to verify the trustworthiness of its client as it does not leak any secrets, it only creates unpredictable random numbers.

The protocol described in this Section offers the following security guarantees for communication between SPM's: authentication of one endpoint, secrecy and integrity of the messages sent and received.

Fig. 3 displays the protocol. In the first step, the client authenticates SecureRandom. It does so by fetching its security report from its SPublic section and validating it. This operation can be performed without leaving the client SPM as SEntry and SPublic sections are world-readable (see Section 3.2).

Next, the generation of a new random number is requested. This request can be made similar to an ordinary function call; by jumping to the correct location in the SEntry section of SecureRandom and passing arguments in registers. However, unlike a function call, execution cannot return directly to the instruction following the call instruction, as this would provide SecureRandom with a way of (re-)entering the calling SPM at an address that is not in the SEntry list, thus enabling return-into-libc-like attacks [17]. The access control on the SPM will prevent such jump instructions into the SPublic section as it originated from outside the SPM. Instead, returning from a service call is implemented by creating a new entry point, `client_entry`, in the SEntry section and sending it as an argument with the request. After the random number is created, SecureRandom will then issue a jump instruction to the specified entry point. There control flow is directed to the correct, fixed, location, as allowed by the access control. This is similar to continuation-passing-style programming.

In the third step of the protocol, the random generator returns the random number k, by placing it in a register and jumping to the return entry point specified by the client.

Placing sensitive information in registers is an inexpensive solution as it does not require encryption and signing. Unfortunately it can only be used when a small amount of data needs to be transferred from one SPM to another. When bulk data needs to be exchanged, it can either be divided and transported using multiple jump instructions, or it can be communicated in untrusted, unprotected memory after appropriate encryption and signing. The keys used can than be exchanged securely in registers.

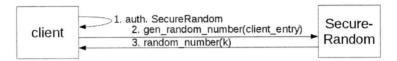

Fig. 3. One-way authentication between SPM's. A client authenticates the random number generator before requesting a new random number.

Mutual Authentication. The protocol presented in Section 3.6 can be modified easily to authenticate both communication endpoints (see Fig. 4). As before, the client initiates the protocol and authenticates the vault. Next, a message is sent requesting the secret data. The entry point to be used to return the data, `client_entry`, is added as well as the location of the security report of the client, `client_sec_rep`.

At the reception of the message, vault must verify that the security report of the client is valid and trusted. To prevent sending the secret to an unprotected location or to an incorrect SPM, vault also has to check that the given entry point is located within the SPM described by the security report. Only when both tests are valid, the secret information, k, will be returned.

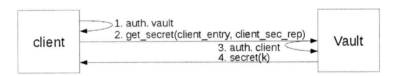

Fig. 4. Two-way authentication between SPM's

Mutual Authentication with Support of Both Endpoints. The previous protocol is inefficient in case multiple authenticated communication events between the same SPM's occur. With support of both endpoints, performance overhead can be reduced by avoiding repeated checks of the security reports.

Fig. 5 displays the protocol where SPM's A and B wish to communicate. The protocol establishes a persistent secure channel in only two passes.

First, A authenticates endpoint B. After trust is established, the `notify_destruction` entry point of B is called providing an entry point of A, $notify_A$ that should be called when B is about to be destroyed. A freshly generated cryptographic nonce N_{BA} is also added to the request. As only B has knowledge of the nonce, any message containing N_{BA} must be sent by B. This avoids repeated authentication of B.

In the second part of the protocol endpoint B performs identical steps, providing A with the entry point $notify_B$ and the fresh nonce N_{AB}. Now A and B are able to communicate securely without repeated authentication events. As before, entry points of the other SPM can be called passing secret data in registers. Providing the received nonce with each communication event, proves the origin of the message.

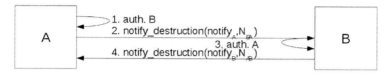

Fig. 5. Two-way authentication between SPM's with support

3.7 Vault: Bootstrapping Trust

After loading the SEntry and SPublic sections into unprotected memory and calling the `setProtected` instruction (step 1 and 2 in Fig. 1a respectively), the SSecret section of newly created SPM's is blank. As described in Section 3.4, SPM's can be easily initialized using public data (step 3). However, in some cases secret data, for example a cryptographic key, of a previous instance of an SPM needs to be restored. A special SPM called *vault* provides such functionality. It is able to store secret data securely in persistent but untrusted memory and guarantees that the secret data will only be returned to the same SPM that requested its storage.

Requesting storage goes as follows. First, an SPM establishes an one-way authenticated channel to the vault. Next, the secret data is transferred to the vault where it is appended with the security report of the requesting SPM, encrypted and signed with the vault's cryptographic keys and stored in persistent storage. Note that vault only stores secret data from other SPM's. As it does not provide any of its own secrets, it does not have to trust its clients.

A different instance of the same SPM, for example after the system is rebooted, is now able to retrieve the stored secrets from the vault. First, it establishes a two-way authenticated channel with the vault. The secret data is fetched from persistent storage[3], its signature checked and decrypted by the vault. Only when the stored security report matches the requesting SPM's, the secret data is passed over the secure channel.

This leaves the problem of how the vault itself gets initialized with its keys. For this we trust (a part of) the boot process: the system is modified to create the vault as early in the boot sequence as possible. Unlike any other SPM, its secret data is provided directly by hardware by copying it from protected memory that is only accessible at boot time.

3.8 Destruction

Before protection on the module is disabled, the SPM's destruction should be prepared. In general two cases need to be considered. First, the stored secret data in the SPM. When access control is disabled, it can be accessed from any location. To avoid disclosing it in unprotected memory, it needs to be overwritten.

---

[3] How the secret data is found on persistent storage is not relevant from a security point of view and is omitted for clarity. However, the vault could return an identifier, for example a filename, when storage is requested and stored unprotected.

Second, other SPM's may assume the presence of the trusted, protected module at a certain memory location. These SPM's need to be notified of the imminent destruction to prevent them from issuing jump instructions to unprotected and/or untrusted code while passing secret data in registers.

3.9   Discussion

Limitations of the Current Design. The proposed solution reduces the TCB to only the SPM's used, a small part of the boot process and the hardware. By eliminating the kernel from the TCB, its correct behavior can no longer be trusted upon and access in *any* way conflicting with the access control model presented in Section 3.2 needs to be prevented. As a result, support of many advanced features, such as interrupts, virtual memory and others, must be implemented in the SPM's, in collaboration with the hardware. Supporting these features is considered to be out of the scope of this paper.

- *interrupts*: when an interrupt occurs during the execution of an SPM, sensitive information stored in registers will be accessible to the kernel. Therefore SPM's should be executed in the highest interrupt level, preventing interrupts from being handled during execution. Hence, SPM implementors should make sure that SPM calls return within a reasonable amount of time.
- *swapping*: in case more memory is required than is available on the machine, the kernel will swap chunks of memory to disk. This may not only prevent the correct memory location from being called, as secret data is stored at an unprotected location, confidentiality and integrity may be compromised. Therefore, swapping of SPM's should be prevented.
- *direct memory access (DMA)*: peripheral devices often use DMA to access memory locations directly; protected memory locations must be excluded.
- *paging*: paging allows the same physical page to be mapped to different address spaces, even at different addresses. In itself this does not pose a security problem as long as access control remains correctly enforced. In practice this may be difficult, as an SPM may span multiple pages and additional pages may be injected at runtime. Support for paging is considered to be out-of-scope, SPM's are currently expected to use physical addresses.
- *concurrent execution of SPM's*: When multiple SPM's exchange secret data, authentication of endpoints does not suffice. In the limited amount of time between authentication and a communication event, one of the endpoints may have been removed. Issuing jump instructions in that case, may leak secret data stored in registers. For this reason, concurrent execution of SPM's is currently not supported.

Note that these assumptions are only made during the execution of self-protecting modules. Execution of unprotected code, including concurrent execution on a different core, are not restricted as long as the access rights presented in Section 3.2 are enforced. By using a multi-core processor to execute the kernel on a different core than the SPM's, the system will remain responsive.

Proof Sketches of Security Guarantees

Security of module code. After installation, an SPM contains all the code that implements its functionality. It cannot be modified nor influenced, not from outside nor from within the SPM, and can only be called using the entry points into the module as defined by the module's provider.

This property almost directly follows from access control enforced on SPM's. Only the SEntry section is executable from outside the module. A user has no other option than to use these specified entry points. After calling an entry point, the SPM is entered and control flow is directed to the SPublic section. Both SPublic as SEntry sections are now executable. As both sections are not writable from any location, an attacker is not able to modify the stored instructions.

Only modification of control data still needs to be considered. In the SSecret section, a return stack may be built to allow easy implementation of the SPM's functionality. Implementation vulnerabilities may allow this data to be overwritten, for example by exploiting a buffer overflow vulnerability [9,10]. Modification of a return address, frame pointer, or other control data may result in modified behavior of the SPM as defined by the SPM's provider. However, it is assumed that code stored in the SPM does not contain such vulnerabilities.

While an attacker is able to modify the code of the SPM before access control is enabled, such modification will be detected during authentication.

Security of module data. Sensitive data such as keys stored in the module must be protected. Access must be restricted to the SPM and unless explicitly specified, secret data must not leak. For example, a key may only leave the SPM when it is securely passed to another, trusted, SPM or when it is encrypted and signed.

Isolation of data stored in the SSecret section is directly provided by the access control model enforced upon it. Any access attempt from outside the SPM is prevented. In contrast, instructions within the SPM are allowed to read and modify data stored in the SSecret section. Considering that the code of the module is secure and cannot be modified nor influenced after installation, as stated by the previous security guarantee, we conclude that secret data can only leave the SPM as implemented by the SPM's provider.

Finally the destruction of an SPM needs to be considered. As access control only allows an SPM to disable its own protection and the SPM is able to enforce the conditions under which the `resetProtected` instruction is issued, any secret data can be overwritten prior to the destruction of the SPM.

Secure communication between modules. Combining the strong isolation of data and code with a secure communication scheme between SPM's, will result in a modular and secure subsystem. Only the existence of such a secure communication mechanism still needs to be argued. In order to pass secret data between modules securely, (mutual) authentication and a secure channel are required.

To authenticate an SPM, its implementation needs to be verified. Access control restricts execution of code within the SPM to the SEntry and SPublic sections. As these sections are world-readable, the functionality of an SPM can be checked easily. The presence of self-modifying code or code injection attacks does not have to be considered; in a previous paragraph it is already argued that after installation the code of an SPM cannot be modified. Finally, the `isProtected` instruction can be issued to check the correct setup of the SPM's protection.

Authentication can only consider the SEntry and SPublic sections as the SPM's protection will prevent access to the SSecret section. Without proper security measures, an attacker may still carefully craft an SSecret section. This could, for example, trick the trusted code into storing received secret data at an unprotected location encrypted using a key under the attackers control. Such spoofing attacks are prevented by automatically clearing the entire SSecret section when the `setProtected` instruction is issued. After initialization the SPM's are responsible to prevent injection of false data.

Next, a secure channel between two modules can be established. Authenticity and confidentiality of the exchanged messages must be provided. SPM's can be called like ordinary functions; by directly modifying the program counter of the processor. Messages can be passed using registers. It is assumed that the execution of modules cannot be interrupted. Therefore, the secrecy of data passed in registers cannot be breached and both requirements are met.

Finally, it must be assured that the secure channel is set up between the correct SPM's. Between authentication and the first message, an endpoint may be destroyed. In that situation, secrecy of the data stored in registers cannot be ensured. An attacker may have replaced the SPM with malicious code.

To prevent such situations, control flow must not leave the SPM between authentication and the communication event. Because SPM's can only be destroyed by themselves, the authenticated SPM must have been entered between the two events. However, it is enforced that at any time no two SPM's can be executing simultaneous. Therefore such attacks are prevented.

Minimal trusted computing base (TCB). The hardware and implementation of *vault* forms the root of trust of the systems. Because modules are able to control the flow of secret data to authenticated modules or to unprotected memory under specific conditions, a chain of trust can be built. This trust does *not* include the kernel. As a result, the TCB only consists of the trusted modules, a small part of the boot process creating a root of trust and the hardware.

3.10 Extensions

The current design does not allow SPM's to be interrupted during execution or swapped to disk. Leveraging these limitations, an attacker is able to execute a denial-of-service attack (DoS), for example, by installing an SPM that goes into an infinite loop. On devices that support multiple privilege levels, the chances of such an attack can be reduced easily. By restricting the `setProtected` instruction to kernel mode, an attacker with only user privileges must request the kernel for the protection of an SPM. Before this request is validated, security checks can be performed. For example, only SPM's of trusted issuers could be allowed. Note that an attacker who compromised the kernel to avoid these restrictions, is also able to power the system down, executing a similar denial-of-service.

4   Applications

Many embedded systems, for instance payment terminals and mobile phones running third-party applications including m-banking applications, have strong security requirements. For example, sensitive data such as cryptographic keys must not leak. To assure these requirements, secret data is stored and computed on a physically separated co-processor and memory, packaged together on a single chip called a *hardware security module (HSM)*. Many modern PC's are already being shipped with such a chip [1]. Similar hardware for mobile devices is being developed.

However, isolation can also be guaranteed by SPM's in software. This reduces manufacturing cost as a separate co-processor and memory is no longer required. For the same reason power consumption is reduced, making secure isolation possible for low-end devices or improve mobility. Prime examples are multi-application smartcards and shared sensor networks.

However, there are differences between HSM's and SPM's. First, a Trusted Platform Module (TPM) [1], the HSM found on many desktop PC's, can only execute the cryptographic algorithms installed on the chip when it was manufactured[4]. Other algorithms on secret data still need to be executed in unprotected memory under a huge TCB. In contrary, SPM's are able to isolate *any* module.

Second, many HSM's do have advantages over SPM's. Secret data can also be protected against physical attacks. However, in many situations the user with physical access to the device can be trusted. A user trying to access his banking account, for example, is only interested to keep his/hers login data secure.

Third, HSM's could also be used to improve performance. As they are built with a specific purpose, they can be more easily optimized for performance. However, when the HSM chips can be omitted, it could be replaced by an additional, general-purpose processor core. This would allow a performance improvement of any process, not just cryptographic algorithms.

5   Related Work

Many security measures have been proposed to increase the security of computing devices. Early work proposed hardware support for multiple privilege modes in the processor to separate trusted from untrusted code [18]. From these added hardware features, a balance between secure and performant architectures have been investigated, leading to a whole design-space ranging from micro-kernels to large monolithic kernels [19].

The Dyad HW[2] and other architectures [3,4] uses hardware features more extensively. Executing trusted code on a co-processor provides strong isolation, even protecting against physical attacks.

Hardware security modules such as the TPM [1], allow integrity measurements during boot process. While it is able to attest a trusted boot sequence, it

---

[4] However, there exist HSM chips that are able to execute custom algorithms within the secured boundaries.

relies on the correctness of the entire code base [6]. An infeasible secure solution considering the millions lines of code of modern monolithic kernels.

Recently, virtualization techniques, with or without hardware support, are considered to provide isolation between trusted and untrusted code. For example, Nizza [5], uses a minimal, trusted kernel to run both trusted AppCores and a legacy operating system running untrusted processes. However, its TCB still consists of hundred of thousands lines of code.

Oslo [6] takes advantage of virtualization instructions found in recent AMD^{TM} and Intel® processors to establish a dynamic root of trust, providing more flexibility. Flicker [7,8] also takes this approach. Running trusted code as virtualized machines, called PAL's and taking advantage of the functionality of a TPM, strong isolation is provided with a small TCB. However, maintaining state between a PAL's executions incurs a large performance overhead. In addition, the requirement of both a TPM as hardware supported virtualization make it ill-equipped for mobile and embedded devices.

6   Conclusion

Many embedded systems, for instance payment terminals and mobile phones running third-party applications including m-banking applications, have relatively strong security requirements.

We propose a novel access control model where access to memory locations also depends on the value of the program counter. Using this approach a secure subsystem can be built and isolated in software instead of hardware, reducing manufacturing cost and offering strong security guarantees to low-end devices such as multi-party smartcards and sensor-networks.

Acknowledgments. This research is partially funded by the Interuniversity Attraction Poles Programme Belgian State, Belgian Science Policy, and by the Research Fund K.U.Leuven.

References

1. Trusted Computing Group: Tpm main specification,
   http://www.trustedcomputinggroup.org/
2. Yee, B.: Using secure coprocessors. PhD thesis (1994)
3. Smith, S., Weingart, S.: Building a high-performance, programmable secure coprocessor. Comput. Networks 31(8), 831–860 (1999)
4. Chen, B., Morris, R.: Certifying program execution with secure processors. In: USENIX HotOS Workshop, pp. 133–138 (2003)
5. Singaravelu, L., Pu, C., Härtig, H., Helmuth, C.: Reducing TCB complexity for security-sensitive applications: Three case studies. In: Proceedings of the 1st ACM SIGOPS/EuroSys European Conference on Computer Systems 2006. ACM, New York (2006)
6. Kauer, B.: OSLO: improving the security of trusted computing. In: Proceedings of 16th USENIX Security Symposium, pp. 1–9. USENIX Association (2007)

7. McCune, J., Parno, B., Perrig, A., Reiter, M., Isozaki, H.: Flicker: An execution infrastructure for TCB minimization. In: Proceedings of the 3rd ACM SIGOPS/EuroSys European Conference on Computer Systems 2008. ACM, New York (2008)

8. McCune, J., Perrig, A., Reiter, M.: Safe passage for passwords and other sensitive data. In: Proceedings of NDSS (2009)

9. Aleph1: Smashing the stack for fun and profit. Phrack 49 (1996)

10. Younan, Y., Joosen, W., Piessens, F.: Code injection in c and c++: A survey of vulnerabilities and countermeasures. Technical report, Departement Computerwetenschappen, Katholieke Universiteit Leuven (2004)

11. Halderman, J., Schoen, S., Heninger, N., Clarkson, W., Paul, W., Calandrino, J., Feldman, A., Appelbaum, J., Felten, E.: Lest we remember: Cold boot attacks on encryption keys. In: USENIX Security Symposium, pp. 45–60 (2008)

12. Longley, D., Rigby, S.: An automatic search for security flaws in key management schemes. Computers & Security 11(1), 75–89 (1992)

13. Strackx, R., Younan, Y., Philippaerts, P., Piessens, F., Lachmund, S., Walter, T.: Breaking the memory secrecy assumption. In: EUROSEC 2009: Proceedings of the Second European Workshop on System Security, pp. 1–8. ACM, New York (March 2009)

14. Erlingsson, Ú.: Low-level software security: Attacks and defenses. In: Aldini, A., Gorrieri, R. (eds.) FOSAD 2007. LNCS, vol. 4677, pp. 92–134. Springer, Heidelberg (2007)

15. Microsoft Corporation: Changes to functionality in microsoft windows xp service pack 2,
    http://www.microsoft.com/downloads/
    details.aspx?FamilyID=7bd948d7-b791-40b6-8364-685b84158c78

16. The PaX Team: Documentation for the pax project,
    http://pax.grsecurity.net/docs/pax.txt

17. Shacham, H.: The geometry of innocent flesh on the bone: Return-into-libc without function calls (on the x86). In: Proceedings of the 14th ACM conference on Computer and communications security, p. 561. ACM, New York (2007)

18. Corbato, F., Vyssotsky, V.: Introduction and overview of the Multics system. In: Proceedings of the fall joint computer conference, part I, November 30-December 1, pp. 185–196. ACM, New York (1965)

19. Liedtke, J.: Toward real microkernels. Communications of the ACM 39(9) (1996)

Enhancing Host Security Using External Environment Sensors

Ee-Chien Chang[1,*], Liming Lu[1], Yongzheng Wu[1,2,**],
Roland H.C. Yap[1], and Jie Yu[3,***]

[1] School of Computing, National University of Singapore, Singapore
{changec,luliming,wuyongzh,ryap}@comp.nus.edu.sg
[2] Temasek Laboratories, National University of Singapore, Singapore
[3] Department of Computer Science
National University of Defense Technology, China
yj@nudt.edu.cn

Abstract. We propose a framework that uses environment information to enhance computer security. We apply our framework to: enhance IDS performance; and to enrich the expressiveness of access/rate controls. The environment information is gathered by external (w.r.t the host) sensors, and transmitted via an out-of-band channel, and thus it is hard for adversaries not having physical access to compromise the system. The information gathered still remains intact even if malware use rootkit techniques to hide its activities. Due to requirements on user privacy, the information gathered could be coarse and simple. We show that such simple information is already useful in several experimental evaluations. For instance, binary user presence indicating at a workstation can help to detect DDoS zombie attacks and illegal email spam. Our framework takes advantage of the growing popularity of multimodal sensors and physical security information management systems. Trends in sensor costs suggest that it will be cost-effective in the near future.

Keywords: intrusion detection, spam, sensors, access control, host security.

1 Introduction

Securing computers against malware is increasingly difficult today. Anecdotes abound that the survival time of an unpatched PC running Windows XP connected to the Internet is in the order of minutes [1,2]. The recent Conficker worm [3] is estimated to have infected 6% of computers on the Internet.

Often the goal of the attackers is to infect a host to make it part of a botnet. The malware may be mostly dormant until it is activated, as such, it can be difficult to detect that the host is infected. The detection problem is made worse

---

* Chang is supported by Grant R-252-000-413-232 from TDSI.
** Wu and Yap are supported by Grant R-394-000-037-422 from DRTech.
*** This work was done during internship at the National University of Singapore.

S. Jajodia and J. Zhou (Eds.): SecureComm 2010, LNICST 50, pp. 362–379, 2010.

since malware can exploit rootkit techniques to hide its presence and also any activity. For example, the Mebroot rootkit infects the master boot record of the hard disk allowing it to infect the Windows kernel during boot. After that it hides the changes to the master boot record to make it difficult for antivirus software to detect its presence.

Most security mechanisms tend to be host-based, and are often part of the operating system or interact with it. A primary exception is network-based security mechanisms which analyze network data and traffic. While there are some successes in detecting the presence or activity of malware by network-based security mechanisms, there are many other sources of information outside the host that are also useful for improving detection.

In this paper, we propose fusing environment information in decision making so as to enhance security. Our framework is designed to protect stationary machines (e.g. workstation) which users work on rather than servers controlled remotely or mobile laptops. We take advantage of the growth in pervasive computing and sensor technology providing relatively cheap sensors which can take a variety of physical measurements. We use the sensors in a variety of ways. As a measurement of how a resource is being used on the host, e.g. correlating CPU usage (the resource) with CPU temperature (the sensor measurement). The sensors allow us to determine the presence or absence of the user on the host and physical user activity such as keyboard usage. We remark that "user" means the human using the host and although there may be more than one user, we simply say user. Although it is possible to obtain comprehensive user activity information, e.g. user identity and key strokes from surveillance cameras, due to concerns of user privacy, we generally only consider sensors that only provide binary information like the presence of a user or keyboard activity or other coarse-grained indirect data. Another source of environment information could be from physical security information management systems. Such systems are already in-place in many organizations and could provide relevant environment information whereby user activities can be derived, e.g. the door entry control system gives evidence that a particular user is in the machine room.

One usage of environment information is in enhancing IDS performance by providing an external source that is difficult to be accessed or compromised by malwares or intruders. The results of an environment sensing based malware detector can be correlated with alerts from an IDS to reduce false positives. While existing IDS may incorporate network traffic information in gateways which are external to the host, the difference is that we make further use of other tamper-proof sensors and fuse it with user presence and activity. The following example shows the difference from the network intrusion problem. Consider the case of a single email being sent. At the network level, there is insufficient information to be able to identify whether it is a spam email generated by malware. Whereas, in our framework, suppose that the email is sent in the absence of the user and user activity, we can conclude that the email has been sent automatically. Furthermore, in the absence of any additional information, it is reasonable for a default rule to classify this email as spam activity. In this paper, we give some application scenarios of malware detection – detecting when a botnet is using the host for email spam, distributed denial of service (DDoS) attack, and as a compute engine for offline dictionary attacks.

Environment information is also useful in other security applications. It increases the expressivity of access control and rate control policies by requiring privileged actions on a host to be correlated with physical user presence and physical activity. This prevents remote attacks which escalate privileges, e.g. enforce privileged actions to be only be performed if the administrator is present and using the console.

One advantage of our framework is that we are able to give reliable security guarantees even when the host is compromised. Without the fusion of sensor data from the environment surrounding the host, the attacker can simply hide inside the host or erase traces of an attack or intrusion. Some malware may even be able to shut down IDSs deployed in the host. A limitation of our framework is that the sensor data obtained is coarse grained and possibly noisy. Nevertheless, our evaluations show such coarse data is already useful in identifying certain mismatches between the host's and user's physical activities.

The rest of this paper is organized as follows. Sec. 2 introduces the framework of integrating the data from external sources to the access control or intrusion detection logic. We apply the framework to malware detection in Sec. 3 to demonstrate that information external to the host enhances the detection of malware activity. The framework is extended to rate and access control in Sec. 4. Related work is discussed in Sec. 5 and Sec. 6 concludes.

2   The Framework

Fig. 1 illustrates the relationship among different entities in our framework. The host considered in this paper is a stationary computer which typically includes keyboard, mouse, hard-disk, CPU, monitor, etc., and is operated through keyboard and mouse. Under this framework, *users* are persons who are directly accessing the computing resources. To access the computing resources, a user needs to be in the proximity of the host and interacting with it directly through the keyboard, mouse and display. Alternatively, users or attackers could be accessing the host remotely through a network connection. All network traffic in and out of the host is channeled through some routers. We consider all information processed and stored in the host as *internal* information. Potentially, internal information can be manipulated by an adversary if the host is compromised. We are more interested in the *external* information. In general, we call sensors installed outside the host *external* sensors, and the information gathered *external* information. External sensors could be an infrared sensor detecting whether a user is sitting in-front of the host's display, or a sensor installed in the router logging traffic information. The infra-red sensor is an example of an *environment sensor* gathering information from the physical environment, instead of the computed data from the host or routers. Information gathered can be classified into two types:

1. Information obtained from measuring computing resource usages, e.g. a temperature sensor measuring temperature near the motherboard (corresponding to CPU load), and a microphone to listen to sounds from the disk.
2. Information measuring user's activities, e.g. infrared sensors to detect user presence, pressure sensor to measure keyboard typing, etc. One method uses infra-red in a similar way as the common shop entrance alarm system. A reliable method is to derive the user presence from video captured by camera [14,15] but that may raise privacy concerns. However, video privacy was found to be an acceptable tradeoff to users [15].

Although we do not exclude the use of surveillance cameras as the environment sensors in our framework, the issue of user privacy must be taken into consideration in an implementation of the framework. A microphone not only can detect keyboard activity, but it can also record conversation among the users. A camera recording the user or display can also violate workplace privacy policies. Hence, we mainly consider binary information on user activities, such as whether a user is present, or detecting keyboard activities. Such information can be captured by sensors that are designed to give binary output or other coarse information, which alleviates privacy concerns, e.g. an infra-red sensor that detects user presence, or a camera that only outputs the detection outcomes.

All information gathered is channeled to a monitor which makes decisions. External sensors should communicate to the monitor securely to ensure the host is unable to compromise its integrity, authenticity and confidentiality. One solution is to have a separate private network for the sensors, e.g. a wireless sensor network with the external sensors as the nodes. Alternatively, the communication can still be tunneled through the host using cryptographic means. The privacy requirements and the need for a separate private network fit well with wireless sensor networks equipped with multi-modality sensors. There are many commercial wireless multi-sensor boards which fit our purposes, e.g. SBT80 from the EasySen [4] contains a number of sensors including infra-red, temperature and acoustic.

Besides wireless sensor networks, many physical security systems can provide relevant information for our monitor. For example, the door entry control system

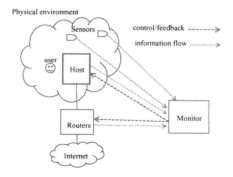

Fig. 1. The components of the framework

can give information about who gained access to a machine room, while surveillance cameras could reliably detect the presence of users near a console or other devices like scanner and printer. Although physical security systems are costly, some organizations could already have such systems in-place, together with a management system that is able to collect and process the data.

It is possible for an attacker to gain information similar to the sensory data, if the host is compromised, e.g. CPU temperature can be collected by the host and user presence can be inferred from keyboard or mouse events. Nevertheless, the CPU temperature and user presence information collected by sensors are still authentic and not subject to tampering.

3   Applying to Malware Detection

We now apply our framework to malware detection and give three malware detection implementations which detect email spamming, DDoS attack and password cracking.

A simple setup is to use two kinds of environment sensors. One detects whether the user is using the host, i.e. sitting at the machine. This can be done in a variety of ways, ranging from motion sensors to infrared sensors to video cameras. Another sensor records the temperature near the CPU. The first class of sensor records user activities while the second class measures the usage of computing resources. Network traffic of the host is also monitored at the router.

In our experiments, the malicious activities are carried out by a modified Agobot worm (also known as Gaobot). The worm sends spam email to other email accounts using the SMTP protocol, carries out a DDoS attack by flooding a target with UDP packets, and consumes CPU resources on the host to perform password cracking by hashing a dictionary of possible passwords.

The basic idea behind our detection rule is simple: the patterns of legitimate resource usage when the user is interacting with the host, is different from that when no user is present. If malware does not have the user presence information, its behavior will not be correlated with the user presence. We divide the time into intervals, in each interval, the user is either present or absent. The changepoint detection algorithm [5,6] is then applied to each interval to detect malicious activity. Table 1 gives an overview of the detection rules.

Table 1. Overview of malware detection rules

Malware Threat	Rules for triggering alarms
Email Spammer	(i) No user is present, and at least one email is sent; or (ii) A user is present, and changepoint detection decides that the cumulative sum of email sent exceeds a threshold.
DDoS Zombie	Changepoint detection detects the cumulative sum of the net outgoing packet rate exceeds thresholds for user present and absent
Password Cracker	Changepoint detection detects the cumulative sum of CPU temperature exceeds a certain threshold when user is absent

Table 2. Detection time of different spam worms. (Detection threshold $N = 120$ emails in $t = 6$ hours at user presence, and $N = 1$ during user absence.)

Spam worm	User present (min)	User absent (sec)
Storm	6.1	4
Rustock	3.6	3
Srizbi	0.07	< 1

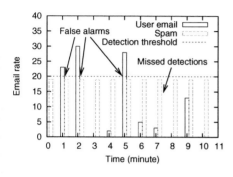

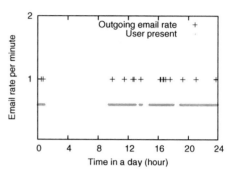

Fig. 2. False detections caused by email rate based spam detection

Fig. 3. Samples of user email rate

3.1 Changepoint Detection

The problem of changepoint detection [6] is to detect changes from normal behavior. We use a customized version of CuSum [7] to do such detection. In our model, behaviors are described as a real-valued time series of x_n. Normal behavior is estimated to have a value a or smaller. To detect an increase from the normal behavior, the following cumulative sum S_n is computed.

$$\begin{cases} S_0 = 0, \\ S_n = S_{n-1} + \max(0, x_n - a), \quad n \geq 1, \end{cases}$$

where x_n is the observation at time n from the sampling process. The value of a can be determined by the system administrator, or by observing samples of normal behaviors to select the smallest acceptable normal upper bound of x_n. If S_n exceeds the threshold N, a change point is detected at time n and the alarm will be triggered. Note that a can be exceeded when normal behavior is violated, so a is a lower detection threshold of abnormal behavior, S_n is the actual signal and N is the changepoint detection threshold. CuSum can be shown to be optimal under certain conditions [6]. As it is simple and efficient, it is suitable for real-time processing of streaming sensor data.

We use spam detection to show the difference between rate based detection and changepoint detection. Fig. 2 illustrates situations where rate based detection causes false positives and false negatives. Occasionally, a user email rate exceeds the spam detection threshold, causing false alarms, even though the high rate is a transient. On the other hand, spam malware can control its email rate to just below the threshold, by spreading the operation over a long period of time. Rate based spam detection do not report such cases correctly, while changepoint detection can. With changepoint detection, we can set the upper bound of normal email rate as a baseline, e.g. one email per minute, then accumulate the excess amount of emails over a time period. Thus, it computes within a time interval, the area in the graph enclosed below by the baseline and bounded above by the email rate curve. With changepoint detection, occasional high email rates do not cause false alarms, and constant medium email rates cannot evade detection.

Changepoint detection relies on empirical or administrative thresholds, advanced attackers may gain information on user presence and adapt their behavior accordingly. Our mechanism cannot fully stop such malware, but it effectively mitigates the malicious activity.

3.2   Experimental Setup

Our experimental setup consists of one router and several hosts connected by 100Mbps connections to the Internet through the router. First, we gather normal data from three uncompromised hosts for a period of 12 days. Next, we "compromise" one host by installing the modified Agobot on it and control it from another machine. The compromised host carries out different activities on demand: generate spam email, start a DDoS attack and perform password cracking. More experimental details are described in the relevant section.

Three types of sensor data are collected on the hosts: (i) user presence; (ii) CPU temperature; and (iii) network traffic. User presence is represented by a binary-valued time series, indicating whether the user is sitting at the host. We use infrared sensors to detect user presence. This is more reliable compared to using acoustic sensors to detect keyboard typing or mouse clicks. One reason is that a user can be simply looking at the monitor. Another reason is that malware can fool the sensor by playing back clicks. The CPU temperature is represented by a real-valued time series measuring temperature at the processor, which correlates to CPU load. In principle, the CPU temperature should be measured with a sensor between the CPU heat sink and fan, but we had difficulty in doing so with our sensor. To prove the concept, we used the CPU temperature obtained from the host's operating system as a proxy.[1] We remark that the sensor data should be measured and sent to the monitor via a secure channel, and thus our temperature readings is only a simulation to simplify the experiments. For network traffic, headers of all packets and partial payload passing through the router are logged.

3.3   Spam Detection

Spam can be sent out at different rates. Some worms like Storm and Rustock have been reported to send at lowish rates of 20 and 33 emails/min while others

---

[1] We use the system call $IDebugDataSpaces\text{->}ReadMsr()$ in Windows.

like Srizbi's rate is 1800 emails/min [12]. While 20 emails/min is probably too high for humans, malware could also send at lower rates. We remark that humans might also send email at high rate, e.g. when using a script to send emails to a group of recipients.

Our experiment is meant to show reliable spam detection when data from external sensors is included. We also experiment on different modes of sending email, namely, SMTP-based clients and also webmail clients.

Spam Detection Using the Framework. To detect bots that send spam, we use the following rules: (i) when the user is absent, any outgoing email flags a spamming activity; and (ii) when the user is present, changepoint detection is applied on the number of emails sent. Essentially, if over N emails are sent within a time interval of length t, the algorithm flags it as spamming activity, where N and t are the two tunable parameters.

The first rule relies on the fact that emails are usually directly sent to the mail servers when the user hits send. Any scheduled delay in delivery is based on the server itself. The actual value of N and t in the second rule can be learned from the normal traffic for each host. Although the rules are simple, no matter how slow the spam rate is, we can detect spam when the user is absent. So if a stealthy spam program sends out only a single email at night, this could slip out unnoticed by normal email rate based spam detection while we would detect it.

We apply CuSum to detect changes in the amount of emails sent when the user is present. We incorporate a limit on the accumulation time t, and set $a = 0$, $N = 120$ and $t = 6$ hours. The effect is that whenever there is an outgoing email, we accumulate the count, and no more than $N = 120$ emails can be sent in 6 hours. If the accumulated sum exceeds 120, we raise a spam alarm for the host. The allowable average email rate is three minutes per email. It is high for a human user, since users do not consistently send an email every 3 minutes for 6 hours. When user is absent, we set $N = 1$, meaning any outgoing email indicates a spam.

Experimental Results on Spammer Detection. The detection of outgoing email is done by matching packets with a list of signatures. Table 3 shows the signatures of email sent using SMTP and webmail. Email sent using SMTP protocol is relatively easy to detect, since an SMTP command `MAIL` indicates the user is submitting email. Webmail interfaces are more complex – Table 3 summarises how we identify emails sent using Hotmail, Gmail, NetEase, and SquirrelMail. The destination IP is first matched with a set of possible known servers. Next, we examine the first few bytes of packet payload to look for HTTP request method `POST`. Existence of such a method indicates that the client could be submitting email, logging into the mail server, making a request to retrieve email, requesting for the email listing, or requesting housekeeping operations. To determine whether the client is sending an email, different checks are carried out for different mail services. For Hotmail, we look for URI that starts with `mail/SendMessageLight.aspx?`. For NetEase, the request URI ends with `&func=mbox:compose`. For Gmail, the request URI contains `&view=up&act=sm`.[2]

---

[2] Gmail uses HTTPS from late Jan. 2010, but our experiments were performed earlier.

Table 3. Rules for email detection

SMTP	the SMTP request command is `MAIL`.
`hotmail.com`	The destination IP is in the set of `hotmail.com` server IPs, the protocol is HTTP, the HTTP request method is `POST`, and the HTTP request URI starts with `/mail/SendMessageLight.aspx?`
`netease.com`	The destination IP is in the set of `netease.com` server IPs, the protocol is HTTP, the HTTP request method is `POST`, and the HTTP request URI ends with `&func=mbox:compose`
`gmail.com`	The destination IP is in the set of `gmail.com` server IPs, the protocol is HTTP, the HTTP request method is `POST`, and the HTTP request URI contains `&view=up&act=sm`
SquirrelMail	A particular HTTP request immediately after an email is sent.

To perform these checks, we need to read 33 bytes into the HTTP message for Hotmail, 64 bytes for NetEase and 80 bytes for Gmail. Hence during packet captures, the packet payload needs to be logged partially. Detecting SquirrelMail is less straightforward as the payload is encrypted. We found that immediately after an email is sent, there is an HTTP Get request in plain text of a large size to fetch the listing of the current folder. The signatures enable us to identify the sending of email reliably. Compared to a typical spam filter that inspects the email content, our method has less privacy concerns.

Fig. 3 shows the typical email activity of a user in a day. About 10 to 20 emails are sent daily. It shows that our hypothesis that all emails are sent with the user present is reasonable.

In our experiment, spam is sent from the monitored host using the modified Agobot. We tested the detection of spam at rates corresponding to Srizbi, Rustock and Storm worms. Table 2 shows the detection time when the user is present and absent. Note that threshold N is set on the parameter of the accumulated email amount. It is easy to see the detection time is inversely proportional to the spam rate. Since the spam rate of Srizbi is much higher than Rustock or Storm, it takes least time to detect. When the user is present, the detection time of Srizbi is less than 0.1 minute and about 4 and 6 minutes for Rustock and Storm respectively. When the user is absent, all three spam worms are detected instantly, because the detection threshold $N = 1$ at user absence.

3.4 Detecting DDoS Zombie Attacks

This experiment deals with detecting zombies which carry out UDP packet flooding for a DDos attack. In this attack, the compromised host sends out UDP packets to a victim to consume the victim's network bandwidth. When the user is absent, legitimate network traffic rate is low and thus we can potentially detect the malicious UDP packet flood by observing the traffic rate. However, there could be background processes that generate network traffic, e.g. automated updates. Another scenario in our experiment is a legitimate P2P program. The P2P program constantly generates network traffic even when the user is absent.

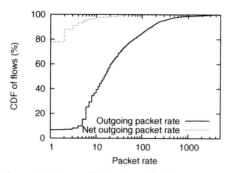

Fig. 4. Difference in the outgoing packet rate and the net outgoing packet rate of 2351 active TCP flows during user presence

Hence, it is desirable to derive another feature, instead of the overall rate, to distinguish UDP flood.

We observe that the UDP flood generates one-way traffic, whereas typical legitimate processes generate two-way traffic. This motivates us to consider the net outgoing packet rate p_{net},

$$p_{net} = \max(p_{out} - p_{in}, 0),$$

where p_{out} and p_{in} are the outgoing and incoming packet rate respectively. We apply CuSum on p_{net}, but with a different threshold a when the user is absent and present.

In addition to p_{net}, we also monitor the ratio r of outgoing packets that are not responded to,

$$r = p_{net}/p_{out}.$$

We have $0 \le r \le 1$ where $r = 1$ if the flow has only outgoing packets; and $r = 0$ if $p_{out} \le p_{in}$. The excess of p_{net} over a is accumulated only if $r \approx 1$.

Fig. 4 compares the maximum net outgoing packet rate p_{net} and the outgoing packet rate p_{out} of 2,351 non-attack TCP flows, observed in 10 minutes. A flow is identified by (local IP, remote IP, transport protocol) – port numbers are not differentiated as attackers may open multiple ports to flood the same victim. Over 60% of the flows have the maximum $p_{out} > 10$ packets a minute; whereas less than 5% of the flows have the maximum $p_{net} > 10$. In some flow, maximum p_{out} is 2,443 packets per minute, but the maximum p_{net} is as low as 10 packets.

Fig. 5 shows the distribution of p_{net} for 13,620 flows. Fig. 5(a) shows the net outgoing packet rate is close to 0 for most flows. When the user is present, 35% of the flows have $p_{net} = 0$; and 80% flows have p_{net} less than 10 packets a minute. When the user is absent, 90% of the flows have $p_{net} = 0$. Fig. 5(b) shows that the difference in p_{net} when user is present and absent, it can be as large as 600 for some flows, so different upper bounds of normal p_{net} should be used for user presence and absence and for each flow.

From Fig. 5(a), initializing the upper bound of normal p_{net} to be $a = 60$ packets per minute is sufficient for most flows. Parameter a can be lowered by

372   E.-C. Chang et al.

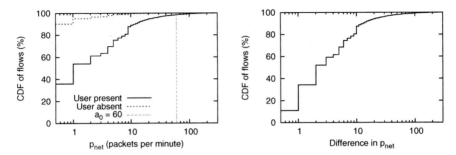

(a) Distribution of flow net outgoing (b) Difference in the flow rates when user
packet rates   is present and absent

Fig. 5. Distribution of the maximum net outgoing packet rate p_{net} with 13,620 TCP and UDP flows, each flow is observed for 10 minutes during user presence and absence

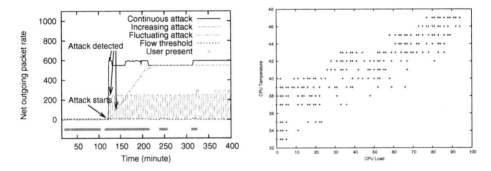

Fig. 6. Net outgoing packet rate of the DDoS attack flow in different attack patterns

Fig. 7. Correlation of CPU load and CPU temperature

examining the online traffic. To accumulate the excess of p_{net} over a, r must be close to 1 and we set it at 0.95. The threshold to trigger an alarm is $N = 800$ packets, accumulated over 20 minutes. It ensures an attack flow can be detected if at least 2 UDP packets are sent a second on average.

Some non-attack flows have large net outgoing packet rate. However, they do not cause false alarms, because the outgoing packets are responded to, or r is not close to 1. In terms of absolute value, $p_{net} = 1278$ is high, but its $p_{out} = 2,812$, making $r = 0.45$, so there is 1 response in about 2 packets, the ratio is reasonable and hence the high net outgoing packet rate is also accepted.

Fig. 6 shows the net outgoing packet rate p_{net} of the attack flow under 3 different attack scenarios. The upper bound a of normal p_{net} is 10 and 2 packets a minute for user present and absent respectively. These bounds are determined from analyzing the training data of the flow. The attack starts at the 125th minute. For the continuous attack, p_{net} sharply increases to around 600. After

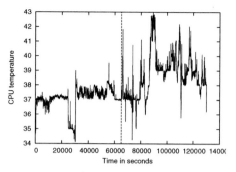

Fig. 8. CPU temperature variation during user absence and presence. User is absent from 0 to 64,000 second; and present from 64,000 second onwards. The vertical line separates user absence from presence.

1.36 minutes, the alarm is triggered. The increasing rate attack increases its attack intensity very slowly to delay detection. This attack might not be detected if the detector adapts to the flow rate in near real time. Our approach detects the attack in about 15 minutes, long before it reaches its peak rate. The fluctuating attack in Fig. 6 constrains the attack intensity, and releases attack traffic in pulses. This is to avoid detection if average traffic rate or peak rate is used by the detector. Our approach detects the fluctuating attack within 3 minutes.

3.5   Detecting Misuse of Compute Resources

Bots are often recruited to invert cryptographic functions to break passwords. Inverting such functions requires extensive computations which are distributed to the bots. To detect such activities, we look for increases in the CPU load after user has been absent for a while. As CPU load is internal to the host, we rely on CPU temperature as a measure of the CPU load.

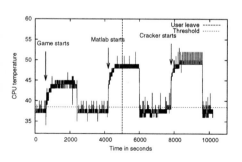

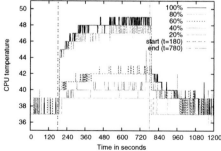

Fig. 9. CPU temperature variation during various activities

Fig. 10. Correlation of attack intensity and CPU temperature

Fig. 7 shows the correlation between CPU load and temperature. The correlation is good but it includes fluctuation and noise. Fig. 8 shows the temperature when a user is present and absent. Note when the user is absent, the temperature is around 37°C, and varies less. We measured the temperature during automated software update and found the temperature increase of 2-3°.

We employ CuSum to detect the increase in CPU temperature. Fig. 8 shows normal temperature variations during user presence and absence. From the observation of Fig. 8, we set the upper bound of system idle temperature to be $a = 38.5$°C. We set the threshold for the accumulated increase in temperature as $N = 2400$ in 30 minutes. This threshold N is chosen to allow software update that increases the CPU temperature by 2°and lasts for 20 minutes. We set a grace period of $g = 10$ minutes at the transition from user presence to absence, that is, if the changepoint is detected within 10 minutes after a user leaves, the alarm is not activated.

Fig. 9 shows the temperature during various computation tasks. The changepoints in temperature for playing games and running matlab are detected 10.4 minutes and 5.2 minutes respectively after they start. Since the user is present or just left when the changepoint occurs, the activities are considered initiated by the user and accepted as normal. The password cracker activity triggers an alarm 4.5 minutes after it starts. Since the changepoint is detected when user is absent, it is considered as malicious computation. If the malicious computation executes during user presence, it can be noted by the user.

We also conducted an experiment which varies the intensity of the CPU usage. This investigates if the CPU usage can be detected when the malware throttles its computation at a lower rate. CPU usage is controlled as follows: for each one-second interval, the bot computes at full speed for x seconds and then sleep for $1 - x$ seconds, where $x < 1$. We denote the CPU usage to be $100x\%$ in Fig. 10. We carry out the attack for 600 seconds (starts at 180 seconds and ends at 780 seconds). Fig. 9 shows the temperature under intensity variation. Note that after the attacks stop, the temperature gradually returns to normal. For the password computation running at 100% usage, we detect the change after about 4.5 minutes. For the computation at 20% usage, we can also detect the change if the computation lasts for more than 20 minutes. To evade detection, the malicious computation can only further reduce its CPU usage or shorten its execution time. Thus, our system effectively limits the amount of malicious computation.

We need to handle carefully the non-malicious programs that commonly run when no user is present. Besides system auto-updates, these programs include nightly backup, nightly virus scan, remote desktop and user scheduled computation. Backup and virus scan are regular tasks. Their resource consumption can be profiled, in terms of the start time, duration, and the increase in CPU temperature. Based on our measurement, system backup only increases the CPU temperature by 1-3°. Virus scan usually increases the CPU temperature by 2-3°. These host profiles are basis of a whitelist kept by the monitor to suppress false alarms. Even if attacker tries to hide the malware execution by running it at the same time as these tasks, the excess increase in temperature or duration will still trigger the alarm.

User scheduled computations may cause irregular behavior. As the execution of scheduled computation can be planned ahead, the user simply declares in advance to the monitor the estimated process start time, duration and CPU load (converted to temperature increases by the monitor). The monitor suppresses any false alarm within the specified resource consumption. The user is advised to give a conservative estimation, for it is better for the user to intervene if excess resources are consumed, than allowing the attacker to free ride.

4 Application to Access Control and Rate Control

Here we investigate how environment information can be useful in controlling and allocating resources. A security policy may require administrators to be physically inside the machine room to access server consoles and administrative tools. In order to mitigate malware from sending spam email, we could implement rate control in the router or the mail server, and the rate limit is based on user presence. In both cases, environment information is used as a condition to access certain resources. Note that the first case is on access control, while the second is on rate control.

4.1 Access Control

Our framework can be used to implement location-based access control. One location-based access control scheme was proposed by Ardagna et al. [8] to restrict access to certain resources based on physical location of the user. In their work, the physical location is obtained from mobile devices, such as mobile phones carried by users. Our framework also implements location-based access control, but in a different way. Their work adopts a user-centric approach where the device is attached to the user and user's location is measured in order to figure out which resources can be accessed. We adopt a resource-centric approach where the device is attached to the resource and user presence is observed near the resource in order to decide whether to grant the access. Both approaches have advantages and disadvantages.

Our access control policy not only incorporates user presence information but also user activity information. For example, the user activity information can be "the user has typed some keys". Enforcement is implemented both on the host and router depending on the type of the resource. Enforcement implemented on the host implicitly assumes that malware is not in control of the host and the host decides the access based on environmental information gathered by the monitor, but the malware cannot affect access control policies at the environment level. Here we give two access control policies as examples.

1. *The user can execute the* `/usr/bin/sudo` *program only if he is sitting at the host.* This policy is used to mitigate the problem of remote attacks - it requires that there is a human present before the sudo operation is allowed.

This policy has to be enforced on the host. A remote attacker who does not yet have control of the host would be prevented from performing actions which could be used to infect the operating system.

2. *The user can send email only if he is sitting at the computer and has mouse or keyboard activity.* This policy is used to prevent malware from sending email while the user is away. Since user activity is enforced in the policy, it also prevents sending email while the user is idle, e.g. watching a movie. The intuition is that the user must have performed some typing or mouse action in order to send an email. Unlike user presence, which can be thought of as being a continuous signal, mouse and keyboard input are discrete events which may happen at time points which do not overlap with the email sending time interval. Thus, the precise meaning of the policy is "An email can be sent at time t if user presence is observed at that t and there is mouse or keyboard input between $[t - \Delta, t + \Delta]$". This policy is enforced in the router or the mail server instead of the host and thus provides enforcement even when the host is compromised.

4.2   Rate Control

Previously we showed that abnormal resource usage when the user is absent can be easily detected under several scenarios. This can be easily extended to controlling the resource usage rate in the case of activities involving external resources. Two natural scenarios of external rate control are:

- **Shaping Network Traffic**
  To mitigate computers being used as bots to perform DDoS attacks, router can shape network traffic based on user presence information. By limiting the traffic on flows, this becomes a form of inverse quality of service, providing reduced quality when the user is not present. If P2P programs are being used, this would save some network bandwidth, e.g. if the host uses Skype and becomes a Skype supernode, it could lose its supernode status under the reduced network flow.
- **Sending Email**
  Similarly, the emails could be simply denied when the user is absent. If the threshold is above zero, then for both webmail and SMTP, the router can simply rate limit the protocol. Alternatively for an SMTP server, it could quarantine email beyond the threshold. In both cases, outgoing spam emails are rate limited possibly to zero.

  The email rate can also be rate limited when the user is present. The idea is that email is based on typing and/or mouse clicks. This data can also be recorded using environmental sensors. The email rate can then be based on a function of the detected keystrokes and/or mouse clicks.

The framework can make resource rate limiting policies more flexible and usable. The idea is to have feedback if a usage is too high for a resource. External sensors can then be used as a secure channel to request a higher resource rate.

For example, a monitor on the host can display the resource usage and warn the user if he is reaching the limit. The user can have something as simple as a button which is pressed to function as the secure request channel to obtain more network bandwidth or more emails. Notice that such a policy cannot be done securely without the help of external environment information.

In the access and rate control application discussed above, to control the resource utilization, essentially we need to verify whether an entity is "human". Instead of using external environment to infer user presence, alternatively, CAPTCHA [9] or graphical Turing test could be implemented to verify that the user is human. Using the environment information has the advantage that the users are not interrupted by the challenges issued by the graphical Turing test.

5   Related Work

If we consider a computer host to include the host, the user channel and the network channel, then host security can be divided into: (*i*) software security, which ensures the software running in the host is authentic, e.g. antivirus [19], system call filtering [16] and binary authentication [17]; (*ii*) user security, which ensures the user is authentic, e.g. password/biometric authentication, physical perimeters and surveillance camera monitoring; and (*iii*) network security, which ensures the network communication is authentic, e.g. personal firewalls [18]. Our approach to enhance host security is substantially different from the existing designs in three aspects. Firstly, the model we propose fuses data from a few channels of external environment sensors to monitor the host activity. Secondly, as our model does not require controlling or modifying the host OS or software, it is able to provide some security even when the host is compromised. Thirdly, our system detects outbound or on-host malware execution, which complements intrusion detection.

There are a few works which correlates information from different channels to improve host security. The system BINDER [10] correlates user events (user input), process events (process creation and process termination), and network events (connection request, data arrival and domain name lookup) to detect malware. Both our malware detection system and BINDER correlate user presence information and system behaviour to detect malware. BINDER uses information collected by the user's machine, which potentially could be manipulated by the compromised host.

The systems proposed by Gu et al. [11] and Yen et al. [13] detect botnets by analyzing and correlating network traces. The two systems and our malware detection system use information from the network router rather than the host in question so as to be able to deal with the case when the host is compromised and gives false information. The difference with our malware detection system is that we have user presence and activity information in addition to network information.

Kumar et al. proposed a system [14] which continuously monitors user's biometric identity and locks up the computer if it cannot detect the correct user.

Both their system and our access control system use physical user information to provide additional factor for authentication. There are two main differences between the two. Firstly, our system only detects user presence information, while their system detects user's biometric information which is much stronger but gives less privacy. Secondly, their system runs entirely in the user's machine, thus it cannot guarantee the authentication once the machine has been compromised.

Location-based access control (LBAC) has been actively researched on wireless networks, e.g. [20]. The model in LBAC assumes user devices are mobile, their locations are tracked for service continuity, or verified before granting access. The problem we address is different in that we are not dealing with mobile devices, instead our focus is on utilizing a combination of environment data to enhance security, such as to detect malware on the host and to regulate the usage of resources by the host.

6   Conclusion

In this paper, we proposed a framework that incorporates environment information in securing host computers in a few ways: by using the environment information as an additional source of information for malware detection, or by integrating the environment information with existing conditions in rate-control mechanisms and access control policies. We argued that, since the sensors are "external" with respect to the host, they are difficult to be accessed and tampered by a compromised host. Furthermore, by investigating several applications, we showed that the simple and coarse information on user activities and resource usages is sufficient to provide good performance in malware detection, and is useful in expressing certain rate-control and access control policies. We have also identified a few important requirements of the sensors, in particular, the concerns of user-privacy and the need of a secure channel. Thus, we have proposed a simple and effective framework for security enhancement which is arguably safe against compromise by attackers.

The framework also takes advantage of the growing popularity of pervasive computing and sensor networks. As the trend in cost of wireless multi-modality sensors is decreasing, applications of our framework are feasible for cost-effective deployment in the near future.

References

1. The Myth of The Four-minute Windows Survival Time,
   http://www.edbott.com/weblog/?p=2071
2. Unpatched PC 'Survival Time' Just 16 Minutes,
   http://www.informationweek.com/news/
   showArticle.jhtml?articleID=29106061
3. Conficker, http://en.wikipedia.org/wiki/Conficker
4. EasySen SBT80 Product Page, http://www.easysen.com/SBT80.htm

5. Wang, H., Zhang, D., Shin, K.G.: Detecting SYN Flooding Attacks. In: IEEE InfoCom (2002)
6. Basseville, M., Nikiforov, I.V.: Detection of Abrupt Changes: Theory and Application. Prentice-Hall, Englewood Cliffs (1993)
7. Page, E.S.: Continuous Inspection Schemes. Biometrika (1954)
8. Ardagna, C.A., Cremonini, M., Damiani, E., di Vimercati, S.D.C., Samarati, P.: Supporting Location-Based Conditions in Access Control Policies. In: ACSAC (2006)
9. Von Ahn, L., Blum, M., Hopper, N.J., Langford, J.: CAPTCHA: Using hard AI problems for security. In: Biham, E. (ed.) EUROCRYPT 2003. LNCS, vol. 2656. Springer, Heidelberg (2003)
10. Cui, W., Katz, R.H., Tan, W-.T.: Design and Implementation of an Extrusion-based Break-In Detector for Personal Computers. In: ACSAC (2005)
11. Gu, G., Porras, P., Yegneswaran, V., Fong, M., Lee, W.: BotHunter: Detecting Malware Infection Through IDS-Driven Dialog Correlation. In: USENIX Security (2005)
12. John, J.P., Moshchuk, A., Gribble, S.D., Krishnamurthy, A.: Studying Spamming Botnets Using Botlab. In: NSDI (2009)
13. Yen, T.-.F., Reiter, M.K.: Traffic Aggregation for Malware Detection. In: GI Intl. Conf. on Detection of Intrusions and Malware, and Vulnerability Assessment (2008)
14. Kumar, S., Sim, T., Janakiraman, R., Zhang, S.: Using Continuous Biometric Verification to Protect Interactive Login Sessions. In: ACSAC (2005)
15. Kwang, G.K., Yap, R.H.C., Sim, T., Ramnath, R.: An Usability Study of Continous Biometrics Authentication. In: IAPR/IEEE Intl. Conf. on Biometrics (2009)
16. Provos, N.: Improving Host Security with System Call Policies. In: USENIX Security (2003)
17. Halim, F., Ramnath, R., Sufatrio Wu, Y., Yap, R.H.C.: A Lightweight Binary Authentication System for Windows. In: IFIPTM (2008)
18. Ingham, K., Forrest, S.: A History and Survey of Network Firewalls. Tech. Rep. TR-CS-2002-37, University of New Mexico Computer Science Department (2002)
19. Post, G., Kagan, A.: The Use and Effectiveness of Anti-Virus Software. Computers & Security 17(7) (1998)
20. Ardagna, C.A., Cremonini, M., Damiani, E., di Vimercati, S.D.C., Samarati, P.: Supporting Location-Based Conditions in Access Control Policies. In: ASIACCS (2006)

FADE: Secure Overlay Cloud Storage with File Assured Deletion

Yang Tang[1], Patrick P.C. Lee[1], John C.S. Lui[1], and Radia Perlman[2]

[1] The Chinese University of Hong Kong
[2] Intel Labs
{tangyang,pclee,cslui}@cse.cuhk.edu.hk, radiaperlman@gmail.com

Abstract. While we can now outsource data backup to third-party cloud storage services so as to reduce data management costs, security concerns arise in terms of ensuring the privacy and integrity of outsourced data. We design *FADE*, a practical, implementable, and readily deployable cloud storage system that focuses on protecting deleted data with policy-based file assured deletion. FADE is built upon standard cryptographic techniques, such that it encrypts outsourced data files to guarantee their privacy and integrity, and most importantly, assuredly deletes files to make them unrecoverable to anyone (including those who manage the cloud storage) upon revocations of file access policies. In particular, the design of FADE is geared toward the objective that it acts as an overlay system that works seamlessly atop today's cloud storage services. To demonstrate this objective, we implement a working prototype of FADE atop Amazon S3, one of today's cloud storage services, and empirically show that FADE provides policy-based file assured deletion with a minimal trade-off of performance overhead. Our work provides insights of how to incorporate value-added security features into current data outsourcing applications.

Keywords: Policy-based file assured deletion, cloud storage, prototype implementation.

1 Introduction

Cloud storage (e.g., Amazon S3 [2], MyAsiaCloud [11]) offers an abstraction of infinite storage space for clients to host data, in a pay-as-you-go manner [3]. For example, SmugMug [19], a photo sharing website, chose to host terabytes of photos on Amazon S3 in 2006 and saved about 500K US dollars on storage devices [1]. Thus, instead of self-maintaining data centers, enterprises can now outsource the storage of a bulk amount of digitized content to those third-party cloud storage providers so as to save the financial overhead in data management. Apart from enterprises, individuals can also benefit from cloud storage as a result of the advent of mobile devices (e.g., smartphones, laptops). Given that mobile devices have limited storage space in general, individuals can move audio/video files to the cloud and make effective use of space in their mobile devices.

S. Jajodia and J. Zhou (Eds.): SecureComm 2010, LNICST 50, pp. 380–397, 2010.
© Institute for Computer Sciences, Social Informatics and Telecommunications Engineering 2010

However, privacy and integrity concerns become relevant as we now count on third parities to host possibly sensitive data. To protect outsourced data, a straightforward approach is to apply cryptographic encryption onto sensitive data with a set of encryption keys, yet maintaining and protecting such encryption keys will create another security issue. One specific issue is that upon requests of deletion of files, cloud storage providers may not completely remove all file copies (e.g., cloud storage providers may make multiple file backup copies and distribute them over the cloud for reliability, and clients do not know the number or even the existence of these backup copies), and eventually have the data disclosed if the encryption keys are unexpectedly obtained, either by accidents or by malicious attacks. Therefore, we seek to achieve a major security goal called *file assured deletion*, meaning that files are reliably deleted and remain permanently unrecoverable and inaccessible by any party.

The security concerns motivate us, as cloud clients, to develop a secure cloud storage system that provides file assured deletion. However, a key challenge of building such a system is that cloud storage infrastructures are externally owned and managed by third-party cloud providers, and hence the system should never assume any structural changes (in protocol or hardware levels) in cloud infrastructures. Thus, it is important to design a secure *overlay* cloud storage system that can work seamlessly atop existing cloud storage services.

In this paper, we present FADE, a secure overlay cloud storage system that ensures file assured deletion and works seamlessly atop today's cloud storage services. FADE decouples the management of encrypted data and encryption keys, such that encrypted data remains on third-party (untrusted) cloud storage providers, while encryption keys are independently maintained by a key manager service, whose trustworthiness can be enforced using a quorum scheme [18]. FADE generalizes time-based file assured deletion [5,14] (i.e., files are assuredly deleted upon time expiration) into a more fine-grained approach called *policy-based file assured deletion*, in which files are associated with more flexible *file access policies* (e.g., time expiration, read/write permissions of authorized users) and are assuredly deleted when the associated file access policies are revoked and become obsolete.

A motivating application of FADE is cloud-based backup systems (e.g., JungleDisk [7], Cumulus [21]), which use the cloud as the backup storage for files. FADE can be viewed as a value-added security service that further enhances the security properties of the existing cloud-based backup systems.

In summary, our paper makes the following contributions:

- We propose a new *policy-based file assured deletion* scheme that reliably deletes files with regard to revoked file access policies. In this context, we design the key management schemes for various file manipulation operations.
- We implement a working prototype of FADE atop Amazon S3 [2]. Our implementation aims to illustrate that various applications can benefit from FADE, such as cloud-based backup systems. FADE consists of a set of API interfaces that we can export, so that we can adapt FADE into different cloud storage implementations.

- We empirically evaluate the performance overhead of FADE atop Amazon S3, and using realistic experiments, we show the feasibility of FADE in improving the security protection of data storage on the cloud.

The remainder of the paper proceeds as follows. In Section 2, we present the design of policy-base file assured deletion, a major building block of FADE. In Section 3, we explain the implementation details of FADE. In Section 4, we evaluate FADE atop Amazon S3. Section 5 discusses the limitations of FADE and possible enhancements. In Section 6, we review related work on protecting outsourced data storage. Finally, Section 7 concludes.

2   Policy-Based File Assured Deletion

We present *policy-based file assured deletion*, the major design building block of our FADE architecture. Our main focus is to deal with the cryptographic key operations that enable file assured deletion. We first review time-based file assured deletion. We then explain how it can be extended to policy-based file assured deletion.

2.1   Background

Time-based file assured deletion, which is first introduced in [14], means that files can be securely deleted and remain permanently inaccessible after a predefined duration. The main idea is that a file is encrypted with a *data key*, and this data key is further encrypted with a *control key* that is maintained by a separate key manager service (known as *Ephemerizer* [14]). In [14], the control key is *time-based*, meaning that it will be completely removed by the key manager when an expiration time is reached, where the expiration time is specified when the file is first declared. Without the control key, the data key and hence the data file remain encrypted and are deemed to be inaccessible. Thus, the main security property of file assured deletion is that even if a cloud provider does not remove expired file copies from its storage, those files remain encrypted and unrecoverable.

Time-based file assured deletion is later prototyped in Vanish [5]. Vanish divides a data key into multiple key shares, which are then stored in different nodes of a peer-to-peer network. Nodes remove the key shares that reside in their caches for 8 hours. If a file needs to remain accessible after 8 hours, then the file owner needs to update the key shares in node caches.

However, both [14] and [5] target only the assured deletion upon time expiration, and do not consider a more fine-grained control of assured deletion with respect to different file access policies. We elaborate this issue in Section 2.2.

2.2   Policy-Based Deletion

We associate each file with a single atomic *file access policy* (or *policy* for short), or more generally, a Boolean combination of atomic policies. Each (atomic) policy is associated with a control key, and all the control keys are maintained by the key manager. Similar to time-based deletion, the file content is encrypted with a data key, and the data key is further encrypted with the control keys corresponding to the policy combination. When a policy is revoked, the corresponding control key will be removed from the key manager. Thus, when the policy combination associated with a file is revoked and no longer holds, the data key and hence the encrypted content of the file cannot be recovered with the control keys of the policies. In this case, we say the file is deleted. The main idea of policy-based deletion is to delete files that are associated with revoked policies.

The definitions of policies vary depending on applications. Time-based deletion is a special case under our framework, and policies with other access rights can be defined. To motivate the use of policy-based deletion, let us consider a scenario where a company outsources its data to the cloud. We consider four practical cases where policy-based deletion will be useful:

- **Storing files for tenured employees.** For each employee (e.g., Alice), we can define a *user-based* policy *"P: Alice is an employee"*, and associate this policy with all files of Alice. If Alice quits her job, then the key manager will expunge the control key of policy P. Thus, nobody including Alice can access the files associated with P on the cloud, and those files are said to be deleted.

- **Storing files for contract-based employees.** An employee may be affiliated with the company for only a fixed length of time. Then we can form a combination of the user-based and time-based policies for employees' files. For example, for a contract-based employee Bob whose contract expires on 2010-01-01, we have two policies *"P_1: Bob is an employee"* and *"P_2: valid before 2010-01-01"*. Then all files of Bob are associated with the policy combination $P_1 \wedge P_2$. If either P_1 or P_2 is revoked, then Bob's files are deleted.

- **Storing files for a team of employees.** The company may have different teams, each of which has more than one employee. As in above, we can assign each employee i a policy combination $P_{i1} \wedge P_{i2}$, where P_{i1} and P_{i2} denote the user-based and time-based policies, respectively. We then associate the team's files with the disjunctive combination $(P_{11} \wedge P_{12}) \vee (P_{21} \wedge P_{22}) \vee \cdots \vee (P_{N1} \wedge P_{N2})$ for employees $1, 2, \ldots, N$. Thus, the team's files can be accessed by any one of the employees, and will be deleted when the policies of all employees of the team are revoked.

- **Switching a cloud provider.** The company can define a *customer-based* policy *"P: a customer of cloud provider X"*, and all files that are stored on cloud X are tied with policy P. If the company switches to a new cloud provider, then it can revoke policy P. Thus, all files on cloud X will be deleted.

Policy-based deletion follows the similar notion of *attribute-based encryption (ABE)* [6,16,17], in which data can be accessed only if a subset of attributes (policies) are satisfied. However, our work is different from ABE in two aspects. First, we focus on how to *delete* data, while ABE focuses on how to *access* data based on attributes. Second, because of the different design objectives, ABE gives users the decryption keys of the associated attributes, so that they can access files that satisfy the attributes. On the other hand, in policy-based deletion, we do *not* share with users any decryption keys of policies, which instead are all maintained in the key manager. Our focus is to appropriately remove keys in the key manager so as to guarantee file assured deletion, which is an important security property when we outsource data storage to the cloud. This guides us into a different design space in contrast with existing ABE approaches.

2.3   Participants in the System

Our system is composed of three participants: the *data owner*, the *key manager*, and the *storage cloud*. They are described as follows.

Data owner. The data owner is the entity that originates file data to be stored on the cloud. It may be a file system of a PC, a user-level program, a mobile device, or even in the form of a plug-in of a client application.

Key manager. The key manager maintains the policy-based control keys that are used to encrypt data keys. It responds to the data owner's requests by performing encryption, decryption, renewal, and revocation to the control keys.

Storage cloud. The storage cloud is maintained by a third-party cloud provider (e.g., Amazon S3) and keeps the data on behalf of the data owner. We emphasize that we do *not* require any protocol and implementation changes on the storage cloud to support our system. Even a naive storage service that merely provides file upload/download operations will be suitable.

2.4   Threat Models and Assumptions

Our main design goal is to provide assured deletion of files produced by the data owner. A file is deleted (or permanently inaccessible) if its policy is revoked and becomes obsolete. Here, we assume that the control key associated with a revoked policy is reliably removed by the key manager. Thus, by assured deletion of files, we mean that any existing file copy that are associated with revoked policies will remain permanently encrypted and unrecoverable.

The key manager can be deployed as a minimally trusted third-party service. By minimally trusted, we mean that the key manager reliably removes the control keys of revoked policies. However, it is possible that the key manager can be compromised. In this case, an attacker can recover the files that are associated with existing active policies. On the other hand, files that are associated with revoked policies still remain inaccessible, as the control keys are removed. Hence, file assured deletion is achieved.

It is still important to improve the robustness of the key manager service to minimize its chance of being compromised. To achieve this, we can use a quorum of key managers [18], in which we create n key shares for a key, such that any $k < n$ of the key shares can be used to recover the key. While the quorum scheme increases the storage overhead of keys, this is justified as keys are of much smaller size than data files.

Before accessing the active keys in the key manager, the data owner needs to present authentication credentials (e.g., based on public key infrastructure certificates) to the key manager to show that it satisfies the proper policies associated with the files. We assume that the data owner does not disclose any successfully decrypted file to unauthorized parties.

2.5   The Basics - File Upload/Download

We now introduce the basics of uploading/downloading files to/from the cloud storage. We first assume that each file is associated with a single policy, and then explain how a file is associated with multiple policies in Section 2.7.

Our design is based on *blinded RSA* [14,20], in which the data owner requests the key manager to decrypt a blinded version of the encrypted data key. If the associated policy is satisfied, then the key manager will decrypt and return the blinded version of the original data key. The data owner can then recover the data key. In this way, the actual content of the data key remains confidential to the key manager as well as to any attacker that sniffs the communication between the data owner and the key manager.

We first summarize the major notation used throughout the paper. For each policy i, the key manager generates two secret large RSA prime numbers p_i and q_i and computes the product $n_i = p_i q_i$[1]. The key manager then randomly chooses the RSA public-private control key pair (e_i, d_i). The parameters (n_i, e_i) will be publicized, while d_i is securely stored in the key manager. On the other hand, when the data owner encrypts a file F, it randomly generates a data key K, and a secret key S_i that corresponds to policy P_i. We let $\{m\}_k$ denote a message m encrypted with key k using symmetric-key encryption (e.g., AES). We let R be the blinded component when we use blinded RSA for the exchanges of cryptographic keys.

Suppose that F is associated with policy P_i. Our goal here is to ensure that K, and hence F, are accessible only when policy P_i is satisfied. Note that we only present the operations on cryptographic keys, while the implementation subtleties, such as metadata, will be discussed in Section 3. Also, when we raise some number to exponents e_i or d_i, it must be done over modulo n_i. For brevity, we drop "mod n_i" in our discussion.

File upload. Figure 1 shows the file upload operation. The data owner first requests the public key (n_i, e_i) of policy P_i from the key manager, and caches (n_i, e_i) for subsequent uses if the same policy P_i is associated with other files. Then the data owner generates two random keys K and S_i, and sends $\{K\}_{S_i}$, $S_i^{e_i}$, and $\{F\}_K$ to the cloud[2]. Then the data owner can discard K and S_i.

File download. Figure 2 shows the file download operation. The data owner fetches $\{K\}_{S_i}$, $S_i^{e_i}$, and $\{F\}_K$ from the storage cloud. Then the data owner

---

[1] We require that each policy i uses a distinct n_i to avoid the common modulus attack on RSA [10].

[2] We point out that the encrypted keys (i.e., $\{K\}_{S_i}$, $S_i^{e_i}$) can be stored in the cloud without creating risks of leaking confidential information.

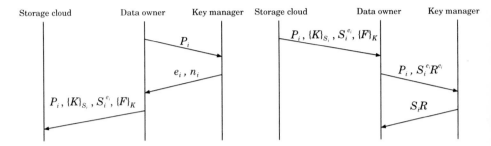

Fig. 1. File upload   **Fig. 2.** File download

generates a secret random number R, computes R^{e_i}, and sends $S_i^{e_i} \cdot R^{e_i} = (S_i R)^{e_i}$ to the key manager to request for decryption. The key manager then computes and returns $((S_i R)^{e_i})^{d_i} = S_i R$ to the data owner. The data owner can now remove R and obtain S_i, and decrypt $\{K\}_{S_i}$ and hence $\{F\}_K$.

Integrity. To protect the integrity of a file, the data owner needs to compute an HMAC on every encrypted file and stores the HMAC, together with the encrypted file, in the cloud storage. When a file is downloaded, the data owner will check whether the HMAC is valid before decrypting the file. We assume that the data owner has a long-term private secret for the HMAC computation.

2.6 Policy Revocation for File Assured Deletion

If a policy P_i is revoked, then the key manager completely removes the private key d_i and the secret prime numbers p_i and q_i. Thus, we cannot recover S_i from $S_i^{e_i}$, and hence cannot recover K and the file F. We say that the file F, which is tied to policy P_i, is assuredly deleted. Note that the policy revocation operations do not involve interactions with the storage cloud.

2.7 Multiple Policies

In addition to one policy per file, FADE supports a Boolean combination of multiple policies. We mainly focus on two kinds of logical connectives: (i) the conjunction (AND), which means the data is accessible only when every policy is satisfied; and (ii) the disjunction (OR), which means if any policy is satisfied, then the data is accessible.

- **Conjunctive Policies.** Suppose that F is associated with conjunctive policies $P_1 \wedge P_2 \wedge \cdots \wedge P_m$. To upload F to the storage cloud, the data owner first randomly generates a data key K, and secret keys $S_1, S_2, \ldots, S_m$. It then sends the following to the storage cloud: $\{\{K\}_{S_1}\}_{S_2} \cdots_{S_m}$, $S_1^{e_1}$, $S_2^{e_2}$, $\ldots, S_m^{e_m}$, and $\{F\}_K$. On the other hand, to recover F, the data owner generates a random number R and sends $(S_1 R)^{e_1}$, $(S_2 R)^{e_2}$, $\ldots, (S_m R)^{e_m}$ to the key manager, which then returns $S_1 R, S_2 R, \ldots, S_m R$. The data owner can then recover $S_1, S_2, \ldots, S_m$, and hence K and F.

– **Disjunctive Policies.** Suppose that F is associated with disjunctive policies $P_{i_1} \vee P_{i_2} \vee \cdots \vee P_{i_m}$. To upload F to the cloud, the data owner will send the following: $\{K\}_{S_1}, \{K\}_{S_2}, \ldots, \{K\}_{S_m}, S_1^{e_1}, S_2^{e_2}, \ldots, S_m^{e_m}$, and $\{F\}_K$. Therefore, the data owner needs to compute m different encrypted copies of K. On the other hand, to recover F, we can use any one of the policies to decrypt the file, as in the above operations.

To delete a file associated with conjunctive policies, we simply revoke any of the policies (say, P_j). Thus, we cannot recover S_j and hence the data key K and file F. On the other hand, to delete a file associated with disjunctive policies, we need to revoke all policies, so that $S_j^{e_j}$ cannot be recovered for all j. Note that for any Boolean combination of policies, we can express it in canonical form, e.g., in the disjunction (OR) of conjunctive (AND) policies.

2.8   Policy Renewal

We conclude this section with the discussion of policy renewal. Policy renewal means to associate a file with a new policy (or combination of policies). For example, if a user wants to extend the expiration time of a file, then the user can update the old policy that specifies an earlier expiration time to the new policy that specifies a later expiration time. However, to guarantee file assured deletion, policy renewal can be performed only when the following condition holds: *the old policy will always be revoked first before the new policy is revoked.* The reason is that after policy renewal, there will be two versions of a file: one is protected with the old policy, and one is protected with the new policy. If the new policy is revoked first, then the file version that is protected with the old policy may still be accessible when the control keys of the old policy are compromised, meaning that the file is not assuredly deleted.

It is important to note that it is a non-trivial task to enforce the condition of policy renewal, as the old policy may be associated with other existing files. In this paper, we do not consider this issue and we pose it as future work.

Suppose that we have enforced the condition of policy renewal. A straightforward approach of implementing policy renewal is to combine the file upload and download operations, but without retrieving the encrypted file from the cloud. The procedures can be summarized as follows: (i) download all encrypted keys from the storage cloud, (ii) send them to the key manager for decryption, (iii) recover the data key, (iv) re-encrypt the data key with the control keys of the new policies, and finally (v) send the newly encrypted keys back to the cloud.

In some special cases, optimization can be made so as to save the operations of decrypting and re-encrypting the data key. Suppose that the Boolean combination structure of policies remain unchanged, but one of the atomic policies P_i is changed $P_{i'}$. For example, when we extend the contract date of Bob (see Section 2.2), we may need to update the particular time-based policy of Bob without changing other policies. In this case, the data owner simply sends the blinded version $S_i^{e_i} R^{e_i}$ to the key manager, which then returns $S_i R$. The data owner then recovers S_i. Now, the data owner re-encrypts S_i into $S_i^{e_{i'}}$ (mod $n_{i'}$),

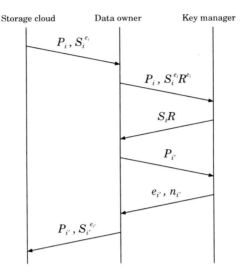

Fig. 3. Policy renewal

where $(n_{i'}, e_{i'})$ is the public key of policy $P_{i'}$, and sends it to the cloud. Note that the encrypted data key K remains intact. Figure 3 illustrates this special case of policy renewal.

3   The FADE Architecture

We implement a working prototype of FADE using C++ on Linux, and we use the OpenSSL library [13] for the cryptographic operations. In addition, we use Amazon S3 [2] as our storage cloud. This section is to address the implementation issues of our FADE architecture, based on our experience in prototyping FADE. Our goal is to show the practicality of FADE when it is deployed with today's cloud storage services.

Figure 4 shows the FADE architecture. In the following, we define the metadata of FADE attached to individual files. We then describe how we implement the data owner and the key manager, and how the data owner interacts with the storage cloud.

3.1   Representation of Metadata

For each file protected by FADE, we include the metadata that describes the policies associated with the file as well as a set of encrypted keys. In FADE, there are two types of metadata: *file metadata* and *policy metadata*.

File metadata. The file metadata mainly contains two pieces of information: file size and HMAC. We hash the encrypted file with HMAC-SHA1 for integrity checking. The file metadata is of fixed size (with 8 bytes of file size and 20 bytes of HMAC) and attached at the beginning of the encrypted file. Both the file

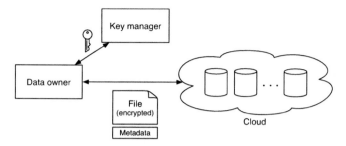

Fig. 4. The FADE architecture

metadata and the encrypted data file will then be treated as a single file to be uploaded to the storage cloud.

Policy metadata. The policy metadata includes the specification of the Boolean combination of policies and the corresponding encrypted cryptographic keys. Here, we assume that each single policy is specified by a unique 4-byte integer identifier. To represent a Boolean combination of policies, we express it in *disjunctive canonical form*, i.e., the disjunction (OR) of conjunctive policies, and use the characters '*' and '+' to denote the AND and OR operators. Then we upload the policy metadata as a separate file to the storage cloud. This enables us to renew policies directly on the policy metadata without retrieving the entire file from the storage cloud.

In our implementation, individual files have their own policy metadata, although we allow multiple files to be associated with the same policy (which is the expected behavior of FADE). In other words, for two data files that are under the same policy, they will have different policy metadata files that specify different data keys, and the data keys are protected by the control key of the same policy. In Section 5, we discuss how we may associate the same policy metadata file with multiple data files so as to reduce the metadata overhead.

3.2   Data Owner and Storage Cloud

Our implementation of the data owner uses the following four function calls to enable end users to interact with the storage cloud:

- `Upload(file, policy)`. The data owner encrypts the input file using the specified policy (or a Boolean combination of policies). It then sends the encrypted file and the metadata onto the cloud. In our implementation, the file is encrypted using the 128-bit AES algorithm with the cipher block chaining (CBC) mode, yet we can adopt a different symmetric-key encryption algorithm depending on applications.
- `Download(file)`. The data owner retrieves the file and the policy metadata from the cloud, checks the integrity of the file, and decrypts the file.
- `Delete(policy)`. The data owner tells the key manager to permanently revoke the specified policy. All files associated with the policy will be assuredly deleted.

- Renew(file, new_policy). The data owner first fetches the policy metadata for the given file from the cloud. It then updates the policy metadata with the new policy. Finally, it sends the policy metadata back to the cloud.

The above function calls can be exported as library APIs that can be embedded into different implementations of the data owner. In our current prototype, we implement the data owner as a user-level program that can access files under a working directory of a desktop PC.

The above exported interfaces *wrap* the third-party APIs for interacting with the storage cloud. As an example, we use LibAWS++ [9], a C++ library for interfacing with Amazon S3. We note that the LibAWS++ library uses HTTP to communicate with the cloud, and it does not provide any security protection on the data being transferred. To interact with different cloud storage services, we can use different third-party APIs, provided that the APIs support the basic file upload/download operations.

3.3 Key Manager

We implement the key manager that supports the following four basic functions.

- *Creating a policy.* The key manager creates a new policy and returns the corresponding public control key.
- *Retrieving the public control key of a policy.* If the policy is accessible, then the key manager returns the public control key. Otherwise, it returns an error.
- *Decrypting a key with respect to a policy.* If the policy is accessible, then the key manager decrypts the (blinded) key. Otherwise, it returns an error.
- *Revoking a policy.* The key manager revokes the policy and removes the corresponding keys.

We implement the basic functionalities of the key manager so that it can perform the required operations on the cryptographic keys. In particular, all the policy control keys are built upon 1024-bit blinded RSA (see Section 2.5). To make the key manager more robust, we can extend the key manager to a quorum of key managers as stated in [18], and implement a PKI-based certification system for policy checking (see Section 2.4).

4   Evaluation

We implement a prototype of FADE atop Amazon S3 [2], and we now evaluate the empirical performance of FADE. It is crucial that FADE does not introduce substantial performance overhead that will lead to a big increase in data management costs. In addition, the cryptographic operations of FADE should only bring insignificant computational overhead. Therefore, our experiments aim to answer the following issue: *What is the performance overhead of FADE, and is it feasible to use FADE to provide file assured deletion for cloud storage?*

Our experiments use Amazon S3, residing in the United States, as the storage cloud. Also, we deploy the data owner and the key manager within an organization's network that resides in an Asian country. In the experiments, we evaluate FADE when it operates on an individual file of different sizes: 1KB, 10KB, 100KB, 1MB, and 10MB.

4.1 Experimental Results on Time Performance of FADE

We now measure the time performance of FADE using our prototype. In order to identify the time overhead of FADE, we divide the running time of each measurement into three components:

- *data transmission time*, the data uploading/downloading time between the data owner and the storage cloud. We further divide it into two components: the *file* component, which measures the transmission time for the file body and the file metadata, and the *policy* component, which measures the transmission time for the policy metadata (see Section 3.1). We upload/download these two components as two separate copies to/from the storage cloud.
- *AES and HMAC time*, the total computational time used for performing AES and HMAC on the file.
- *key management time*, the time for the data owner to coordinate with the key manager on operating the cryptographic keys. For the file upload operation (see Figure 1 in Section 2.5), we require the data owner to obtain the public control key for the corresponding policy; for the download operation (see Figure 2 in Section 2.5), the data owner works with the key manager to obtain the data key.

We average each of our measurement results over 10 different trials.

Experiment 1 (Performance of file upload/download operations). First, we measure the running time of the file upload and download operations for different file sizes. Table 1 shows the results. We find that the transmission time is the dominant factor (over 99%). The AES and HMAC time increases linearly with the file size. However, the key management time stays constant on the order of milliseconds, regardless of the file size. In other words, compared with the basic encryption and integrity check provided by AES and HMAC, FADE only involves a small time overhead in key management.

We note that when the file size is small, the transmission time for the policy metadata is comparable with the transmission time for the file. To understand this, we capture and analyze the data traffic, and find that the round-trip time between our network (in Asia) and Amazon S3 (in the United States) is 200-300 milliseconds. Because the file and the policy metadata are stored on the cloud as two separate copies, they are transferred through two different TCP connections, and a significant portion of data transmission time is actually due to the TCP connection setup. In Section 4.2, we will show that the actual number of bytes stored for the policy metadata is in fact much less than that for the file.

Experiment 2 (Performance of policy updates). Table 2 shows the time used for renewing a single policy of a file (see Figure 3 in Section 2.8), in which

Table 1. Experiment 1 (Performance of upload/download operations)

(a) Upload

File size	Total time	Data transmission				AES+HMAC		Key management	
		File	(%)	Policy	(%)	Time	(%)	Time	(%)
1KB	1.260s	0.724s	57.4%	0.537s	42.6%	0.000s	0.0%	0.000s	0.0%
10KB	1.552s	1.020s	65.7%	0.532s	34.3%	0.001s	0.0%	0.000s	0.0%
100KB	2.452s	1.903s	77.6%	0.546s	22.3%	0.002s	0.1%	0.001s	0.0%
1MB	4.194s	3.646s	86.9%	0.527s	12.6%	0.022s	0.5%	0.000s	0.0%
10MB	16.275s	15.463s	95.0%	0.595s	3.7%	0.218s	1.3%	0.000s	0.0%

(b) Download

File size	Total time	Data transmission				AES+HMAC		Key management	
		File	(%)	Policy	(%)	Time	(%)	Time	(%)
1KB	0.843s	0.485s	57.5%	0.355s	42.1%	0.000s	0.0%	0.003s	0.4%
10KB	0.912s	0.615s	67.4%	0.294s	32.2%	0.000s	0.0%	0.003s	0.3%
100KB	1.968s	1.682s	85.5%	0.282s	14.3%	0.002s	0.1%	0.002s	0.1%
1MB	4.696s	4.360s	92.8%	0.317s	6.7%	0.017s	0.4%	0.002s	0.1%
10MB	33.746s	33.182s	98.3%	0.395s	1.2%	0.166s	0.5%	0.002s	0.0%

Table 2. Experiment 2 (Performance of policy updates). We do not show the AES+HMAC time as it is not involved in policy renewal.

File size	Total time	Data transmission				Key management	
		Download	(%)	Upload	(%)	Time	(%)
1KB	0.923s	0.315s	34.1%	0.605s	65.5%	0.004s	0.4%
10KB	0.805s	0.266s	33.0%	0.536s	66.6%	0.004s	0.4%
100KB	0.821s	0.271s	33.0%	0.546s	66.5%	0.004s	0.5%
1MB	0.813s	0.273s	33.5%	0.537s	66.0%	0.003s	0.4%
10MB	0.832s	0.266s	32.0%	0.562s	67.6%	0.004s	0.5%

we update the policy metadata on the storage cloud with the new set of crypto-graphic keys. Our experiments show that the total time is generally small (less than a second) regardless of the file size, as we operate on the policy metadata only. Also, the key management time only takes about 0.004s in renewing a policy, and this value is again independent of the file size.

Experiment 3 (Performance of multiple policies). We now evaluate the performance of FADE when multiple policies are associated with a file (see Section 2.7). Here, we focus on the file upload operation, and fix the file size at 1MB. We look at two specific combinations of policies, one on the conjunctive case and one on the disjunctive case.

Table 3a shows different components of time for different numbers of conjunctive policies, and Table 3b shows the case for disjunctive policies. A key observation is that the AES and HMAC and the key management time remain very low (on the order of milliseconds) when the number of policies increases.

Table 3. Experiment 3 (Performance of multiple policies)

(a) Conjunctive policies

Number of policies	Total time	Data transmission				AES+HMAC		Key management	
		File	(%)	Policy	(%)	Time	(%)	Time	(%)
1	5.141s	4.562s	88.7%	0.557s	10.8%	0.022s	0.4%	0.000s	0.0%
2	4.970s	4.352s	87.6%	0.595s	12.0%	0.022s	0.4%	0.000s	0.0%
3	4.667s	3.983s	85.3%	0.662s	14.2%	0.022s	0.5%	0.001s	0.0%
4	4.976s	4.397s	88.4%	0.557s	11.2%	0.022s	0.4%	0.001s	0.0%
5	4.962s	4.406s	88.8%	0.533s	10.7%	0.021s	0.4%	0.001s	0.0%

(b) Disjunctive policies

Number of policies	Total time	Data transmission				AES+HMAC		Key management	
		File	(%)	Policy	(%)	Time	(%)	Time	(%)
1	3.927s	3.364s	85.7%	0.541s	13.8%	0.022s	0.6%	0.000s	0.0%
2	4.015s	3.460s	86.2%	0.534s	13.3%	0.021s	0.5%	0.000s	0.0%
3	3.923s	3.390s	86.4%	0.511s	13.0%	0.022s	0.6%	0.001s	0.0%
4	3.859s	3.322s	86.1%	0.515s	13.3%	0.022s	0.6%	0.000s	0.0%
5	4.118s	3.559s	86.4%	0.536s	13.0%	0.022s	0.5%	0.001s	0.0%

4.2 Space Utilization of FADE

We now assess the space utilization. As stated in Section 3.1, there are file metadata and policy metadata for each file, and this metadata information is the space overhead introduced by FADE. For the file metadata, it is always fixed at 28 bytes. On the other hand, for the policy metadata, its size differs with the number of policies. For instance, we need 128 bytes for the policy-based secret key $S_i^{e_i}$ for some policy i. The size of an encrypted copy of K is 16 bytes, and this size increases with the number of terms in the case of disjunctive (OR) policies (see Section 2.7). Table 4 shows the different sizes of the policy metadata based on our implementation prototype for a variable number of (a) conjunctive policies ($P_1 \wedge P_2 \wedge \cdots \wedge P_m$), and (b) disjunctive policies ($P_1 \vee P_2 \vee \cdots \vee P_m$). For instance, if the file size is 1MB and there is only one policy, then the size of the file metadata is 28 bytes and the policy metadata is 149 bytes, and hence the space overhead is 0.017%.

4.3 Lessons Learned

In this section, we evaluate the performance of FADE in terms of the overheads of time, space utilization, and data transfer. It is important to note that the performance results depend on the deployment environment. For instance, if the data owner and the key manager all reside in the United States as Amazon S3, then the transmission times for files and metadata will significantly reduce; or if the policy metadata contains more descriptive information, the overhead will increase. Nevertheless, we emphasize that our experiments can show the feasibility of FADE in providing an additional level of security protection for today's cloud storage.

Table 4. Size of the policy metadata

(a) Conjunctive policies

Number of policies	Policy metadata size (bytes)
1	149
2	282
3	415
4	548
5	681

(b) Disjunctive policies

Number of policies	Policy metadata size (bytes)
1	149
2	298
3	447
4	596
5	745

We note that the performance overhead of FADE becomes less significant when the size of the actual file content increases (e.g. on the order of megabytes or even bigger). Thus, FADE is more suitable for enterprises that need to archive large files with a substantial amount of data. On the other hand, individuals may generally manipulate small files on the order of kilobytes. In this case, we may consider the techniques of associate the same policy metadata with multiple files (see Section 5) to reduce the overhead of FADE.

5   Discussion

In this section, we discuss several design limitations that we do not address in this paper. We suggest possible enhancements that we can make to FADE.

Adding an Additional Layer of Encryption. In our current design of FADE, if the key manager colludes with the storage cloud, then the storage cloud can decrypt the files of data owner. To prevent this from happening, one solution is to add an additional layer of encryption in the data owner. The idea is that the data owner first encrypts a file with a long-term secret key, and then encrypts the encrypted file with the data key. In this way, even if the key manager colludes with the storage cloud, the files of the data owner remain encrypted.

Multiple Files with the Same Policy Metadata. In our current implementation, the operations of FADE are on a per-file basis, such that each data file has one corresponding policy metadata file (see Section 3). To reduce the metadata overhead of FADE, we can associate a batch of multiple data files (e.g., files under the same directory) with the same policy metadata and the same set of cryptographic keys (including the data key and the control keys of policies). The advantage of the batch-based approach is that we can use one single policy metadata for multiple data files. Thus, if the data files are of small size, then the batch-based approach can reduce the storage overhead due to the policy metadata.

It is possible to add a new data file into the batch of files that are currently associated with the same policy metadata. To achieve this, the data owner first downloads the policy metadata from the storage cloud and recovers the data key.

Then it uses the same data key to encrypt the new file. Note that the content of the policy metadata remains unchanged. Also, the data key can be cached in the data owner's volatile storage so as to include new files into the batch later.

Reliability of the key manager. This work assumes several reliability features of the key manager (see Section 2.4), including: (i) implementation of the quorum scheme that improves the robustness of key management, (ii) removal of keys of revoked policies, and (iii) secure and reliable storage of keys of active policies that are not yet revoked. We plan to address these issues in future work.

6   Related Work

In Section 2.1, we discuss time-based deletion in [5,14], which we generalize into policy-based deletion. In this section, we review other related work on protecting outsourced data storage.

Cryptographic protection on outsourced data storage has been considered (see survey in [8]). For example, Wang et al. [23] propose secure outsourced data access mechanisms that support changes in user access rights and outsourced data. Ateniese et al. [4] and Wang et al. [22] propose an auditing system that verifies the integrity of outsourced data. However, all the above systems require new protocol support on the cloud infrastructure, and such additional functionalities may make deployment more challenging.

Security solutions that are compatible with existing public cloud storage services have been proposed. Yun et al. [24] propose a cryptographic file system that provides privacy and integrity guarantees for outsourced data using a universal-hash based MAC tree. They prototype a system that can interact with an untrusted storage server via a modified file system. JungleDisk [7] and Cumulus [21] are proposed to protect the privacy of outsourced data, and their implementation use Amazon S3 [2] as the storage backend. Specifically, Cumulus focuses on making effective use of storage space while providing essential encryption on outsourced data. The above systems mainly put the protocol functionalities on the client side, and the cloud storage providers merely provide the storage space.

The concept of attributed-based encryption (ABE) is first introduced in [17], in which attributes are associated with encrypted data. Goyal et al. [6] extend the idea to key-policy ABE, in which attributes are associated with private keys, and encrypted data can be decrypted only when a threshold of attributes are satisfied. Pirretti et al. [16] implement ABE and conduct empirical studies. Nair et al. [12] consider a similar idea of ABE, and they seek to enforce a fine-grained access control of files based on identity-based public key cryptography. Perlman et al. [15] also address the Boolean combinations of policies, but they focus on digital rights management rather than file assured deletion and their operations of cryptographic keys are different from our work because of the different frameworks. As argued in Section 2.2, ABE and our work have different design objectives and hence different key management mechanisms.

7   Conclusions

We propose a cloud storage system called FADE, which aims to provide assured deletion for files that are hosted by today's cloud storage services. We present the design of policy-based file assured deletion, in which files are assuredly deleted and made unrecoverable by anyone when their associated file access policies are revoked. We present the essential operations on cryptographic keys so as to achieve policy-based file assured deletion. We implement a prototype of FADE to demonstrate its practicality, and empirically study its performance overhead when it works with Amazon S3. Our experimental results provide insights into the performance-security trade-off when FADE is deployed in practice.

Acknowledgment

The work of Patrick P. C. Lee was supported by project #MMT-p1-10 of the Shun Hing Institute of Advanced Engineering, The Chinese University of Hong Kong.

References

1. Amazon. SmugMug Case Study: Amazon Web Services (2006),
   http://aws.amazon.com/solutions/case-studies/smugmug/
2. Amazon Simple Storage Service (Amazon S3), http://aws.amazon.com/s3/
3. Armbrust, M., Fox, A., Griffith, R., Joseph, A.D., Katz, R.H., Konwinski, A., Lee, G., Patterson, D.A., Rabkin, A., Stoica, I., Zaharia, M.: Above the Clouds: A Berkeley View of Cloud Computing. Technical Report UCB/EECS-2009-28, EECS Department, University of California, Berkeley (February 2009)
4. Ateniese, G., Pietro, R.D., Mancini, L.V., Tsudik, G.: Scalable and Efficient Provable Data Possession. In: Proc. of SecureComm. (2008)
5. Geambasu, R., Kohno, T., Levy, A., Levy, H.M.: Vanish: Increasing Data Privacy with Self-Destructing Data. In: Proc. of USENIX Security Symposium (August 2009)
6. Goyal, V., Pandey, O., Sahai, A., Waters, B.: Attribute-Based Encryption for Fine-Grained Access Control of Encrypted Data. In: Proc. of ACM CCS (2006)
7. JungleDisk, http://www.jungledisk.com/
8. Kamara, S., Lauter, K.: Cryptographic Cloud Storage. In: Proc. of Financial Cryptography: Workshop on Real-Life Cryptographic Protocols and Standardization (2010)
9. LibAWS++, http://aws.28msec.com/
10. Menezes, A.J., van Oorschot, P.C., Vanstone, S.A.: Handbook of Applied Cryptography. CRC Press, Boca Raton (October 1996)
11. MyAsiaCloud, http://www.myasiacloud.com/
12. Nair, S., Dashti, M.T., Crispo, B., Tanenbaum, A.S.: A Hybrid PKI-IBC Based Ephemerizer System. In: IFIP International Federation for Information Processing, vol. 232, pp. 241–252 (2007)
13. OpenSSL, http://www.openssl.org/
14. Perlman, R.: File System Design with Assured Delete. In: ISOC NDSS (2007)

15. Perlman, R., Kaufman, C., Perlner, R.: Privacy-Preserving DRM. In: IDtrust (2010)
16. Pirretti, M., Traynor, P., McDaniel, P., Waters, B.: Secure Attribute-Based Systems. In: ACM CCS (2006)
17. Sahai, A., Waters, B.: Fuzzy Identity-Based Encryption. In: Cramer, R. (ed.) EUROCRYPT 2005. LNCS, vol. 3494, pp. 457–473. Springer, Heidelberg (2005)
18. Shamir, A.: How to Share a Secret. CACM 22(11), 612–613 (1979)
19. SmugMug, http://www.smugmug.com/
20. Stallings, W.: Cryptography and Network Security. Prentice-Hall, Englewood Cliffs (2006)
21. Vrable, M., Savage, S., Voelker, G.M.: Cumulus: Filesystem backup to the cloud. ACM Trans. on Storage (ToS) 5(4) (December 2009)
22. Wang, C., Wang, Q., Ren, K., Lou, W.: Privacy-preserving public auditing for storage security in cloud computing. In: Proc. of IEEE INFOCOM (March 2010)
23. Wang, W., Li, Z., Owens, R., Bhargava, B.: Secure and Efficient Access to Outsourced Data. In: ACM Cloud Computing Security Workshop (CCSW) (November 2009)
24. Yun, A., Shi, C., Kim, Y.: On Protecting Integrity and Confidentiality of Cryptographic File System for Outsourced Storage. In: ACM Cloud Computing Security Workshop (CCSW) (November 2009)

A New Information Leakage Measure for Anonymity Protocols

Sami Zhioua

King Fahd University of Petroleum and Minerals
Saudi Arabia
zhioua@kfupm.edu.sa

Abstract. The main goal of anonymity protocols is to protect the identities of communicating entities in a network communication. An anonymity protocol can be characterized by a noisy channel in the information-theoretic sense. The anonymity of the protocol is then tightly related to how much information is being leaked by the channel. In this paper we investigate a new idea of measuring the information leaked based on how much the rows of the channel probabilities matrix are different from each other. We considered each row of the matrix as a point in the n-dimensional space and we used statistical dispersion measures to estimate how much the points are scattered in the space. Empirical results showed that the two proposed measures KLSD and KLMD are sensitive to the modifications of the attacker capabilities and most importantly they are stable when the a priori distribution on the secret events changes. We show that a variant of KLSD coincides with the classical notion of mutual information which gives the latter an interesting geometric interpretation. The same idea of statistical dispersion is used in a new decision function when the protocol is re-executed several times.

1 Introduction

The ubiquitous popularity of the Internet as a means of communication and information dissemination is creating regularly during the last few decades several security concerns. Most of the security efforts have been devoted to the privacy of communications. Although encrypting communication can help protect the privacy of data, the identities of the communicating entities remain generally known. For example, in the Internet Protocol (IP), each IP packet carries the IP addresses of the sender as well as the receiver. Even if this information is made invisible, an attacker can still reveal the identities of the communicating entities by using traffic analysis (e.g. tracking encrypted packets, analyzing the time delays between packets, comparing the payload size, etc.).

A variety of methods have been proposed to provide anonymous connections over the Internet. These include protocols such as Mix based systems [1] Crowds [2], Onion-routing [3], DC-Net [4], Hordes [5], etc. Most of these protocols use the idea of blending into a crowd, that is, hiding a user's action within the actions of many others. On the positive side, this idea suggests that the mere availability of other users offers the actual initiator some degree of deniability. On the negative side, a user may be incorrectly suspected of initiating a message.

In the last decade and with the increasing need to analyze anonymity systems in more formal and mathematical-based approaches, a significant number of works have been

S. Jajodia and J. Zhou (Eds.): SecureComm 2010, LNICST 50, pp. 398–414, 2010.

dedicated to exploring the notion of anonymity from an information-theoretic point of view. In this regard, we see a natural progression from anonymity set [4], to entropy-based measures [6,7] then to mutual information [8] and finally to capacity [9,10]. A detailed account of related work is given in the next section.

In this research, we adopt the same information theory based approach where a protocol is considered as a noisy channel. A noisy channel is a concept from information theory [11] which represents the link between a set of anonymous events A and a set of observable events O. Events in A represent the information to hide from a potential attacker while events in O are the ones that the attacker actually observes. A good anonymity protocol should make it hard to the attacker to guess the anonymous event given the observable event. The extreme case is when the distributions A and O are completely independent. This is called *noninterference* and achieving it, unfortunately, is often not possible because in most of the cases the protocol needs to reveal information about A. For example, in an election protocol, the individual votes should be secret but ultimately, the result of the votes must be made public which reveals information about individual votes. Hence the degree of anonymity of a protocol is tightly related to the amount of information leaked about the anonymous event when an observation is observed.

In information theory, the information leaked by a noisy channel is given by the notion of mutual information which measures the amount of information that one random variable (O) contains about another random variable (A). Recently, Smith [12] showed through an interesting example that when an adversary tries to guess the value of the anonymous event in a single try, an information-leak measure based on Renyi min-entropy [13] is more suitable than mutual information. However, both mutual information and Smith's measure depend on the knowledge of the a priori distribution (the probabilities that a user did some action) while in general this distribution is not known. Capacity on the other hand is an abstraction of mutual information obtained by maximizing over the possible a priori distributions. Unfortunately, it has been argued that the capacity is too strong [14] and there is no analytical formula to compute it for arbitrary channels.

The contributions of this paper are threefold:

- Starting from the fact that a noisy channel can be represented as a matrix of the conditional probabilities $p(o|a)$ for $o \in O$ and $a \in A$, we present a new family of measures based on how much the rows of the matrix are different from each others and we adopt a geometric approach to assess how much the corresponding points in the n-dimensional space are scattered. Empirical analysis show very promising properties of this measure compared to mutual information and Smith's measure. In particular we strongly think that these measures hold the promise of much less dependence on the a priori distribution.
- We illustrate an interesting relationship between the new measure and the classical concept of mutual information. To the best of our knowledge, this is the first time that such geometric interpretation is given to mutual information.
- The same idea of statistical dispersion is used in a new decision function when the protocol is re-executed several times. The decision function turns out to be more reliable than the one based on maximum likelihood (ML).

2 Related Work

Chaum [4] introduced the notion of anonymity set which is the set of users who are likely to be the sender or receiver of a particular message. Naturally, the anonymity of the users increases if the size of the anonymity set increases. Serjantov and Danezis [6] defined the effective set size based on the concept of entropy after they showed that the simple anonymity set is inadequate when not all the users are equally likely to have sent a particular message. For instance, an attacker analyzing emails will assign a lower probability to a German sender of an email in arabic which arrived in Dubai. Diaz et al. [7] proposed independently a similar measure and took the next step in attempting to normalize the entropy and thus define a degree of anonymity as a number between 0 and 1. These two simple entropy measures were the first to explore the anonymity notion from an information theoretic point of view and as such they have since been the subject of various discussions and comparisons. Newman et al. [15] argued that those measures focused on how well protected the actions of a particular user are and do not examine how much protection a system provide to its users collectively. Toth et al. pointed out that by using simple entropy the focus is to quantify how many bits of information an adversary needs in order to perfectly match a message to a respective use [16]. They refer to this approach as global and propose another approach that uses the maximal probability of the distribution that they refer to as local measure and they show through several interesting examples that from the user's point of view, the local approach is more appropriate. The main difference with respect to our approach is that in those works, the measure reflects the lack of information (uncertainty) that an attacker has about the distribution of users whereas in this paper, we focus on measures that reflect the capability of protocol to disguise this information given the attacker's knowledge about the observables. In other words, we focus on the difference between the a priori and a posteriori distributions and not on analyzing the a posteriori distribution only.

In information theory, the notion of mutual information quantifies the information leaked by a noisy channel and can be seen as the difference between the a priori distribution (Shannon) entropy and the a posteriori distribution (Shannon) entropy. In [8], Zhu and Bettati proposed to use mutual information as a measure of anonymity and applied it to several mix based anonymity systems. Recently, Smith [12] showed that if the attacker tries to guess the value of the anonymous event in a single try, mutual information is not a suitable measure. The example he used is very close to the examples of Toth et al. [16]. He proposed then a new information leak measure which is the difference between the Reny Min-entropies [13] of the a priori and a posteriori distributions. The main problem with these two measures, mutual information and Smith's measure, is that they require the knowledge of the a priori distribution which is generally not possible in practice. Channel capacity which is an important notion in information theory have been used as an anonymity measure [9,14]. Capacity is the maximum mutual information over all possible a priori distributions and hence it is an abstraction of mutual information which is independent from the a priori distribution. However, it has been argued that capacity in some cases is too strong and most importantly, for arbitrary channels, there is no analytical formula to compute its value. The best one can do is to approximate it using for example Blahut-Arimoto algorithm [11].

In this paper we still consider an anonymity protocol as a noisy channel which can be represented as a conditional probabilities matrix. The main contribution is to propose a new anonymity measure based on the vector configuration of the matrix. This is to the best of our knowledge the first attempt to establish a connection between the information leaked and the vector configuration of the matrix. Edman et al. [17] proposed an anonymity metric based on the permanent of a matrix. The matrix in their case represents possible input-output correlations in a network of mixes. The permanent of that matrix will give the number of perfect input-output matchings in the system. The main difference with our work lies in the interpretation of the matrix. In their matrix, the inputs are the messages entering a mix node or a mix network and the outputs are the messages leaving the mix. In our matrix, the inputs are information to keep secret and the output are the observations the attacker observes. Newman et al. [15] used a matrix they called traffic matrix to assess how good a Traffic Analysis Prevention (TAP) system is. Intuitively, the matrix will represent all observations made by an attacker in a period of time and if the number of possible matrices is large enough this indicates a good amount of protection. Clearly, this is very different from our interpretation of the matrix.

Finally we mention that Chatzikokolakis et al. [18] proposed to consider the probability of error as a measure of leakage. In our view, this work falls in the same class as [12] and [16].

3   Anonymity Protocols as Noisy Channels

Information theory turns out to be very useful in analyzing anonymity protocols [19,9]. Indeed, an anonymity protocol can be represented as a memoryless noisy channel where the input is the information to be kept secret and the output is the observed events. The attacker's challenge is then to guess the secret information based on the observed event. The set of observables depends on the capabilities of the attacker. So each attack scenario can be represented by a different channel.

A channel is a tuple $(A, O, p(\cdot|\cdot))$ where A is a random variable representing the inputs with n values $\{a_1, \ldots, a_n\}$, O is a random variable representing the outputs (observables) with m values $\{o_1, \ldots, o_m\}$, and $p(o|a)$ is a conditional probability of observing $o \in O$ given that $a \in A$ is the input.

The channel is noisy because an input might lead to different outputs with different probabilities. The probability values $p(o|a)$ for every input/output pair constitutes the channel matrix. Typically, the inputs are arranged by rows and the outputs by columns.

Generally, the channel matrix and its conditional probabilities $p(o|a)$ can be easily computed manually. It can also be computed analytically or by means of a model-checking tool like PRISM [20]. The first step is to define the sets A of secret inputs and O of observables. The inputs are generally the identities of the senders (assuming the goal is sender anonymity) and the outputs are the attacker's observables. Chatzikokolakis [21] gives a detailed description of how channel matrices are computed.

The probability distribution $p(\cdot)$ over A is called the a priori distribution and is generally not known in advance. When an output o is observed, the probability that the input is a certain a is given by the a posteriori probability of a given o ($p(a|o)$).

As example, let us determine the channel matrix for Crowds protocol under the collaborators attack[1] [2].

Consider a Crowds protocol with n users among them c are compromised (c collaborators) and with p_f as probability of forwarding. The set of inputs is the set of the identities of the users $\{u_1, u_2, \ldots, u_n\}$. Recall that in collaborators attack, a set of corrupted users collaborate to figure out the identity of the initiator. An observable action in the protocol happens when a (honest) user i forwards the message to a collaborator. This action is denoted d_i and means that user i is detected. Hence, the set of observable actions is the set $\{d_1, d_2, \ldots, d_n\}$. It is easy to note that there is a form of symmetry in the corresponding channel matrix. Indeed, once a user is detected, the probability that it is actually the initiator is the same regardless of which user is the actual initiator. According to the proof of Theorem 5.2 in [2], this probability is

$$\alpha = c \, \frac{1 - \left(\frac{n-c-1}{n}\right) p_f}{n - (n - c)\, p_f}.$$

The probability of detecting a user other than the initiator is the same for all other users and is $\beta = \alpha - \frac{c}{n}$. Hence the conditional probabilities of the matrix are[2]:

$$p(o_j|a_i) = \begin{cases} \dfrac{\alpha}{s} & \text{if } i = j \\[2ex] \dfrac{\beta}{s} & \text{otherwise} \end{cases}$$

where $s = \alpha + (n - 1)\beta$.

Crowds protocol with $n = 10$ users, $c = 3$ collaborators, and $p_f = 0.8$ has the following channel matrix:

	d_1	d_2	$\ldots$	d_{10}
a_1	0.4462	0.0615	$\ldots$	0.0615
a_2	0.0615	0.4462	$\ldots$	0.0615
$\vdots$	$\vdots$	$\vdots$	$\ddots$	$\vdots$
a_{10}	0.0615	0.0615	$\ldots$	0.4462

3.1   Channel Matrix Analysis

Anonymity protocols can be seen as noisy channels where the noise is a manifestation of the efforts of the protocol to hide the link between the inputs and the outputs[3].

---

[1] Sometimes called predecessor attack.

[2] The matrix probabilities are computed by conditioning on the event that some user was detected. The situation when no user is detected corresponds to absolute privacy and anonymity is not an issue in that case.

[3] In the rest of the paper, the terms secret information and input will be used interchangeably and so are observation and output

The more noise there is in the channel, the more anonymous the protocol is. One promising approach to analyze these protocols is the quantitative theory of information flow which focuses on "how much" information is being leaked. Indeed, initially, there is an initial uncertainty about the secret information. After the protocol executes and the adversary observes the output, the uncertainty might decrease. The idea of the quantitative approach of information theory is to quantify the amount of initial uncertainty (a priori), the remaining uncertainty after observing the observation (a posteriori) and then deduce the amount of information leaked.

In Shannon information theory, the information leaked by a noisy channel is given by the notion of mutual information. Mutual Information of A and O, noted $I(A;O)$, represents the correlation of information between A and O and is defined as:

$$I(A;O) = H(A) - H(A|O) \tag{1}$$

where $H(A)$ is the Shannon entropy of A and $H(A|O)$ is the conditional entropy of A given O. Channel capacity is the maximum mutual information over all a priori distributions.

$$C = \max_{p} I(A;O) \tag{2}$$

Most of previous works [4,6,7] use a different interpretation of the anonymity degree which is based only on the capabilities of the attacker after the protocol executes, that is, the uncertainty (entropy) of the a posteriori distribution on the inputs. The approach we use in this paper which is based on how much information is being leaked by the protocol is more adequate and more reliable than the simple a posteriori entropy approach. Indeed, it is easy to think of two channels with significantly different a priori distributions but with the same a posteriori uncertainty. For example, consider the following two channels (recall that the inputs are arranged by rows and the outputs by columns):

$$C_1 = \begin{pmatrix} 0 & 1 & 0 \\ 0.5 & 0.5 & 0 \\ 0.5 & 0 & 0.5 \end{pmatrix} \qquad C_2 = \begin{pmatrix} 0 & 1 & 0 \\ 0 & 0 & 1 \\ 0 & 0 & 1 \\ 0 & 1 & 0 \\ 1 & 0 & 0 \end{pmatrix}$$

In channel C_1 the number of inputs is 3 so if we assume a uniform a priori distribution $[\frac{1}{3}, \frac{1}{3}, \frac{1}{3}]$, the entropy $H(A)$ will be equal to 1.58. In channel C_2, the number of inputs is 5 so the uniform distribution is $[\frac{1}{5}, \frac{1}{5}, \frac{1}{5}, \frac{1}{5}, \frac{1}{5}]$ and the corresponding entropy is $H(A) = 2.32$. Hence, initially there is more uncertainty in channel C_1 than in C_2. The a posteriori distributions in C_1 and C_2, however, have very similar uncertainty values. Indeed, $H(A|O)$ in C_1 is equal to 0.79 and in C_2 it is 0.8. That is, after observing an observation, an attacker in C_1 will have the same uncertainty as an attacker in C_2. So measures that rely only on the a posteriori distribution will declare both protocols with similar anonymity degrees. This is not accurate because C_1 is clearly better than C_2 since it leaks less information and preserves better the uncertainty on the input distribution. Mutual information as well as the measures we propose in this paper reflects this difference. For instance, Mutual Information for C_1 is 0.79 while it it 1.52 in C_2.

As an alternative to Shannon entropy, one can use the concept of probability of error of an adversary [18]. In an anonymity protocol, the attacker tries to guess the secret information based on the information she observes. Her goal is to use a decision function so that to minimize the probability of error (probability of guessing wrong). The decision function $f : O \rightarrow A$ gives for every output o, the guessed input a. The probability of error associated to f is the averaged sum over all outputs of making a wrong guess:

$$P_e = \sum_{o \in O} p(o)(1 - p(f(o)|o)) \tag{3}$$

The two most known decision functions are MAP (Maximum A Posteriori Probability) and ML (Maximum Likelihood).

If an observation o has been observed, the MAP decision function chooses the input that maximizes the a posteriori probability $p(a|o)$:

$$f(o) = a \quad \Rightarrow \forall b \in A, \ p(a|o) \geq p(b|o).$$

The probability of error with the MAP criterion is then:

$$1 - \sum_{o \in O} \max_{a \in A}(p(o|a) \, p(a)). \tag{4}$$

The ML decision function chooses the input that maximizes the likelihood $p(o|a)$:

$$f(o) = a \quad \Rightarrow \forall b \in A, \ p(o|a) \geq p(o|b).$$

The corresponding probability of error is thus:

$$1 - \sum_{o \in O} \max_{a \in A}(p(o|a)) \, p(a). \tag{5}$$

It is well known that the best decision function is based on the MAP rule and the corresponding probability of error is called Bayes risk. It is known also that ML is only an approximation of MAP when the a priori distribution is not available. This explains why in some cases the ML deviates considerably from MAP [22].

The probability of error is not a measure of information leakage. Instead, it can be used to measure the attacker's initial capability (based on the a priori distribution) and also the attacker capability after observing the output (based on the a posteriori probability). A notion of "difference" between these probabilities of error can give rise to an information leakage measure. Smith [12] introduced an information leakage measure along this idea but in his formulation, he used Rényi entropy [13]:

$$InformationLeak = H_\infty(A) - H_\infty(A|O) \tag{6}$$

where
$$\bullet \ H_\infty(A) = \log \frac{1}{\max_{a \in A} p(a)}$$

$$\bullet \ H_\infty(A|O) = \log \frac{1}{\sum_{o \in O} \max_{a \in A} p(o|a)p(a)}$$

Equation (6) can be formulated as follows :

$$InformationLeak = \log \frac{\sum\limits_{o \in O} \max\limits_{a \in A} p(o|a) p(a)}{\max\limits_{a \in A} p(a)} \qquad (7)$$

In this paper we refer to this measure as min-entropy information leak. Smith showed through an interesting example that when an adversary tries to guess the value of the input in a single try, min-entropy information leak is more suitable than mutual information. The example features two systems with the same mutual information, the same a priori uncertainty, but with very different MAP probabilities of error.

4   Scattering of the Channel Matrix Rows

The new family of measures we present in this paper are based on how much the rows of the matrix are different from each others. Since the inputs are arranged by rows, every row of the matrix is a probability distribution on the observations for a given input : $(p(o_1|a), p(o_2|a), \ldots, p(o_m|a))$. Intuitively, the more these rows are similar to each other, the more the protocol is anonymous because the observation of the output in that case does not help much the attacker to guess the right input. On the other hand, the more the rows are different from each other, the less anonymous the protocol is because the knowledge of the output carries significant information about the input. To measure how much the rows are different from each others, we consider every row as a point in the $m-$dimensional space. If the rows are different, then the associated points will be very scattered in the space and if they are similar they will be close to each others. We consider two measures of statistical dispersion: mean difference and standard deviation and we propose variants of theses measures we call Kullback-Leibler mean difference (KLMD) and Kullback-Leilbler standard deviation (KLSD).

Definition 1. *Let M be a channel matrix where* $|A| = n$ *and* $|O| = m$.

$$KLMD(M,p) = \frac{1}{n(n-1)} \sum_{a \neq b \in A} p(a) \, p(b) \, D_{KL}(\overrightarrow{R_a} \, || \, \overrightarrow{R_b}) \qquad (8)$$

$$KLSD(M,p) = \sqrt{\sum_{a \in A} p(a) \, D_{KL}(\overrightarrow{R_a} \, || \, \overrightarrow{Mean_p})^2} \qquad (9)$$

where

- D_{KL} *is the Kullback-Leibler distance (know also as relative entropy)*
- $\overrightarrow{R_a}$ *denotes the matrix row associated to input a*
- $\overrightarrow{Mean_p}$ *is the mean distribution with respect to the prior distribution p. $Mean_p(o) = \sum_a p(a) \, p(o|a)$.*

   In addition to mean difference and standard deviation, we tried other statistical dispersion measures such as variance but the most promising empirical results were obtained with the selected two measures. On the other hand, the choice of relative entropy is motivated by the fact that in information theory, the divergence between two probability distributions is given by the relative entropy. We tried also to use Euclidean norm but again the empirical results were clearly better with relative entropy. That said, our plans for future work include the investigation of other statistical dispersion measures and probability distribution metrics and different combinations of them.

The measures (8) and (9) have a geometric flavor and they are based on relative entropy. Interestingly, we could establish a link between a variant of KLSD and the classical mutual information notion. This gives an interesting geometrical interpretation to mutual information. To the best of our knowledge, this fact has not been mentioned in the literature so far.

Theorem 1.

$$I(A;O) = \sum_a p(a) \, D_{KL}(\vec{R_a} \, || \, \overrightarrow{Mean_p})$$

Proof.

$$\sum_a p(a) \, D_{KL}(\vec{R_a} \, || \, \overrightarrow{Mean_p}) = \sum_a p(a) \sum_o p(o|a) \, \log\left(\frac{p(o|a)}{Mean_p(o)}\right)$$

$$= \sum_a p(a) \sum_o p(o|a) \, (\log(p(o|a) - \log(Mean_p(o)))$$

$$= \left(\sum_a p(a) \sum_o p(o|a) \log(p(o|a))\right)$$

$$\quad - \left(\sum_a p(a) \sum_o p(o|a) \log(Mean_p(o))\right)$$

$$= -\sum_a p(a) H(\vec{R_a}) - \left(\sum_o \sum_a p(a) p(o|a) \log(Mean_p(o))\right)$$

$$= -\sum_a p(a) H(\vec{R_a}) + H(\overrightarrow{Mean_p})$$

$$= H(\overrightarrow{Mean_p}) - \sum_a p(a) H(\vec{R_a})$$

$$= H(O) - H(O|A)$$

$$= I(A;O) \qquad\qquad (10)$$

4.1   Empirical Analysis

To see how these new measures compare to mutual information and Smith's min-entropy information leak, we performed empirical study on Crowds [2], Onion-routing [3], and ring-based DC-Net [4] anonymity protocols under the collaborators attack [2,23]. Two types of experiments are performed. The first experiment aims at showing how the different measures behave as the capabilities of the attacker increase. The second experiment focuses rather on the impact of changing the a priori distribution on the different measures.

For Crowds, the experiment consists in considering a crowd of 20 users, a fixed probability of forwarding of 0.8 and then computing the different measures while increasing

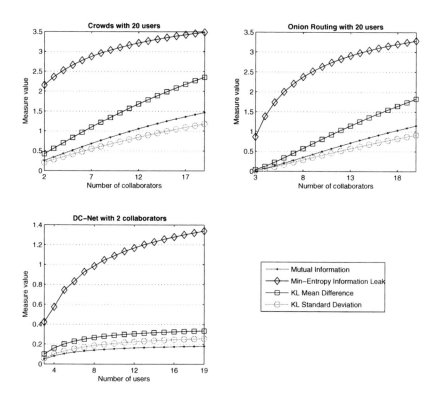

Fig. 1. Comparison of the four different measures on three protocols under collaborators attack while increasing the number of collaborators

the number of collaborators from 2 to 19. The upper left plot of Figure 1 shows how the four measures behave. The upper right plot of the same figure shows the result of the same experiment but on Onion-routing (20 users and the number of collaborators increasing from 3 to 19). For the ring-based DC-Net an attack with more than 2 collaborators is difficult to analyze. To avoid dealing with this complexity, a slightly different experiment is carried out which consists in fixing the number of collaborators to 2 and decreasing the number of users from 19 to 3. This is equivalent to increasing the attacker capabilities. The results are depicted in the lower left plot of Figure 1.

A good information leak measure should be sensitive to the increase of the attacker capabilities. If the number of collaborators increases, for instance, this should be reflected by the measure. Overall, min-entropy information leak is the more sensitive to the attacker capabilities increases. For Crowds and Onion-routing, KLMD is interestingly sensitive to the attacker capabilities modification. For all protocols mutual information and KLSD behave very similarly. This can be explained by the Thoerem 1.

In experiment 2, we fix the attacker capabilities and play on the a priori distribution. For each protocol, the different measures are computed for different a priori distributions starting from a distribution peaked in one input and then flattering until reaching

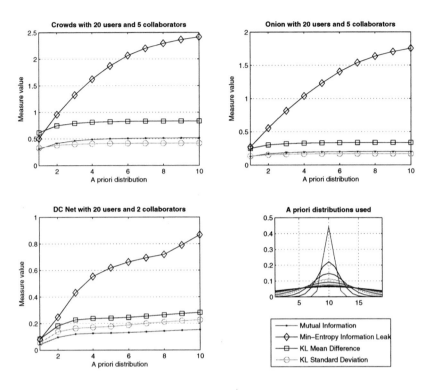

Fig. 2. Comparison of the four different measures on three protocols under collaborators attack using different a priori distributions

the uniform distribution. The lower left plot of Figure 2 illustrates the distributions graphically. It is easy to see from the rest of plots of Figure 2 that the min-entropy information leak is very sensitive to the a priori distribution unlike the other measures. This does not constitute a desirable property for an anonymity measure. Indeed, generally, the a priori distribution is not assumed to be known and hence a good anonymity measure should be as independent as possible from that distribution. Such good measure should be determined uniquely by the matrix. Dependence on the a priori distribution has always been an argument against the MAP rule because this makes it look as an artificial rule. The fact that min-entropy information leak measure is inspired by the MAP probability of error explains the sensitivity of this measure with respect to the a priori distribution as depicted in Figure 2. The rest of the measures: mutual information, KLMD, and KLSD are more stable when the a priori distribution changes.

To further see how each measure behaves for each protocol under the collaborators attack, we combined the results of experiment 1 and experiment 2 in a single 3-d chart. Figure 3 illustrates the measures for Crowds: the x axis represents the a priori distribution, the y axis the number of collaborators and the z axis the different measures values. Note that on the x axis, only the min-entropy information leak values increase considerably while on the y axis, the slope is neat for all measures, in particular the KLMD measure.

5   Re-executing the Protocol Multiple Times

Most of anonymity attacks are passive attacks in the sense that they don't draw attention to themselves and consequently may continue for a long period of time. In particular, a collaborators attack that last for a long period of time may detect several messages from the same session (initiated by the same user). If the path used in that session does not change, then the collaborators will not gain additional information even if the attack lasts forever because it is always the same user which is detected. However, protocols such as Crowds, Onion-routing, and Hordes change their paths periodically because some users join the protocol, some others leave and also to improve the performance of the protocol by balancing the load among all users. By changing the path during the same session, the collaborators will have more information to identify the initiator since several users will be detected and it is easy to see that the true initiator will be more likely to be detected than any other user. The same situation happens if the path is fixed but the set of collaborators (compromised users) change periodically which corresponds to a second variant of the collaborators attack called called Roving adversary [24].

From an information theoretical standpoint, changing the path several times during the same session can be regarded as re-executing the protocol several times with the same input. Since an anonymity protocol is typically represented as a noisy channel, re-executing the protocol will yield to a sequence of possibly different observations. It is assumed that the protocol is memoryless, that is, each time it is re-executed, it works according to the same probability distribution, independently from what happened in previous sessions.

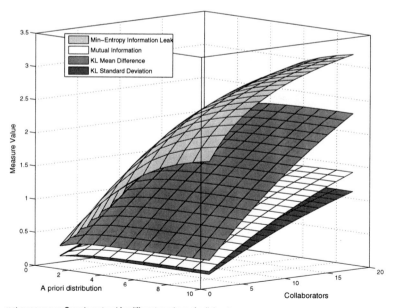

rent measures on Crowds protocol for different numbers of collaborators
different a priori distributions.

Fig. 3. The four measures applied on Crowds in a 3-d graphics

Let $a \in A$ be the input and suppose that the protocol is re-executed k times with the same input a. The attacker has to infer the input a based on the k observations she obtains. Let $\overrightarrow{o}$ denotes the sequence of k observations $o_1, o_2, \ldots o_k$. The total number of possible sequences is :

$$ns = \frac{(m+k-1)!}{k!\,(m-1)!}$$

where $m = |O|$ is the number of observations. The probability of an observation sequence $\overrightarrow{o}$ given an input a is :

$$p(\overrightarrow{o} \mid a) = \Pi_{i=1}^{k} p(o_i|a).$$

Re-executing the protocol k times can be represented by a bigger channel matrix where the n inputs $a_1, a_2, \ldots, a_n$ are arranged by rows and the ns possible sequences $\overrightarrow{o_1}, \overrightarrow{o_2}, \ldots, \overrightarrow{o_{ns}}$ are arranged by columns. The probability at row i and column j represents $p(\overrightarrow{o_j}|a_i)$.

Let f_k be a decision function adopted by the attacker to infer the input from the sequence of k observations. Similarly to the the single execution case, there are mainly two types of decision functions: one based on the MAP rule and one based on ML rule. A MAP rule based decision function returns the input that maximizes the a posteriori prbability :

$$p(a|\overrightarrow{o}) = \frac{p(\overrightarrow{o}|a)\,p(a)}{p(\overrightarrow{o})}.$$

That is,

$$f_k(\overrightarrow{o}) = a \quad \Rightarrow \quad p(\overrightarrow{o}|a)p(a) \geq p(\overrightarrow{o}|a')p(a') \ \forall a' \in A.$$

According to the ML rule, the decision function returns the input that maximizes the likelihood $p(\overrightarrow{o}|a)$. That is,

$$f_k(\overrightarrow{o}) = a \quad \Rightarrow \quad p(\overrightarrow{o}|a) \geq p(\overrightarrow{o}|a') \ \forall a' \in A.$$

Hence the probability of error after k executions according to the MAP rule is:

$$1 - \sum_{\overrightarrow{o}} \max_{a} (p(\overrightarrow{o}|a)p(a)).$$

According to ML rule, it is:

$$1 - \sum_{\overrightarrow{o}} \max_{a} (p(\overrightarrow{o}|a))p(a).$$

In the same spirit as the new anonymity measures introduced in Section 4, we propose an alternative decision function based on how close $\overrightarrow{o}$ is from the channel matrix's rows. Let $freq(\overrightarrow{o})$ be a vector composed of the frequencies of each o in $\overrightarrow{o}$. $freq(\overrightarrow{o})$ can be seen as a probability distribution on O and consequently a point in the m-dimentional space. Hence, we can think of a decision function that chooses the input a whose row is the closest to the point associated to $freq(\overrightarrow{o})$. The proposed decision function is as follows:

$$f_k(\overrightarrow{o}) = a \quad \Rightarrow \quad D_{KL}(\overrightarrow{R_a} \,\|\, freq(\overrightarrow{o})) \leq D_{KL}(\overrightarrow{R_{a'}} \,\|\, freq(\overrightarrow{o})) \ \forall a' \in A$$

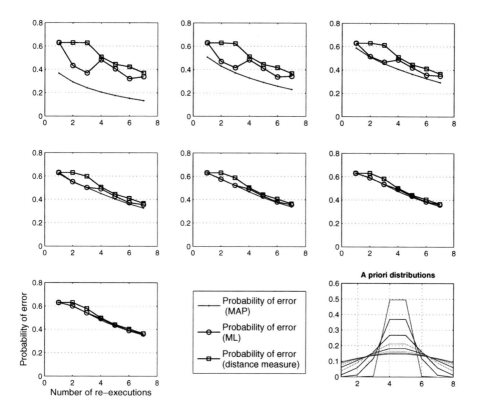

Fig. 4. Comparison of the three probabilities of error using different a priori distributions

where $D_{KL}(\cdot \,||\, \cdot)$ is the KL divergence (relative entropy).

The probability of error based on this decision function is:

$$1 - \sum_{\overrightarrow{o}} p(\overrightarrow{o}\,|a_{min\,\overrightarrow{o}})\, p(a_{min\,\overrightarrow{o}})$$

where

$$\forall \overrightarrow{o}, \ a_{min\,\overrightarrow{o}} = \arg\min_a D_{KL}(\overrightarrow{R_a}||freq(\overrightarrow{o})).$$

To compare these probabilities of error, we did a set of empirical experiments on Crowds protocol. We considered a Crowds protocol (8 users, 2 collaborators, and $p_f = 0.9$) and a set of a priori distributions ranging from a distribution peaked in 2 inputs to the almost uniform distribution as shown in the lower right plot of Figure 4. The experiment consists in repeating the execution of the protocol 1 time, 2 times, etc. until 8 times and seeing how the 3 probabilities of error compare to each others. Each plot of Figure 4 shows the result of the experiment for a different a priori distribution. The first plot (upper-left), for instance, corresponds to the distribution peaked in two inputs. In all plots, the probabilities of error are decreasing. This is expected because the more the protocol is re-executed, the less uncertain the attacker will be about the input.

The only exception concerns the probability of error with ML as the 3 first plots exhibit a strange situation where an increase in the number of re-executions yields to a larger probability of error which is clearly counter intuitive. This can be explained by the inconsistent values of ML probability of error in some extreme situations as discussed in Section 3.1.

According to Figure 4, MAP rule yields the best decision function. This confirms a result in [9] stating that even when the protocol is re-executed, the MAP rule based decision function remains the best. As of the probability of error we proposed, according to Figure 4, it is not minimal but it is more reliable than ML. Also, from the same figure we can note that as the a priori distribution approaches the uniform distribution, the different probabilities of error become almost the same.

6 Conclusion

In this paper we have investigated a new idea of measuring the information leaked by a protocol by analyzing the vector configuration of the channel probabilities matrix. We considered each row of the matrix as a point in the n-dimensional space and we used statistical dispersion measures to estimate how much the points are scattered in the space. Empirical results showed that the two proposed measures KLSD and KLMD are sensitive to the modifications of the attacker capabilities and most importantly they are stable when the a priori distribution on the secret events changes. In the light of this second property, we strongly think that this new approach holds the promise of much less dependence on the a priori distribution on secret events. On the other side, compared to existing information-theoretic anonymity measures ([6,?]) which focus on the lack of information that an attacker has about the identities of users, the proposed approach focuses rather on the capability of the protocol to disguise this information given the attacker's knowledge about the observables. In other words, we focus on the difference between the a priori and a posteriori distributions and not on analyzing the a posteriori distribution only. This makes our approach more general. We mention also that the proposed measures are easy to compute compared for instance to channel capacity.

In this paper, we compared the proposed measures with mutual information by trying them on Crowds, Onion-Routing, and DC-Net protocols. It turns out that the channel matrices for these particular protocols are symmetric and hence the capacity reaches its maximum in the uniform distribution. We plan to carry out comparisons on other protocols and attack scenarios where capacity reaches its maximum in a non-uniform distribution. It is important to mention however that in order to fairly compare the proposed measures as well as Smith's measure with Capacity, one has to find the distribution that maximizes every one of these measures. This is part of our future work.

In both proposed measures, we used relative entropy (or Kullback-Leibler divergence) to compute the "distance" between two probability distributions (rows the matrix). Our plans for future work include the investigation of other statistical dispersion measures such as average (mean) deviation and interquartile range and also other probability distribution metrics such as Hellinger distance and Levy metric [25]. Our goal is to find the best combination of statistical dispersion measure and probability distribution metric that reveals the connection between the vector configuration of the matrix and the information leaked. We plan also further analyze the proposed family of measures when applied on other anonymity systems, in particular Mix-based ones [26] and Tor [27].

Acknowledgement

This research has been initiated by an informal discussion with Catuscia Palamidessi and a large part of it took place under the supervision of Prakash Panangaden. We sincerely thank them for their help and their support. Research funded in part by FQRNT (McGill University, Canada) and Junior Faculty Grant (KFUPM, Saudi Arabia).

References

1. Chaum, D.: Untraceable electronic mail, return addresses, and digital pseudonyms. Communications of the ACM 24(2), 84–90 (1981)
2. Reiter, M., Rubin, A.: Crowds: Anonymity for web transactions. ACM Transactions on Information and System Security 1(1), 66–92 (1998)
3. Syverson, P., Goldschlag, D., Reed, M.: Anonymous connections and onion routing. In: Proceedings of the 1997 IEEE Symposium on Security and Privacy (SP 1997), Washington, DC, USA. IEEE Computer Society, Los Alamitos (1997)
4. Chaum, D.: The dining cryptographers problem: unconditional sender and recipient untraceability. Journal of Cryptology 1(1), 65–75 (1988)
5. Shields, C., Levine, B.: A protocol for anonymous communication over the internet. In: Proceedings of the 7th ACM Conference on Computer and Communications Security, pp. 33–42. ACM, New York (2000)
6. Serjantov, A., Danezis, G.: Towards an information theoretic metric for anonymity. In: Dingledine, R., Syverson, P.F. (eds.) PET 2002. LNCS, vol. 2482, pp. 41–53. Springer, Heidelberg (2003)
7. Diaz, C., Seys, S., Claessens, J., Preneel, B.: Towards measuring anonymity. In: Dingledine, R., Syverson, P.F. (eds.) PET 2002. LNCS, vol. 2482, pp. 54–68. Springer, Heidelberg (2003)
8. Zhu, Y., Bettati, R.: Anonymity vs. information leakage in anonymity systems. In: Proceedings of the 25th IEEE International Conference on Distributed Computing Systems (ICDCS 2005), Columbus, Ohio, pp. 514–524 (2005)
9. Chatzikokolakis, K., Palamidessi, C., Panangaden, P.: Anonymity protocols as noisy channels. Information and Computation 206(2-4), 378–401 (2008)
10. Moskowitz, I., Newman, R., Crepeau, D., Miller, A.: Covert channels and anonymizing networks. In: WPES 2003: Proceedings of the 2003 ACM workshop on Privacy in the electronic society, pp. 79–88. ACM, New York (2003)
11. Cover, T., Thomas, J.: Elements of Information Theory. Wiley-Interscience, New York (1991)
12. Smith, G.: On the foundations of quantitative information flow. In: de Alfaro, L. (ed.) FOSSACS 2009. LNCS, vol. 5504, pp. 288–302. Springer, Heidelberg (2009)
13. Rény, A.: On measures of entropy and information. In: Proceedings of the 4th Berkeley Symposium on Mathematics, Statistics, and Probability, pp. 547–561 (1960)
14. Moskowitz, I., Newman, R., Syverson, P.: Quasi-anonymous channels. In: IASTED CNIS, pp. 126–131 (2003)
15. Newman, R., Moskowitz, I., Syverson, P., Serjantov, A.: Metrics for traffic analysis prevention. In: Dingledine, R. (ed.) PET 2003. LNCS, vol. 2760, pp. 48–65. Springer, Heidelberg (2003)

16. Tóth, G., Hornák, Z., Vajda, F.: Measuring anonymity revisited. In: Liimatainen, S., Virtanen, T. (eds.) Proceedings of the Ninth Nordic Workshop on Secure IT Systems, Espoo, Finland, pp. 85–90 (November 2004)
17. Edman, M., Sivrikaya, F., Yener, B.: A combinatorial approach to measuring anonymity. In: 2007 IEEE Intelligence and Security Informatics, pp. 356–363 (2007)
18. Chatzikokolakis, K., Palamidessi, C., Panangaden, P.: On the bayes risk in information-hiding protocols. Journal of Computer Security 16(5), 531–571 (2008)
19. Clark, D., Hunt, S., Malacaria, P.: Quantitative analysis of the leakage of confidential data. Electrical Notes in Theoretical Computer Science 59, 238–251 (2001)
20. University of Oxford: Prism, http://www.prismmodelchecker.org
21. Chatzikokolakis, K.: Probabilistic and Information-Theoretic Approaches to Anonymity. PhD thesis, Laboratoire d'Informatique (LIX), École Polytechnique, Paris (October 2007)
22. MacKay, D.: Information Theory, Inference and Learning Algorithms. Cambridge University Press, Cambridge (2003)
23. Wright, M., Adler, M., Levine, B., Shields, C.: An analysis of the degradation of anonymous protocols. In: Proceedings of the Network and Distributed Security Symposium (NDSS 2002). IEEE Computer Society, Los Alamitos (2001)
24. Syverson, P., Tsudik, G., Reed, M., Landwehr, C.: Towards an analysis of onion routing security. In: Proceedings of the international workshop on Designing privacy enhancing technologies, pp. 96–114. Springer, New York (2001)
25. Gibbs, A., Su, F.: On choosing and bounding probability metrics. International Statistical Institute 70, 418–435 (2002)
26. Danezis, G., Diaz, C.: A survey of anonymous communication channels. Technical Report MSR-TR-2008-35, Microsoft Research (January 2008)
27. Dingledine, R., Mathewson, N., Syverson, P.: Tor: the second-generation onion router. In: Proceedings of the 13th Usenix Security Symposium (August 2004)

Hidden Markov Models for
Automated Protocol Learning

Sean Whalen[1,2], Matt Bishop[1], and James P. Crutchfield[1,2,3]

[1] Department of Computer Science
University of California, Davis
{whalen,bishop}@cs.ucdavis.edu
[2] Department of Physics
University of California, Davis
chaos@cse.ucdavis.edu
[3] Santa Fe Institute
1399 Hyde Park Road
Santa Fe, New Mexico 87501

Abstract. Hidden Markov Models (HMMs) have applications in several areas of computer security. One drawback of HMMs is the selection of appropriate model parameters, which is often ad hoc or requires domain-specific knowledge. While algorithms exist to find local optima for some parameters, the number of states must always be specified and directly impacts the accuracy and generality of the model. In addition, domain knowledge is not always available or may be based on assumptions that prove incorrect or sub-optimal.

We apply the ϵ-machine—a special type of HMM—to the task of constructing network protocol models solely from network traffic. Unlike previous approaches, ϵ-machine reconstruction infers the minimal HMM architecture directly from data and is well suited to applications such as anomaly detection. We draw distinctions between our approach and previous research, and discuss the benefits and challenges of ϵ-machines for protocol model inference.

Keywords: Statistical Inference, Reverse Engineering, Network Protocols, Markov Models, Computational Mechanics.

1 Introduction

Understanding the structure of a network protocol allows us to "speak" its language and converse with other systems on the network that use it. The structure of commonly used protocols, such as HTTP and FTP, are provided by their specification. In addition, these protocols use fragments of English as well as other ASCII text such as domain names. As a result, the presence of HTTP or FTP traffic can be identified by visual inspection of a network trace, assuming the channel is not encrypted. One can then use its specification, or one of many free or commercial tools, to understand the traffic present in the trace.

S. Jajodia and J. Zhou (Eds.): SecureComm 2010, LNICST 50, pp. 415–428, 2010.
© Institute for Computer Sciences, Social Informatics and Telecommunications Engineering 2010

The task becomes more difficult when the protocol in question uses non-ASCII representations of state to establish connections and exchange data. Still, there are many approaches to identify the protocol such as using port numbers, unique payload signatures, or machine learning techniques [1]. Once the protocol is identified, the traffic can again be understood by using the specification.

In contrast to protocol identification, consider the scenario where we do not have access to the protocol's specification—it is either proprietary, undocumented, or otherwise obfuscated. We can treat the protocol as a black box, where a hidden state machine governs the transmission of packets on the network. To understand the structure of the packets, the task of protocol inference is to approximate this hidden state machine with only the observed packets as a guide.

Hidden Markov Models (HMMs) [2] are a common statistical model for systems with hidden internal states that can be measured only indirectly by observation. These models have numerous applications in computer science, including several in computer security. An HMM is specified by a state transition matrix and a symbol emission matrix. This means that, for an N-state HMM with a discrete alphabet of size M, there are $N(N-1) + N(M-1)$ free parameters to be specified. These parameters can be trained using the Baum-Welch algorithm [2], but training is often slow and gets stuck in local optima. In addition, the number of states must still be specified. A model with too many states tends to over-fit the data, while too few states may not fit the data at all. Worse, when dealing with an unknown protocol, there is little if any knowledge available for selecting appropriate model parameters.

To address this problem, we turn to the ϵ-machines of *computational mechanics* [3]. An ϵ-machine is the minimal deterministic HMM of a stochastic process. A *reconstruction algorithm* creates an ϵ-machine from a set of finite strings, and infers the parameters of the minimal HMM that generates those strings. Here, we treat a network protocol as a stochastic process and the traffic it generates as input strings for the reconstruction algorithm. With the ϵ-machine in hand, we can perform different tasks such as protocol mimicry, intelligent fuzzing, traffic generation, and anomaly detection.

We next discuss recent work done on protocol inference and the benefits of our approach. We follow this with background on HMMs and ϵ-machines, and demonstrate our reconstruction technique using several simple protocols. Finally, we discuss future applications and the limitations of our approach. Our discussion assumes familiarity with stochastic processes and information theory at the level of Cover and Thomas [4].

2   Related Work

Current approaches to protocol inference can be divided into two primary groups: those that infer partial or complete protocol formats [5, 6, 7, 8, 9, 10], and those that infer a state machine model [11, 12]. Both groups can be further divided into those that examine network traces [5, 11, 6, 7], and those that additionally examine how a protocol implementation processes those traces [8,9,10,12]. Each approach has different strengths and weaknesses, but both must identify the location and size of protocol headers.

Much of the recent work can be traced back to Protocol Informatics, which attempted to "determine the location and length of fields within protocol packets" using sequence alignment algorithms typically found in bioinformatics [5]. This approach was extended by RolePlayer, which used heuristics identify the locations of IP addresses and domain names in a packet, in order to "successfully replay one side of a [protocol] session" [6].

This work led to Discoverer, which focused on "reverse engineering the [complete] message format specification" [7]. In this work, Cui et al. found that selecting robust parameters for sequence alignment was difficult, and that alignment has trouble identifying variable length fields in messages of the same format. In response, they developed a type-based alignment algorithm that infers the semantics of different fields, and used these semantics to cluster messages of the same format. Inference of the state machine, which is the focus of our approach, was left to future work.

Prospex addressed this issue by inferring non-probabilistic state machines from execution traces of a protocol implementation [12]. Their state machine "reflects the sequences in which messages may be exchanged". They converted their machines into input specifications for the fuzzing tool Peach, and found several known and unknown flaws in open source software.

In contrast, our ϵ-machine approach infers the minimal HMM from passively observed network data without using execution traces. This strikes a middle ground between Discoverer and Prospex, with several unique contributions. These include using a probabilistic model that enables anomaly detection via model comparison techniques, and avoiding ad hoc specification of model parameters by inferring them from the data.

We continue with a brief overview of HMMs and ϵ-machines, and refer the reader to references [2] and [3] for further detail.

3   Background

A discrete stochastic process is a sequence $\ldots X_1, X_2, X_3 \ldots$ of random variables X_n indexed by time; realizations $\ldots x_1, x_2, x_3 \ldots$ are often referred to as *time series* data. Here, we use time series and *string* interchangeably. The set of strings a process generates forms a stochastic language in which each string occurs with some probability. We treat a network protocol as a stochastic process, transmitting packets in the protocol's language with varying probabilities. Several well known model classes, such as Markov Chains and Hidden Markov Models, are commonly used to represent finite-memory stochastic processes. We will consider these in turn, eventually introducing ϵ-machines as a useful alternative.

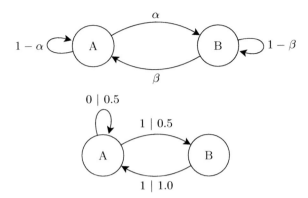

Fig. 1. *Top:* The general form of a two-state Markov Chain. *Bottom:* An HMM for the Even Process. A state transition occurs with some probability p and generates a symbol s, displayed as the edge label $s \mid p$. For example, the label $1 \mid 0.5$ indicates symbol 1 is generated with probability 0.5.

3.1   Markov Models

A Markov Chain is a representation of a stochastic process that assumes the conditional probability of a future state X_{n+1} depends only on the present state X_n [13]:

$$\Pr(X_{n+1} = x \mid X_n = x_n, X_{n-1} = x_{n-1}, \ldots, X_1 = x_1)$$
$$= \Pr(X_{n+1} = x \mid X_n = x_n) , \quad (1)$$

where $X_1 \ldots X_n$ is a sequence of random variables representing process state over time. While this dependency can be extended to include a fixed number of past states, a finite state Markov Chain can only represent a stochastic process that has a limited dependence on history.

Transitions between states are random, occurring with probabilities specified in a row-normalized transition matrix T of size $|X| \times |X|$. Here, $|X|$ is the number of states. The probability of transitioning from state i to state j is denoted T_{ij}. As an example, a Markov Chain with two states $X = \{A, B\}$ has the form:

$$T = \begin{pmatrix} 1 - \alpha & \alpha \\ \beta & 1 - \beta \end{pmatrix} , \quad (2)$$

where $\alpha, \beta \in [0, 1]$ are parameters. This corresponds graphically to the state machine diagram shown in Fig. 1.

Due to their limited history dependence, Markov Chains represent only a subset of stochastic processes. Consider the Even Process which generates binary strings in which the number of consecutive 1s, bounded by 0s, is always even. For example, the strings 0110 and 011110 are in its language, but the string 010 is not. It turns out that this process is not equivalent to a Markov Chain of any finite order [14]. In such cases, one must employ a more sophisticated model class such as Hidden Markov Models (HMMs).

3.2   Hidden Markov Models

An HMM is a Markov Chain in which the states, now denoted $\mathcal{S}$, are not observed directly but indirectly through measurement symbols X_n. Each observed symbol is generated by a transition between hidden states according to some distribution.

Since multiple transitions can generate the same observed symbol, the internal transitions and states of the system typically are not directly revealed by observation. Nonetheless, given an HMM, several quantities of interest can be calculated [2], including the probability of observing a particular string, the most likely hidden-state sequence for a given string, and the state transition and symbol emission probabilities that maximize the probability of a particular string.

The Even Process is exactly represented by the two-state HMM given in Fig. 1. By distinguishing internal states from observed symbols, HMMs can finitely represent a much wider class of stochastic processes than Markov Chains.

3.3 ϵ-Machines

In fact, Fig. 1 shows a special HMM representation for the Even Process—one with a minimal number of states. Moreover, the transitions are *deterministic*, meaning that the measurement symbols occur on at most one transition leaving a state. This property guarantees that, although there is not a one-to-one relationship between internal states and measurement symbols, there is a one-to-one relationship between sufficiently long measurement *words* and internal state *paths*. Thus, internal state information is present, if very indirectly, in the observed process.

An HMM with these properties is called an ϵ-*machine*. An ϵ-machine is the minimal, optimal predictor for a stochastic process and so captures all of the latter's causal structure [3]. For these reasons, this is the model class we will use.

Formally, an ϵ-machine consists of a set of *causal states* $\mathcal{S}$, a measurement alphabet $\mathcal{A}$, and a set of transition matrices $\{T^{(s)} : s \in \mathcal{A}\}$. There are several *reconstruction algorithms* that one can use to infer an ϵ-machine from a time series. We use the state splitting algorithm of Shalizi et al., whose time complexity is $O(|\mathcal{A}|^{2L_{max}+1}) + O(N)$ [15]. Separate from the mathematical theory, different reconstruction algorithms make specific assumptions about the underlying process. The type of process being modeled thus affects the choice of algorithm.

Given an ϵ-machine, we can calculate certain important properties of a process. In particular, the determinism of the state transitions enables direct calculation of information-theoretic quantities, such as the process's rate of information production (source entropy rate) and the amount of historical information it stores (statistical complexity) [3,14]. Such properties cannot be calculated from an HMM representation that is not an ϵ-machine.

To estimate an HMM from time series, the number of states and transitions must be guessed a priori. In contrast, ϵ-machine reconstruction algorithms infer the minimal deterministic HMM architecture directly from time series data [16, 15]. This is a critical distinction if one wishes to discover the structure embedded in a process, as opposed to guessing it ahead of time. This is advantageous when reverse engineering protocols where prior information is unavailable.

4   Protocol Inference

4.1   Approach

We first define a network protocol as a set of *message types*. Each message type consists of a sequence of bits, and related bits are often grouped into *headers*. A particular message type may contain a set of headers, as well as a data *payload*. This payload may contain data provided by the user, or may *encapsulate* messages of a higher level protocol. Thus, we can think of a protocol message at several levels of abstraction: as a sequence of bits, bytes, or headers and payloads.

By changing the level of abstraction, we can adjust the order of the underlying Markov Chain as well as its alphabet size $|\mathcal{A}|$. In addition, we are interested in the structure of the protocol and not highly entropic user data such as images or movies, so we attempt to detect and ignore payloads. This further reduces the alphabet size, and is essential to the practical use of ϵ-machines.

Consider a minimal protocol having a single message type, consisting of a 2-byte length header and a payload. The length header specifies the number of bytes in the payload as an unsigned 16-bit integer. A four byte message sending the ASCII characters for "no" could then be viewed as a sequence of bits:

$$00000000\ 00000010\ 01101110\ 01101111$$

or of bytes:

$$0\ 2\ 110\ 111$$

or of headers and payloads:

$$2\ \text{"no"}$$

The binary sequence has $|\mathcal{A}| = 2$, but requires a prohibitive order-16 model to capture the first header. At the byte level this becomes order-2, but $|\mathcal{A}|$ increases to 4. Finally, if we know where the separation between header and payload is, we can use an order-1 model with $|\mathcal{A}| = 2$. If more messages are observed, the alphabet size of the byte representation could increase to 256, so operating at the header level is desirable. Of course, knowing the location and size of message headers requires either the protocol specification or heuristics.

Protocols such as HTTP and FTP use ASCII tokens, so header boundaries are easily identified by inspection—typically tabs, spaces, newlines, and carriage returns. For more difficult binary protocols, Beddoe aligns bytes across different messages using bioinformatics algorithms and then uses simple statistics as a boundary detection heuristic [5]. Cui et al. discuss difficulties with sequence alignment and devise a significantly improved type-based alignment algorithm [7]. Both methods are compatible with our approach, though we use minimum entropy clustering [17] to group messages of the same type and then apply the simple statistics of Beddoe to identify likely header boundaries. This method is adequate for the protocols discussed here, but complex protocols may require additional sophistication.

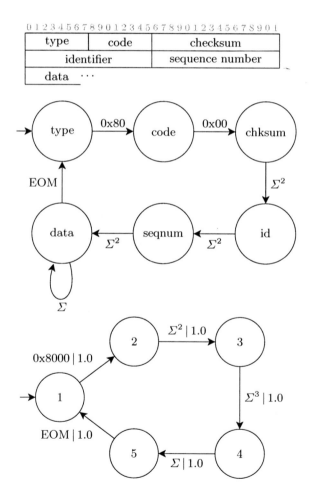

Fig. 2. *Top:* Specification of an ICMP echo request [18], *Middle:* HMM representation, *Bottom:* ϵ-Machine representation. The symbol Σ represents a random byte of data, with Σ^n denoting n consecutive random bytes.

Thus, our inference approach can be separated into three primary tasks: 1) grouping bytes into headers, 2) filtering highly entropic data, and 3) reconstructing the ϵ-machine. Tasks 1 and 2 exist primarily to reduce the alphabet size, and can be changed independently of task 3. For example, type-based alignment could be exchanged with minimum entropy clustering to transparently improve the accuracy of the inferred model.

4.2   Results

We introduce protocol ϵ-machines and their accompanying notation using two simple binary protocols, followed by two more complex protocols. The first of these, the Internet Control Messaging Protocol (ICMP) [18] defines several message types used for network diagnostics. One of these types, the echo request/reply, finds common use in the ping command line utility bundled with most operating systems. For this discussion we focus on echo requests, consisting of a 1-byte type set to 0x80, 1-byte code set to 0x00, 2-byte checksum whose contents are a function of the message, 2-byte identifier, 2-byte sequence number, and zero or more bytes of payload.

The message specification, a corresponding 6-state HMM, and the ϵ-machine are shown in Figure 2. A state is created in the HMM for each header, with transitions between states whose headers are adjacent in the specification. Transition are labeled with the symbols to be generated. The symbol Σ^n denotes n consecutive random bytes. The symbol EOM signals the message is complete and ready for transmission.

The ϵ-machine inferred from captured echo requests is shown below the HMM. Transitions are labeled with the symbol s generated by the transition and the probability p of the transition being taken, denoted $s \mid p$. This intentionally simple example has no branching between states, resulting in transition probabilities of 1. The type and code headers are constant values, causing their separate HMM states to be merged in the ϵ-machine.

Many protocols contain a sequence number header represented as a 16-bit integer. However, the first byte of this header changes very rarely compared to the second byte that is incremented with each message. In the requests captured for this example, the identifier header and the first byte of the sequence number remained constant, resulting in their grouping into a single value by the boundary detection heuristic (see the $\mathcal{A}^3$ transition between state 3 and 4). While this does not match the specification, it is a reasonable grouping to make based solely on the statistics of the observed messages. Given enough data, the bytes will be grouped into the correct fields.

We next examine Modbus, a protocol commonly used in supervisory control and data acquisition (SCADA) systems for managing industrial and infrastructure processes such as power generation and waste management. Designed in the late 70s to operate on simple programmable logic controllers, it has gained recent notoriety due to its lack of security. These issues have escalated due to the Modbus/TCP variant [19] connecting these systems to standard TCP/IP networks.

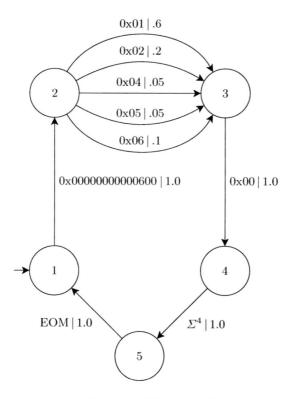

Fig. 3. *Top:* Specification of a Modbus/TCP request [19], *Bottom:* ε-Machine representation

The specification of Modbus/TCP requests and an inferred ε-machine are shown in Figure 3. A request consists of a 2-byte transaction id, 2-byte protocol id set to 0x00, 2-byte length, 1-byte unit id, 1-byte function code, and variable length payload.

The captured traffic, generated by a protocol simulator, consists of 150 requests where all transaction ids and unit ids are set to 0x00. Traffic generated by the simulator is actual Modbus traffic, and not a statistical approximation. Observed function codes include 0x01 for reading coils, 0x02 for reading discrete inputs, 0x04 for reading input registers, 0x05 for writing single coils, and 0x06 for writing single registers. Each payload contains 4 bytes specifying the range of coils or registers to read or write. Branching occurs between state 2 and 3, with each transition probability representing the maximum likelihood estimate of a different function code.

FTP

Sample Size	Recurrent States	Time (Seconds)
300	6	0.18
600	9	0.20
900	10	0.23
1200	10	0.11
1500	11	0.32

HTTP

Sample Size	Recurrent States	Time (Seconds)
14337	12	0.18
28674	14	0.35
43011	18	0.84
57348	20	1.16
71685	22	1.86

Fig. 4. Scaling of inferred states and inference time as a function of data length, for FTP (top) and HTTP (bottom). Time is not necessarily monotonically increasing due to finite sample effects. State counts are given for non-deterministic presentations of the ϵ-machine.

Reconstruction also works with more complex protocols such as FTP and HTTP. Model size prevents including the full ϵ-machines here, so we present summaries of their reconstruction in Figure 4. Shown is the scaling of inferred states and reconstruction time as a function of data length, performed on a single core of an Intel Core 2 Duo 2.4GHz CPU under OS X 10.6.3. A Python implementation of the state splitting reconstruction algorithm [15] was used, and will soon be available in the open source Computational Mechanics in Python (CMPy) library. Captured traffic was obtained from the UCDavis Honeynet Project.

An 18-state ϵ-machine can be inferred from 60,000 symbols in less than a second using an interpreted language. A random walk on the machine generates new packets that are accepted by a remote protocol implementation as valid, indicating the structure of the protocol is correctly captured. Together, these results show that probabilistic reconstruction of both binary and text-based protocols is possible when alphabet size is managed. Given this, we next discuss future applications of probabilistic models to protocol inference.

5   Future Work

Capturing probabilities enables an ϵ-machine to model normal behavior and detect anomalies using model comparison techniques. This is an advantage of ϵ-machines over non-probabilistic state machines such as minimized prefix tree acceptors [20].

We employ relative entropy [4] for model comparison between ϵ-machines, as well as measuring the model's fit. Relative entropy, also known as the Kullback-Liebler

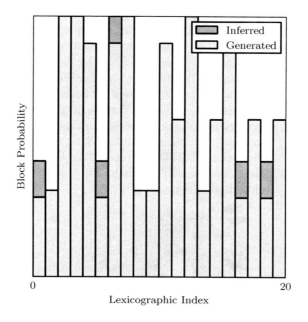

Fig. 5. Overlayed distributions of block length 4 symbols using an ϵ-machine inferred from Modbus traffic (dark gray) to generate new traffic (light gray). Relative entropy between the distributions is 0.09 bits, indicating the distributions are close.

divergence, measures the distance between two probability distributions P and Q and is defined as:

$$D_{KL}(P||Q) = \sum_i P(i) \log \frac{P(i)}{Q(i)} \ , \tag{3}$$

and $D_{KL}(P||Q) = 0$ when P and Q are equal. Thus, a large relative entropy between machines may indicate anomalous behavior. More work is needed to determine appropriate thresholds for flagging behavior as anomalous with an acceptable false positive rate.

A random walk on an ϵ-machine generates new traffic, useful for both protocol mimicry and traffic simulation. We measure the fit of the model by taking the relative entropy between the new and original traffic distributions as shown in Figure 5. An ϵ-machine inferred from 500 captured Modbus requests was used to generate new traffic with a distribution almost identical to the original, having 0.09 bits of relative entropy.

Random walks on the machine can also be used for intelligent fuzzing. Fuzzing tests the robustness of a program by feeding it invalid input values, often in the form of random inputs or mutated valid inputs. If the program does not correctly handle invalid input, it may crash or leave the system vulnerable to attack.

While generally considered effective for finding bugs, a substantial drawback
to this approach is code coverage. For example, if the code's execution path
depends on the value of a 32-bit integer, a random input has a 1 in 2^{32} chance of
evaluating that code path [21]. Working with mutated valid inputs enables more
targeted testing, but requires some knowledge of the specification. The inferred
ϵ-machine enables such targeted fuzzing when no specification is available.

Consider a previously known flaw in Golden FTP Server 2.70 for Windows [22].
A CWD command sent from the client with certain large arguments crashes the
server and enables remote code execution. Using an ϵ-machine inferred from FTP
traffic and tuned to produce longer runs of random data, this flaw was reproduced
by a random walk on the machine. The subgraph of the ϵ-machine relating to the
crash is given in Figure 6. We plan to investigate if probabilistic models confer
additional benefits to intelligent fuzzing.

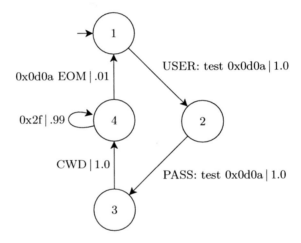

Fig. 6. Subgraph of the ϵ-machine used for fuzzing Golden FTP Server 2.70, crashing
the server when a CWD command is followed by more than 150 bytes. Symbol probabilities in the inferred ϵ-machine were tuned to produce longer sequences of random
data for guided fuzzing.

6   Conclusion

We presented a novel HMM-based approach for inferring the state machine of
network protocols using only their traffic. While generally applicable to any
non-encrypted protocol stream, our emphasis is on protocols without a publicly
available specification.

Our approach uses ϵ-machine reconstruction [3] to infer the minimal deterministic HMM of a protocol. The parameters of the HMM are inferred directly
from the data, which avoids the typical pitfalls involved in parameter selection.
We demonstrated our approach using ICMP, Modbus, FTP, and HTTP, and use
the inferred ϵ-machines for protocol mimicry, fuzzing, and traffic generation. We

plan to use the probabilistic nature of our models for anomaly detection, and have early success doing so in high performance computing environments.

Due to the limitations of traffic-based approaches, as well as sensitivity to alphabet size, more work remains to adapt reconstruction to high complexity protocols. In some cases where domain knowledge is available, traditional HMMs may scale better than ϵ-machines, and we leave this investigation to future work. However, our approach is well suited to protocol inference where domain knowledge is lacking for manual construction of state machine models.

Acknowledgements

This work was partially supported by the DARPA Physical Intelligence Program, as well as the Director, Office of Computational and Technology Research, Division of Mathematical, Information, and Computational Sciences of the U.S. Department of Energy, under contract number DE-AC02-05CH11231.

References

1. Erman, J., Mahanti, A., Arlitt, M.: Internet traffic identification using machine learning. In: Proceedings of the 49th IEEE Global Telecommunications Conference, pp. 1–6 (2006)
2. Rabiner, L.: A tutorial on Hidden Markov Models and selected applications in speech recognition. Proceedings of the IEEE 77, 257–286 (1989)
3. Crutchfield, J.P., Young, K.: Inferring statistical complexity. Phys. Rev. Let. 63 (1989); Crutchfield, J.P.: Physica D 75 11–54 (1994); Crutchfield, J. P., Shalizi, C. R.: Phys. Rev. E 59(1), 275–283, 105–108 (1999)
4. Cover, T.M., Thomas, J.A.: Elements of Information Theory, 2nd edn. Wiley Interscience, New York (2006)
5. Beddoe, M.: Network protocol analysis using bioinformatics algorithms. Technical report, McAfee Inc. (2005)
6. Cui, W., Paxson, V., Weaver, N., Katz, R.: Protocol-independent adaptive replay of application dialog. In: Proceedings of the 13th Annual Symposium on Network and Distributed System Security (2006)
7. Cui, W., Kannan, J., Wang, H.: Discoverer: Automatic protocol reverse engineering from network traces. In: Proceedings of 16th USENIX Security Symposium on USENIX Security Symposium, pp. 1–14 (2007)
8. Lin, Z., Jiang, X., Xu, D., Zhang, X.: Automatic protocol format reverse engineering through context-aware monitored execution. In: Proceedings of the 15th Annual Network and Distributed System Security Symposium (2008)
9. Wondracek, G., Milani Comparetti, P., Kruegel, C., Kirda, E.: Automatic network protocol analysis. In: Proceedings of the 15th Symposium on Network and Distributed System Security (2008)
10. Caballero, J., Poosankam, P., Kreibich, C., Song, D.: Dispatcher: enabling active botnet infiltration using automatic protocol reverse-engineering. In: Proceedings of the 16th ACM conference on Computer and Communications Security, pp. 621–634 (2009)

11. Leita, C., Mermoud, K., Dacier, M.: Scriptgen: An automated script generation tool for honeyd. In: Proceedings of the 21st Annual Computer Security Applications Conference, pp. 203–214 (2005)
12. Milani Comparetti, P., Wondracek, G., Kruegel, C., Kirda, E.: Prospex: Protocol specification extraction. In: IEEE Symposium on Security and Privacy (2009)
13. Norris, J.R.: Markov Chains. Cambridge University Press, Cambridge (1997)
14. Crutchfield, J., Feldman, D.: Regularities unseen, randomness observed: Levels of entropy convergence. Chaos 15, 25–54 (2003)
15. Shalizi, C.R., Shalizi, K.L.: Blind construction of optimal nonlinear recursive predictors for discrete sequences. In: Proceedings of the 20th conference on Uncertainty in Artificial Intelligence, pp. 504–511 (2004)
16. Shalizi, C., Shalizi, K., Crutchfield, J.: Pattern discovery in time series, Part I: Theory, algorithm, analysis, and convergence, 2002 Santa Fe Institute Working Paper 02-10-060; arXiv.org/abs/cs.LG/0210025
17. Li, H., Zhang, K., Jiang, T.: Minimum entropy clustering and applications to gene expression analysis. In: Computational Systems Bioinformatics Conference, International IEEE Computer Society, pp. 142–151 (2004)
18. Postel, J.: Internet Control Message Protocol (1981), Updated by RFCs 950, 4884
19. Modbus Organization: Modbus Messaging Implementation Guide 1.0b (2006)
20. Bugalho, M., Oliveira, A.L.: Inference of regular languages using state merging algorithms with search. Pattern Recognition 38 (2005)
21. Godefroid, P.: Random testing for security: blackbox vs. whitebox fuzzing. In: Proceedings of the 2nd international workshop on Random testing, p. 1 (2007)
22. Infigo Information Security: Multiple FTP Servers vulnerabilities (2006) (accessed October 29, 2006)

Epistemic Model Checking for Knowledge-Based Program Implementation: An Application to Anonymous Broadcast*

Omar I. Al-Bataineh and Ron van der Meyden

School of Computer Science and Engineering,
University of New South Wales

Abstract. Knowledge-based programs provide an abstract level of description of protocols in which agent actions are related to their states of knowledge. The paper describes how epistemic model checking technology may be applied to discover and verify concrete implementations based on this abstract level of description. The details of the implementations depend on the specific context of use of the protocol. The knowledge-based approach enables the implementations to be optimized relative to these conditions of use. The approach is illustrated using extensions of the Dining Cryptographers protocol, a security protocol for anonymous broadcast.

Keywords: Formal methods, anonymity, model checking.

1 Introduction

In distributed systems, we generally would like agent's actions to depend upon the information that they have. However, the way that information flows in such systems can be quite complex. It has been proposed to address this complexity by the use of formal logics of knowledge [4].

In particular, *knowledge based programs* have been proposed as a level of abstraction that directly captures the relationship between an agent's knowledge and its actions, by allowing branching statements to contain formulas of the modal logic of knowledge, expressing what the agent knows about the global state of the system. This has several advantages. By focusing on what information is required, rather than how it is encoded, knowledge-based programs can be more intuitive and more easily verified to be correct. They can also provide a common description that is independent of assumptions such as the failure modes of

---

* This material is based on research sponsored by the Air Force Research Laboratory, under agreement number FA2386-09-1-4156. The U.S. Government is authorized to reproduce and distribute reprints for Governmental purposes notwithstanding any copyright notation thereon. The views and conclusions contained herein are those of the authors and should not be interpreted as necessarily representing the official policies or endorsements, either expressed or implied, of the Air Force Research Laboratory or the U.S. Government.

S. Jajodia and J. Zhou (Eds.): SecureComm 2010, LNICST 50, pp. 429–447, 2010.

communication channels in the system. Finally, knowledge-based programs lead us to implementations that are *optimal* in their use of information, in the sense that agents do not overlook opportunities to use relevant information that is available in their local states.

A cost of the abstraction that knowledge-based programs provide, is that they are more like specifications than concrete programs, so cannot be directly executed. To obtain an executable program, it is necessary to replace the tests for knowledge in the knowledge based program by equivalent concrete predicates of the agent's local state. Because of the complexity of information flow in distributed systems, such concrete predicates can be difficult to find. To date, this task has generally been carried out by pencil and paper reasoning. Perhaps for this reason, there remain only a handful of worked out examples of the development of concrete implementations of knowledge-based programs (e.g., [1,3,7,9]).

The difficulty can be addressed through the use of model checking technology for the logic of knowledge. Model checkers are systems that take as input a formal model of a system, together with a specification, and determine whether that specification is satisfied by the model [11]. The specification language used in model checkers is generally a form of temporal logic, but in recent years work has begun on the development of model checkers based on logics of knowledge [5,12,19]. We describe a methodology for the use of this latter class of model checkers to the development of implementations of knowledge based programs. The methodology is partially automated. It assists users in finding a concrete predicate that is equivalent to a knowledge condition in a knowledge-based program by means of an iterative process, in which automatically computed counterexamples to a user's guess for the concrete predicate are used by the user to construct an improved concrete predicate, until one is found that is equivalent to the knowledge condition.

We illustrate the methodology by means of an example in which we use the epistemic model checker MCK [5], to develop concrete implementations of a knowledge-based program for anonymous broadcast, based on multiple rounds of Chaum's Dining Cryptographers Protocol [2].

The Dining Cryptographers Protocol enables a message to be broadcast anonymously, under the assumption that only one agent is attempting to broadcast a message. The objective of the extension that we consider is to remove this assumption, so that any number of agents may broadcast their messages anonymously. One of the main difficulties in this is that, since agents operate independently, it is possible for simultaneous broadcasts to interfere with each other, causing a failure in the transmission. Thus, a key issue is to enable the agents to detect conflicts in the transmission, and to respond appropriately when a conflict is detected.

In our analysis, we express the expected behaviour using a knowledge based program that conditions the agent's actions on whether it knows that there is a conflict. We then use our model checking supported methodology to identify exactly the concrete conditions under which an agent knows whether there is a conflict. These conditions turn out to have a surprising level of complexity. In particular, we find that these conditions can differ, depending on the assumptions that we make about the number of agents wishing to broadcast.

Our approach leads to the discovery (assisted by automation) of a number of subtleties concerning the protocol that, to our knowledge, have not been previously noticed. In particular, we find that it is possible for agents to detect conflicts (or lack of conflict) in some quite unexpected situations. Moreover, we discover situations where, even though the protocol terminates, an agent cannot be sure that its message has been successfully transmitted (although it may have a high subjective probability that this is the case). Our results both show that there are previously unnoticed opportunities to optimize the protocol, and help to clarify what should be the specification of the protocol (the previous literature generally describes the protocol without providing a formal specification beyond the statement that it is intended for anonymous broadcast.)

The structure of the paper is as follows. We give a brief introduction to the logic of knowledge and epistemic model checking in Section 2. In Section 3 we discuss knowledge-based programs and describe our methodology for the development of their implementations using epistemic model checking. The Dining Cryptographers problem and its extensions are introduced in Section 4. In Section 5, we describe the application of our methodology to this protocol. Finally, some conclusions are drawn in Section 6.

2   Model Checking Epistemic Logic

Epistemic logics are a class of modal logics that include operators whose meaning concerns the information available to agents in a distributed or multi-agent system. We describe here briefly a version of such a logic combining operators for knowledge and linear time, and its semantics in a class of structures known in the literature as *interpreted systems* [4]. We then discuss the model checker MCK [5], which is based on this semantics.

Suppose that we are interested in systems comprised of n agents and a set *Prop* of atomic propositions. The syntax of the fragment of the logic of knowledge and time relevant for this paper is given by the following grammar:

$$\phi ::= \top \mid p \mid \neg\phi \mid \phi \wedge \phi \mid K_i\phi \mid X\phi$$

where $p \in Prop$ is an atomic proposition and $i \in \{1 \ldots n\}$ is an agent. (We freely use standard boolean operators that can be defined using the two given.) Intuitively, the meaning of $K_i\phi$ is that agent i knows that ϕ is true, and $X\phi$ means that ϕ will be true at the next moment of time.

The semantics we use is the *interpreted systems* model for the logic of knowledge [4]. For each $i = 0 \ldots n$, let S_i be a set of states. For $i = 0$, we interpret S_i as the set of possible states of the environment within which the agents operate; for $i = 1 \ldots n$ we interpret S_i as the set of *local states* of agent i. Intuitively, a local state captures all the concrete pieces of information on the basis of which an agent determines what it knows. We define the set of *global state* based on such collection of environment and local states, to be the set $S = S_0 \times S_1 \times \ldots \times S_n$.

We write s_i for the i-th component (counting from 0) of a global state s. A *run* over S is a function $r : \mathbf{N} \rightarrow S$. An *interpreted system* for n agents is a tuple $\mathcal{I} = (\mathcal{R}, \pi)$, where $\mathcal{R}$ is a set of runs over S, and $\pi : S \rightarrow \mathcal{P}(Prop)$ is an interpretation function.

A *point* of $\mathcal{I}$ is a pair (r, m) where $r \in \mathcal{R}$ and $m \in \mathbf{N}$. We say that two points $(r, m), (r', m')$ are *indistinguishable* to agent i, and write $(r, m) \sim_i (r', m')$, if $r(m)_i = r'(m')_i$, i.e., if agent i has the same local state at these two points. We define the semantics of the logic by means of a relation $\mathcal{I}, (r, m) \models \phi$, where $\mathcal{I}$ is an intepreted system, (r, m) is a point of $\mathcal{I}$ and ϕ is a formula. This relation is defined inductively as follows:

- $\mathcal{I}, (r, m) \models p$ if $p \in \pi(r(m))$,
- $\mathcal{I}, (r, m) \models \neg\phi$ if not $\mathcal{I}, (r, m) \models \phi$
- $\mathcal{I}, (r, m) \models \phi_1 \wedge \phi_2$ if $\mathcal{I}, (r, m) \models \phi_1$ and $\mathcal{I}, (r, m) \models \phi_2$
- $\mathcal{I}, (r, m) \models X\phi$ if $\mathcal{I}, (r, m + 1) \models \phi$
- $\mathcal{I}, (r, m) \models K_i\phi$ if for all points (r', m') of $\mathcal{I}$ such that $r(m) \sim_i r'(m')$ we have $\mathcal{I}, (r', m') \models \phi$

We note that the semantics of the knowledge operator depends not just on the run at which the formula is being evaluated, but also the set of all possible runs. Changing the set of runs (e.g., by making changes to the protocol), can change what an agent knows. Since knowledge-based programs change agent behaviours based on what the agent knows, this makes the semantics of knowledge-based programs somewhat subtle.

MCK is a model checker based on this semantics for the logic of knowledge. For a given interpreted system $\mathcal{I}$, and a specification ϕ in the logic of knowledge and time, MCK computes whether $\mathcal{I}, (r, 0) \models \phi$ holds for all runs r of $\mathcal{I}$.

Since interpreted systems are infinite structures, MCK allows an interpreted system to be given a finite description in the form of a program from which the interpreted system can be generated. This description is given using:

1. A list of global variables making up states of the environment, and their types.
2. A listing of the agents in the system, together with the global variables that they are able to access. For each agent, we may also introduce local variables. If v is a local variable of agent A, then we may refer to this variable in specification formulas as $A.v$. Local variables may be aliased to global variables.

   A subset of the local variables is specified as being *observable* to the agent. This means that it will be taken into account in the definition of the indistinguishability relation for the agent.
3. A statement `init_cond` ϕ, where ϕ is a boolean formula. All assignments satisfying this formula represent an initial state of the system.
4. A program that describes the protocol executed by each agent. The protocol describes how the agent chooses its actions depending on its history.

Executing the agent protocols starting at an initial state generates a set of runs, that we take to be the set of runs of the interpreted system generated by input script. (The agents operate in lock-step, each agent executing a single action in each step. Write-conflicts are syntactically prevented.) If V is the set of all local and global variables in the system, then the component $s_0 = r(n)_0$ of the global state at each point (r, n) of a run r is a well-typed assignment of values to the variables V. The local states s_i of agent i in these runs are defined using the variables declared to be local. MCK allows this to be done in a number of ways, each giving a different semantics for the knowledge operators. The construction of local states relevant to the present paper is the *perfect recall interpretation*. Writing $s_0 \upharpoonright V_i$ for the restriction of the assignment s_0 to the variables V_i that are observable to agent $i = 1 \ldots n$, the local states are defined to be the sequence

$$r(n)_i = (r(0)_0 \upharpoonright V_i)\,(r(1)_0 \upharpoonright V_i) \ldots (r(n)_0 \upharpoonright V_i),$$

i.e., the local state is the history of all values of the variables observable to the agent.

This perfect recall intepretation of knowledge is particularly relevant for analyses in which security or the optimal use of information are of concern. In both cases, we are interested in determining the maximal information that an agent is able to extract from what it observes. Both issues are significant in the example that we study in this paper. MCK is the only model checker currently available that supports *symbolic* model checking for the perfect recall interpretation of knowledge. (DEMO [19] uses a less scalable explicit state algorithm.)

3   Implementation of Knowledge-Based Programs

Knowledge-based programs [4] are like standard programs, except that expressions may refer to agent's knowledge. That is, in a knowledge-based program for agent i, we may find statements of the forms if ϕ then P_1 else P_2 and $v := \phi$, where ϕ is a formula of the logic of knowledge that is a boolean combination of atomic formulas concerning the agent's local variables and formulas of the form $K_i\psi$, and P_1, P_2 are knowledge-based programs for agent i.

Unlike standard programs, knowledge-based programs cannot in general be directly executed, since, as noted above, the satisfaction of the knowledge subformulas depends on the set of all runs of the program, which depends on the actions taken, which in turn depends on the satisfaction of these knowledge subformulas.

This apparent circularity is handled by treating knowledge-based programs as specifications, and defining when a concrete standard program satisfies this specification. Suppose that we have a standard program P of the same syntactic structure as the knowledge-based program $\mathbf{P}$, in which each knowledge-based expression ϕ is replaced by a concrete predicate p_ϕ of the local variables of the agent. In order to handle the perfect recall semantics, we also allow P to add local *history variables* v and code fragments of the form $v := e$, where e is an expression, that update these history variables, so as to make information about past states available at the current time. The predicate p_ϕ may depend on the history variables.

The concrete program P generates a set of runs that we can take to be the basis of an interpreted system $\mathcal{I}(P)$. We now say that P is an *implementation* of the knowledge-based program $\mathbf{P}$ if for each formula ϕ in a conditional, we have that in the interpreted system $\mathcal{I}(P)$, the formula $p_\phi \Leftrightarrow \phi$ is valid (at times when the condition is used). That is, the concrete condition is equivalent to the knowledge condition in the implementation. In general, knowledge-based programs may have no implementations, a behaviourally unique implementation, or many implementations. Some conditions are known under which a behaviourally unique implementation is guaranteed to exist. One of these conditions is that agents have perfect recall and all knowledge formulas in the program refer to the present time (rather than to the past or future). This case will apply to the knowledge-based programs we consider in this paper, so we are guaranteed behaviourally unique implementations.

We now describe a partially automated process, using epistemic model checking, that can be followed to find implementations of knowledge-based programs $\mathbf{P}$ (provide these terminate in a finitely bounded time: this applies to our examples) The user begins by introducing a local boolean variable v_ϕ for each knowledge formula $\phi = K_i\psi$ in the knowledge-based program, and replacing ϕ by v_ϕ. Treating v_ϕ as a history variable, the user may also add to the program statements of the form $v_\phi := e$, relying on their intuitions concerning situations under which the epistemic formula ϕ will be true. This produces a standard program P that is a candidate to be an implementation of the knowledge-based program $\mathbf{P}$. (It has, at least, the correct syntactic structure.)

To verify the correctness of P as an implementation of $\mathbf{P}$, the user must now check that the variables v_ϕ are being maintained so as to be equivalent to the knowledge formulas that they are intended to express. This can be done using epistemic model checking, where we verify formulas of the form

$$X^n(pc_i = l \Rightarrow (v_\phi \Leftrightarrow K_i\psi))$$

where n is a time at which the test containing ϕ may be executed, pc_i is the program counter of agent i and l is a label for the location of the expression containing ϕ. (This conditioning on the program counter can be dispensed with when the expression is known to always occur at particular times n, as it always is in our examples. More generally, we would write a formula that checks equivalence at *all* times for nonterminating programs, but the resulting model checking problem is undecidable with respect to the perfect recall semantics.)

In general, the user's guess concerning the concrete condition that is equivalent to the knowledge formula may be incorrect, and the model checker will report the error. In this case, the model checker can be used to generate an *error trace*, a partial run leading to a situation that falsifies the formula being checked. The next step of our process requires the user to analyse this error trace (by inspection and human reasoning) in order to understand the source of the error in their guess for the concrete condition representing the knowledge formula. As a result of this analysis, a correction of the assignment(s) to the variable v_ϕ is made by the user (this step may require some ingenuity on the part of the user.) The model checker is then invoked again to check the new guess. This process is iterated until a guess is produced for which all the formulas of interest are found to be true, at which point an implementation of the knowledge-based program has been found.

In many cases, this process can proceed monotonically. Starting from an initial assignment $v_\phi := e$, where e is a condition that the user can easily see to be *sufficient* for $K_i\psi$, the error trace leads to the identification of a situation where i may know ψ, which is not covered by the condition e. (That is, where $K_i\psi \Rightarrow e$ does not hold.) An analysis of this condition may lead to the discovery of another sufficient condition e'. In this case, the user can take as the next guess the assignment $v_\phi := e \vee e'$. Continuing in this way, we obtaining an increasing sequence of concrete lower approximations to the knowledge formula, eventually converging to the correct implementation. (We note that such a condition e' can always be found, since we may always take it to be a complete description of the run producing the counter-example. Finding a good generalization that remains a sufficient condition for the knowledge formula may be more difficult.)

In general, monotonicity is not guaranteed, but it obtains in our example in this paper. We leave the question of characterizing the situations where monotonicity applies to future work, and turn to a demonstration of the process on a particular example, introduced in the next section.

4   Chaum's Dining Cryptographers Protocol

Chaum's dining cryptographers protocol [2, p. 65] is an example of a protocol for secure multiparty computation: it enables the value of a function of a group of agents to be computed while revealing nothing more than that value. Chaum introduces the protocol with the following story:

> Three cryptographers are sitting down to dinner at their favourite restaurant. Their waiter informs them that arrangements have been made with the maitre d'hotel for the bill to be paid anonymously. One of the cryptographers might be paying for the dinner, or it might have been NSA (U.S National Security Agency). The three cryptographers respect each other's right to make an anonymous payment, but they wonder if NSA is paying. They resolve their uncertainty fairly by carrying out the following protocol:
> Each cryptographer flips an unbiased coin behind his menu, between him and the cryptographer on his right, so that only the two of them can see the outcome. Each cryptographer then states aloud whether the two coins he can see–the one he flipped and the one his left-hand neighbor flipped–fell on the same side or on different sides. If one of the cryptographers is the payer, he states the opposite of what he sees. An odd number of differences uttered at the table indicates that a cryptographer is paying; an even number indicates that NSA is paying (assuming that the dinner was paid for only once). Yet if a cryptographer is paying, neither of the other two learns anything from the utterances about which cryptographer it is.

This version of the dining cryptographers protocol has frequently been the focus of studies of verification of security protocols, but it is just one of many variants discussed in Chaum's paper. One of Chaum's considerations is the use of the protocol for more general anonymous broadcast applications, and he writes:

> The cryptographers become intrigued with the ability to make messages public untraceably. They devise a way to do this at the table for a statement of arbitrary length: the basic protocol is repeated over and over; when one cryptographer wishes to make a message public, he merely begins inverting his statements in those rounds corresponding to 1's in a binary coded version of his message. If he notices that his message would collide with some other message, he may for example wait for a number of rounds chosen at random from some suitable distribution before trying to transmit again.

He notes that "undetected collision results only from an odd number of synchronized identical message segments". As a particular realization of this idea, he discusses grouping communication into blocks and the use of the following *2-phase broadcast* protocol using *slot-reservation*:

> In a network with many messages per block, a first block may be used by various anonymous senders to request a "slot reservation" in a second block. A simple scheme would be for each anonymous sender to invert one randomly selected bit in the first block for each slot they wish to reserve in the second block. After the result of the first block becomes known, the participant who caused the ith bit in the first block sends in the ith slot of the second block.

This idea has been implemented as part of the Herbivore system[6]. (Herbivore also adds mechanisms for dividing the group of participants into cliques of sufficient size to provide reasonable anonymity guarantees, as well as protocols for joining and leaving the group of participants - we will not discuss these extension here.) The Herbivore authors note that

> If an even number of nodes attempt to reserve a given slot, the collision will be evident in the reservation phase, and they will simply wait until the next round to transmit. If an odd number of nodes collide, the collission will occur during the transmission phase.

The remarks above do not constitute a concrete definition of the protocol, and leave a number of questions concerning the implementation open. For example, what exact test is applied to determine whether there is a collision? Which agents are able to detect a collision? Are there situations where some agent expects to receive a message, but a collision occurs that it does not detect (although some other agent may do so?)

Note that each round of the DC protocol has been proved correct, but what about the way in which the rounds are combined? It is not immediately clear that there are not subtle flows of information!

Prior knowledge of the participants may also affect the flow of information. For example, suppose that the protocol is being used for the participants in a referendum to anonymously announce their votes. In this case it is known that all particpants will attempt to reseve a slot - does this information change the flow of information in any way? If so, does it affect the security of the protocol? One of the benefits of verification by epistemic model checking is that it permits such questions about variants of a protocol, and its application in a particular setting to be investigated efficiently without requiring reconstruction of possibly complex proofs.

5   The 2-Phase Broadcast Protocol as a Knowledge-Based Program

It is interesting to note that the descriptions of the 2-phase protocol above are, in their level of abstraction, more like knowledge-based programs than like concrete implementations. In this section, we explicitly study the protocol from this perspective, and apply our partially automated methodology to derive the concrete implementations. We consider a setting with 3 agents who use 3 slots for their broadcast. Each slot permits the transmission of a single-bit message.

5.1   The Knowledge-Based Program

Figure 1 represents the 2-phase protocol as a knowledge-based program. The parameters of the protocol in the first line alias certain local variables to global variables in the environment. Variable i is a number in the range 1..3 used to index the present instance of the protocol, and variables keyleft and keyright represent keybits (referred to as "coins", above), which are shared between by agents in the appropriate pattern. Note that since a fresh set of keybits needs to be used for each instance of the basic Dining Cryptographers protocol (which we run 6 times here), we assume that an external process generates fresh values for these keybit variables at each step; we omit the details. The final variable said in the parameters represent the array of public announcements by the agents at each step. All arrays are assumed to be indexed starting from 1. The local variable slot-request records the slot number (in the range 1..3) that this agent will attempt to reserve. If slot-request=0, then the agent will not attempt to reserve any slot. The variable message records the single bit message that the agent wishes to anonymously broadcast (if any). Variables for which an initial value is not explicitly specified can take any initial value. We write '⊕' for the exclusive or operation.

The term conflict(s) in the knowledge-based program represents that there is a conflict on slot s. This is a global condition that is defined as

$$\texttt{conflict}(s) = \bigvee_{i \neq j} (i.\texttt{slot-request} = s = j.\texttt{slot-request}) \; .$$

i.e., there exist two distinct agents i and j both requesting slot s.

```
protocol dc_agent(i:[1,3], keyleft,keyright,said[3]:Bool) {
local variables:
      slot-request:[0,3],
      message:Bool,
      rcvd0[3], rcvd1[3], dlvrd: Bool (initially false);
//reservation phase
for (s = 1; s ≤ 3; s++)
{
   said[i] := (keyleft⊕ keyright⊕ (slot-request=s));
}
//transmission phase
for (s = 1; s ≤ 3; s++)
{
   if (slot-request = s ∧ ¬Kᵢ(conflict(s))
       then said[i] := (keyleft⊕ keyright⊕ message)
       else said[i] := (keyleft⊕ keyright⊕ false);
   rcvd0[s] := Kᵢ(sender(i,0,s));
   rcvd1[s] := Kᵢ(sender(i,1,s))
};
dlvrd:= ⋀ₓ∈Bool,t=1..3((message = x ∧ slot-request = t) ⇒
                            Kᵢ(⋀ⱼ≠ᵢ Kⱼsender(j,x,t)))
}
```

Fig. 1. The knowledge-based program CDC

The term $\mathtt{sender}(i,x,s)$ represents that an agent other than i is sending message x in slot s; this is defined as

$$\mathtt{sender}(i,x,s) = \bigvee_{j\neq i} (j.\mathtt{message} = x \wedge j.\mathtt{slot\text{-}request} = s) \ .$$

Thus, the variable $\mathtt{rcvd0[s]}$ is assigned to be true if in round s, the agent learns that someone else is trying to send the bit 0, and similarly for $\mathtt{rcvd1[s]}$. This addresses an issue that is not explicitly mentioned in the discussion of the two-phase protocol above, viz., how does an agent know whether it has received a transmission from another? Note that this is pertinent because the knowledge-based program allows that, although an agent has declared that it wishes to reserve a slot, it may still back off from the transmission if it discovers that there is a conflict. But will the receiver always know that it has done so?

We note that this representation of the 2-phase protocol as a knowledge-based program is *speculative*: an agent transmits in a slot so long as it does not know that there is a conflict. This allows that a collision will occur during the transmission phase. One of the benefits of the knowledge-based approach is that it makes explicit the difference between this and another interpretation of the protocol where, in place of the condition $\neg K_i(\mathtt{conflict}(s))$, we use the condition $K_i(\neg\mathtt{conflict}(s))$. In this *conservative* version, an agent would broadcast only if it is certain that there is not a conflict on its desired slot. Both versions may be appropriate depending on the circumstances, but we focus our discussion here on the speculative version.

Since an agent may attempt to reserve a slot, and then back off, or may send in a reserved slot without success, the protocol does not guarantee that the message will be delivered. In this case, the agent is required to retry the transmission in the next run of the protocol. So that it can determine whether a retry is necessary, the final assignment to the variable dlvrd captures whether the agent knows that its (anonymous) transmission has been successful. This is the case if all other agents know that *some* agent sent the bit i.message in slot j.slot-request. (Subtleties about the semantics of the logic of knowledge prevent simplification of this formula by substitution of these expressions for x and t.)

In order to set up the appropriate configuration of the 3 agents and to alias their parameters to variables in the environment, we use the following declaration block:

```
agent C2 : dc_agent(1,k31,k12,said)
agent C3 : dc_agent(2,k12,k23,said)
agent C3 : dc_agent(3,k23,k31,said)
```

where the kij are boolean variables that represent the keybit shared between agent i and agent j.

In Figure 2, we give the generic structure of a possible implementation of the knowledge-based program, as we seek using our partially-automated process. The lines marked with (+) indicate places of difference with CDC.

Here we have introduced some history variables rr[s] that record the *round results* said[0] ⊕ said[1] ⊕said[2] obtained from each round s of the basic Dining Cryptographers protocol. Note that, because of the pattern of sharing of the keybits between the agents, this expression contains each keybit value twice, so that the keybits cancel out, leaving just the exclusive-or of the actual content being transmitted by each of the agents (in each assignment to said[i], this is the final term in the exclusive-or). In particular, under the assumption that just one agent has a genuine message x to transmit in round j, and the others transmit *false*, we obtain that rr[j]=x.

The variable kc[s] is used to represent the epistemic condition concerning conflict in the knowledge-based program (either $\neg K_i(\text{conflict}(s))$ or $K_i(\neg\text{conflict}(s))$, depending on whether we are dealing with the speculative or the conservative version). Thus, in verifying that we have an implementation, the key condition to be checked is whether kc[s] $\Leftrightarrow \neg K_i(\text{conflict}(s))$ (respectively, kc[s] $\Leftrightarrow K_i(\neg\text{conflict}(s))$) is valid at the times the if statement is executed. The main difficulty in finding an implementation is to find the appropriate concrete assignment for this variable that will make this condition valid. Similarly we seek assignments to the variables rcvd0[s], recvd1[s] that give these the intended meaning.

```
protocol dc_agent(i:[0,2], keyleft,keyright,said[3]:Bool) {
local variables:
      slot-request:[0,3],
      message:Bool,
      rcvd0[3], rcvd1[3]:Bool (initially false),
      rr[6]:Bool,                                                    (+)
      kc[3]:Bool (initially false);                                  (+)
//reservation phase
for (s = 1; s ≤ 3; s++)
{
   said[i] := (keyleft⊕ keyright⊕ (slot-request== s));
   rr[s] :=said[0]⊕ said[1]⊕ said[2];                                (+)
}
//transmission phase
for (s = 1; s ≤ 3; s++)
{
   kc[s] :=???;                                                      (+)
   if (slot-request== s ∧ kc[s])
      then said[i] := (keyleft⊕ keyright⊕ message)
      else said[i] := (keyleft⊕ keyright⊕ false);
   rr[s+3] := said[0]⊕ said[1]⊕ said[2];                             (+)
   rcvd0[s] := ???;                                                  (+)
   rcvd1[s] := ???;                                                  (+)
}
dlvrd:= ???                                                          (+)
}
```

Fig. 2. A generic implementation of CDC

5.2 Verification Conditions

In order to apply our methodology, it is necessary for the user to substitute a guess for parts of the implementation marked '???', and then to use model checking to check the correctness of the guess. We now discuss the formulas that are used to verify the implementation. In general, the conditions need to be verified only at specific times n, straightforwardly determined from the structure of the program. We generally omit discussion of this.

The first formula of interest concerns the correctness of the guess for the knowledge condition $\neg K_i(\text{conflict}(s))$ (in case of the speculative implementation, or $K_i(\neg\text{conflict}(s))$ (in the case of the conservative implementation). In the implementation, this condition is represented by the variable kc[s].

Specification 1: kc[s] *correctly represents knowledge of the existence of a conflict in slot $s = 1..3$.* In case of the speculative interpretation, we use the formula

$$X^n(i.\text{kc[s]} \Leftrightarrow \neg K_i(\text{conflict}(s))) \qquad (1s)$$

and in case of the conservative implementation, we use the formula

$$X^n(i.\texttt{kc[s]} \Leftrightarrow K_i(\neg\texttt{conflict}(s))) \qquad (1c)$$

(In both cases, the appropriate values of n are 7, 12 and 17, where we treat the
`for` loops as macros and the `if` conditions as taking zero time.)

As remarked above, it has been claimed that the 2-phase protocol is guaranteed to detect a conflict either in the slot-reservation phase or else in the transmission phase. To verify this, we can use the following specification:

Specification 2: A conflict is always detected.

$$X^n(\texttt{conflict}(s) \Rightarrow K_i(\texttt{conflict}(s)))$$

where we may take time n to correspond to the final time in the protocol. We remark that the converse implication is trivial from the semantics of knowledge.

As will discuss below, Specification 2 is arguably too strong, since agents may not be able to learn about conflicts on slots they do not reserve. Thus, the following weaker specification is also of interest.

Specification 3: If there is a slot conflict involving agent i, then agent i detects it.

$$X^n((\texttt{conflict}(s) \wedge i.\texttt{slot-request} = s) \Rightarrow K_i(\texttt{conflict}(s)))$$

where again we take n to correspond to the end of the protocol.

Next, the protocol has some positive goals, viz., to allow agents to broadcast some information, and to do so anonymously. Successful reception of a bit by the time n immediately after the transmission in slot s is intended to be represented by the variables `rcvd0[s]` and `rcvd1[s]`. To ensure that the assignments to these variables correctly implement their intended meaning in the knowledge-based program, we use specifications of the following form.

Specification 4: reception variables correctly represent transmissions by others

$$X^n(i.\texttt{rcvd0}[s] \Leftrightarrow K_i(\texttt{sender}(i, 0, s))) \qquad (4a)$$

and

$$X^n(\texttt{rcvd1}[s] \Leftrightarrow K_i(\texttt{sender}(i, 1, s))) \qquad (4b)$$

Similarly, we need to verify correct implementation of the agent's knowledge about whether its transmission is successful.

Specification 5: delivery variables correctly represent knowledge about delivery

$$X^n(i.\texttt{dlvrd} \Leftrightarrow \bigwedge\nolimits_{x \in Bool, t=1..3}(i.\texttt{message} = x \wedge i.\texttt{slot-request} = t \\ \Rightarrow K_i(\bigwedge\nolimits_{j \neq i} K_j \texttt{sender}(j, x, t))))$$

Finally, the aim of the protocol is to ensure that when information is transmitted, this is done anonymously. An agent may know that one of the other two agents has a particular message value, but it may not know what that value is for a specific agent. We may write the fact that agent i knows the value of a boolean variable x by the notation $\hat{K}_i(x)$, defined by $\hat{K}_i(x) = K_i(x) \vee K_i(\neg x)$. Using this, we might first attempt to specify anonymity as $\bigwedge_{j \neq i}(\neg \hat{K}_i(j.\texttt{message}))$, i.e., agent

i knows no other's message. Unfortunately, the protocol cannot be expected to satisfy this: suppose that all agents manage to broadcast their message and all messages have the same value x: then each knows that the other's value is x. We therefore write the following weaker specification of anonymity:

Specification 6: The protocol preserves anonymity

$$X^n(\bigvee_{x=0,1} K_i(\bigwedge_{j\neq i}(j.\text{message} = x)) \vee \bigwedge_{j\neq i}(\neg \hat{K}_i(j.\text{message})))$$

to be evaluated with n set to the final time of the protocol.

5.3   Finding an Implemention of the Knowledge-Based Program

We now illustrate how we find an implementation of the knowledge-based program using our methodology. We focus here on the speculative version, and consider a scenario where the number of agents that are seeking to broadcast— is initially unknown, and could be any value from the set $\{0..3\}$.

Our first task in implementing the knowledge-based program is to find an appropriate assignment for the variables $kc[s]$, and to verify that this assignment correctly represents knowledge about slot conflicts and validates *Specification 1*. It is plain from the discussion above that if an agent attempts to reserve slot s, but sees that the round result for that reservation attempt is not *true*, then this must be because some other agent also attempted to reserve the slot. Thus, in this case the agent detects a conflict. A reasonable guess for the assignment to $kc[s]$ to represent $\neg K_i(\text{conflict}(s))$ is therefore

$$kc[s] := \neg(\text{slot-request} = s \wedge \neg rr[s] = \mathit{false}) .$$

Indeed, this proves to be the correct choice: if we now model check *Specification 1s* then we find that this specification is true.[1]

The next question of interest is then whether *Specification 2* holds , as claimed. The answer obtained by model checking is that it does not, and the counter-example discovered is the following:

Example 1: (None of the agents discover conflict) Suppose that all agents (C1, C2, C3) would like to reserve slot 2 and each has message 1. The round results $rr[s]$ are shown in on the left in Figure 3, where we show for each agent the contribution other than keybits (which cancel out).

Now from agent $C1$'s perspective, this run of the protocol is indistinguishable from another run where only $C1$ attempts to reserve slot 2, and it still has message 1, shown on the right in Figure 3. Hence we have a situation where although there is a conflict agent $C1$ cannot know that there is a conflict, and *Specification 2* fails, contra to what one might have expected from the quote

---

[1] Strictly, in order to model check this claim, we first need to fill in the other '???' assignments. We remark that because of independencies, the outcome of model checking *Specification 1s* is the same *whatever* we choose for the other '???' assignments. We omit a detailed argument for this here.

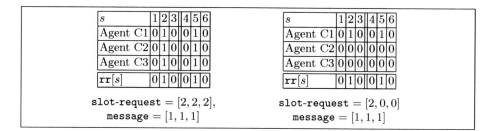

Fig. 3. Runs indistinguishable to C1

from [6] above.[2] Indeed, we see that the more liberal *Specification 3* also fails in this example.

In the discussion above, we have focused on the agent's knowledge that there is a conflict. From the point of view of determining the appropriate assignments to the variables rcvd0 and rcvd1, it would be helpful to determine under what circumstances an agent knows that there will be a transmission on a slot but there is *not* a conflict on that slot. Thus, it would be helpful to have a predicate $i.\texttt{conflict-free}(s)$ that is equivalent to $K_i(\bigvee_j j.\texttt{slot-request} = s \land \neg\texttt{conflict}(s))$. We now investigate this question, and use it to illustrate the iterative procedure to obtain local predicates that are equivalent to knowledge formulas.

Plainly, a round-result of 1 during the reservation phase implies that someone wishes to send in that slot. However, Example 1 also shows that $K_i\neg\texttt{conflict}(s)$ cannot hold in case agent i obtains round result 1 in a slot it intends to transmit in, and 0 in all other slots, since it is possible that all agents are attempting to transmit in the same slot. Hence a reasonable guess is

$$\texttt{conflict-free1}(s) = \texttt{rr}[s] = 1 \land \neg(\wedge_{t \in \{1,2,3\}\setminus\{s\}}\texttt{rr}[t] = 0) \ .$$

When we model check

$$X^n(i.\texttt{conflict-free1}(s) \Leftrightarrow K_i(\bigvee_j j.\texttt{slot-request} = s \land \neg\texttt{conflict}(s))$$

at time n after the transmission phase, we find that this formula is false. A counter-example produced by the model checker shows that this happens when $C1$ and $C3$ request slot 3, and $C2$ requests slot 1. Note that in this case the reservation round results are $(1, 0, 0)$. Here $C1$ and $C3$ detect a conflict in slot 3. Since there are only three agents, they are able to reason that the conflict must have been 2-way (else we have the scenario of Example 1). This means that they are able to deduce that there is *not* a conflict in slot 1.

---

[2] It is unclear if the authors of [6] intended to imply that all conflicts would be detected. They also state that messages are sent with an MD5 checksum, so most conflicts of messages somewhat longer than a single bit would in fact be detected with high probability through corruption of this checksum. However, even with this device, collisions of 3 identical messages would still go undetected, as noted by Chaum.

This example motivates a second guess for the predicate conflict-free(s), viz., (when all variables are local to agent i)

conflict-free2(s) = conflict-free1(s) $\lor$
    (rr[s] = 1 $\land$ slot-request $\in \{1,2,3\} \setminus \{s\}$ $\land$ rr[i.slot-request] = 0) .

Model checking this predicate for equivalence to $K_i(\bigvee_j j$.slot-request $= s \land \neg$conflict(s)), we still find that the equivalence does not hold. The counterexample produced this time is the situation where agents $C1$ and $C2$ do not request a slot, but agent $C3$ requests slot s so that the round result of slot s is 1. Note that here, agents $C1$ and $C2$ know that any slot collision must be 2-way, since they cannot be a participant. Since the reservation request on slot s gave round result 1, there must be exactly one agent requesting slot s. With some reflection, we note that agent $C1$ would have been able to draw the same conclusion about slots 2 and 3 in case the round result pattern were $(0,1,1)$. Thus, we are led to the following improved guess:

conflict-free3(s) = conflict-free2(s) $\lor$ (rr[s] = 1 $\land$ slot-request $\neq s$)

At this point, model checking shows that we have found the predicate we seek.

Returning now to the question of when agents learn the bit that another agent is transmitting, we guess the assignment

$$\text{rcvd1}[s] := \text{rr}[s] = 1 \land \text{conflict-free3}(s) \land \text{slot-request} \neq s .$$

That is, the agent sees that there will be a conflict free transmission on slot s, but it is not itself using that slot. We now model check Specification 4b. Somewhat surprisingly, this specification turns out to be false! The counter example returned is one in which the agent is $C1$, all agents reserve slot 1, and the agents have messages $(1,1,0)$. Note that here, the round result obtained for the transmission is 0, so agent $C1$ detects the collision, which it knows must have been 3-way. It can also reason that the other agents cannot both have had messages 0, since this would have produced round result 0, thus, at least one must have had message 1! This observation leads to the revised guess

rcvd1[s] := (rr[s] = 1 $\land$ conflict-free3(s) $\land$ slot-request $\neq s$)$\lor$
    (slot-request = 1 $\land$ rr[$s+3$] $\neq$ message $\land$ $\bigwedge_{t \in \{1,2,3\} \setminus \{s\}}$ rr[t] = 0) .

We now find that Specification 4b holds, so we have correctly implemented this part of the knowledge-based program. A similar assignment works for the assignment to rcvd0 and *Specification 4a*.

This process can also be carried out also for the final specification *Specification 5*, which concerns the circumstances under which a sender knows that their message (if any) has been received by the others. One obvious situation when this is the case is when the sender i knows that the slot on which they are sending is conflict-free. Recall that this occurs only when two or more of the reservation round results equal 1, and note that this implies that all other agents also know that the slot on which i is sending is conflict-free. Thus the others will receive the message that i is sending (anonymously) on this slot. This suggests the assignment

$$\texttt{dlvrd} := \texttt{slot-request} = 0 \lor \bigvee_{s \in \{1,2,3\}} \texttt{slot-request} = s \land \texttt{conflict-free3}(s) \, .$$

When we model check this with respect to *Specification 5*, we find that that the specification holds, and we have a complete implementation of the knowledge-based program. Finally, we may also model check *Specification 6* and verify that the protocol preserves anonymity in the appropriate sense. This proves to be the case.

6   Conclusion

We have demonstrated the application of our partially automated methodology for knowledge-based program implementation on a protocol for anonymous broadcast. While, like related studies [8,10,18,17,15,16], we verify that an anonymity property holds, the focus of our effort lies in other aspects of the protocol.

One of the main outcomes of the analysis is that the flows of information in the protocol are considerably more subtle than one might have expected. In particular, we find that there are circumstances, that go beyond those that have been identified in the literature, where agents are able to obtain knowledge of each other's bits. Significantly, we make this discovery not manually, but using automated support. We also address in our work a number of questions that have not been considered in the prior literature, viz., under what circumstances can a receiver be confident that they are receiving a transmission, and under what circumstances a sender can know that its transmission has been successful, and find complete answers to these questions in a particular scenario.

On the other hand, being based on model checking of a concrete model under very particular assumptions, our approach lacks generality: it does not yield an immediate answer to how our conclusions are affected by changing the number of agents, their topology, or the initial assumptions concerning the number of agents wishing to transmit. However, the methodology provides an efficient means to experiment with such questions. We are presently investigating further variants using our methodology, in order to obtain an empirical basis from which theoretical results may be generalized. Our present models are also starting to press the limits of the model checking technology (run times of the order of hours for some queries, for protocols of around 20 steps), so we are also investigating optimizations to increase the scale and complexity of the problems we can address. We plan to report on this in future work.

In work conducted independently, Luo et al [13] have also model checked knowledge in the 2-phase protocol, but they focus on a number of formulas concerning conflict detection, rather than attempting to implement a knowledge-based program, as we have done in this paper. They consider larger numbers of agents, but they do not consider the questions we have studied concerning reception and termination, nor do they try to find exact conditions under which knowledge properties of interest hold. They also use observational rather than perfect recall semantics, and justify this by an informal argument that what they do is equivalent to perfect recall. We believe their claim of equivalence to be correct, and it would be an interesting topic for future work to provide a more formal and systematic justification. (Some initial steps on optimizing models of the 2-phase protocol were already taken in [14].)

References

1. Baukus, K., van der Meyden, R.: A knowledge based analysis of cache coherence. In: Davies, J., Schulte, W., Barnett, M. (eds.) ICFEM 2004. LNCS, vol. 3308, pp. 99–114. Springer, Heidelberg (2004)
2. Chaum, D.: The dining cryptographers problem: Unconditional sender and recipient untraceability. Journal of Cryptology, 65–75 (1988)
3. Dwork, C., Moses, Y.: Knowledge and common knowledge in a Byzantine environment: crash failures. Information and Computation 88(2), 156–186 (1990)
4. Fagin, R., Halpern, J.Y., Moses, Y., Vardi, M.Y.: Reasoning about Knowledge. MIT Press, Cambridge (1995)
5. Gammie, P., van der Meyden, R.: MCK: Model checking the logic of knowledge. In: Alur, R., Peled, D.A. (eds.) CAV 2004. LNCS, vol. 3114, pp. 479–483. Springer, Heidelberg (2004)
6. Goel, S., Robson, M., Polte, M., Sirer, E.: Herbivore: A scalable and efficient protocol for anonymous communication. Technical report, Cornell University, Ithaca, NY (February 2003)
7. Hadzilacos, V.: A knowledge-theoretic analysis of atomic commitment protocols. In: PODS 1987: Proc. 6th ACM Symp. on Principles of Database Systems, pp. 129–134. ACM, New York (1987)
8. Halpern, J.Y., O'Neill, K.R.: Anonymity and information hiding in multiagent systems. In: Proc. 16th IEEE Computer Security Foundations Workshop, pp. 75–88 (2003)
9. Halpern, J.Y., Zuck, L.D.: A little knowledge goes a long way: knowledge-based derivations and correctness proofs for a family of protocols. Journal of the ACM 39(3), 449–478 (1992)
10. Hughes, D., Shmatikov, V.: Information hiding, anonymity and privacy: a modular approach. Journal of Computer Security 12(1), 3–36 (2004)
11. Clarke Jr., E.M., Grumberg, O., Peled, D.A.: Model Checking. The MIT Press, Cambridge (1999)
12. Lomuscio, A., Qu, H., Raimondi, F.: MCMAS: A model checker for the verification of multi-agent systems. In: Bouajjani, A., Maler, O. (eds.) CAV 2009. LNCS, vol. 5643, pp. 682–688. Springer, Heidelberg (2009)
13. Luo, X., Su, K., Gu, M., Wu, L., Yang, J.: Symbolic model checking the knowledge in Herbivore protocol. In: van der Meyden, R., Smaus, G. (eds.) MoChArt 2010: 6th Int. Workshop on Model Checking and Artificial Intelligence, LNCS. Springer, Hiedelberg (2010) (to appear), AAAI Working Notes
14. Nhu, L.L.V.: Enhancing an epsitemic logic model checker for application to extensions of the dining cryptographers protocol. Honours thesis, School of Computer Science and Engineering, University of New South Wales (November 2005)

15. Ryan, P., Schneider, S.: The modelling and analysis of security protocols: the CSP approach. Addison-Wesley Professional, Reading (2000)
16. Schneider, S., Sidiropoulos, A.: CSP and anonymity. In: Proc. of the European Symposium on Research in Computer Security (ESORICS), pp. 198–218. Springer, Heidelberg (1996)
17. Syverson, P., Stubblebine, S.: Group principals and the formalization of anonymity. In: Wing, J.M., Woodcock, J.C.P., Davies, J. (eds.) FM 1999, Part I. LNCS, vol. 1708, pp. 814–833. Springer, Heidelberg (1999)
18. van der Meyden, R., Su, K.: Symbolic model checking the knowledge of the dining cryptographers. In: Proc. 17th IEEE Computer Security Foundation Workshop, pp. 280–291. IEEE Computer Society, Los Alamitos (2004)
19. van Eijck, J.: Dynamic epistemic modelling. Technical report, Centrum voor Wiskunde en Informatica, Amsterdam (2004), CWI Report SEN-E0424

Surveying DNS Wildcard Usage
among the Good, the Bad, and the Ugly

Andrew Kalafut, Minaxi Gupta, Pairoj Rattadilok, and Pragneshkumar Patel

School of Informatics and Computing, Indiana University
{akalafut,minaxi,prattadi,patel27}@cs.indiana.edu

Abstract. A DNS wildcard can be used to point arbitrary requests for host names within a domain to a specific host name or IP address. Wildcards offer administrators the convenience of not having to change DNS entries when host names change. However, we are not aware of any work that documents how wildcards are used in practice. Such a study is particularly important now, because Internet miscreants are starting to exploit DNS wildcards for convenience and possibly for evading blacklists based on exact host names. In this paper, we study the prevalence and uses of wildcards among the good, bad, and ugly domains in the Internet. We find that wildcards are in extensive use among businesses that monetize unregistered domains, domains hosted by large web-hosting providers, blogging sites, and websites connected to scam, phishing, and malware.

Keywords: DNS, Wildcard, Security.

1 Introduction

The Domain Name System (DNS) [16] serves the basic purpose of translating human-readable host names into the IP addresses. While conceptually a simple mapping, the DNS is complex in reality. Several record types exist for different types of mappings, and several features exist to improve convenience and functionality beyond this basic description. One such feature, which we examine in this paper, is *wildcards.*

Wildcards are one of the original features of DNS, defined in the original standard. The role of wildcards in DNS is a many to one mapping, allowing all names within a single domain or subdomain to map to a single value. This can be used for example to map all host names in a domain to a single IP address, or to assign a single DNS or mail server to all possible subdomains of a domain. In both of these and other similar cases, the single catch-all wildcard record saves the DNS administrator from having to maintain many different records that all return the same value.

Despite their usefulness, very little is known about who uses wildcards, and for what purposes. There are signs that Internet miscreants have discovered the convenience of wildcards. Recently, Netcraft released two advisories that point to the use of wildcards in setting up phishing campaigns [15,19]. Wildcards may be

S. Jajodia and J. Zhou (Eds.): SecureComm 2010, LNICST 50, pp. 448–465, 2010.

attractive to miscreants because they allow mapping multiple host names in their campaigns to the same IP address, for example. This can be useful in evading host name based blacklists with minimal effort. Given this, understanding the use of wildcards becomes even more important.

In this paper, we undertake the first systematic study to investigate the use of wildcards in the Internet. We specifically work towards two goals. Our primary goal is to survey wildcard usage among good, bad, and ugly domains in the Internet. Toward this goal, we query approximately 8 million domains for wildcard entries in the four most popular DNS record types. Our second goal is to investigate if malicious uses of wildcards can be differentiated from their benign uses. The ability to do so may be helpful in identifying and effectively blacklisting malicious domains.

Working towards these goals, we arrive at the following key results:

- **Prevalence:** We find that a surprisingly large percentage of Internet domains use wildcards. Specifically, 25-75% of domains in various data sets use wildcards, making this a much more popular DNS feature than one would expect.
- **Type:** An overwhelming majority of domains using wildcards use them in their address records, which map arbitrary host names to a IP address.
- **Uses:** Prominent users of wildcards include domain-parking businesses that wish to monetize unregistered domains and subdomains, web-hosting companies, and blogging and social-networking sites.
- **Malicious sites:** Malicious sites also make extensive use of wildcards, with spammers leading the pack with 75% of the scam-related domains in our data wildcarded. We also find that Google knows more host names matching wildcards in malicious domains than are in our data sets, implying that the coverage of blacklists could be improved by including wildcard entries.
- **Distinguishing malicious uses:** Our preliminary investigation shows that IP addresses contained in wildcard records typically spread across many ASes. Additionally, they tend to have lower TTLs than wildcards for benign purposes. These features can be used to differentiate wildcard usage among malicious domains, particularly those associated with spam, from the benign ones

The rest of this paper proceeds as follows: Section 2 presents background on the syntax and behavior of DNS wildcards. The data we use throughout the paper is described in Section 3. We discuss the prevalence of wildcards in Section 4. We examine what they are being used for in Section 5. Section 6 explores differences between wildcards used for malicious purposes and others. We discuss related work in Section 7 and conclude in Section 8.

2   Background

The primary goal of DNS is to translate host names into IP addresses. The most popular types of host names resolved are mail servers, DNS servers (also known as name servers) and all other types of servers, including web servers. Mail and

DNS servers have dedicated DNS record types, MX and NS respectively, that map the queries for those servers to host names. These host names are then mapped to IP addresses through A records[1]. Web and other kinds of servers do not have dedicated types of DNS records and a mapping between their exact name and the corresponding IP addresses is accomplished directly through the A records. A fourth popular DNS record type is the CNAME record, which aliases a host name to another host name. In total, 59 DNS record types are defined as of now but only 42 of these are in wide use [9]. Figure 1(a) shows an example of DNS provisioning for a domain with one MX, one NS, and three A records.

www.foo.com	A	129.79.245.53
foo.com	MX	mail.foo.com
foo.com	NS	ns1.foo.com
mail.foo.com	A	129.79.247.191
ns1.foo.com	A	129.79.247.191

www.foo.com	A	129.79.245.53
foo.com	MX	mail.foo.com
foo.com	NS	ns1.foo.com
*.foo.com	A	129.79.247.191

(a) without wildcards   (b) with wildcards

Fig. 1. Example of DNS provisioning of a domain with and without wildcards

Wildcards in DNS were first defined in RFCs 1034 [16]. Later, RFC 4592 [10] updated and clarified the specification, providing more details and examples of intended behavior, and the interactions of wildcards with specific record types. A wildcard record is a DNS record of any type with a minor change to the left hand side of the record. In a wildcarded DNS record, instead of the name being an exact host name, its least significant (leftmost) label in the name consists of a single asterisk character, as shown in Figure 1(b). Conceptually, the asterisk matches one or more labels at the left end of the DNS name. In this example, *.foo.com is being used in place of mail.foo.com and ns1.foo.com. When a DNS query is made for mail.foo.com, seeing no match, the server will return results for *.foo.com, substituting mail for the *. Specific records override the wildcard records. Since the record for www.foo.com is still present, the wildcard would not be considered when responding to a query for this host name.

The client receiving a DNS response can not directly tell if the response was generated from a wildcard record or not; their use is transparent to the client systems. If a query for host name name.foo.com were matched from the wildcard record *.foo.com, the name on the record returned in the response will still be name.foo.com instead of *.foo.com as it is stored on the DNS server. We can however still tell if a wildcard is in use by directly querying for the wildcard name, in this case, *.foo.com. Since the wildcard record is the only one that would match such a query, if a response is given to such a query, it would let us know a wildcard record is present. Note that wildcard matches only work in one direction. Although the query for *.foo.com looks like the client has a wildcard in the query, it will only match an explicit wildcard record, not an arbitrary name in foo.com on the server.

---

[1] AAAA records are used to map host names to IPv6 addresses.

3   Data Sets

Our goal is to study DNS wildcard usage in three contexts: domains judged as worthwhile or useful by Internet users (*the good*), domains from several blacklists (*the bad*), and a large general collection of domains, including both good and bad domains (*the ugly*). Table 1 shows an overview of the data sets.

Table 1. Overview of the data sets

	DMOZ	ZONE_FILES	PHISH	MALWARE	SPAM
Start Date	Sept. 17	Sept. 27	Sept. 22	Sept. 22	Sept. 22
End Date	N/A	N/A	Oct. 21	Oct. 21	Oct. 21
Frequency	Once	Once	Daily	Daily	Daily
Hosts	3,038,928	N/A	16,496	18,570	N/A
Domains	2,737,326	5,536,475	10,575	12,854	548,041
TLDs	3,235	7	306	259	327

The good: One context in which we study wildcards is the domains determined to be useful by Internet users. We use data from the DMOZ Open Directory Project [?] for this purpose. The Open Directory Project is a large directory of user submitted and editor approved Web URLs. We assume that those links submitted and approved are those someone has judged to be worthwhile, and are therefore in some sense good. We consider 2.7 million domains contained in this data set on September 17th, 2009. We refer to this data set as DMOZ throughout this paper.

The Bad: Another context in which we study wildcards is domains known to be associated with malicious activity. For this context, we use host names extracted from two real-time feeds of known phishing URLs [2, 22], three feeds of known malware-serving URLs [5, 11, 20], and one feed of domains for scam sites seen in spam mails [26]. We examine each of these feeds every day for a period of 30 days, extracting a total of 571,470 domains that were alive at the time of our receiving the feed. We refer to these data sets respectively as PHISH, MALWARE, and SPAM throughout this paper.

The Ugly: The last context we consider is a large general list of domains on the Internet. We refer to these as "ugly" since they could be used for any purpose, good or bad or something in between. The data source for this context is the zone files[2] from seven generic top-level domains (gTLDs), .asia, .biz, .com, .info, .mobi, .net, and .org [28,18,4,24,1,21], on September 27th, 2009. There were 110,728,143 domains contained in these TLDs, 58% of the total 192 million domains in the Internet at the time of our study [27]. From these, we randomly sample at a rate of 5%, or 5,536,475, which we examine in this paper. We refer to this data set as ZONE_FILES throughout this paper.

---

[2] Zone files are text files listing all DNS records directly contained in a domain.

4   Wildcard Prevalence

Wildcards can occur at all levels of the DNS hierarchy. We concentrate on the
domain level, instead of TLDs or subdomains, since this is generally the start
or administrative control. We look for wildcards in four DNS record types: A,
NS, MX, and CNAME. From the entries in each data set, we determine the domain
name part of each host name using the Public Suffix List [17]. For all domain
names in these data sets, for example, foo.com, we query for *.foo.com for the
four record types. All queries were run once for each domain in the DMOZ and
ZONE_FILES data sets, but daily for the others that changed often in real-time.
We also query for the NS record for each domain to ensure that the domain exists
at the time of the query.

A large fraction of domains we surveyed used wildcards. Table 2 presents
an overview of the number and types of wildcards present in each data set
at the domain level. *Between 1/4 and 3/4 of domains use wildcards, with the
DMOZ data set showing the least prevalence of wildcards and the SPAM data set
showing the most.* Not only is the A wildcard overwhelmingly popular, its usage
mimics general wildcard usage trends. Some domains have more than one type
of wildcard, causing the percentages in the last four rows of Table 2 to exceed
the total percentage of domains using wildcards.

Table 2. % of active domains with wildcards of each record type in each data set

	DMOZ	ZONE_FILES	PHISH	MALWARE	SPAM
Domains					
Checked	2,737,326	5,536,475	10,575	12,854	548,041
Active	2,717,186	4,861,053	9,044	11,312	226,060
Inactive (%)	0.73%	12.2%	14.5%	12%	58.7%
Wildcards					
total %	24.52%	45.15%	32.09%	31.39%	75.10%
% A	18.76%	42.72%	27.79%	26.59%	72.30%
% NS	0.32%	5.53%	0.20%	0.19%	1.60%
% MX	5.72%	6.44%	4.10%	6.14%	6.83%
% CNAME	3.40%	3.75%	3.37%	4.49%	2.34%

4.1   Overridden Wildcards

Some wildcards may be overridden by specific entries. For example, a domain
foo.com, may have a wildcard entry for *.foo.com, and a more specific entry
for host name a.b.foo.com. This allows the domain to point a.b.foo.com to a
different value than any other host name fitting *.foo.com. Now that we have
seen how often wildcards are occurring, an important consideration is if they are
overridden by a more specific DNS entry. If latter, then our conclusion about
wildcard usage in the Internet would be different.

Toward the goal of identifying overrides, we proceed as following. For the
DMOZ, PHISH, and MALWARE data sets where we have host names in the feeds, we
query the DNS for A and CNAME records corresponding to the host names and
check if the results of this lookup match the results of the wildcard lookup. If

they are not the same answers, we consider the exact match to be overriding the wildcard. If we have multiple host names for one wildcard, we count it as an override if any of them do not match the wildcard entry. For ZONE_FILES and SPAM, we do not have exact host names, so we simply prepend www to the domain name. Though we do not know for sure that the host name so generated is being used, it is commonly used for web servers and may catch some overrides.

Notice that since our data sets are for web servers only, they do not contain name servers or mail servers. As a result, we cannot establish the presence of overrides for MX and NS wildcards by querying each domain for MX and NS wildcards and comparing the result to host names in the feed. This limitation is not severe since MX and NS are the two least popular type of wildcards per Table 2.

Table 3 shows the percentage of A and CNAME wildcards being overridden in each data set. Wildcards are overridden in 2.8-31.6% of cases. The SPAM data set sees the least overrides.

Table 3. Percentage of A and CNAME wildcards being overridden by specific entries

	DMOZ	ZONE_FILES	PHISH	MALWARE	SPAM
A	10.7%	31.6%	19.0%	19.9%	6.7%
CNAME	17.4%	8.8%	17.5%	30.0%	2.8%

Some data sets witness overrides for CNAME wildcards more often than those for A wildcards and vice versa. The difference is most striking for the ZONE_FILES data set. Examining the overrides in this data set closely, we find that 25.4% (557,949) of wildcards in the ZONE_FILES data set are hosted on name servers in domaincontrol.com. Of these, 99.7% are A wildcards being overridden by a specific CNAME record. These account for 88.9% of the overrides of A wildcards in this data set. If we ignore wildcard entries on this name server, only 6.6% of remaining A wildcards in this data set are overridden, much closer the percentage of overridden CNAME wildcards in this data set. *We conclude that wildcards are not frequently overridden in most data sets.*

5   Wildcard Usage

We now investigate the specific uses of wildcards by the good, bad, and ugly domains. To group related wildcarded domains, we considered several options and found it best to aggregate them by the DNS servers serving them. This grouping is intuitive because provider of DNS services, for example hosting companies, often provide a default configuration which most domains may choose. Similarly, large organizations running many of their own domains are likely to use similarly-provisioned servers. In fact, we aggregate even more by grouping wildcarded domains in terms of the domain of the DNS server.

5.1   Wildcard Usage among Good Domains

The first data set we analyze is DMOZ, our set of good domains from a user edited directory. From this data set, we saw a total of 666,334 domains (24.5%)

using wildcards. These were served by DNS servers belonging to 28,883 domains. Figure 2 shows a CDF of the wildcarded domains and the corresponding DNS server domains for this and ZONE_FILES data sets. *A key observation from this Figure is that just a few DNS servers are responsible for a disproportionate number of wildcarded domains.* Specifically, 29.1% of domains in the DMOZ data set are served by just top ten DNS server domains.

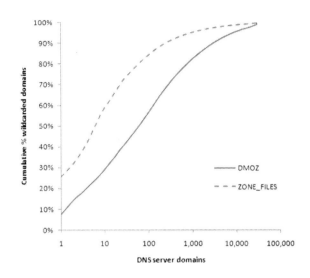

Fig. 2. CDF of wildcarded domains served by each DNS server domain

We now consider the top ten DNS server domains serving the most wildcarded domains. Table 4 shows the total domains and wildcarded domains served by each. *In looking over the domains accounting for most wildcard usage, we find that all are operated by registrars or web-hosting providers. Both these entities tend to provide a default configuration to users which includes a wildcard record.* Even users who override these with specific records for individual hosts may choose to keep the wildcard record.

5.2   Usage among the Ugly

We now change our focus to the ZONE_FILES data set, a large collection of domains taken from several TLD zone files. In this data set, we saw 2,194,565 domains using wildcards (45.2%). These domains are also served by a small number of DNS server domains, only 32,644. *Overall, we find that wildcarded domains are even more concentrated at a few name server domains than in the DMOZ data set.* Table 5 shows the top ten name server domains serving the most wildcarded domains in the ZONE_FILES data set. Four of the domains listed are in common with those in Table 4.

Table 4. Top 10 DNS server domains serving the most wildcarded domains in the DMOZ data set

	Domains served	Wildcarded domains
worldnic.com	55,947	48,484
rzone.de	47,913	47,771
yahoo.com	23,194	21,835
namespace4you.de	17,611	17,409
kasserver.com	13,313	13,227
name-services.com	17,529	10,595
b-one.nu	9,471	9,406
ipower.com	9,058	9,057
register.com	13,853	8,077
mediatemple.net	7,869	7,705

Table 5. Top 10 DNS server domains serving the most wildcarded domains in the ZONE_FILES data set

	Domains served	Wildcarded domains
domaincontrol.com	1,138,877	557,949
name-services.com	179,130	147,697
worldnic.com	137,696	116,759
sedoparking.com	96,790	96,789
dsredirection.com	91,796	91,796
yahoo.com	82,747	80,669
register.com	72,827	62,137
secureserver.net	62,672	60,063
fabulous.com	39,166	39,137
parked.com	37,529	37,522

100% of the domains served by **sedoparking.com** and **dsredirection.com** are wildcarded. *These two, along with the two others that have the highest percentage of wildcarded domains, fabulous.com and parked.com, belong to companies involved in domain parking*[3]. Wildcards are very useful for parked domains. By directing visitors to a parking page, they allow monetization of all possible subdomains of a domain. However, not all parked domains are wildcarded. At least one provider of parking services we know of serves over 700,000 domains but uses wildcards on less than 1%. The other major user of wildcards in this data set are web-hosting providers, as we saw in DMOZ. In fact, four of these are the same ones we saw in the top 10 from the DMOZ data set.

5.3   Usage among the Bad

Next, we look for wildcard usage in bad data sets, PHISH, MALWARE, and SPAM. As we saw in Table 2, 32.1% of active phishing domains, 31.4% of active malware hosting domains, and 75.1% of active spam domains were using wildcards. The

---

[3] A parked domain is a domain with no actual useful content, just a template page filled with ads redirecting the user to other pages, mostly for the purpose of monetizing chance-visitors to the domain.

top ten DNS server domains serving wildcarded domains in PHISH, MALWARE, and SPAM, are shown in Tables 6, 7, and 8. They account for 21.67%, 22.95%, and 21.82% of the wildcard domains in these data sets respectively. This indicates a slightly lower concentration on the top name servers than we saw in the DMOZ data set, and much lower than we saw in the ZONE_FILES data set. *The other key observation from these tables is that many of the top-10 domains serving wildcarded domains are shared across all data sets.* This happens because many of the registrars and web-hosting providers are common across the three types of data sets.

Table 6. Top 10 DNS server domains serving the most wildcarded domains in the PHISH data set

	Domains served	Wildcarded domains
ixwebhosting.com	151	151
nshost.com.ve	139	139
rzone.de	63	60
yahoo.com	98	55
name-services.com	54	47
hosteurope.com	100	44
worldnic.com	48	42
hrnoc.net	33	32
register.com	32	30
namebay.com	128	29

Table 7. Top 10 DNS server domains serving the most wildcarded domains in the MALWARE data set

	Domains served	Wildcarded domains
freeservers.com	203	203
ixwebhosting.com	93	92
ipower.com	83	83
name-services.com	101	81
northsky.com	73	73
everydns.net	173	67
yahoo.com	63	59
servage.net	58	57
sorpresor.com	51	51
sitelutions.com	54	49

Examining the domains listed in these three tables, some of the top ten from these data sets are in common with the top ten from the other two data sets. Some of these from the SPAM data set are associated with domain parking, and are probably there due to spam domains that have been taken down but still appear in our data set. These are less than 5% of the wildcards in SPAM so are certainly not the primary reason it has a higher proportion of wildcards than the others. Others are present because they are hosting providers. The most prominent example of this is name-services.com, which appears in the top ten from every data set. This and the few others from the three malicious data sets

Table 8. Top 10 DNS server domains serving the most wildcarded domains in the SPAM data set

	Domains served	Wildcarded domains
name-services.com	16,699	14,764
tutby.com	6,167	5,966
domainservice.com	4,640	4,555
domainsite.com	3,202	3,200
domaincontrol.com	6,278	2,045
dsredirection.com	1,778	1,777
sedoparking.com	1,323	1,323
netstandardconsulting.com	1,296	1,296
peak-communications.net	1,180	1,180
dzcamera.net	941	940

that are also top users in the other data sets may be large providers of malicious wildcards just because they are large providers who use wildcards by default and miscreants happen to use them. However, a majority that are the top users in these three data sets are not among the top users in the other two, making it likely that the miscreants are configuring wildcards intentionally.

Churn of Hosts Among Bad Wildcarded Domains: Miscreants can exploit the flexibility of wildcards to their advantage by simply swapping a blacklisted host name with a new one without having to change DNS entries. This can be useful in evading blacklists, which are based on exact host names today. We now attempt to determine if such is the case. In this analysis, we focus on the PHISH and MALWARE data sets, since the SPAM data set only includes domains, not host names.

We examine if new host names matching an existing wildcard entry are being added to our feed of bad data sets over time. Toward this goal, we calculate the daily churn of host names for each wildcarded domain in PHISH and MALWARE

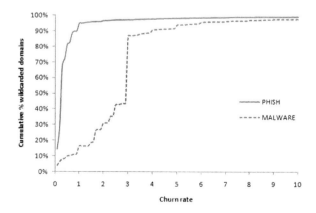

Fig. 3. CDF of churn rate of malicious domains over 30 days

data sets. For this, we compare the host names for a domain with those listed the previous day. The sum of the additions and deletions is the churn rate for the day. We average this over all days the domain is alive. We do not count the initial set up or take down of the domain since some domains may have existed before or continued to exist after our data collection. Domains only seen for one day are also not counted since there is no second day to compare to derive a churn. Figure 3 depicts the CDF of churn over a period of 30 days.

For the PHISH data set, the average churn rate is 0.64, a little more than one change every 2 days, and the maximum is 52. For malware, the average is 2.87 with a maximum of 32.5. *Clearly, these numbers indicate that miscreants whose domains are active for more than a day, especially those serving malware, are taking advantage of the wildcard records to use new host names over time.*

6   Identifying Malicious Wildcard Usage

Thus far, we have seen that wildcards are in wide-spread use among all types of domains in the Internet. Even though some types of bad domains use wildcards more commonly than good or ugly domains, it is unclear if there are any trends that would distinguish wildcard usage among such domains from others. The primary reason for this is that the largest wildcard users are domain registrars and web-hosting providers and many of them are common across all data sets. This is somewhat unsurprising, given that a recent report examining phishing attacks from the first half of 2009 [25], found that only 14.5% of domains used in phishing were actually registered by the phishers, the remaining were compromised domains that could belong to a known service provider.

In this section, we take the first step and examine features of wildcard usage in an attempt to find ones that can distinguish their malicious usage from benign ones. Specifically, we examine time to live (TTL) values on wildcard DNS records and autonomous systems (ASes) corresponding to the wildcarded domains. We also use the Google search engine to discover new hosts matching known wildcards.

6.1   TTLs of Wildcarded Records

We examined the TTLs for each type of wildcarded records to see if malicious domains set different TTLs on their DNS records than benign ones. We compared the TTLs across the three data sets focusing on A wildcards since they were the most common type. A histogram of TTLs for A records is shown in Figure 4.

A few TTLs are most popular in our data sets: 5 minutes, 30 minutes, 1 hour, and 1 day. The most significant difference we see among data sets is at 30 minutes, where the PHISH domains have a large spike but none other do. *In general, we find that wildcards in the PHISH, MALWARE, and SPAM data sets have shorter TTLs than those in good and ugly data sets, with 30 minutes and 1 hour being most popular values for malicious wildcarded domains.* This is intuitive because shorter TTLs allow miscreants to quickly update the IP addresses corresponding

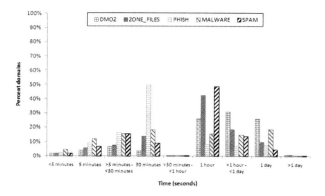

Fig. 4. TTLs for A records in each data set

to malicious host names. Given that it is well known that miscreants are increasingly *fluxing* through IP addresses using short TTLs in an attempt to escape detection [12], examining TTLs corresponding to wildcarded records appears to be a promising avenue for investigation.

6.2 Autonomous Systems Pointed to by Wildcards

Many of the malicious domains are hosted on bots in geographically diverse Internet locations. ASes are one way to measure such diversity. Here, we examine how often the IP addresses corresponding to the wildcard records for each domain are spread over multiple ASes. This test only applies when there are multiple wildcard records for the same name pointing to different IP addresses. This is straightforward to do for A wildcards, since the right hand side of these records directly provides an IP address. For CNAME, MX, and NS records, which point to a host name instead of an IP address, we simply resolve the hosts on the right hand side to IP addresses. For all wildcard types, we see some difference in the results among the various data sets, however, we focus on A and CNAME wildcards in this discussion since these show the greatest difference, enough that they could be used to distinguish benign and malicious use of wildcards.

A histogram of the ratio of ASNs to IP addresses for wildcarded A records is shown in Figure 5. *The most notable observation here is that a majority of SPAM wildcard domains with multiple IP addresses have a ratio of ASNs to IP addresses between 0.6 and 0.7. Very few of the good data sets are in this range. In fact, PHISH and MALWARE A wildcards are much more likely than ZONE_FILES and somewhat more likely than DMOZ to be in the 0.9 to 1.0 range.*

Figure 6 shows the ASN/IP ratio for wildcarded CNAME records. Here, the SPAM data set almost all ends up in the 0.9-1.0 range, while less than 10% of the good data sets do so. Phishing and malware sites are significantly more likely than good ones to fall into the ranges from 0.1 to 0.4.

Overall, this method looks like a good one for identifying wildcards associated with spam sites, and can also be used with wildcards associated with phishing

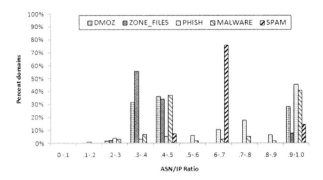

Fig. 5. Ratio of number of ASNs associated with each wildcard A record to number of IP addresses pointed to by record

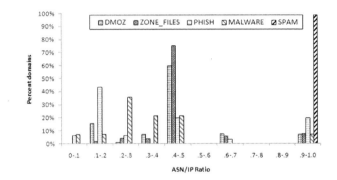

Fig. 6. Ratio of number of ASNs associated with each wildcard CNAME record to number of IP addresses pointed to by record

and malware sites. The only issue with it is that it relies on the wildcard entry pointing to multiple IP addresses, since otherwise, the notion of geographical diversity makes no sense. Wildcard entries point to multiple IP addresses in 1.6 - 4.2% of domains with CNAME wildcards and 0.5 - 27.2% of A wildcards depending on the data set. In the SPAM data set, this happens for 18.2% of A wildcards and 41.2% of CNAME wildcards. This data set is also the one where the ratio is most different from the good data sets, indicating that it would be effective a significant amount of the time for identifying wildcards associated with spam.

6.3   Host Names Represented by Wildcards

Technically, a wildcard entry in the DNS can match any host name. However, in practice, a site may only use some of these host names. Blogging and social networking sites often provide a subdomain for each user. Out of 170 such sites we investigated, 52 support subdomains for each user and all do so using wildcard entries. Of these 52, 37 use `A` wildcards, and the rest use `CNAME`. As a specific example of this, `Windows Live Spaces` provides a subdomain for each user, all handled by a single wildcard entry, and claims 175 million users [14]. Even the smallest blog site we have found using wildcards supports over 10,000 subdomains.

We now investigate if Google searches can reveal new host names covered by our wildcards. Using this method, we would like to see if malicious and benign domains use the wildcard for differing numbers of host names in practice. Toward this goal, we queried the Google search API [6] for a sampling of the domains with `A` or `CNAME` wildcards from each data set, using site restriction to make sure all responses were from the domain we were interested in, not external pages with the domain in their text. This gives us an idea of how the wildcard is being used, subject to a maximum of 64 results imposed by the Google API. Table 9 shows how many domains were queried from each data set, and what percentage were found in the Google index.

Table 9. Wildcarded domains from each data set queried at Google

	DMOZ	ZONE_FILES	PHISH	MALWARE	SPAM
Domains checked	6,717	9,867	1825	2321	4,057
Domains responding	6,587	4,596	1089	1263	475
% indexed	98.1%	46.6%	59.7%	54.4%	11.7%

We find that a large percentage of domains we queried were indexed by Google. Over half from `ZONE_FILES` were not indexed, probably due to the large amount of sites devoid of useful content, such as parking pages. Over half of the `MALWARE` pages were indexed. From `SPAM`, a large majority were not indexed by Google. This is perhaps because the URLs associated with them are only advertised though email, so the Google crawler would have never seen them. It is possible that Google to intentionally excludes some pages with known malicious content.

Out of the domains that did return Google results we examine how many results were returned. Results are shown in Figure 7. The most notable result here is that wildcards from `PHISH` correspond to a higher number of hosts known by Google than wildcards from other data sets. For the other data sets, meaningful distinctions are hard to make, since `SPAM` and `ZONE_FILES` results are similar to each other, as are `MALWARE` and `DMOZ`. While it can not be said with certainty that wildcards representing large numbers of host names are associated with phishing, it is certainly an indication that further scrutiny is required to see if they are phishing sites. While a client could not directly determine the number of hosts a wildcard represents, any organization who crawls the Web should be able to provide data on how many host names they have seen in a domain name, making this check practical.

Figure 8 shows how many host names Google returned that were not found in out data sets. Here, only those data feeds that contained host names are considered since no conclusions can be drawn from data sets containing only

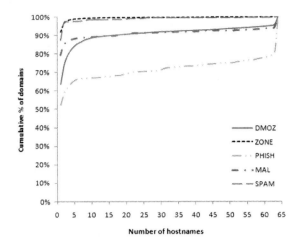

Fig. 7. Cumulative percent of wildcarded domains in each data set with the given number of host names found in the Google index

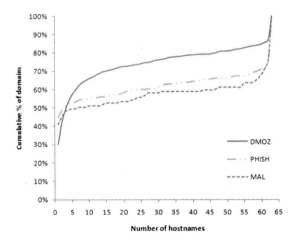

Fig. 8. Cumulative percent of wildcarded domains in each data set with new host names found in the Google index

domain names. *For most domains Google indexed in the PHISH and MALWARE data sets, it knows of several host names not in our data set. This indicates that blacklisting could be improved by directly including wildcard entries instead of exact host names.*

Since overridden wildcards may indicate the wildcard entry itself is not actually used, just present as a default, we wanted to see if the wildcarded domains where we found specific DNS records overriding the wildcarded entry appeared less than others in Google. This does in fact appear to be true. 8.8% of overridden domains we looked up from DMOZ, 20.4% from PHISH, 6.8% from MALWARE, and 1.0% from SPAM appear in Google. Compared to the percent responding for wildcarded domain in general from Table 9, the percent responding for domains with overridden wildcards is an order of magnitude less, for all but PHISH, which is still significantly lower. The fact that Google does not know about these domains indicates their wildcard may not be used to represent as many hosts, giving Google less of a chance to find them. This is further reinforced by the observation that of the ones with overriding found in Google, only 4.8% from DMOZ, 7.2% from PHISH and 2.4% from MALWARE return any new results not from our data feed. This is far lower than seen in Figure 8. *This observation implies that the presence of DNS records overriding wildcarded records may be an indication that the wildcard is not used for purposes such as evading blacklists.*

7   Related Work

Wildcard records have been a part of DNS from the original specification [16]. This specification is ambiguous and unintuitive, so RFC 4592 [10] was created to clarify the intended behaviors of wildcard records. In addition to issues arising from the specification being non-intuitive, it has been argued that they violate common assumptions on how DNS should operate. An Internet Architecture Board (IAB) commentary [8] describes the way wildcards violate this assumptions and the issues that can arise from it. It recommends only using MX type wildcards since they are the only ones that only affect a single protocol. It also recommends not ever using wildcards for domains that have subdomains. Nonetheless, wildcards are in widespread use, as our study finds.

Previous work by Kalafut *et al.* [9] took a more general look at the contents of all DNS records in 5 million DNS domains. In this paper, we focus in more detail on a specific subset of the records, just the wildcards, and search for such records in a larger set of domains. Pappas *et al.* [23] also examined DNS configurations, looking specifically for three types of errors that could impact availability. The Measurement Factory also has done surveys of DNS configurations [13], focusing on software version and deployment of features such a source port randomization.

8   Discussion

Our study found that wildcards are popular among all types of Internet domains, including those involved in malicious behaviors. Among malicious users, spammers use wildcards the most. They are also the least likely to override them. There is a significant churn among host names matching wildcards belonging to malware and phishing domains, implying that they too are likely taking advantage of the wildcards to escape exact host-name-based blacklists.

We found some distinguishing features of the malicious wildcards, such as short TTLs, distinct ratios of IP addresses to ASes when the wildcard pointed to multiple IP addresses, and a low likelihood of appearing in Google results, especially for wildcard domains associated with spam. None of these observations on their own may be enough to distinguish a benign wildcard use from a malicious one. However, these characteristics may be useful in conjunction with others and with each other to identify some malicious sites, a direction we plan to pursue in future work.

Finally, the observations in this paper point to a specific immediate improvement that can be made in blacklists. Many blacklists currently list individual host names. One prominent example, the Google Safe Browsing API [7], uses a system somewhat similar to regular expressions, but this is not common for other blacklists. In the blacklists we use for data feeds, only individual host names were listed, which often ended up matching wildcards. Such blacklists could be easily improved by checking for a wildcard DNS entry and adding it instead of the host name where appropriate. Miscreants could evade detection based on wildcards and still use a large number of host names by creating separate DNS entries for each. However, these cases could still be dealt with by a wildcard entry in the blacklist, added once some threshold number of individual host names in a domain has been seen involved in malicious activity.

References

1. Afilias Limited: How can I get access to Afilias' TLD zone file for .INFO domains? http://www.info.info/faq/ how-can-i-get-access-afilias-tld-zone-file-inf%o-domains
2. APWG: Anti-phishing working group, http://www.antiphishing.org/
3. DMOZ, Open directory project, http://www.dmoz.org/
4. DotAsia Organization Limited. ASIA Zone File Access Agreement, http://www.dotasia.org/info/DAO.ZONE-2007-10-24.pdf
5. eSoft Inc., http://www.esoft.com/
6. Google: Google AJAX Search API, http://code.google.com/apis/ajaxsearch/
7. Google: Google Safe Browsing API, http://code.google.com/apis/safebrowsing
8. Internet Architecture Board: Architectural concerns on the use of DNS wildcards. IAB Commentary (September 2003), http://www.iab.org/documents/docs/2003-09-20-dns-wildcards.html
9. Kalafut, A., Shue, C., Gupta, M.: Understanding implications of DNS zone provisioning. In: ACM SIGCOMM Internet Measurement Conference, IMC (2008)
10. Lewis, E.: The role of wildcards in the domain name system (July 2006)
11. MalwarePatrol: Malwarepatrol - malware block list, http://www.malwarepatrol.net/lists.shtml
12. McGrath, D.K., Kalafut, A., Gupta, M.: Phishing infrastructure fluxes all the way. IEEE Security and Privacy Magazine Special Issue on DNS Security (2009)
13. Measurement Factory: DNS survey (October 2008), http://dns.measurement-factory.com/surveys/200810.html
14. Microsoft: Windows Live Fact Sheet, http://www.microsoft.com/presspass/newsroom/msn/factsheet/WindowsLive.mspx
15. Miller, R.: Phishers use wildcard DNS to build convincing bait URLs (March 2005)

16. Mockapetris, P.: Domain names - concepts and facilities. IETF RFC 1034 (November 1987)
17. Mozilla Foundation: Public suffix list, `http://publicsuffix.org`
18. mTLD, Ltd.: dotMobi Zone File Access Agreement,
    `http://mtld.mobi/domain/zonefile`
19. Mutton, P.: New phishing attacks combine wildcard DNS and XSS, `http://news.netcraft.com/archives/2009/02/17/new_phishing_attacks_combi%ne_wildcard_dns_and_xss.html` (February 2009)
20. NETpilot GmbH: Viruswatch mailing list, `http://lists.clean-mx.com/cgi-bin/mailman/listinfo/viruswatch`
21. NeuStar Registry Services: BIZ Zone File Distribution,
    `https://www.neulevel.biz/zonefile/`
22. OpenDNS: PhishTank, `http://www.phishtank.com/`
23. Pappas, V., Xu, Z., Lu, S., Massey, D., Terzis, A., Zhang, L.: Impact of configuration errors on DNS robustness (2004)
24. Public Interest Registry. ORG Registry - Zone File Access,
    `http://pir.org/index.php?db=content/Website&tbl=Registrars&id=7`
25. Rasmussen, R., Aaron, G.: Apwg global phsihing survey: Trends and domain name use in 1h2009 (Oct.ober 2009)
26. SURBL: `http://www.surbl.org/`
27. VeriSign: Domain name industry brief (February 2010),
    `http://www.verisign.com/domain-name-services/domain-information-center/%domain-name-resources/domain-name-report-feb10.pdf`
28. VeriSign, Inc.: TLD Zone Access Program,
    `http://www.versign.com/information-services/naming-services/page_001052.html`

The Hitchhiker's Guide to DNS Cache Poisoning

Sooel Son and Vitaly Shmatikov

The University of Texas at Austin

Abstract. DNS cache poisoning is a serious threat to today's Internet. We develop a formal model of the semantics of DNS caches, including the bailiwick rule and trust-level logic, and use it to systematically investigate different types of cache poisoning and to generate templates for attack payloads. We explain the impact of the attacks on DNS resolvers such as BIND, MaraDNS, and Unbound and their implications for several defenses against DNS cache poisoning.

Keywords: DNS, cache poisoning, formal model.

1 Introduction

The Domain Name System (DNS) is an essential part of the Internet. The primary purpose of DNS is to resolve symbolic domain names to IP addresses [17,18,10]. Many Internet security mechanisms, including host access control and defenses against spam and phishing, implicitly or explicitly depend on the integrity of the DNS infrastructure. Unfortunately, security was not one of the design considerations for DNS, and many attacks on DNS were reported over the years [19,3,12,15].

Cache poisoning is arguably the most prominent and dangerous attack on DNS. DNS cache poisoning results in a DNS resolver storing (*i.e.*, caching) invalid or malicious mappings between symbolic names and IP addresses. Because the process of resolving a name depends on authoritative servers located elsewhere on the Internet (see Section 2.2), DNS protocol is intrinsically vulnerable to cache poisoning [3]. An attacker may poison the cache by compromising an authoritative DNS server or by forging a response to a recursive DNS query sent by a resolver to an authoritative server.

Many non-cryptographic defenses (surveyed in Section 8) focus solely on blind response forgery and attempt to solve the problem by increasing the entropy of DNS query components such as transaction IDs, query labels, and port numbers. This makes blind response forgery more difficult. Unfortunately, blind response forgery is just one of the possible attack vectors for DNS cache poisoning and, unlike cryptographic solutions, these defenses are vulnerable to trivial eavesdropping attacks. Therefore, they do not address the root causes of DNS cache poisoning and provide only partial protection.

Our goal is to develop a formal model for the semantics of DNS caches and use it to study cache poisoning attacks. Our analysis focuses on the *internal* operation of DNS resolvers and is thus complementary to the analyses of network protocols used to deliver DNS messages, success rate of forgery attempts, network-level defenses, and so forth. For instance, in a concurrent work [4], Bau and Mitchell formally modeled the cryptographic operations involved in the DNSSEC protocol, discovering a vulnerability that allows an attacker to add a forged name into a signed zone.

S. Jajodia and J. Zhou (Eds.): SecureComm 2010, LNICST 50, pp. 466–483, 2010.

By contrast, we analyze the internal bailiwick rules (used by DNS resolvers to decide whether to accept a mapping from a given authority) and the trust levels of DNS data (used by resolvers to decide whether to overwrite an existing record). The bailiwick rule in particular, while critical for DNS security and reliability, is not part of the DNS standard and left to the resolver implementation. Its subtleties are often exploited by cache poisoning attacks, regardless of the actual mechanism (such as blind response forgery) used to deliver attack packets. To the best of our knowledge, internal operations of DNS resolvers have not been formally modeled before.

Our contributions. We explain the nature of DNS cache poisoning attacks and present a precise, formal model of the bailiwick rule and the record overwriting mechanism of modern DNS resolvers, including BIND v9.4.1, Unbound v1.3.4, and MaraDNS v1.3.07.09. We use our model to systematically enumerate and analyze different types of cache poisoning attacks and to explain the damage to different aspects of DNS resolution resulting from each attack. Using the ProVerif protocol analysis tool [6], we automatically construct attack templates for all attacks in our taxonomy, verifying that the attacks work against actual implementations.

The objective of this study is to develop a precise understanding of the semantics of modern DNS caches, including their bailiwick rules and trust-level logic. We do *not* propose a new defense against DNS response forgery since defending against specific types of DNS compromise is largely orthogonal to our goals. (In general, the only reliable protection is provided by cryptographic authentication schemes such as DNSSEC; unfortunately, these schemes are not yet deployed widely.) Instead, we use our model to enumerate the consequences of different types of DNS forgery exploits, regardless of whether they are perpetrated via server compromise, birthday attack, eavesdropping, or some other attack vector. We also show that our model is useful for evaluating the effectiveness of some non-cryptographic defenses against DNS response forgery.

2   DNS Background

2.1   Resource Record Set

DNS is a distributed storage system for Resource Records (RR). Each DNS resolver or authoritative server stores RRs in its cache or local zone file. A Resource Record includes a label, class, type, and data [10]. The label of an RR is a symbolic domain name used when accessing an Internet resource [17]. The class is either IN, or CH; the class of most RRs is IN, which means the Internet system. The type can have many possible values, but we will focus on records of type A, CNAME, and NS. An A record holds a mapping from a domain name to an IP address, a CNAME record holds a mapping from a domain name to an alias, and an NS record holds a mapping from a domain name to the name of an authoritative name server for that domain. Each record has a time-to-live (TTL) parameter and is purged from the cache once its TTL expires.

No two RRs in the cache may have the same label, class, type, and data, but it is possible to have multiple records with the same label, class, and type. Such a group is called a Resource Record Set (RRset).

2.2 Caching and Recursive Resolution

When a DNS resolver or authoritative server receives a query, it searches its cache for a matching label. If there is no matching label in the cache, the server may instead retrieve from the cache and return a referral response, containing an RRset of NS type whose label is "closer" to the domain which is the subject of the query [17].

Instead of sending a referral response, the DNS resolver may also be configured to initiate the same query to an authoritative DNS server responsible for the domain name which is the subject of the query [17]. Each query is identified by a random 16-bit transaction ID (TXID). The authoritative server can respond with an answer, a referral, or a failed response. In general, a response is comprised of the query, answer, authority, and additional sections. Each section may have none, one, or multiple RRsets.

The authoritative server's response—or a forged message pretending to be the authoritative server's response—is accepted by the DNS resolver and stored in its cache only if the RRset of each section passes a set of conditions known as the *bailiwick rule*. These conditions are not part of the DNS specification and depend on the implementation of the resolver. Furthermore, in certain circumstances (see Section 5), the received records may even *overwrite* those already stored in the cache.

Poisoning the DNS cache by adding false records is a serious threat, but DNS records corresponding to popular domains are likely to be already stored in the cache prior to an attack and are thus not vulnerable to the basic forgery exploit (this observation underlies the naive defense of increasing the time-to-live parameter of these records). It is the ability to overwrite existing records that makes DNS response forgery such a devastating attack. To understand record overwriting, we need to understand (1) the mechanism through which an attacker may introduce forged records into the cache of a DNS resolver (Section 3) and (2) the bailiwick and trust-level rules that govern addition and overwriting of records in DNS caches (Sections 4 and 5).

3 DNS Response Forgery

3.1 Cache Poisoning without Response Forgery

Before BIND adopted the bailiwick rule in 1993, the owner of any DNS authoritative server could compromise records corresponding to any domain name [22, 23]. When responding to a query from the resolver, a malicious authoritative server can send, in the additional section of its response, an arbitrary mapping from any domain name (including those outside its authority) to an IP address.

For instance, consider a malicious authoritative server for bad.com. When a client asks its DNS resolver to resolve www.bad.com, the resolver queries the server. The server's response contains in its additional section the mapping from, say, ns1.good.com to a malicious IP address. Without the bailiwick rule (described in Section 4), this mapping would have been cached by the resolver, even though good.com was neither part of the query, nor under the malicious server's authority (see Fig. 2(a)).

3.2   Blind Response Forgery Using Birthday Attack

The basic DNS protocol does not authenticate responses to recursive queries. The only checks are: (1) the query section and 16-bit transaction ID (TXID) of the response must match those of the query, and (2) the source IP address and destination port of the response must match, respectively, the destination IP address and source port of the query. The first arriving UDP packet which satisfies these conditions is treated as a valid response from the authoritative server.

Prior to recent patches [8], many DNS resolvers used a fixed port to send queries. Therefore, with the exception of a random TXID, all values used by the resolver to determine the validity of a packet received in response to its query are predictable. To generate a valid-looking response, it is sufficient to guess the TXID used in the query.

Attacks on DNS exploiting the "birthday paradox" have been known since at least 2002 [21]. If the TXID has only N bits of entropy (in practice, $N = 16$), a network attacker needs only $O(2^{\frac{N}{2}})$ trials on average to generate a forged response which matches the TXID of the query and will thus be accepted as valid by the target resolver. The answer section of the forgery contains a malicious mapping from a domain name to an IP address (see Fig. 1).

For the attack to succeed, the forgery must arrive to the target resolver before the response from the legitimate authoritative server. If the legitimate response arrives first, it will be cached by the re-

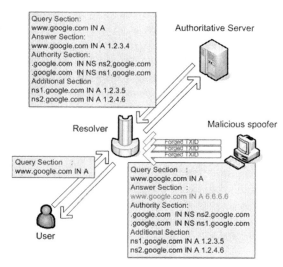

Fig. 1. Overview of the cache poisoning attack

solver and until its time-to-live (TTL) expires, the resolver will not ask the authoritative server to resolve the same domain name, preventing the attacker from poisoning the mapping for that domain.

Kaminsky's exploit. At Black Hat 2008, Kaminsky presented a new extension of the birthday attack [13]. While the basic mechanism is the same (using the birthday attack to forge a response with the same transaction ID as the query), three observations make Kaminsky's attack more serious than "conventional" DNS forgery [19].

First, the attacker can force the target resolver to initiate a query to an authoritative server of his choice. Second, modern attackers have enough network bandwidth to generate a large number of spoofed responses, each with a different guess of the transaction ID. Third, the malicious "payload" of the forged response is the additional section (as opposed to the answer section in the conventional attack), for reasons explained below.

The basic scheme of the exploit is as follows. The attacker chooses the domain name that he wants to compromise (*e.g.*, www.google.com). He then queries the target

Query Section : www.bad.com IN A	Query Section : xyx12.google.com IN A
Answer Section : www.bad.com IN A 6.6.6.6	Answer Section :
Authority Section:	NONE
.bad.com IN NS ns1.yahoo.com	Authority Section:
.bad.com IN NS ns1.google.com	.google.com IN NS www.google.com
Additional Section	Additional Section
ns1.yahoo.com IN A 6.6.6.6	www.google.com IN A 6.6.6.6
ns1.google.com IN A 6.6.6.6	

(a) A forged response without considering bailiwick

(b) Kaminsky's exploit

Fig. 2. Payloads of various cache poisoning attacks

resolver with any subdomain which is not already cached on the resolver (*e.g.*, a non-existent subdomain such as xyz12.google.com). Because the name is not in the cache, this causes the target resolver to send a query to the authoritative server(s) for this domain. At this point, the attacker floods the resolver with a large number of forged responses, each containing a different guess of the query's transaction ID.

A typical forged response is shown in Fig. 2(b). Note that it is a *referral*, not an answer, and the false information is contained in the additional section rather than the answer section. This greatly increases the efficacy of the attack. Instead of hijacking a mapping for a single domain name, the attack, if successful, introduces into the target resolver's cache a false mapping for an authoritative server. Future queries from the compromised resolver will be sent directly to an attacker-controlled IP address, enabling the attacker to provide malicious responses without blind response forgery.

If a forgery attempt fails, the attacker can immediately start a new race, using a different domain name, and continue until he actually wins the race, *i.e.*, a forgery with a valid transaction ID arrives to the resolver before the legitimate answer.

3.3 Response Forgery Using Eavesdropping

A number of recently proposed defenses against DNS cache poisoning, including source port randomization, 0x20-bit encoding, XQID, and WSEC-DNS, fundamentally depend on the *asymmetric accessibility* of the components used for authenticating responses to DNS queries [7, 8, 11, 20].

These defenses ensure neither confidentiality of DNS queries, nor authentication of responses (in contrast to cryptographic defenses such as DNSSEC) and thus prevent only *blind* forgery. DNS remains vulnerable to trivial attacks by compromised servers and/or network eavesdroppers: in a non-switched subnet environment, the attacker can run an eavesdropping tool in the promiscuous mode; in a switched environment, ARP poisoning [14] or any similar technique can be used to force all packets from the target resolver to pass through a malicious computer on the same subnet.

4 The Bailiwick Rule

The purpose of the bailiwick rule is to prevent malicious authoritative servers from providing DNS mappings for domains outside their authority as part of a referral response (see Section 3.1). For example, the authoritative server for .com can return a mapping for any .com domain, while the authoritative server for bad.com should only be able to provide mappings for subdomains of bad.com.

The RFC specifying the DNS protocol does not define a concrete bailiwick rule. For the purposes of this paper, we analyze the bailiwick rules of three open-source implementations: BIND v9.4.1 [1], Unbound v1.3.4 [16], and MaraDNS v1.3.07.09 [24].

BIND. The key data structure used by the bailiwick-checking algorithm of BIND v9.4.1 to keep track of the bailiwick at any given point in the recursive DNS resolution is Query.zone. If a BIND resolver cannot resolve a query locally, it finds the RRset whose label is the "closest" to the received query among all RRsets of type NS in its cache. This label is stored in Query.zone, and the resolver sends the query to the name server indicated by the NS record.

If the response holds an RRset in the answer section, the resolver caches it after checking that its domain label matches the query. NS records in the authority section are cached only if their domain label is a subdomain of or equal to Query.zone.

If the response is a referral (i.e., the answer section does not contain a record), the resolver must resend the query to another name server, as indicated in the referral. At this point, the bailiwick check is performed. First, the resolver checks whether the domain label of the query is a subdomain of the label in the authority section of the received response. If it is, the resolver next checks whether the domain label in the authority section is a subdomain of the current value of Query.zone. Only if both conditions hold, the resolver caches the NS-type RRset received in the referral.

The next step is to determine whether to cache the RRsets in the additional section of the referral. If the domain label of each record in the additional section is a subdomain of Query.zone, the additional section is cached; otherwise, it is not cached and the resolver will initiate new queries for the labels of the records from the additional section.

This prevents a malicious name server from referring a query to a name server in a different bailiwick along with a false IP address mapping for that server (as in Fig. 2(a)), since the resolver will not cache the additional section containing the false mapping.

Finally, the value of Query.zone is changed to the label of the RRset in the authority section of the received referral response. The BIND resolver then initiates queries for the names which were not cached in the previous steps.

Unbound. The bailiwick checking algorithm of Unbound is very different from BIND. All records whose labels are out of the bailiwick are removed from the received responses. The remaining records are cached, provided the response contains at least one answer record which comes from an authoritative server.

Unbound also differs in how it decides whether a response is a referral or not. If the label of the authority record in a response is below the resolver's bailiwick zone, Unbound labels the response as a referral even if there is a record in the answer section. The resolver caches all records from the additional and authority sections of a referral response, but, by default, does not send them to clients [26].

MaraDNS. The bailiwick logic of MaraDNS is significantly simpler. MaraDNS does not cache the authority and additional section of responses containing an RRset in the answer sections, thus eliminating the need to perform bailiwick checks on them. Furthermore, even for referral responses, MaraDNS caches neither the NS mapping from the domain name to an authoritative server name (authority section), nor the A mapping from the latter name to an IP address (additional section). Instead, MaraDNS simply stores an authority section with a mapping from the domain name to the IP address. This eliminates the need to perform a bailiwick check on the name of the authoritative server, since this name is not cached (with a potential loss in efficiency).

Differences between resolver implementations. Table 1 summarizes the differences between DNS resolver implementations. There is an important difference between BIND's and Unbound's default caching policies for RRsets in the additional section. To shorten query resolution times, BIND caches all such mappings, including domain labels and IP addresses from the additional section. By default, Unbound, too, caches the additional section, but these mappings are not sent to the client as the answer for a query. Therefore, from the client's viewpoint, the default behavior of Unbound is similar to that of MaraDNS. All three implementations can be compromised by different types of cache poisoning attacks (the implementations are semantically correct, but the protocols they use for updating the DNS cache are intrinsically weak). In Section 7, we show which implementation is vulnerable to which attack.

Table 1. Differences between resolver implementations

Functionality	BIND 9.4.1	Unbound 1.3.4	MaraDNS 1.3.07
RRset trust rules	O	O	X
Caching answer section	O	O	O
Caching authority section from a referral response	O	O	O
Caching authority section from an answer response	O	O	X
Caching additional section from a referral response	O	O	X
Caching additional section from an answer response	O	O	X
Additional section data sent to clients	Default O	Default X	X

Kaminsky's exploit and the bailiwick check. Kaminsky's exploit does not violate the bailiwick rule. The forged referral in this attack contains an authority section with a (possibly fake) *in-bailiwick* name server, along with an additional section mapping this server to an attacker-controlled IP address. This invalid mapping is cached by the target BIND resolver. If the attacker wants to compromise the mapping of an existing name server (as opposed to introducing a fake one), there is a complication. The mappings for the name servers of popular domains tend to have long TTLs; they are likely to be already present in the victim's cache and must be overwritten. In Section 5, we explain the conditions under which an existing record may be overwritten.

Unbound caches RRsets from the additional section, but, by default, does not send them to clients. These RRsets are used internally by the resolver to find IP addresses of authoritative servers and can be overwritten, facilitating certain attacks (see Section 7).

MaraDNS will accept the malicious authority section, but the mapping from the fake name server to an attacker-controlled IP address will not be cached. The IP address of an authoritative server can be changed only by overwriting an existing mapping.

5   Cache Overwriting

Cache poisoning attacks are especially dangerous because they enable the attacker not just to add false mappings to the cache of vulnerable DNS resolvers, but also to *over-write* existing mappings, including long-lived mappings for popular domains.

The rules for overwriting cache records are defined in RFC 2181 [10]. They depend on the *trust level* of an RRset. Table 2 shows trust levels used by BIND resolvers. The trust level of an RRset contained in a response depends on whether it comes from an authoritative server and whether the response is a referral. Trust level 8 is for records in a local zone setup file provided by a DNS server administrator, while trust level 7 is used by DNSSEC. We focus on records whose trust levels are from 2 to 6.

Table 2. Trust levels in BIND 9.4.1.

Define symbol	Trust level	Description
dns_trust_ultimate	8	This server is authoritative
dns_trust_secure	7	Successfully DNSSEC validated
dns_trust_authanswer	6	Answer from an authoritative server
dns_trust_authauthority	5	Received in the auth section as an authority response
dns_trust_answer	4	Answer from a non-authoritative server
dns_trust_glue	3	Received in a referral response
dns_trust_additional	2	Received in the add section of a response

BIND and Unbound. In BIND, a cached RRset is overwritten if the trust level of the received RRset is higher or equal to the cached one and its TTL is longer. NS-type RRsets received in a referral are an exception: they have the trust level 8 for the purposes of overwriting (*i.e.*, they always overwrite the records already present in the cache), but are stored with the trust level 3.

In Unbound, the absolute trust levels are different, but the relative order is the same. Therefore, we use the same trust-level model for BIND and Unbound.

MaraDNS. MaraDNS does not use trust levels. A new record contained in the response simply overwrites the existing record. In practice, however, only NS records can be overwritten by forged responses. Because MaraDNS does not cache the additional section of responses, in order to overwrite an A or CNAME record the forged response should contain the replacement mapping in the answer section and its label must be exactly the same as the label of the record to be overwritten. Such a forgery would only be accepted in response to a query with the same label. Observe, however, that since a record with this label is already present in the cache, a MaraDNS resolver would never initiate a recursive query for this label. Therefore, there is no query that would give the attacker an opportunity to overwrite an existing A or CNAME record.

6   Formal Model of DNS Resolver

6.1   Modeling Methodology

As shown in Sections 4 and 5, the semantics of DNS caches are quite complicated. To understand the potential impact of cache poisoning attacks, we construct a formal

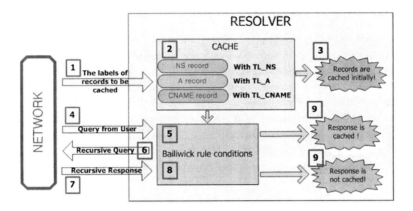

Fig. 3. Generic model of a DNS resolver

model of the default bailiwick-checking and cache-overwriting rules of BIND v9.4.1 and Unbound v1.3.4. We do not build a formal model for MaraDNS because it does not cache the authority and additional sections of responses containing an answer RRset and does not use trust levels for overwriting existing records. We do show attacks against all three implementations, including MaraDNS, in Table 4

We use the ProVerif protocol analysis tool, due to its success in practical formal verification of security protocols (*e.g.*, [2]). The details of ProVerif are beyond the scope of this paper and can be found in [6]. The behavior of each protocol participant is modeled as a set of Horn clauses, which represent sending or receiving messages on specified communication channels. ProVerif then uses a sound, resolution-based algorithm to determine whether a specified property holds over all executions of the protocol.

Fig. 3 shows the abstract model of DNS resolver. We use it to check whether or not a cached resource record with a certain label and trust level is secure against cache poisoning conducted by the active adversary who has complete control of the network. This attacker model may appear strong, but we emphasize once again that our goal is to model the *internal behavior of DNS resolvers*, not the details of the network protocol through which DNS messages are exchanged. By modeling the network as a public channel, we can focus on the semantics of the cache and abstract from the particulars of the forgery method through which attacker packets are introduced.

The initial state of the model asserts that three valid records of types A, NS, and CNAME, respectively, have been cached. Their labels are determined via network inputs. (In reality, the attacker can insert an arbitrary label into the cache by tricking a client of the resolver into asking to resolve the corresponding name.) Trust levels are specified manually. The model then receives a query from the network. If recursive resolution is required, the model sends out a recursive query and receives a response from the network. The bailiwick rule in the model determines which records in the response should be cached. If a malicious record satisfies the bailiwick conditions, the model asserts that a cache poisoning event has occurred.

6.2   Base Data Types

We use a simplified model of DNS records with only three components—type (A, NS, or CNAME), domain name, and data—and ignore other aspects such as authority RRsets in the answer section, lame resolution, and zone delegation. Events model critical points in the resolution process. The *evInitCache* event occurs when the model is initialized. It asserts that a record is cached with a verifier-specified trust level prior to the attack (in our analysis, we vary the trust level to determine whether or not a particular record can be overwritten). The *evRecursiveQueryStart* event occurs when the cache does not have a record matching a given query and the resolver must send a recursive query to an authoritative server responsible for the bailiwick zone. The *evPoison* event occurs when an invalid record passes all checks and is about to be cached.

6.3   Cache Initialization

Our model assumes that the CNAME, A and NS resource records for a certain name are already present in the cache. The model then generates a query, waits for a response from the network, and decides whether or not the response should be cached.

The following property says that the *evPoison* event does not occur unless the *evInitCache* event has occurred. More precisely, in the resolver which already caches *cachedns*, *cacheda* and *cachedcname* labels, a resource record whose label is *poisonedlabel* and whose type is *rectype* is cached with the trust level *tl* only if there has occurred an *evInitCache* event in which the resource record whose label was *cachedlabel* and whose type was *cachedtype* was cached with the trust level *cachedtl*.

query ev: evPoison(rectype, poisonedlabel, poisoneddata, tl,
                          cachedns, cacheda, cachedcname)
⟶ ev: evInitCache(Record(cachedtype, cachedlabel, data), cachedtl)

6.4   Non-overwritability

Recall from Section 5 that a cached record can only be overwritten by a record with an equal or higher trust level. The following properties model "non-overwritability" of A records with various trust levels:

query ev: evPoison(At, cacheda, wrongdst, tl, cachedns, cacheda, cachedcname)
    ⟶ ev: evInitCache(Record(At, cacheda, validdst), tl6) ∧ tl6 > tl
query ev: evPoison(At, cacheda, wrongdst, tl, cachedns, cacheda, cachedcname)
    ⟶ ev: evInitCache(Record(At, cacheda, validdst), tl4) ∧ tl4 > tl
query ev: evPoison(At, cacheda, wrongdst, tl, cachedns, cacheda, cachedcname)
    ⟶ ev: evInitCache(Record(At, cacheda, validdst), tl3) ∧ tl3 > tl
query ev: evPoison(At, cacheda, wrongdst, tl, cachedns, cacheda, cachedcname)
    ⟶ ev: evInitCache(Record(At, cacheda, validdst), tl2) ∧ tl2 > tl

Each of these properties says that whenever a poisoning event occurs, the target record is already cached with a certain trust level which is higher than the trust level of the forged response. If the property holds, the existing record cannot be overwritten.

Question any1.abc.com. ?	Question any1.abc.com. ?	Question any1.abc.com. ?	Question any1.sub.abc.com. ?
Answer NULL	Answer any1.abc.com A 1.2.3.4	Answer NULL	Answer NULL
Authority sub.abc.com. NS www.abc.com	Authority abc.com. NS www.abc.com	Authority abc.com. NS www.abc.com	Authority sub.abc.com. NS www.abc.com
Additional www.abc.com A 6.6.6.6	Additional www.abc.com A 6.6.6.6	Additional www.abc.com A 6.6.6.6	Additional www.abc.com A 6.6.6.6

| sub.abc.com is a sub domain name under abc.com excluding abc.com itself. Payload 1 | abc.com is a sub domain name under abc.com including abc.com itself. Payload 2 | abc.com is a sub domain name under abc.com including abc.com itself. Payload 3 | abc.com is a sub domain name under abc.com including abc.com itself. Payload 4 |

* AA bit means that a reponse comes from an authoritative server.

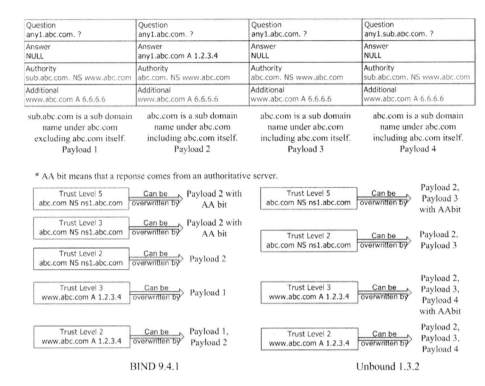

Fig. 4. All ways to overwrite an existing RRset in the cache

If the property cannot be provable, then the model contains at least one path in which the trust level of the forged record is higher than the trust level of the cached record. Therefore, the cached record can be successfully overwritten by the forgery.

ProVerif analysis shows that in both BIND and Unbound, non-overwritability holds only for trust levels 4 and 6. All cached records whose trust level is 2, or 3 *can* be overwritten. For all interesting trust levels of an A or NS record, Fig. 4 shows the (automatically generated) templates for malicious payloads to be used in the forged response. In Fig. 4, we assume that the NS record of abc.com and the A record of www.abc.com are already cached by the victim resolver.

The following property is always false in our model, showing that CNAME records cannot be overwritten.

query ev: evPoison(CNAMEt, cachedc, invalid, tl, cachedns, cacheda, cachedc)

6.5 Bailiwick Rule

The primary purpose of the bailiwick rule is to prevent an authoritative server from claiming the mappings from domain names belonging to other authorities. To determine whether the bailiwick-checking logic of BIND and Unbound resolvers achieves this, we used ProVerif to verify the following three properties:

query ev: evPoison(NSt/At/CNAMEt, targetname, dst, tl, cachedns, cacheda, cachedc)
$\longrightarrow$ ev: evRecursiveQueryStart(query, bailiwick, bailiwickAAserver)
$\wedge$ isSubName: query, bailiwick
$\wedge$ isSubName: targetname, bailiwick

These properties say that a record can enter the cache (represented by the cache poisoning event, since in our model all responses arrive from the network attacker) only in response to a recursive query and if *targetname* and *query* are subdomains of *bailiwick*. Here *bailiwick* is the authority name closest to the domain label in the query.

According to ProVerif, these three properties hold in our model. Therefore, the domain name of both legitimate and forged responses must be a subdomain of the proper bailiwick, as determined by the DNS resolver. Note, however, that the bailiwick depends on the label of the current query. An attacker may initiate a query for a domain of his choice or manipulate the resolver into issuing such a query (*e.g.*, by tricking one of the resolver's users into visiting a webpage with a link to the domain), thus ensuring that forged responses do not violate the bailiwick rule.

7   Taxonomy of Cache Poisoning Attacks

We use our model to systematically enumerate several types of cache poisoning attacks, the corresponding payloads of forged DNS responses, and their effect on the compromised resolver. Our taxonomy is shown in Table 3. It is *complete* for A, NS, and CNAME records. We assume that the resolver has already fixed the bailiwick zone (abc.com) for incoming responses. Every name which can be a target of cache poisoning belongs to one of three categories: domain outside abc.com, subdomain of abc.com, or abc.com itself. There are two types of cache poisoning: adding a new name and overwriting the mapping for an existing name. Table 3 covers all possibilities.

Table 4 summarizes the feasibility of different types of cache poisoning attacks against different resolver implementations. Because BIND and Unbound use different

Table 3. Taxonomy of cache poisoning attacks on BIND and Unbound (abc.com is the bailiwick zone)

Target domain name	Type	Type of poisoning	
		Adding a new mapping	Overwriting an existing mapping
Domain name outside abc.com	CNAME	Impossible (Section 6.5)	Impossible (Section 6.5)
	A		
	NS		
abc.com	NS	Target name is already in the cache	Possible (Section 7.4)
Subdomain of abc.com	CNAME	Possible (Section 7.1)	Impossible (Section 6.4)
	A	Possible (Sections 7.1, 7.2, 7.5, 7.6)	Possible for trust levels 2, 3 (Sections 7.3, 6.4)
	NS	Possible (Section 7.4)	Possible (Section 7.4)

Table 4. Cache poisoning attacks on different resolvers. All attacks have been tested against actual implementations.

Type of attack	BIND 9.4.1	Unbound 1.3.4	MaraDNS 1.3.07
Adding a new CNAME record (Section 7.1)	Effective	Effective	Effective
Adding a subdomain under an existing authority (Section 7.2)	Effective	Possible, but ineffective with the default policy	Impossible by forging additional data
Overwriting an existing A record (Section 7.3)	Effective	Effective	Impossible *
Overwriting an existing NS record (Section 7.4)	Effective	Effective	Effective
Creating fake domains (Section 7.5)	Effective (by forging additional section)	Effective (requires prior overwriting of IP addresses of authoritative servers)	Effective (requires prior overwriting of IP addresses of authoritative servers)
Stealing a popular domain name by hijacking subauthorities (Section 7.6)	Effective	Effective	Effective

* IP addresses of authoritative servers can be overwritten without overwriting an A record.

caching policies by default and MaraDNS does not cache the additional section, the effective attack payload varies from resolver to resolver. For BIND and Unbound, our analysis is based on our formal model and experimental attacks against the resolver implementation. For MaraDNS, we analyzed the bailiwick-checking logic manually (it is significantly simpler than in either BIND, or Unbound).

7.1 Adding a New CNAME Record

Our model shows that the only way to add a malicious CNAME mapping to the cache is to forge an answer section whose label is exactly same as the query (the reason is that the authority section contains only NS records and the additional section only A records). This is captured by the following property:

query ev: evPoison(CNAMEt, newname, invalidlabel, tl, cachedns, cacheda, cachedc)
⟶ ev: evInitCache(Record(At, cacheda, validlabel), cachedtl)

The disadvantage of this attack is that it cannot be easily perpetrated via blind, brute-force forgery. If the attacker fails in a single race, the resolver will cache the failed label and the attacker must change the target name. If, however, the attacker poisons the IP addresses of authoritative servers for a certain zone, he controls all names in this zone and adding any CNAME mapping is trivial. The IP addresses of authoritative servers are usually cached with the trust level 2 or 3 and can thus be overwritten (Section 7.3).

7.2   Adding a Subdomain under an Existing Authority

This exploit adds a record for a fake subdomain under an existing authority in the victim's cache. It is modeled by the following property:

query ev: evPoison(At, makeSubName(bad, goodZone), invalid, tl,
                  goodZone, makeSubName(good, goodZone), cname)
   $\longrightarrow$ev: evInitCache(Record(At, makeSubName(good, goodZone), valid), cachetl)

As shown in Fig. 4, payloads 1 and 2 can add a new domain name to a BIND cache. By default, the RRsets in the additional section will be used as the answer to the query. Payloads 2, 3, and 4 can add a new domain name to an Unbound cache, but Unbound's default policy does not send this information to clients.

This attack is dangerous to clients using BIND resolvers because many Web security policies are vulnerable to attacks from subdomains. For example, many websites set the path and domain name of cookies as, respectively, '/' and the top two levels of the site's domain (*e.g.*, example.com rather than www10.example.com). An attacker who uses cache poisoning to introduce a fake subdomain can use phishing to lure naive users to this subdomain and then overwrite and/or read cookies set by legitimate subdomains.

7.3   Overwriting an Existing a Record

One may assume that address mappings for popular domain names are already cached by most resolvers with the trust level 4 or 6. Therefore, they cannot be overwritten until their TTL expires. This is the basis of a common defense against DNS forgery: simply increase TTL for legitimate DNS records.

A cleverer attack exploits the fact that it is uncommon for clients to directly initiate queries about authoritative name servers such as ns1.google.com. Records with addresses of authoritative name servers are typically received by resolvers as part of referral responses, which are cached with the trust level 2 or 3. Therefore, they can be overwritten. In our model, this is captured by the following property:

query ev: evPoison(At, targetname, invaliddata, tl, ns, targetname, cname)
   $\longrightarrow$ ev: evInitCache(Record(At, targetname, validdata), tl2) $\wedge$ tl2 > tl
query ev: evPoison(At, targetname, invaliddata, tl, ns, targetname, cname)
   $\longrightarrow$ ev: evInitCache(Record(At, targetname, validdata), tl3) $\wedge$ tl3 > tl

Our formal analysis shows that payloads 1 and 2 for BIND and payloads 2, 3, and 4 for Unbound (see Fig. 4) can accomplish this attack.

This attack is dangerous to clients of both BIND and Unbound. It results in changing the IP addresses of authoritative servers and enables the attacker to compromise *any* domain in the server's zone. Furthermore, IP address mappings for the names of root DNS servers such as A.ROOT-SERVERS.NET can be stored in the cache with the trust level 2. Although there are only 13 root servers, making forgery harder, if the attack does succeed, their addresses can be overwritten.

7.4   Overwriting an Existing NS Record

Unlike Kaminsky's attack, which uses the authority and additional sections of the forged response to compromise the mapping from a domain name to an IP address, forged responses can also be used to overwrite existing NS records in the resolver's cache [25]. In our formal model, this is represented by the following property:

query ev: evPoison(NSt, targetname, invalidlabel, tl, targetname, a, cname)
    $\longrightarrow$ ev: evInitCache(Record(NSt, targetname, validlabel), cachetl) $\land$ cachetl $>$ tl

Payload 2 from Fig. 4 works against BIND, payloads 2 and 3 against Unbound.

The consequence of this attack is that any query for a domain name under the compromised authority is sent by the resolver directly to an attacker-controlled authoritative server(s). This exploit is more serious than Kaminsky's exploit because it effectively hijacks *every* domain name under the compromised authority. We emphasize that the attacker can overwrite any NS record in the cache, even those with non-expired TTL.

7.5   Creating Fake Domains

Cache poisoning enables the attacker to insert a mapping for any domain name into the victim resolver's cache even if the domain does not exist in reality. For example, the attacker can create mappings for plausible domain names such as www.google.edu and www.university.gov, making it easier to carry out phishing attacks. To stage this exploit, the forged packet must look like a valid response from the authoritative server for a top-level domain such as .edu or .gov. Against BIND, it is sufficient to forge RRsets in the additional section. Technically, the attack is modeled by the same rules and uses the same payloads as in Section 7.2.

The attack against Unbound is more sophisticated because Unbound by default does not send the additional section to clients. The attacker must change the authority section for the target zone or the IP addresses of the zone's authoritative servers. Once that's done, adding a new name under this zone is trivial. Technically, this attack is modeled by the same rules and uses the same payloads as in Section 7.3 (respectively, 7.4).

7.6   Hijacking a Popular Domain via a Sub-authority

A common objective of DNS attacks is to compromise the mappings for popular domain names such as www.paypal.com and www.google.com. As mentioned above, such mappings are difficult to compromise because they are likely to be already cached with a long TTL. In practice, popular domain names are usually mapped to subdomains via long-lived CNAME records. For example, www.google.com may be mapped to www.1.google.com. Even if the attacker succeeds in forging an A record which maps www.google.com to a malicious IP address, the resolver will use the unexpired CNAME record rather than the forged A record, foiling the attack.

Subdomain names, however, are mapped to actual IP addresses by A records with relatively short TTL values. For example, the record mapping www.1.google.com to an IP address may have a 300-second TTL. Suppose the attacker poisons the authority section for 1.google.com. Once the A record for www.1.google.com expires, the victim will ask an attacker-controlled server to resolve www.1.google.com, giving him complete control over the mapping. This attack is effective against both BIND and Unbound because it targets the authority section of a zone or the IP address of the zone's authoritative server, not the records in the additional section. Therefore, Unbound's default policy does not prevent the attack. Technically, this attack is modeled by the same rules and uses the same payloads as in Section 7.3 (respectively, 7.4).

8 Defenses

The objective of our formal model is to understand the nature and impact of cache poisoning attacks at the level of DNS resolvers, *not* the protocol through which poisoned packets are delivered. By contrast, the defenses surveyed below (with the exception of cryptographic defenses) focus solely on preventing blind response forgery, which is simply one of the many vectors for cache poisoning attacks. Therefore, they are largely complementary and orthogonal to the goals of this paper.

Cryptographic solutions include DNSSEC [9] and DNSCurve [5]. DNSSEC uses digital signatures to authenticate and protect integrity of responses to DNS queries. So far, cryptographic solutions have not been widely deployed due to their impact on DNS performance, as well as political and infrastructural issues.

The most popular non-cryptographic defense against blind response forgery is UDP source port randomization [8]. It increases entropy of recursive DNS queries by randomizing the source port number in addition to the transaction ID, thus making the birthday attack more difficult. This patch depends on the configuration of the local network such as the firewall imposing strict constraints on inbound connections. Other solutions aiming to prevent blind response forgery by increasing entropy of queries are 0x20-bit encoding [7], which randomizes capitalization of letters in the query (the amount of entropy depends on the length of the query), and WSEC-DNS [20] and XQID [11], which use a challenge-response scheme with random nonces.

While these solutions may be effective for blocking a particularly dangerous attack vector (namely, blind response forgery), they do not actually authenticate responses to recursive DNS queries and should be viewed only as a temporary patch until proper authentication mechanisms are deployed. As long as there exist other attack vectors (see Section 3) and modern resolver implementations such as BIND and Unbound cache information provided in the authority and additional sections of unauthenticated responses (see Section 4), DNS cache poisoning will remain a serious issue.

Other proposed solutions include increasing TTLs of legitimate records and limiting the number of simultaneous recursive queries (the latter to decrease the number of simultaneous races that may be staged by the attacker). Our model helps evaluate such defenses because their efficacy depends on a detailed understanding of the semantics of DNS caches. For example, our analysis shows that increasing TTL does not help against a large class of attacks that involve overwriting of existing DNS records.

9 Conclusion

We presented a formal model of DNS cache semantics, including the bailiwick and trust-level rules used by common resolver implementations, and analyzed it with the

ProVerif protocol analysis tool. The result is a comprehensive taxonomy of cache poisoning attacks, showing (1) which parts of the cache can be poisoned, (2) conditions necessary for each attack, and (3) consequences of each attack. Furthermore, our analysis enabled us to produce payload templates for each attack. We argue that our formal model is an essential tool for understanding the subtle caching rules used by modern DNS resolvers and developing robust defenses against DNS cache poisoning.

References

1. Internet Systems Consortium BIND 9.4.1, http://www.isc.org/downloadtables
2. Abadi, M., Blanchet, B.: Computer-assisted verification of a protocol for certified email. Sci. Comput. Program. 58(1-2), 3–27 (2005)
3. Atkins, D., Austein, R.: Threat Analysis of the Domain Name System (DNS). RFC 3833, Informational (August 2004)
4. Bau, J., Mitchell, J.: A security evaluation of DNSSEC with NSEC3. In: NDSS (2010)
5. Bernstein, D.J.: DNSCurve, http://DNSCurve.org
6. Blanchet, B.: Automatic verification of correspondences for security protocols. J. Computer Security (2009)
7. Dagon, D., Antonakakis, M., Vixie, P., Jinmei, T., Lee, W.: Increased DNS forgery resistance through 0x20-bit encoding. In: CCS (2008)
8. Doughety, C.R.: Vulnerability note vu#800113 (2008), https://www.kb.cert.org/vuls/id/800113
9. Eastlake, D.: Domain Name System Security Extensions. RFC 2535 (Proposed Standard) (March 1999), Obsoleted by RFCs 4033, 4034, 4035, updated by RFCs 2931, 3007, 3008, 3090, 3226, 3445, 3597, 3655, 3658, 3755, 3757, 3845
10. Elz, R., Bush, R.: Clarifications to the DNS Specification. RFC 2181 (Proposed Standard) (July 1997), Updated by RFCs 4035, 2535, 4343, 4033, 4034
11. Høy, J.: Anti DNS spoofing - extended query ID (XQID) (April 2008), http://www.jhsoft.com/dns-xqid.htm
12. Jackson, C., Barth, A., Bortz, A., Shao, W., Boneh, D.: Protecting browsers from DNS rebinding attacks. In: CCS (2007)
13. Kaminsky, D.: Black ops 2008-it's the end of the cache as we know it. Presented at Black-Hat 2008 (2008)
14. King, T.: Packet sniffing in a switched environment (August 2002), http://www.sans.org/reading_room/whitepapers/networkdevs/
15. Klein, A.: BIND 9 DNS cache poisoning (March 2007), http://www.trusteer.com/bind9dns
16. NLnet Labs. Unbound 1.3.4, http://www.unbound.net/download.html
17. Mockapetris, P.V.: Domain names - concepts and facilities. RFC 1034 (Standard) (November 1987), Updated by RFCs 1101, 1183, 1348, 1876, 1982, 2065, 2181, 2308, 2535, 4033, 4034, 4035, 4343, 4035, 4592
18. Mockapetris, P.V.: Domain names - implementation and specification. RFC 1035 (Standard) (November 1987), Updated by RFCs 1101, 1183, 1348, 1876, 1982, 1995, 1996, 2065, 2136, 2181, 2137, 2308, 2535, 2845, 3425, 3658, 4033, 4034, 4035, 4343
19. Olnet, M., Mullen, P., Miklavcic, K.: Dan Kaminsky's 2008 DNS vulnerability (2008), http://www.ietf.org/mail-archive/web/dnsop/current/pdf2jgx6rzxN4.pdf
20. Perdisci, R., Antonakakis, M., Luo, X., Lee, W.: WSEC DNS: Protecting recursive DNS resolvers from poisoning attacks. In: DSN-DCCS (2009)

21. Sacramento, V.: Vulnerability in the sending requests control of Bind version 4 and 8 allows DNS spoofing (November 2002),
   `http://www.rnp.br/cais/alertas/2002/cais-ALR-19112002a.html`
22. Schuba, C.: Addessing weaknesses in the domain name system protocol (1993),
   `http://ftp.cerias.purdue.edu/pub/papers/christoph-schuba/`
23. Secure Works. DNS cache poisoning - the next generation (2007),
   `http://www.secureworks.com/research/`
   `articles/dns-cache-poisoning`
24. S. Trenholme. MaraDNS 1.3.07.09, `http://www.maradns.org`.
25. Computer Academic Underground,
   `http://www.caughq.org/exploits/CAU-EX-2008-0003.txt`
26. Wijngaards, W.: Resolver side mitigations (August 2008),
   `http://tools.ietf.org/html/`
   `draft-wijngaards-dnsext-resolver-side-mitiga%tion-00`

A Formal Definition of Online Abuse-Freeness[*]

Ralf Küsters[1], Henning Schnoor[2], and Tomasz Truderung[1]

[1] Universität Trier, Germany
{kuesters,truderung}@uni-trier.de
[2] Christian-Albrechts-Universität zu Kiel, Germany
schnoor@ti.informatik.uni-kiel.de

Abstract. Abuse-freeness is an important security requirement for contract-signing protocols. In previous work, Kähler, Küsters, and Wilke proposed a definition for *offline* abuse-freeness. In this work, we generalize this definition to *online* abuse-freeness and apply it to two prominent contract-signing protocols. We demonstrate that online abuse-freeness is strictly stronger than offline abuse-freeness.

Keywords: contract signing, cryptographic protocols, formal verification.

1 Introduction

In a (two-party) contract-signing protocol (see, e.g., [4,3,9]), two parties, A (Alice) and B (Bob), aim to exchange signatures on a contractual text that they previously agreed upon. In this paper, we consider *optimistic* contract-signing protocols. In such protocols, a trusted third party T (TTP), serving as an impartial judge, is not involved in every protocol run, but in case of a problem only.

A central security property for optimistic contract-signing, introduced in [9], is abuse-freeness: This property (formulated for the case of the honest signer Alice) requires that there is no state in a protocol run in which dishonest Bob (the prover) can convince an outside party, Charlie (the verifier), that the protocol is in an unbalanced state, i.e., a state in which Bob has both (i) a strategy to prevent Alice from obtaining a valid contract and (ii) a strategy to obtain a valid contract himself. In other words, if a contract-signing protocol is not abuse-free, then Alice can be misused by Bob to get leverage for another contract (with Charlie). Obviously, abuse-freeness is a highly desirable security property.

In [12], Kähler, Küsters, and Wilke presented the first rigorous and protocol-independent definition of abuse-free for (two-party) optimistic contract-signing. However, their definition focusses on an *offline* setting: Charlie is not actively involved in the protocol run and may receive a single message from Bob only, based on which he has to make his decision.

---

[*] This work was partially supported by *Deutsche Forschungsgemeinschaft* (DFG) under Grant KU 1434/5-1.

S. Jajodia and J. Zhou (Eds.): SecureComm 2010, LNICST 50, pp. 484–497, 2010.
© Institute for Computer Sciences, Social Informatics and Telecommunications Engineering 2010

The goal of this work is to generalize the definition from [12] to the setting in which Charlie may be *online*, i.e., may be actively involved in the protocol run, and to apply the definition to prominent contract-signing protocols.

Contribution of this Work. We propose a definition for *online* abuse-freeness, generalizing the definition of Kähler et al., who considered *offline* abuse-freeness. As theirs, our definition is protocol-independent. More precisely, we define two variants of online abuse-freeness: *Weak* abuse-freeness requires that there is no way for dishonest Bob to convince the verifier that the protocol is *currently* in an unbalanced state. As will be explained in Section 3, in the setting of *offline* abuse-freeness, every contract-signing protocol is weakly abuse-free. *Strong* abuse-freeness requires that Bob cannot even prove to Charlie that the protocol was in an unbalanced state at some point of the run.

We apply our definitions to two prominent contract signing protocols: a protocol by Asokan, Shoup, and Waidner [3] (ASW protocol), and one by Garay, Jakobsson, and P. MacKenzie [9] (GJM protocol). The latter was explicitly designed with abuse-freeness in mind. Depending on whether the verifier is allowed to eavesdrop on the network connection between the signers or on the channel between the signers and the TTP, and whether the initiator or responder in the protocol is dishonest, the protocols behave differently: We show that if the verifier can read the messages between the signers and the TTP, and the initiator is dishonest, then the ASW protocol is vulnerable to a very strong attack, i.e. it is not even weakly abuse-free. In this attack, the online aspect of our definition plays a crucial role, as the verifier "dictates" parts of the messages sent by the dishonest signer. In all other situations, ASW is weakly, but not strongly abuse-free. The GJM protocol shows a stronger resistance against abuse: It is weakly abuse-free in all situations, and strongly abuse free if the verifier cannot eavesdrop on the network channel between the signers.

Related Work. As mentioned above, Kähler et al. [12] introduced the first rigorous and protocol-independent definition of offline abuse-freeness.

Kremer et al. [13] analyzed the ASW and GJM protocol w.r.t. abuse-freeness using a finite-state model checking tool. They explicitly needed to specify the behavior of dishonest principals and which states are the ones that are convincing to Charlie.

Chadha et al. [5] introduce a stronger notion than abuse-freeness, namely *balance*: A protocol is balanced, if unbalanced states (see above) do not occur at all. Obviously, a balanced protocol is abuse-free as well. However, balance is very difficult to achieve. In fact, as shown by Chadha et al. [6], if principals are optimistic, i.e., they are willing to wait for messages of other parties, balance is impossible to achieve.

Procedures for deciding properties of contract-signing protocols, including balance, were presented in [11] and [10].

Shmatikov and Mitchell [16] employ the finite-state model checker Murφ to automatically analyze contract-signing protocols. They approximate the notion of abuse-freeness by a notion similar to balance.

A cryptographic definition of the balance property was presented by Cortier, Küsters, and Warinschi in [7].

Aizatulin, Schnoor, and Wilke [2] introduced a contract signing protocol which satisfies a probabilistic notion of balance. Wang [17] introduces an abuse-free contract signing protocol based on the RSA signature scheme.

Structure of the Paper. In Section 2, we introduce our protocol model. The definition of abuse-freeness is then given in Section 3, and applied to the ASW and GJM protocols in Sections 4 and 5, respectively. Proofs of our results can be found in our technical report [14].

2   Protocol Model

In this section, following [15], we present a quite abstract symbolic protocol model. In this model, processes are represented as functions that from a sequence of input messages (the messages received so far) produce output messages. This model is the basis of our definition of abuse-freeness provided in the next section. We note, however, that the details of the model are not essential for the definition. The main motivation for using this model is brevity of presentation. We could as well have used another protocol model, such as the applied pi calculus [1].

2.1   Terms and Messages

Let Σ be some signature for cryptographic primitives (including a possibly infinite set of constants for representing participant names, etc.), $X = \{x_1, x_2, \dots\}$ be a set of variables, and Nonce be an infinite set of *nonces*, where the sets Σ, X, and Nonce are pairwise disjoint. For $N \subseteq$ Nonce, the set T_N of *terms* over $\Sigma \cup N$ and X is defined as usual. Ground terms, i.e., terms without variables, represent messages. We assume some fixed equational theory associated with Σ and denote by $\equiv$ the congruence relation on terms induced by this theory. The exact definition of Σ and the equational theory will depend on the cryptographic primitives used in the protocol under consideration. A simple example of a signature Σ_{ex} and its associated equational theory is provided in Figure 1. A term of the form $\mathsf{sig}(\mathsf{sk}(k), m)$ represents a message m signed using the (private) key $\mathsf{sk}(k)$. Checking validity of such a signature is modeled by equation (1). The fact that signatures do not necessarily hide the signed message is expressed by equation (2). A term of the form $\{x\}^r_{\mathsf{pk}(k)}$ represents the ciphertext obtained by encrypting x under the public key $\mathsf{pk}(k)$ using randomness r. Decryption of such a term using the corresponding private key $\mathsf{sk}(k)$ is modeled by equation (3). A term of the form $\langle x, y \rangle$ models the pairing of terms x and y. The components x and y of $\langle x, y \rangle$ can be extracted by applying the operators $\mathsf{first}(\cdot)$ and $\mathsf{second}(\cdot)$, respectively, as modeled by the equations (4) and (5). A term of the form $\mathsf{hash}(m)$ represents the result of applying a hash function to a message m. Note that $\mathsf{hash}(\cdot)$ is a free symbol, i.e. there is no equation involving this symbol in the given equational theory. For example, let $\equiv_{ex}$ denote the congruence relation induced by the equational theory in Figure 1, then we have that $\mathsf{dec}(\{a\}^r_{\mathsf{pk}(k)}, \mathsf{first}(\langle \mathsf{sk}(k), b \rangle)) \equiv_{ex} a$.

$$\mathsf{checksig}(\mathsf{sig}(\mathsf{sk}(k), m), \mathsf{pk}(k)) = \mathsf{T} \tag{1}$$

$$\mathsf{extractmsg}(\mathsf{sig}(\mathsf{sk}(k), m)) = m \tag{2}$$

$$\mathsf{dec}(\{x\}^r_{\mathsf{pk}(k)}, \mathsf{sk}(k)) = x \tag{3}$$

$$\mathsf{first}(\langle x, y \rangle) = x, \tag{4}$$

$$\mathsf{second}(\langle x, y \rangle) = y \tag{5}$$

Fig. 1. The equational theory associated with the signature $\Sigma_{ex} = \{\mathsf{sig}(\cdot, \cdot), \langle \cdot, \cdot \rangle, \{\cdot\}\cdot,$
$\mathsf{T}, \mathsf{checksig}(\cdot, \cdot), \mathsf{extractmsg}(\cdot), \mathsf{first}(\cdot), \mathsf{second}(\cdot), \mathsf{hash}(\cdot), \mathsf{pk}(\cdot), \mathsf{sk}(\cdot)\}$

2.2   Event Sequences and Views

Let Ch be a set of *channels* (*channel names*). An *input/output event* is of the
form $(c : m)$ and $(\bar{c} : m)$, respectively, for $c \in \mathsf{Ch}$ and a message m (note that
$\bar{c} \notin \mathsf{Ch}$). A finite or infinite sequence of events is called an *event sequence*. For a
sequence $\rho = (c_1 : m_1)(c_2 : m_2), \ldots$ of input events, we denote by $\mathsf{chan}(\rho)$ the
sequence $c_1, c_2, \ldots$ of channels in this sequence. For $C \subseteq \mathsf{Ch}$, we denote by $\rho_{|C}$
the subsequence of ρ containing only the events of the form $(c : m)$ with $c \in C$.

Let $\tau \in T_N$ be a term, which may contain variables $x_1, x_2, \ldots$. Then, with
ρ as above, we denote by $\tau[\rho]$ the message $\tau[m_1/x_1, m_2/x_2, \ldots]$, where x_i is
replaced by m_i. For example, assume that $\tau_{ex} = \mathsf{dec}(x_1, \mathsf{first}(x_2))$ and $\rho_{ex} = (c_1 :$
$\{a\}^r_{\mathsf{pk}(k)}), (c_2 : \langle \mathsf{sk}(k), b \rangle)$. Then $\tau_{ex}[\rho_{ex}] = \mathsf{dec}(\{a\}^r_{\mathsf{pk}(k)}, \mathsf{first}(\langle \mathsf{sk}(k), b \rangle)) \equiv_{ex} a$.

Borrowing the notion of static equivalence from [1], we call two event sequences
ρ and ρ' *statically equivalent w.r.t. a set* $C \subseteq \mathsf{Ch}$ *of channels and a set* $N \subseteq \mathsf{Nonce}$
of nonces, written $\rho \equiv^C_N \rho'$, if (i) $\mathsf{chan}(\rho_{|C}) = \mathsf{chan}(\rho'_{|C})$ and (ii) for every $\tau_1, \tau_2 \in$
T_N we have that $\tau_1[\rho_{|C}] \equiv \tau_2[\rho_{|C}]$ iff $\tau_1[\rho'_{|C}] \equiv \tau_2[\rho'_{|C}]$. Intuitively, $\rho \equiv^C_N \rho'$
means that a party listening on channels C and a priori knowing the nonces in
N cannot distinguish between the inputs received according to ρ and ρ'. We call
the equivalence class of ρ w.r.t. $\equiv^C_N$, the (C, N)-*view* on ρ. For example, if a and
b are different constants, k, k', r and r' are nonces, $C = \{c_1, c_2\}$, and $N = \emptyset$,
then it is easy to see that $\rho^1_{ex} = (c_1 : \{a\}^r_{\mathsf{pk}(k)}), (c_2 : \langle \mathsf{sk}(k'), b \rangle), (c_3 : \mathsf{sk}(k))$ and
$\rho^2_{ex} = (c_1 : \{b\}^{r'}_{\mathsf{pk}(k)}), (c_2 : \langle \mathsf{sk}(k'), b \rangle)$ yield the same (C, N)-view w.r.t. $\equiv_{ex}$.

2.3   Processes

A process is, basically, a function that given a sequence of input events (representing the history so far) produces a sequence of output events. We require
that a process behaves the same on inputs on which it has the same view. More
precisely, a *process* is a tuple $\pi = (I, O, N, f)$ where

(i) $I, O \subseteq \mathsf{Ch}$ are finite sets of *input* and *output* channels, respectively,
(ii) $N \subseteq \mathsf{Nonce}$ is a set of *nonces used by* π,
(iii) f is a mapping which assigns a sequence $f(U) = (c_1 : \tau_1) \cdots (c_n : \tau_n)$ with
     $c_i \in O$ and $\tau_i \in T_N$ to each (I, N)-*view* U.

We note that (iii) guarantees that π performs the same computation on event sequences that are equivalent according to $\equiv_N^I$, and hence, on which π has the same view.

For an event sequence ρ, we write $\pi(\rho)$ for the output produced by π on input ρ. This output is $(c_1 : \tau_1[\rho']) \cdots (c_n : \tau_n[\rho'])$, where $\rho' = \rho_{|I}$ and $(c_1 : \tau_1) \cdots (c_n : \tau_n) = f(U)$ for the equivalence class U of ρ w.r.t. $\equiv_N^I$. For example, let $I = \{c_1, c_2\}$, $N = \emptyset$, U be the equivalence class of ρ_{ex}^1, and assume that $f(U) = (c_4 : \langle x_1, \mathsf{first}(x_2)\rangle)$. Then, $\pi(\rho_{ex}^1) = (c_4 : \langle \{a\}_{\mathsf{pk}(k)}^r, \mathsf{first}(\langle \mathsf{sk}(k'), b\rangle)\rangle)$, which modulo $\equiv_{ex}$ can be written equivalently as $(c_4 : \langle \{a\}_{\mathsf{pk}(k)}^r, \mathsf{sk}(k')\rangle)$ and $\pi(\rho_{ex}^2) = (c_4 : \langle \{b\}_{\mathsf{pk}(k)}^{r'}, \mathsf{first}(\langle \mathsf{sk}(k'), b\rangle)\rangle)$, which modulo $\equiv_{ex}$ can be equivalently written as $(c_4 : \langle \{b\}_{\mathsf{pk}(k)}^{r'}, \mathsf{sk}(k')\rangle)$. Note that since ρ_{ex}^1 and ρ_{ex}^2 yield the same (I, N)-view w.r.t. $\equiv_{ex}$, π performs the same transformation on ρ_{ex}^1 and ρ_{ex}^2. We refer to I, O and N by I_π, O_π, and N_π, respectively. We note that the sets I_π and O_π do not have to be disjoint, i.e., π can send messages to itself. By $\mathsf{Proc}(I, O, N)$ we denote the set of all processes π with $I_\pi \subseteq I$, $O_\pi \subseteq O$, and $N_\pi \subseteq N$.

2.4   Systems and Runs

A *system* S is a finite set of processes with disjoint sets of input channels and sets of nonces, i.e., $I_\pi \cap I_{\pi'} = \emptyset$ and $N_\pi \cap N_{\pi'} = \emptyset$, for distinct $\pi, \pi' \in S$. We will write $\pi_1 \parallel \cdots \parallel \pi_n$ for the system $\{\pi_1, \cdots, \pi_n\}$.

Given a system S and a finite sequence s_0 of output events, a *run ρ of S initiated by* s_0 is a finite or infinite sequence of input and output events which evolves from s_0 in a natural way: An output event is chosen non-deterministically (initial from s_0). Once an output event has been chosen, it will not be chosen anymore later on. By definition of systems, there exists at most one process, say π, in S with an input channel corresponding to the output event. Now, π (if any) is given the input event corresponding to the chosen output event, along with all previous input events on channels of π. Then, π produces a sequence of output events as described above. Now, from these or older output events an output event is chosen non-deterministically, and the computation continues as before.

We emphasize that s_0 may induce many runs, due to the non-deterministic delivery of messages. In what follows, we assume *fair* runs, i.e., every output event in a run will eventually be chosen. A run is *complete* if it is either infinite or else all output events have been chosen at some point. For runs ρ, ρ', we write $\rho \leq \rho'$, if ρ' is an extension of ρ, i.e., is obtained by continuing the run ρ.

2.5   Protocols

A *protocol* is a tuple $P = (A, in, out, nonce, s_0, \Pi)$, where

(i) A is a finite set of *agent names*. An agent $a \in A$ has access to his/her nonces $nonce(a)$, input and output channels $in(a)$, $out(a) \subseteq \mathsf{Ch}$, respectively, such that $nonce(a) \cap nonce(a') = \emptyset$ and $in(a) \cap in(a') = \emptyset$, for $a \neq a'$,

(ii) s_0 is a finite sequence of output events, the *initial output sequence*, for initializing parties,

(iii) for every $a \in A$, $\Pi(a) \subseteq \mathsf{Proc}(in(a), out(a), nonce(a))$ is the set of *programs* or *processes of a*. We will write $P(a)$ for $\Pi(a)$.

If $A = \{a_1, \ldots, a_n\}$ and $\pi_i \in \Pi(a_i)$, then the system $(\pi_1 \parallel \cdots \parallel \pi_n)$ is an *instance of P*. A *run of P* is a fair run of some instance of P initiated by s_0. A *property* γ of P is a subset of runs of P.

We note that our model allows to express nondeterminism: To make a nondeterministic choice, a program can simply send two (or more) messages to itself, and change its behaviour depending on which message arrives first.

3   Online Abuse-Freeness

We define (online) abuse-freeness of a protocol $P = (A, in, out, nonce, s_0, \Pi)$ with respect to two distinct agents of P: the prover $\mathsf{p} \in A$ and the verifier $\mathsf{v} \in A$. Both agents are considered to be dishonest, and hence, the sets of programs of these agents will typically contain all possible processes, i.e., $P(\mathsf{p}) = \mathsf{Proc}(in(\mathsf{p}), out(\mathsf{p}), nonce(\mathsf{p}))$ and $P(\mathsf{v}) = \mathsf{Proc}(in(\mathsf{v}), out(\mathsf{v}), nonce(\mathsf{v}))$; these processes are only limited by their network interfaces, i.e., the set of input/output channels available to them.

Moreover, we define abuse-freeness of P with respect to two properties of P: γ^+ and γ^-. The property γ^+ is supposed to contain all the runs of P in which p obtains a valid contract from an honest signer a and γ^- is supposed to contain all runs where the honest signer a is prevented from obtaining a valid contract from p.

To define abuse-freeness, we first need to formalize the notion of an unbalanced run. Intuitively, a run of an instance of a protocol P is unbalanced with respect to the properties γ^+ and γ^- if p has both a strategy to achieve γ^+ (i.e., enforce a continuation of the run so that the overall run belongs to γ^+) and a strategy to achieve γ^-. In other words, in an unbalanced state, the prover can unilaterally determine the outcome of the protocol: i) obtain a signed contract from the honest signer a or ii) prevent a from obtaining a signed contract from p.

To model the choice made by the prover to either achieve γ^+ or γ^-, we introduce the following notation. We assume that the prover p has a distinct input channel $\mathsf{ch_{choice}}$ which is not an output channel of any agent in the protocol P. Moreover, we assume that the events $(\overline{\mathsf{ch}}_{choice} : 0)$ and $(\overline{\mathsf{ch}}_{choice} : 1)$ belong to the initial event sequence s_0 of P. Intuitively, if in a run p receives 1 on $\mathsf{ch_{choice}}$, then p will try to achieve γ^+. If p receives 0 on $\mathsf{ch_{choice}}$, then p will try to achieve γ^-. More precisely, a run ρ in which neither $(\mathsf{ch_{choice}} : 0)$ nor $(\mathsf{ch_{choice}} : 1)$ has been delivered is called *open*; intuitively, in such a run the prover has not yet made a decision. Otherwise the run is called *closed*. In such a run, p tries to achieve γ^+ or γ^- depending on the message received; note that only the first message received on $\mathsf{ch_{choice}}$ will set p's goal.

In the following definition, given a finite open run ρ, we denote by $\rho^{(\mathsf{ch_{choice}}:0)}$ the run obtained from ρ by delivering 0 on channel $\mathsf{ch_{choice}}$ to p, i.e., in $\rho^{(\mathsf{ch_{choice}}:0)}$

the prover p is now determined to achieve γ^-. The run $\rho^{(\mathsf{ch_{choice}}:1)}$ is defined analogously. We say that a run ρ' is a *complete extension* of ρ if ρ' is an extension of ρ and is complete.

We are now ready to formally define unbalanced runs.

Definition 1. *Given an instance S of a protocol P as above with a prover p and two properties γ^+ and γ^-, we say that a finite open run ρ of S is* unbalanced, *if the following two conditions hold true:*

(i) γ^- holds in every complete extension of $\rho^{(\mathsf{ch_{choice}}:0)}$.
(ii) γ^+ holds in every complete extension of $\rho^{(\mathsf{ch_{choice}}:1)}$.

Now, intuitively, a protocol is abusive if a prover p can convince the verifier v that the current run is unbalanced. In other words, p can convince v that in the current run he, the prover, has a strategy to obtain a valid contract from the honest signer (and hence, close the deal) and a strategy to prevent the honest signer from obtaining a valid contract (and hence, cancel the deal). This may convince v to agree into a deal with p that for p is more profitable than the one with the honest signer. Thus, in an abusive protocol, p can take advantage of the honest signer.

Since we consider *online* abuse-freeness in this paper, we allow v to be actively involved in the protocol run. In particular, p and v can freely exchange messages during a run. For example, v could dictate (parts of the) messages p is supposed to send to the honest signer, and v could request to receive the private keys of p. The verifier v may even control some of the network traffic. However, this is not hard-wired in our definition. The power of p and v can be modeled in a flexible way in terms of the programs p and v may run and the network interface they have.

We will consider two forms of abuse-freeness, namely strong and weak abuse-freeness. In the strong form, p merely needs to convince v that the run was unbalanced at some point. In contrast, for the weak form, p needs to convince v that the run is unbalanced in the *current state* of the run. Since in the latter case, the task of p is harder, the latter form of abuse-freeness is weaker. It is desirable that a protocol is abuse-free in the strong sense since the fact that a run was and potentially still is unbalanced might already be sufficient incentive for v to agree into a deal with p.

In the formal definition of (online) abuse-freeness, we assume that the verifier v can *accept* a run by sending the message accept on the designated channel $\mathsf{ch_{accept}}$, indicating that v is convinced that the run is/was unbalanced. We say that a finite run is *freshly accepted*, if the message accept is sent by v in the last step of this run.

We also use the following notation in the definition of abuse-freeness: Let $P = (A, in, out, nonce, s_0, \Pi)$ be a protocol. For a program $v \in \Pi(\mathsf{v})$ of the verifier, we write $P_{|v}$ for the protocol that coincides with P except that the set $\Pi(\mathsf{v})$ of programs of v is restricted to $\{v\}$. In particular, in every instance of $P_{|v}$ the verifier runs the program v.

We are now ready to define (online) abuse-freeness. We start with the strong form of abuse-freeness.

Definition 2. Let $P = (A, in, out, nonce, s_0, \Pi)$ with $\mathsf{p}, \mathsf{v} \in A$. Let γ^+ and γ^- be properties of P. Then, the protocol P is called (γ^+, γ^-)-*abusive* w.r.t. the prover p and the verifier v, if there is a program $v \in \Pi(\mathsf{v})$ of v such that the following conditions are satisfied:

(i) If an open run ρ of $P_{|v}$ is accepted by v, then there is an unbalanced run ρ' with $\rho' \leq \rho$.

(ii) There exists an open, freshly accepted, unbalanced run ρ of $P_{|v}$.

The protocol P is *(strongly)* (γ^+, γ^-)-*abuse-free* w.r.t. p and v, if P is not (γ^+, γ^-)-abusive w.r.t. p and v.

Condition (i) in the above definition says that if v accepts a run, i.e., is convinced that the run was unbalanced at some point, then this is in fact the case. Note that according to the definition of unbalanced runs, v may help p to achieve his goals (γ^+ or γ^-). One could as well consider a variant where p has to achieve these goals against v (and in fact, our negative results, presented in Sections 4 and 5, use a prover that works without the help of the verifier). However, this would make the definition only weaker. We note that it would not make sense to consider closed runs in Condition (i): The definition of unbalanced runs only applies to open runs. Moreover, the restriction to open runs does not limit the power of any agent.

While Condition (i) is the core of the above definition, it would not make sense without Condition (ii): A verifier who never accepts a run would satisfy Condition (i) trivially. Moreover, a verifier who only accepts runs which are not unbalanced anymore would potentially also suffice to meet Condition (i). By Condition (ii) we require that the strategy of the verifier for accepting a run is reasonable in the sense that there is at least one run which is accepted and which is still unbalanced.

Altogether the above definition says that a protocol is abuse-free if there is no program a verifier could run which i) reliably tells, for any dishonest prover (which the verifier does not trust), whether a run was unbalanced and ii) accepts an actual unbalanced run.

We note that the above definition is possibilistic. It does, for example, not take into account the probability with which unbalanced runs occur or a verifier accepts an (unbalanced) run. As mentioned in the introduction, a cryptographic, in particular probabilistic definition of the balance property, which is stronger than abuse-freeness in that it does not require a dishonest signer to convince an outside party of the fact that he is in an unbalanced state, was presented in [7].

Given Definition 2, it is now straightforward to define weak abuse-freeness:

Definition 3. Let $P, \mathsf{p}, \mathsf{v}, \gamma^+$, and γ^- be given as in Definition 2. Then protocol P is *strongly* (γ^+, γ^-)-*abusive* w.r.t. p and v, if there is a program v such that the following conditions are satisfied:

(i) If an open run ρ of $P_{|v}$ is freshly accepted, then ρ is unbalanced,

(ii) There exists an open, freshly accepted, unbalanced run ρ of $P_{|v}$.

The protocol P is *weakly* (γ^+, γ^-)-*abuse-free* w.r.t. p and v, if P is not strongly (γ^+, γ^-)-abusive w.r.t. p and v.

This notion differs from the (strong) abuse-freenes only in Condition (i): Now we require that the accepted run *is* unbalanced, not only that it was unbalanced at some previous point. Clearly, (strong) abuse-freeness implies weak abuse-freeness.

Note that a notion like weak abuse-freeness does not make sense in the offline setting considered in [12]: If the verifier receives only a single message from the prover, this message can only prove that the protocol was in an unbalanced state at some point during the protocol run; since the prover may withhold that evidence for as long as he wishes, it does not prove that the current state is unbalanced.

4   The ASW Protocol

In this section, we study abuse-freeness of the contract-signing protocol proposed by Asokan, Shoup, and Waidner (ASW protocol) in [3].

In [12], it has been shown (in a *synchronous* communication model without optimistic honest parties, see below) that the ASW protocol is *offline* abusive. Not surprisingly, the protocol is also abusive in the online setting. More precisely, we show that the protocol is weakly abusive. Interestingly, we can show that the protocol is, in some cases, even *strongly abusive*. For this attack, it is crucial that the verifier is online, i.e., can interact with the prover. In fact, the verifier will dictate part of the message the prover sends to the honest signer.

4.1   Description of the Protocol

The ASW protocol assumes the following scenario: Alice and Bob want to sign a contract and a TTP is present. The following two types of messages, the *standard contract (SC)* and the *replacement contract (RC)*, will be recognized as valid contracts between Alice and Bob with contractual text text: $SC = \langle me_1, N_A, me_2, N_B \rangle$ and $RC = \mathsf{sig}(\mathsf{sk}(k_t), \langle me_1, me_2 \rangle)$ where N_A and N_B stand for nonces, $me_1 = \mathsf{sig}(\mathsf{sk}(k_a), \langle A, B, \text{text}, \mathsf{hash}(N_A) \rangle)$, and $me_2 = \mathsf{sig}(\mathsf{sk}(k_b), \langle me_1, \mathsf{hash}(N_B) \rangle)$, with $\mathsf{sk}(k_t)$, $\mathsf{sk}(k_a)$, and $\mathsf{sk}(k_b)$ denoting the private keys of the TTP, Alice, and Bob, respectively. In addition to SC and RC, the variants of SC and RC which one obtains by exchanging the roles of A and B are regarded as valid contracts.

There are three interdependent parts to the protocol: an exchange protocol, an abort protocol, and a resolve protocol. The *exchange protocol* consists of four steps, which, in Alice-Bob notation, are displayed in Fig. 2. The first two messages, me_1 and me_2, serve as respective *promises* of Alice and Bob to sign the contract, and N_A and N_B serve as *contract authenticators*: After they have been revealed, Alice and Bob can compose the standard contract, SC.

The *abort protocol* is run between Alice and the TTP and is used by Alice to abort the contract signing process when she does not receive Bob's promise. Alice will obtain (from the TTP) an abort receipt or, if the protocol instance has already been resolved (see below), a replacement contract. The first step is $A \rightarrow$ T: ma_1, where $ma_1 = \mathsf{sig}(\mathsf{sk}(k_a), \langle \mathrm{aborted}, me_1 \rangle)$ is Alice's *abort request*; the second step is the TTP's reply, which is either $\mathsf{sig}(\mathsf{sk}(k_t), \langle \mathrm{aborted}, ma_1 \rangle)$, the *abort receipt*, if the protocol has not been resolved, or the replacement contract, RC.

$$A \rightarrow B : me_1$$
$$B \rightarrow A : me_2$$
$$A \rightarrow B : N_A$$
$$B \rightarrow A : N_B$$

Fig. 2.   ASW   exchange protocol

The *resolve protocol* can be used by Alice and Bob to resolve the protocol, which either results in a replacement contract or, if the protocol has already been aborted, in an abort receipt. When Bob runs the protocol (because Alice has not sent her contract authenticator yet), the first step is $B \rightarrow T$: $\langle me_1, me_2 \rangle$; the second step is the TTP's reply, which is either the abort receipt $\mathsf{sig}(\mathsf{sk}(k_t), \langle \mathrm{aborted}, ma_1 \rangle)$, if the protocol has already been aborted, or the replacement contract, RC. The same protocol (with roles of A and B exchanged) is also used by Alice.

4.2   Modeling

Our modeling of the ASW protocol uses the equational theory presented in Section 2 (however, without encryption, which is not used in the protocol). We consider, besides the regular protocol participants of the protocol—Alice, Bob, and the trusted third party—two additional parties, the verifier and a key distribution center. We will consider four cases depending on (a) which signer (Alice or Bob) is dishonest and plays the role of the prover and (b) which part of the network is controlled by the verifier.

In each case we assume that the honest signer is *optimistic* in the sense that he/she only contacts the TTP if the dishonest signer allows the honest signer to do so. In other words, the dishonest signer can buy himself as much time as he needs, before the honest signer contacts the TTP. This assumption, also made in [6], seems realistic. In any case, it only makes the dishonest party more powerful, and hence, strengthens our positive results.

Let $P^A_{ASW\text{-}Net}$ denote the specification of the ASW protocol, as a protocol in the sense of our definition (see Section 2.5), with dishonest Alice and honest Bob, where the verifier can eavesdrop on (but not block) the network traffic between Alice and Bob. Analogously, $P^B_{ASW\text{-}Net}$ denotes the protocol with dishonest Bob and honest Alice, where again the verifier can eavesdrop on the network traffic between Alice and Bob. Let $P^A_{ASW\text{-}TTP}$ ($P^B_{ASW\text{-}TTP}$) be the protocols with dishonest Alice (Bob) and honest Bob (Alice), where the verifier can eavesdrop on (but not block) the communication between the signers and the TTP.

In the modeling of these protocols (see below), we allow an honest signer to *not* be engaged in the protocol run. This is of course realistic; also, otherwise the initial state of the protocol would already be unbalanced before a signer has committed to the contract. To model this, we assume that an honest signer decides nondeterministically (see end of Section 2.5) as to whether he/she will participate in the protocol run.

More formally, the set of programs of the protocol participants are defined as follows:

Key Distribution Center. The set of programs for this party consists of exactly one program, which generates key pairs (using its set of nonces) for all other parties. Private keys, modeled as terms of the form $\mathsf{sk}(k)$, where k is a nonce, are sent, via dedicated channels, only to the respective parties. Public keys, modeled as terms of the form $\mathsf{pk}(k)$, are distributed to all parties, including the verifier. Honest parties will first wait to receive their public/private key pair and the public keys of the other protocol participants. In the specification of honest parties below this is assumed implicitly.

Dishonest parties (prover and verifier). The sets of programs of dishonest parties contain all the possible processes, only constrained by the network configuration and, possibly, some additional constrains, as described below. We allow the prover and verifier to communicate directly with each other via a direct (asynchronous) channel.

Network configuration. In the protocols $P^A_{ASW\text{-}TTP}$ and $P^B_{ASW\text{-}TTP}$ (in which the verifier can eavesdrop on messages between the signers and the TTP) we assume that the messages that Alice and Bob want to send to the TTP are routed through the verifier. We require the verifier to forward these messages to the recipient, i.e. we restrict the set of program of the verifier to those programs which comply with this constraint. However, we assume direct (asynchronous) channels between Alice and Bob.

Similarly, in $P^A_{ASW\text{-}TTP}$ and $P^B_{ASW\text{-}TTP}$ messages between Alice and Bob are routed through the verifier, who, as above, can only eavesdrop on these messages. Message between the signers and the TTP can be sent via direct (asynchronous) channels.

TTP. The set of programs of TTP consists of only one program (process), namely the one that performs exactly the steps defined by the protocol as described in Section 4.1.

Honest Alice or Bob. The set of programs of Alice in $P^A_{ASW\text{-}TTP}$ and $P^A_{ASW\text{-}Net}$ consists of only one program, namely the one described in Section 4.1. As mentioned above, at the beginning Alice first nondeterministically chooses whether to participate in the contract signing. Also, she contacts the TTP only if she receives a message from Bob that she is allowed to contact the TTP. The case of honest Bob is analogous.

Remark 1. One could also study the case where the verifier can eavesdrop on all channels. However in this case, both the ASW and GJM protocols clearly are strongly abusive, since the verifier always knows the exact stage of the protocol run.

4.3   Security Analysis

We define γ^+ as the set of all runs where the prover is able to construct the standard contract or has received the replacement contract. Analogously, γ^- consists of those runs in which the honest signer is not able to construct the standard contract and has not received the replacement contract. For the ASW protocol, we prove the following results (see our technical report [14] for the proof).

Theorem 1. *The protocol $P^A_{ASW\text{-}TTP}$ is not weakly (γ^+, γ^-)-abuse-free (and hence also not abuse-free). $P^B_{ASW\text{-}TTP}$, $P^A_{ASW\text{-}Net}$, and $P^B_{ASW\text{-}Net}$ are weakly (γ^+, γ^-)-abuse-free but not abuse-free.*

We note that the first result exhibits a particularly devastating attack, which makes heavy use of the fact that the verifier is an online agent. This result shows that under certain conditions the ASW protocol is not even weakly abuse-free. The above results also show that weak abuse-freeness is a much weaker security property than strong abuse-freeness.

Remark 2. The proofs for $P^A_{ASW\text{-}Net}$ and $P^B_{ASW\text{-}Net}$ easily carry over to the case when the verifier not only eavesdrops on the channels between Alice and Bob, but also controls these channels.

5   The GJM Protocol

In [12], it has been shown that, in a *synchronous* communication model, the GJM protocol is *offline* abuse-free. In this section, we show that whether it is *online* abuse-free depends on assumptions about what part of the network the verifier can eavesdrop on. In particular, we show that in some cases the GJM protocol is not online abuse-free, which, again, illustrates the fact that online abuse-freeness is stronger than offline abuse-freeness.

5.1   Informal Description and Model of the Protocol

The structure of the GJM protocol is the same as the one of the ASW protocol. However, the actual messages exchanged are different. In particular, the exchange protocol of the GJM protocol the first two messages are so-called private contract signatures (PCS) [9] and the last two messages are actual signatures (obtained by converting the private contract signatures into universally verifiable signatures). For the GJM protocol we consider the signature $\Sigma_{GJM} = \{$ $\mathsf{sig}(\cdot, \cdot, \cdot)$, $\mathsf{sigcheck}(\cdot, \cdot, \cdot)$, $\mathsf{pk}(\cdot)$, $\mathsf{sk}(\cdot)$, $\mathsf{fake}(\cdot, \cdot, \cdot, \cdot, \cdot)$, $\mathsf{pcs}(\cdot, \cdot, \cdot, \cdot, \cdot)$, $\mathsf{pcsver}(\cdot, \cdot, \cdot, \cdot, \cdot)$, $\mathsf{sconv}(\cdot, \cdot, \cdot)$, $\mathsf{tpconv}(\cdot, \cdot, \cdot)$, $\mathsf{sver}(\cdot, \cdot, \cdot, \cdot)$, $\mathsf{tpver}(\cdot, \cdot, \cdot, \cdot)$, $\langle \cdot, \cdot \rangle$, $\mathsf{first}(\cdot)$, $\mathsf{second}(\cdot)$, A, B, T, text, initiator, responder, ok, pcsok, sok, tpok, aborted$\}$.

The equational theory for GJM contains, in addition to the equations for pairing and signatures, equations for modeling private contract signatures, as depicted in Figure 3. A term of the form $\mathsf{pcs}(u, \mathsf{sk}(x), w, \mathsf{pk}(y), \mathsf{pk}(z))$ stands for

$$\mathsf{pcsver}(w, \mathsf{pk}(x), \mathsf{pk}(y), \mathsf{pk}(z), \mathsf{pcs}(u, \mathsf{sk}(x), w, \mathsf{pk}(y), \mathsf{pk}(z))) = \mathsf{pcsok}, \qquad (6)$$
$$\mathsf{pcsver}(w, \mathsf{pk}(x), \mathsf{pk}(y), \mathsf{pk}(z), \mathsf{fake}(u, \mathsf{sk}(y), w, \mathsf{pk}(x), \mathsf{pk}(z))) = \mathsf{pcsok}, \qquad (7)$$
$$\mathsf{sver}(w, \mathsf{pk}(x), \mathsf{pk}(z), \mathsf{sconv}(u, \mathsf{sk}(x), \mathsf{pcs}(v, \mathsf{sk}(x), w, \mathsf{pk}(y), \mathsf{pk}(z)))) = \mathsf{sok}, \qquad (8)$$
$$\mathsf{tpver}(w, \mathsf{pk}(x), \mathsf{pk}(z), \mathsf{tpconv}(u, \mathsf{sk}(z), \mathsf{pcs}(v, \mathsf{sk}(x), w, \mathsf{pk}(y), \mathsf{pk}(z)))) = \mathsf{tpok}. \qquad (9)$$

Fig. 3. Equations for private contract signatures.

a PCS computed by x (with $\mathsf{sk}(x)$) involving the text w, the party y, and the TTP z, while u models the random coins used to compute the PCS. Everybody can verify the PCS with the public keys involved (equation (6)), but cannot determine whether the PCS was computed by x or y (equation (7)): instead of x computing the "real" PCS, y could have computed a "fake" PCS which would also pass the verification with pcsver. Using sconv and tpconv, see (8) and (9), a "real" PCS can be converted by x and the TTP z, respectively, into a universally verifiable signature (verifiable by everyone who possesses $\mathsf{pk}(x)$ and $\mathsf{pk}(z)$).

We study the version of the GJM protocol with the modification proposed in [16] to obtain fairness. In the protocol, the following messages are exchanged: The initial messages containing the private contract signatures are $me_1 = \mathsf{pcs}(u, \mathsf{sk}(A), \mathsf{contract}, \mathsf{pk}(B), \mathsf{pk}(TTP))$ and $me_2 = \mathsf{pcs}(u', \mathsf{sk}(B),$ $\mathsf{contract}, \mathsf{pk}(A), \mathsf{pk}(TTP))$, where $\mathsf{sk}(A)$, $\mathsf{pk}(A)$, $\mathsf{sk}(B)$, $\mathsf{pk}(B)$, and $\mathsf{pk}(TTP)$ are the private and public keys of Alice, Bob, and the TTP. The abort request sent by Alice is of the form $ma_1 = \mathsf{sig}(w, \mathsf{sk}(A), \langle \mathsf{contract}, A, B, \mathsf{aborted} \rangle)$, where w are random coins (for the GJM protocol, we consider randomized signatures). The resolve request sent by Alice is $\langle me_1, me_2 \rangle$, the resolve request from Bob is $\langle me_2, me_1 \rangle$. As mentioned earlier, the structure of the protocol is the same as for the ASW protocol (see Section 4).

5.2 Security Analysis

We study the cases $P^A_{GJM\text{-}TTP}$, $P^B_{GJM\text{-}TTP}$, $P^A_{GJM\text{-}Net}$ and $P^B_{GJM\text{-}Net}$, which are defined analogously to the case of ASW (see Section 4.2). The properties γ^+ and γ^- are also defined analogously to the case of the ASW protocol (see Section 4.3). The proof of this result can be found in our technical report [14].

Theorem 2. *1. $P^A_{GJM\text{-}TTP}$ and $P^B_{GJM\text{-}TTP}$ are (γ^+, γ^-)-abuse-free.*
2. $P^A_{GJM\text{-}Net}$ and $P^B_{GJM\text{-}Net}$ are weakly (γ^+, γ^-)-abuse-free but not (γ^+, γ^-)-abuse-free.

As made precise by this theorem, abuse-freeness of the GJM protocol in the online setting depends on the assumptions about what part of the network the verifier can eavesdrop on. In the offline case, the verifier was not allowed to easvesdrop on any part of the network (and of course, was also not allowed to be actively involved in the protocol run). Therefore, and just as in the case of the ASW protocol, our positive results are stronger than those shown for offline abuse-freeness. Conversely, our negative results exhibit the extra power of online verifiers.

References

1. Abadi, M., Fournet, C.: Mobile Values, New Names, and Secure Communication. In: POPL 2001, pp. 104–115. ACM Press, New York (2001)
2. Aizatulin, M., Schnoor, H., Wilke, T.: Computationally Sound Analysis of a Probabilistic Contract Signing Protocol. In: Backes, M., Ning, P. (eds.) ESORICS 2009. LNCS, vol. 5789, pp. 571–586. Springer, Heidelberg (2009)
3. Asokan, N., Shoup, V., Waidner, M.: Asynchronous protocols for optimistic fair exchange. In: IEEE Symposium on Research in Security and Privacy, pp. 86–99 (1998)
4. Ben-Or, M., Goldreich, O., Micali, S., Rivest, R.L.: Fair protocol for signing contracts. IEEE Transactions on Information Theory 36(1), 40–46 (1990)
5. Chadha, R., Kanovich, M.I., Scedrov, A.: Inductive methods and contract-signing protocols. In: CCS 2001, pp. 176–185. ACM Press, New York (2001)
6. Chadha, R., Mitchell, J.C., Scedrov, A., Shmatikov, V.: Contract Signing, Optimism, and Advantage. In: Amadio, R.M., Lugiez, D. (eds.) CONCUR 2003. LNCS, vol. 2761, pp. 361–377. Springer, Heidelberg (2003)
7. Cortier, V., Küsters, R., Warinschi, B.: A cryptographic model for branching time security properties – the case of contract signing protocols. In: Biskup, J., López, J. (eds.) ESORICS 2007. LNCS, vol. 4734, pp. 422–437. Springer, Heidelberg (2007)
8. Dolev, D., Yao, A.C.: On the Security of Public-Key Protocols. IEEE Transactions on Information Theory 29(2), 198–208 (1983)
9. Garay, J.A., Jakobsson, M., MacKenzie, P.: Abuse-free optimistic contract signing. In: Wiener, M. (ed.) CRYPTO 1999. LNCS, vol. 1666, pp. 449–466. Springer, Heidelberg (1999)
10. Kähler, D., Küsters, R.: Constraint Solving for Contract-Signing Protocols. In: Abadi, M., de Alfaro, L. (eds.) CONCUR 2005. LNCS, vol. 3653, pp. 233–247. Springer, Heidelberg (2005)
11. Kähler, D., Küsters, R., Wilke, T.: Deciding Properties of Contract-Signing Protocols. In: Diekert, V., Durand, B. (eds.) STACS 2005. LNCS, vol. 3404, pp. 158–169. Springer, Heidelberg (2005)
12. Kähler, D., Küsters, R., Wilke, T.: A Dolev-Yao-based Definition of Abuse-free Protocols. In: Bugliesi, M., Preneel, B., Sassone, V., Wegener, I. (eds.) ICALP 2006. LNCS, vol. 4052, pp. 95–106. Springer, Heidelberg (2006)
13. Kremer, S., Raskin, J.-F.: Game analysis of abuse-free contract signing. In: CSFW 2002 (2002)
14. Küsters, R., Schnoor, H., Truderung, T.: A Formal Definition of Online Abuse-freeness. Technical Report, University of Trier (2010), http://infsec.uni-trier.de/publications.html
15. Küsters, R., Truderung, T.: An Epistemic Approach to Coercion-Resistance for Electronic Voting Protocols. In: Security and Privacy 2009, pp. 251–266. IEEE Computer Society, Los Alamitos (2009)
16. Shmatikov, V., Mitchell, J.C.: Finite-state analysis of two contract signing protocols. Theoretical Computer Science (TCS), special issue on Theoretical Foundations of Security Analysis and Design 283(2), 419–450 (2002)
17. Wang, G.: An Abuse-Free Fair Contract-Signing Protocol Based on the RSA Signature. IEEE Transactions on Information Forensics and Security 5(1), 158–168 (2010)

Author Index

9 783642 161605